Meetings, Expositions, Events, & Conventions

An Introduction to the Industry

Seventh Edition

George Fenich | Kristin Malek

Cover images © Shutterstock, Inc.

www.kendallhunt.com
Send all inquiries to:
4050 Westmark Drive
Dubuque, IA 52004-1840

Copyright © 2021, 2024 by Kendall Hunt Publishing Company

Text ISBN 979-8-7657-6082-6
eBook ISBN 979-8-3851-1532-7

All rights reserved. No part of this publication may be reproduced, stored in a retrieval system, or transmitted, in any form or by any means, electronic, mechanical, photocopying, recording, or otherwise, without the prior written permission of the copyright owner.

Published in the United States of America

CONTENTS

PREFACE XV
ACKNOWLEDGMENTS XVII
ABOUT THE AUTHORS XXI

CHAPTER 1: INTRODUCTION TO THE MEETINGS, EXPOSITIONS, EVENTS, AND CONVENTIONS INDUSTRY (MEEC) 1

WHAT IS THE MEEC INDUSTRY? 2
   Industry Terminology and Practice 4
   The Organizational Structure of the Tourism and Hospitality Industry: In support of the Global Business Events Industry and How MEEC Fits In 7

HISTORY OF THE INDUSTRY 9

EVOLUTION AND MATURATION OF THE MEEC INDUSTRY 13
   MBECS 13
   CMP International Standards (CMP-IS) 15
   Use of the MBECS and CMP International Standards 17

IN SUPPORT OF THE INDUSTRY 19
   EIC's APEX Commission 19

CMP CODE OF ETHICS 20
   Careers in and Around the MEEC Industry 21
   Which Career Is Right for You? 28

TRENDS IN 2023 29
   The Impact of Unforeseen Calamities 29
   Transforming Role of Technology 30
   Pivot From Event Logistics to Event Strategists 31
   Sustainability and Social Impact 32

REFERENCES 1 40

KEY WORDS AND TERMS 40

REVIEW AND DISCUSSION QUESTIONS 40
   About the Chapter Contributor 41

III

CHAPTER 2: MEETING, EXHIBITION, EVENT, AND CONVENTION ORGANIZERS AND SPONSORS 43

Who Holds Gatherings? 44
Corporations 44
Associations 50
Government 58
Other Organizations Arranging Gatherings 61

Entities That Help Organize Gatherings 62
EMCS 62
Association Management Companies (AMCs) 64
Meeting Management Companies 65
Independent Meeting Managers 66

Trends and Best Practices 67
Summary 70
Professional Preparation for a Career in the MEEC Industry 71

Key Words and Terms 73
Review and Discussion Questions 73
About the Chapter Contributor 74

CHAPTER 3: DESTINATION MARKETING ORGANIZATIONS (DMOs) 75

The Role and Function of DMOs 76
What Is a DMO? 76
The Purpose of a DMO 77
If DMOs Do Not Charge for Their Services, How Do They Make Money? 78
Attracting Leisure Travelers 79
Promoting the Destination 80

What a DMO Can Do for Meeting Professionals 81
What Meeting Planners Need to Know About DMOs 81

Activities of DMOs Relative to Convention Marketing and Sales 85
Sales Processes 85
Site Review and Leads Process 86
Site Inspections 88
DMO Services for Meeting Professionals 89
Changing Scope of DMO Responsibilities 90

Destinations International (DI) 91
DI Professional Development Offerings 92
Certified Destination Management Executive (CDME) 92
Professional in Destination Management (PDM) Program 92
DI Research and Advocacy 93
DI Destination Tools 93
Event Impact Calculator 94

    Accreditation 94
    Destination and Travel Foundation 95
TRENDS 96
SUMMARY 101
KEY WORDS AND TERMS 104
REVIEW AND DISCUSSION QUESTIONS 104
    Websites for Reference 104
    About the Chapter Contributor 104

CHAPTER 4: MEETING, EXPOSITIONS, EVENT, AND CONVENTION VENUES: AN EXAMINATION OF FACILITIES USED BY MEETING AND EVENT PROFESSIONALS 105

HOTELS 106
    Physical Characteristics 106
    Financial Structure 107
    Negotiating Your Event 108
    Room Rates 108
CONVENTION CENTERS 111
    Financial Structure 117
    Negotiating for Your Event 118
CONFERENCE CENTERS 119
    Meeting Room Spaces 119
    Associations and Consortia 121
    F&B 121
    Negotiating Your Event 122
CRUISE SHIPS 126
    Negotiating Your Event 126
SPECIFIC USE FACILITIES 132
    Financial Structure 132
COLLEGE AND UNIVERSITIES 133
    Negotiating Your Event 134
RETREAT FACILITIES 135
UNUSUAL VENUES 137
OUTDOOR EVENTS 138
    Outdoor Venue Challenges 139
    Outdoor Tents 139
    Outdoor Venue Permits 140
TRENDS 140
SUMMARY 141
    Case Study Assignment 144
KEY WORDS AND TERMS 146
REVIEW AND DISCUSSION QUESTIONS 146
    About the Chapter Contributors 147

CHAPTER 5: EXHIBITIONS AND TRADE SHOWS 149
HISTORY 150
TYPES OF SHOWS AND EXHIBITIONS 152
    Trade Shows or B2B Shows 152
    Consumer Show or Business-to-Consumer (B2C) Shows 155
    Consolidation Shows (Also Called "Combined" or "Mixed" Shows) 156
EXHIBITION MANAGEMENT: KEY PLAYERS 156
    Exhibition Organizer 157
    Facility Manager 157
    OSC 158
KNOWLEDGE, SKILLS, AND ABILITIES (KSAs) OF AN EXHIBITION MANAGER 159
CONSIDERATIONS IN MANAGING THE SHOW 161
    Location 161
    Shipping and Storage 163
    Marketing and Promotion 164
    Technology 165
    Risk and Crisis Management 166
EXHIBITOR PERSPECTIVE 167
    Why Exhibit? 167
    Exhibit Design Principles 167
    Staffing the Exhibit 171
    Measuring ROI 173
SUMMARY 176
KEY WORDS AND TERMS 177
REVIEW AND DISCUSSION QUESTIONS 177
    About the Chapter Contributor 178

CHAPTER 6: SERVICE CONTRACTORS 179
DEFINITION OF A GENERAL SERVICES CONTRACTOR (GSC) 180
    GSC Responsibilities 181
LABOR/TRADE UNIONS 185
EVOLUTION OF SERVICE CONTRACTORS 188
ORGANIZATION OF A GENERAL SERVICES CONTRACTING COMPANY 191
TYPES OF SERVICE CONTRACTORS 193
    Specialty Service Contractors 193
    Exhibitor-Appointed Service Contractors 196
RELATIONSHIP BETWEEN CONTRACTORS AND EVENT ORGANIZERS 197
RESOURCES IN THE SERVICE CONTRACTOR INDUSTRY 198
HOW DOES IT ALL WORK? 199
    Best Practices 200

Summary 201
    Review and Discussion Questions 203
Key Words and Terms 204
Review and Discussion Questions 204
    About the Chapter Contributor 205

CHAPTER 7: DESTINATION MANAGEMENT COMPANIES (DMCs) 207

DMC: Definition, Structure, and Services 208
    Services Provided by DMCs 209
    DMC Versus Destination Marketing Organization 211
    Business Structure of DMCs 212
The DMC Organization 213
    Independent Operator 214
    Multiservices Operator 214
    Destination Management Networks 214
Business Model of DMCs 215
    Clients 216
DMC Operations 218
    The Sales Process 220
    Identifying New Business Opportunities 221
    RFP 222
    Site Inspections 225
    Program Development 225
    Program Execution 226
    Transportation Services 227
    Production of Events 231
    Wrap-Up and Billing 233
Finding and Selecting a DMC 234
    Association of Destination Management Executives 234
Best Practices in DMCs 235
The COVID-19 Impact on Business Destinations and DMCs 237
Summary 238
Key Words and Terms 241
Review and Discussion Questions 241
    About the Chapter Contributors 242

CHAPTER 8: SPECIAL EVENTS MANAGEMENT 243

History and Overview of Special Events 244
    A Working Definition of a Special Event 244
    History and Background 245
    It All Begins With a Relationship 246
    Examples of Special Events 249

PLANNING TOOLS FOR SPECIAL EVENTS 250
    Understanding Community Infrastructure 252
SPECIAL EVENT MARKETING CONSIDERATIONS 252
    Merchandising and Promoting 252
    Promotional Mix 253
    Sponsorships for Special Events 257
    Working With the Media for an Event 260
    Understanding the Target Market for Your Special Event 262
PREPARING FOR THE SPECIAL EVENT 264
    Software and Tools for Special Events 265
THE BUDGET 267
    Rental Costs 267
    Security Costs 268
    Production Costs 268
    Labor Costs 268
    Marketing Costs 269
    Talent Costs 269
BREAKDOWN OF THE SPECIAL EVENT 269
TRENDS AND BEST PRACTICES IN SPECIAL EVENTS 270
SUMMARY 271
KEY WORDS AND TERMS 275
REVIEW AND DISCUSSION QUESTIONS 275
    About the Chapter Contributor 276

CHAPTER 9: FOOD AND BEVERAGE (F&B) 277

CATERED EVENTS 278
    On-Premise Catering 279
    Off-Premise Catering 280
    Style of Service 283
    Menus 289
    Food Consumption Guidelines 291
    Contracts 293
BEVERAGE EVENTS 294
    Reasons for a Beverage Event 294
    Categories of Liquor 295
    How Beverages Are Sold 297
    Labor Charges 299
HOSPITALITY SUITES 300
ROOMS 302
    Room Setups 302
    Tablescapes 303
    Room Rental Charges 304

SERVICE REQUIREMENTS 305
    Set Over Guarantee 306
    Cocktail Servers 306
    Service Timing 307
TRENDS AND BEST PRACTICES BEFORE COVID-19 307
SUMMARY 308
KEY WORDS AND TERMS 311
REVIEW AND DISCUSSION QUESTIONS 311
    About the Chapter Contributors 312

CHAPTER 10: LEGAL ISSUES IN THE MEETINGS, EVENTS, EXHIBITIONS, AND CONVENTIONS (MEEC) INDUSTRY 313

NEGOTIATION 314
    General Negotiation Strategies 315
    Negotiating Hotel Contracts 317
    Naming Names 318
CONTRACTS 323
    Statute of Frauds 326
    Parol Evidence 327
    Key Hotel Group Meeting Contract Clauses 327
    Attrition 328
    Cancellation 330
    Force Majeure 332
    Dispute Resolution 333
CRISIS PREPAREDNESS AND MANAGEMENT 335
    What Is Risk? Crisis Preparedness? 335
    Crisis Management 336
AMERICANS WITH DISABILITIES ACT 338
INTELLECTUAL PROPERTY 341
    Patents 341
    Trademarks 342
    Copyrights 342
LABOR ISSUES 344
ETHICS IN MEEC 346
    Supplier Relations 347
TRENDS AND BEST PRACTICES REGARDING LEGAL ISSUES IN MEEC 348
SUMMARY 349
KEY WORDS AND TERMS 350
CASE STUDY 350
REVIEW AND DISCUSSION QUESTIONS 351
    About the Chapter Contributor 352

CHAPTER 11: TECHNOLOGY AND THE MEETING PROFESSIONAL 353

INTRODUCTION 354

VIRTUAL SITE SELECTION AND RESEARCH 355
- Online RFPs 355
- Virtual Tours 356
- Meeting Industry Portals and Information Resources 357

MARKETING AND COMMUNICATIONS 359
- Websites and Strategic Communications 359
- Event Websites 360
- Mobile Websites 361
- E-Blasts 362
- Video Marketing 364
- Room Design Software 364
- Selling the Show Floor 365
- Online Registration 365

SOCIAL MEDIA 366
- Primary Social Channels 366
- Livestreaming 368
- Blogging 369
- Podcasting 370
- Hashtags 370
- Social Selling 371

EVENT APPS 372

DESKTOP AND MOBILE TOOLS 373
- Accepted Practices Exchange (APEX) 374
- Virtual Trade Shows 374

ON-SITE EVENT TECH INFRASTRUCTURE 374
- Facial Recognition at On-Site Registration 375
- Bandwidth 376
- Wired Versus Wireless 377
- Streaming Media 378
- Digital Recordings of Sessions 379
- Drones 380

ATTENDEE INTERACTION AND COMMUNICATIONS 380
- Beacons 381
- Near Field Communications (NFC) and Radio Frequency Identification (RFID) 381
- Lead Retrieval Systems 382
- Audience Response Systems (ARSs) and Speaker Interaction 382

POSTCONFERENCE TECHNOLOGY APPLICATIONS 383
- Evaluations and Surveys 383
- Marketing the Media 384

MIXED REALITY 385
    AR 386
    Virtual Reality/360° Videos 387
AI 388
    ChatGPT 390
    AI, Chat GPT, and Hospitality 391
VIRTUAL AND HYBRID MEETINGS 392
    Hybrid Meetings 392
    Online Meetings and Webinars 393
    Large-Scale Virtual Meetings 394
THE ROARING TECH TWENTIES 395
SUMMARY 397
KEY WORDS AND TERMS 398
    About the Chapter Contributor 398

CHAPTER 12: SUSTAINABLE MEETINGS AND EVENTS 399

INTRODUCTION TO GREEN & SUSTAINABLE MEETINGS 401
WHY DO IT? 404
    The Triple Bottom Line 404
    Benefits of Sustainability 409
SUSTAINABLE MEETING STANDARDS AND GUIDELINES 410
    Sustainable Meeting Standards 410
    United Nations (UN) Sustainable Development Goals 411
    ISO 20121 411
GREENWASHING 413
CREATING A PROCESS FOR SUSTAINABLE PRACTICES 414
    Best Environmental Practices 416
EVALUATION OF SUSTAINABLE EFFORTS 418
    MeetGreen® Calculator 2.0 418
SUSTAINABLE MEETING PROFESSIONAL 419
TRENDS AND BEST PRACTICES 422
SUMMARY 423
KEY WORDS AND TERMS 425
REVIEW AND DISCUSSION QUESTIONS 425
    Recommended Websites 426
    About the Chapter Contributor 426

CHAPTER 13: PLANNING MEEC GATHERINGS 429

NEEDS ANALYSIS 430
    Setting Goals and Objectives 431
EVENT BUDGETING 438
    Establish Financial Goals 438
    Identify Expenses and Revenue Sources 439

BUDGET ASSEMBLY   441
PROGRAM PLANNING   442
    Program Types   444
    Program Content   446
    Session Scheduling   447
LOGISTICAL CONSIDERATIONS   449
    Registration   449
    Housing   451
    Refreshment Breaks and Meal Functions   454
    Speaker Arrangements   454
    Inclusion Through Speaker Selection   457
    A/V Equipment   458
MARKETING AND PROMOTION   459
    Types of Promotion for Events   461
SUMMARY AND BEST PRACTICES   464
KEYWORDS AND TERMS   467
REVIEW AND DISCUSSION QUESTIONS   467
    About the Chapter Contributors   468

CHAPTER 14: PRODUCING MEETINGS AND EVENTS   469

ON-SITE MANAGEMENT   470
    Registration and Housing   470
    F&B   471
    Function Room Layouts   472
    Common Issues Faced On-Site   477
    Speakers and Entertainers   480
    On-Site A/V   481
    Ancillary Events   482
    Meeting and Event Specification Guide   483
    Controlling Costs   484
MANAGING THE ON-SITE TEAM   485
    Employees   485
    Temporary Staff   486
    Volunteers   486
ON-SITE COMMUNICATIONS   487
    Personal Communications   487
    Technology   489
PUBLIC RELATIONS   493
    What Is Public Relations?   493
    Develop and Manage Media Relations   493
    News Releases   494
    Attract and Accommodate Media   495
    Media Outlets   497
    Select and Manage Spokespersons   498

Preconvention Meetings   499
Postconvention Review   500
   Evaluation   500
Summary and Best Practices   502
Key Words and Terms   504
Review and Discussion Questions   504
   About the Chapter Contributors   505

CHAPTER 15: INTERNATIONAL ASPECTS IN MEEC   507

How MEEC Varies Around the Globe   508
   Europe   511
   Asia   515
   Australia   522
   Africa   523
   Middle East   525
   Latin America   526
Ownership, Sponsorship, and Management Models   527
   Professional Congress Organizer (PCO)   527
Important International Meeting and Trade Fair Associations   528
International MEEC Considerations   530
   Lessons to Be Learned   530
   Methods of Exhibiting   531
   Terminology   532
   Contractual and Procedural Issues   532
   Customs Clearance   533
   Protocol   533
Virtual and Hybrid Events   539
   ESC Congress 2020—The Digital Experience   539
   Canton Fair   540
   UFI Global Congress 2020   540
Summary and Best Practices   541
Key Words and Terms   544
Review and Discussion Questions   544
   About the Chapter Contributors   545

CHAPTER 16: PUTTING IT ALL TOGETHER   547

The Association   548
Goals   550
Budget   550
Income   554
Request for Proposals (RFP)   555

FIRST SITE INSPECTIONS—EXPLORING TWO POSSIBLE CONFERENCE LOCATIONS 557
    Day 1   557
    Day 2   558
    Day 3   559

DESTINATION SELECTION 560

SECOND SITE INSPECTION: FINALIZING DETAILS 560
    Day 1   560
    Day 2   562
    Day 3   562

MARKETING COMMITTEE 562

CREATION OF THE CONFERENCE PROGRAM 564

PARTNERSHIPS 565

CONTRACTS 567

MEETING TIMELINE 567
    1 Year to 6-Month Countdown   567
    6 Months Before to Day of the Meeting   569
    Meeting Day Activities   573

AFTER THE MEETING 573
    Immediate Postmeeting Activities   573
    2-Month Postmeeting Activities   574

SUMMARY 575

REVIEW AND DISCUSSION QUESTIONS 575

KEY WORDS AND TERMS 577
    About the Chapter Contributor   577

REFERENCES 579

INDEX 581

PREFACE

The meetings, expositions, events, and conventions (MEEC, pronounced like *geese*) industry continues to grow and garner increasing attention from the hospitality industry, colleges and universities, and communities. This book gives a broad overview of the industry and is thus an introduction. It is not meant to provide a hands-on or step-by-step method for handling gatherings. The latter is addressed in two books by Fenich: *Planning and Management of Meetings, Expositions, Events, and Conventions* and *Production and Logistics in Meetings, Expositions, Events, and Conventions*. Both of these books are based on and align with the Meeting and Business Event Competency Standards.

This book is being produced at this time for a number of reasons. One is the continued growth of this industry; in spite of the ebbs and flows of the economy, the MEEC segment of the hospitality industry remains resilient. Communities continue to build or expand MEEC venues unabated, and the private sector has also become a player in convention center construction and operation. People still need face-to-face meetings. The MEEC industry appears to be on a growth curve and is of interest to many people.

Also, college faculties have indicated a need for a book such as this. The authors have been teaching introductory MEEC courses for many years and found that they need to continually supplement existing books to make them both current and more complete in addressing the various segments of the industry. This book concept originated at a meeting of the Convention Special Interest Group at the International Council on Hotel, Restaurant, and Institutional Education (ICHRIE) Convention in 2001, when the need for a new text was discussed. The members of this group all noted the need, and Fenich volunteered to spearhead an effort, using faculty and industry experts to write various chapters. This book is a culmination of that effort. The result is a text where some of the best and most notable people in the MEEC industry have made contributions.

The approach to deciding on topics was unusual. Rather than have a list of topics or chapters based on people's willingness to contribute, a more scientific method was used. Fenich began by reviewing books, both theoretical and practical, to ascertain which topics to cover. Topics that appeared in more than one text were compiled into a list. Then a number of meetings were held with educators to discuss the relative importance of topics, which led to developing a comprehensive list that was sent to educators and practitioners, who were asked to rank each topic as critically important, important, or not important. The results were used to pare down the list, and this iterative voting procedure (Delphi technique) was used to reach the decision as to the topics to include. This seventh edition not only has updated material and statistics but also relied on feedback from adopters and reviewers to make improvements.

This industry is referred to in many ways: "Meetings and Events," "Events," "Meeting Planning," and others. A very common acronym, and one used extensively in Asia, is "MICE," which stands for "Meetings, Incentives, Conventions, Events" and is pronounced like the plural of mouse. That acronym was purposely *not* chosen for the title of this text, because most programs of study deal with the Incentives or Incentive Travel very little, if at all. Furthermore, the Incentive Travel segment has evolved significantly in the past number of years, moving away from trips that were strictly for pleasure (as a reward for performance) and much more into trips that have notable education and training components. They are now much more like sales training meetings, motivational meetings, or team building exercises, but on a more grandiose scale. Thus, this book deals with MEEC.

NEW IN THIS EDITION

- The last edition had separate callouts specific to real-time information about pandemics. This edition replaces this with trends and incorporates the long-standing effects to our industry.
- All chapter case studies have been updated.
- Several chapters have been substantially rewritten.
- New authors for many chapters have made the chapters their own with industry perspectives.
- The chapter discussing international aspects of MEEC includes additional regions.
- The glossary has been expanded to include all key terms found in the chapters.
- Teaching materials have been updated.

Meetings, Expositions, Events, and Conventions should be of interest to practitioners, educators, students, and the general public. It is the most up-to-date book on the MEEC industry and will provide users with an overview of the industry; it is also comprehensive and covers a wider range of topics than any other book available. It can easily serve as the basis for an introductory college course on the subject or for orientation sessions for new employees in the industry. It should meet the needs of anyone interested in knowing more about the MEEC industry.

George G. Fenich, Ph.D. and Kristin Malek, Ph.D.

ACKNOWLEDGMENTS

We would like to thank the chapter contributors for their work and insights and students everywhere for their interest in the MEEC industry. Also, thank you to the educators in the MEEC field for helping develop the concept for this book and continuing support through adoptions of this text. The contributors are the following.

PART 1: INTRODUCTION

Chapter 1: Introduction to the Meetings, Expositions, Events, and Conventions Industry

Ann D. Summerall-Jabro, Ph.D.
Professor of Communication and Organizational Leadership, Robert Morris University
Principal, ATEC Enterprises
Pittsburgh, Pennsylvania

Chapter 2: Meeting, Expositions, Events, and Convention Organizers

Thomas Padron, Ph.D., CMP
Associate Professor and Program Coordinator
Cal State East Bay
Hayward, CA

PART 2: KEY PLAYERS

Chapter 3: Destination Marketing Organizations (DMOs)

Jonathon Day, Ph.D.
Associate Professor and Graduate Program Director
School of Hospitality and Tourism Management

Purdue University
West Lafayette, Indiana

Chapter 4: Meeting and Convention Venues

Lisa Young, Ph.D.
Director of the School of Hospitality Leadership and Associate Professor
DePaul University
Chicago, IL

Juan Mendez
Instructor
DePaul University
Chicago, IL

Chapter 5: Exhibitions

Marsha Flanagan, M.Ed., CEM
Senior Vice President Events & Learning Experiences
International Association of Exhibition and Events®
Dallas, Texas

Chapter 6: Service Contractors

Shinyong (Shawn) Jung, Ph.D., MBA
Assistant Professor
White Lodging—J.W. Marriott, Jr. School of Hospitality and Tourism Management
Purdue University
West Lafayette, IN

Chapter 7: Destination Management Companies

Dr. Alan Fyall
Associate Dean, Academic Affairs
Visit Orlando Endowed Chair of Tourism Marketing
Rosen College of Hospitality Management
University of Central Florida
Orlando, FL 32819

Steve Brinkman, M.Ed.
Instructor

Rosen College of Hospitality Management
University of Central Florida
Orlando, FL 32819

Chapter 8: Special Events Management

David L Smiley, MS, PGA
Indiana University Bloomington
School of Public Health, RPTS
Bloomington, IN 47405

PART 3: IMPORTANT ELEMENTS IN MEETING, EXPOSITION, EVENT, AND CONVENTION PLANNING

Chapter 9: Food and Beverage in Meetings and Events

Kristin Malek, Ph.D., CMP, CED, DES, CHE
Event Management Specialist and Assistant Professor
University of Nebraska—Lincoln
Lincoln, NE

George G. Fenich, Ph.D.
Professor Emeritus
School of Hospitality Leadership
East Caroline University
Greenville, NC

Chapter 10: Legal Issues in Meetings and Events

Tyra Warner, Ph.D., J.D., CMP
Department Chair and Associate Professor
Hospitality, Tourism, & Culinary Arts at College of Coastal Georgia
College of Coastal Georgia
Brunswick, GA

Chapter 11: Technology

Jim Spellos
Meeting U.
50-26 206th Street
Bayside NY 11364

Chapter 12: Sustainable Meetings and Events

Carole B. Sox, Ph.D.
Associate Professor
Columbia College
Columbia, SC

Chapter 13: Planning Meetings and Events & Chapter 14: Producing Meetings and Events

Amanda Cecil, Ph.D., CMP
Professor
Department of Tourism, Conventions and Event Management
Indiana University
Indianapolis, Indiana USA

Erica Shonkwiler, M.B.A., CMP
Senior Lecturer
Department of Tourism, Event, and Sport Management
Indiana University
Indianapolis, Indiana USA

Chapter 15: International Aspects in MEEC

Mady Keup
Retired
SKEMA Business School
France

Chapter 16: Putting It All Together

M.T. Hickman, CMP, CPECP
Senior Lecturer, Hospitality, Event, and Tourism Management
University of North Texas
Denton, TX

ABOUT THE AUTHORS

George G. Fenich, Ph.D., is a professor emeritus in the School of Hospitality Leadership at East Carolina University. Dr. Fenich worked in the hospitality industry for 15 years before joining academe. He teaches and researches in the area of conventions and meetings and has written over 70 academic articles and presented at over 150 conferences—including the International Council on Hotel Restaurant and Institutional Education, Destination Marketing Association International, Association for Convention Operations Management, International Association of Assembly Managers, AHTMM in Istanbul, Taipei, and Mauritius, International Conference on Meetings & Events (Shanghai China), and Professional Convention Management Association. He is on the editorial board of six academic journals—and the retired editor in chief for *Journal of Convention and Event Tourism*. He is also the principal of the consulting firm Fenich & Associates LLC.

Source: George Fenich

Kristin Malek, Ph.D., CMP, CED, DES, CHE is an event management extension specialist and assistant professor in the Hospitality, Restaurant, and Tourism Management program at the University of Nebraska. Dr. Malek worked in the hospitality industry for over 10 years before joining academia and still remains active with industry groups and consulting. She teaches and researches on meetings and events with a focus on engagement, cocreation, and ROI. She has been named as a Top 20 Meeting Industry Trendsetter by *Meetings Today Magazine* (2016), has been recognized as an Emerging Leader of the Year by PCMA (2018), won the International Educator of the Year award by IAEE (2022), and earned the prestigious Excellence in Teaching and Training Award by ICHRIE (2022). She has achieved designations as a certified meeting professional, certified event designer, digital event strategist, and certified hospitality educator.

Source: Kristin Malek

XXI

CHAPTER 1

INTRODUCTION TO THE MEETINGS, EXPOSITIONS, EVENTS, AND CONVENTIONS INDUSTRY (MEEC)

CONVENTIONS AND TRADE SHOWS ARE A SIGNIFICANT ELEMENT OF THE MEEC INDUSTRY

CHAPTER OBJECTIVES

- Understand the scope, roles, profit, direct and indirect economic impact of the MEEC industry—an industry founded on collaboration and partnerships.
- Define the fundamental concepts related to the MEEC industry.
- Establish the context of the global events industry's role as a part of the tourism and hospitality ecosystem.
- Explore the history, scope, scale, and collaborative aspects of the events industry.
- Articulate the significance of standards, certifications, best practices, codes of conduct, risk assessment, and ethical practices in the events industry.
- Present and highlight career definitions and opportunities for event professionals.
- Outline current and ongoing trends in the MEEC industry.

Contributed by Ann D. Summerall-Jabro. © Kendall Hunt Publishing Company.

The MEEC industry is intricate, comprised of interrelated components and collaborations that synergize to deliver diverse, tailored, and innovative experiences to specific audiences. Simultaneously, it is a multifaceted business encompassing numerous specializations. Professionals supporting the industry are highly skilled and creative multitaskers. They develop a diverse skill set and continually evolve their knowledge and technological tools for successful event planning, execution, and evaluation.

WHAT IS THE MEEC INDUSTRY?

The MEEC industry is vast, affecting nearly every facet of the hospitality sector. It includes travel and hospitality, convention and visitors' bureaus, corporate event planning, event venues, technology service providers, virtual platforms, and more. Events span a wide range, from sporting spectacles, such as the Olympics and Super Bowl, to social gatherings, such as family reunions and weddings, and from corporate functions, such as sales meetings and product launches, to business events, such as meetings, incentives, conventions, and exhibitions, hosted in on-site, digital, and hybrid environments.

The industry represents a series of interconnected complexities and multifaceted partnerships. Professionals supporting event planning and execution require a diverse skill set and knowledge base. They must grasp interpersonal dynamics and appreciate the significance of cultivating and maintaining relationships. Proficiency in the foundational aspects of in-person, digital, and hybrid event execution that align with organizational strategy, drive business outcomes, and promote human capital is crucial. Moreover, they should comprehend the direct and indirect economic impacts that events have on the communities they serve and know how to gauge and communicate these effects.

The industry thrives on relationship-building, fostering successful and enduring partnerships and collaborations throughout the industry and its supply chain. Consider the multitude of partnerships required to orchestrate a Super Bowl or a live music event: talent, transportation, signage, venue selection, catering, security, sanitation, and more. This dedication to collaboration is imperative for event success and a return on investment for all stakeholders—the participants, hosting organization, and event partners. Events need to stand out amidst competition by expressing a commitment to creating inviting environments through empathy, customization, and a devotion to constructing an experience that bolsters community and value.

The olympic and paralympic games are an example of one of the many aspects of the meec industry

In 2023, the **Events Industry Council (EIC)** unveiled commissioned findings on the global economic significance of business events, a study conducted by Oxford Economics. This marks the most recent and comprehensive global report. The key findings underscore the industry's scale, intricacy, and impact.

DIRECT IMPACTS OF GLOBAL BUSINESS EVENTS (2019):

- Business events engaged 1.6 billion participants across over 180 countries.
- Direct Expenditure (business sales): Business events generated a staggering $1.15 trillion in direct spending. This includes planning and executing, associated travel, and exhibitor expenditures.
- Direct Gross Domestic Product (GDP) and Employment: Globally, business events supported 10.9 million direct jobs and contributed $662.6 billion to direct GDP.
- Average Spending per Participant: This was $707.
- Leading Countries: The top 50 countries accounted for $1.11 trillion of direct spending in business events, constituting 96.5% of the global total.
- Country-Level Studies: Country-level analyses of business events activity, including U.S. research within this study, encompassed almost two-thirds of the estimated global total, providing a robust research foundation.

TOTAL IMPACTS OF GLOBAL BUSINESS EVENTS (2019):

Taking into account indirect and induced effects, business events underpinned a total global economic impact of

- $2.8 trillion in output (business sales);
- 27.5 million jobs;
- $1.6 trillion in GDP (representing a contribution to the global GDP);
- more output (business sales) than numerous prominent global sectors, including telecommunication equipment and air transport;
- total GDP of $1.62 trillion supported by global business events positioning the sector as the 13th largest economy worldwide;
- a direct GDP impact of $662.6 billion, making it the 21st largest economy globally; and
- $2.8 trillion in total output bolstered by global business events, indicating a 9.1% surge compared to 2017, the last year reported by the EIC.

For the complete report and regional fact sheets, visit the EIC website at www.eventscouncil.org.

INDUSTRY TERMINOLOGY AND PRACTICE

Gatherings involving two or more individuals have been commonly labeled "**meetings**." This term could encompass gatherings referred to as "conventions," "congresses," and "symposia," some of which could draw tens of thousands of people. When elements such as displays of materials or products are incorporated into a meeting, it gains an **exposition** or **exhibition** (trade show) component. Collectively, a meeting that integrates a trade show is designated as a **convention**. Upon the addition of sporting, social, or life cycle activities, the overarching term is "events." A broader and more comprehensive term is "gathering."

One should be mindful of how stakeholders or the intended audience will perceive the nomenclature assigned to a specific gathering. To enhance clarity, it becomes vital to explicitly define the scope of these generic terms when referencing impact data. As an illustration, in the case of the EIC Global Economic Significance Study of 2017, the following definition was introduced for the business events included in the study: "A gathering of 10 or more participants for a minimum of four hours in a contracted venue. This includes business events, but excludes social, educational (formal educational activities at primary, secondary, and university level education), and recreational activities, as well as consumer exhibitions."

The ensuing list of terms is significant for anyone engaged in the MEEC industry. These terms were developed by the terminology panel of the **Accepted Practices Exchange** (APEX), an initiative by the EIC. They constitute a small sampling of the multitude of words relevant to this industry. The complete glossary of terms used in the MEEC industry can be accessed online at www.eventscouncil.org. The terms and other content sourced from the EIC are consistently employed throughout this book, used with its permission.

> *Meeting:* An event where the primary activity of the participants is to attend educational and/or business sessions, participate in discussions, social functions, or attend other organized events, with no exhibit component.
>
> *Exposition:* A large public show, exhibit, or trade show. These events focus primarily on business-to-consumer (B2C) relationships. *Primarily used in North America.*
>
> *Exhibition:* An event at which products, services or promotional materials are displayed to attendees visiting exhibits on the show floor. These events focus primarily on business-to-business (B2B) relationships. Related terms: "trade fair," "trade show."
>
> *Event:* An organized occasion, such as a meeting, convention, exhibition, special event, gala dinner. An event is often composed of several different yet related functions.
>
> *Convention:* Gathering of delegates, representatives, and members of a membership or industry organization convened for a common purpose. Common features include educational sessions, committee meetings, social functions, and meetings to conduct the governance business of the organization. Conventions are typically recurring events with specific, established timing. Related terms: "congress," **"conference."**
>
> *Trade Show:* An exhibition of products and/or services held for members of a common or related industry. Not open to the public. Related terms: "exhibition."

Seminar: (a) Lecture and dialogue allowing participants to share experiences in a particular field under the guidance of an expert discussion leader. (b) A meeting or series of meetings of a small group of specialists with different skills who have a specific common interest and come together for training or learning purposes.

Workshop: (a) Meeting of several persons for intensive discussion. The workshop concept was developed to compensate for diverging views in a particular discipline or on a particular subject. (b) Informal and public session of free discussion organized between formal plenary sessions or commissions of a congress or of a conference, on either a subject chosen by the participants themselves or a special problem suggested by the organizers. (c) Training session in which participants, often through exercises, develop skills and knowledge in a given field.

Conference: (a) Participatory meeting designed for discussion, fact-finding, problem solving and consultation. (b) An event used by any organization to meet and exchange views, convey a message, open a debate, or give publicity to some area of opinion on a specific issue. No tradition, continuity, or timing is required. Conferences are usually short, have specific objectives, and are generally on a smaller scale than congresses or conventions. Related terms: "congress," "convention."

Clinic: Workshop-type educational experience where participants learn by doing.

Breakout Sessions: Small group sessions, panels, workshops, or presentations, offered concurrently within an event. Breakout sessions occur apart from the general session.

Assembly: (a) A general or formal meeting of an organization attended by representatives of its members to decide legislative direction, discuss policy matters, hold elections, or conduct governance business. An assembly usually observes certain rules of procedure for its meetings, generally prescribed in its articles and bylaws. (b) The process of erecting display component parts into a complete exhibit.

Congress: (a) The regular coming together of large groups of individuals, generally to discuss a particular subject. A congress will often last several days and have several simultaneous sessions. Congresses are usually annual, although some are less frequent. Most international or world congresses are the latter type; national congresses are more often annual. (b) European term for convention. Related terms: "conference," "convention." *Primarily used in Europe.*

Forum: Open discussion with audience, panel, and moderator. A meeting or part of a meeting set aside for an open discussion by recognized participants on subjects of public interest.

Symposium: A meeting of a number of experts in a particular field, at which papers are presented and discussed by specialists on particular subjects with a view to making recommendations concerning the problems under discussion.

Institute: In-depth instructional meeting providing intensive education on a particular subject.

Lecture: Informative and educational presentation to an audience.

Panel Discussion: Instructional technique using a group of people chosen to discuss a topic in the presence of an audience, or for a virtual event, such as a webinar.

Social Event: (a) An event to facilitate networking among attendees. (b) Life cycle celebration (e.g., a wedding, bar/bat mitzvah, anniversary, birthday).

THE ORGANIZATIONAL STRUCTURE OF THE TOURISM AND HOSPITALITY INDUSTRY: IN SUPPORT OF THE GLOBAL BUSINESS EVENTS INDUSTRY AND HOW MEEC FITS IN

The tourism and hospitality industry is multifaceted. The framework offered is meant to help provide a basic understanding and not intended to be an all-inclusive inventory. MEEC professionals rely on partners to support the successful outcomes of each event. To understand how MEEC is connected to the hospitality and service industry, one must understand the key segments of the tourism and hospitality industry itself.

It has four major segments: lodging, food and beverage (F&B), transportation and travel, and tourism and recreation.

LODGING

The lodging segment consists of all types of places where travelers may spend the night. These can include hotels, conference centers, resorts, motels, bed-and-breakfasts, Airbnb, Vrbo, accommodations, and college dormitories. The important characteristics of this segment are that they are available to the public and charge a fee for usage.

F&B

As the name would indicate, this segment contains two subsegments: food service and beverage operations. The former can include table service facilities that can be further broken down by price (high, medium, and low), type of service (i.e., luxury, quick service), or cuisine (i.e., American, East Asian, Italian). It also embraces other types of operations, including caterers and institutional operations (i.e., hospitals, schools, nursing homes). Beverage operations can also be broken down by price or type of service. This includes whether alcoholic beverages are served.

Transportation and Travel

This segment includes any means or modality that people use to get from one place to another, including walking. The better known subsegments include air, water, and ground transportation.

- *Air:* includes regularly scheduled airline carriers, such as Delta or American, and charter air service that can involve jets, propeller aircraft, and helicopters.
- *Water:* includes cruise ships, paddle wheelers, charter operations, ferries, and water taxis. Cruise ships are a significant element because they provide not only transportation but lodging, F&B, entertainment, and meeting facilities.
- *Ground:* includes private automobiles, taxis, limousines, ride-share services, jitneys, buses, trains, cog railways, cable cars, monorails, horse-drawn vehicles, and even elephants and camels.

Tourism and Recreation

This segment includes anything that attracts people to a destination.

- *Natural attractions:* includes national parks, mountains, seashores, lakes, forests, swamps, and rivers.
- *Person-made attractions:* includes things made or constructed by human beings, such as monuments, museums, theme parks, zoos, and aquariums.
- *Entertainment:* includes anything that provides entertainment value, such as movie theaters, playhouses, orchestras, bands, and festivals.

The categories have many overlaps: A hotel may be an attraction, such as the Broadmoor Resort in Colorado Springs. Hotels often have F&B outlets, attractions, and entertainment. Furthermore, some of the businesses mentioned cater to tourists, meeting-goers, and local residents alike.

Understanding the interactions and complexities of the hospitality and tourism industry helps explain why it is difficult to determine their size and scope. Until the late 1990s, the U.S. government, using its North American Industry Classification System (NAICS) codes, did not even track many elements of these industries. Because travel and tourism are not a single industry producing a single product, they cannot be measured accurately by a singular NAICS code. Travel and Tourism Satellite Accounts are a relatively new economic statistical method to more accurately measure the impact on the U.S. economy. Similarly, meetings and events cannot be captured by a single industry measure. EIC undertakes a research project every 3–4 years to measure the economic significance of the meetings and events industry.

HISTORY OF THE INDUSTRY

Gatherings, meetings, events, and conventions (of sorts) have been a part of people's lives since the earliest recorded history. Archeologists have found primitive ruins from ancient cultures that were used as meeting areas where citizens would gather to discuss common interests, such as government, war, hunting, or tribal celebrations. Once humans developed permanent settlements, each town or village had a public meeting area, often called a "town square," where residents could meet, talk, and celebrate. Under the leadership of Alexander the Great, over half a million people traveled to what was then Ephesus (now Turkey) to see exhibitions that included acrobats, magicians, animal trainers, and jugglers. In Rome, the forum was a type of organized meeting to discuss politics and decide the fate of the country. Ancient Rome had the Coliseum, which was the site of major sporting events, such as gladiatorial contests. Think about it—someone had to organize them! Using excellent roadways, the Romans were able to establish trade markets to entice people to visit their cities. Old England had stories of King Arthur's Round Table, another example of a meeting to discuss the trials and tribulations of the day. Religious gatherings of various faiths and pilgrimages are examples of ancient religious meetings and festivals. The Olympics began as an ancient sporting event that was organized as similar events are today. World's Fairs and Expositions are still another piece of the MEEC industry.

The First Continental Congress in Philadelphia is an example of a "formal meeting," to decide the governance of the 13 colonies. Political conventions have a long history in the United States and are part of the MEEC industry. U.S. people have also created festivals and celebrations of every sort. Mardi Gras in New Orleans and events like it are also a part of the MEEC industry.

Today, structures supporting the MEEC industry are integral parts of major cities. It is a well-known fact that to be considered a *world class city*, a community must have a convention center and a stadium/arena for sports and events. All of the largest cities have these venues, including New York City, Washington DC, Barcelona, Chicago, London, Moscow, Pretoria, and Hong Kong. These public facilities attract out-of-town attendees for conventions and events and are an important economic driver for the community.

Although the history of meetings is long, storied, and varied, meeting planning as a recognized profession and established set of practices is a more recent development. The first U.S. academic program was developed and approved by the state of Colorado in September 1976 and implemented by Metropolitan State College (now a university) in Denver. It was closely followed by the program at Northeastern Oklahoma University in Tahlequah. In 1979, Patti Shock started hotel convention service management and meeting planning classes at Georgia State University. In 1983, trade show classes were added with the financial support of the National Association of Exposition Managers (now the International Association of Exhibitions and Events—IAEE) and International Association of Fairs and Expositions. Today, almost 700 academic programs worldwide and over 150 in the United States alone have MEEC programs.

One factor that contributed to the rapid development of both industry education and academic programs during the 1980s was the development and implementation of the Certified Meeting Professional (CMP) examination and designation by the Convention Liaison Council (now the EIC). It gives both status and credence to the person who achieves it. Additional certificate programs have followed, including the following:

- American Hotel and Lodging Educational Institute Certified Hotel Administrator and Certified Hospitality Facilities Executive;
- American Society of Association Executives Certified Association Executive;
- Association of Collegiate Conference and Events Directors—International Collegiate Conference and Events professional Certification and One-Stop Shop Certification;
- Association for Destination Management Executives Destination Management Certified Professional;
- Destinations International Certified Destination Management Executive;
- EIC's CMP and Certified Meeting Professional healthcare subspecialty (CMP-HC) program;
- Hotel Sales and Marketing Association International Certified Hospitality Revenue; Management Executive, Certified Hospitality Digital Marketer, Certified in Hospitality Business Acumen;
- IAEE Certified in Exhibition Management;
- International Association of Venue Managers Certified Venue Executive and Certified Venue Professional;
- International Live Events Association Certified Special Events Professional;
- Meeting Professionals International Certificate in Meeting Management;
- National Association for Catering & Events Certified Professional in Catering and Events;
- National Speakers Association Certified Speaking Professional;
- Professional Convention Management Association Digital Event Strategist Certification;
- Religious Conference Management Association Certified Faith-Based Meeting Professional;
- Society for Incentive Travel Excellence Certified Incentive Specialist and Certified Incentive Travel Professional; and
- Society of Government Meeting Professionals Certified Government Meeting Professional.

The organization now known as the "Event Industry Council" was founded in New York in 1949 by four organizations: the American Society of Association Executives (ASAE), American Hotel and Motel Association (now the American Hotel Lodging Association), Hotel (now Hospitality) Sales and Marketing

Association International (HSMAI), and International Association of Convention and Visitor Bureaus (now Destinations International). EIC is a cross-industry effort and has led its constituent organizations in the professionalizing of the industry through certification, establishing best practices, and education.

AMC Institute
American Hotel & Lodging Association (AH&LA)
ASAE & The Center for Association Leadership (ASAE & The Center)
Association of Collegiate Conference and Events Directors-International (ACCED-I)
Association of Destination Management Executives International (ADMEI)
Convention Sales Professionals International (CSPI)
Corporate Event Marketing Association (CEMA)
Destinations International
Event Service Professionals Association (ESPA)
Exhibition Services & Contractors Association (ESCA)
Federacion De Entidades Organizadoras De Congresos Y Afines De America Latina (COCAL)
Financial & Insurance Conference Professionals (FICP)
Hospitality Sales & Marketing Association International (HSMAI)
IACC
Incentive Research Foundation
International Association of Exhibitions & Events (IAEE)
International Association of Professional Congress Organisers (IAPCO)
International Association of Speakers Bureaus (IASB)
International Association of Venue Managers (IAVM)
International Congress and Convention Association (ICCA)
International Exhibition Logistics Association (IELA)
International Live Events Association (ILEA)
Meeting Professionals International (MPI)
National Association for Catering and Events (NACE)
National Coalition of Black Meeting Professionals (NCBMP)
National Speakers Association (NSA)
Professional Convention Management Association (PCMA)
Religious Conference Management Association (RCMA)
Society for Incentive Travel Excellence (SITE)
Society of Government Meeting Professionals (SGMP)
Society of Independent Show Organizers (SISO)
Southern African Association for the Conference Industry (SAACI)
U.S. Travel Association (U.S. Travel)

FIGURE 1:
EIC Member Organizations

In 1895, the basis of today's convention and visitor bureaus (CVBs)—also called "destination marketing organizations" (DMOs)—was put forth when journalist Milton Carmichael suggested in *The Detroit Journal* that local businessmen get together to promote the city as a convention destination and represent it and its many hotels to bid for that business. Shortly thereafter, the Detroit Convention and Businessmen's League was conceived to do just that. Carmichael was the head of the group that evolved into the Detroit Metro CVB that is now *VisitDetroit*.

The role of CVBs has changed over time. As in Detroit, most began by trying to attract only conventions and business meetings. Later, they realized leisure visitors were an important source of business and added the "V" to the name. Today, virtually every city in the United States and Canada, and many throughout the world, has a CVB, DMO or convention and visitors association (CVA). The CVBs, DMOs, and CVAs are membership organizations that help promote tourism, meetings, and related business for their cities. In some international destinations, the CVB is a division of government. Many CVBs have now evolved to not only market but help develop and manage tourism in their destinations. In this text, CVB and DMO are synonymous and interchangeable.

EVOLUTION AND MATURATION OF THE MEEC INDUSTRY

The textbook *Planning and Management of Meetings, Expositions, Events, and Conventions,* 1st edition, by George Fenich, serves as the foundation for the content in the next section.

As an industry evolves and matures, it has an increasing need to formalize a set of competency standards to which professionals must adhere, such as law and accounting. Until recently, no common set of knowledge, skills, and abilities (**KSAs**) existed for event professionals. As the global business events industry continues to adapt and transform, they need engage in continuing education to ensure the relevance and reliability of their skills and experiences.

This dearth of standards changed in 2011 with the development of several competency standards, all building off a common platform—the **Meetings and Business Events Competency Standards** (MBECS), Canadian Human Resources Council Competency Standards, and CMP International Standards. Although all are slightly different for their individual purposes, they all contain a similar set of knowledge, skills, and ability statements required of event professionals at the different levels of position or purpose. Each will be addressed in separate sections of this chapter along with correlating resources available to the professional through certifications and industry associations.

MBECS

Using MBECS as an example, the standards are divided into 12 domains or blocks with 33 skills and almost 100 subskills or subsegments.

> **A. STRATEGIC PLANNING**
> 1. Manage Strategic Plan for Meeting or Event
> 2. Develop Sustainability Plan for Meeting or Event
> 3. Measure Value of Meeting or Business Event
>
> **B. PROJECT MANAGEMENT**
> 4. Plan Meeting or Event
> 5. Manage Meeting or Event Project

C. RISK MANAGEMENT
  6. Manage Risk Management Plan

D. FINANCIAL MANAGEMENT
  7. Develop Financial Resources
  8. Manage Budget
  9. Manage Monetary Transactions

E. ADMINISTRATION
  10. Perform Administrative Tasks

F. HUMAN RESOURCES
  11. Manage Human Resource Plan
  12. Acquire Staff and Volunteers
  13. Train Staff and Volunteers
  14. Manage Workforce Relations

G. STAKEHOLDER MANAGEMENT
  15. Manage Stakeholder Relationships

H. MEETING OR EVENT DESIGN
  16. Design Program
  17. Engage Speakers and Performers
  18. Coordinate Food and Beverage
  19. Design Environment
  20. Manage Technical Production
  21. Develop Plan for Managing Movement of People

I. SITE MANAGEMENT
  22. Select Site
  23. Design Site Layout
  24. Manage Meeting or Event Site
  25. Manage On-site Communications

J. MARKETING
  26. Manage Marketing Plan
  27. Manage Marketing Materials
  28. Manage Meeting or Event Merchandise
  29. Promote Meeting or Event
  30. Contribute to Public Relations Activities
  31. Manage Sales Activities

K. PROFESSIONALISM
  32. Exhibit Professional Behavior

L. COMMUNICATIONS
  33. Conduct Business Communications

MEETINGS, EXPOSITIONS, EVENTS, AND CONVENTIONS

CMP INTERNATIONAL STANDARDS (CMP-IS)

The **CMP International Standards (CMP-IS)** define the exam leading to the CMP credential. Developing these common standards marked a milestone in the MEEC industry. They represent the first time that the industry knowledge base has been codified. This has been a great advancement for the profession, the individuals who work in it, and academics, students, and individuals who train the next generation of professionals. The CMP International Standards are divided into nine domains or blocks with 28 skills and almost 100 subskills.

The CMP program was launched in 1985 to enhance professionals' knowledge and performance, promote the status and credibility of the profession, and advance uniform standards of practice. Today, it is recognized globally as the badge of excellence in the industry. The qualifications for certification are based on professional experience, education, and a rigorous exam.

Benefits of CMP Certification

Meeting planners who hold the CMP earn (on average) more than $10,000 annually than their noncertified counterparts. CMP certification is the mark of excellence in comprehensive events management. It opens the door to better and more opportunities. Client expectations for meetings are higher than ever, and recruiters and prospective employers recognize CMP certification in our growing industry.

Created by and for Meeting Professionals

The CMP exam was developed and is maintained by meeting professionals worldwide who volunteer their time to ensure that the program reflects the best practices in the field. More than 11,000 professionals in 55 countries hold the CMP designation. This unique community represents every sector of the industry—from corporations and associations to government and institutional organizations.

The CMP program aims to increase professionalism in all sectors of the industry by

- identifying a comprehensive body of knowledge in the meeting management profession.
- promoting industry standards, practices, and ethics.
- stimulating the advancement of the art and science of meeting management.

- increasing the value of CMPs to their employers.
- maximizing the value received from the products and services provided by CMPs.

The CMP-HC subspecialty

The CMP-HC program was launched in 2014 to address the needs of a growing segment of CMPs who manage the production of meetings in the healthcare industry. Those seeking it must first pass the CMP exam. The CMP-HC credential was designed to validate CMPs who have demonstrated a superior understanding and mastery of the specific regulations, laws, and best practices that must be followed when conducting a healthcare-focused meeting.

DOMAIN A: STRATEGIC PLANNING
- SKILL 1 Create Strategic Plan for Meeting or Event
- SKILL 2 Develop Sustainability Plan for Meeting or Event
- SKILL 3 Develop Business Continuity or Long-Term Viability Plan of Meeting or Event

DOMAIN B: PROJECT MANAGEMENT
- SKILL 4 Plan Meeting or Event Project
- SKILL 5 Manage Meeting or Event Project

DOMAIN C: RISK MANAGEMENT
- SKILL 6 Manage Risk Management Plan

DOMAIN D: FINANCIAL MANAGEMENT
- SKILL 7 Manage Event Funding and Financial Resources
- SKILL 8 Manage Budget
- SKILL 9 Manage Monetary Transactions

DOMAIN E: HUMAN RESOURCES
- SKILL 10 Recruit Staff and Volunteers
- SKILL 11 Train Staff and Volunteers

DOMAIN F: STAKEHOLDER MANAGEMENT
- SKILL 12 Manage Stakeholder Relationships

DOMAIN G: MEETING OR EVENT DESIGN

- SKILL 13 Develop Program
- SKILL 14 Engage Speakers and Performers
- SKILL 15 Coordinate Food and Beverage Services
- SKILL 16 Design Environment
- SKILL 17 Manage Audiovisual and Technical Production
- SKILL 18 Develop Plan for Managing Movement of Attendees

DOMAIN H: SITE MANAGEMENT

- SKILL 19 Select Site
- SKILL 20 Design Site Layout
- SKILL 21 Manage Meeting or Event Site
- SKILL 22 Manage On-Site Communications

DOMAIN I: MARKETING

- SKILL 23 Manage Marketing Plan
- SKILL 24 Create and Manage Marketing Materials
- SKILL 25 Create and Manage Meeting or Event Merchandise
- SKILL 26 Promote Meeting or Event
- SKILL 27 Contribute to Public Relations Activities
- SKILL 28 Manage Meeting-Related Sales Activities

USE OF THE MBECS AND CMP INTERNATIONAL STANDARDS

Uses for Event Professionals

These competencies represent all the KSAs an event professional needs to acquire, and be proficient in, during their career. Innovations in different aspects of the KSAs requires continuous education to conform to best practices. Industry professionals can perform a personal skills assessment of these standards and skills at which they are adept and those that they are not. The resulting gap analysis can guide their professional and personal development. MBECS and the CMP International Standards can also help plot career paths. Being able to provide an assessment that shows a broad mastery of the subject will enhance employability and mobility across sectors and countries. This also allows an industry professional to promote the attainment of this knowledge and associated skills to employers or clients.

Standards are of great value to employers and managers. They can aid in developing job descriptions and job specifications. This leads to improvements in determining workforce requirements and producing worker solicitations. The standards can also help in developing a sequence of training for employees as well as a basis for performance assessment and feedback.

Uses for the Academic Community

These standards provide the internationally accepted basis for developing courses of study and their requisite content. It is up to a given program or institution to determine how the content is delivered: meetings/events-specific courses, business courses, general education, or a combination. The significant advantage of using a standard is that it is not prescriptive: One size does not fit all. Existing programs can benchmark themselves against the standards with resulting global recognition. These standards also provide a platform for dealing with governmental authorities and accrediting bodies. Using MBECS, a program can show the relevance of its course offerings and justify the content based on an international body of knowledge. Students can use the standards to develop their educational pathways, validate their employability to recruiters, and determine which educational programs best meet their learning needs. For academics, the standards can help delineate areas or topics that need research.

Uses for Associations

First and foremost, standards provide recognition of the KSAs required by the industry. This can help guide in developing program content and delivery that is consistent with international standards. They can also be used by the members of an association to determine their educational or professional development needs and how the association can best fulfill those needs.

IN SUPPORT OF THE INDUSTRY

EIC'S APEX COMMISSION

Throughout this book, you will hear about EIC (formerly the Convention Industry Council) and its APEX.

EIC is at the forefront of efforts to advance the MEEC industry. It represents a broad cross-section of the industry with more than 30 related associations as members, representing more than 103,500 individuals and more than 19,000 firms and properties. Formed in 1949, it provides a forum for member organizations to advance the industry. It facilitates this by enabling the exchange of information among members via developing programs to promote professionalism and educating the public on the industry's profound economic impact. The council provides an impartial and inclusive forum for the APEX initiative and developing accepted practices.

APEX brings together stakeholders in developing and implementing industrywide accepted practices to create and enhance efficiencies, solve common problems, and address industry issues. APEX also creates resources and tools to address these issues, such as education, white papers, and sample documents.

Some of the results of accepted practices implementation include the following:

- time and cost savings,
- easier communication and data sharing,
- enhanced customer service,
- streamlined systems and processes,
- less duplication of efforts and increased operational efficiencies,
- better educated and more professional employees, and
- solutions to common issues and problems.

CMP CODE OF ETHICS

EIC has published the CMP Code of Ethics, available with permission for your reference.

It establishes basic standards of values and conduct for applicants and CMPs; it applies only to CMPs.

As a recipient of the CMP designation by the EIC ("Certificant"), a CMP must pledge to

- maintain exemplary standards of professional conduct at all times.
- actively model and encourage the integration of ethics into all aspects of the performance of my duties.
- perform my responsibilities in accordance with the laws and regulations of the local, state, or national governments under which I reside.
- maintain the confidentiality of all privileged information, including the identity or personal information of other CMP candidates and the contents of the CMP examination, except when required to do so by law or by court order.
- never use my position for undue personal gain and to promptly disclose to appropriate parties all potential and actual conflicts of interest.
- communicate all relevant information to my employer in a truthful and accurate manner in order to facilitate the execution of my fiduciary responsibilities.
- not use the CMP designation or service mark in any way other than that which is authorized by the Events Industry Council, and to immediately cease using the designation should I fail to maintain the requirements of the CMP certification or for any other reason have my certification revoked, including payment of required fees.
- to abide by all policies and procedures of the CMP program as outlined in the CMP Handbook or those that may be set by the CMP Governance Commission in the future.
- to be truthful in all information provided to the Events Industry Council in all applications and recertification applications at all times.

Any action of a certificant or applicant that compromises the reliability of the certification process may be subject to the process described by the procedures.

CAREERS IN AND AROUND THE MEEC INDUSTRY

The MEEC industry is a vibrant, dynamic, and exciting part of the travel, tourism, and hospitality industry.

Wedding planning is a career in MEEC

Some of the critical aspects are strategic planning and visioning, business acumen (financial and people management, legalities and risk management, **sales and marketing**, ethics, risk management, safety and security and duty of care), execution of ideas into concepts, and knowledge of adult learning techniques. In addition to knowledge and ability for preparing and delivering virtual, hybrid, and on-site meetings, industry professionals must know more about sustainability, social impact, and technology for meetings and events.

Many careers in MEEC involve multiple aspects of the tourism and hospitality industry. For example, someone who works in convention or group sales in a facility must interface with, be knowledgeable about, and manage people who work with guest rooms, front desk, F&B, catering, and all the meeting facilities. EIC members are actively developing tools and resources to support the careers and wellness of our workforce.

American Hotel and Lodging Association (AHLA) Career Development Resources

AHLA's resources, supported by the AHLA Foundation, include the following:

- apprenticeship and empowering youth programs,
- debt-free college program, career center, and
- career development program.

ASAE Association Career HQ

ASAE's Career headquarter site includes the following:

- job summaries and salaries;
- coaching, mentoring, and other services;
- article, webinar, and video collections; and
- resources for employers.

Association of Collegiate Conference and Events Directors—International (ACCED-I) Career Center

ACCED-I's Career Center resources include the following:

- resume tips and review,
- interviewing recommendations,
- resources for networking in the digital world, and
- career advancement and coaching.

Association Management Company (AMC) Institute Talent Center

AMC's Talent Center resources include the following:

- AMC career paths,
- job seeker resources,
- a day in the life video series, and
- Association Management Company 101.

Financial & Insurance Conference Professionals (FICP) Mentorship Programme

FICP's mentorship program resources include the following:

- FICP Hospitality partner mentorship program webinar, and
- mentor and mentee interest form.

Hospitality, Sales, & Marketing Association International (HSMAI)

HSMAI's foundation offers an interviewing resource guide, including the following:

- insights for interviews: hospitality sales,
- insights for interviews: hospitality revenue management, and
- insights for interviews: hospitality digital marketing.

IACC Scholarships and Internships

IACC offers the following programs:

- student scholarships,
- global internships, and
- job opportunities.

Incentive Research Foundation (IRF)

Research reports from IRF include the following:

- wellness in meetings and incentives travel study, and
- solving the wellness engagement challenge using mobile apps.

IAEE Career Center

IAEE's Career Center resources include the following:

- job search tools,
- employer/recruiter resources,
- getting started in exhibitions and events, andprofessional development resources.

International Association of Venue Managers (IAVM) Career and Learning Resources

IAVM's resources include the following:

- career center,
- mentor program,
- college partnership program, and
- job shadowing program.

Meeting Professionals International (MPI) Resources

MPI's well-being resources include the following:

- a free white paper on quarantine survival strategies;
- tips for self-care from the World Health Organization;
- a list of regional and national crisis hotlines; and
- resources for financial, mental, and physical well-being.

PCMA Recovery Discovery

PCMA's Recovery Discovery campaign includes the following:

- COVID-19 Recovery Dashboard,
- Accelerating Reskilling PCMA Foundation Donation Campaign,
- Business Events Compass: Insights and Strategies for the Next Normal, and
- Convening Asia Pacific Global Recovery Forum.

Society of Incentive Travel Excellence (SITE)

SITE's career center includes the following:

- resume and interviewing recommendations, and
- career advancement and digital networking resources.

Roles Within the Global Business Event Industry and Organizations That Support These Subspecialties

Business Events Strategist/Meeting Professional: Organizes meetings and other gatherings for companies, corporations, and associations. These can include a small board of directors meeting, a stockholders meeting, new product introductions and training, educational seminars, and regional or national conventions. Corporate meeting/event planners fall into this category.

Exhibition Manager: organizes and manages trade shows.

Sales Executives/Hotel or Conference Center Sales: The majority of sales and convention or catering services positions in hotels and conference centers deal with groups, and MEEC covers most of those groups.

F&B Manager/Restaurant Sales: Although most people think of restaurants as attracting walk-in clientele, many rely heavily on the MEEC industry for business. F&B venues employ significant numbers of people on their group sales staff. In New Orleans, Arnaud's and Emeril's, for example, have group or convention sales teams.

Entertainment/Sporting Venue Sales & Services: Although these places primarily attract individual patrons, most also devote much time and effort to selling, providing space for, and producing events for groups. These off-site venues are often good alternatives for experiential learning.

Destination Management Professional: **A destination management company** (DMC) functions as the "local expert" for companies and associations in organizing gatherings and events, arranging, and supervising transportation, and securing entertainers. People employed for DMCs usually work in either sales or production.

Hotel Operations: Hotels are one of the primary locations where MEEC events are held, using ballrooms, meeting rooms, breakout rooms, and so on, for their gatherings along with sleeping rooms and F&B for their attendees. The hotel departments that deal with the MEEC industry are sales, catering, and convention services.

Convention Centers/Facilities Management: These venues include dedicated facilities, such as McCormick Place in Chicago, the Jacob K. Javits Convention Center in New York, the Congress Center Messe in Frankfurt Germany and the Canton Fair in Guangzhou, China—the world's biggest.

Venue Management/Multipurpose Venues: The venues include arenas such as the Superdome in New Orleans or the Astrodome in Houston. Careers are often found in sales or operations.

Exposition Services Contractors: If you like to build things or have thought about being an engineer or architect, you should consider being an exposition services contractor (ESC). ESCs design and erect the booths, backdrops, staging, etc. for exhibitions, meetings, and conventions. One may have created the decorations and backdrops for your school prom. Again, career paths exist in sales and production and increasingly in design of sustainable products and services.

CVB DMOs: CVBs represent a wide range of MEEC companies and market the destination to business and leisure travelers. CVBs have many departments and careers, including convention sales, tourism sales, housing bureaus, convention services, marketing, research, and member services.

Special Events Professional: These specialize in organizing events such as galas and award ceremonies. They are highly creative and often design unique experiences for their clients. They may be hired by other event professionals to design a special event within a larger program, such as an awards ceremony within an annual conference.

Housing Specialists and Site Selection Specialists: A housing bureau coordinates group reservations and manages hotel rooming blocks on behalf of the event organizers. Site selection specialists source hotels and venues for events, including managing the requests for proposals and negotiating and facilitating contracts on behalf of their clients. Career opportunities in these areas include reservations agents and site selection associates.

Virtual and Digital Event Strategist: These specialize in designing and executing events that include virtual or digital elements. Careers include production specialists, digital platform specialists, developers, and graphic designers. As more in-person events include hybrid elements, having skills in this area are beneficial for all event professionals.

Key Event Stakeholder Groups: It is often said that MEEC is a "relationship industry," that is, one built on who you know and with whom you do business. As in many industries, we depend on those we know to help us learn and grow and to provide accurate information. These relationships are built over time and always with the understanding that first and foremost, ethical business practices will be the most important aspect of how we relate.

Think for just a moment about all the individuals and businesses involved in the execution of a single meeting or event. They could include the following:

The Meeting Sponsor

- association or corporation sponsor; marketing leadership;
- staff specialists in departments that include marketing, governance and government affairs, education/professional development/training, membership, information technology, and accreditation;
- meeting professional;
- executive director or chief executive officer;
- administrative and logistical support and others who staff call centers, copy materials, process registrations, manage human resources, control purchasing, and more;
- volunteer leadership, board of directors, committees; and
- strategic partners and sponsors.

The Facility

- owners
- executive staff, including general manager, revenue manager, resident or hotel manager, directors of sales, marketing, convention services, catering, housekeeping, engineering, maintenance, purchasing, human resources, F&B, front office operations, sustainability, social responsibility, and security; and·
- thousands of other full- and part-time, year-round, and seasonal staff: groundskeepers, animal handlers, housekeepers, food servers (for banquets, room service, or outlets), maintenance, security, and engineering.

The Destination

- CVB/DMO (president, directors of sales, marketing, convention services, membership, registration, social responsibility, and all support staff);
- restaurants;
- attractions;
- off-site venues;
- theaters (movie and legitimate);
- copy and printing companies;
- transportation (buses, airport shuttles, taxicabs, limousines);
- airport concessions;
- doctors, medical personnel, and emergency workers;
- pharmacies;
- florists;
- DMCs;
- audiovisual suppliers;
- general services contractors;
- specialty services contractors;
- dry cleaners and tailors;
- city, county, and state employees; and
- IT division and telecommunications department.

All Others Who Provide Services for Meetings

- talent (entertainers, disc jockeys, bands, magicians),
- education (speakers, trainers, facilitators),
- sound and lighting,
- transportation (air, rail, car, boat, and travel agencies),
- printing,
- shipping,

CHAPTER 1   INTRODUCTION TO THE MEETINGS, EXPOSITIONS, EVENTS, AND CONVENTIONS INDUSTRY (MEEC)

- promotional products,
- off-property F&B,
- translators for those who speak American Sign Language and other languages,
- Americans with Disabilities Act equipment,
- carpentry,
- national sales (hotels, conference centers), and
- third-party or independent meeting planners.

Even the president of the United States and Congress impact our industry by determining trade regulations, travel restrictions, security issues, visa requirements, and whether our country goes to war.

Is there anyone who does not have some influence on the meetings and events industry? A case can be made that every person has an impact, in some way, on each and every meeting—even those meetings of two or three that take place in an office or restaurant. Take a few minutes and add to these jobs or functions that might affect a meeting. Then think again. Also, create a career pathway for at least one of these careers.

WHICH CAREER IS RIGHT FOR YOU?

The following are some of the career planning questions you might ask yourself to determine if this may be the right profession for you:

- Do you like to plan work or social events, or adjust your day, down to the last detail, ensuring everything is locked in?
- Do you have and regularly update a date book or Outlook or Google calendar that includes everything you need to do for weeks or even months into the future?
- Have any of the activities or skills outlined in this chapter struck a chord and made you say, "this sounds like me" or "I have that ability or strength" and "I want to be part of that"?
- Do you ask good questions, rarely taking anything as a given? Do you think about contingencies or what if X happened? How would I adjust?
- Do you thrive in environments where multiple tasks and diverse people are under your direction and control on different projects concurrently?

If you answered "yes" to some of these questions, you may just have the aptitude to be a good event professional.

TRENDS IN 2023

In 2023, meetings and events are not just face-to-face gatherings solely to exchange business information. Rather, they are enriching, one-of-a-kind experiences where attendees create community engagement and drive brand awareness and loyalty.

In this section, we will focus on the following key areas: the impact of unforeseen calamities; the transforming role of technology, content and community; the pivot from event logistics to event strategists; and sustainability and social impact.

THE IMPACT OF UNFORESEEN CALAMITIES

Responding to Environmental, Social, and Cultural Occurrences

Globalization has generated an interdependency on goods and services that allows for economies of scale and greater efficiencies. However, political unrest in one country may impact another country's ability to move product seamlessly across borders. Weather conditions may impact livestock, crops, and transport of these goods. Various health crises, some of which originate outside the United States, create significant disruption in supply chain vendors and lead to quarantine. COVID-19 created unprecedent disruption and job loss and propelled innovation and the use of new technologies in our industry. The pandemic caused sector job losses in the millions, decreased travel, canceled and postponed meetings and events, closed businesses, and closed borders across the global events ecosystem. Recovery requires a commitment to unity, adaptation, and transformation. In response, the EIC, a global federation of more than 30 member organizations, formed the APEX COVID-19 Business Recovery Task Force. Its work groups are focused on aggregating and curating accepted practices across the events ecosystem and providing a framework for recovery and resilience as the industry adapts to its most significant disruption. Its work is grounded in principles for recovery that are based on the Sustainable Development Goals. This guidance is intended to be global. The work continues to evolve through regional workshops led by task force members to ensure it is either applicable or customized to each region.

https://www.eventscouncil.org/Industry-Insights/Principles-for-Recovery

FIGURE 2: EIC Principles for Recovery

Changes to Event Protocols and Design in Response to Unforeseen Calamities

Event professionals have had a long-standing commitment to health and safety. The frequency, visibility, and communication of cleaning and sanitization practices has increased. Event organizers partner with other providers to develop protocols that support safe social engagement and leverage technology to provide digital options for event participation.

Increase in Advocacy for the Events Industry's Workforce

The need to advocate on behalf of our industry's workforce was enhanced during the pandemic and is now commonplace. Coordinated efforts and campaigns have been developed to encourage our industry to speak with a unified voice to emphasize to governments around the world about the importance of supporting it. This will not only benefit our industry but support all industries that depend on the power of human connections to accelerate the global economic recovery.

TRANSFORMING ROLE OF TECHNOLOGY

Increased Technology Use for Engagement

Technology use in the events industry continues to evolve from production technology to human-centered engagement technology, with significant innovations in virtual meeting software packages and enhancements to existing packages, such as Zoom, GoogleMeet, and Microsoft Teams. Great care is being taken to develop exceptional experiences for participants by leveraging technology to drive engagement with event content, facilitate networking, and amaze participants through creative and inspiring design. Event professionals are also taking into consideration the "second screen," the personal devices that attendees carry to provide far more than a simple schedule at a glance. These can also integrate location-based wayfinding in a trade show, encourage connections with exhibitors and sponsors through gamification, and provide extended learning opportunities.

The Transition to Omnichannel Events

Innovations in technology, participant needs, and event planners' sophistication has propelled event professionals to understand and promote omnichannel experiences for participants, who selected one option: in-person, digital/virtual, or hybrid (combining elements of both). More recently, events are being described as omnichannel, where participants can seamlessly transition between in-person or digital experiences. This approach is beneficial for participants on limited budgets, with conflicting schedules and work commitments, and facing times of uncertainty. Omnichannel events help to encourage participation. As a result of this, event venues will likely need to continue to expand wireless internet capabilities and security.

Data Security, Trust, and Responsibility

Event professionals collect data from participants through registration processes, travel reservations, and integrations of event apps with social media platforms. With the rise of new technologies and mobile applications in events, such as facial recognition software, event professionals need to take measures to ensure data security and compliance with all applicable regulations. Given that data privacy and security regulations vary by jurisdiction, they need to consider the regulations that apply to not only the event location but also all the jurisdictions that participants reside. This is important from a legal compliance aspect and also builds trust with stakeholders.

Content and Community

An important shift in the last decade has been toward community-led content development. This means that it is no longer simply the event organizers, speakers, and facilitators determining the content and marketing. Participants are increasingly filling this role. More specifically, social media engagement during an event provides crowd-sourced context for the information shared by presenters. This form of participation also helps create a community and promote the event and the ability to connect with the social networks of their participants.

PIVOT FROM EVENT LOGISTICS TO EVENT STRATEGISTS

Event professionals are also continuing to increase their value to their organizations by serving as event strategists, in addition to being well versed in logistics. This important shift means that event professionals and their supplier partners are focusing on the organization's strategic objectives and designing experiences and services that support these goals.

SUSTAINABILITY AND SOCIAL IMPACT

The Sustainable Development Goals are an important framework for event professionals. They provide guidance on how we can support achieving our goals through socially and environmentally responsible practices. The EIC Sustainable Event Standards, which assess events and suppliers on a wide range of sustainability criteria in support of environmental and social responsibility, provide specific guidance for event organizers and suppliers to improve their sustainability impacts.

Seven standards represent different sectors of the industry: event organizer, accommodations, A/V and production, destination, exhibitions, F&B, and venue.

| Event Planner | Accommodations | Audio Visual & Production | Destination | Exhibitions | Food and Beverage | Venue |

© Kendall Hunt Publishing Company

SUSTAINABILITY

Sustainability in the events industry has greatly evolved in the past 10 years, with considerable opportunity for us to improve. Focus areas include evolving to a circular economy approach for materials, managing environmental impacts of food choices and food waste, and accelerating toward carbon neutrality.

DIVERSITY, EQUITY, INCLUSION, AND ACCESSIBILITY

As an industry, we strive to create environments that are welcoming for all. Although designing inclusive events is neither new nor a trend, it is included here as a priority area. Event professionals are becoming better able to understand how their unconscious bias affects the way they design events and marketing and actively rethinking how elements can be designed to encourage diversity, equity, inclusion, and accessibility. This is also a focus area in the development of meaningful and equitable career pathways in our industry.

SOCIAL IMPACT

Events are also being increasingly designed and recognized for their social impact. Although you may first think of this as including a community service project, it can be much broader. For example, events have a social impact on a community by creating jobs and opportunities to learn and make new connections. Many venues are also supporting their communities as emergency evacuation centers or temporary hospitals during a crisis.

CASE STUDY A CHALLENGING SPECIAL EVENT: UNIVERSITY PRESIDENT INAUGURATION PREPARED BY COMMITTEE

ABOUT ROBERT MORRIS UNIVERSITY

Robert Morris University (RMU) is steeped in tradition, change and growth. Founded as the Pittsburgh School of Accountancy in 1921 in downtown Pittsburgh, it soon expanded its popular curriculum to include business and secretarial studies and evolved to offer graduate degrees and achieve college and university status. Numerous factors contributed to transitioning to a university in 2002, including the diversification of curriculum to five schools and the development and execution of three doctoral programs: communications and information systems, education, and engineering (later a DNP in nursing). During this time of continuous growth, on-site events, such as meetings, dinners, and receptions, were planned and executed by the Conference and Facility Services (CFS) unit. CFS supported university events, such as commencement exercises, but was not positioned as a profit center or additional revenue stream. More recently, RMU outsourced to a unit focused on bringing meetings, exhibitions, and events on campus for the explicit purpose of generating revenue for a 2,400-seat arena and 300-seat meeting room with additional meeting facilities that were not used much after May graduation through the August Convocation. The team was charged with identifying other ways the university could serve a niche market in the MEEC industry over the years. The growth of university on-campus spaces for meetings and events is discussed in more detail in Chapter 4.

Special Events at RMU

Commencement exercises and presidential inaugurations are special events in the life of a university. A special event is one marked by unique circumstances and conditions. Commencement exercises were the major events that occurred at RMU's Sewall Center annually. A commencement is a special event guided by a protocol established by the American Council on Education (ACE). Academic participants wear special regalia defined by the Academic Costume Code and Academic Ceremony Guide, and various ceremonies occur within the larger ceremony, such as hooding of doctoral and masters' degree-confirmed students, awarding of honor cords and stoles, medals and medallions, and awarding of diplomas. Two individuals cochaired the commencement committee and were involved in planning the May event in a space that served primarily as the University's Division I basketball arena. Sewall Center's capacity was 2,400, or 3,200 when seating could be provided on the floor and stage areas. Registrar Frank Perry and his team of three planned all university-related events before 2004, and the dean of academic services, Larry Tomei. A commencement committee comprising individuals from each of the university's five schools and representatives from the Academic Media Center, Office of University Relations, Marketing, Public Safety, American Federation of Teachers Faculty Federation, Alumni Relations, president's office, CFS, Catering/Parkhurst Dining Services, Bands and Performing Ensemble, Athletics, Student Body, Student Life, and Finance initially met biweekly to plan the event. As months from the event shifted to weeks and days, meetings became weekly to almost daily. A carefully constructed script and activities check sheet, comparable to a GANTT chart, depicted what every person was responsible for doing and their locations throughout the event. Action items were listed in the right column so each participant was reminded of what they needed to address. Each member was responsible for articulating the needs of the constituencies represented and listening carefully to what others needed to ensure no conflicting movements or toes stepped on. The Catering Department supported commencement with meal preparation and delivery for board members, snacks for faculty during robing, and eventually, a reception for graduates' families under a large tent. University support personnel worked the event in lieu of compensation; they earned comp time. Part-time facilities workers, some of whom were employed as work-study, set up and tore down the center based on a floor plan designed by CFS and the facilities coordinator. Eventually, Becky Diana was appointed to oversee event facilities. Her role will be detailed later in the case. But first, the case will review the emergence of cochairs for the special event: the inauguration of RMU's eighth president.

Lessons Learned Serving as Cochair of the Inauguration Event Committee: Larry Tomei, Retired Vice Provost for Academic Affairs and Professor of Education

A person responsible for event planning handles logistics, coordinating permanent and auxiliary personnel, confirming and coordinating that key talent, stage fixtures, and technology are ordered, produced, positioned and operational. Larry Tomei distinguished himself as a successful jack-of-all-trades with respect to executing successful graduation ceremonies. "I knew the right people to call to get a job done that we couldn't do in-house," stated Dr. Tomei. "Over the years, I worked with different vendors (audiovisual, media, printing, transportation, etc.), and I had a team in place that was dependable and I could trust to do things the right way," he shared. Dr. Tomei began his career in the United States Air Force; he was unit commander on two different occasions. He planned change-of-command ceremonies with 450+ participants. He suggests that his service to his country made him a good project manager, and his position as director of administrative technology at Duquesne University aided his understanding of the multiple uses of technology for diverse situations. Dr. Tomei joined RMU's administration in 2004, and 1 year later, he was supporting Frank Perry in commencement planning and special projects. "When I was asked to plan and execute the inauguration of the seventh president of RMU, Greg Dell'Omo, I met with him and his wife, Polly. They indicated anything I would do to celebrate the occasion would be wonderful." Dr. Tomei established base ground rules to keep the myriad members working in unison. Script changes were not allowed in the final 48 hours. Different participant groups (platform party, distinguished guests and family members of the president, faculty, students, band, technology run-through, etc.) rehearsed in the days before the event to allow time for revisions/corrections to the procession and seating arrangements. Dr. Tomei and Perry successfully executed numerous graduations with the aid of Catering and Banquet Services; the same team also created a warm, thoughtful, and intimate inauguration celebration of RMU's seventh president.

The carefully crafted plans, scripts, and arrangements would soon be past practice. Dr. Tomei would enhance his project management skills and design a unique multievent celebration when he accepted the new president's prestigious invitation to cochair a committee for his inauguration. Dr. Tomei had advanced to vice provost for academic affairs. He was introduced to a new cochair, who was a member of the presidential search committee and a faculty colleague, Yasmin Purohit, chief diversity and inclusion officer. Together with an invited 34-member team and the team's subgroups, RMU's eighth president and first African American president was determined to plan and execute the inauguration of a lifetime. The rest of Dr. Tomei's experiences will conclude this case study.

LESSONS LEARNED ON SERVING AS COCHAIR OF THE INAUGURATION EVENT COMMITTEE: YASMIN PUROHIT, RETIRED CHIEF DIVERSITY AND INCLUSION OFFICER, PROFESSOR OF HUMAN RESOURCE MANAGEMENT

According to April L. Harris in her 2005 book, *Academic Ceremonies: A Handbook of Traditions and Protocols,* inaugurations are large celebrations where a new president expresses their vision for the future. The celebration is built around a theme and encompasses multiple public events, such as theatrical productions, musical performances, and lectures. Dr. Purohit commented, "I was asked to serve as cochair of the Inauguration Committee because of my position on the president's cabinet, to add gender diversity to the team, my expertise in inclusion and the unique perspective as I am of foreign origin. I understand how those who are not native Americans may interpret culture, customs and information. I also served on the presidential search committee, which provided a relatively more in-depth understanding of the president and his family since I spent some time with them during their visits to RMU." Dr. Purohit learned about the president's wife and her philanthropic interests in her homeland, South Africa. The planning experience was multifaceted on a number of levels for Dr. Purohit, who, in addition to her duties as cochair, also maintained the Inauguration Tracking Document (the GANTT chart for the entire weekend). "I have strong project management, computing, people and organization skills," shared Dr. Purohit as she explained why she was selected as a cochair. Unlike other university events, this event had a nonuniversity member participating in every aspect of the planning process: the president's wife. Decisions were often changed by the new president and/or his wife, sometimes after significant decisions had been made and plans were in progress. An example was the initial $30,000 budget. The costs escalated to over $100,000, and line-item budgeting was no longer part of the cochairs' job duties. The cochairs were paired to plan a task that continued to evolve and increase in complexity without the requisite time to consider how they would approach their responsibilities. "We experienced communication drop-out when a committee member would share information with one of us and not the other and we would forget to share the information with the other," explained Dr. Purohit. The planning model conformed to that used for the university's commencement exercises. A committee of 34 RMU colleagues from the same key areas was invited to participate in planning in February for an event during the first weekend in October. "We were learning our strengths and weaknesses while we were putting the evolving event together and had to work to delegate to each other and to the committee," shared Dr. Purohit. "The key to effective event planning is communication, organization, and development of a Plan B when the first plan hits a snag," she stated.

The cochairs were charged with overseeing not one event but a series of events with different attendees simultaneously welcoming the new president and celebrating the annual homecoming weekend. Some external constituencies included representatives from Pennsylvania colleges and universities, which sent representatives who robed and marched in the inaugural party procession; family and guests of the president who were identified for special seating; key political and community representatives; and the internal RMU audience of board members, faculty, staff, and students, all of whom were identified according to where they were seated. As an illustration of the agility required for this event, Dr. Purohit shared that "hours before the event, a request for additional plants for the stage and changes in critical stakeholder seating arrangements were made that impacted the videographer and photographer's abilities to identify the correct individuals to project images at critical moments in the script."

The inauguration commenced Thursday evening with Rita Moreno, an Oscar-winning actress, singer, and dancer, performing at an off-campus location. An invitation-only reception for president's council members before the event and significant donors who made contributions that impacted student lives was held at a Pittsburgh-based hotel. Two prestigious awards were presented at the reception. On campus, two one-act plays were performed at the Colonial Theatre. The next morning turned into a facilities challenge, with one large space and multiple meeting rooms redesigned and reset multiple times quickly over 2 days. "The facilities crews were working literally around the clock to set up and tear down spaces," explained Dr. Purohit. A Celebration of Excellence kicked off the inauguration day at 9:00 a.m., with RMU's five schools showcasing areas of expertise and influence within their academic and service communities. By noon, a VIP luncheon for 225 invited guests was set in one location, and a large picnic on campus for delegates and faculty was accommodating all the guests and faculty robing for the inaugural procession. After the inauguration, a large celebration with different F&B stations occurred in tents behind the center. The VIP luncheon space was reset for a 5:30 panel discussion on "Empowering Women" and the inauguration space reset and decorated for a homecoming dance. "Keeping track of the number of participants became a challenge because a response confirmation wasn't requested for each activity from some attendees. We were uncertain what the final number of attendees would be. We planned for between 2,500 and 3,200 guests," said Dr. Purohit. She explained that performing all of her duties and overseeing the activities related to the inauguration was challenging, and a lot of complex, intricate and time-consuming hard work. The weekend far exceeded expectations. The take-away from the experience is be transparent, understand how much power you have, and understand what your client wants. I was happy we made the event memorable. The committee members were outstanding, but the real heroine was Becky Diana, said Dr. Purohit.

A Day in the Life for Event Professional Becky Diana, Director of Conferences and Event Services, Point Park University

Sometimes, you know what you want to be; sometimes, you take an interesting path to confirm your choice or in my case, identify what I wanted as my career," said Ms. Diana. She sold copy machines after completing a bachelor's degree in business. She held a position in the admissions office while in college, which turned out to be a career-changing move. During a sales visit to RMU, she was informed that a position in admissions was available. Joining the admissions team introduced and led her to a career that she was unaware existed. Twenty years ago, admissions events planning consisted of a single student's campus visit that included meeting with faculty, financial aid, and admissions. With time, the process evolved. Ms. Diana found herself planning open houses in conjunction with placement testing, registrations days, transfer days, and campus tours and working closely with the catering and banquets unit. She realized that her on-the-job training was a great start, but she wanted a more solid foundation. Her boss, Don Smith, strongly urged her to pursue MPI affiliation and potentially earn CMP certification. She chose the Association of Collegiate Conference and Events Directors—International (ACCED-I) because she knew the education industry was her passion and lifelong career ambition. She also earned an M.A. in marketing. "I am always marketing something, and it seemed like a good fit with my career aspirations to also teach part time." With time, effort, and continuous education and experience, Ms. Diana's career path accelerated; she became assistant director, sales manager, and finally, events manager at RMU. According to Drs. Tomei and Purohit, there would not be any events without Becky Diana. "Becky Diana was our rock. She was unbelievably good, patient and positive throughout the planning and execution process," exclaimed Dr. Purohit.

Ms. Diana was invited to serve on the Inauguration Committee to work with Dr. Ann Summerall-Jabro and Registrar Frank Perry on the inauguration ceremony component. Realistically, Ms. Diana was in charge of every activity for the weekend, as she was the director of events; everything was happening in the Events Center or on the RMU campus. "I am either responsible for the design, planning, and execution of the event or I am involved in specific elements of an event contingent upon who has jurisdiction of a space." Ms. Diana feels that "event planners who are adept at the soft skills, such as relationship-building and maintenance, conflict resolution, creative thinking and adaptability" will enjoy successful careers. "There were a lot of different personalities with whom I interacted when planning the inauguration. We adapt our style to the clients' needs," said Ms. Diana. "The inauguration had a lot of different technology needs, some of which we contracted in for and some of which we could manage on-site." Ms. Diana commented that "technology use in events has shifted significantly and with the virtual component commonplace, technology integration in events will continue to evolve." A number of individuals served food at the inauguration for the first time. The part-time labor pool was extensive; people to set up and tear down, people to deliver, set up, and replenish food in remote locations, and then the stakeholder groups' ushers, coordinators, and event producers. "The president wanted ice carvings atop the appetizer tables to keep food cold and look stunning. Another component of my job was to determine how to make that happen and think about what happens when the ice melts. There was no doubt in my mind that the event would be spectacular. We had a phenomenal team who was committed to doing the very best. When I learned of last-minute changes, which were substantial and impacted multiple areas, I did my best to think through the impact to the master plan and adjust accordingly," shared Ms. Diana. She used technology and word of mouth to communicate changes. "Of course, there's always departures from the master plan. Creative and insightful event planners have alternatives thought through before the event. All our key people were on walkie-talkies so we could get immediate access to them. Drs. Tomei and Purohit were in constant contact about changes or problem areas and we functioned as a thoughtful team," shared Ms. Diana.

LESSONS LEARNED SERVING AS COCHAIR OF THE INAUGURATION EVENT COMMITTEE: LARRY TOMEI, RETIRED VICE PROVOST FOR ACADEMIC AFFAIRS AND PROFESSOR OF EDUCATION (FINAL THOUGHTS)

Dr. Tomei believed strongly in the importance of empowering people to do their jobs. His approach to planning and execution was simple: "Once the committee agreed on a plan and it was approved by the president, the committee heads and their working group members interpret and implement the plan. If there is a problem, the information needs to be communicated to me and Dr. Purohit immediately." He was enthusiastic that most of the committees adhered to the empowerment advice and reached out when they needed support. "We avoided making a fatal mistake," stated Dr. Tomei. According to Dr. Tomei, every activity on the Inauguration Tracking Document was achieved. All the meeting spaces were turned around and dressed in a timely manner according to the plan. The F&B and entertainment were spectacular. Feedback on the weekend was generally positive. The committee was disbanded, and RMU's eighth president enjoyed a memorable celebration.

REFERENCES 1

American Council on Education (ACE). (n.d.). Academic Costume Code and Academic Ceremony Guide. https://www.acenet.edu/Programs-Services/Pages/Academic-Regalia.aspx

Harris, A. L. (2005). *Academic ceremonies: A handbook of traditions and protocol*. Council for Advancement and Support of Education (CASE).

KEY WORDS AND TERMS

For definitions, see the glossary or https://insights.eventscouncil.org/Industry-glossary.

Accepted Practices Exchange
conference
convention
CMP International Standards
destination management companyEICexhibition
exposition

KSAs
meetings and business events competency standards
meetings, expositions, events, and conventionsmeeting
MPI
sales and marketing

REVIEW AND DISCUSSION QUESTIONS

1. How do meetings, events, and exhibitions differ?
2. Why is this industry interdependent with other businesses?
3. Describe some current aspects of MEEC industry jobs.
4. How have unforeseen calamities altered meeting planning and events?
5. What KSA do you demonstrate proficiency in?
6. What are key jobs in a facility (hotel, resort, conference center) that contribute to the successful outcome of a meeting?
7. What is the EIC?
8. What is APEX, and what is its impact?
9. What is the impact of meetings on the global. economy?

10. What is MBECS?

11. What are the EIC Principles for Recovery?

12. Create your own career pathway in the MEEC Industry.

13. Create a list of situations in the MEEC industry where ethics would come into play.

ABOUT THE CHAPTER CONTRIBUTOR

Ann D. Summerall-Jabro, Ph.D., is a professor of communication and organizational Leadership at RMU, Pittsburgh, Pennsylvania.

Previous Edition Chapter Contributors

Amy Calvert, CEO of EIC

Mariela McIlwraith, vice president of sustainability and industry advancement of EIC

Joan L. Eisenstodt, president of Washington, DC-based Eisenstodt Associates, LLC

Kathryn Hashimoto, Ph.D., faculty member in the School of Hospitality Leadership at East Carolina University

Karen Kotowski, CAE, CMP, former CEO of the EIC

CHAPTER 2

MEETING, EXHIBITION, EVENT, AND CONVENTION ORGANIZERS AND SPONSORS

COMING TOGETHER FOR A COMMON PURPOSE

CHAPTER OBJECTIVES

- Understand the major types of organizations that hold gatherings.
- Differentiate the types of meetings and the planning required for each organization.
- Identify the associations that support the professional development of those responsible for producing gatherings.
- Summarize the major trends facing MEEC organizers and sponsors.

Contributed by Thomas C. Padron. © Kendall Hunt Publishing Company.

This chapter is dedicated to explaining the entities responsible for organizing and sponsoring various types of gatherings. Each hosts gatherings to meet its distinct needs and reach its intended audience. Whether it is a corporate entity, a nonprofit association, a government agency, or a private company focused on producing exhibitions, each has specific objectives that might lead to planning an MEEC gathering to commemorate an event. The purpose of this chapter is to identify these organizing and sponsoring organizations, delve into the types of gatherings they host, explore their average event planning timeline, define their target attendees, and examine their methods for attracting participants. Additionally, the individuals who play pivotal roles in orchestrating these gatherings are highlighted, alongside the professional associations that offer them support and opportunities for professional growth.

WHO HOLDS GATHERINGS?

The three most prominent entities engaged in organizing and sponsoring MEEC gatherings are (a) corporations, (b) associations, and (c) government bodies. This chapter also discusses other organizations.

CORPORATIONS

Although a multitude of corporations exist, within this chapter, the term "**corporation**" will specifically pertain to legally chartered enterprises engaged in business activities on behalf of their proprietors, aiming to generate profits and enhance their value. This categorization can be further divided into public and private. Public corporations issue stock on the open market and are overseen by a board of directors, responsible for managing corporate affairs on behalf of the shareholders who elected them. Private corporations share the same fundamental objectives, but their stock is not publicly traded.

Practically all businesses encounter requirements that necessitate planning and executing gatherings. Publicly traded companies are legally obligated to conduct annual shareholders' meetings. Numerous companies arrange press conferences or ribbon-cutting ceremonies. Organizations also consistently need to provide training on policies and procedures and develop new policies to enhance operational efficiency. Client groups might convene for focus groups to gather opinions or to introduce new products/services. Incentive meetings are convened to reward high achievers. Executive retreats may enhance communication or establish long-term business strategies. Gatherings are also organized to recognize employee achievements (promotions or retirements), celebrate holidays, and bolster overall organizational morale. Moreover, companies often host clients in VIP areas at events such as concerts or major sporting occasions, such as the U.S. Open or the Super Bowl.

Numerous corporate meetings are scheduled based on necessity, usually less than 6 months in advance. When a corporation opts to convene a gathering, it delineates the budget, venue, and guest list. As the corporation bears the expenses linked to attending the meeting, it retains complete authority over the proceedings. The decision to initiate a meeting typically rests with individuals in key positions within the corporate hierarchy. Executives and senior managers in sales and marketing may summon regional sales managers to formulate sales strategies for new product lines; senior financial managers and controllers may assemble their distributed teams to discuss budgets for upcoming year. Predominantly, attendees at corporate gatherings comprise corporate associates and individuals with close business affiliations. Participation from corporate personnel is typically obligatory.

Although attendance might be mandatory for the majority, marketing efforts are still imperative. The purpose should be meticulously articulated, and company websites need to be updated with pertinent details, encompassing the event's theme and objectives. Although formal invitations may not be issued, notifications and RSVP registration websites are generally established. The company should use internal marketing strategies to generate anticipation. This ensures that attendees arrive with a sense of eagerness to absorb, engage, and relish their time away from the office. Even for of "command performances," the imperative remains intact: The meeting must deliver information, productivity, and enjoyment.

Corporate meetings can vary greatly, mirroring the diversity within corporations. Achieving success hinges on meticulous attention to detail, a wholehearted embrace of the corporate culture, and a clear understanding of the meeting's objectives.

Types of Corporate Gatherings and Events—Their Purposes and Objectives

Corporate meetings encompass a wide spectrum, ranging from intimate VIP board of directors sessions to expansive sales conferences, customer incentive gatherings, and more modest staff training assemblies. A unifying element among these diverse meetings is their sponsorship by the corporation itself. Financial backing is typically allocated from specific departmental or individual budgets within the organization.

The objectives typically include motivational talks, training sessions, team-building exercises, camaraderie, brainstorming sessions, and the review of overarching goals. Additionally, the meetings often place significant emphasis on social events. Although these occasions might appear leisure oriented, they present valuable networking opportunities across various departments and hierarchical levels, with potential repercussions for future corporate strategies. Therefore, meticulous planning is crucial to strategically unite appropriate individuals during activities, such as dinners or golf outings.

Corporations convene for a myriad of reasons, each gathering tailored to meet specific needs. The following compilation should not be mistaken for an exhaustive list; rather, it offers a panoramic glimpse into the array of corporate-sponsored events.

Stockholder Meetings

Voting shareholders of a corporation receive invitations to the annual stockholders meeting. Traditionally, it has been hosted in the city with the company headquarters. However, a growing trend among many companies involves rotating the location to enhance accessibility for all stockholders. During the event, attendees are provided with comprehensive reports detailing the corporation's state and can cast their votes on matters of significant corporate importance.

Although the majority of stockholders typically do not attend in person, they actively engage in governance by submitting a "proxy statement." This document outlines their preferences for voting their shares. These meetings may adopt virtual or hybrid formats, allowing for participation from afar, or be recorded, permitting stockholders to view them at a later time.

Management Meetings

Companies convene management meetings for an array of compelling reasons. Each significant division within a corporation might find it imperative to gather its key decisionmakers and vital personnel. The primary objectives range from devising strategic plans and evaluating performance to refining operational processes. These meetings might adhere to a predetermined schedule, but others could be impromptu, initiated to swiftly tackle emergent issues and address situations demanding immediate attention.

Board Meetings

Among the spectrum of management meetings, board meetings are distinct. They are orchestrated by the governing body of a corporation—the board of directors. Scheduled multiple times throughout the year, these sessions usually take place near the corporation's operational base. Although the headquarters might host, the magnitude of such gatherings often necessitates supplementary arrangements, including accommodations, dining arrangements, and ancillary events, which frequently unfold at local hotels and various venues.

Training Meetings

When companies change, it may become necessary to conduct training meetings, which bring managers and key employees up to date with improved methods of job performance or equip them with the skills needed to operate new systems and equipment and can serve as a platform to introduce new managers to corporate procedures and culture. Some meetings may be held on a regular schedule, but others might be convened as dictated by the prevailing conditions.

Sales Training and Product Launches

Among the various types of training meetings, sales training and product launches are distinct. They aim to enhance the performance of the sales staff, distributors, and retailers or introduce new products and services to distribution networks and the broader public. The objective is to educate and motivate individuals with significant influence over the corporation's success.

Corporation meeting attendees gathering information

Professional and Technical Training

Professional technical training represents yet another specialized form of training meeting. These gatherings are often convened to ensure that managers and other stakeholders are well informed about matters directly pertinent to their roles within the company. Simultaneously, they enrich the understanding of service providers. For instance, a company might organize a meeting involving its unit and regional controllers to discuss alterations in tax laws and company policies.

Incentive Trips

Numerous corporations offer **incentive trips** to recognize and reward their top performers based on specific criteria. A significant amount of time is devoted to "fun" activities that employees perceive as a commendation for their outstanding work, such as golf tournaments, sightseeing tours, and outdoor adventures. The recipients could encobempass employees, distributors, and/or customers. These events often provide an opportunity to bring these high achievers together with corporate leadership, fostering a more synergistic organization. Although these trips typically feature exciting and glamorous destinations, organizations are incorporating tailored activities to enhance collaboration and bring additional value to the sponsoring corporation.

According to the 2022 Incentive Travel Index (previously the Incentive Travel Industry Index), a remarkable 80% of companies concur that incentive travel is gaining strategic significance. With the evolving landscape of the generational workforce, travel has emerged as one of the most popular and rapidly growing strategies for motivating employees. A notable 72% find that prioritizing relationship-building holds the utmost importance for the success of such programs. Additionally, more than 65% of firms worldwide have expressed intentions to expand their existing incentive travel initiatives.

Public Shows

Public shows, also known as "consumer shows," are gatherings where businesses directly sell their products to the general public. They are often trade shows, where exhibitors showcase products tailored to local interests, creating an atmosphere of excitement that draws attendees. This attribute gives rise to the label "public shows." Examples include boat shows, car shows, winter sports shows, and art exhibitions. Generally, attendees are required to pay an admission fee. The corporations selling the showcased goods typically own and sponsor these occasions.

To attract public attendance, organizers employ various promotional channels, including social media, local radio and television stations, newspapers, and often local billboards. A growing trend in relation to the show's theme involves specific exhibitors incorporating scheduled entertainment and educational sessions within their booths. This strategy aims to not only drive attendance but also enhance awareness of their products or services.

Department and/or Individual Responsible for Organizing and Planning

In the realm of corporate planning, a diverse array of positions, titles, and backgrounds have long been prevalent. Many individuals have duties that extend beyond or complement their meeting planning roles. Approximately three-quarters of their time is allocated to organizing meetings, with nearly half of them titled explicitly as meeting planners or convention managers.

The landscape has undergone transformations catalyzed by the pandemic, directly impacting corporate planners, such as budget adjustments, shifts in corporate hierarchies, and evolving job responsibilities. A case in point is the evolution of virtual and hybrid events, which once constituted a minor aspect of existing job descriptions but have escalated into full-time positions. This evolution birthed professions such as event technologists, virtual engagement specialists, online event facilitators, moderators, and various roles integral to the domain of online engagement activities, all of which continue to be pivotal within the industry.

In smaller corporations, it is common for a single individual to have a diverse array of responsibilities, so a dedicated "Meetings and Events Department" might not exist. Most professionals engaged in meeting planning within smaller corporations usually function within the departments hosting the meetings (such as sales and marketing, human resources, or finance). They often take on meeting planning responsibilities at the behest of their supervisors. Conversely, larger corporations, such as Microsoft, Coca-Cola, Salesforce, ExxonMobil, and Google, have independent meeting planning departments. Given the extensive number of large and small gatherings these corporations host annually, such specialized units are necessary.

A significant number of corporate meeting planners opt to become members of professional associations to bolster their ongoing learning and development, which offers them avenues for expanding their network, staying abreast of the latest advancements in their field, and carving out a reputation within their organization and the wider industry. Prominent associations are

Meeting Professionals International (MPI), Professional Convention Management Association (PCMA), Society for Incentive Travel Excellence (SITE), and Corporate Event Marketing Association.

United States	Europe	Latin America	Asia Pacific
1. Las Vegas	1. Madrid	1. Bogota	1. Tokyo
2. Orlando	2. Barcelona	2. Mexico City	2. Osaka
3. New York	3. London	3. Cartagena	3. Sydney
4. Dallas	4. Paris	4. Buenos Aires	4. Seoul
5. Atlanta	5. Manchester	5. Cancun	5. Taipei

TABLE 1. Top cities that hosted meetings in 2022

ASSOCIATIONS

Within the United States, more than 300,000 association meetings and events take place annually, drawing a crowd of over 60 million attendees. This constitutes a segment of the industry that demands attention. The term "**association**" denotes a collective of individuals organized for shared objectives, whether professional, industrial, educational, scientific, or social, which holds true within the Meetings, Events, Exhibitions, and Conventions (MEEC) domain as well. Various gatherings, such as annual conventions, focused conferences, global congresses, topical workshops, and seminars, convene for the benefit of the association's members. Internally, meetings also advance its interests, including sessions such as board of directors meetings, committee meetings, and leadership development workshops. Often, associations accompany their annual **conventions** with affiliated exhibitions, showcasing products and services of interest to attendees through various vendors. These gatherings not only deliver value to association members and potentially amplify the association's recognition but also generate a significant revenue stream.

Associations extend opportunities for enriching members' professional growth through conferences, seminars, and workshops. These events often blend structured educational sessions with informal networking occasions, such as receptions, golf tournaments, and dinners. Associations actively encourage their members to participate, ensuring that member-oriented meetings are conceptualized with inputs from the members themselves. The meeting planner collaborates closely with member committees from initial planning to final execution. Committee members play a pivotal role by proposing program themes and speakers resonating with their peers. Local committee members may even recommend suitable local venues for social gatherings, tourist attractions, entertainment options, and golf courses for conference tournaments. Their involvement adds substantial value and forms an integral aspect of the planning process, contributing to the event's appeal and success.

Association meetings, including conventions, vary widely, from hundreds to tens of thousands of attendees. Around two-thirds of conventions are held alongside trade shows. On average, conventions feature 250 exhibitors and require 50,0001 square feet of exhibit space. This size constraint limits options for smaller cities, driving demand for larger venues in major urban centers. This competitive landscape prompts major associations to secure venues 5–10 years in advance to ensure space availability. Smaller associations have more choices, even in regional cities, requiring less lead time. Regardless of size, most associations finalize their meeting locations at least a year ahead.

The decision-making process for association meetings is intricate and comprises several distinct stages. After confirming the intent to hold a meeting (often by the board of directors or in accordance with the association's constitution or bylaws), the initial focus is on defining the objectives, which must be established before planning. The next step is selecting the venue. Some organizations employ a regional rotation strategy to distribute hosting duties across their membership. Determining the specific city for the event can rest with the association's board of directors or be guided by the executive director, influenced by feedback from site visits conducted by either the association's internal meeting planner or an external contracted provider. This report offers a summary outlining the rationale for recommending a particular destination, considering factors such as hotel and convention center prices, air transportation (daily flight frequency and seat availability), expected weather during the event, room availability, cost per attendee, precedent of holding the meeting there, labor rates, and overall business friendliness.

Once the decision is made for a specific city, the meeting planner, supported by site visits and inspections, identifies a venue based on factors such as date availability and alignment with the meeting's requirements. The meeting planner presents their recommendation to the association's board and leadership. Following approval, negotiations ensue with the facility, encompassing financial terms and logistical arrangements. This culminates in a contract, which is eventually signed by both the venue and a senior representative of the association, often the executive director or chief financial officer. Association events serve as vital revenue streams. The magnitude of revenue is inherently tied to the number of paid attendees, rendering the event more financially rewarding. However, as attendees are obliged to cover registration costs, travel, and lodging expenses, associations are compelled to curate programming that they consider indispensable, encouraging their active participation.

Types of Associations

As outlined by the preeminent association for association planners, PCMA, the association category has been categorized into four distinct types: professional, medical or health, trade, and **social, military, educational, religious, and fraternal** (SMERF).

Professional

Membership consists of individuals from the same industry. It is established at the individual level, and each member is responsible for their own membership dues. According to PCMA Convene Magazine's 29th Annual Meetings Market Survey (2020), professional associations make up 48% of all associations. Notable examples include MPI and SITE.

Medical or Health

This type of association is composed of individuals specifically from the medical or health sector. Although still a "professional" field, it merits its own category due to its substantial influence and stringent requirements. According to PCMA, it is 21% of all associations. Prominent examples are the American Medical Association and American Hospital Association.

Trade

Membership comprises organizations from the same industry. It is established at the company level: Employees of the member company automatically become members. According to PCMA, this sector constitutes 19% of all associations. Notable examples include Hospitality Sales and Marketing Association International and the International Franchise Association.

SMERFs

Educational groups may include universities, for-profit education institutions, or high schools. Fraternal groups might encompass organizations such as Kiwanis, Elks, or university fraternities and sororities. Attendees typically cover their own expenses, making this category highly cost sensitive. According to PCMA, this segment accounts for 7% of all associations.

Association events provide opportunities for their members

Any of these association segments can operate on a local, state, regional, national, or international scale, depending on members' geographical distribution. Moreover, within the United States, any of these categories can attain a special tax-exempt status conferred by the Internal Revenue Service. Despite not being driven by profit, tax-exempt associations need to be managed efficiently, with revenues surpassing expenses. Given that all income supports the mission, any surplus funds, equivalent to corporate profits, are allowed to remain with the organization, exempt from taxation. On average, associations draw about one-third of their annual operational revenues from surplus income generated by annual meetings and conventions.

Types of Association Gatherings and Events—Their Purposes and Objectives

Conventions

As defined by the Accepted Practices Exchange (APEX), a convention is a gathering of an industry organization for a shared objective. Association conventions are often annual and commonly include educational sessions, committee meetings, social functions, and sessions dedicated to the organization's governance matters. A prevalent feature of many conventions is an accompanying exhibition or trade show, which frequently serves as a primary revenue stream for the association. Exhibitors participate in these events by paying, as conventions offer them a platform to present their products and services to a precisely targeted audience of potential buyers. This avenue proves more cost effective compared to individual sales trips aimed at meeting association members separately. Conventions are bolstered, in part, by sponsors—companies or entities that stand to gain from exposure to convention attendees. Conventions, and other forms of gatherings, can be in person, hybrid, or entirely online.

Regional Conferences

Organizations structured regionally often arrange one or more events annually to unite members from the same geographic area and might host distinct regional social gatherings during the larger annual convention.

Board Meetings

The board of directors typically convenes multiple times a year to provide counsel and guidance to the organization. These meetings are typically the smallest of the association's gatherings, serving to offer updates on association operations and conference planning endeavors.

Committee Meetings

Numerous association committees conduct their own smaller meetings to address matters relevant to their respective missions (e.g., government relations, convention host committee, national conference program committee, and publications committee). Depending on the committee, these meetings can often be conference calls.

Training Meetings and Educational Seminars

Associations frequently provide members with opportunities to enhance their professional skills and knowledge through meetings focused on specific topics. In numerous fields, continuing education is obligatory (e.g., continuing medical education for various medical specialties). Attending training meetings enables members to accumulate **continuing education units**. Certain associations organize training meetings aimed at nurturing the leadership potential of elected national and regional officers. These seminars are often led by experts, allowing participants to exchange viewpoints and share experiences.

Attendance and Marketing

A notable distinction between association and corporate gatherings is that attendance at association meetings is voluntary, so they must offer engaging programs to entice members. Another distinction is that many attendees pay their own registration, transportation, lodging, and related expenses. Occasionally, employers might finance employees' attendance at industry and professional association events deemed work related and beneficial to employee education.

Effective marketing is crucial to the success of association meetings. All marketing initiatives should start with a comprehensive understanding of the members' identities and requirements. This focus should be seamlessly integrated into the development of all meetings. In today's business landscape, especially with the proliferation of online meetings, attendees might hesitate to dedicate significant time away from their work environment. Hence, the association must meticulously design a robust program that captivates attendees and furnishes them with a compelling and valuable rationale to commit to traveling. Many attendees need to substantiate the meeting's worth to their superiors to secure permission to participate. Well-crafted marketing materials are indispensable in doing so.

When the meeting genuinely provides avenues for members to address their needs, the promotional facet of marketing becomes less arduous. Given that the primary attendee group comprises association members, key marketing elements are providing advance notice of the meeting's date and location and insights into the planned content, speakers, and special activities. Subsequently, detailed registration information and an initial program should be presented.

Traditionally, this information was disseminated through direct mail, notices, or advertisements in the association's newsletter and magazine. However, evolving technology and cost considerations have prompted many associations to shift toward electronic media. The use of emails and social media for promoting meetings has experienced rapid growth, guiding recipients to explore the association's website for details. Additionally, promoting and marketing the subsequent year's meeting or convention during the current year's event through a "save the date" announcement is advisable. This empowers attendees to note those dates on their calendars and generates excitement well in advance.

To broaden the attendee base, numerous associations extend promotional materials and notifications to nonmembers who have been pinpointed as sharing an affinity for the meeting's objectives. Given that the nonmember registration fee is typically higher, if this endeavor proves successful, it could draw in fresh members and generate supplementary revenue.

Department and/or Individual Responsible for Organizing and Planning

Within associations, the event planner is typically an internal paid employee, a member committee overseen by an executive director, or an **association management company**. This determination often hinges on the association's size. Roughly two-thirds of association planners have an undergraduate degree; approximately 20% have a postgraduate degree.

They are more likely to join professional associations compared to their corporate counterparts. Over 20 associations exist in specific industries, conveniently accessible through the Event Industry Council (EIC) website under EIC—Association Members. The most widely recognized associations spanning industries include PCMA, American Society of Association Executives, and MPI. These organizations also feature regional chapters, and various local meeting planner associations offer valuable support and professional development opportunities.

	Corporation	Association	Government
Definition	Legally chartered enterprises that conduct business on behalf of their owners with the purpose of making a profit and increasing its value	A group of people organized for certain common purposes, whether that be for professional, industry, educational, scientific, or social reasons	Subdivisions of federal, state, or local government
Purpose	Training, team building, and incentives	Primarily educational and networking with some having trade show components	Primarily training and educational
Decision Makers	Centralized (typically leaders in the corporate hierarchy)	Decentralized (oftentimes committee decision)	Managers who decide to have the meeting and fund it from their departmental budget

TABLE 2. Comparison

Attendees	Members of the corporation or have a close business relationship with the company	Members of, or people interested in, that particular industry	Government employees and, depending on the event, the general public
Spouse Attendance	Rare	Common	Rare
Attendance	Mandatory	Voluntary	Mandatory for personnel; voluntary for public
Size	Varies by company; typically less than ten to one thousand	Several hundred to tens of thousands	Varies by event
Marketing	Minimal; invitation or notice to all attendees	Crucial; often mailers, magazines, and electronically	Internally similar to corporate, when public is invited similar to association
Location and Site Selection	Convenience, service, and security are valued	Seek attractive locations to help build attendance, amenities and nearby attractions are important	Convenience, service, and security are valued
Lead Time	Less than six months	Large associations—Five to 10 years or more; smaller associations—minimum one year	Less than three to four months
Payment	Corporation pays for everything	Attendee pays for travel, hotel, and registration; registration and sponsorships cover cost of the conference	Funding is awarded through the legislative process; department allocates meeting budget
Planner	Corporate planner, most likely a part of someone's job, could be any department in the company	Association planner and board or outsourced to association management company	Similar to corporate planners who are spread throughout the agency, will outsource an independent planner if outside of their internal capabilities
Professional Associations	Meeting Professional International (MPI), Professional Convention Management Association (PCMA), Society of Incentive and Travel Executives (SITE), and the Association of Insurance and Financial Services Conference Planners	Professional Convention Management Association (PCMA), the American Society of Association Executives (ASAE), Meeting Professionals International (MPI), the Center for Association Leadership, and the Religious Conference Management Association	Society of Government Meeting Professionals (SGMP), Professional Convention Management Association (PCMA), and Meeting Professionals International (MPI). If responsible for organizing exhibitions—International Association of Exhibitions and Events (IAEE).

TABLE 2. Comparison (continued)

GOVERNMENT

Government entities across all levels frequently convene gatherings to address their ongoing need for communication and interaction with diverse constituent bodies. These meetings span a wide spectrum—ranging from sessions attended by world leaders, accompanied by sizable groups of protestors and supporters, to more intimate gatherings featuring local officials engaged in legislative retreats. In contrast to corporate and association meetings, government meetings are subject to a spectrum of rules and regulations. Recognizing that it is impractical to cover information specific to every one of the 1901 countries worldwide, this section offers a broader overview applicable to the fundamental job responsibilities of government meeting planners. Specific links and statistics will be oriented toward the United States.

Typically, managers within government agencies are tasked with identifying the necessity for a meeting and secure funding through their departmental budget procedures or alternative avenues. Similar to other components of an agency's budget, meeting funding primarily hinges on allocations provided via the legislative process. Hence, as political interest in an agency's mission shifts, so does the budget—fluctuating in tandem with its capacity to host gatherings. Recent years have demonstrated that public backlash and U.S. policies can impact off-site meetings and the attendance of government agency employees. Although such incidents have also occurred historically, they are more prominent in contemporary times due to the swift dissemination of information through media outlets and greater coverage in mainstream media.

Government meetings have characteristics that align with both corporate and association meetings. A prevalent objective of numerous such meetings is training government personnel. At the federal level, many of these meetings are replicated across various regions to curtail travel expenses for employees in different branches of an agency. Other meetings encompass agency personnel and members of the general public who share an interest in the subject matter. For instance, gatherings focused on discussing prescription drug proposals or the future of Social Security often go "on the road" to solicit input from the public. Employee participation is generally obligatory, necessitating adequate advance notice to enable participants to accommodate their schedules accordingly. On the other hand, attendance by the general public is voluntary and might require enhanced promotion efforts.

MEETINGS, EXPOSITIONS, EVENTS, AND CONVENTIONS

Some government agencies have embraced the concept of virtual meetings. Beyond the cost-cutting aim, additional constraints add an extra layer of stringency to government meetings. In the United States, venues must adhere to specific provisions for accommodating individuals with particular physical needs under the Americans with Disabilities Act and satisfy fire safety certifications. Moreover, both the federal government and numerous state governments have instituted **per diem rates**, which establish caps on the daily expenditure allowed for government attendees covering lodging and meals. Given the extensive array of rate tables, those seeking the current federal domestic per diem rates are recommended to consult the General Services Administration website at http://www.gsa.gov/. These considerations have collectively contributed to the growing acceptance of online programming as an alternative solution.

Government meetings have characteristics of both corporate and association meetings

Financial Rules and Regulations

Government meetings stand apart from association and corporate meetings due to their adherence to government regulations and operational policies that may not be applicable to other meeting types. Given that most government activities are financed through taxpayer funds, stringent financial rules and regulations govern government meetings.

First, rates are established for hotel rooms. To economize, the government establishes per diem rates (including meals and other incidentals) for travelers across all locations in the continental United States. These rates are generally below those offered to conference groups in most cities. Furthermore, government meetings can only be hosted in properties that adhere to the stipulations outlined in the Hotel Motel Fire Safety Act of 1990. Even after identifying a hotel that agrees to the requested terms and rates, the hotel contracts are not "official." Although a contract might be appended to the paperwork submitted to the procurement official, the prevailing authority is the government contract rather than a contract from the private sector. Funding *must* be secured *before* service provision, not after. Additionally, the government *must* retain the ability to terminate without penalties if event funding is withdrawn, government facilities are furloughed or closed, or other governmental actions render the meeting inadvisable.

Federal procurement policies further distinguish government meetings. For most purchases, bids for meeting supplies and services must be secured from *at least* three vendors. Additionally, the individuals responsible for arranging meetings often are not the ones authorized to allocate funds. Hence, it is crucial to ascertain who holds the actual authority to commit funds and endorse contracts on behalf of the government.

Security

Within the MEEC industry, the government segment exhibits an unparalleled commitment to safety and security. In the United States, organizers of government meetings are in constant collaboration with the Department of Homeland Security, primarily due to the presence of high-profile leaders among their attendees. Although this list is not exhaustive, the following recommendations can assist in implementing security measures:

- plan and prepare,
- refine the preconvention meeting to emphasize security issues,
- be sure there is coordination of all parties involved,
- establish a security team and its decisionmakers,
- provide education on security for attendees,
- be proactive rather than reactive, and
- stay informed and alert to incidents.

Considering that government meetings frequently convene representatives from both the Uniformed Services and agencies outside the Department of Defense, they are often classified. If so, they might have to be held within a "secure" facility, be it a government building or a public venue fortified by trained personnel.

Department and/or Individual Responsible for Organizing and Planning

Government meetings are notably more intricate compared to most private-sector conferences. When assigned internally, they are often coordinated by individuals who are not full-time meeting planners, such as budget analysts, public affairs officers, scientists, secretaries, or administrative officers. If a department has the resources to have a dedicated meeting planner, these are similar to their corporate counterparts.

Due to the absence of in-house expertise, numerous government agencies enlist meeting management companies or independent meeting planners to oversee gatherings that exceed their internal capacities. In the Washington,

DC area, several meeting planning companies specialize in this. Stringent government guidelines dictate what a meeting planner can offer in terms of food and beverage (F&B) and extracurricular activities. Government planners must acquaint themselves with these regulations and remain ready for financial audits afterward.

Meeting planners within government agencies or independent meeting management firms are also inclined to join associations that foster their professional development. In the government (and health) sectors, where regulations frequently evolve, this commitment to ongoing education is particularly crucial. These associations facilitate government planners in grasping these precise guidelines and financial/sponsorship protocols. Prominent organizations are the Society of Government Meeting Professionals and its local or regional chapters, PCMA, and MPI. Those responsible for arranging exhibitions are also likely to affiliate with the International Association of Exhibitions and Events (IAEE).

OTHER ORGANIZATIONS ARRANGING GATHERINGS

Political Organizations

Except for their subject matter, political events share many similarities with nonpolitical events, differing mainly in aspects such as security, press coverage, and venue management. Political events encompass a wide range, from major conventions to special occasions, such as inaugurations, trade shows, fundraising events, and local gatherings. Conventions often tend to be notably larger than their nonpolitical counterparts, which can pose challenges in terms of crowd control. Attendees' fervent passion for their causes and speakers' potentially polarizing nature necessitates engaging specialized security agencies. Disruptive guests are managed more sternly, with the possibility of formal legal action. Press presence is expected to be prominent, so dedicated areas, such as press boxes, press risers, and spaces accommodating multiple cameras, should be allocated. In essence, although security, press coverage, and venue management are the primary distinctions, political events closely mirror nonpolitical events in most aspects.

Labor Unions

The labor union market has witnessed a sharp decrease in private-sector membership, plummeting from 24.3% in 1973 to approximately 6%. By 2022, the highest rates were in the public sector, specifically within protective service, education, training, and library occupations. Despite this transformative shift, the United States still has over 60 unions, representing more than 16 million members, who regularly convene meetings. Prominent examples include Carpenters, Decorators, Electricians, Riggers, Stagehands, and Teamster Unions. Union gatherings generally occur biennially and are exclusively held at unionized venues, often boasting substantial attendance because they encompass all members. Such events frequently showcase notable political speakers. National conventions include sponsored events, social programs, significant spouse attendance, and considerable per-person expenditures. Surprisingly, 2022 marked the first annual surge in union membership since 2017. Despite a persistent decline, those advocating for unionization have observed a general upswing. This evolving perspective and a range of activities notwithstanding, the trajectory of union membership remains uncertain.

ENTITIES THAT HELP ORGANIZE GATHERINGS

Beyond internal meeting planners, various entities play pivotal roles in facilitating the organization of meetings and events for corporations, associations, government bodies, and other entities. These include **exhibition management companies** (EMCs), association management companies, meeting management companies, and independent meeting managers.

EMCS

EMCs specialize in owning and operating trade shows and expositions. These companies not only conceive and orchestrate events that contribute to their own profits but also manage events for corporations, associations, or government clients. Although both trade shows and public shows showcase products and services to potential buyers, **trade shows** (or **exhibitions**) typically are not accessible to the general public. Their focus is on a well-defined market within a particular trade or profession. Conversely, **public shows** (or **expositions**) are open to the public, often with an admission fee. Depending on the nature of the exposition, attendees can vary significantly, primarily determined by their interests and geographical proximity.

EMCs operate as profit-oriented enterprises, identifying economic niches that attract either the general public (such as auto, boat, home, or garden shows) or specific industry members (such as high-technology communications networking). Exhibitions serve as platforms for face-to-face marketing, offering valuable opportunities for direct interaction. Owners and senior managers of company-operated shows determine the "where, when, and frequency" of their events. This decision-making process is largely driven by profit considerations. Offering too many shows risks market saturation, but too few could pave the way for competitors. Prominent EMCs often oversee multiple events each year. They typically organize their teams according to the various shows, enabling focused efforts on understanding, expanding, marketing, and eventually executing each event on-site. Smaller EMCs may have a unified staff working together on all aspects of the exhibition. The primary association supporting the production side of the exhibition management industry is IAEE. Other relevant associations include the Exhibit Designers and Producers Association, Exposition Services and Contractors Association, and Healthcare Convention and Exhibitor Association. These associations play crucial roles in fostering professional growth and development within the exhibition management industry.

Certain associations choose to engage EMCs to oversee various aspects of their exhibitions. These companies receive compensation for their services rendered. Among EMCs, Reed Exhibitions and Emerald Expositions are prominent players. Their diverse array of shows caters to a wide range of industries, both domestically and internationally, across aerospace, art and entertainment, electronics, hospitality, security, sports and health, and travel. Other notable EMCs include International Gem and Jewelry Inc., Cygnus Expositions, and National Event Management Inc.

Despite playing a crucial role in the event planning sector, EMCs are primarily marketing entities that cultivate an environment conducive to fulfilling exchanges. Their core objectives are selling exhibit space, orchestrating events that ensure exhibitor satisfaction and recurring participation, and fostering buyer attendance. These companies must cater to two distinct yet interdependent audiences. The first is exhibitors seeking to engage potential buyers for their offerings. The second is trade professionals or the general public who need or want to explore, discuss, and acquire the products and services presented by exhibitors. The trade sector necessitates awareness of the exhibition or trade show's dates and location. Established shows may rely on means such as direct mail, email, and social media postings. In contrast, events appealing to the general public demand extensive media advertising involving social media, television, online platforms, magazines, and radio to disseminate specifics within the geographic region. Promotional strategies, including distributing discount coupons, are common. In both scenarios, the pivotal marketing outcome is generating robust foot traffic at the exhibition, thereby fulfilling exhibitors' requirements effectively.

ASSOCIATION MANAGEMENT COMPANIES (AMCS)

In line with the title, an AMC is engaged by an association to undertake full or partial management responsibilities, tailored to its requirements. A designated individual is the primary liaison for the association, engaging with the board of directors and members to advance the association's mission. For

AMCs
Caitlin Condie
Manager, Meetings and Expositions at Kellen

As a planner at an AMC, your role may be similar to those at stand-alone associations. The key difference is that you will work on multiple client events with varying needs. You will provide full-service planning—from consulting with the volunteer committees on site selection all the way up to meeting execution. What makes working at an AMC unique compared to working internally at an association is that you are constantly in different phases of each of your client events and each phase is just slightly different from your other clients. One event might be in the RFP process, and another is just wrapping up its annual convention. Because you are working with many different clients at the same time, your days are hardly ever the same. Challenges that arise are usually easier to handle because it is likely your other clients have already faced it or are going through the same issues.

Being a planner at an AMC has its perks—no two days are alike, you work on different staff teams and interact with them almost daily, and you have your own tiny network of other planners right next to you in the trenches. However, an AMC can also have its challenges. When you are working on multiple clients, you typically keep a full schedule throughout the entire year without much downtime because when one client is slow, you are usually weeks out from another client's annual meeting. The AMC environment tends to be a little more fast paced and, in many situations, you are the sole meeting planner on that client's association. This may sound frightening or too much to handle for some people. But, if you are someone who thrives in a fast-paced and steady environment, enjoys working with a team of people, and still wants the responsibility and role as *the* planner for an association, an AMC could be the place for you.

smaller associations with limited financial resources, this point of contact might fulfill similar duties for two or more associations. These were labeled "multimanagement companies" due to their management of multiple associations, but that was revised to avoid confusion regarding their target audience.

The AMC's team comprises additional staff members who support the main contact and provide contracted services, including functions such as membership management, financial oversight, publications, government relations, and meeting planning services. The association's administrative hub is often situated within the premises of the AMC. Renowned examples of such firms include SmithBucklin & Associates and the Association Management Group.

MEETING MANAGEMENT COMPANIES

These entities, also referred to as "**third parties**," function through contractual arrangements. Comparable to AMCs, **meeting management companies** offer a spectrum of services, either comprehensive or tailored to specific needs, that span numerous aspects of meeting planning, from premeeting support to "day-of assistance," encompassing city and venue research (also called "**sourcing**"), hotel negotiations and contracting, exhibit and sponsorship sales, on-site exhibit floor management, registration and housing services, lead retrieval equipment/platforms, meeting apps, marketing services, online meeting platforms, online moderation and coordination, or combinations thereof. Their events might occur at convention centers, conference centers, special venue facilities, or hotels. Prominent examples of MMCs are Conference Direct, Meeting Management Group, and Experient Inc.

For on-site events, a significant portion of revenue often originates from a 10% commission on each room night reserved at the hotel. In exchange for generating these bookings, a comprehensive third-party service provider might employ portions of these commissions to offset fees charged to the client for other services. For virtual events or events with a direct fee structure, the meeting management company might impose a flat fee or a percentage of the overall event cost.

Professional Congress Organizers (PCOs)

Beyond the United States, a meeting management company is commonly called a "PCO." In international settings, a "congress" encompasses conferences or conventions. As per the EIC APEX Glossary, a PCO is a local supplier capable of arranging, managing, and/or planning any function or service for an event. PCOs strongly resemble destination management companies in the United States. For international events organized by sponsors from North America, a PCO from the host region is often engaged to assist with local logistics. In certain countries, it is a requirement to contract with a domestic company for the management of the event.

INDEPENDENT MEETING MANAGERS

Experienced meeting professionals often leverage their expertise and industry connections to establish their own businesses focused on managing meetings or specific components of events. These independent meeting managers offer their services to a wide range of entities, including associations, corporations, and individuals. Their scope of work can encompass diverse tasks, such as planning and executing weddings, coordinating golf tournaments as part of larger events, providing on-site management, or acting as a full-service meeting management firm. They might also be called upon to address last-minute crises within the meetings department. When sudden personnel changes occur shortly before a meeting, hiring a capable professional to salvage and successfully execute it becomes crucial. This model is particularly suitable for professionals who have garnered substantial knowledge and respect within the industry while working full time for an organization. By venturing out on their own, they can take charge of their schedules and choose the clients they wish to work with. Independent meeting managers operate on a contract basis and enjoy the flexibility to select their engagements. The area of the industry that they are associated with will determine the type of professional organization they are likely to join for their ongoing development. Many may opt for associations such as PCMA or MPI. Alternatively, some might prefer to be part of organizations such as the International Live Events Association, National Association of Catering Executives, or Association of Bridal Consultants.

Independent Meeting Planners
Melissa Whitaker, CMP
Meetings Consultant

Independent meeting planners have unique benefits that employed planners do not, such as creating their own clientele base, setting their own schedules, and being their own boss. Personally, I love working with several clients, who vary from corporate to association to incentive, because it provides me with a variety of work so that every day looks different. Also, setting my own schedule allows me more flexibility in balancing my work and family responsibilities. Self-employment gives me the opportunity to work from home, build my own company, and direct my career accordingly.

Independent meeting planners get to choose their own work projects and what they want their particular focus to be. My projects vary daily and include sourcing RFPs, site selection, negotiating contracts, creating budgets, preparing event specifications, planning logistics for off-site events, and on-site assistance/travel directing. Independent meeting planners also get to dictate if they want to travel, and if they do, how much they would like to. I travel about 30% of the time and get to experience many places that I have never been before.

In the event industry, networking is important, but it is especially critical for the independent meeting planner. It is key to the success of my business, so I always make sure that colleagues know that I am available to help whenever they or someone they know needs assistance. Although it is up to the planner where they want to focus their own time and energy, I have found that it is important to me to be involved in my local associations. These are excellent opportunities to give back to my professional community, stay on top of industry trends, and network with colleagues.

TRENDS AND BEST PRACTICES

The advancement of technologies has ushered in more virtual interactions, alleviating meeting and event planners' concerns that online conferences might replace face-to-face meetings. The pandemic's effects presented planners with chances to view virtual and hybrid interactions as assets. Contrary to their apprehensions, what transpired was quite the opposite—planners developed a newfound appreciation for virtual interactions. Substantial research over the years has revealed that online meetings have not harmed in-person gatherings. In fact, they have aided in extending their reach to audiences who might otherwise have been unable to attend, enabling attendees to try out conferences before converting to face-to-face experiences. Experts firmly believe that the allure of face-to-face meetings will persist. Although technology allows people to join online communities and engage more frequently, human nature dictates a fundamental need for genuine, in-person interactions.

People not only enjoy but also require the opportunity to come together, exchange ideas, reconnect, and build networks.

In the realm of meetings and events, several recent trends have emerged, which are anticipated to persist in the near future. As a "before" and "after" examination, the following trends were identified as imminent in the previous edition of this textbook (2021). These trends have become integral to the fabric of the meeting and event industry, and their influence continues to endure.

- *budgetary constraints,*
- *shortening meetings,*
- *changing frequency of annual meetings,*
- *creating more value for their members,*
- *increasing the interactivity of meeting sessions,*
- *merging of sponsoring organizations,*
- *virtual conferences,*
- *virtual trade shows,*
- *outsourcing,*
- *focus on ROI, and*
- *limiting government meetings/events.*

Sustainability and sustainable practices require a strategy

What are the trends we are seeing now in the industry?

Attendee personalization. Personalized attendee experiences have emerged as a significant trend. Much like individuals customizing their products and services, attendees seek tailored events that cater to their preferences and requirements. With the aid of event technology, participants can now personalize their engagement and connection in various meetings and events, irrespective of their scale or style.

Event experience design versus traditional planning. A shift from traditional planning to event experience design has taken center stage. The industry now distinguishes between event coordinators, who focus on logistics, and event designers/strategists who craft experiences aligned with a broader strategy. The later demonstrate a return on investment (ROI) for the event itself.

More collaboration during meetings/fewer presentations. Meetings and events are shifting toward greater collaboration and reduced emphasis on presentations. In the context of an experience and transformation-oriented economy, they prioritize curating moments for attendees. Recent research reveals that almost 75% of meetings include workshop components. The new objective is to foster environments where participants engage, collaborate, and discuss, with deliberate outcomes, takeaways, and tools that can be applied within their organizations.

Consolidation will dominate. The surge in mergers and acquisitions encompasses event-related organizations and suppliers. As larger corporations amass more resources, smaller counterparts and rival associations face challenges in competing and must strategically position themselves within their market to ensure their success.

Sustainability. The integration of sustainability initiatives and practices has gained momentum, with attendees increasingly conscious of such efforts at every event. According to recent research, 80% of respondents indicated that their organizations consider sustainability when planning gatherings. Among them, 76% have already implemented a well-defined sustainable meeting program or strategy.

Diversity and inclusion. The significance of diversity and inclusion has grown, with a strong emphasis on its communication. More than half of North American event websites now feature information about their diversity and inclusion policies.

Embrace last-minute attendees. Attendees are waiting longer and longer to make the decision to attend. Although scheduling constraints might play a role, financial considerations and the fear of missing out on alternative opportunities are also contributing factors. Event professionals should warmly welcome last-minute attendees, reevaluate early bird pricing strategies, and ensure continuous promotion leading up to the event.

Hybrid events are increasing. Time has officially been acknowledged as one of the most precious resources globally. Although events hold value, the inconvenience of travel may not be deemed essential. Hybrid events offer a solution for individuals seeking either an in-person experience or the convenience of virtual attendance. The approach extends the event's reach beyond the confines of the physical meeting room to a global audience.

Event technology. Event technology has seamlessly integrated itself into virtually every kind of gathering. With widespread public acceptance, its

Event technology is essential to the future of the MEEC industry

offerings have expanded rapidly. Artificial intelligence, augmented reality, virtual reality, the advent of the metaverse, and innovations such as ChatGPT have collectively disrupted the industry. As technological advancements continue, they will consistently shape gatherings of varying sizes and types.

SUMMARY

The array of organizations that sponsor gatherings is as diverse as the events themselves and the attendees who partake in them. A significant portion of the population will engage in some form of gathering at least once in their lifetime. For many, attending meetings, conventions, exhibitions, and other events—whether in person, hybrid, or virtual—becomes a regular aspect of their lives, reflecting their personal and professional interests.

Those aiming to pursue careers in meeting planning within sponsoring organizations need to employ targeted strategies to locate suitable opportunities. Although such positions are distributed across the country, they are most concentrated in areas where these organizations are headquartered. The metropolitan Washington, DC region, recognized as the meetings capital of the world, houses numerous associations in and around the city. With the federal government also situated in Washington, DC, it employs a substantial number of individuals in the meetings field to manage and host numerous events annually. State capitals are hubs for state and regional associations and government agencies, all of which organize multiple annual meetings. Major corporations are often based in large cities, and though they might have branches in smaller locales, their event planning is typically centralized at their headquarters. Opportunities for employment can be found in both prominent urban centers and smaller towns among organizations and venues that facilitate gatherings.

As the baby boomer generation, the second-largest age group in the U.S. population, enters retirement, it is projected that a growing number of employment openings will emerge in the MEEC industry. This trend will be evident in the roles of both planners and suppliers.

PROFESSIONAL PREPARATION FOR A CAREER IN THE MEEC INDUSTRY

The Pineapple Corporation is a hospitality management company that develops and delivers management training for a range of hospitality and tourism businesses. Its leadership has proposed to host a launch event for the entire company showcasing a new program that has been in development. This event will include 3 days of professional development, meetings, social gatherings, and entertainment, culminating on Day 3 with the launch event gala. A series of pre-event meetings will take place beginning 6 months before.

LAUNCH EVENT
- Attendees: company personnel and the media;
- Location: local luxury hotel with ample event space;
- Travel arrangements: lodging and air, for some;
- F&B: fine dining, featuring local/regional cuisine; and
- Entertainment: local artists.

You have been with the Pineapple Corporation for just under a year and are still new to corporate meetings and events after completing your degree. This is your first time planning an event of this type and caliber. Your responsibilities including site selection, layout and design, programming, including all F&B, and execution of the launch event gala.

The company's leadership has informed you that they have a specific date; it is just over a year away. Normally, the lead time is less than 6 months, but to ensure quality, they are providing you with an *extra* 6 months to plan this exciting event. This is a new initiative that will include future associated meetings and events.

The leadership recognizes that you are developing as an event professional and wishes to support your growth by sponsoring your membership in an industry association, which includes completing an industry certification. This will assist you in planning the launch event.

Questions

1. Given the scenario, what training/education would *you* need to enhance your professional acumen for this particular position? Explain.
2. Use the Table below to answer a–b.
    a. Research three professional meetings and events associations. MPI and PCMA are included. Select a third association.
       Compare and contrast the associations. What are your findings?
    b. What types of *meeting and event certifications and certificates* are available through each of these associations?

Associations—Compare & Contrast		
MPI	PCMA	
Certifications & Certificates		

3. Which professional association do *you* feel would assist in further developing your skills for your role with the Pineapple Corporation? Why?
4. Which *certification(s) and/or certificate(s)* would be best for *you* in this type of organization? Explain.

KEY WORDS AND TERMS

For definitions, see the glossary, http://glossary.conventionindustry.org, or http://www.exhibitoronline.com/glossary/index.asp.

associations
association management company
continuing education units
conventions
corporation
exhibitions
expositions
exhibition management companies
incentive trips
per diem rates
public shows
meeting management companies
social, military, educational, religious, and fraternal
sourcing
third parties
trade show

REVIEW AND DISCUSSION QUESTIONS

1. Identify the type of sponsoring organization that holds the greatest number of gatherings and the type that generates the greatest economic benefit.

2. Which type or types of sponsoring organizations have the greatest marketing challenges to ensure the success of their gatherings?

3. What changes are occurring with incentive trips to provide more value for the corporation sponsoring the gathering?

4. How do not-for-profit associations differ from for-profit organizations?

5. What types of organizations comprise SMERFs, and what similarities do they share with each other?

6. Compare and contrast trade shows and expositions.

7. What efficiencies do AMCs bring to the management and operation of small associations?

8. Name three careers that were created for virtual and hybrid events.

ABOUT THE CHAPTER CONTRIBUTOR

Thomas C. Padron, Ph.D., CMP, CHE, CWP

Dr. Padron is an associate professor of hospitality and tourism and the undergraduate and graduate program coordinator at Cal State East Bay in California. He has been a hospitality educator for more than 20 years, teaching courses on campus, hybrid, and online. Dr. Padron has held many positions in the hospitality industry, including chef, sous chef, banquet chef, director of catering, banquet sales director, foodservice director, and foodservice manager.

He has a Ph.D. in business organization and management with a specialization in leadership from Capella University; a master of science in hospitality and tourism management with a specialization in education, and a bachelor of science in hospitality and tourism management with a concentration in F&B, both from the University of Wisconsin-Stout; and an associate's degree in culinary arts and a vocational diploma in food service production, both from Madison College (formerly Madison Area Technical College). Dr. Padron is also a certified hospitality educator and certified wedding planner through the Certified Wedding Planner Society.

Dr. Padron is active in the PCMA, where he chaired the Faculty Committee; MPI Northern California Chapter, where he chaired the Emerging Professionals Committee; IAEE, where he chaired the Faculty Committee; and the California Restaurant Association and National Restaurant Association. He is also a member of the International Council on Hotel, Restaurant, and Institutional Education, and West Federation CHRIE, where was the director of conferences, secretary, and treasurer.

Contact information:
California State University, East Bay
25800 Carlos Bee Boulevard, Hayward, CA 94542
thomas.padron@csueastbay.edu

Previous Edition Chapter Contributors

Kristin Malek, University of Nebraska—Lincoln
Nancy DeBrosse, senior vice president at Experient
Howard E. Reichbart, emeritus from Northern Virginia Community College.

CHAPTER 3

DESTINATION MARKETING ORGANIZATIONS (DMOs)

CONVENTION AND VISITORS BUREAUS (CVBS)/DESTINATION MARKETING ORGANIZATIONS (DMOs) ARE FOUND THROUGHOUT THE WORLD

CHAPTER OBJECTIVES

- Articulate the roles and functions of a DMO.
- Outline the needs and opportunities a DMO can meet for a meeting professional.
- Illustrate the convention marketing and sales activities expected of a DMO.
- Describe the tools and associations available through Destination International.
- Discuss trends in the field of designation market organizations.
- Identify ways the COVID-19 pandemic is impacting DMOs.

Contributed by Dr Jonathon Day. © Kendall Hunt Publishing Company.

If a destination were merely a location—a dot on a map, a bump in the road, or just another stop along the way—then its significance would be diminished. However, destinations are significant. They are referred to as "destinations" for a reason: people have a desire or a need to visit them. In many cases, people go to great lengths to reach these places. They have a magnetic pull, and for some, they symbolize the realization of lifelong dreams. Whether by boat, car, plane, or train, people embark on these journeys. Why? Because, contrary to the age-old adage, it is not solely about the journey; the destination has its own importance. The motivations for these journeys are as diverse as the people making them. Whether for business, conventions/meetings, or leisure, individuals seek them out in anticipation of a gratifying experience.

In essence, a destination must offer distinctive experiences that compel individuals to invest their time and money in traveling there. Travel and tourism play a crucial role in enhancing the quality of life within destination communities. They create employment opportunities, stimulate fresh economic activities, and contribute tax revenue that can be used for public services and to sustain cultural and recreational establishments that cater to both tourists and locals. Convention facilities are frequently leased by groups that cater to local residents. For instance, home and garden shows, boat shows, car shows, golf exhibitions, comic book expositions, and a plethora of other events draw in audiences from near and far.

THE ROLE AND FUNCTION OF DMOs

WHAT IS A DMO?

A **destination marketing organization (DMO)** goes by various names, such as "national tourism board," "state tourism office," or "convention and visitor bureau" (CVB). These not-for-profit or hybrid government entities represent specific destinations, fostering economic growth through travel and tourism strategies. Across cities, regions, or countries, DMOs promote their locales to leisure and business travelers and event planners seeking meeting spaces. They also aid event hosts in preparation. DMOs entice visitors to engage with a destination's historical, cultural, and recreational offerings. Serving as exclusive marketers, they shape the destination's brand, uniting diverse audiences. Achieving this requires effective communication, collaboration with locals, and a keen grasp of unique attributes. Through strategic marketing, DMOs create an alluring image that draws people in, driving them to explore the destination personally.

Although a DMO does not typically organize meetings, events, and conventions, it plays a vital role in aiding event planners to fully leverage the destination's services and facilities. This assistance enables planners to explore the destination's attractions and make optimal use of available resources. DMOs trace back to 1895, when a group of Detroit businessmen dispatched a full-time salesman to invite conventions to their city. This endeavor expanded over time, leading to the establishment of convention bureaus. Today, DMOs operate globally, focused on generating "new revenue" for the communities they represent by attracting visitor spending.

Initially centered on selling and servicing conventions, DMOs gradually diversified into tourism promotion. What were once convention bureaus extended their reach to include tourism, adopting the term "CVB." This evolutionary process of expanding roles and functions is ongoing. Many CVBs now use "DMO" interchangeably to better encompass their efforts in selling and promoting their destinations to a wide array of customers. DMOs and CVBs are synonymous, encompassing the same essential functions.

THE PURPOSE OF A DMO

DMOs significantly enhance the quality of life within their communities by contributing to long-term economic development, preserving local heritage and culture, and promoting responsible environmental practices. Some DMOs operate on a membership basis, uniting local businesses reliant on tourism and meetings for revenue. These organizations are the official point of contact for their destinations. Although certain DMOs function as departments of local government—akin to libraries or highway departments—this is more prevalent outside the United States. In these cases, DMOs might either be independent organizations with government support or divisions of local government referred to as "authorities." Many U.S. DMOs are not-for-profit organizations and categorized as either "501(c)(3)" or "501(c)(6)" entities, enabling them to effectively serve their communities and promote economic growth, cultural preservation, and sustainable environmental practices.

For visitors, DMOs are a key to unlock the city's treasures. They serve as impartial guides and experts about their destinations. Acting as a comprehensive resource hub, they streamline local tourism interests, saving both visitors and event professionals valuable time and effort. DMOs offer a comprehensive spectrum of information about a destination, and their services are free.

In the realm of conventions, DMOs frequently act as intermediaries between hosting organizations and hospitality businesses, such as coordinating site visits, facilitating the distribution and collection of **requests for proposals**, and crafting promotional materials. Some DMOs also secure funding to attract major conventions and even provide direct financial support to present the most enticing proposal, especially when the business's value justifies the investment. Often, cities compete against one another to attract business, which can translate into millions of dollars injected into the local economy from a single event. Ultimately, when competing cities offer comparable facilities, the most appealing financial arrangement often secures the deal.

An inherent value of most DMOs is their commitment to delivering impartial information on amenities and offerings. Their primary objective is to outshine competitors by skillfully aligning customers' precise meeting requirements with the available services and facilities. To illustrate, a student group may prioritize cost effectiveness and exhibit greater interest in budget-friendly hotels and economical meeting spaces. In contrast, corporate gatherings often gravitate toward the most upscale hotels and premium venues. A DMO assesses the client's needs and financial considerations, presenting viable options that resonate with their preferences. The DMO's task is to secure business for the entire community, ensuring equitable representation for all stakeholders. A DMO operates as a facilitator, orchestrating a harmonious match between customer requirements and the diverse array of local offerings.

IF DMOs DO NOT CHARGE FOR THEIR SERVICES, HOW DO THEY MAKE MONEY?

DMOs extend their services to leisure visitors, business travelers, and event planners for free. In the United States, they are primarily funded through a combination of sources. These include a portion of the hotel occupancy taxes, membership dues, and occasionally contributions from a tourism improvement district (TID). A TID designates a specific community area where any increase in property taxes is allocated for a designated purpose. Various forms of TIDs exist. For instance, if hotels, restaurants, and other hospitality establishments undergo expansion, improvement, or addition, the DMO benefits financially. The rationale is that these new facilities are direct outcomes of the DMO's marketing and promotional endeavors. Another variation of a TID arises when hotels within the district levy an extra user fee for each occupied room night. The revenue generated often funds the DMO's marketing initiatives.

When the DMO is a government agency, its funding is from governmental sources. This multifaceted funding approach enables DMOs to diligently pursue their mission of promoting and enhancing the destination's appeal.

> Memphis boasts a rich tapestry of over 60 tourist attractions, including renowned sites, such as Graceland, Beale Street, and the Memphis Pyramid, complemented by a vibrant array of restaurants, theaters, and art museums. The Memphis CVB adeptly harnesses the allure of these iconic destinations to promote the city to a global audience.
>
> Beyond its leisure draws, the Memphis Renasant Convention Center commands the attention of over 500,000 annual visitors, who gather for conventions, trade shows, and performing arts events. In 2020, the convention center concluded a remarkable $200 million renovation, transforming it into a cutting-edge facility designed to attract fresh business to the city.
>
> To sustain its competitive edge and finance the convention center's enhancements, the bureau, along with city hoteliers, orchestrated a groundbreaking collaboration—the first TID in Tennessee. This innovative effort capitalized on their shared commitment and involved working alongside the city to channel new bed tax funds exclusively toward convention center improvements. The Memphis TID was inaugurated on January 1, 2016, featuring a modest assessment of $2.00 per occupied room per night. This initiative infuses $5.3 million annually into the district, fueling a range of destination marketing endeavors.
>
> *Used with permission by Civitas Advisors*

ATTRACTING LEISURE TRAVELERS

Although various stakeholders, such as hotels, attractions, and organizations play roles in destination marketing, the DMO is the primary tourism marketer for most locales. Its chief objectives are promoting the destination and bolstering the influx of overnight guests. At the forefront of community efforts, the DMO spearheads creating a destination brand and comprehensive marketing strategy.

Beyond conventional advertising and promotional campaigns, DMOs can actively contribute to product development tailored for specific market segments.

They harness the distinctive attributes and unique strengths of the community to compel individuals to explore the destination. Often, DMOs curate bundles of attractions, tailored to specific demographic groups. For instance, if a destination features a zoo, children's museum, and amusement park, the DMO will target families—primarily mothers—offering curated itineraries for enjoyable family vacations. Similarly, it might use a city's shopping venues, spas, and local eateries to promote "girls' getaway" weekends or market sporting events and craft beer festivals to distinct demographics. In essence, DMOs strategically assemble the most captivating collection of assets to draw the highest number of leisure visitors—who not only spend but also foster repeat visits.

PROMOTING THE DESTINATION

Although certain cities, such as Las Vegas and Orlando, have earned reputations as tourist hot spots, most cities need to educate potential visitors about the compelling reasons to plan a trip.

A DMO must select the most effective ways to reach its target audience and often employs a combination of marketing strategies based on its overall advertising budget and insights into the spending habits of its intended customers. These strategies might encompass traditional avenues, such as television, radio, newspapers, and magazines, or extend to digital advertising on platforms such as Facebook and an array of other available options.

DMOs skillfully employ public relations initiatives to amplify positive narratives about their destinations. One impactful technique involves inviting travel journalists for an all-expenses-paid visit to experience their community firsthand. During this typically 3-day immersive experience, the DMO hosts the travel writer, blogger, or influencer, aiming for them to produce favorable stories. This unprejudiced "third-party" endorsement proves highly effective in capturing the curiosity of their devoted readership, who regard these sources as reliable founts of travel information. This approach significantly enhances the destination's appeal and credibility.

Website

One of the most potent marketing tools in a DMO's arsenal is a well-crafted and all-encompassing website, showcasing the premier attractions and amenities. The finest websites boast captivating visuals, engaging videos, and insightful blogs that paint vivid narratives of the community's offerings.

DMOs are adept at narrating the destination's tale, and their most impactful blogs spotlight riveting encounters and unforgettable events that render the locale irresistible. These blogs delve into various aspects, including culinary delights, local communities, natural beauty, and authentic interactions with the residents. In essence, they bring the destination to life through firsthand experiences and genuine human connections.

WHAT A DMO CAN DO FOR MEETING PROFESSIONALS

WHAT MEETING PLANNERS NEED TO KNOW ABOUT DMOS

Many individuals remain unaware of DMOs, overlooking the abundant information and resources that they generously provide. They are best compared to real estate agents. Much like realtors, DMOs identify potential prospects (event planners) interested in acquiring the goods and services available within the destination. They act as intermediaries, facilitating the interaction between the buyer (event planner) and seller (destination services) to eliminate obstacles that could hinder a successful transaction.

A DMO has numerous responsibilities. Most important, it assumes the role of *the* official point of contact for convention and event planners. In situations involving a convention center, the DMO often manages bookings, extending 18 months or more in advance. The DMO endeavors to entice groups to select their destination for events and lends assistance with various aspects of meeting preparations. This includes furnishing promotional materials, giveaways, and video "teasers" to boost attendance and coordinating room blocks (reserved hotel rooms for a group).

For event planners, DMOs offer a gamut of services, packages, and additional perks. However, before delving into the specifics of how DMOs support event planners, it is pertinent to address a few common misconceptions.

> *Misconception 1:* DMOs only handle hotel room and convention space bookings.
>
> *Fact:* DMOs encompass a wide spectrum of visitor-oriented businesses, ranging from restaurants and retail to car rentals and entertainment venues. They introduce planners to the full array of meeting-related products and services available in the city.

Misconception 2: DMOs exclusively cater to large groups.

Fact: Over two-thirds of DMO efforts are dedicated to meetings with fewer than 200 attendees. Larger DMOs even designate staff members solely for managing small meetings, group tours, leisure travelers, and transient business trips.

Misconception 3: DMOs own and operate convention centers.

Fact: Only about 10% of DMOs manage their local convention centers, such as the Las Vegas Convention and Visitor Authority. Nevertheless, DMOs maintain close collaborations with these centers and can assist planners in obtaining necessary support from their staff.

Misconception 4: Planners need to pay DMOs for their services.

Fact: Most of the services offered are free.

Some might question the necessity of involving a DMO in planning a meeting, especially when the majority of it is in one hotel or solely within a convention center. However, a DMO's contribution goes beyond these venues. It assists planners in collaborating with these entities and also enriches the convention schedule by incorporating off-site activities, such as spouse tours and pre- or posttours. Being an impartial resource, the DMO adeptly guides planners toward the optimal products and services that align with attendees' needs and financial considerations.

DMOs are pivotal in streamlining meeting planning and execution, affording direct access to essential services. Armed with an intimate understanding of their destination, DMOs provide event planners with an array of services, packages, and value-added perks. DMO sales managers assist in locating suitable meeting spaces, verifying hotel availability, and coordinating site inspections. DMOs forge connections between planners and suppliers, from motor coach companies and catering services to off-site entertainment venues that cater to diverse demands.

Furthermore, DMOs act as intermediaries between planners and community officials, facilitating processes such as securing special permits and arranging street closures. They also extend suggestions to attendees on maximizing their free time, crafting companion programs, and curating pre- and postconvention tours. The DMO's role optimizes the overall event experience, making it more seamless and enriching for both planners and attendees.

A Business Case for DMOs

How DMOs Provide Return on Investment to Their Communities

DMOs must forge and skillfully promote the destination's brand to potential visitors, effectively assuming the roles of sales, marketing, and public relations firms for the entire community.

Much like any business entity, DMOs must constantly prove their value to stakeholders, including hotels, attraction members, and governmental bodies. These organizations are entrusted with judiciously using revenue, often from tax dollars, and held accountable for delivering a substantial return on investment (ROI). Most DMOs present their performance against key performance indicators (KPIs) during annual meetings.

Examples of KPIs include the following:

- communications: media contacts, press releases, media coverage, press tours, and media impressions;
- convention Sales: trade shows attended, familiarization tours conducted, sales calls, site inspections, leads sent, definite bookings, definite room nights, definite convention attendance, and lost opportunities;
- services: citywide events, welcome booth referrals, planning bulletins, registrar hours, site visits, housings, reservations processed, and room nights processed; and
- marketing: web statistics, social media statistics, tracked visitors, inquiries, retail revenue, visitor satisfaction, advertising expenditure, and ad value gained.

KPIs with a significant focus typically include those linked to the industry's overall economic impact, job creation, and the local taxes contributed by out-of-town visitors.

In addition to operational efficiency, DMOs must ensure key stakeholders—including tourism enterprises, policymakers, legislators, and the local community—grasp the intrinsic value of their endeavors. Garnering such understanding and support is pivotal to their sustained success.

Photo of light bulbs with shining fibers in shapes of Marketing Sales, Advertising, Promotion and Strategy concept related words isolated on black background

DMO Departments and Staff

Although departments, job titles, and responsibilities vary from one DMO to another, most with convention facilities have the following:

- president and CEO/executive director,
- vice president of convention sales,
- vice president of convention services,
- vice president of marketing,
- vice president of finance,
- vice president of communications, and
- vice president of membership.

Within each department of a DMO, dedicated staff members provide crucial support to the vice president. These roles include directors, managers, coordinators, and assistants; their distribution depends on the DMO's focus, with more leisure-oriented organizations allocating greater support for marketing and public relations and DMOs with substantial convention facilities assigning more staff to selling and servicing conventions.

In specific destinations, additional roles, such as research director, community relations director, or government relations director, might also be present.

DMOs are keenly interested in engaging both current and aspiring professionals in the field. Many offer a diverse range of internships, primarily targeted at college students. Often, these interns are given priority consideration for entry-level positions. Aspiring professionals are encouraged to explore DMO websites for available internship opportunities, which may be open year-round. Internships offer valuable insights and experiences, serving as stepping-stones for those aspiring to build careers within the field of destination marketing and management.

ACTIVITIES OF DMOs RELATIVE TO CONVENTION MARKETING AND SALES

Professionals who work in a DMO serve as the sales representative for their destination. A DMO undertakes an entire process with a meeting professional to bring a meeting to its destination.

SALES PROCESSES

DMOs are actively invested in capturing a portion of the thriving events and meetings market. They enlist skilled sales professionals to advocate for their destinations. Employing an array of sales strategies and tactics, DMOs aim to attract conventions, trade shows, meetings, and various events. Some larger not-for-profit industry shows include the following:

- American Bus Association,
- American Society of Association Executives,
- Destinations International Destinations Showcase,
- International Travel Association,
- National Association of Sports Commissions,
- National Coalition of Black Meeting Planners,
- NCAA Convention,
- Professional Conference Management Association Annual Meeting, and
- Religious Conference Management Association.

The largest for-profit trade show in the United States and Germany is organized by IMEX, based in London, England. Each of its shows attracts more than 12,000 attendees.

BERLIN, GERMANY - MARCH 8, 2014: attendees walking around California stand in the Section 2.1 at ITB Travel Trade Show in the fairgrounds of Messe Berlin

DMOs have a range of options for participating in numerous local, regional, and national expositions. Their choice hinges on aligning their community strengths with the attendee profile. For instance, a destination lacking sports facilities would not find the NCAA Convention as beneficial.

Most industry events allow DMOs to engage in multiday trade shows, coupled with educational and networking events. The overarching aim is to cultivate personal relationships with both current and potential customers, facilitating the process of promoting their destination.

DMO sales professionals also rely on conventional sales solicitation methods, such as phone calls, emails, and mail, to connect with new event planner customers. In this era of abundant information, DMO salespeople can access customer lists and market insights to streamline their outreach efforts effectively.

SITE REVIEW AND LEADS PROCESS

Assessing the suitability of a site or venue for hosting a meeting is of utmost importance. The DMO assumes a pivotal role as the central repository of information, providing invaluable guidance on location selection, transportation options, and local services, all without any cost or commitment for the event organizer. DMO representatives have comprehensive knowledge and data, offering real-time insights into the region's current status and future developmental plans.

Regardless of the event's scale, the DMO can be the initial destination for the site assessment process. When an event planner contacts a DMO, a designated sales manager is assigned to facilitate the acquisition of essential information to ensure the event's success. This sales contact collects details about preferred event dates, available facilities, sufficiency of lodging and meeting spaces, and the availability of convention facilities for the entire event duration, including setup and teardown times for exhibitors.

To cater to the diverse needs of their stakeholders, most DMOs employ a lead management process. The sales contact disseminates the meeting specifications to facilities and accommodations providers capable of fulfilling the requirements. Vital details essential for the DMO are documented on the convention lead sheet and distributed electronically.

Lead distribution can also be tailored by imposing specific criteria, such as requesting locations near the downtown area or the airport; the lead is exclusively shared with properties that fulfill the requirements. This could encompass various factors, regardless of their scale, such as the number of rooms, meeting space square footage, options for off-site meal functions, or proximity to sports facilities. If an event planner is well acquainted with certain properties in the destination, they might express interest in those venues, prompting lead distribution only to those establishments.

Upon receiving a lead, the DMO sales contact may prompt the property to directly furnish information to the event planner. Alternatively, the contact could gather the essential details, compile them into a comprehensive package, and forward it. In the United States, federal antitrust regulations restrict DMOs from discussing pricing policies with hotels. All pricing negotiations must be between the planner and hotel. Although a DMO sales contact may indicate that an event planner seeks a specific range of rates, they are not authorized to negotiate on the planner's behalf.

Throughout the process, DMO sales professionals frequently engage with customers to ensure that the destination extends the most enticing offer in terms of available venues, services, and expenses. Certain DMOs and destination venues allocate dedicated funds to offer financial incentives to defray event costs. These incentives are quite influential, often swaying groups in their decision.

Convention Lead Sheet

The convention lead sheet used by DMOs will usually contain the following information:

- name of the DMO sales contact,
- distribution date of convention lead sheet,
- name of event planner and title,
- name of the group or organization,
- address information for group or organization,
- email and telephone number of the event planner,
- total number of room nights anticipated,
- peak room nights and day of peak,
- dates for the event or meeting,
- decision date,
- total anticipated attendance,
- occupancy pattern
  - day
  - date
  - rooms
- meeting space requirements
  - exhibit space
  - food functions
- history
- competing cities
- bedroom rate history
- bedroom pickup history
- meeting rotation pattern (south, north, east, west, central)
- decision steps
- additional information, and
- name of person who prepared the sheet and date of preparation.

The lead management process occurs well before the actual event. For associations, the average time frame between considering a destination and the event varies. For sizable groups and major cities, it can span years or even decades. A notable example is the Morial Convention Center in New Orleans, which regularly secures commitments from large groups up to 25 years in advance.

The DMO's sales manager is pivotal in orchestrating communication between the event planner and venues. They ensure that all vital information is shared, received, and comprehended. Any additional queries from the planner are promptly addressed, and they are encouraged to visit the city and personally inspect the venues and hotels. The DMO's role is crucial during that review, facilitating site inspections and coordinating visits to potential locations. This active involvement enhances the planner's familiarity with the destination and the facilities being considered.

SITE INSPECTIONS

A site inspection involves physically evaluating potential venues and services before the actual event. It can be a crucial step at any stage of the sales process. Planners might conduct site inspections before or after receiving a proposal or after contracting for space.

- preproposal site inspection: Allows the client to gather information. Often, the DMO hosts.
- postproposal site inspection: Takes place after proposal submission but before the client's decision; addresses queries about the proposed execution.
- postcontract site inspection: Occurs after contract signing; initiates event finalization.

Site inspections vary in duration and detail. Careful planning is essential to showcase venues and services and introduce the destination team, including community contacts, to the customer. These inspections must be meticulously orchestrated to highlight offerings and allow customers to interact with the destination team. Site inspections can profoundly impact customer decisions, offering the DMO a chance to build relationships and gain confidence. Often, seemingly simple lunch conversations can sway the outcome.

DMO SERVICES FOR MEETING PROFESSIONALS

DMOs offer an array of general services to support meeting professionals. One crucial category is "connecting planners and attendees to the destination." DMOs furnish essential data, such as hotel room counts and meeting space statistics, and maintain a central database of other ongoing meetings, aiding planners in preventing scheduling conflicts and space shortages.

DMOs excel in ensuring meeting facility availability, offering information about the readiness of hotels, convention centers, and other venues. They also facilitate access to the local transportation network, assisting planners with shuttle services, ground transportation, and airline details. Moreover, DMOs can grant access to unique venues. With their connections to city departments and influence on local government officials, DMOs can secure a range of assistance, from official welcome letters from the mayor to road closures for street events.

DMOs extend their role to help meeting attendees optimize their free time by crafting pre- and postconference activities, spouse tours, and special evening events. Last, DMOs are liaisons in destination government and community relations. They serve as local resources, offering insights into legislative, regulatory, and municipal matters that could impact meetings or the broader meetings industry.

Another service category can be termed "information." DMOs are impartial sources of comprehensive information about various destination services and facilities. They act as extensive information hubs, offering a one-stop resource that saves planners time, effort, and money during the process. DMOs are also intermediaries between planners and the community. For instance, they are aware of local events that might align well with a meeting's schedule, such as festivals or sporting events. Additionally, DMOs furnish destination information, covering local events, attractions, activities, restaurants, and aiding in tour and event planning.

A third service category involves assisting with the meeting or event itself. DMOs contribute to creating collateral materials and handling on-site logistics and registration. They can also design pre- and postconference activities, spouse tours, and special events. Furthermore, DMOs can support site inspections, familiarization tours, and site selection. They may also offer speakers and local educational opportunities. Last, DMOs can assist in securing auxiliary services, such as production companies, catering, and security.

CHANGING SCOPE OF DMO RESPONSIBILITIES

A primary goal of DMOs is to ensure the satisfaction of their clients by matching event planners with the perfect setting and services for their events.

Traditionally, DMOs have concentrated on boosting hotel occupancy and the number of meetings and conventions held in their destinations. However, the rapid growth in global tourism has led to a shift in some communities, altering the ratio of visitors to locals; residents are raising concerns about when the influx of tourists might start to negatively impact their quality of life.

In response, DMOs are adapting their roles, transitioning from solely marketers to destination managers. They are actively cultivating stronger ties with governments and planning authorities to include tourism perspectives in decision-making. A pivotal step is creating a tourism master plan, which outlines a long-term framework (10–20 years) for tourism development, emphasizing policy, strategy, planning, institutional strengthening, legislation, regulation, product development, and diversification.

Increasingly, DMOs are assuming the role of community partners, collaborating to bolster the tourism infrastructure. For instance, many DMOs collaborate with local airport authorities to enhance air travel options. They also work alongside hotel developers to ensure that new properties align with the city's unique assets, contributing to the overall enhancement of the destination.

The popularity of both amateur and professional sports has grown significantly, prompting many DMOs to establish sports development departments or sports commissions to tap into this market. With a youth component prevalent in every sport, destinations have effectively attracted tournaments to their locales. An advantageous aspect of youth sports events is their weekend and summer scheduling, complementing the typical Monday to Thursday convention schedule. Sports facilities, such as baseball diamonds, swimming pools, soccer fields, and ice arenas, have become sought-after venues for teams seeking to compete while traveling. This benefits not only the visiting teams but also the local community, which can also use these facilities. This trend translates into substantial gains for local hotels, restaurants, and attractions, making it a profitable venture for all involved.

A significant number of DMOs employ dedicated research directors to collect an array of pertinent data from the tourism industry, including the following:

- hotel occupancy rates, average daily rates, and revenue per available room;
- count of local tourism-related jobs;
- amount of local and state taxes generated by the tourism sector;
- total direct spending associated with tourism;
- economic and social impact analyses for various groups, festivals, and sporting events; and
- surveys measuring traveler satisfaction with the destination.

These statistics are meticulously compiled and shared with local community partners, government bodies, and stakeholders. This data serves as a powerful tool to substantiate the DMO's contributions within the broader context of the local tourism endeavor.

DESTINATIONS INTERNATIONAL (DI)

As the global trade association for official DMOs, DI plays a vital role in safeguarding and advancing the achievements of destination marketing on a global scale.

With a membership roster exceeding 800 official DMOs, over 6,750 individual members across 23 countries and territories, and a collective annual budget of more than $2 billion, DI is a unifying force. Membership is open to all recognized official DMOs, spanning the spectrum from the smallest towns to the largest countries. This encompasses convention and visitor bureaus, regional tourism boards, state and provincial tourism offices, and national tourism boards.

DI delivers an array of valuable offerings to its members, including information, resources, research insights, networking avenues, professional development, and certification programs.

Mission

We empower destinations so their communities thrive.

Vision

Our members are essential to the success of destinations worldwide.

Value Proposition

> We inform, connect, inspire, and educate our members to drive destination economic impact, job creation, community sustainability, and quality of life through travel.
>
> *Brand Promise*
>
> DI educates, equips, and empowers its members to grow the success of their destinations and to excel professionally.

DI actively promotes DMOs worldwide, highlighting the value of using a DMO's services to the media and the general public.

DI PROFESSIONAL DEVELOPMENT OFFERINGS

DI provides professional development to DMOs and their employees via an annual convention, an online learning center, forums, summits, sales academy, and certification.

CERTIFIED DESTINATION MANAGEMENT EXECUTIVE (CDME)

The CDME is akin to the CMP designation in the event professional realm. Widely recognized within the DMO industry as the pinnacle of educational achievement, the CDME program is tailored for seasoned DMO executives seeking advanced professional growth. The curriculum is designed to equip senior-level executives and managers with the tools to navigate evolving landscapes and intensified competition.

Centered around vision, leadership, productivity, and strategic implementation, the CDME program emphasizes enhancing the effectiveness of both destination teams and individual performance through adept organizational and industry leadership. It is a testament to DI's commitment to fostering enduring excellence within the DMO community.

PROFESSIONAL IN DESTINATION MANAGEMENT (PDM) PROGRAM

DI's PDM certificate program, although not a formal designation like CDME, enjoys industrywide recognition for its immense value as a skill set. The PDM program is designed for those at the entry level of their career journey or new to the field of destination management, who gain the knowledge and skills required to excel as effective and accomplished destination management practitioners.

DI RESEARCH AND ADVOCACY

DI presents an abundance of research and resources with indispensable statistical data and insights necessary for various aspects of destination management, including economic impact assessment, budgeting, strategic planning, marketing, promotion, and stakeholder education. Its nonprofit Destination and Travel Foundation offers destination management professionals a gateway to comprehensive and industry-specific information. This wealth of resources assists professionals in enhancing the efficiency of their DMO's daily operations and business planning endeavors.

A significant research endeavor under the auspices of the Destination and Travel Foundation involves a series of commissioned reports, aiming to examine future trends that will shape the landscape of tourism and destination marketing. This comprehensive initiative, the **DestinationNEXT Futures Study**, is meticulously crafted to equip DMOs with actionable insights and strategies aimed at enhancing their performance and achieving future objectives.

The core purpose of DestinationNEXT is to address a crucial question: How will the DMOs of the future be configured, and how can today's leaders guide their organizations toward a trajectory that safeguards the advantages of tourism, strengthens their position in the marketplace, and fosters meaningful community engagement? The outcomes of this research have been integral in guiding DI's efforts to provide DMOs with the tools and knowledge necessary to advocate for the significance of their role within their communities and the broader tourism ecosystem.

DI DESTINATION TOOLS

DI also provides a range of tools that support DMOs in their operations. DI gathers information on DMO operations through two reporting platforms:

> *DMO Compensation and Benefits Reporting Platform:* collects information on compensation and benefits from DMOs; and

> *DMO Organizational Performance Reporting Platform:* dynamic and the most comprehensive of its type for DMOs, provides standards for a variety of operations while also allowing DMOs to compare their operations with their peers.

Other tools include an equity, diversity, and inclusions (EDI) assessment tool, designed to assist DMOs in implementing EDI programs in their communities, and the DestinationNEXT assessment tool that helps destinations track stakeholder attitude and assess their place in the local community.

EVENT IMPACT CALCULATOR

The *Event Impact Calculator* serves as a robust tool for quantifying the economic value of events and assessing their ROI in terms of local taxes. By leveraging this tool, DMOs are equipped to advocate effectively for the continual advancement and expansion of the meetings sector to policymakers. The calculator, which is updated annually, draws from an array of 10 distinct data sources, establishing an industrywide benchmark with the following attributes:

- Credible: Requiring minimal user inputs, DMOs can generate impactful analyses rooted in the latest survey data and economic statistics available.
- Localized: Each DMO gains access to a model meticulously tailored to the nuances of their specific destination.
- Comprehensive: The calculator meticulously gauges events' direct impacts on various aspects, including businesses, employment, income generation, and tax contributions.

With its robust capabilities, the Event Impact Calculator equips DMOs with a persuasive tool to communicate the value of events, enabling them to effectively advocate for the growth and development of the meetings sector in collaboration with policymakers.

ACCREDITATION

Introduced in 2006, the Destination Marketing Accreditation Program was pioneered by DI, and it has garnered substantial adoption, with over 200 DMOs attaining it. Its comprehensive standards cover a diverse spectrum of crucial aspects, encompassing governance, finance, management, human resources, visitor services, group services, sales communications, membership, brand management, destination development, research/market intelligence, innovation, and stakeholder relationships. This meticulous accreditation process serves as a vital tool for DMOs, ensuring that they follow superior practices. Moreover, it is a prominent indicator to external stakeholders of the organization's professionalism and commitment to excellence.

DESTINATION AND TRAVEL FOUNDATION

Established in 1993, the Destination and Travel Foundation emerged to enhance and amplify the influence of both DI and the destination management sector. Its mission encompasses research, education, visionary initiatives, and cultivating resources and collaborations to support these endeavors. The DI Foundation integrated with the U.S. Travel Association's Foundation, culminating in the formation of the Destination and Travel Foundation. It is classified as a charitable entity according to Section 501(c)(3) of the U.S. Internal Revenue Service Code; donations directed toward it are eligible for tax deductions as charitable contributions.

ASSOCIATION OF AUSTRALIAN CONVENTION BUREAUX

The Association of Australian Convention Bureaux Inc. (AACB) serves as a unifying force that assembles city and regional bureaus with a shared goal of promoting distinct regions as prime destinations for business events on both domestic and international scales. Leveraging its influential position among stakeholders, including government bodies, AACB is committed to fostering the expansion of business events. AACB's strategic priorities are the following:

- Enhancing Australia's competitive edge in global business events: AACB endeavors to bolster Australia's position as a prominent contender in the global business events landscape.
- Demonstrating the impact of business events through research and storytelling: AACB aims to showcase the profound influence of business events.
- Leading a vibrant and interconnected business events industry: AACB seeks to spearhead a dynamic and cohesive industry, fostering connections and collaboration.
- Operating as an agile, high-performing, and unified organization: AACB strives for agility, high performance, and unity, positioning itself as a potent force in business events.

TRENDS

DMOs' roles and responsibilities are significantly expanding. Many DMOs have begun actively "managing" the destination itself: participating in various facets of tourism development, policy formulation, infrastructure enhancement, urban planning, and the expansion of convention centers. They are also instrumental in attracting hotel developers and facilitating a range of initiatives.

A dual perspective exists on the acronym "DMO." It denotes either destination *marketing* organization or destination *management* organization. Moreover, experts within the industry have proposed a more comprehensive and descriptive compromise term: destination marketing and management organizations (DMMOs). It encapsulates the evolving multifaceted roles these organizations play in not only marketing but also actively managing and fostering the growth of their respective destinations.

DMMOs

The following is a synopsis of a presentation by Chris Fair of Resonance Consultancy at the European Cities Marketing Meeting in Gdansk

The transformation of the DMOs is so profound that the organization's name itself needs to change. How should the DMMOs evolve into the future?

At this juncture, DMOs face a critical choice as they chart the course for their destination's success. Historically, their focus and success metrics have revolved around boosting hotel occupancy and increasing the number of meetings and conventions held within the destination. However, the rapid surge in global tourism has led to a substantial shift in the visitors-to-locals ratio in cities across the world. As tourism grows, residents in many cities are starting to question when the influx of tourists might start to impact *their* local quality of life adversely. To illustrate, cities such as Savannah, Georgia have initiated research studies to investigate this very issue. The perception of tourism can rapidly shift from being an economic boon to a potential threat to the community's well-being. Consequently, DMOs can transition from being perceived as contributors to the local community to being seen as detractors. DMOs that neglect to address this concern might find themselves on the unfavorable end of this discourse.

As DMOs contemplate their evolution into DMMOs, they need to scrutinize all facets of a destination's needs and holistic development. DMOs possess limited influence over city planning, policy formulation, and program implementation. A pivotal step in the transition is to forge stronger connections with government bodies and planning authorities, thereby ensuring that tourism is represented in important discussions. Crafting a collaborative *tourism master plan* with the city can serve as an initial stride in this direction. This can be facilitated by organizations such as DI through initiatives such as *Destination Next*. Another integral aspect involves delineating roles and responsibilities within the organization, backed by appropriate funding, to guarantee the implementation and ongoing monitoring of the plan's recommendations. Last, DMMOs can play an elevated role in managing the overall guest experience within the destination. This extends beyond staffing visitor centers and delves into how tourism impacts the lives of residents as well.

DMOs commonly assess visitor satisfaction with their destinations, yet engaging with residents is often overlooked. The transition into a DMMO necessitates a shift in focus, requiring organizations to allocate as much effort toward communicating with, monitoring, and gauging resident satisfaction as they currently do with visitors.

The travel industry has undergone remarkable disruption due to technological advancements, substantially altering DMOs' marketing strategies. However, attention has been limited for harnessing technology as a marketing channel and exploring its potential to enrich and manage visitors' experiences postarrival. DMMOs should adapt their existing digital platforms or establish distinct websites, apps, and booking systems specifically tailored for visitors to access upon their arrival. This empowers visitors to take charge of their experiences. Concurrently, DMMOs should strengthen their connection with and understanding of visitors in real time.

By striking this balance between visitor empowerment and enhanced connection, DMMOs can effectively manage the complex landscape of both visitor satisfaction and resident engagement, thereby ensuring that the destination thrives for all stakeholders.

DMOs must broaden their roles within cities and destinations and position themselves as guardians and curators of the city's brand. This extends beyond just tourism and encompasses talent attraction and investment. Unlike any other entity in a destination, DMOs possess the funding and expertise required to do this and can greatly enhance the value proposition to the communities they serve.

Establishing a shared vision with the community to define strategic direction involves envisioning the destination's future. A comprehensive plan is crafted to outline the pathway toward that future. However, that is merely the first step. The most challenging aspect is its execution, which demands dedicated budget and personnel. Some DMOs have introduced specialized administrative roles within their structures to facilitate this process. Two notable titles are chief experience officer and vice president of destination development.

Through this evolved approach, DMOs can elevate their contributions by actively shaping the destination's identity, enhancing resident engagement, and driving sustainable growth across multiple sectors. This comprehensive perspective ensures that the destination thrives holistically and remains a desirable place for visitors, residents, and investors alike.

map with Pin Pointers 3d rendering image

Another term gaining prominence is "destination stewardship." The Destination Next Report (2019) highlighted that this term better encapsulates the role of DMOs in influencing stakeholders and fostering collaborations within the community, rather than simply "managing" the extensive array of activities in a tourism destination. Destination stewardship places greater emphasis on the DMO's responsibility to enhance the well-being and quality of life of community members in the context of tourism. This concept necessitates DMOs to consider the social, environmental, and economic impacts of tourism on their destinations.

In recent years, DMOs have significantly increased their efforts to engage with their local communities. This trend will persist as more residents seek an active role in shaping their destination's strategic direction. DMOs must expand these collaborations, extending beyond the confines of the traditional tourism industry. As tourism continues to grow, DMOs will continue to advocate for it while elucidating its benefits to a range of stakeholders, including policymakers, legislators, businesses, and residents. Community support is pivotal for the effective functioning of tourism, and DMOs are vital to conveying the positive impact of tourism within the community.

DMOs are also becoming increasingly involved in destination development and enhancing the visitor experience. For instance, organizations such as DI have developed a variety of support materials focusing on EDI to assist in creating welcoming environments for diverse visitors.

The journey of DMOs in adapting to and adopting new technologies remains ongoing. Staying ahead of trends in digital marketing, including harnessing the potential of social media and other online promotional avenues, has proven to be a significant challenge for many DMOs in recent times. Nonetheless, numerous DMOs have effectively used these innovative tools to advance their destination marketing objectives.

The dynamic technology landscape, marked by the rise of new AI technologies, expansion of the metaverse, and immersive experiences offered by augmented and virtual reality, is poised to present even more intricate challenges in the years to come. Nevertheless, DMOs will undeniably continue to leverage these cutting-edge tools to create substantial benefits for not only themselves but also their destination communities and the visitors they serve.

Visit http://www.destinationmarketing.org, DI's official website.

Beautiful of Aerial panoramic view in an Autumn season at a historic city of Salzburg with Salzach river in beautiful golden evening light sky and colorful of autumn at sunset, Salzburger Land, Austria

Vienna Convention Bureau

The Vienna Convention Bureau is your neutral partner. Our job is to promote Vienna as Central Europe's leading conference city. We offer our services free of charge to any national or international organizer of meetings, conventions, and incentives.

The Vienna Convention Bureau was set up in 1969 as a department of the Vienna Tourist Board with financial support from the Vienna City Council and Chamber of Commerce. Additional funding comes from sponsors. To hold its corner in today's networked global markets, the Vienna Convention Bureau belongs to a number of international convention and meeting industry associations.

In a recent year, the meetings industry accounted for 9% of all overnights in Vienna. The exceptional meeting infrastructure, the excellent service standard of the meeting service sector as well as the cultural attractiveness of the city are all factors that contribute to making Vienna a top destination worldwide for international meetings.

The Vienna Convention Bureau has set itself the task of promoting awareness on sustainable actions in the sector and supports initiatives and projects on the topics of green meetings, sustainability, and corporate social responsibility.

Courtesy of the Vienna Convention Bureau

Airport screen indicating canceled flights due to the Coronavirus pandemic

SUMMARY

DMOs play an integral role within the meetings, conventions, and travel industry. For over a century, DMOs have diligently worked to attract meetings and conventions to their destinations and extended free services to support these events. Their role has expanded from being solely marketers to becoming comprehensive destination managers, engaging in every facet of their destinations to enhance the overall experience for all visitors. The concept of destination stewardship aptly captures the emerging role of DMOs in improving the overall quality of life in their communities through their actions.

DI is the professional association for DMO employees, offering a plethora of member services to support DMOs since its inception in 1914.

As DMOs look ahead, they will confront various challenges, including the increasing need to advocate for tourism within their communities, effectively manage intricate stakeholder relationships within the broader tourism ecosystem, and seamlessly integrate evolving technologies into their operations. Nevertheless, DMOs remain a pivotal resource for the meetings industry, continuously working to enhance the success and growth of the destinations they serve.

CASE STUDY: GLASGOW CONVENTION BUREAU (GCB)'S COMMITMENT TO POSITIVE IMPACT

Sustainability has gained increasing importance among event planners and their clients and attendees. DMOs play a pivotal role in facilitating the connection between planners and local resources, ensuring that sustainability goals are met.

An exemplary case is Glasgow, Scotland, where GCB, a division of Glasgow Life, is dedicated to advancing sustainable practices in both meetings and tourism. GCB's Sustainable Tourism and Conventions Action Plan is strategically designed to "develop the tourism and convention sector to benefit our citizens, our economy, and the environment." GCB recognizes that achieving sustainable meetings and events necessitates collaborative efforts from the CVB, visitors, and the entire conference supply chain.

GCB empowers and educates event planners by offering an online sustainability toolkit that equips conference organizers with the tools to identify businesses and services committed to sustainability, access green activities for delegates, and explore sustainable food initiatives. One valuable resource is the downloadable brochure titled "Go Greener: Sustainable Conference Ideas," which offers insights into offsetting conference carbon emissions through local projects, such as the Clyde Climate Forest, and suggests attendee gifts that contribute to green initiatives, fostering a more environmentally conscious approach to events. Through these efforts, DMOs such as GCB are contributing to a more sustainable future within the industry.

GCB's commitment extends to ensuring that conventions have a lasting positive impact on their host communities. In the past, conferences would often come and go, without engaging deeply with the local community. GCB has transformed this approach by providing a platform for meeting organizers to connect with the local community, businesses, and academic institutions.

Moreover, GCB has initiated campaigns in collaboration with conference organizers to enhance Glasgow's identity as a welcoming and beneficial destination. An illustrative instance is the partnership between GCB and the organizing associations of major events, such as the World Federation of Hemophilia World Congress, World Down Syndrome Congress, and International Symposium on ALS/MND in 2018. The collaboration developed educational materials and training programs to ensure that Glasgow was well prepared to provide a welcoming environment for attendees.

In subsequent years, GCB launched the "People Make Glasgow Healthier" campaign, catering to health-related conferences. This initiative aimed to engage with the local population in ways that not only elevated the profile of the participating associations but also contributed to improving its health and well-being. By fostering these connections and collaborative efforts, GCB demonstrates a proactive approach to making conventions more impactful, beneficial, and enriching for both visitors and the local community.

KEY WORDS AND TERMS

For definitions, see glossary or http://glossary.conventionindustry.org.
certified destination management executive
Destinations International
destination marketing organization
DestinationNEXT Futures Study
requests for proposals

REVIEW AND DISCUSSION QUESTIONS

1. Define the role and function of a DMO.
2. Name the different ways that DMOs can be funded.
3. Name two things that a DMO does for meeting professionals.
4. Name two things that DI does for meeting professionals.
5. What can DI do for DMOs?
6. What trends are facing DMOs?

WEBSITES FOR REFERENCE

1. http://www.destinationmarketing.org
2. https://www.ustravel.org/
3. https://aacb.org.au/
4. https://convention-europe.com/
5. https://www.europeancitiesmarketing.com/
6. https://glasgowconventionbureau.com/plan-your-meeting/meeting-planners-toolkit/sustainability/

ABOUT THE CHAPTER CONTRIBUTOR

Dr. Jonathon Day is an associate professor in Purdue University's School of Hospitality and Tourism Management. Before joining academia, he was a destination marketing professional with Tourism Queensland, Australia.

Previous Chapter Contributors

Craig Davis, CEO, Visit Dallas

Karen M. Gonzales, CMP, Destinations International

CHAPTER 4

MEETING, EXPOSITIONS, EVENT, AND CONVENTION VENUES: AN EXAMINATION OF FACILITIES USED BY MEETING AND EVENT PROFESSIONALS

Interior photography of a large hotel ballroom decorated for a special event

CHAPTER OBJECTIVES

- Discuss the physical characteristics and financial structure of hotels.
- Identify the types of events best suited to a convention center and the reasons behind that solution.
- Discuss the space, functions, consortia, and financing involved in using conference centers for events.
- Identify the similarities, differences, and benefits of cruise ships and other event venue options.
- Articulate the benefits of specific use facilities as event venues.
- Outline the appeal and uses of colleges and universities as event venues.
- Cover the unique needs and uses that differentiate retreat facilities from other kinds of venues.
- Discuss the expanded use and growth of unique and unusual venues to create memorable event experiences.
- Illustrate the typical needs and obstacles specific to an outdoor event.

Contributed by Dr. Lisa Young. © Kendall Hunt Publishing Company.
Contributed by Juan Mendez. © Kendall Hunt Publishing Company.

Meeting planners and event professionals operate within a diverse range of venues. (Throughout this chapter, terms such as "meeting planner," "event professional," "planner," and "professional" are used interchangeably.) These venues encompass a broad spectrum, spanning from intimate **hotel** suites capable of accommodating only a few individuals to expansive convention centers and open-air festival sites designed for tens of thousands. Essentially, any location where two or more individuals gather qualifies as a meeting event site. Regardless of whether it is a sprawling multimillion-square-foot convention center or a modest local restaurant, people always manage to find a suitable place for congregating.

Event professionals match an event to a venue by assessing two fundamental aspects about it: (a) the identity of the participants and (b) the purpose behind it. Planners comprehensively research facilities to ensure that the chosen venue aligns with the group's requirements and anticipations. Before finalizing a venue, a comprehensive **needs analysis** must be conducted. Refer to Chapter 12 for an in-depth elaboration on planning Meetings, Expositions, Events, and Conventions (MEEC) events and the significance of needs analysis.

The majority of meetings take place within conference rooms and offices located on the organization's premises. Typically, one room within a suite of offices is designated as a conference room, allowing a small group of colleagues to convene to discuss ongoing matters. Although these meetings, whether scheduled or impromptu, often do not involve a dedicated full-time planner, they are frequently organized by an employee who handles such responsibilities as part of their job description. As these meetings expand in scale and involve more participants, the individual responsible for on-site meetings inevitably starts planning events beyond the company's office, selecting the most suitable venue to achieve the objectives.

HOTELS

PHYSICAL CHARACTERISTICS

Meeting Room Spaces

Hotels consistently emerge as the primary preference for numerous corporate events. Any hotel with at least one compact **boardroom** becomes integrated into the realm of meetings and events. On one end of the spectrum, we find modest meeting rooms—often styled as boardrooms—primarily tailored for a limited number of participants. These spaces come furnished with a dedicated table and chairs. Conversely, at the opposite extreme, we encounter grand, formally appointed ballrooms designed to accommodate several thousand guests. A conventional floor layout features larger sections flanked by smaller ones, accessible through side corridors. The smaller segments, often referred to as "**breakout rooms**," have lower ceilings.

Other Hotel Meeting Spaces

Attendees seek distinctive avenues to foster engagement, maximize interactions, and establish interactive meetings characterized by a high degree of customization and personalization. They often search for spaces that enable them to concentrate on specific subjects within dedicated rooms, each crafted to serve different objectives, including small group discussions, spaces for attendee contemplation, casual gatherings, and formal presentations. Hotels offer various public spaces, such as pools, patios, atriums, lobbies, lawns, and gardens, that can be seamlessly transformed into MEEC settings. For instance, numerous resort hotels boast splendid outdoor patios and pool areas that regularly host events and continue to gain popularity.

Besides the use of outdoor venues, **prefunction spaces**—such as corridors or lobbies adjacent to meeting rooms—provides an ideal setting for supplementary meeting or event requirements. These areas conveniently accommodate refreshment breaks, registration desks, and cocktail receptions, ensuring vital services are provided without taking up valuable meeting rooms. As planners and attendees' demands veer toward experiential events, similar to breakout rooms and ballrooms, a hotel is more competitive when it can infuse nontraditional spaces with uniqueness, intrigue, and creativity, thus setting it apart from its competitors.

FINANCIAL STRUCTURE

Hotels can be owned by prominent branded hotel companies or operate as owned and franchised establishments managed by real estate investment firms that enlist hotel management companies to oversee operations in accordance with corporate brand standards. For the majority of hotels, meetings and events are not necessarily their primary focus. Almost all hotels primarily sell accommodations for overnight stays. A hotel's meeting space is often used to attract meeting customers to fill what would otherwise be empty sleeping rooms, especially on **shoulder** nights when the hotel does not have its core corporate or leisure business demand. Although room occupancy remains a crucial goal, meetings, events, and food and beverage (F&B) services more substantially affect the profit and loss equation of numerous hotels.

Additional revenue streams that contribute significantly to a hotel's earnings encompass restaurants, bars, and coffee kiosks frequented by MEEC attendees. A smaller portion of revenue also stems from **concessionaires** operating at **amenities**, such as pools, beaches, or spas.

NEGOTIATING YOUR EVENT

As the negotiation phase commences, key discussion points between the meeting planner and the venue are sleeping room rates, F&B offerings and associated costs, meeting space expenses, and charges for audiovisual (A/V) equipment and technology usage. Additional minor concessions might need to be discussed, such as parking, transportation, or supplementary hotel services, but these should be broached only once agreement on the main aspects has been reached.

ROOM RATES

When reserving meetings and events, the primary customer for hotels is the meeting planner. Their needs and preferences are important during sales and negotiations. It is commonly believed that meeting planners do not bear the cost of using meeting spaces in hotels, and these incur substantial expenses for hotels. Costs such as interest payments on the capital invested in constructing the hotel and the resources required for maintaining, cleaning, and operating the meeting rooms constitute some of the most significant outlays and need to be financed through either sleeping room bookings or banquet services.

Hotel banquet catering departments design menus and catering services that align with the specific demands of each meeting or event. In some instances, hotels link banquet revenue with meeting space use; a meeting planner who reaches a certain spending threshold within the catering department might be entitled to a reduced cost for the meeting room.

Often, the expenses for meetings and events are offset by stipulating that it commits to reserving a minimum number of sleeping rooms and nights. This arrangement, commonly referred to as a "room block," is an essential requirement for the meeting planner to fulfill and typically associated with complimentary rooms and/or room discounts. The industry standard is that for every 50 rooms reserved, one room is complimentary. As a negotiation point, this ratio could be revised to one complimentary room for every 30 reserved.

The room block method makes it possible to reduce the cost associated with reserving meeting rooms. However, this approach presents a challenge, primarily due to the precision required when projecting the number of sleeping rooms. Before negotiations, meeting planners research the nightly rates listed on online travel agencies for the specific hotel. Planners are keenly aware that their attendees often consult these platforms to secure rates lower than the negotiated rate. These room nights are excluded from the contracted room block, potentially leading the planner to incur **attrition** penalties for failing to meet the room block commitments. Contract clauses can be introduced to address this concern, and consulting an attorney experienced in these matters is advised. The planner's objective is to receive credit for every room night sold as a result of the event. This particular issue can often prove to be the most challenging aspect of negotiating with hotels. To mitigate attrition, certain associations require their attendees to book within the room block or face significantly higher registration fees.

F&B

F&B represent another substantial revenue stream for the majority of hotels. The hotel's restaurants and bars are typically designed to cater to its regular guests, a mix of business travelers and tourists. Both meeting planners and hotels recognize that specific periods during a meeting or event will cause an uptick in business at the hotel's dining outlets. For instance, attendees may gather at the hotel bar before and after a meeting or event in the ballroom. During negotiations, it is crucial to incorporate this aspect into the discussion about F&B expenditure.

OTHER REVENUE-GENERATING DEPARTMENTS

Hotels generate revenue through a diverse array of nonmeeting services, which form an integral part of negotiations with the meeting planner. Hotels frequently establish agreements with exclusive vendors to provide services within their premises. In addition to revenue from catering services, hotels can also earn commissions from other vendors who pay for the privilege of operating within them. These vendors may include **exposition service contractors** (ESCs), A/V providers, disc jockeys, florists, limousine services, and entertainers. Commissions to the hotel can sometimes reach as high as 40%, and certain hotels also impose attrition charges.

The underlying principle from the hotel's standpoint is that both it and the vendors have invested resources in the facility and equipment for the benefit of the meeting planner; should they choose not to use these services, they may still be subject to charges because these were made available. This scenario is particularly prevalent with A/V services. Hotels often stipulate that planners must either use the in-house A/V department or an exclusive vendor. If a planner insists on an external company, they might be required to pay a higher fee. Addressing these expectations and commission-related matters early in negotiation prevents confusion down the line.

Local Meetings and Events

Numerous meetings and events do not necessitate booking sleeping rooms, and some hotels are open to these, particularly in the month or two leading up to the event when their event spaces remain unoccupied. To secure **complimentary** meeting space for a **local event**, the planner usually needs to guarantee a minimum amount of catering revenue.

Seasonality

Seasonality and the fluctuating levels of occupancy can exert a significant influence on the cost of using a facility. In destinations marked by seasonal shifts, the off-season rates can plummet to as little as half of peak rates. By attentively observing a facility's seasonal patterns of occupancy, meeting planners can unearth some truly advantageous deals. Meeting attendees often believe that their ability to secure an incredibly affordable rate at an exclusive resort reflects their planner's negotiation prowess. In reality, the attractive rate often stems from the strategic selection of a venue that experiences pronounced seasonal variations.

Apart from these factors to consider when reserving meeting space in hotels, planners must also account for move-in and move-out schedules and the presence of other groups on-site. Depending on the scale of the event, the setup or dismantling of the physical aspects can span from a few hours to a week, particularly if an exhibition component is involved. This time frame represents an opportunity cost for the hotel, as it cannot host another group that could generate revenue. To offset this loss, hotels may impose a rental fee for the space, given that additional profit via catering or other revenue sources is not feasible. Planners should anticipate the need to negotiate move-in and move-out dates, as hotels prioritize optimizing the use of their meeting spaces. Additionally, hotels often host meetings for multiple groups simultaneously, which becomes particularly relevant when a corporation is orchestrating a product launch or discussing proprietary information, as it prefers to maintain exclusivity by avoiding the presence of competitors within the same facility.

Efficient space coordination becomes vital, especially when groups exhibit conflicting behaviors. A serious conflict could arise if, for instance, a professional organization conducting a certification exam is placed in a meeting room adjacent to a daylong band rehearsal or an alcoholic beverage trade show is scheduled alongside a religious convention. Planners should be aware of and consider such conflicts during the negotiation and contracting phases to ensure successful planning and execution.

When meeting planners engage in negotiations with hotels, they need to factor in the comprehensive financial package their event will bring to the venue. The closer the financial structure of the event aligns with the hotel's needs, the more favorable the pricing the planner can secure. This financial package extends beyond just the event's revenue; it encompasses income generated from sleeping room bookings, restaurants, bars, and exclusive vendors. The presence and cost of specific amenities often shape attendee expectations of the venue. Hence, planners must align attendee expectations with the quality of service offered by the hotel, all within a cost framework that the meeting planner deems reasonable.

CONVENTION CENTERS

Convention centers are meticulously designed to accommodate significantly larger events than what could be feasibly hosted within a hotel setting. Some convention centers boast expansive meeting and exhibit spaces exceeding one million square feet. Their sheer size is both an advantage and a limitation. Convention centers are event venues without accommodations for sleeping, often characterized by grand architectural marvels that embody astonishing feats of engineering, accompanied by breathtaking vistas.

The global landscape is peppered with hundreds of convention centers, prompting meeting planners to seek out those that offer distinctive features aligned with their event's requirements for space and destination appeal. Moreover, the spectrum continually evolves, as several centers expand each year, leading to a dynamic and ever-changing array of available exhibition and meeting space. Refer to Table 4-1 for a list of the 15 largest convention centers worldwide and Table 4-2 for the 20 largest convention centers in the United States.

	Name	City	Square Meters	Square Footage
1	Messegelände Hannover	Hannover, Germany	496,000	5,340,000
2	National Exhibition and Convention Center	Shanghai, China	400,000	4,306,000
3	Messegelände Frankfurt	Frankfurt, Germany	366,637	3,946,500
4	Crocus Expo	Moscow, Russia	366,100	3,940,670
5	Fiera Milano	Milan, Italy	345,000	3,713,550
6	Canton (China Import & Export) Fair Complex	Guangzhou, China	338,000	3,638,200
7	Kunming Dianchi Conv. & Exhibition Center	Kunming, China	310,000	3,336,800
8	Koelnmesse (Cologne Trade Fair)	Cologne, Germany	284,000	3,057,000
9	Düsseldorf Messe	Düsseldorf, Germany	262,000	2,820,150
10	Paris-Nord Villepinte	Paris, France	242,082	2,605,750
11	McCormick Place	Chicago, USA	241,500	2,600,000
12	Fira Barcelona – Gran Via	Barcelona, Spain	240,000	2,584,000
13	Feria Valencia	Valencia, Spain	230,000	2,475,700
14	Paris Expo Porte de Versailles	Paris, France	216,000	2,325,000
15	Messe München	Munich, Germany	200,000	2,152,780

TABLE 4.1. Largest Convention Centers in the World (by Total Indoor Exhibition Space)

	Convention Center Name (City)	Exhibition Space	Total Exhibition & Meeting Space
1	McCormick Place (Chicago)	2,600,000	3,800,000
2	Las Vegas Convention Center	2,543,000	4,600,000
3	Orange County Convention Center (Orlando)	2,055,000	7,000,000
4	Georgia World Congress Center (Atlanta)	1,500,000	3,900,000
5	Mandalay Bay Convention Center (Las Vegas)	1,100,000	2,100,000
6	New Orleans Morial Convention Center	1,100,000	1,671,000
7	Anaheim Convention Center	1,013,000	1,800,000
8	Kay Bailey Hutchison Convention Center Dallas	1,000,000	1,390,000
9	Venetian Convention & Expo Center (Las Vegas)	936,600	2,250,000
10	Jacob K. Javits Convention Center (New York City)	850,000	1,200,000
11	Donald E Stephens Convention Center (Rosemont, IL)	840,000	840,000
12	Moscone Center (San Francisco)	800,000	2,000,000
13	George R. Brown Convention Center (Houston)	770,000	1,012,000

TABLE 4.2 Largest Convention Centers in the United States (by Square Foot)

14	Indiana Convention Center (Indianapolis)	750,000	1,030,000
15	Huntington Place (Detroit)	723,000	1,145,000
16	Los Angeles Convention Center	720,000	860,000
17	Walter E Washington Conv. Center (Wash. DC)	703,000	2,300,000
18	San Diego Convention Center	616,000	2,600,000
19	Colorado Convention Center (Denver)	584,000	670,000
20	Pennsylvania Convention Center (Philadelphia)	528,000	1,100,000

TABLE 4.2 Largest Convention Centers in the United States (by Square Foot) continued

In contrast to hotels, convention centers tend to allocate a larger proportion of their space to **exhibit halls** and functional areas. However, recent expansions of convention centers have incorporated additional elements of comfort and design. Their lobbies are meticulously designed to facilitate the seamless movement of several thousand attendees. Given the multitude of convention centers worldwide, meeting planners actively seek out venues that present distinctive attributes catering to their event's requirements for space and destination allure.

Exterior of the Las Vegas, Convention Center during the Consumer Electronic Show

© RYO Alexandre/Shutterstock.com

Conversations about convention centers typically address aspects such as the count of meeting rooms, available square footage, adaptability of the space, and infusion of local elements, all of which are important. The central emphasis is on diverse configurations, innovative space use, and an anticipation that all areas will be more captivating, pertinent, and enjoyable. The spotlight is on establishing hubs, education centers, interactive zones, and technology hubs.

Show floor of IMEX Frankfurt Trade Show

Similar to hotels boasting an array of space dimensions, convention centers also offer a wide variety of spaces. Within a conventional full-service hotel, the ballrooms are the largest meeting areas, followed by breakout rooms. In a convention center, exhibit halls are typically the most expansive spaces, followed by carpeted ballrooms and then breakout and meeting rooms.

Industry Spotlight: Associations Are the Driving Force Behind the Business Events Industry

Please tell us your title, the organization you work for, and a brief description of your job.

As a meeting associate with American Association of Oral and Maxillofacial Surgeons (AAOMS), I plan and execute logistics for the association's annual meetings, dental implant conferences, off-site board meetings, regional meetings, affiliate meetings, and all in-house meetings. I work very closely with our vendors and venues to successfully plan meetings and events that include interacting with A/V companies, catering, hotels, and convention centers. I am currently the housing lead for all our association's meetings by working with a third-party housing company for our large annual meeting and manage the remaining housing needs for our meetings in house.

Cassie Mancera, Meetings Staff Associate, American Association of Oral and Maxillofacial Surgeons

MEETINGS, EXPOSITIONS, EVENTS, AND CONVENTIONS

Can you describe the types of events you plan?

I plan educational conferences. Our annual conference brings in between 3,000–4,000 people in person and online. Our regional programs have 100–200 people in attendance. I also plan all in-house committee meetings and small educational programs at our innovation center located in our headquarters in Rosemont, IL.

During our annual conference, we hold business meetings for our delegates, and we also provide education for our members. There are multiple receptions held during this week including a welcome reception at the beginning and a closing reception during our President's Event. Most of the programs I plan also include special event receptions to provide networking opportunities for our members.

What types of venues do you use?

I typically work with convention centers as the venue for our annual conferences, hotels for most regional programs, and our internal building for department in-house meetings. Occasionally, I work with unique venues for off-site special events.

What are some challenges and benefits of using convention centers?

Some of the challenges that come with using convention centers are related to staffing. It can be difficult for them to retain good staff with the skills needed, even more so post-COVID-19. Many staff are unionized, which can cause logistical issues if not planned correctly. Because every convention center is different, I increase my knowledge and skills throughout each planning cycle.

What changes have you seen in event venues and event planning from the pandemic?

In general, the pandemic has brought multiple challenges and opportunities to the events industry. One change is many venues have reduced the number of contract concessions that are available for negotiation, such as attrition and cancellation policies. Another change is the staff shortage in many venues, with someone often doing a job that was done by three people pre-COVID. The upside is that there are many open positions throughout the events industry allowing for career mobility.

The pandemic has also allowed us to be more creative and conscious of our ecological footprint throughout the event planning process, especially event design and décor. We are focused on being more sustainable, such as offering fewer buffets, which can often be wasteful if not ordered properly. We are replacing traditional printed conventional signage, which gets thrown away at the end of an event, with digital signs. Other changes have included reducing plastic flatware and taking advantage of existing recycling programs at our venues. Most importantly, we have been educating attendees on how they can reduce their own environmental impact at our meetings.

The COVID-19 pandemic showed us that digital interactions are possible and can help reduce carbon emissions generated by travel. We implement a virtual component to most of our meetings, allowing people to earn their continuing education credits online, which reduces their costs and time traveling to a destination. Yet, as we saw during quarantine, even high-quality virtual experiences may not be as impactful as attending an event in person. As industry professionals, we are always looking for ways to do things better and the pandemic showed us that we can do just that. Overall, many great improvements have come out of the pandemic for the event industry.

What is a favorite event venue that you have used, and why?

During our recent annual meeting, we had our President's Event at the Country Music Hall of Fame and Museum, located in Nashville. I assisted with the event's logistics, and it was an incredible experience to be in person at the event. We booked multiple levels of entertainment throughout the venue and paired each section with innovative food and drinks. That venue is fascinating!

What advice do you have for hospitality students?

Just go for it! There is a place for everybody in the meetings and events industry. My advice to students is get your foot in the door by trying something as simple as being a part-time server in a restaurant's private dining room or in a hotel's conference space. You are able to get industry and customer service experience while you are taking classes toward your college degree. Whatever position you have, there is always something new to learn each day that will get you one step closer to your dream job. Take time to learn about different types of events, meetings, and associations, explore other options, and reach out to mentors for advice. Find a way to incorporate what you love and the skills that you are good at into your events.

Once you have some basic hospitality experience, stretch yourself and go beyond hotel and restaurant positions. Complete internships in diverse areas, try different roles, belong to event planning organizations, and spend time volunteering your event skills. When you understand more about shows and events, you can make better choices about what you want your career to look like. There will be multiple event management opportunities to choose from when you get involved in the industry once you graduate.

I work as a meeting planner, but I do so much more than that. Sometimes I feel like I work in finance, sometimes I am doing logistics, other times I am teaching--there is never a dull moment. There are many skills that I use throughout my day, so there is bound to be something that interests everyone. Associations are a great segment of the industry to work for because they allow for a better work-life balance. There are endless opportunities within the hospitality industry, so my advice is to go for it!

FINANCIAL STRUCTURE

Unlike hotels, which are frequently part of corporate entities, many convention centers are owned by government entities. Governments aim to see a return on their investment and often enlist private convention facility management companies to oversee their operations. Numerous convention centers receive active support from local destination marketing organizations and convention and visitors bureaus, with some of these even managing convention centers themselves. As with most government investments, the management of these facilities is ultimately accountable to taxpayers. The success of a planner's event hinges on their relationship with the facility's management and the level of meticulous planning. Particularly for convention centers, thorough planning directly correlates with the success of the event.

One distinguishing aspect of convention centers is their energy budget. They often allocate more funds for utilities than for full-time staff. This does not reflect excessive staffing levels but rather underscores the significant expenses involved in maintaining proper climate control within vast facilities. Hotels also contend with substantial energy bills, but unlike convention centers, they do not need to regulate vast spaces with high ceilings and large doors that remain open throughout the day. In newly constructed convention centers, sustainability practices are paramount. Ceilings are made of transparent materials, windows are positioned to maximize natural sunlight, and thermal heat pumps are installed to reduce heating expenses. Water runoff and reclaimed water are recycled for irrigation purposes.

How do convention centers generate revenue? They are not expected to turn a profit in the traditional sense; their primary goal is to cover operational costs. Typically, the government entities that build these facilities intend for them to serve as economic drivers for the entire community, so they can host events that benefit the community without necessarily focusing on driving demand for sleeping room bookings in nearby hotels. This is partly why convention centers, unlike hotels, host events, such as local consumer shows, that may not generate overnight stays. The funding for convention centers might also involve a hotel sleeping room tax.

NEGOTIATING FOR YOUR EVENT

Convention centers adopt a comprehensive pay-per-use approach, charging for every service they provide. Each square foot carries a price tag. Room rentals, calculated per square foot per day, represent the most substantial revenue source. Every piece of furniture, including chairs and tables, and every service also has a specific cost. F&B services, catering, and concessions are typically outsourced to external vendors, who pay the convention center a percentage of their revenue. Unlike hotels that often bundle services into packages of room rates, F&B, and other amenities, convention centers meticulously itemize each expense. This approach allows them to charge for precisely the services used.

The financial arrangements between vendors and convention centers vary. Some vendors might remit a commission based on their revenue. Others may own equipment that is installed within the facility. For instance, the vending equipment for soft drinks might be owned and serviced by the soft drink company that holds exclusive rights within the facility, in exchange for a pre-defined level of product sales.

Historically, catering was the sole exclusive service, but power, rigging, A/V equipment, security, and telecom services may also be. Some of these exclusive relationships stem from government regulations, and others are aimed at mitigating liability-related legal actions. Conversely, some convention centers allow planners to engage vendors not on the recommended list but impose an additional fee.

Pricing transparency is a hallmark of most convention centers. Information regarding services offered, associated costs, and specific details about the facility's size and capabilities are typically accessible on their websites, so the onus falls on the planner to access and use these resources rather than the facility needing to guide a newcomer planner through the process.

CONFERENCE CENTERS

A **conference**, characterized by an agenda and defined objectives, serves as a platform for consultation, education, fact-finding, problem-solving, and information exchange. Conferences encompass a diverse array of purposes, including tasks such as auditing, budgeting, marketing and sales forecasting, product launches, strategic planning, team-building, and training. Conferences are generally shorter and more modest in scale compared to conventions.

MEETING ROOM SPACES

Given the multifaceted nature and diverse goals of conferences, a **conference center** is designed to accommodate the varied needs of the numerous organizations that use it. Vital design considerations include meeting rooms, spaces for refreshments, restrooms, isolated seating areas, and a staffed on-site business center. Conference centers are purposefully crafted to cater to conference activities, with acoustics, wall surfaces, lighting, and color schemes tailored to enhance attendee productivity and comfort.

Room Layouts

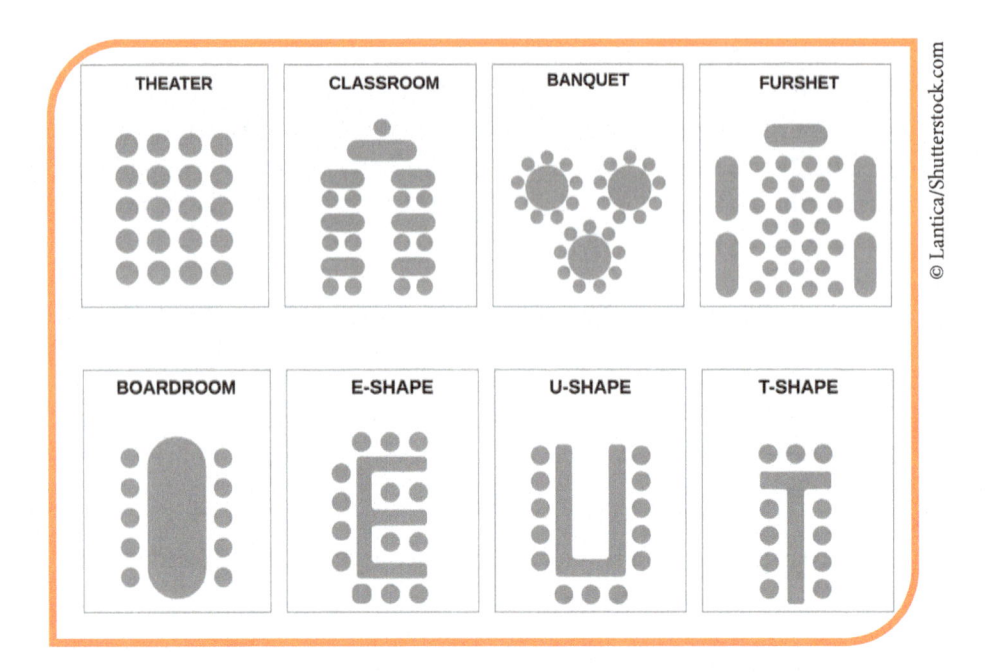

THEATER | CLASSROOM | BANQUET | FURSHET

BOARDROOM | E-SHAPE | U-SHAPE | T-SHAPE

© Lantica/Shutterstock.com

Conference center meeting rooms are specifically designed to optimize the learning experience and commonly set up in a **classroom-style** configuration. Chairs are chosen to provide both comfort and attentiveness, often featuring ergonomic executive-style designs. Tables are robust and steady, with smooth surfaces conducive to note-taking, and ample space to accommodate laptops and other essential meeting materials, and often electrical outlets to facilitate charging computers and phones. Notably, conference centers are recognized for their comprehensive inventory of in-house A/V technology and dedicated full-time media technicians. This translates into superior equipment quality and expedited response times for technical support.

Conference centers are dedicated to delivering exceptional service levels to cater to their diverse clientele, all of whom rely on an optimal meeting environment. When an organization reserves space, a designated manager is assigned to oversee all aspects of their meeting. This manager takes on responsibilities ranging from coordinating program specifics to providing attentive support during the meeting and even managing the postconvention evaluation, which ensures a seamless service experience for both the organization and its attendees. Some conference centers are integrated into corporate office complexes, and others are exclusively used by a single corporation.

ASSOCIATIONS AND CONSORTIA

The **International Association of Conference Centers** has crafted specific guidelines designed to guarantee that IACC conference centers offer consistent, high-quality meeting facilities worldwide. These guidelines encompass essential aspects, such as lighting, technology, and sound barrier standards, that organizations depend on to create an optimal learning environment and ensure that the facility is conducive to immersive group learning settings, managed by event professionals with certain meeting planning certifications. Certain conference centers feature overnight guest rooms, referred to as "**residential** conference centers"; others, known as "**nonresidential** conference centers," do not. IACC also stipulates guidelines for guest rooms, including providing a dedicated workspace with internet connectivity. Prominent corporations, such as Aramark, Dolce, Hilton, Marriott, and Sodexo, operate conference centers. IACC website conveniently offers a list of its global conference centers, complete with facility details and provided services, simplifying the initial search process for planners.

Various other associations and consortia focus on enhancing conference center offerings. A consortium signifies an association, partnership, or alliance formed by its members to extend services to regional, national, and global clients. Members typically pay an annual fee, which is pooled to market the consortium as a whole, ultimately driving customers to individual member facilities. Similar to associations, consortia often establish guidelines that all members must adhere to, ensuring consistent, high-quality products and services. Some conference facilities might belong to multiple associations and consortia, strategically maximizing their marketing.

F&B

Conference centers endeavor to provide attendees with a premium dining experience characterized by flexible options and elevated service levels in their on-site restaurants and bars. Menus are thoughtfully curated to align with the preferences anticipated by attendees and planners. This often encompasses an array of choices, spanning international cuisine, vibrant networking luncheons, and formal award dinners.

NEGOTIATING YOUR EVENT

Key areas of negotiation between the meeting planner and the conference center are meeting space costs, sleeping room rates (for a residential conference center), F&B menus and associated expenses, and A/V and technology offerings.

Many conference centers employ a pricing approach termed the "**complete meeting package**," which essentially grants planners access to the facility's inventory of equipment without additional charges. It places an array of resources—such as easels, projectors, microphones, and sound systems—at planners' immediate disposal, which provides flexibility, streamlining the process by eliminating the need to schedule external A/V companies for technological requirements and last-minute supply purchases.

Attrition takes on a new meaning in a conference center. It is not uncommon for conference centers to impose a fixed price for a predetermined number of delegates. If some delegates fail to attend, the planner is still accountable for the full contracted amount. This fee is not contingent upon the facility's ability to resell the rooms; rather, it is based on 100% of the negotiated facility fee, regardless of the extent to which the facility is used. Although the planner's on-site responsibilities may be less intense compared to a convention center, their capacity to accurately forecast room night use becomes exceedingly critical.

INDUSTRY SPOTLIGHT: CRUISES INSPIRE, INDULGE, AND INTRIGUE YOUR GROUP CLIENTS WITH EXQUISITE STYLE

What is your title, the organization you work for, and a brief description of your job?

I am Silversea's Senior Director of National Accounts. As part of the industry's ultraluxury sales organization, I oversee the cruise line's relationships with North America's top travel advisers, agencies, and networks. I manage my national account sale team and their strategy, training, and marketing initiatives to achieve successful sales in the industry. As the 'jewel in the crown' of the Royal Caribbean Group, Silversea Cruises is the leading ultraluxury and expedition cruise line—acclaimed for both its all-inclusive lifestyle offerings and its

Source: Laurie K. Bohn

Laurie K. Bohn, CTIE, Senior Director National Accounts, Silversea

MEETINGS, EXPOSITIONS, EVENTS, AND CONVENTIONS

global destination portfolio. Launched in 1994 as the world's first all-inclusive, ultraluxury global cruise line, Silversea guests travel deep into 900+ destinations from pole to pole, across all seven continents, enjoying a curated selection of immersive experiences in the world's most remarkable places. Voyages include butler service in every suite category; a choice of restaurants on every ship, as well as in-suite dining around the clock, complimentary sustainable caviar on-demand 24/7 and premium beverages served throughout the ship. Silversea is passionate about discovering our planet from the furthest reaches of the Arctic Circle to an iconic Mediterranean square. These voyages enable guests to unlock once-in-a-lifetime experiences.

What are some benefits of using cruise ships?

First and foremost, a cruise is an excellent value proposition that creates extraordinary experiences for group attendees. The small, exclusive ships of Silversea prove to be surprisingly reasonable. Unlike land-based resorts or mass-market vessels, there are no hidden fees or extra charges. There's no charge for coffee breakout sessions, breakfast in bed, or late-night snacks. Silversea's all-inclusive pricing means just that–gratuities, wines and spirits, entertainment, enrichment–even an in-suite bar setup with premium liquors is included in our fares. That means better budget control. Attendees are all onboard the ship and can easily connect throughout the trip. It creates a more fluid, cohesive experience that allows for better conversation and collaboration.

What are the types of events held aboard your ships?

We have unique venues throughout the ships to hold memorable events. Group customization is available from an extensive array of options for private receptions, meetings, team-building, shore excursions, and turndown gifts. Nothing makes group attendees feel more special than having a wonderful dessert or framed photo from the day waiting for them in their stateroom after a busy day. From customized theme parties and meetings for your group, we can be as creative as you want to be.

Professional associations enjoy creating unique continuing education for all types of professionals onboard our ships. Event planners can weave the association's learning experience throughout the cruise itinerary, either onboard the ship or at the destinations. Learning opportunities can be created to include the local sea life, the ship's sustainability efforts, and the local cuisine. This means that clients can spend the day with a famous chef, learning cooking techniques and then tasting the food. Or enjoying a tour of the vineyards and savoring the local wine. Or learning the secrets of the local sea life or native animals with park rangers and naturalist guides while learning about local sustainability efforts to ensure they are here for future generations. Silversea offers guests the opportunity to be curious and experience an in-depth, holistic way of visiting the destination, where it becomes a life-long memory.

A full ship charter for a large company, organization, or association is also an option. Popular full ship charters are university fundraising cruises, where a portion of the cruise fee goes to the university. It is a great networking opportunity for graduates to reconnect with former classmates and make new friends. Attendees have the chance to collaborate with alumni board members and find ways to get more involved. These alumni events typically sell out within a few days of being announced as guests love the experience onboard our ships and want to enjoy it again, year after year.

What changes have you seen with your company as we come out of the pandemic?

Meetings are the number one reason why consumers are returning to travel since the pandemic. Spending quality time with people who share similar goals and interests is what consumers missed during the pandemic. They want to meet in person again, now more than ever. Additionally, Silversea ships are smaller than other cruise lines, with less than 600 guests onboard and a higher space-guest ratio giving everyone plenty of room to move around.

Silversea has always had the highest standards of cleanliness and sanitation, as the health and well-being of our guests is, and has always been, a top priority. Handwashing stations and gel sanitization were always part of our protocol before COVID-19. Now, post-COVID, there are even more stations along with complimentary masks available for anyone who wants them to ensure that they feel safe. Full medical facilities have always been available to our guests. These facilities have been expanded for isolation area for guests who may be unwell with a contagious illness. Guests can cruise in confidence knowing that their health and everyone's health is a top concern for us.

Staying fit is also important, now more than ever, and our ships have wonderful health clubs and spas. For many guests, the impromptu option to get in their steps by taking a brisk walk around the ship, gives them the chance to clear their head and breathe in the sea air before heading to their next meeting.

What is your favorite event venue on board, and why?

Anytime we do a poolside party it always creates a unique experience! My personal favorite event area is the gas-lit firepit on the deck of our ship, *Silver Origin*. The fire pit is something that you will not find on other cruise lines. The fire pit offers an intimate opportunity for groups to celebrate after a busy day of meetings, as we have been gathering around a fire since the beginning of time. When your group gathers with one another at sunset or after dark, it is a special feeling to be celebrating under the stars as we soak up the wonder of the sea.

What advice do you have for hospitality students?

Always be curious and continue to learn as the industry (and life) is constantly changing. Stay fresh by gaining new knowledge and expertise. I am a Board of Trustee for The Travel Institute, the education destination for travel professionals. For over 50 years, the Travel Institute training and certification designations have given travel professionals industry expertise, from learning about travel wellness to becoming a certified travel consultant. The Travel Institute fulfills its nonprofit mission to promote a standard of trade knowledge and excellence for the travel industry. Being curious about the world makes it a better place for everyone and a more joyful life for ourselves.

CRUISE SHIPS

Cruise ships embody a fusion of hotels, conference centers, and full-service resorts on water. Hosting a meeting on a cruise ship requires meticulous planning, as the quality of the planning has a profound impact on the meeting's success. Unlike other venues, cruise ships adhere to their own itineraries, making it imperative to ensure that all attendees' transportation aligns with the ship's schedule. Late arrivals may be left behind when the ship departs, with the added expense of catching up at the next port.

Meetings while the ship is in port will exhibit distinct attendance patterns compared to those while it is at sea. Event scheduling is synchronized with the ship's itinerary, as it significantly influences attendance. Many cruise lines offer well-structured children's programs, allowing attendees to concentrate on their events. Furthermore, meeting attendees are essentially a captive audience while the ship is sailing, reducing the likelihood of missed meetings.

NEGOTIATING YOUR EVENT

Beyond repurposing ship facilities, a trend is emerging where new ships are purposefully designed and constructed to cater to the MEEC industry. These ships can be tailored for groups ranging from as few as 16 to over 5,000 guests. Opting for a cruise program can yield significant cost savings, as the majority of event expenses are included in the fare. This includes accommodations, meals, entertainment, onboard activities, fitness amenities, meeting spaces, A/V equipment, and coffee breaks, and a section of the ship's main dining room is typically allocated for each group.

Most cruise lines feature dedicated, purpose-built meeting facilities across their fleet. The seating capacities and configurations of these spaces can vary based on the ship. Conference center rooms can usually be adjusted to accommodate various meeting setups, ranging from theater-style and classroom setups to boardrooms, card rooms, or minitrade show arrangements. These conference facilities come equipped with a suite of A/V resources, including LCD projectors, overhead projectors, slide projectors, screens, TVs, DVD players, flipcharts, laser pointers, microphones, and podiums. A technical fee might assessed if the group requires a technician to operate the equipment. Prepaid Wi-Fi packages can be integrated into group packages to ensure seamless connectivity, allowing participants to share experiences on social media.

Each ship is has a dedicated onboard group coordinator who is available to provide assistance throughout all stages of the program, culminating in the postconvention report. In many ways, the collaboration process closely resembles working with a traditional conference center.

Cruise ships boast a multitude of versatile venues that lend themselves perfectly to group events. Many ship features are intentionally incorporated into the vessel's design to cater to large gatherings. For instance, the ice-skating rink, theaters, and lounges can be seamlessly transformed into spaces suitable for receptions, general sessions, or meetings. Outdoor spaces an idyllic backdrop for evening receptions beneath the stars, adding a touch of spectacle to the occasion.

Chartering an entire cruise ship presents an optimal solution for events demanding paramount privacy and customization for groups of 3,000–5,500 attendees. Ships are typically reserved 1–2 years in advance. A smaller vessel is also an option, such as yachts capable of accommodating 12–20 passengers, European barges, or river cruises tailored to groups numbering around 100–200. Given that the ship exclusively serves your group during the charter, virtually all aspects of the experience can be tailored to your preferences.

Customization extends to the ship's dining timings, daily activities, and entertainment offerings, all designed to align with the objectives of your event. With a solitary group onboard, your company logo can be prominently displayed throughout the ship—whether on room keys or desserts—instilling a sense of prestige and brand loyalty in attendees. Exclusive use of onboard facilities and function spaces allows for a VIP experience, providing distinctive opportunities for attendees to learn, network, and foster connections.

Whether it is an annual event for a major corporation, a university alumni reunion, a nonprofit fundraising initiative, or even a poker cruise with entire dining rooms transformed into poker tournament arenas, a ship can be the ideal choice.

Seasonality

Multiple factors contribute to the fluctuation of group or charter cruise prices. First, a general industry guideline is that the newer the ship, the higher the pricing. Second, more appealing pricing is often available during nonpeak travel seasons, such as January, September, October, and early December. In contrast, peak demand is from May to August, including major holiday periods, such as Christmas and New Year's Eve. Additionally, cruises in high-demand destinations, such as Alaska, Bermuda, and Europe, may also come with elevated pricing. Last, the choice of stateroom influences the per-guest price, ranging from budget-friendly inside cabins with no outside views to a diverse selection of suites. When chartering an entire ship, the combined price usually encompasses all guest cabins.

INDUSTRY SPOTLIGHT: BEHIND EVERY MEMORABLE EVENT IS AN EVENT PROFESSIONAL WITH A CREATIVE IDEA

Please tell us your title, the organization you work for, and a brief description of your job and the types of events you plan.

I am the director of events for the Kansas City Chiefs. I lead a team of five whose goal is to make GEHA Field at Arrowhead Stadium *the destination for events*. We plan around 330 small to large events each year at Arrowhead Stadium in addition to our K.C. Chiefs football games. We also plan other public facing events for the Chiefs, such as the Super Bowl welcome party and the postgame celebration, the Super Bowl Victory Parade, and the Super Bowl Ring Ceremony. We are also in the planning stages of hosting several 2026 FIFA World Cup games, which will end up being an 8-year project once the games are held. I am passionate about sports and providing guests with an unforgettable experience at Arrowhead Stadium and celebrating the Chiefs. As event planners, we live each event step-by-step. Being a great event manager means being very detail-oriented, customer friendly, and the ability to think on your toes.

What types of events do you hold at Arrowhead?

Because the K.C. Chiefs football players are relatable to people from all walks of life, we get a lot of organizations, associations, and companies who want to hold a memorable event here in our facilities. Our facilities are popular with a wide range of companies from agriculture to finance. We host many nonprofit galas and weddings. We hold 5K runs, from color runs to black-light runs. The Chiefs have many corporate partners who enjoy using our facilities for events for their

Jacquelyn (Luedtke) Carroll, CMP, Director of Events, Kansas City Chiefs Football Team

Source: Jacquelyn (Luedtke) Carroll

customers or vendors. We are also popular with photo and video shoots, from TV shows to commercials. My favorite part of the event process is when people walk into the event space and the attendees light up when they see all the amazing work that has been done to transform it to reach the event's goals.

What types of venues do you offer at Arrowhead?

Holding an event here at Arrowhead is completely different than a traditional upscale hotel ballroom. It is not a traditional rectangle shape. Instead, it is a football stadium which is curved and has columns. It is a working building, 365 days of the year. There's construction and improvements that are ongoing to keep the facilities state-of-the art.

Arrowhead offers more than 20 flexible event spaces with multiple room options to accommodate as few as 10 to over a thousand guests. The North Club is the venue's largest and most versatile space with 18,860 square feet of event space making it ideal for banquets, receptions, trade shows, and larger conference sessions. It is a contemporary space with floor to ceiling windows overlooking the stadium and a combination of dining, bar, and spectacular fireside lounge seating. The adjacent North Club Reserve is a popular meeting space, breakout, green room, or bridal party gathering place. Additional adjacent suites are available for small breakout rooms, board meetings, interviews, or a bridal dressing room.

We also have spaces that are not available at hotels or convention centers. Captivate your audience when you hold a meeting in the Chief's Locker Room where guests feel like a player, with a breakout session in the Press Conference auditorium. Then move to the Locker Room Club for reception style events. Stadium tours are also offered in conjunction with booked events. Events are a human experience, so holding an event where attendees become emotionally invested means the memories last a lifetime.

For the past decade, we have found success through creative sustainability initiatives by becoming a more environmentally conscious organization. Our stadium uses a lot of energy and we are finding ways to be more efficient as a charter member of the Green Sports

Alliance, including integration of composting and recycling receptacles throughout the stadium. In the event space we are focused on being proactive and thinking ahead to ensure that events run smoothly throughout the entire event.

What is the favorite event that you have planned, and why?

I love to create life-long memories for people and the K.C. Chiefs ring ceremony did just that. It still brings a smile to my face to think about it. We did a lot of research to ensure that the experience was memorable to everyone. First was the design. Who are we doing this for—the owners, the players, and the employees who made this Super Bowl win possible. Next, we reviewed other sports teams' ceremonies as every sports team does their ring ceremony differently. The ceremony was also a chance to properly celebrate our Super Bowl LVII victory as we could not do three years prior when we won Super Bowl LIV. That year we had a socially distanced ring ceremony at Arrowhead Stadium, which was special in its own right.

Therefore, the 2023 event needed to be a huge party with a combination of luxury and elegance to elevate all the guests in attendance. It began with a red-carpet experience with a huge logo hanging above entrance at Union Station, an iconic Kansas City destination. Inside, Union Station was decked inside and out in Chiefs colors for the occasion. We wanted the event to be something that the Hunt family and players could be proud of as we celebrated the win and the ring.

The Chiefs' ring highlights all three of Kansas City's Super Bowl wins on one side of the ring and pays tribute to Chiefs Kingdom above the Super Bowl LVII logo on the other side. The top of the ring slides off to reveal a miniature Arrowhead Stadium inside the ring itself. The interior of the main part of the ring includes a miniature version of the stadium in yellow gold. Encircling the stadium is a quote from Chiefs Founder Lamar Hunt that reads, "Arrowhead Stadium is my favorite place on earth." The backside of the ring top pendant piece displays the championship years that the recipient has spent with the Chiefs organization as well as the

50th anniversary logo and an image of the trophy. Having a ring that highlights our stadium has created even more excitement for holding events at Arrowhead Stadium.

What is a favorite event venue that you have used, and why?

Outside of holding events at Arrowhead Stadium, my favorite event venue is the Ziegfeld Ballroom in New York City. It is the mecca event spot for society galas with state-of-the-art technology all wrapped up in the art deco elegance of a 1920s movie palace. It is where the U.S. Ski and Snowboard team has held their annual Gold Medal Gala for the past five years. We were involved in creating our unique event, not long after the ballroom was being renovated back to its original grandeur. We toured the space in construction hard hats when it had been stripped to its barebones of four white walls. This event space allows you to be as creative as you like with the décor and food with the ability to 3-D map different images to create a unique space for the U.S. athletes and guests to experience. This memorable experience is what makes it possible for the organization to raise over a million dollars annually for the U.S. Ski team.

What advice do you have for hospitality students?

Get involved with everything that interests you while you are in still college. I was active in university events, from fashion shows, rodeos, sports related events, and even bacon-fest, which earned us the award for university event of the year. I enjoyed the process of how both sports and event planning bring people together. Be active in your university and find a part-time job to give you the skills to build your resume and prepare you for your future career. Take interesting internships where you can travel for work to gain new experiences, meet new people, and experience new destinations. Then upon graduation, continue exploring your career options by pursuing opportunities with organizations you are passionate about.

After college, I worked for the United States Olympic Committee as a Program Coordinator for several years. That experience gave me the skills to be a successful Director of Special Events & Hospitality in the

KANSAS CITY, UNITED STATES - Nov 11, 2015: The famous Kansas City Chiefs NFM Stadium, USA

Development Department for the U.S. Ski & Snowboard team. While there, I was actively involved with the Winter Olympics in South Korea and had the opportunity to spend time in Pyongyang. In turn, all these experiences gave me the wide range of skills I needed to create memorable events as the director of events for the Kansas City Chiefs. It is been a whirlwind career since my 2013 graduation from Iowa State University with a Bachelor of Science in Event Management. Creating memorable experiences for others has given me the opportunity to experience a life full of lasting memories. And it is just the start of a career that continues to bring me a life of adventure.

SPECIFIC USE FACILITIES

Theaters, **amphitheaters**, **arenas**, **stadiums**, and **sports facilities** also serve as excellent options for hosting large meetings and events. Designed for public assembly, they can accommodate spectacular and impressive gatherings. Entertainment venues range from expansive outdoor stadiums to more intimate settings. Success with these venues hinges on understanding that their primary focus is entertainment rather than meetings. Some services considered standard in hotels or convention centers may not be available.

FINANCIAL STRUCTURE

Many of these facilities primarily cater to the general public through ticketed events, making closed events for invited audiences a refreshing change for their staff. Although the front-office staff may welcome meeting planners, it is essential to assess whether adequate house and technical staff are available. Entertainment events often occur during evenings and weekends, resulting in a staff predominantly comprised of part-time employees or retirees available during the day. Whether staff availability and demographics pose challenges or not, these factors should be addressed with the facility management before finalizing a contract.

Similar to convention centers, larger arenas and amphitheaters are frequently owned by government bodies or operate as public–private partnerships. As with convention centers, these venues demand meticulous planning. Depending on the venue's public event schedule, extended rehearsal and setup times might not be feasible. For instance, if the venue hosts a resident sports team, event planners must work around its practice sessions and game schedules or consider holding their event during the off-season.

Finances within a special use facility often combine aspects from both convention centers and conference centers. Typically, a predetermined fee covers facility usage and a specified selection of equipment and services. Basic cleanup, akin to that after a public event, is usually incorporated. Additionally, the facility might mandate a minimum staffing level, with an hourly charge based on a specified minimum duration. All other labor, equipment, and services are generally structured similar to a convention center, employing a per-item billing system.

COLLEGE AND UNIVERSITIES

"From quaint, private college galleries to Big Ten stadiums, college and university venues offer diverse meeting spaces for events of any size and budget."

Numerous university programs have gained a strong reputation as exceptional meeting venues, with some boasting renowned hospitality and tourism programs. Purdue University, for instance, is a premier choice, offering top-tier conference and meeting spaces, lodging accommodations, and dining services all year round. Nestled in the Midwest, its picturesque campus and excellent conference center and coordination services render it an ideal destination for a wide range of events, including corporate, religious, association, and fraternal gatherings.

Another noteworthy option is the UMass Amherst Hotel and Conference Center. Set in the scenic Pioneer Valley, it provides comprehensive, year-round conference and hotel accommodations, along with availability in summer residence halls. With a staggering 32 meeting spaces, the largest of which can host up to 10,000 guests, it caters to diverse event needs.

The University of Nebraska—Lincoln is another standout, with one of the most extensive U.S. summer conference operations. With capacity for up to 5,500 guests, it offers complete meeting, dining, and overnight lodging solutions and an impressive array of 200 meeting spaces.

The Oregon State University Conference Center is a gem in the captivating city of Corvallis, set against the backdrop of the picturesque Willamette Valley wine region and nestled along the Willamette River's west bank. The university showcases cutting-edge technology and elegant event spaces, complemented by fine dining and catering options, and the capacity to accommodate up to 2,000 attendees for overnight stays.

NEGOTIATING YOUR EVENT

Universities offer ample lodging space, particularly during nonclassroom periods, such as summer breaks. However, they differ significantly traditional convention hotels or conference centers. Dorm rooms typically feature single beds, often in extralong sizes that require specialized linen services for proper bedding and towels. Although some dorms offer single rooms, the majority are designed for double occupancy, necessitating the meticulous process of assigning and managing roommates. For larger events, hiring an intern for this role can be beneficial.

Dorms usually feature shared bathrooms. Although this arrangement might suit high school and college athletes, it may not be ideal for professional gatherings, such as those of doctors or accountants. Newer and renovated dorms may have elevators, but many older ones lack elevator access to upper floors.

College campuses can yield substantial cost savings, especially if the athletic facilities are integrated into the meeting plan. However, it is essential to consider the nature of the event, as not all types of meetings are well suited for university settings.

F&B

University food services have evolved into a significant business often managed by large corporations. This shift means that experienced chefs, many with backgrounds in top restaurants, bring the quality of campus dining services on par with that of hotels and large convention centers. These chefs can craft custom event menus. However, external staffing companies are often required to provide waitstaff, ensuring that attendees receive the expected level of service.

Certain universities and colleges offer academic programs focused on hospitality, food service, and cuisine. They might possess food labs with multiple cooking and preparation stations, which can be excellent spaces for food-oriented meetings, team-building exercises, or nonmeeting activities. Although some colleges can adequately accommodate major events, their staff might not be as skilled in responding to immediate needs as dedicated meeting facilities. Planners should be prepared to navigate and coordinate with various segments of the organizational structure.

College art museums and student centers are captivating options. Art museums, in particular, offer unique opportunities for engaging conversations that can enhance networking events. The diverse opinions on the art can naturally initiate discussions among attendees who may be strangers. Additionally, art centers and theaters possess a special attribute often overlooked by planners and the general public. Unlike staff members at many other meeting and event venues, those at these facilities view their roles not just as jobs but as passions. They take immense pride in and deeply care about the facility's condition and contents. Planners looking to use such facilities must grasp the sensitivities involved and effectively communicate this understanding to their own staff.

RETREAT FACILITIES

Retreat facilities offer a welcome escape from workplace pressures, providing a serene and inspiring environment. Unlike other types of facilities, these tend to be owned by families, closely held corporations, not-for-profit organizations, charitable entities, or religious groups.

Beyond the standard classroom-style learning found in conference centers, retreat facilities often specialize in unique extracurricular learning experiences. These venues can be located at places such as dude ranches, woodland cabins, where nature becomes a part of the educational journey, or religious centers, where spiritual elements are integrated into the program. Regrettably, some planners may disregard retreat facilities due to concerns that their attendees might not fully embrace the distinctive environment.

Retreat centers serve as perfect settings for corporate or nonprofit teams seeking respite and new connections. The relaxed ambiance complements the goals of corporate retreats. A mountain lodge, coastal hideaway, or tranquil dude ranch can provide an ideal backdrop for strategic planning, leadership training, and team-building. These venues offer surprisingly affordable options for customizable conference services, featuring rejuvenating and inspiring facilities.

A Unique Guest Experience

Not all potential event venues are immediately obvious choices, but unconventional locations can offer attendees a one-of-a-kind and extraordinary experience, such as the Giraffe Manor in Nairobi, Kenya, which is part of the Safari Collection, a luxury accommodations group in East Africa. Since its establishment in 1972, the Giraffe Manor has been one of four lodges under this collection, situated within a 140-acre indigenous forest on a 12-acre property.

Giraffe Manor, Nairobi, Kenya

What sets the Giraffe Manor apart is its remarkable interaction opportunities with giraffes. It and the neighboring Garden Manor feature 12 uniquely themed bedrooms, immersing guests in local aesthetics. Guests can have breakfast accompanied by giraffes, which often approach the manor's windows. Throughout the day, guests can engage in various activities, including breakfasts, lunches, wine sessions, or afternoon tea, surrounded by these magnificent creatures. Feeding and closely observing the giraffes within the manor's grounds are some of the experiences offered. Moreover, the Garden Manor offers spa treatments for guests' relaxation.

A significant aspect of staying at the Giraffe Manor is that all F&B needs are provided. The Sanctuary, the organization behind this unique venue, also allows groups to reserve the entire manor for exclusive use during their stay. These extraordinary experiences create lasting memories for event attendees, making their time at the Giraffe Manor truly unforgettable.

MEETINGS, EXPOSITIONS, EVENTS, AND CONVENTIONS

USS Midway Museum in San Diego, CA

UNUSUAL VENUES

The rising demand for events that stand out and offer unique experiences has driven the popularity of nontraditional venues. Organizations aim to set themselves apart from competitors and create memorable experiences that leave a lasting impact on attendees and members. The allure of hosting events that are larger-than-life and filled with unexpected elements provides that "wow" factor, contributing to a memorable and exceptional event.

Even venues that were not initially accustomed to hosting such events are now embracing the opportunity. For instance, the Ngala Private Animal Reserve in Naples, Florida, constructed event venues on its property to cater to group business due to increased interest. Prominent examples of this trend include the PCMA annual convention, which has rented out unconventional spaces, such as SeaWorld in Orlando, an aircraft carrier in San Diego, Chase Arena in San Francisco, and museums, creating exclusive experiences.

Restaurants have long been a popular choice for event venues, and the growing demand for unique experiences has prompted many to offer private rooms for special events. When groups are using hotels or conference centers, planners often incorporate off-premise meals at local restaurants to showcase regional cuisine and provide an intimate dining experience with exceptional F&B. Many restaurants now have dedicated group sales managers who facilitate seamless group dining experiences, offering event planners a single point of contact for all details. This streamlined approach yields a successful and memorable event for all involved.

Organizations have various options to host MEEC events through membership in private clubs. These exclusive venues require a member to sponsor and cover the costs of the event, but attendees do not necessarily need to be members. Typically, someone within the hosting organization, corporation, association, or nonprofit is the sponsor. They collaborate with the organization and club's event professionals to design and coordinate the event. These private facilities offer a range of settings, from historic urban clubs with sophisticated conference spaces and elegant dining rooms to country clubs with sprawling golf courses, spa facilities, and multiple dining options.

Beyond serving as meeting and reception venues, private clubs are also gaining popularity for personal events, particularly weddings. Destination weddings, where a couple chooses to marry in a distant location, often take place in unique venues. Beaches, botanical gardens, castles, sailboats, theme parks, and renowned restaurants are among these diverse locations. For instance, Walt Disney World in Florida hosts over 2,500 weddings annually, some even in Cinderella's castle. The options are virtually limitless when planners embrace creativity and think outside the box.

Event planners seeking unique venues can tap into associations and consortia that specialize in locating them worldwide. For instance, the Westminster Venue Collection is a consortium of distinctive venues in the United Kingdom, including townhouses, private members' clubs, famous attractions, historic institutions, and museums. Among the exceptional venues is the House of Commons, a historic setting where the U.K. government operates. It is available for events when the House is not in session. Another remarkable venue is Westminster Abbey, with a thousand years of royal history as the coronation church for British monarchs. It provides a grand backdrop for events with a rich heritage of hosting prestigious occasions.

OUTDOOR EVENTS

For many event planners, holding an outdoor event is the ideal choice. However, numerous outdoor venues lack permanently installed equipment, which means that virtually everything must be brought in. Moreover, these venues typically have limited or no staff to assist with logistics.

Although public parks can offer beautiful settings, they can also pose challenges for private events due to their openness to the public. For public events, such as art shows, a park's regular foot traffic might be advantageous, making it an ideal location. However, if an event is more private, especially if alcohol is involved, a public park may not be a suitable option.

OUTDOOR VENUE CHALLENGES

Outdoor sports arenas might seem like convenient venues due to their existing bleachers and restrooms. However, they come with their own set of challenges. Professional or competition fields often have delicate irrigation systems beneath the surface that can be damaged by heavy vehicles. Some venues have restrictions on the weight of vehicles allowed on the grounds, and stages might require padding with plywood sheeting to protect the grass. Similar limitations can apply to golf courses and resorts with extensive landscaping.

In addition to the typical concerns that event planners handle, those using outdoor facilities must arrange support services that are typically provided by the venue. This could include portable restrooms, parking facilities, and waste removal, as many outdoor venues lack these amenities. Logistics and catering become even more complex due to these challenges. Accessibility can be compromised by weather conditions, such as flooding during the rainy season or impassable roads in winter. Even if roads are suitable for delivery trucks, it is important to ascertain if a loading dock is available or a forklift is necessary. For the latter, the planner must determine who will provide the driver and address other logistical considerations.

OUTDOOR TENTS

Tents are a common solution, and they generally fall into three categories: pole, frame, and clear span. These types offer versatile options for setting up event spaces both indoors and outdoors. An open-sided pole or **frame tent** set up on a grassy area provides a straightforward venue. Planning for such a venue is relatively simple, usually involving coordinating with tent rental services to ensure timely setup. To mitigate weather concerns, sides and air conditioning can be added. If rain is a concern, it might be necessary to lay down a floor that facilitates proper rain drainage, preventing water from flowing over attendees' feet.

Clear span tents feature a robust roof structure that enables suspending lighting from its beams through specialized clamps. It is advisable to hang the lights before installing the floor. Many tent floors may not support the weight of scissor lifts used by lighting and decoration crews during setup. When dealing with **pole tents**, hanging lighting may necessitate special brackets to affix lights to the poles, provided the poles are strong enough to support them. As an alternative, supporting lighting from the floor using boom stands or truss towers might be more feasible.

The primary purpose of setting up a tent is to create an environment that did not exist. This means that other essential services, such as power, water supply, and restroom facilities, may not be readily available and will need to be arranged separately for the event.

OUTDOOR VENUE PERMITS

Obtaining the necessary permits is a challenge that often takes event planners by surprise. Many local governments require permits for events held in or even on private properties. Neglecting to secure them can lead to the abrupt shutdown of an event. The process involves notifying various authorities, including the police and fire departments and sometimes the building code office.

For events featuring tents, fire department inspections are typically required. However, the specifics can vary by location. Generators are another potential concern. In some areas, fire departments oversee generators, but others have specialized offices dedicated to electrical matters. These offices might be part of the Building and Zoning department or operate independently within a designated special events office.

When alcohol is involved, a one-time-use liquor license may be mandatory to comply with local regulations. Navigating the complexities of these requirements is crucial to ensure that the event proceeds without any unforeseen disruptions.

TRENDS

The industry is always evolving, making it an exciting field. One notable aspect of this evolution is the increasing demand for and use of unique venues. Planners continuously seek out fresh and innovative ideas to differentiate their events from the competition. The choice of venue is the most overt method. Equally, attendees anticipate being captivated, desiring an experience beyond the repetitive formats they have encountered year after year. With each location, attendees are treated to a distinct encounter, fostering the sentiment that their event was truly exceptional.

In a similar vein, a recent trend is the burgeoning expansion of new venues under the ownership and operation of décor, catering, and A/V companies. Established and successful enterprises have recognized the financial advantages of incorporating event venues into their existing portfolios. In some instances, companies have extended their offerings to encompass catering or décor services, creating a comprehensive solution for all event requirements. This kind of company structure affords clients the convenience of liaising with a single point of contact for all their event essentials, akin to the comprehensive provisions of a hotel, encompassing event venues, décor, catering, and A/V amenities.

SUMMARY

Recommendations for Working With All Venues

When selecting a venue, it is imperative for planners to assess the facilities from the perspective of attendees' expectations. Who constitutes the attendee base? What objectives are central to the event? If all attendees are local, a venue without accommodations might be suitable. Conversely, for a conference where attendees will leave during sessions, a remote venue could prove advantageous. Analyziing the event's history is important in identifying the most fitting venue.

Research and Understand Venue Options

Gathering accurate information about venue options is a crucial aspect of planning successful meetings and events. The initial phase of this process entails in-depth and meticulous research. Many exceptional facilities boast comprehensive websites with intricate details. Some venues even provide 360-degree visual tours, enabling planners to virtually explore the premises.

Naturally, weather proves to be a concern for all events, with outdoor venues especially vulnerable. When orchestrating an outdoor function, establishing an indoor backup plan or contingency strategy is paramount to ensuring success. A seasoned planner must consistently acknowledge the potential impact of weather on the event and enact the preparations for worst-case scenarios.

Communication and Verification

Once the event planner has conducted thorough research and identified a suitable venue, the next step involves reaching out to the facility's sales department. The linchpin of collaborating with any venue is cultivating an open, honest, and trustworthy relationship among all stakeholders. Regrettably, certain venues might exploit this relationship, just as planners might fail to uphold integrity in their dealings with suppliers. Despite these potential pitfalls, it remains imperative to build this relationship, given that the triumph of each event hinges upon the synergy between the planner and all involved parties. This rapport commences with a mutual comprehension of the contributions and requisites of each participant.

Effective communication commences with a comprehensive set of requirements. Their accuracy significantly impacts the quality of communication. However, precision and thoroughness are not synonymous. For instance, in a contractual context, the hotel needs an estimate of attendee numbers, but specific names might only be necessary closer to the event date. Submitting precise and well-timed requirements is the foundation of a successful partnership. Equally vital is verifying documentation provided by the venue in response to these requirements. The planner must furnish their stipulations and the venue acknowledge its comprehension of these requirements and strategy for fulfilling them appropriately.

An invaluable resource for event planning, aiding in the determination of required venue services, is a needs analysis. Accessing the Event Industry Council website and obtaining its request for proposals (RFP) workbook from the Accepted Practices Exchange (APEX) section is immensely beneficial. By adhering to industry-standard templates, event planners can ensure the inclusion of all requisite particulars, facilitating the path to a triumphant event.

The four keys to working with any venue are research, understand, communicate, and verify. This chapter furnishes meeting planners with insights crucial for undertaking the initial two phases. The subsequent stages are what distinguish exceptional planners from the rest.

CASE STUDY: MASTER OF CEREMONIES TO THE WORLD'S CELEBRITIES AND HIGH ROLLERS

Gary McCreary is the vice president of catering and convention operations for the Venetian and Palazzo Hotels in Las Vegas, Nevada. Mr. McCreary was on the opening team of the Venetian. He oversees banquet operations, which generates over $100M annually in banquet revenue.

The Venetian Palazzo Congress Center and adjacent Sands Expo and Convention Center have been awarded the *Meetings and Conventions* Magazine's Gold Platter Award as a "Best of the Best" meeting property for excellence in creativity, culinary experience, quality, and professionalism and the *Meeting and Conventions* Magazine's Gold Key Award annually since 2000 for professionalism and quality. They have also won the Gala Award by *Special Events Magazine* for multiple years.

Beyond the basics of staying organized, monitoring vendors, and all the mechanical components of running a large-scale event, Mr. McCreary draws inspiration from all aspects of an event to make it memorable, including history, art, and pop culture to infuse a deeper meaning or level of passion for attendees. He was the mastermind behind the grand opening party of the Tony-award-winning Jersey Boys musical at the Venetian's Las Vegas Resort. "Oh, what a night!" was both the theme and the enthusiastic response by the 1,900 celebrity and VIP attendees. The gala not only celebrated the launch of the popular musical but also honored the legendary musical group the Four Seasons and its lead singer Frankie Valli's birthday.

Guests were directed to the postperformance gala site by models in 1950s costumes. Outside the Palazzo ballroom, waiters were clad in white Eisenhower dinner jackets and served up signature cocktails themed to Four Seasons' musical hits. Upon entering, guests were photographed as they walked through a series of three-dimensional, eight-foot-tall letters spelling out "Jersey Boys." Anchoring the corners of the room were $1.2 million classic cars from the 50s. The room's centerpiece was a 180-by-20-foot Kabuki curtain displaying vintage footage of Valli and the Four Seasons. At the big reveal, the curtain plummeted to the floor to expose the true entertainment stage, where 1950s costumed dancers came alive to the audience's cheers.

Menu design and food presentation was a modern twist on classic 1950s fare. Passed items, including Dungeness crab canapés and pigs in a blanket, were served on trays resembling vinyl records with the Jersey Boys logo. Sleek, stainless-steel tables with minimal décor held a "no-chafing-dish" menu. Hot food items were finished to order by chefs behind main service buffets, and attendants assembled plates in front of the guests. Every aspect was designed for the feel of a high-end diner. American Kobe beef and lobster sliders, beef and sausage meatloaf, chicken pot pie with duck confit, and clams casino with citrus fennel salad were served. Guests were nostalgic over the handcrafted milkshake station with penny candy that was popular during that point in history. "Working on the Jersey Boys grand opening party at the Palazzo was exciting," explained Mr. McCreary. "The event was created to fit the theme and concept of the show, and in doing so, we stretched our creative legs and had fun with the food, drink, and atmosphere."

CASE STUDY ASSIGNMENT

As one of the newest team members of the catering and convention services team at the Venetian Resorts, which has one of the world's largest hotel event spaces, you have been asked to create an event for a new show. Individually, or in student teams, follow each of the case study steps.

Step 1. Go to the website for the event and convention services: https://www.venetianlasvegas.com/meetings/services.html.

Review each section of the website, and download the PDFs so that you are aware of the many options available: Culinary, Floral Creations, Signage, Technical Services, and Spaces (Venue Floorplans).

Step 2: You are on the committee to help select the next show that is coming to the Venetian Resorts. Choose the show, and research it to get ideas for themes, décor, and menus.

Step 3: Create a broad outline of your grand opening event using the APEX guide http://www.eventscouncil.org/APEX/RequestsforProposals.aspx.

Select the document titled "Function Set-Up Order, MS Word version—without exhibits."

Step 4: Using your creative ideas for the grand opening event, complete the RFP. Select the room that you feel is the best fit for the celebration. Your boss has high expectations of you, so be sure to come up with a creative theme, a memorable décor, and an innovative menu. Use the knowledge from the chapter and online resources to create a memorable grand opening event.

Step 5: Submit your completed RFP to your professor by the due date. On a poster, use pictures that give examples of your décor ideas of the venue space and catering menu items, along with the venue and your room layout. During the class session, hang the posters on the wall. Each class member votes for their favorite poster with a sticky note with their initials on it. (You cannot vote for your own poster.)

Step 6: Discuss in class the highlights of the top voted posters. Using the best ideas from all of the posters, create a combined class concept for this case study that your class feels is up to the high standards of the Venetian's meetings operations team.

KEY WORDS AND TERMS

For definitions, see the glossary or http://glossary.conventionindustry.org.

amenities	frame tent
amphitheater	hotel
arenas	International Association of Conference Centers
attrition	
boardroom	local event
breakout room	needs analysis
classroom-style	nonresidential
clear span tents	pole tents
complete meeting package	prefunction space
complimentary	residential
concessionaires	seasonality
conference	shoulder
conference center	sports facilities
exposition service contractors	stadiums
exhibit halls	theater

REVIEW AND DISCUSSION QUESTIONS

1. Compare and contrast a hotel's and a convention center's meeting space. Include the differences and/or similarities of the spaces, financial structure, and F & B options.

2. What are the differences between a conference center and a convention center? Include the meeting room spaces, the financial structure, and F & B options.

3. What are some additional benefits to using a cruise ship as an event venue?

4. What are the benefits of using a college or university as a venue? What are the challenges? Does your college or university have a conference center that it markets to the public?

5. How is the financial structure of a hotel different from that of other facilities? What is a hotel's biggest source of revenue? A convention center's?

6. How can a planner use seasonality to their advantage?

7. Describe the differences between the types of event space layouts.

8. What should be a planner's greatest concern for an outdoor event? What should they do about it?

9. What is the name and location of the nearest convention center to you? How much total meeting space does it have? What is one of the largest conventions or expositions that it holds each year?

ABOUT THE CHAPTER CONTRIBUTORS

Dr. Lisa Young is an associate professor and is the director for the School of Hospitality Leadership at DePaul University. Dr. Young has over 20 years of experience in planning and hosting events throughout her sales and marketing career with top hospitality brands, such as Sandals Reports and Celebrity Cruises. She frequently created special events and participated in industry conventions and trade shows to introduce clients to resorts, ships, and/or destinations. Her research interests include how special events are emerging as a strategic tool to increase revenue for resorts and how hotels use large citywide conference and festivals to increase key performance metrics.

Juan Mendez, M.S. has been a full-time instructor at the School of Hospitality Leadership in the Driehaus College of Business at DePaul University since 2017. Earlier, he was an event planner at nonprofit universities for over a decade. His primary focus was on development and fundraising events, specializing in donor recognition events.

Previous Edition Chapter Contributors

Kathryn Hashimoto, East Carolina University
Kelly Virginia Phelan, University of Queensland
Bob Cherny, Paradise Light and Sound
Mary Jo Dolasinski, DePaul University

CHAPTER 5

EXHIBITIONS AND TRADE SHOWS

Young businesspeople at a digital marketing exhibition and trade show

CHAPTER OBJECTIVES

- Define the different types of exhibitions.
- Identify the key players of exhibition management.
- Categorize the components of exhibition planning.
- Identify the role of the exhibitor and the fundamentals of exhibit planning.

Contributed by Marsha L. Flanagan. © Kendall Hunt Publishing Company.

With tens of thousands of exhibitions taking place worldwide, trade shows and exhibitions have evolved into a thriving and ever-changing industry. This chapter presents an overview of the historical and current state of the exhibition industry, examining it from the perspectives of both show organizers and exhibit managers.

HISTORY

The **trade fair** has its origins in biblical times and gained popularity in Medieval Europe and the Middle East. These fairs provided craftsmen and farmers with the opportunity to showcase and sell their products in town and city centers as a means of sustenance. These early events marked the emergence of "public" trade fairs and offered handmade crafts, agricultural products, and other specialties. The earliest recorded instances of organized fairs can be traced back to Germany and France. Notable examples include the Leipzig Fair in 1165, the Dublin Fair of 1215, Cologne's biannual fair, commencing in 1259, and Frankfurt's Book Fair, established in 1445. Such trade fairs persisted through the Renaissance period, transitioning into the Industrial Revolution, when mass production of goods commenced.

Over time, businesses came to recognize the significance of convening, exchanging information, and offering sneak peeks of their products to potential customers. This facet of the industry flourished in the late 1800s, leading to the construction of numerous venues exclusively designed for world-class exhibitions. This model, where buyers and sellers interacted, came to be known as an "**exhibition**" and typically unfolded in major cities within purpose-built facilities. For instance, the Crystal Palace in London gained prominence as the venue for the "Great Industrial Exhibition of All Nations." This event showcased an impressive array of 13,000 exhibits from across the globe and drew more than 6 million attendees. In the United States, specialized facilities emerged in Chicago and Philadelphia to commemorate "world's fairs." These events, essentially exhibitions, highlighted the industrial advancements of participating nations. Detroit kick-started collective efforts to attract exhibition business in 1895, and in 1914, the National Association of Convention Bureaus (now Destinations International) was established.

During the early to mid-20th century, trade associations expanded and recognized the potential of coupling exhibitions with their annual meetings. This approach fostered industry communication and augmented revenue streams linked to these gatherings. However, the 20th century was marked by both promising and challenging times for the exhibition sector. Notable setbacks occurred during World War I, World War II, and the Great Depression. To amplify awareness and the value of exhibitions, a cohort of industry experts founded the National Association of Exposition Managers, which evolved into the International Association of Exhibitions and Events (IAEE) in 1978. It now boasts members who sponsor, host, and organize exhibits on a global scale.

For decades, exhibitions and events across the globe have played a pivotal role in brand establishment, partnership cultivation, knowledge dissemination, and much more. However, when a crisis, such as the COVID-19 pandemic, emerges, its reverberations affect not only the Meetings, Expositions, Events, and Conventions industry but also the brands that exhibit and the attendees seeking to explore emerging trends and plan future procurements. On March 11, 2020, the World Health Organization officially designated the COVID-19 outbreak as a pandemic. By April 2020, it had issued guidelines regarding adjustments to public health and social measures, including large-scale movement restrictions commonly referred to as "lockdowns." The cancellations commenced in February 2020, originating in Asia, with U.S. shows following suit in mid-March 2020. Many companies found themselves compelled to enable remote work for their employees, aside from essential workers. Corporations such as Amazon and Facebook declared their intention to make remote work a permanent option.

The U.S. exhibitions industry bore the brunt, experiencing a profound and devastating impact. In the initial quarter of 2020, a staggering 72.6% of U.S. exhibitions were forced to cancel their scheduled events for the year, as reported by the Center for Exhibition Industry Research (CEIR). The CEIR Index, which gauges the performance of **business-to-business** (B2B) exhibitions, encompassing factors such as **exhibitor** and attendee counts, net square footage of paid exhibit space, and organizer gross revenues, registered a disheartening decrease of 15.1%. The subsequent quarter witnessed almost no B2B exhibitions, leading to a historic Index plummet of nearly 100%.

In spring 2020, the **Go LIVE Together** Coalition emerged as an advocacy campaign, harnessing collective efforts to communicate a crucial message to U.S. legislators that emphasized that exhibitions are managed environments that can be conducted safely. Although governmental restrictions were imposed on large gatherings, the coalition put forth a narrative that aimed to clarify the distinction between such gatherings and controlled business events. Unlike venues characterized by fixed seating or other pre-existing structures necessitating adaptations to align with social distancing directives, the exhibitions industry could conceive each event while factoring in social distancing measures from the outset. Moreover, it had the flexibility to incorporate safety precautions in line with CDC guidance to mitigate transmission risks, such as heightened sanitation, personal protective equipment, and reduced physical interactions.

As of 2023, CEIR has reported a steady resurgence in the U.S. B2B exhibition sector, showcasing ongoing progress during the third quarter of 2022, extending the positive trend observed over the past 10 quarters. Although the cancellation rate for in-person, physical events remains modest, it has had a slight uptick, from 2.0% in the second quarter to 3.1% in the third quarter. These rates represent a significant improvement compared to the staggering 97.8% in the third quarter of 2020 and the 20.6% in the same quarter of 2021. Projections suggest that the B2B exhibition cancellation rates will continue their remarkable decline and successfully executed events increase, which is expected to culminate in a comprehensive recovery for the industry, forecasted to materialize in the year 2024.

TYPES OF SHOWS AND EXHIBITIONS

TRADE SHOWS OR B2B SHOWS

B2B exhibitions, also known as "trade fairs" or "trade shows," are private events and not open to the public. The definitions have become close enough that the terms are used interchangeably. The term "trade fair" is more commonly used outside the United States. Trade fairs are discussed in more detail in Chapter 15. Although the historical definition of "exhibition" was quite different, this term has also evolved to mean a trade show or trade fair. "**Exposition**" has also evolved to be similar in meaning. An association meeting may include an exposition as the trade show segment. This chapter refers to trade shows, trade fairs, expositions, and exhibitions interchangeably.

The exhibitor, often a manufacturer or distributor of products or services closely aligned with the industries represented by the sponsor or organizer, occupies a central role. Attendance is often confined to industry buyers, requiring business credentials during registration. Recent times have seen an expanding trend toward incorporating educational content to entice attendees. Generally, the sponsorship or management falls under the jurisdiction of a trade association or has transitioned to being overseen by a management company. Certain exhibitions are created with a clear intent to generate profits. Typically, exhibitions are annual. Major entities might also host regional exhibitions of smaller scale compared to their primary national or international counterparts. Attendees and exhibitors converge from diverse geographic origins, necessitating the consideration of factors such as lodging and transportation when determining the event's location.

A growing number of organizations are contemplating a transition to a **hosted buyer** exhibition format. Attendees are prequalified, ensuring they have purchasing influence and the authority to make procurement decisions. These attendees benefit from the show management company or exhibitors/sponsors covering a substantial portion of their travel costs. In exchange, the **exhibition organizer** coordinates meetings with suppliers, facilitating business interactions.

In 1988, when Ray Bloom, chairman of the IMEX Group, secured space at Geneva's PalExpo for his inaugural non-U.K. trade show, he worried that the target audience of incentive travel buyers might be hesitant to make the cross-border journey. However, he channeled this apprehension into proactive measures. Bloom approached industry trade publications with a proposition: they could host the premier buyers from their readership, with their travel and lodging expenses covered. Remarkably, each publication readily accepted, due to cultivated relationships. This injected fresh energy into his event and introduced an innovative mechanism for trade shows to thrive.

What began with a few trade media intermediaries in Europe has expanded into a global network encompassing over 3,500 intermediaries in Frankfurt and over 2,500 America. These intermediaries span a diverse spectrum, including hotel chains, representation and destination marketing firms, airlines, trade publications, and trade associations.

This tripartite relationship does not just create a distinctive experience for the hosted buyers; it also furnishes intermediaries with opportunities to expand their networks, cultivate new or fortified business connections, deliver enhanced value to their foremost clients and prospects, and explore novel business avenues and collaborative partnerships. Bloom succinctly captures the essence of this model, stating, "Once you can ensure that the very best buyers will attend your show, you possess a compelling proposition for exhibitors. One follows the other."

Hosted buyers meeting with suppliers

To qualify for inclusion in the IMEX hosted programs, buyers must hold roles encompassing the planning, organization, recommendation, or financial decision-making for various corporate events, such as meetings, conferences, seminars, exhibitions, road shows, association meetings, and incentive travel programs. In terms of qualification criteria, ideally, buyers would have contributed business to a minimum of two "global" events within 12 months. Recognizing the substantial scale of the U.S. domestic market, IMEX America reserves slots for high-level buyers who engage in business transactions outside their home state rather than internationally.

In return, buyers in the IMEX program receive a package with complimentary travel and accommodations. This comprehensive offering provides them with streamlined access to both domestic and global destinations and a diverse array of suppliers. Furthermore, participants gain access to world-class educational sessions and networking opportunities. They are expected to schedule up to eight appointments daily using the exclusive IMEX online tool, which allows them to choose their preferred counterparts for meetings, which can take various forms, ranging from individual appointments to open-stand presentations and even group meetings, further enhancing the flexibility for hosted buyers. This arrangement results in a mutually beneficial outcome, with many hosted buyers attesting to accomplishing a year's worth of business within the 3-day shows.

A prevalent method of marketing to potential B2B exhibitors involves advertisements within trade publications or targeted electronic communication. Traditionally, established exhibitions encountered minimal marketing challenges, with exhibit halls brimming and regular waiting lists for exhibitors. Nevertheless, recent years have witnessed a shift, as numerous companies have chosen to downsize their exhibit spaces or participate in fewer shows. Management companies have realigned their strategies to intensify efforts in marketing to prospective exhibitors. The landscape has evolved into one of competition for exhibitors, prompting exhibition management companies to put considerable effort into both retaining current exhibitors and enticing new ones.

CONSUMER SHOW OR BUSINESS-TO-CONSUMER (B2C) SHOWS

Business-to-consumer (B2C) **public shows**, commonly referred to as "consumer shows," are exhibitions accessible to the public and showcase a diverse range of products. This category serves as a conduit for consumer-centric industries to present their merchandise directly to their targeted end users. Show management decides whether to charge an admission fee. Typically, public-access shows are scheduled on weekends to accommodate broader attendance. Consumer shows often adopt a regional scope, with exhibitors traveling from one city to another with their displays and merchandise. These events are an excellent avenue for companies to enhance their brand presence or conduct test marketing for new products.

Summary of Characteristics—B2B and B2C

Show Type	Attendee	Registration or Admission	Marketing	Show Days	Location
B2B	International and national	Preregistration, qualified buyers	Targeted electronic communications	Business week (Monday–Friday)	Large markets with significant meeting space, hotel, and transportation
B2C	Regional or local	Ticket purchase on-site, general public	Newspapers, regional magazines, billboards, social media, and TV advertising	Weekends (Friday–Sunday)	Large or secondary markets with large parking areas

Effective promotion is pivotal for the success of public exhibitions. Typically, promotional efforts for public shows entail advertising placements in trade publications or local public media outlets. These ads often extend discounts for early ticket purchases or spotlight special events and speakers anticipated to attract substantial attendee interest. Promotion can be a formidable undertaking due to the expansive potential audience, necessitating substantial investments in print, radio, social media, and television advertising to achieve wide outreach. Event organizers must be confident that their investments will yield the desired outcomes. Producers must remain attuned to concurrent events that might influence attendance. To augment the appeal of B2C shows, many incorporate local and national celebrities to generate added attention and buzz.

Common types of consumer shows include home and garden, travel-related, and sports-specific shows, such as the following:

- *The Central Florida Home and Garden Show* each spring features hundreds of exhibitors showcasing remodeling, home improvement, and outdoor gardening ideas.
- *The Kansas Sports, Boat & Travel Show* has been one of the most popular shows in the Heartland. It features exhibits in ATV, hunting, fishing, camping, or the freedom of traveling in an RV. Tickets for the February event cost $7 for adults.
- *The Michigan Golf Show* hosts more than 350 exhibitors with great deals on every aspect of the golf game. This weekend show costs adult golf lovers around $12.

CONSOLIDATION SHOWS (ALSO CALLED "COMBINED" OR "MIXED" SHOWS)

Consolidation shows adopt an inclusive approach, extending access to both industry buyers and the general public. The exhibitors typically consist of manufacturers or distributors. Operating hours may vary by attendee type, affording trade professionals the opportunity to preview the show ahead of consumer buyers. Industries such as consumer electronics and the automotive sector, characterized by diverse audience requirements, adopt this format to accommodate the distinct needs of both industry buyers and retail consumers.

EXHIBITION MANAGEMENT: KEY PLAYERS

Regardless of the exhibition type, three key players ensure that the components of the show come together to accomplish the objectives of each stakeholder—the exhibition organizer, the facility manager, and the **official service contractor** (OSC).

EXHIBITION ORGANIZER

The **exhibition management company** (organizer) is often a trade association, a company subcontracted by the trade association, or a separate entity organized to generate profits from the venture. The individual overseeing the entire exhibition area is the exhibit manager, with a comprehensive array of responsibilities related to managing all facets of the event. Exhibition managers are like "systems integrators" tasked with orchestrating the show's execution, marketing it to both buyers and sellers, and assembling all requisite resources for success.

In addition to the core event, the exhibition management company must also contemplate supplementary programs aimed at enhancing attendance. These evolved exhibition programs encompass a diverse range of offerings, including the following:

- educational programs;
- entertainment programs;
- availability of exhibitor demonstrations and educational/training programs;
- special sections on the show floor for emerging companies, new exhibitors, or new technologies;
- celebrity or industry-leader speakers;
- meal programs;
- continuing education units or certifications for educational programs;
- spouse and children's programs; and
- internet access and e-mail centers.

FACILITY MANAGER

Facilities are a pivotal component in exhibitions, ranging from modest hotels with limited meeting areas to expansive convention centers. These facilities not only offer the event space itself but also include proximate accommodations and entertainment venues that serve both exhibitors and visitors. The facility manager, often referred to as a "convention service manager" or "event manager," collaborates with the show manager to coordinate the logistical intricacies of the event.

Selecting a suitable facility is multifaceted and influenced by several factors. Exhibition organizers evaluate variables such as facility size, available services (such as telecommunications, dining options, setup and teardown times), cost, contractor availability, exhibitor and attendee preferences, logistical elements (including transportation, parking, and airline services), and the range of lodging and entertainment offerings. Meeting and convention facilities have evolved in tandem with the industry's growth. Destinations, ranging from small regional centers to major cities, recognize the advantages of attracting exhibitions and conventions. Hotels and unconventional venues are also investing in expanded exhibit areas and enlarged meeting spaces. An array of options, including fairgrounds, sports centers, sizable parking lots, museums, nightclubs, and community centers, has emerged. These alternatives must be evaluated, particularly for smaller exhibitions, alongside convention centers and large hotels. The selection process is critical to ensuring the event's success and alignment with its objectives.

OSC

The OSC, formerly referred to as a "general or exhibit service contractor" or "decorator," furnishes products and a comprehensive catalog of services provided itself or from additional subcontractors to both the exhibition management company and the participating exhibitors. These services frequently play a pivotal role in success. OSCs provide services such as the following:

- floor plan development and design;
- aisle carpet and signage;
- custom and modular booths;
- freight handling and shipping;
- storage and warehousing;
- installation, maintenance, and dismantling labor;
- lighting, electronics, and plumbing;
- telecommunication and computer requests;
- sound and audiovisual; and
- coordination with specialty contractors.

Coordinating and overseeing these multifaceted services for a large-scale exhibition can be notably intricate for both the exhibition management company and exhibitors. Convention centers, management entities, and exhibitors have grown accustomed to navigating diverse arrangements and collaborating with a variety of service providers. Operating within a highly competitive sphere, service contractors have recognized that customer service, equitable pricing, and attentiveness to customer requirements are vital components, which reassures organizers and exhibitors, fostering a reliance on service contractors to tackle the challenges of orchestrating a successful exhibition.

Working with the exhibition management company, the OSC typically compiles an exhibitor service manual, which encompasses all the crucial information necessary for exhibitors to plan and execute their program for the show. It incorporates the requisite forms for ordering services from the service contractors and the regulations set forth by the exhibition management company, the venue (convention center or hotel), and local government authorities.

Despite the meticulous oversight and organization maintained by the exhibition management company and service contractors, occasional disputes may arise. It is imperative to involve all relevant parties to collaboratively arrive at a satisfactory resolution. Ultimately, the show manager is responsible for ensuring compliance with show regulations for exhibitors, attendees, and service contractors alike. For more detailed insights on service contractors, refer to Chapter 6.

KNOWLEDGE, SKILLS, AND ABILITIES (KSAs) OF AN EXHIBITION MANAGER

The landscape of event management has significantly transformed in recent years, driven in large part by the integration of emerging technologies that aim to enhance overall event experiences. Various event management software solutions can streamline operations and ensure seamless execution. When leveraged judiciously, these offer exhibition and trade show managers a distinct competitive advantage. By embracing innovative technologies, event managers can optimize their operations and gain an edge over their rivals. These technologies encompass a spectrum of tools, ranging from registration platforms to attendee engagement apps, providing comprehensive solutions to elevate event management.

An event manager's toolkit must encompass exceptional interpersonal skills (KSAs). The collaborative nature of the role necessitates effective interaction with teams and stakeholders. Proficiency in both conveying messages and actively listening is paramount; it facilitates understanding client requirements and devising strategies to meet them, including presenting alternative solutions. Those adept in interpersonal communication excel in not only team leadership but also effectively conveying information, a hallmark of successful event managers.

The significance of meticulous attention to detail cannot be overstated. Often, the minutiae hold the key to success. A proficient exhibition manager possesses a discerning eye, delving into the nuances and intricacies that might otherwise be overlooked, which is instrumental in preventing minor issues from escalating into substantial problems. Attention to detail empowers managers to orchestrate events with precision, ensuring all elements are impeccably organized and in their rightful place.

The role demands exceptional leadership skills. The adage "leaders are born and not made" holds true in this context as well. Innate leadership qualities often signify a natural inclination toward event management and empower managers to effectively guide their teams toward the ultimate goal, contributing significantly to the triumph of their events. The fusion of these leadership skills and an innate drive is the bedrock of successful event management.

Exemplary organizational skills are an indispensable hallmark of an effective exhibition manager. Orchestrating an event hinges on seamless choreography, ensuring every facet unfolds without a hitch. Although it is possible to learn organizational skills, mastery is challenging. Event managers must adeptly synchronize countless moving parts, a feat that demands an innate knack for organization.

The universe of exhibitions and trade shows is characterized by its frenetic pace and whirlwind nature; adept time management skills are indispensable. A successful manager excels at multitasking, which empowers them to allocate priorities adeptly, enabling them to be more efficient and accomplish more within tight time constraints.

Event organization operates within a realm of constant change and fluidity. The ability to adapt to sudden shifts and navigate the unexpected is a hallmark of a skilled event manager. Flexibility is paramount, allowing managers to seamlessly accommodate changes and adjust their strategies accordingly. Thriving amidst dynamic circumstances requires a readiness to face any situation head-on and the capacity to think swiftly and effectively. For those who have cultivated a flexible approach in their work, becoming a successful event manager is much more attainable.

The journey toward becoming a successful event manager involves embracing innovation and creativity. Thinking outside the box is essential, as it empowers managers to approach challenges with fresh perspectives. An event manager skilled at creative problem-solving is equipped to navigate obstacles and hurdles seamlessly, employing innovative solutions to surmount them. This attribute transforms problems into opportunities for growth.

The landscape of event management has undergone a profound transformation fueled by technology's evolution. Successful event managers must be well versed in harnessing the power of technology to streamline operations. This proficiency not only expedites tasks but also enhances overall efficiency and productivity. A plethora of event management software tools, ranging from event ticketing and venue management software to floor plan solutions, provide event managers with the means to simplify their work and maximize their impact.

CONSIDERATIONS IN MANAGING THE SHOW

LOCATION

Exhibition managers carefully weigh several factors when choosing a location. The city and venue significantly influence attendance. A delicate balance is needed between location, cost, and desired attendance. Some organizations stick to one city for consistency and favorable deals, often for association meetings with strong educational programs. Others rotate cities annually to attract diverse attendees, offering cost savings for locals and tourist appeal for out-of-town visitors. The choice hinges on achieving the right blend of factors for a successful event.

2018 bauma CONEXPO India

Source: International Association of Exhibitions and Events®

CHAPTER 5   EXHIBITIONS AND TRADE SHOWS

Organizations and exhibition management firms often survey their members or potential attendees to gauge location preferences. The triumph of convention centers in cities such as Las Vegas, Chicago, Frankfurt, and Guangzhou (China) reflects a focus on accommodating their audience's needs. The expansion of facilities in these cities underscores their recognition of the economic value brought by extensive B2B and B2C shows.

Hotel accommodations also factor into location decisions. Are local options suitable for projected attendance? Do negotiated room rates align with attendees' and exhibitors' budgets? Proximity to the exhibition site and transportation requirements are critical considerations. Additionally, the potential for labor issues at host cities or hotels and compliance with government regulations by convention centers and local hotels must be weighed.

Sizable exhibitions often necessitate extensive parking facilities or dedicated local ground transportation to move visitors and exhibitors between their lodgings and the event site. Event managers now explore a range of ground options, including trolleys, subways, and even bicycles, as they make decisions about meeting sites and venues. In light of growing sustainability concerns, ground transportation has evolved into a pivotal factor influencing the choice of city.

When evaluating the need for dedicated ground transportation, safety stands out as a crucial determinant. Even if hotels are within reasonable walking distance from the convention center, the urban conditions en route may warrant providing transportation. For instance, in New Orleans, many hotels are near the convention center, but sweltering summer temperatures can make walking uncomfortable. Selecting providers involves thoroughly considering their experience, availability, specialized services, insurance coverage, vehicle conditions, labor agreements, and costs.

For B2B exhibitions with a national or international reach, housing and transportation are pivotal factors influencing success. Organizers invest significant time in negotiating hotel room blocks and securing airline and car rental discounts for exhibitors and attendees. Lately, a shift has occurred toward outsourcing housing and transportation logistics to local convention and visitor bureaus or third-party vendors. Nevertheless, the underlying expectation is that these arrangements remain seamless and invisible to event participants.

A further consideration for exhibition organizers is catering to the diverse food and beverage preferences of attendees and exhibitors. Catering options can range from basic concessions serving snacks and drinks to sophisticated caterers providing an array of salads, entrees, and desserts. Addressing these services entails meticulous planning, encompassing budget constraints, menu offerings, space allocation for service and seating, and more. Ensuring that attendees' needs are met while considering logistical and budgetary factors is paramount to success.

Weather conditions emerge as another pivotal selection criterion. B2C exhibitions, relying on local and regional populations for attendance, face unique challenges. Residents and regional visitors are less likely to attend a public show during severe snowstorms or heavy rainfall. A single instance of inclement weather can substantially impact an exhibition's financial performance. A striking example is the National Western Stock Show in Denver, held annually in January. Years marked by extreme cold and snow led to diminished attendance; unseasonably mild weather caused attendance surges. As a result, the show extended its duration to 16 days, making it likely to include both favorable and unfavorable weather days. This approach fosters more consistent attendance levels across the years.

SHIPPING AND STORAGE

Upon finalizing the location, the logistics of transporting booths and other exhibition materials to the site are the next focus. Although air freight may be used on occasion, truck-based over-the-road freight remains the prevailing mode. Charges are generally calculated per hundred pounds, contingent upon the freight's distance of travel.

Given the criticality of on-time freight shipment for an exhibition, exhibitors allocate extra transit time as a precaution. This necessitates arrangements for temporary storage at the destination before the exhibition's move-in date. Additionally, they must consider the storage of freight containers during the event. When the exhibition concludes, the process is reversed. Certain exposition services contractors, such as GES and Freeman, have dedicated divisions that manage shipping and storage aspects. This cyclical process underscores the multifaceted nature of exhibition management, with specialized divisions of major contractors catering to intricate shipping and storage requirements.

MARKETING AND PROMOTION

The success of an exhibition, regardless of its nature, hinges on of both exhibitors and attendees. Without exhibitors, it cannot be successful; without attendees, exhibitors may decline to participate or return. Exhibition managers craft marketing and promotional strategies aimed at filling the exhibition hall with both. It is primarily incumbent upon the exhibition management company to pinpoint and effectively market to the appropriate audience. This is typically achieved through avenues such as direct mail, advertising in trade publications, social media outreach, the official website, and e-marketing.

In addition, exhibition management companies and service providers present exhibitors with supplementary marketing prospects to consider. Exhibitors opt to invest in a particular exhibition due to the presence of their potential clientele. Tailoring their strategies to their specific show objectives, exhibitors can opt to participate in various programs, such as the following:

- *General Sponsorships*: These programs typically include or print the company's name or logo in the promotional materials or display them prominently within the exhibit hall.
- *Special Event Sponsorship*: Special events, such as receptions, press conferences, or entertainment, are often held; companies sponsoring these gain prominent visibility through their name or logo featured in promotional materials and throughout the event.
- Advertising in the Show Daily: In larger exhibitions, a daily newspaper is usually provided to exhibitors and attendees each morning. It recaps the previous day's happenings and provides previews for upcoming events. Exhibitors can advertise in it.
- Advertising in the Show Directory: Nearly all exhibitions offer attendees a comprehensive show directory containing vital information about the event and participating exhibitors. Advertising opportunities are also available within this show directory.
- Promotio*nal Items Sponsorship*: Management companies might extend sponsorship opportunities to firms for items such as badge holders, tote bags, and various other promotional items distributed to registered attendees. These items are often colloquially referred to as "swag."

Management companies responsible for organizing B2B shows are tasked with creating convention programs that encompass more than just the exhibit hall, aiming to entice visitors effectively. Often, these programs feature additional elements, such as educational sessions, strategically provided to serve as incentives. Another approach involves securing notable figures from the industry to deliver keynote addresses, which attracts attendees. To enhance visitor engagement, a spectrum of tools is commonly employed, including contests, giveaways, and discount initiatives. Exhibitors themselves play a pivotal role in bolstering attendance. They typically receive a number of complimentary passes, which they can extend to their most valued clients, and are actively encouraged to either sponsor or organize special events and promote them within their customer base.

TECHNOLOGY

Advances in technology have made managing the show, and the exhibition itself, easier and more productive (for more information, see Chapter 12 on technology).

- Gamification has emerged as a dynamic tool in exhibitions, serving to incentivize and reward attendees for interacting with both exhibitors and fellow attendees. This approach presents a fresh and unconventional means of engagement, fostering an enjoyable way to explore exhibitors' products and services. Numerous exhibitions now feature games that offer attendees the chance to win prizes.
- The internet has revolutionized the marketing strategies employed to attract potential visitors to exhibitions. Virtually all shows boast online platforms that facilitate attendee registration (B2B shows) and advance ticket purchases (B2C shows). Attendees can peruse lists of exhibitors, delve into educational programs, and even organize their travel arrangements. Interactive floor plans are often available, allowing attendees to efficiently plan their schedule by selecting educational programs and special events.
- For exhibitors, **lead retrieval systems** have proven immensely advantageous. These enable exhibit staff to swiftly "swipe" an attendee's card or scan their bar-coded badge, capturing all pertinent contact information. This streamlined process eliminates the laborious task of manually inputting business card data, resulting in significant time savings.
- **Radio Frequency Identification** (RFID) technology is part of the toolkit of convention and exhibition managers, enabling the monitoring of attendees' movements and behaviors. It holds promise for data collection, lead retrieval, and generating comprehensive reports. However, its implementation has sparked significant discussions concerning privacy concerns and the ethical use of personal data.

- In response to the evolving landscape, numerous organizations are introducing the possibility of *virtual* participation. This forward-looking approach not only conserves attendees' time but also mitigates travel expenses.
- Technology has also become a cornerstone in product promotion strategies. Many enterprises now furnish visitors with budget-friendly flash drives or direct them to website links in lieu of cumbersome brochures. The electronic format can accommodate extensive information and intricate presentations, affording potential customers the flexibility to peruse them at their convenience.

RISK AND CRISIS MANAGEMENT

Organizing and participating in a trade show carries inherent risks. Without meticulous execution, a show can fail completely. Therefore, both exhibition organizers and exhibitors must establish robust risk management programs. A risk management plan does the following:

- identifies all potential risks for the exhibition management and the exhibitors;
- quantifies each risk to determine the effect it will have if it occurs;
- assesses each risk to determine which to ignore, avoid, or mitigate;
- provides risk avoidance steps to prevent the risk from occurring; and
- provides risk mitigation steps to minimize potential costs if the risk occurs.

An exhibition is fundamentally a business endeavor that merits every opportunity for success. Familiarity with the application of risk management principles is integral to ensuring this success.

Crisis management is now paramount for exhibition organizers. Distinguishing itself from the concept of risk, a crisis is an acute situation that can endanger the safety of attendees or exhibitors. Recent instances include the Japan tsunami, Nashville floods, and volcanic ash clouds that disrupted European travel. Exhibitions slated during these crises faced cancellations or early terminations, resulting in substantial losses for organizing entities.

Every exhibition organizer should have a crisis management plan that comprehensively covers measures for preempting, controlling, and communicating during emergencies. It should encompass scenarios more likely to occur, such as fires, food-related health concerns, protests, bomb threats, acts of terrorism, and natural calamities. All procedures for addressing emergency situations should be meticulously outlined.

Consider establishing a crisis management team proficient in assessing potential crises, implementing preventive actions, and orchestrating responses. It can have input into site selection, enhancing overall preparedness and safety.

More detail on these processes can be found in Chapter 12.

EXHIBITOR PERSPECTIVE

Exhibitions hinge on exhibitors' business success. Exhibiting is often integral to a company's marketing strategy, with substantial investments aimed at securing a positive return. This section examines challenges faced by exhibitors.

WHY EXHIBIT?

Exhibit booths spotlight offerings and communicate messages. Prior to planning, it is essential for companies to grasp and evaluate exhibition benefits. Unlike other marketing avenues, exhibitions uniquely allow potential buyers to experience products/services. This leads to higher expenditure on exhibitions, surpassing traditional advertising or sales travel.

Additional reasons that companies participate in an exhibition include the following:

- live marketing,
- branding of their name in the industry,
- annual presentation of products to industry analysts,
- new product rollout,
- opportunities to meet with potential and existing customers,
- opportunities to learn about customer needs,
- opportunities to meet with trade media, and
- opportunities to learn about changes in industry trends and competitor products.

EXHIBIT DESIGN PRINCIPLES

Although exhibit design might face limitations set by exhibit management, facility constraints, or cultural norms, it has overarching principles that

> **TOP REASONS EXHIBITORS FAIL**
>
> 1. They did not understand that every show is different.
> 2. No SMART objectives were set for the show:
>   **S**pecific
>   **M**easurable
>   **A**chievable
>   **R**elevant
>   **T**ime constrained
> 3. They did not differentiate their company from their competitors.
> 4. No formal marketing or promotional plan was created or shared.
> 5. Logical planning was poor.
> 6. Attendees had no reason to visit the booth space.
> 7. Staff were not trained to sell the product or service.
> 8. They exhibited for all the wrong reasons—did not ensure the "right" buyers would be there.
> 9. They were unable to measure **return on investment** (ROI).
> 10. They did not follow up on leads generated at the show.

include optimal layout selection, size alignment with budget and objectives, and skillful use of signage, lighting, and staff. Given that exhibits and their space entail significant corporate investments, each factor requires careful attention.

Exhibit size is pivotal, chiefly due to cost implications. Standard booth expenses fluctuate based on industry, show locale, and venue. A larger exhibit commands higher costs for space rental, materials, setup labor, additional staffing, and maintenance. Thus, it is crucial to strike a balance between costs and benefits. A spacious display tends to draw visitor attention and makes a lasting impression when executed skillfully. It also signals a robust financial stance and industry leadership. However, effective use of space is essential to effectively convey the company's intended messages to prospective customers.

Companies engaged in numerous trade shows often present exhibits that can range from the very compact, suitable for less significant or more specialized events, to the very expansive, reserved for their most crucial exhibitions. For instance, consider Xerox, a company actively participating in various shows annually. It sets up substantial exhibits for information technology shows but opts for smaller peninsular or in-line exhibits at specialized or regional events. In some cases, certain companies even manage two or three exhibits within the same show: a prominent one to promote their central theme and intended message, with smaller exhibits in separate sections aimed at highlighting specialized products or services.

Space allocation is often determined by a priority points system; the exhibition management company bestows points based on several factors, including the desired size of the space, total expenditure on exhibit space, number of years of involvement, and participation in sponsorship and advertising. From the perspective of the organizers, this retains exhibitors and also favors loyal and higher paying participants.

When selecting space, the company's exhibit manager should consider the following:

- Traffic patterns within the exhibit hall,
- Location of entrances,
- Location of food facilities and restrooms,
- Location of industry leaders, and
- Location of competitors.

The layout of an exhibit is intricately tied to the objectives that a company sets for the exhibition. If the primary goal is to engage with as many individuals as possible and establish a strong industry presence for its brand, an expansive and open space is fitting. This layout type not only invites people to step into the exhibit but also ensures a smooth flow of high foot traffic. Certain sections will be designed to captivate visitors for an extended duration, such as during product demonstrations. The exhibit manager must inform the show management company if the company plans to host celebrities, deliver vociferous presentations from a stage, or arrange special events within the booth that might attract an unusually large audience.

Conversely, an alternative layout might deliberately discourage general access, with certain parts of the exhibit designated as "by invitation only." Why would a company adopt this approach? If its primary focus is exclusively on connecting with serious buyers or existing customers, it becomes imperative to restrict entry to them. As a result, this exhibit layout aims to minimize overall foot traffic. Another strategic approach involves creating a designated "closing room" within the booth space, providing a private setting to engage with potential buyers more personally.

A standard trade show booth

Most exhibition floor plans in the United States are based on a 10-foot by 10-foot or an 8-foot by 10-foot grid. This is known as the "**standard booth.**"

CHAPTER 5 EXHIBITIONS AND TRADE SHOWS

In the typical setup, standard booths are arranged side by side and back to back, creating an aisle that runs in front of each booth. Alternatively, standard booths might be positioned along the interior walls. These standard booths can also be combined to form a longer **in-line exhibit**.

Island booths have configurations such as blocks of four, nine, or even larger; they are unique in that they have aisles on all four sides and can be particularly advantageous for medium-sized companies. **Peninsula booths**, on the other hand, are four or more standard booths aligned back to back, featuring aisles on only three sides.

Larger companies often opt for **multilevel exhibits** to expand their exhibit space without increasing their footprint. The upper floor can serve specialized purposes, such as meeting areas, private demonstration spaces, or hospitality stations. However, exhibitors must be well versed in the regulations of each convention center pertaining to this exhibit type.

As mentioned, exhibitors must remain cognizant of key factors such as the placement of food facilities, restrooms, entrances, and specialized event zones. Each of these elements affects the flow of traffic within the aisles and can either impede or enhance an exhibit's success. Despite the common desire to be situated directly in front of an entrance for heightened exposure, this strategic choice can yield unexpected challenges due to the sheer volume of foot traffic, which could render it difficult for exhibit staff to distinguish between genuinely interested visitors and those merely seeking entry or exit from the hall. Additionally, food service areas might result in lines forming during meal periods, spilling into exhibit spaces and rendering them essentially unusable.

Smaller exhibitors encounter a distinct array of challenges. With an in-line exhibit, their options for configuring it may be somewhat constrained. Should they wish to maximize interactions with visitors, they might opt to create an "open" layout, ensuring no tables or obstructions obstruct the view between the aisle and their staff. Conversely, if their focus is on engaging with serious potential customers, they might delineate the interior of the exhibit as much as possible, accompanied by designated meeting areas integrated within the exhibit.

Many individuals who pass by or through an exhibit tend to engage primarily with the signage. Therefore, this factor must be meticulously considered in exhibit planning. Signs must effectively and swiftly convey the company's messages. Intricate lists detailing equipment specifications tend to go largely unnoticed on signs. Instead, signs should be strategically designed to concentrate on key selling points and the benefits offered to the user.

Lighting technology has substantially advanced in the past 2 decades. Numerous companies have adopted pinpoint lighting to precisely direct visitors' attention toward their products and signage. Colored lighting is often used to accentuate specific aspects of an exhibit, evoking particular moods for visitors. Furthermore, the importance of lighting extends to areas designated for discussions or meetings with potential customers, necessitating well-considered lighting setups.

STAFFING THE EXHIBIT

Undoubtedly, the crux of any exhibit is its staff members. Although a company might boast an appealing, open, inviting, and informative exhibit space, it falls flat if the staff—those who represent the company—are untrained, ineffectual in communication, and inappropriately dressed. That inadvertently conveys an undesirable message about the company and its offerings. Hence, regardless of exhibit size, staff readiness and training are paramount, ensuring they adeptly champion the company and uphold a professional representation of its products or services.

Staff training should place a special emphasis on the "meet and greet" aspect. Extending a warm welcome and creating an inviting atmosphere is a fundamental practice. Equally crucial is the skill of "qualifying" visitors to discern their potential as customers. Through adept questions and active listening, staff members can swiftly assess whether more time should be invested, a transfer to another staff member is prudent, or polite guidance through the exhibit suffices. Given the value of time, particularly during peak show hours, visitor qualification is a pivotal step that effectively channels staff efforts.

Many companies provide product demonstrations or even elaborate productions about their products or services at the booth. This aspect must be well managed and focus the visitors' attention on the main messages the company wants to communicate.

Strategic allocation of exhibit staff is equally crucial, including comprehensive coverage across all exhibit areas and ensuring that the right individuals are placed in the appropriate positions. For expansive exhibits, deploying

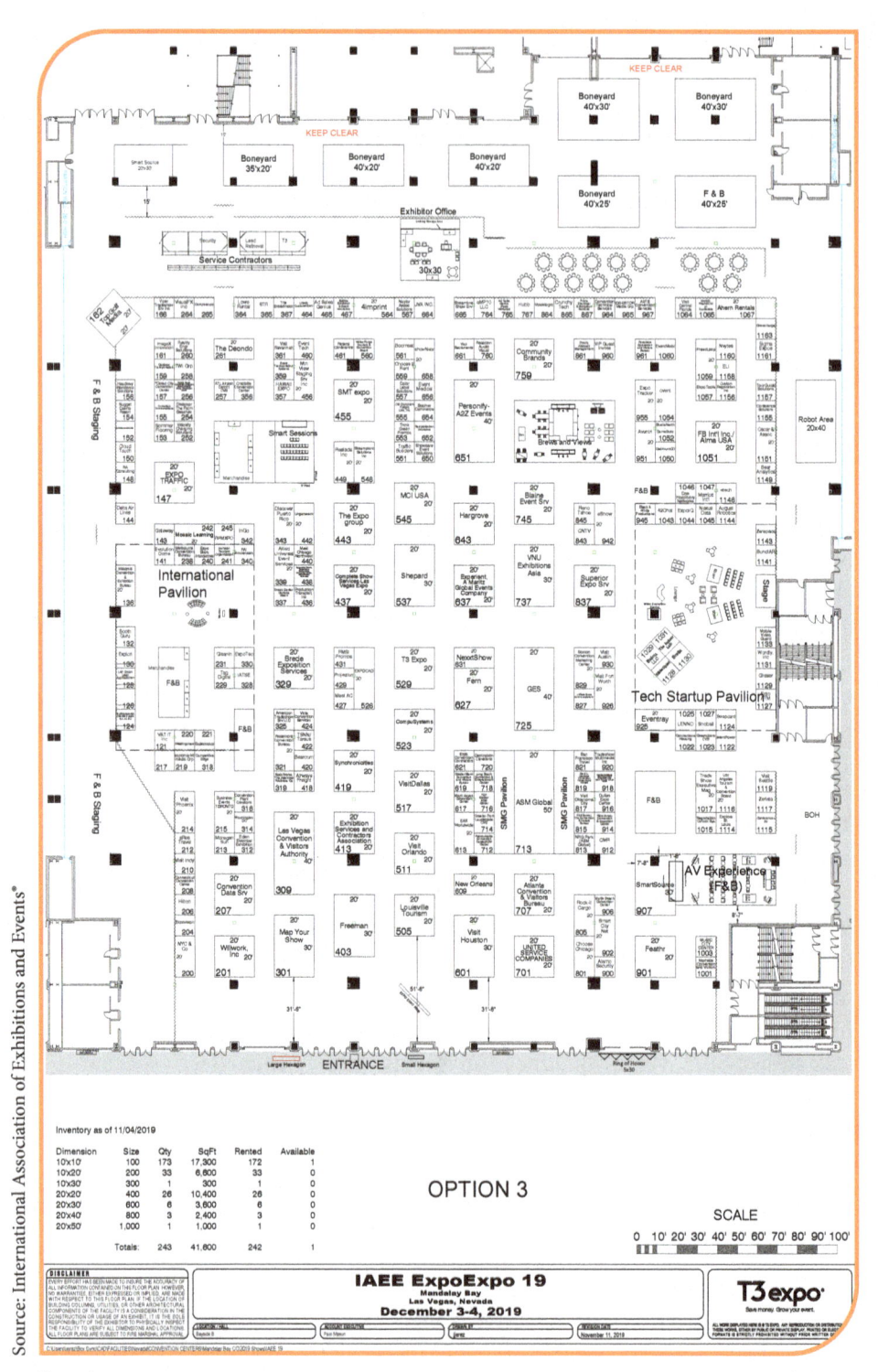

Source: International Association of Exhibitions and Events®

Floor plan

MEETINGS, EXPOSITIONS, EVENTS, AND CONVENTIONS

greeters on the exterior is advisable. They offer initial greetings and steer visitors toward their areas of specific interest. Technical experts can be positioned alongside the products, prepared to address intricate queries. Corporate executives, on the other hand, might adopt a more fluid approach, either moving about the exhibit or congregating near meeting zones to ensure easy availability to staff. Serious customers often express a desire to interact with senior executives, so they need to be readily accessible.

Smaller exhibits present a distinct set of staffing considerations. Primarily, they contend with the challenge of maintaining an adequate staff count during the exhibition's peak periods while also avoiding an excess of staff relative to the exhibit size. Once again, a judicious selection of personnel is essential, tailored to the exhibit's unique requirements. Furthermore, careful planning of staff assignments to align with the show's busiest intervals is vital for effective management.

MEASURING ROI

In the current economic climate, companies find themselves compelled to carefully cherry-pick shows where the right prospective buyers are present. It is all too common for a company to evaluate its ROI and be perplexed by the lackluster outcome. This could be particularly bewildering when the company had participated in the same show for years and experienced declining returns in recent times, which could stem from overlooking changes in the show's theme and attendee profile. The show might now be an unsuitable platform for the company.

Meticulously calculating ROI for each show is more than mere justification—it serves as a pivotal compass in determining whether a company is participating in appropriate shows and implementing effective strategies and planning. Unfortunately, this calculation often takes a backseat due to reasons such as uncertainty about whether a sale was from a show lead or a lack of accurate data, w can be preempted by diligently evaluating the actual expenses incurred and the revenue generated through the exhibit leads.

When calculating ROI, establish all the expenses that are a part of the show. Typical expenses include the following:

- space rental,
- service contractors (electrical, computer, etc.),

- personnel travel, including hotel and meals,
- personnel time for nonmarketing personnel,
- customer entertainment,
- preshow mailings,
- freight charges,
- photography,
- brochure printing and shipment,
- promotional items,
- training, and
- postshow communications.

A simple approach to gauging revenue involves establishing a time frame within which business from show leads can be attributed. Maintaining the lead list and discerning which leads yielded tangible business outcomes is relatively straightforward. Nevertheless, over time, it is plausible that generated business could be attributed to other activities. This underlines the importance of precision. The formula for quantifying ROI is to subtract the incurred expenses (as outlined) from the revenue generated through transactions with buyers encountered at the show. This succinct formula encapsulates the fundamental financial evaluation of an exhibition's effectiveness.

Other methods of measuring ROI include evaluating results versus objectives:

- Cost per lead (total investment divided by the total number of leads)
- Percentage of the sales goal achieved (leads gathered divided by the leads identified in objectives)
- Percentage of leads converted to sales (number of sales divided by the leads generated)

Hence, it remains imperative for exhibitors to consistently assess their show program, confirming alignment with the right shows to effectively engage potential customers. To gauge the success of their efforts, they can tap into an array of tools that are instrumental in quantifying the impact and effectiveness of their exhibition strategies. Notable examples encompass lead retrieval data, surveys conducted both within the booth and postevent, media coverage highlights, and RFID sales tracking mechanisms. Employing these tools offers exhibitors valuable insights into their performance and aids in refining their approach to achieve optimal results.

A company exhibited at a show and collected 400 qualified leads and spent $75,000 to exhibit. In the next 6 months, the company tracked its sales from the show and found it generated 100 new sales, totaling $175,000 in new business. The ROI calculation based on the company's objectives for participation in the show is the following:

- 400 qualified leads
- Total cost to exhibit $75,000
- 100 new sales
- Revenue resulting in show sales $175,000
- Target number of qualified leads to gather from show: 700
- ROI Calculations
- Revenue – Expenses $175,000 – $75,000 5 $100,000
- Total cost per lead $75,000/400 leads: $187.50
- Percentage of goal achieved 5 700/400 57%
- Percentage of leads converted to sales 100/400 5 25%

Trends and Best Practices

- Exhibitions have stood the test of time and are poised to remain a fixture for decades to come. Yet, as the landscape evolves, adapting becomes imperative for the exhibition industry to not only survive but also flourish.
- Although attendees at future shows might dwindle, a silver lining is that their purchasing potential is notably stronger. Many companies and organizations are opting to send decisionmakers instead of multiple representatives to shows and conferences.
- As technology advances, the industry must evolve to adapt to changing times and economic conditions. Although shows might see reduced attendance, the buying power of attendees is increasing. Technology will drive new methods of business, including the growth of virtual shows as a supplement to, not a replacement for, face-to-face events. The human element remains vital in business interactions, but attendees now gather significant information online in advance.
- As information becomes readily available to attendees, exhibitors must be creative for booth design and activities that captivate them. Space use, decor, signage, and displays will be more important as attendees choose which vendors to engage with on-site.

- In response to challenging economic conditions, associations, organizations, and private media firms might need to consolidate shows or events. The constraints encourage inventive business collaborations, the amplification of show quality, and room for innovative event planning.
- Certain exhibitions are downsizing or transitioning to a hosted buyer model. This format proves appealing to both attendees and exhibitors, offering a dynamic setup. Increasingly, show management entities are seriously contemplating this hosted buyer format as an alternative to the traditional tradeshow structure.

SUMMARY

Exhibitions serve as platforms for businesses to showcase and sell their offerings, either to other businesses (B2B) or directly to consumers (B2C). Collaborative efforts between the exhibition organizer, facility manager, general contractor, and other suppliers are integral to cater to exhibitors' needs. Coordinating an exhibition entails selecting an appropriate venue and suppliers, promoting and marketing it, assessing potential risks, and orchestrating logistical aspects, such as move-in/move-out, shipping, and technology integration.

Furthermore, meticulous coordination is essential for each individual booth. Exhibitors must be selective about the exhibitions and set clear objectives. Rigorous planning for booth operation encompasses appropriate staffing, optimizing the spatial arrangement, and devising strategies to effectively engage visitors. These exhibition opportunities are essentially business ventures, necessitating the collection of qualified leads. Postevent, the sales team should follow up with prospects, and the company should assess the ROI.

KEY WORDS AND TERMS

For definitions, see the glossary or http://glossary.conventionindustry.org.

business to business
business to consumer
exhibition
exhibition management company
exhibition organizer
exhibitor
exposition
hosted buyer
in-line exhibit
island booth
lead retrieval systems
multilevel exhibit
official service contractor
peninsula booth
public show
radio frequency identification
return on investment
standard booth
trade fair

REVIEW AND DISCUSSION QUESTIONS

1. What is the difference between a B2B and B2C exhibition?

2. Give some examples of services that exhibition service contractors provide to exhibitors.

3. What attributes of an exhibit layout would a company want if its major objective is branding?

4. Describe the layout of a peninsula exhibit.

5. What kinds of additional marketing opportunities do management companies typically offer?

6. Why is risk management important to an exhibition management company? To an exhibitor?

7. What factors are considered by an exhibition management company when determining the location of an exhibition?

8. What are the three phases of planning that a company exhibit manager must address?

TRADE PUBLICATIONS

Art of the Show—An Introduction to the Study of Exposition, 5th edition
Convene
Exhibit Builder
Exhibitor Magazine
EXPO
Facility Manager
IdEAs
Meetings and Conventions

ABOUT THE CHAPTER CONTRIBUTOR

Marsha L. Flanagan, M.Ed., CEM

Marsha Flanagan is the senior vice president of events and learning experiences at IAEE, where she is responsible for all educational initiatives, including all certification programs: Exhibition Management, Exhibition Management—Advanced Professional, and CEM Fellow. She is also responsible for all membership and chapter relations activities and works with various committees, executive leadership, and boards to identify member needs, and design and execute member experiences. She was named one of the 25 Most Influential People in the Meetings Industry by Successful Meetings in 2017 and named to BizBash's Inaugural Top 500 in the Events Industry in 2018 and 2019.

Flanagan received her bachelor's from Texas Christian University and her master's in education from the University of Arkansas, specializing in meeting, tourism, and recreation management.

PREVIOUS EDITION CHAPTER CONTRIBUTORS

Cathy Breden, CMP, CAE, CEM, EVP and CEO, IAEE, and CEO of CEIR

Amanda Cecil, Ph.D., CMP, professor, Indiana University's Department of Tourism, Conventions and Event Management

Ben McDonald, vice president of BenchMark Learning, Inc.

CHAPTER 6

SERVICE CONTRACTORS

SERVICE CONTRACTORS ARE RESPONSIBLE FOR ERECTING TRADE SHOW BOOTHS, SIGNAGE, CARPET, AND MORE

CHAPTER OBJECTIVES

- Learn the definition of service contractors and their role in Meetings, Expositions, Events and Conventions (MEEC).
- Understand the responsibilities of service contractors.
- Become knowledgeable about the evolution of service contractors.
- Understand the organization of a general services contractor.
- Classify the different types of service contractors, and outline their respective roles.
- Understand the relationship between service contractors and show/event organizers.
- Discover resources in the service contractor sector.

Contributed by Shinyong (Shawn) Jung. © Kendall Hunt Publishing Company.

An event producer or show manager/organizer might possess a wide array of tools for promoting, selling, and executing a show or conference. However, they may often lack critical components, such as specialized knowledge, human resources, and equipment. Consider someone who excels at cooking but does not manufacture frying pans or spatulas—they buy these essential items. To ensure smooth and efficient execution, organizers and managers rely on professional **service contractors** who furnish the necessary resources for both managers and exhibitors to achieve success. These service contractors are pivotal in the process, and this chapter delves into their varied responsibilities, association with organizers, and interactions with one another.

DEFINITION OF A GENERAL SERVICES CONTRACTOR (GSC)

A service contractor encompasses anyone who offers a product or service for exhibitors or show/event management during the actual show or conference. This can include florists, electrical companies, registration firms, and staffing agencies. Some service contractors are enlisted by event professionals, but others are directly hired by exhibitors.

Service contractors, essentially external companies, are engaged by clients to supply specific products or services. For instance, they often provide exhibitor manuals, floor plans, and electronic dance floor layouts, sometimes integrated into an app. The roles and functions of MEEC service contractors have evolved over time. Historically, they were commonly known as "*decorators*," a term rooted in their initial primary role, which involved embellishing the vacant spaces within convention centers or hotel ballrooms. This duty encompassed tasks such as setting up pipe and drape, laying carpets, arranging backdrops, assembling booths, and providing furnishings.

The event manager selects a GSC, also known as the "official service contractor" or "exposition services contractor," to oversee the essential tasks required for on-site show production. It offers a comprehensive range of services that can include various tasks, including installation and dismantling, the creation and installation of signage and banners, carpet installation, **material handling**, provision of booth/stand furniture, and the design and construction of customized client booths.

Three well-recognized GSCs within the industry are Freeman, Global Live Events & Experiential Marketing Company (GES), and Shepard Exposition Services. GSCs set themselves apart from **exhibitor-appointed contractors** (EACs), who are specifically engaged by individual exhibitors—a distinction addressed later in this chapter.

GSC RESPONSIBILITIES

Over time, service contractors have expanded the range of their activities to align with the increasing sophistication of MEEC. In today's landscape, it is highly likely that service contractors are involved in every aspect of the event, from the setup and operation to the teardown and departure phases. Consequently, service contractors are pivotal intermediaries between the event professional and other suppliers, such as hotel convention services, convention centers, exhibitors, local labor, and unions. Service contractors collaborate with the organizer to meticulously plan the layout of trade show floors, based on precise measurements. They are also actively engaged before setup, disseminating exhibitor kits and related information, usually in electronic formats.

GSCs assist with various tasks, including handling graphic treatments for entrance areas and all signage, installing pipe and drape or hard wall exhibits, laying aisle carpets, and creating official booths, such as association centers, registration stations, food and beverage (F&B) areas, lounges, and special zones. Even more crucially, GSCs recruit and manage labor for specific events. They maintain standing contracts with trade unions and possess the expertise to hire an appropriate workforce to facilitate setup and teardown, taking into account the unique requirements of each event. Additionally, GSCs manage the movement of freight in and out of the facility, oversee the flow of trucks entering and exiting (including scheduling the marshaling yards), and handle the storage of crates and boxes during the show. This comprehensive service is referred to as "**material handling**," which may either be a separate contract or included within the general contract.

GCSs provide graphic treatments for entrance and signage for event professionals

CHAPTER 6 SERVICE CONTRACTORS

Material Handling	Services performed by GSC include delivering exhibit materials from the loading dock to assigned space, removing empty crates, returning crates at the end of the event for recrating, and delivering materials back to the dock for carrier loading. It is a two-way charge, incoming and outgoing.

"*Material handling*," often referred to as "drayage," encompasses the costs associated with transporting exhibit materials and products via various means, including trucks and planes. This fee covers a wide range of transportation services provided by GSCs, which may levy charges for tasks such as securely packing an exhibit into a crate or container, using forklifts to load the crate onto a smaller truck destined for a local warehouse or storage facility, and transferring it to an 18-wheeler for long-haul transportation. The reverse process occurs upon arrival, leading to unloading at the event site. The GSC supervises unloading and ensures delivery to the correct booth. After the crate is unpacked, the GSC arranges for its storage until the show concludes, and the entire process is reversed. The cost of **drayage** is determined by weight and not size, calculated per 100 pounds of weight and commonly referred to as "hundredweight." To document this process, the shipper completes a "bill of lading" to outline the contents of the package, its ownership, destination, and any special instructions. It is the official shipping document, and authorities at various checkpoints, such as state or provincial and particularly national borders, may inspect it. For a visual overview of how exhibit materials are handled, see Figure 6-1.

The changing landscape has prompted many GSCs to diversify into specialized areas, expanding beyond their core functions. GSCs provide an array of additional services, including audiovisual (A/V) and production, various event technologies and software, health and safety resources, and event strategy consulting. Several factors drive this diversification. First, GSCs build on the relationships they have cultivated with organizers over years of interaction, leveraging the concept of "relationship marketing." The wide range of services also benefits organizers, providing them with the convenience of "one-stop shopping." By engaging a GSC that offers both general and specialty services, event professionals avoid dealing with multiple companies. Second, in the pandemic era, the evolving business event industry necessitates

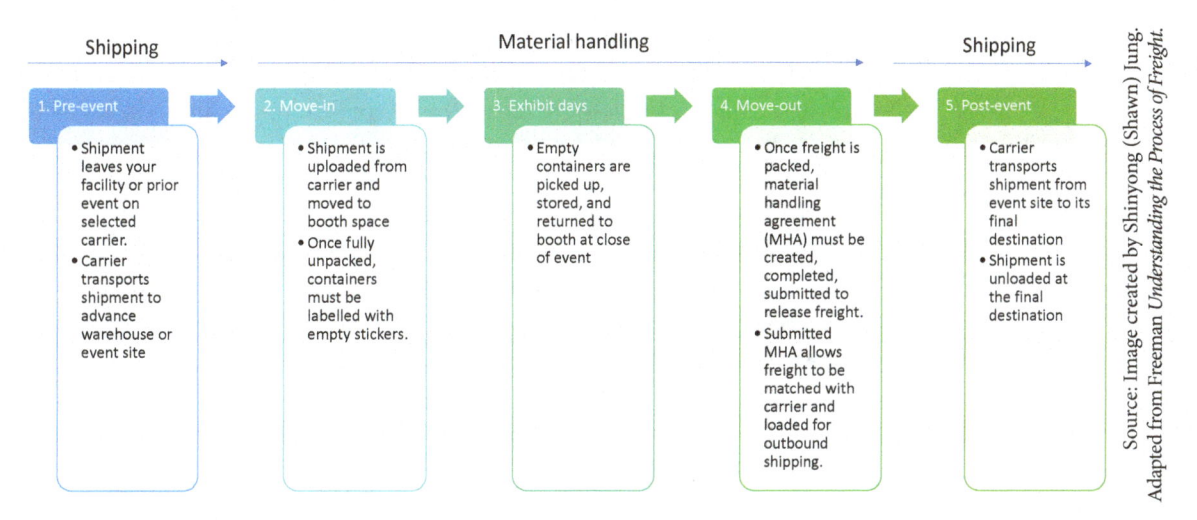

Shipping →	Material handling →	Shipping →
1. Pre-event • Shipment leaves your facility or prior event on selected carrier. • Carrier transports shipment to advance warehouse or event site	**2. Move-in** • Shipment is uploaded from carrier and moved to booth space • Once fully unpacked, containers must be labelled with empty stickers.	**3. Exhibit days** • Empty containers are picked up, stored, and returned to booth at close of event	**4. Move-out** • Once freight is packed, material handling agreement (MHA) must be created, completed, submitted to release freight. • Submitted MHA allows freight to be matched with carrier and loaded for outbound shipping.	**5. Post-event** • Carrier transports shipment from event site to its final destination • Shipment is unloaded at the final destination

Source: Image created by Shinyong (Shawn) Jung. Adapted from Freeman *Understanding the Process of Freight.*

FIGURE 6-1
Overall process of the exhibit freight

that GSCs adapt to changing customer needs, including for virtual and hybrid events. Last, providing a variety of services allows GSCs to not only increase their revenues but also enhance their financial security and stability.

However, a word of caution: it is crucial to compare pricing for individual contractors against consolidating services with one GSC, as discussed. Determine what is the most cost-effective and time-efficient approach for your specific event or show.

GSCs not only serve the event professionals but also function as the official service contractor for exhibitors, who benefit from the convenience of renting a wide range of items needed for their exhibit directly from the GSC. Whether they require a simple chair and table or a fully furnished exhibit, GSCs offer a comprehensive rental service. Some GSCs even construct booths, store them, and arrange for shipping to other shows on behalf of the exhibitor.

GSCs enhance their services by collaborating closely with event professionals to develop the **exhibitor service manual**, often referred to as the "exhibitor services kit." It is typically electronic and customized for each specific event, often taking the form of a dedicated application. It serves as a comprehensive repository of all essential show-related information, including dates, times, rules, and regulations applicable to both the event professional and the host city. Additionally, it includes all necessary forms that exhibitors require to ensure a successful show. These forms typically cover orders for services and products, such as carpeting, furniture, utilities, setup and dismantling, and material handling. Some event professionals go a step further by incorporating promotional

CHAPTER 6 SERVICE CONTRACTORS

opportunities to assist exhibitors with preshow and on-site promotion efforts. The exhibitor service manual is predominantly electronic, accessible through websites, cloud technology, or as dedicated applications, which enables exhibitors to place orders for services and products from anywhere.

On-site, GSCs collaborate with both the event professional and exhibitors to facilitate smooth move-in and move-out processes. They are a vital link to the event facility, ensuring that all rules and regulations are adhered to. GSCs also play a pivotal role in resolving exhibitors' challenges, including locating lost freight, repairing damaged booths or crates, and managing the cleaning of carpets and booths during and after show hours.

The services provided can include the following:

To Event Professionals:

- account management;
- on-site coordination;
- pipe and drape;
- entry areas;
- offices;
- registration areas;
- setup and dismantling of booths;

Signages and riggings are important services

- planning, layout, and design of exhibit area
- carpet
- furniture
- signs
- graphics
- backdrops
- interface with labor and unions
- cleaning
- transportation services
- material handling; and
- customer service.

To Exhibitors:

- exhibit design and construction,
- booth setup and dismantling,
- carpet,
- furniture and accessories,
- signs/signage,
- interface with labor and unions,
- rigging,
- material handling,
- exhibitor kit, and
- customs brokerage when dealing internationally.

LABOR/TRADE UNIONS

Exhibition service managers and event professionals frequently engage local tradespeople to facilitate show setup and teardown, and many of these are members of trade unions. Using union members has advantages and disadvantages. One advantage is that you can be confident that the worker possesses the required knowledge and skills. However, the drawbacks include that union members are typically limited to tasks within their specific *trade*, strict regulations govern their working hours, and the cost is significantly higher.

Everyone involved in a show must be aware of local laws and policies in the city, state/province, or country where it is held, especially regarding unionized personnel. The key issue is whether the community falls within a "right-to-work" state/province. In these regions, individuals in a particular trade are not obligated to join the trade union representing that skill. Therefore, event professionals and participants can hire whomever they choose, regardless of union membership. Conversely, in areas that are not right to work, individuals in trades, such as electricians, plumbers, riggers, and porters, must belong to the relevant union. Failure to comply with these rules can result in significant consequences. In some places, exhibitors are not even allowed to transport their materials from their vehicles to the trade show booth; they must enlist a member of the porters' union. Before signing any contracts, event professionals should ascertain when union contracts are up for negotiation and determine the nature of past negotiations. It is essential to know about any strikes, how long they lasted before resolution, and who oversees the necessary work if a strike is ongoing to ensure the conference or trade show set up and teardown proceed smoothly and without disruption.

In the United States, the Taft-Hartley Act of 1947, officially known as the "Labor Management Relations Act," grants states the authority to enact right-to-work laws. This significant piece of legislation places constraints on labor unions by prohibiting unfair labor practices and delineating the rights of both employers and employees who are union members.

Exhibiting in a Unionized City

Service contractors assume a critical role in managing the complexities of dealing with unionized labor. This is especially problematic because (a) the unions and rules vary throughout the United States and other countries, and (b) local labor is essential for putting together an event or trade show. The following scenario illustrates one exhibitor's experience with unionized labor in a northeastern U.S. city. The exhibit, packed in a crate, was transported to the convention center via a tractor-trailer, as mandated by local regulations requiring Teamsters Union members to operate such trailers. Upon arrival, the driver was restricted from assisting in removing the crate. This task required a forklift, which was categorized as heavy equipment rather than a truck. Consequently, a member of the Heavy Equipment Operators Union was required, and the exhibitor had to wait for the forklift operator, who relocated the crate to the exhibit booth and placed it on the ground. The exhibitor was eager to commence setup, but they could not perform tasks that fell within the domain of union members. They had to wait for a member of the Carpenters Union, who arrived to remove the nails from the crate.

Once the crate was opened, the exhibitor waited again, this time for a member of the Porters Union to remove the exhibit contents. This sequence continued with various union members, each performing their specific, distinct tasks and respecting the boundaries of the other unions' responsibilities and activities. The exhibit frame, constructed from pipes, demanded assembly by a member of the Plumbers Union because only plumbers work with pipes. The arrangement and layout of products and cloth fell under the jurisdiction of the Stagehands Union, as exhibits are considered part of a "show." A member of the Heavy Equipment Operators Union was needed to operate a bucket lift to install the sign above the booth, but a member of the Riggers Union did so for rigging the sign. Even a simple task such as plugging a computer into an electrical outlet, provided by show management, had to be handled by a member of the Electricians Union. Setting up the internet and Wi-Fi required a member of the Communications Workers Union, and flower arrangement was the responsibility of a member of the Agricultural Union. Additionally, essential roles, such as cleaning and security, had to be filled by members of the respective unions. Notably, a portion of a supervisor's pay in each union had to be covered by the exhibitor, corresponding to the time each union spent. Complicating matters further, unless special fees were paid, significant delays could occur between one union member completing a task and the next arriving. Furthermore, if any union rule was violated or the exhibitor attempted to perform a task themselves, all the unions could boycott the booth.

Clearly, a service contractor with in-depth knowledge of local union rules and an established relationship with local labor can prove invaluable to both exhibitors and event professionals. Nevertheless, unions fulfill several commendable roles. They act as representatives for specific groups of workers, such as electricians, when negotiating with management regarding issues such as pay scales and working conditions. Unions wield greater influence than any individual worker could on their own; they also establish precise protocols concerning employee terminations and offer legal support to union members. Furthermore, they are pivotal in maintaining safe and conducive working environments. Last, unions collaborate with government agencies to establish guidelines and standards for the construction trades.

EVOLUTION OF SERVICE CONTRACTORS

GSCs are significantly evolving and adapting to better serve their clients and the changing landscape. One of the most notable changes is broadening their responsibilities to focus more on meeting the requirements of exhibitors. Much like event professionals, GSCs have recognized that exhibitors are the driving force behind the trade show sector of MEEC and have an expanding array of trade shows and vendors to choose from, in addition to an increased number of marketing channels for product promotion and distribution. As a result, both GSCs and event professionals are shifting their attention toward addressing the needs of exhibitors, who are responding by becoming more specific about their desires and requirements and more discerning and selective when choosing a service contractor. Given that exhibitors invest substantial amounts of money in trade shows, they are eager to achieve the best possible return on investment (ROI). In today's economic climate, they must justify the expense of participating in a trade show, and they are looking to service contractors to assist. They are seeking to understand the value added by participating in face-to-face shows, emphasizing the need for demonstrable ROI.

In the long term, service contractors must consistently deliver high-quality services and products to their clients, whether they are event professionals or exhibitors. Failure to do so may prompt both groups to explore alternative marketing avenues and strategies, potentially leaving event professionals at a disadvantage. Some companies have discontinued participation in trade shows they have been a part of for many years. An illustrative example is the transformation of Computer Dealers Exposition, once the largest trade show in the United States, which faced similar challenges and has rebranded as the Interop Show—an annual information technology conference and exposition that adapted to changing circumstances.

Instead of participating in alternative trade shows, some companies are creating private trade shows tailored to specific target markets or customers. Many are also developing social media campaigns that reduce the need for in-person interactions with customers. Another notable change affecting GSCs is that many event venues are now offering in-house services that were traditionally the exclusive domain of GSCs. For instance, convention centers are providing utilities, such as electricity, water, steam, and gas, and may no longer permit GSCs to handle these services. These in-house services are venue exclusive (event professionals must use them). Venues are also extending their offerings to include services such as cleaning, security, A/V, internet connectivity, and room setups. This shift is impacting GSCs' business and revenues, as venues are establishing exclusivity for certain services. Consequently, show and event professionals have limited options when selecting service contractors for specific services, as mentioned.

The rise of EACs significantly impacted the GSC business. This trend gained momentum in the mid-1980s when U.S. courts ruled that service contractors could no longer have exclusive rights to control and negotiate with organized labor, allowing EACs from outside the local area to compete with GSCs and set up booths for exhibitors. EACs represent a subset of GSCs. Unlike traditional GSCs, which operate from a single city or location, EACs work directly for exhibiting companies and travel nationwide to handle booth setups and dismantling. Their success is predicated on establishing long-term relationships with clients, a strategy known as "relationship marketing." Because EACs work with the same company across multiple trade shows and events, they possess an in-depth understanding of the client's specific needs and can offer superior service compared to broader GSCs.

The competition between GSCs and EACs has driven GSCs to enhance their services, making them more specialized, streamlined, and efficient. As an example, one GSC has introduced a dedicated service representative for exhibiting companies, assisting them throughout the entire trade show process, from preparation to postevent activities. This representative helps with various tasks, including inquiries, logistics, and billing and reconciliation. This approach enables customers to interact with a single source for ordering all required services and products—a one-stop service desk. At the end of the trade show, they receive a single master bill that consolidates all the products and services. This is akin to an individual receiving different credit card receipts for each transaction but getting a single, cumulative bill at the end of the month. Several service contractors also offer special programs for their top-tier customers, which may include a dedicated 24/7 customer service representative and a private service center equipped with amenities, such as a lounge, Wi-Fi, phone services, and copying facilities. Sales representatives of service contractors have mobile devices, such as cell phones and tablets, allowing them to provide on-the-spot service at exhibitor booths. Business transactions are conducted in real time, on the spot. Clients can use their own tablets or smartphones to handle most business requests, check freight status, and generate forms, such as order forms, invoice summaries, and shipping labels.

GSCs have evolved to meet exhibitors' evolving needs

GSCs are also diversifying their offerings into the realm of event marketing, which is driven by clients' preference to conduct business with individuals or companies they know and trust (relationship marketing). Although show and event professionals or associations typically arrange sponsored events, it is primarily corporations that host a significant portion of these. Consequently, demand is growing for GSCs to deliver comprehensive event marketing services that cater to the needs of corporate clients that are now responsible for organizing a wide range of events that extend beyond the traditional trade show floor. GSCs, having cultivated long-term relationships with exhibitors, are now developing corporate event programs that encompass various offerings, such as multievent exhibit programs, private trade shows, new product launches, client hospitality events, multicity touring exhibitions, and an array of nontraditional promotional materials. In response to the evolving landscape, GSCs are positioning themselves to meet the diverse and expanding needs of their corporate clients in the realm of event marketing.

The emergence of advanced technology, including artificial intelligence (AI), has profoundly transformed how GSCs operate and conduct their business. Integrating computers, tablets, and smartphones has streamlined and enhanced many traditional tasks and activities. For instance, floor plans can now be easily updated, freight tracking has become more efficient, and small package deliveries are monitored with greater precision. AI technology has played a pivotal role in automating and optimizing these processes, leading to increased efficiency in GSC operations and improved services. GSCs have also developed proprietary software that incorporates floor plans for prominent convention facilities across the United States, Canada, and beyond. This software offers clients a "virtual tour" experience, often with 3D technology and virtual/augmented reality. This immersive virtual tour allows clients to explore the venue and make immediate floor plan adjustments, which empowers clients with a dynamic and interactive means of visualizing and customizing their event space, greatly enhancing the event planning process.

GSCs have also harnessed technology to streamline material handling processes, which enables faster and more precise tracking of shipments of all sizes. Virtually everything is now accessible online or via a mobile app. When a truck enters or departs from a facility, it is immediately logged into the computer system. Freight managers can then access a central computer to check the status of not only the vehicle but also its contents. Many trucks are equipped with Global Positioning Systems (GPS) for satellite tracking of their location. This technological monitoring extends to the trade show floor as well. Exhibitors can easily contact the GSC to ascertain which crates are still on the truck and which have been delivered to their booth. Small packages, such as brochures, can be tracked similarly. Technology relies on GPS tracking devices placed by the exhibitor in each package or container to provide real-time location updates, accessible from a smartphone.

Moreover, GSCs have embraced website development to leverage technology. They create websites for show and event professionals that incorporate interactive floor plans, exhibitor information, booth reservation services, and personalized itineraries for attendees. Social media integration and mobile apps further enable organizers to offer comprehensive online platforms.

ORGANIZATION OF A GENERAL SERVICES CONTRACTING COMPANY

Service contractors, like most other businesses, are structured into functional areas. This organizational approach involves different departments grouped by a shared activity or function that collectively supports the company's mission. The central department responsible for controlling and overseeing the company's operations is "administration." This department typically includes the general manager or chief executive officer, marketing teams, administrative assistants, receptionists, and related roles. Several other departments or divisions exist:

- *Sales:* Typically, this department is divided into national sales and local sales or special events. Some companies also maintain a separate "exhibitor sales" department that takes over from national sales when dealing with exhibitors; that team provides each exhibitor with an inventory of the supplies available and the cost of each item and also actively works to encourage exhibitors to "upgrade" ("upsell") from standard to superior products at a higher price. Typically, exhibitor sales will have an office and maintain a full-time presence at the trade show to facilitate interaction between production and exhibitors and sell additional products and services on the trade show floor.
- *Logistics/Operations:* This department is responsible for an array of critical functions, including planning, scheduling, shipping, labor relations, site inspections with the event professional, and preparation. One key role is to determine the flow and delivery of booth materials, ensuring that booths in the center of the hall are delivered before those near the doors to prevent any access blockages. This department may also collaborate with the exhibit facility to design layouts for various booth sizes, aisles, food service areas, registration zones, and more. In today's digital age, a multitude of software solutions are available, and many companies have developed their own proprietary software to design exhibit floors and conference stages.
- *Material Handling and Warehousing:* This includes transporting materials, booths, exhibits, and related items and their temporary storage within the host city via various modes, including air transport, over-the-road tractor-trailers, and local services.
- *Event Technology:* This department manages technology-related aspects, including A/V systems, special effects, and reports. It plans and install the output of the production department.
- *Event Customer Services:* This department is responsible for exhibitor kits, on-site coordination, and registration. The kit serves as a comprehensive guide, offering essential information about the facility, capacities, rules, regulations, labor, move-in and move-out schedules, and the range of services provided by the service contractor. These processes are primarily managed online and stored electronically, facilitating rapid updates and ensuring that all relevant parties can easily access the information.
- *Production:* The production department encompasses various specialties, such as carpentry, props, backdrops, signs, electrical work, lighting, and metalwork. For instance, at Freeman in New Orleans, clients frequently

request backdrops that resemble the French Quarter or a swamp, which are created on large boards similar to those used in theater productions.
- *Accounting and Finance:* This includes accounts receivable, accounts payable, payroll, and financial analysis.

Two of the largest U.S. GSCs are Freeman and GES. You can find more information about various GSCs by using a search engine and visiting their websites.

Freeman is headquartered in Dallas, Texas, with offices in the United States, Canada, the United Kingdom, China, and Singapore. Founded in 1927, it offers comprehensive services for expositions, conventions, special events, and corporate meetings. Freeman is a privately held company owned by the Freeman family and its employees.

GES is headquartered in Las Vegas and has a presence in 60 countries worldwide, including the United States, Canada, and the United Kingdom. GES operates as a wholly owned subsidiary of Viad Corp.

Shepard Exposition Services is based in Atlanta, Georgia and maintains offices in nine major metropolitan areas across the United States. Established in 1905, Shepard is a full-service event production company specializing in the design, development, and management of trade shows, corporate events, and various other events.

Stronco is an all-Canadian, privately owned company founded in 1952. It specializes in trade shows, conventions, special performances, and sporting events, serving the Canadian market.

TYPES OF SERVICE CONTRACTORS

The discussion has centered on GSCs and their interactions with individual exhibitors and event professionals. Now, the focus will broaden to encompass all potential service contractors.

SPECIALTY SERVICE CONTRACTORS

Specialty service contractors specialize in a specific area, in contrast to the broad and generic services offered by GSCs. they can be either official contractors (appointed by show/event management) or EACs (see next).

They handle all the necessary services, whether it is a special event, trade show, conference, or general meeting:

- *A/V (Technology):* Services and supplies aimed at enhancing the event through A/V technologies, potentially before and after the event. This can include digital and hybrid exhibitions and conferences.
- *Business Services:* Copying, printing, shipping, and other essential services.
- *Catering:* F&B services for event professionals during the event and for individual exhibitors who may wish to offer F&B in their booths or at private client events.
- *Cleaning Services:* Cleaning for public areas, particularly carpets, along with booths, offices, and nonpublic areas.
- *Computers:* Rental services for computers, monitors, and printers.
- *Consulting:* Pre-event planning, coordination, facilitation, layout and design of the event, and booth design. Often referred to as "third-party planners" or "independent consultants."
- *Décor:* Basic décor services to enhance staging and establish a general décor theme. This may also include floral arrangements and entertainment.
- *Electrical:* Electrical power for exhibits and any other areas where it may be required.
- *Entertainment Agency:* An intermediary between entertainers and event professionals, offering entertainment services.
- *Floral:* Rental of plants, flowers, and props.
- *Freight:* Ships exhibit materials from the company to the show and back. Various types of shippers may be involved, including common carriers, van lines, and airfreight.
- *Furniture:* Rental services for furniture, often featuring designs more elaborate than typical household furniture.
- *Internet Access and Telecommunications Equipment:* Rental services for equipment and lines needed on the show floor or any other event area, including Wi-Fi and wired internet access, ensuring sufficient bandwidth. This category may also encompass cell phones, telephones, and walkie-talkies.
- *Labor Planning and Supervision:* Expertise in local rules and regulations, including requirements for tradespeople and unions, and supervises workers on-site.
- *Lighting:* Lighting design, rental services, and lighting operators. This service can sometimes be included with an A/V supplier.
- *Material Handling:* Encompasses over-the-road transportation of materials, transfers, delivery from a local warehouse or depot to the site, airfreight services, and returns.

- *Moderator:* Manages the dialogue between virtual attendees, on-site attendees, and the presenter. This specialist role may be part of the A/V team.
- *Producer:* Ensures all production is designed and delivered without errors or omissions. This specialist role may also be part of the A/V team.
- *Social Media Expert:* A team or individual skilled in social media management to enhance the reach of exhibits/conferences or special events before, during, and after.
- *Staffing:* Temporary hiring of exhibit or demonstration personnel or registration.
- *Utilities:* Plumbing, air, gas, steam, and water for technical exhibits.
- *Photography:* For event professionals to provide publicity and to individual exhibitors.
- *Postal and Package Services:* For both organizers and exhibitors.
- *Registration Company:* An outsourced company responsible for managing the entire registration process. This includes database management, payment processing, badge production, and often on-site staffing.
- *Security:* Security to watch the booth during closed hours and control the entrances when the show is open or general security for an event/conference.
- *Speaker Bureaus:* Finding of ideal keynote speakers, entertainers, performers, etc. to open/close conference.
- *Translators:* Simultaneous translation of speeches and presentations; also work with exhibitors for communication between sales representatives and foreign attendees.

THE TRANSLATOR WHO KNEW TOO MUCH

A small American company decided that it wanted to exhibit at a trade show in Europe. It hired a skilled translator who efficiently handled inquiries from multilingual attendees. However, as the translator became more familiar with the product and began answering questions directly without consulting the sales managers, she unintentionally conveyed the wrong message to attendees, who interpreted her actions as a sign that the products were simplistic and lacked innovation. This misperception resulted in poor attendee responses and low interest in the company's offerings. To rectify this issue and ensure a more favorable impression, the company decided

> to emphasize the involvement of its sales managers in responding to inquiries. This approach aimed to demonstrate that the products were cutting edge and that knowledgeable experts were readily available to provide information. Ultimately, this story underscores the significance of effective communication and perception management when participating in trade shows, highlighting the need to carefully manage how a company presents itself to attendees.

The specific needs of trade shows can vary widely based on the industry and event focus. Tailoring services to these requirements is crucial for the success of any event. For instance, trade shows in the F&B industry may need specialized contractors for services, such as ice and cold storage, to meet their unique demands. Similarly, trade shows in the automotive industry might require contractors specialized in car cleaning and maintenance to keep their exhibits in top condition.

To streamline the process for event professionals and exhibitors, some GSCs offer one-stop shopping solutions that encompass a wide range of services. This approach simplifies the coordination of various suppliers and vendors, providing convenience and efficiency for all involved parties. Notable venues, such as McCormick Place in Chicago, the Metropolitan Toronto Convention Centre in Toronto, and certain hotel chains, such as Marriott, may offer comprehensive one-stop shopping options. However, the availability of these services can vary, so it is essential to confirm with the specific venue or hotel to determine the extent of its offerings.

EXHIBITOR-APPOINTED SERVICE CONTRACTORS

As companies participate in an increasing number of shows, their exhibits tend to become more complex, and they often prefer having a single service provider year round. Alternatively, they may have a vendor they have collaborated with extensively in a city where they hold numerous shows. This preference becomes particularly pronounced when it comes to installing and dismantling the exhibit. Most event professionals are open to this arrangement, provided the company meets the necessary insurance and licensing requirements. These companies are EACs and perform duties akin to specialty contractors but exclusively for the exhibitor.

Certain services may be offered only by the official service contractor, known as **"exclusive services."** The event professional typically makes the decision to designate a service as exclusive, considering the specific needs of the show, facility regulations, and requirement for a smooth setup and teardown process. Imagine the chaos that would ensue if every freight and installation company attempted to move its exhibitors' materials all at once; material handling is often designated as an exclusive service. Many facilities have well-defined guidelines regarding the use of EACs, and in some instances, exhibitors must seek approval from the facility to engage them.

This simple example of rigging was used to attract attention to a booth selling chairs

RELATIONSHIP BETWEEN CONTRACTORS AND EVENT ORGANIZERS

One of the first steps event professionals take is to engage a GSC. This partnership evolves in tandem with the show's development. GSCs often provide recommendations regarding suitable cities for hosting the show, optimal timing during the year, and appropriate venues. It is crucial to secure this company early in the planning process.

The process of hiring service contractors typically involves issuing a **Request for Proposal (RFP)**. The event professional formulates a set of questions and specifications tailored to each show's unique requirements. Factors include the contractor's industry knowledge, familiarity with the chosen facility, experience with similar events, organization size, and budget considerations. Once the professional selects a service contractor and they agree on the proposed services and payments, they enter into a legally binding contract that establishes the terms and conditions of their relationship. Legal action can be pursued after a breach of contract by either party.

Throughout the development of the show, GSCs closely monitor the progress and may provide input on how marketing themes and association logos can be incorporated into entrance treatments and signage to achieve the desired look and feel. Elements such as color schemes, visual designs, and material choices may either be contracted or recommended by the GSC.

Specialty service contractors collaborate with event professionals to assist exhibitors in saving time and money. By examining the historical data of a show, service contractors can identify the types of furniture, floral arrangements, and electrical setups that exhibitors have used. This insight enables specialty contractors to offer cost-effective suggestions, resulting in savings that can be passed on to exhibitors. This approach fosters goodwill among exhibitors, encouraging them to continue participating in the show.

Over time, a service contractor can become intimately familiar with a show, potentially rivaling the event professional's knowledge. This deep understanding can be a valuable asset, especially in the face of staff turnovers, as the service contractor becomes a living repository of the show's history and unique intricacies.

RESOURCES IN THE SERVICE CONTRACTOR INDUSTRY

Numerous national and international associations cater to individuals and companies within the service contractor industry. These organizations serve as valuable resources for event professionals seeking service contractors in specific cities. To gain comprehensive insights into each association's mission, ethical standards, member responsibilities, and contact details, you can visit their websites. Here is a partial list of such associations:

CAEM: Canadian Association of Exposition Management. Canadian association of event professionals and the people who work for service contractors.

CEIR: Center for Exhibition Industry Research.

CEMA: Corporate Event Marketing Association. Advances strategic event marketing and marketing communications for senior-level event marketers and industry professionals.

EACA: Exhibitor-Appointed Contractors Association. Represents EACs and other individual show-floor professionals that provide exhibit services on the trade show floor.

EDPA: Exhibit Designers & Producers Association. Serves companies engaged in the design, manufacture, transport, installation, and service of displays and exhibits primarily for the trade show industry.

The Exhibition and Event Association of Australasia: Peak industry association for those in the business of trade and consumer expos and events.

Exhibition Services & Contractors Association: Serves general and specialty contractors.

Healthcare Convention and Exhibitors Association: Represents organizations united by a common desire to increase the effectiveness and quality of healthcare conventions and exhibitions as an educational and marketing medium.

International Association of Exhibits and Events: Show organizers and the people who work for service contractors.

National Association of Consumer Shows: Public (consumer) event professionals and the suppliers who support them.

UFI The Global Association of the Exhibition Industry: World's leading trade show organizers and fairground owners and the major national and international exhibition associations and selected partners of the exhibition industry.

The professionalism exhibited by organizations such as ESCA is a shining example of the high standards maintained by various industry associations. When searching for a show services contractor, or any contractor, it is crucial to consider their affiliations with industry associations, which can offer valuable insights into their commitment to professionalism, adherence to industry best practices, and dedication to upholding high-quality standards.

HOW DOES IT ALL WORK?

If you examine the organizational chart in Figure 6-2, you can gain a clearer understanding of how the GSC interacts with various stakeholders, including the event professional, the facility, exhibitors, and other contractors. Exhibitions function much like small cities, and the event professional must

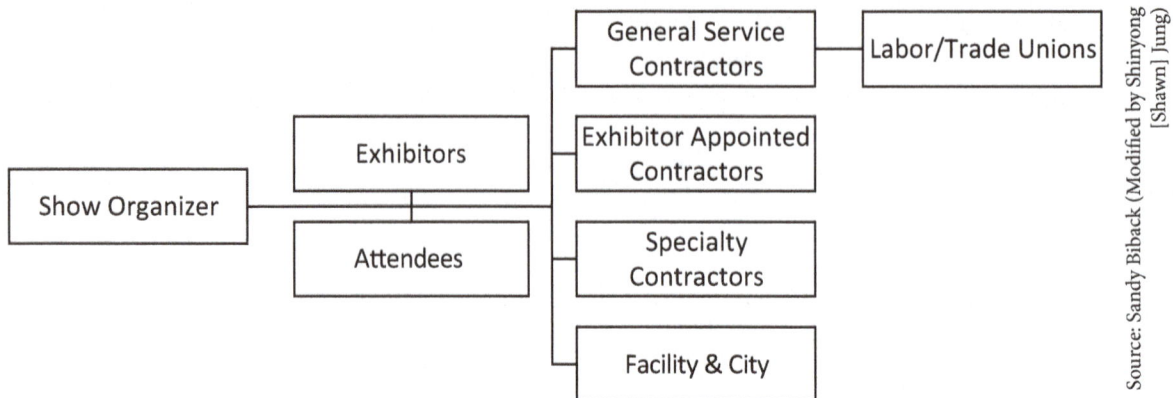

FIGURE 6-2
Relationship between event professional and service contractors

Source: Sandy Biback (Modified by Shinyong [Shawn] Jung)

provide everything a city does, from safety and security to a workspace (think of the exhibits as offices), access to essential utilities, such as electricity and water, and even transportation (including shuttle buses). All of this must be accomplished in a very short time, often less than a week. Effective communication among all parties involved is paramount, and the GSC is frequently the crucial link. Coordinating all the contractors typically falls under the purview of the GSC, effectively acting as the right hand of the event professional.

BEST PRACTICES

Sustainability and corporate social responsibility (CSR) remain significant considerations when selecting a venue. Event planners are increasingly attentive to their suppliers' CSR programs and their supply chain's implications for creating more sustainable programs. Venues play a pivotal role in this by implementing specific policies and procedures to ensure that end users and service contractors meet sustainability requirements. For example, the Colorado Convention Center in Denver has introduced various sustainability initiatives, including a waste management program, the donation of leftover conference materials, and water-efficient landscaping and irrigation. The center actively encourages event planners and contractors to engage in sustainability efforts by incorporating eco-friendly practices. Service contractors can play a key role in sustainability of by reducing the carbon footprint; embracing recyclable materials, using locally produced items, and working with the venues to meet their guidelines for low lighting usage when full lighting is not required and ensure waste management policies are met. Furthermore, event planners, venues, and service contractors should make a concerted effort to understand their supply chains, ensuring fair treatment and payment of migrant workers and the total absence of human slavery. Service contractors often establish lasting relationships with organizers, planners, and sponsors, aiding in the execution of meetings and events across multiple locations while aligning with CSR mandates.

As technology continues to advance, hybrid meetings will become more prominent, especially when they align with events' objectives. This shift will necessitate specialized requirements from A/V and technical service contractors, including increased bandwidth demands.

To ensure the success of these hybrid meetings, specialized consultants, such as producers and moderators, will play crucial roles. Their expertise will ensure that attendees, whether online, in person, or after the event is over, remain engaged throughout. Furthermore, emerging technologies, such as holograms, are becoming increasingly mainstream. They enable exhibitors to provide participants with a more immersive experience showcasing their products and services. Robots are poised to take on more responsibilities, such as heavy lifting and navigating the event floor to attract participants to specific booths. Drones have already made their debut and will soon have rules, regulations, and policies in place; participants will be able to control their own robotic avatars, allowing them to virtually attend shows and interact with exhibitors. These developments signify a dynamic shift in how events are conducted and experienced.

SUMMARY

Service contractors are the backbone of the exhibitions and corporate events industry: their support structure is vital for seamless operation. By understanding the distinct roles and responsibilities of each contractor, event professionals can deliver outstanding service to exhibitors, creating a thriving environment where buyers and sellers can effectively conduct business.

CASE STUDY

Transforming Vision to Reality: The Importance of the Relationship Between Show Organizer and GSC

Introduction:

The Specialty Equipment Market Association (SEMA) offers a renowned trade show in the automotive aftermarket and performance industry. With over 2,400 exhibitors and more than 160,000 attendees, it needed to transform the production concept into a tangible and authentic experience that resonated with the target community. It demonstrates the importance of collaboration between event professionals and GSCs in bringing visionary concepts to life.

SEMA Show exhibit floor, Las Vegas Convention Center

© Steve Lagreca/Shutterstock.com

Challenge:

The primary challenge was to create a central hub at the event where the global community could gather and connect with the association. The goal of the event professional was to craft an immersive space that effectively captured the vibrant and dynamic essence of the automotive industry. A central focus was to thoroughly engage attendees in an authentic experience that deeply resonated with their passion for automobiles and performance enhancements.

Solution:

SEMA collaborated closely with its partners at Freeman, the GSC, to design and implement "SEMA Central." The experiential and A/V team conceptualized a centralized, multisensory space that immediately caught attendees' attention as they entered the Las Vegas Convention Center. The design aimed to create an industrial yet welcoming town square where attendees could engage with SEMA staff and form personal connections with the association.

Leveraging its 20-plus-year partnership with SEMA, Freeman's team brought the vision to life, ensuring that SEMA Central aligned with the show's core values and provided a high-energy experiential environment.

Results:

The success of SEMA Central was evident, as it fulfilled the set design and logistical objectives while effectively managing the budget. Attendees felt a deeper connection to the association, enhancing the sense of community. This success translated into increased attendee engagement with exhibitors, creating a positive ripple effect on the exhibit floor. Throughout the event, attendees actively interacted with products and content, sharing their experiences with customers and enthusiasts worldwide. SEMA Central's impact was measured not just in numbers but also in the emotional connection it fostered with visitors.

REVIEW AND DISCUSSION QUESTIONS

1. What unique challenges do large-scale trade shows, such as SEMA, face in transforming production concepts into experiential realities? What resources are available for the event professionals in addressing these challenges?
2. What are some factors that enabled SEMA to solve its problem?
3. What is the role of a GSC in successfully designing immersive spaces, such as SEMA Central?
4. What are the logistical challenges the event professional encounters when hosting a large-scale trade show, such as SEMA? How can the GSC help overcome these challenges? Discuss the aspects of labor, exhibit freight, layout and design, technology, and other on-site coordination.
5. What other types of service contractors can contribute to the success of a large trade show, such as SEMA, and how?

Note: These discussion questions are designed to prompt critical thinking and foster discussions around the challenges, resources, and coordination involved in organizing large-scale trade shows. They encourage exploring the roles of GSCs and other service contractors in creating experiential environments and ensuring seamless event execution.

KEY WORDS AND TERMS

For definitions, see glossary or https://insights.eventscouncil.org/Industry-glossary

drayage
exclusive service
exhibitor service manual
exhibitor-appointed contractor
general service contractor

material handling
RFP
service contractor
specialty service contractor

REVIEW AND DISCUSSION QUESTIONS

1. What types of services do GSCs provide, and how do they differ from those of specialty contractors?

2. What are some of the questions that should be asked in an RFP when looking to contract with a GSC?

3. Describe the difference between a general (official) and an exhibitor-appointed service contractor.

4. How can the GSC assist the event professional as they prepare?

5. You are the event manager of a large conference that includes a trade show component. The trucks are ready to move and the weather sets in. Winter storms are everywhere on the route. Whom do you contact? What alternative plans can you make? What if the trucks cannot get there in time to set up?

6. With the pandemic and technological advancements, virtual and hybrid events have become more prevalent. How can you, the planner, adapt to a virtual/hybrid trade show? What is the role of service contractors in successfully executing a virtual or hybrid trade show?

ABOUT THE CHAPTER CONTRIBUTOR

Shinyong (Shawn) Jung, Ph.D., MBA, is an assistant professor in the White Lodging-J.W. Marriott, Jr. School of Hospitality and Tourism Management. He has extensive global experiences in the hospitality and events industry, having worked with Shepard Exposition Services, UNLV Student Union & Event Services, and Midas Convention Services in the United States and COEX Intercontinental Hotel in South Korea. With 10 years of teaching experience, he has taught a diverse range of event and meeting management courses, including Introduction to the Event Industry, Festivals and Special Events, Event Support Systems, and Conventions and Tradeshows. He contributes to the field by serving on the faculty committee of the International Association of Exhibitions and Events and maintaining an active membership in the Professional Convention Management Association. His research focuses on sustainable event tourism, and experience design/management in business and social events.

Previous Chapter Contributors

Susan L. Schwartz, CEM.

Sandy Biback, CMP Emeritus, CMM

CHAPTER 7

DESTINATION MANAGEMENT COMPANIES (DMCs)

LONDON IS A MAJOR GLOBAL DESTINATION FOR BUSINESS TRAVEL WITH ITS FAVORABLE LOCATION IN EUROPE CONVENIENT FOR TRAVELERS FROM THE EAST AND WEST

CHAPTER OBJECTIVES

- Define a DMC and its structure and services.
- Outline a DMC's organization.
- Describe the elements involved in the business model of DMCs.
- Discuss strategies and tools for finding and selecting a DMC.
- Describe at least eight best practices in DMCs.
- Outline the COVID-19 impact on DMCs.

Contributed by Dr. Alan Fyall. © Kendall Hunt Publishing Company.
Contributed by Steve Brinkman. © Kendall Hunt Publishing Company.

Within the Meetings, Expositions, Events, and Conventions (MEEC) industry, a wide range of career opportunities exists. One involves providing local destination management services, which are a crucial link between the meeting planner from the host organization and various suppliers. These suppliers can include on-site meeting management, hotel services, convention centers and bureaus, airlines, transportation providers, and catering services. Although many students might not initially think of pursuing a career on the supplier side of the MEEC industry, the services offered at the event destination play a pivotal role in the successful planning and execution. This chapter discusses the business and services provided by a DMC.

DMC: DEFINITION, STRUCTURE, AND SERVICES

A DMC is a professional services business with extensive local knowledge, expertise, and resources at its disposal. DMCs specialize in designing and executing events, activities, tours, transportation arrangements, and program logistics. Depending on the specific DMC and the expertise of its staff, DMCs offer a wide array of services, including creative proposals for special events; guest tours; VIP amenities and transportation; shuttle services; on-site staffing; team-building, golf and sport outings; entertainment; décor and theme development; and on-site registration services, housing, and concierge services.

Originally known as "**ground operator**s," DMCs have evolved significantly to encompass a broader range of services. Another related term is "**professional congress organizer**" (PCO), which is predominantly used in international contexts. PCOs are invaluable when planning international events and often members of the **International Association of Professional Congress Organizers**. DMCs offer an essential layer of services and are sought after by event professionals for their extensive local knowledge, experience, and resources. They collaborate closely with transportation companies, airlines, hotels and resorts, convention centers, and other service providers to deliver and execute MEEC activities seamlessly. Successful events hinge on a deep understanding of the destination's infrastructure, local laws, statutes, and regulations. Event professionals must engage with local experts who can provide verified, firsthand information about supplier availability, capabilities, and capacities, which they have acquired through actual project work. This collaboration is essential to ensure the success of any event.

Within the context of DMCs and their services, the industry commonly refers to the client's engagement as a "**client project**." This project, which could be a meeting, exhibition, event, or convention, is typically termed a "program." A program encompasses all the activities and services that the DMC provides to during a visit to a specific destination over a defined period.

SERVICES PROVIDED BY DMCS

Event professionals work closely with DMCs to provide recommendations for local destination resources that will best fit and satisfy the goals for a gathering. After these services are determined, a contract is written for the DMC to plan, set up, and deliver them. Services typically offered by DMCs include the following:

- budgeting and resource management,
- concierge services (e.g., restaurant reservations, theme park/attraction tickets, off-site tours),
- creative itineraries,
- creative theme design,
- dining programs,
- entertainers,
- event production,
- event venue selection,
- hotel selection,
- incentive travel,
- meeting support services,
- sightseeing and tour options,
- speakers,
- special event concepts,
- sport events (e.g., golf, tennis, fishing tournaments),
- staffing services,
- team-building activities,
- transportation planning and delivery, and
- VIP services.

DMCs may make special arrangements for models or entertainers; this one in costume

DMCs are pivotal in the world of meetings and events, facilitating connections among attendees, celebrating achievements, and introducing new ideas or products. In today's highly competitive environment, where the success and return on investment (ROI) of meetings and events are meticulously scrutinized, professionals turn to DMCs to craft unique and imaginative event concepts. These must not only align with the event's specific objectives but also seamlessly integrate with other activities in the client's program while staying within budget constraints. Full-service DMCs offer comprehensive meeting management support services, which encompass a wide array of responsibilities, including transportation, on-site staffing, and overseeing all aspects of event production, such as staging, sound, décor, and lighting. DMCs also serve as a dependable resource for entertainment solutions, ranging from small musical ensembles for background ambiance at intimate cocktail parties to headline entertainment for grand special events. Their familiarity with and access to local musicians and entertainers are crucial factors when choosing a DMC. Furthermore, DMCs frequently provide and suggest décor elements, such as props, floral designs, and decorations, to enhance event spaces and venues.

Transportation logistics represent a cornerstone service offered by DMCs. These services encompass airport "meet-and-greet," seamless hotel transfers, efficient baggage management, and shuttles. Ensuring the smooth movement of participant groups—whether large or small—is a critical component of most events. It demands precision in timing, execution, local expertise, and overall management responsibility, all of which are best handled by a professional DMC. Its involvement guarantees attendee comfort, convenience, and safety. Additionally, many DMCs offer tailored sightseeing tours and recreational activities, such as golf and tennis tournaments.

Due to the inherently creative nature of meetings and events, coupled with the diverse needs and expectations of each group, the spectrum of services offered by DMCs is virtually limitless. Although one client may enlist a DMC to oversee and execute the entire event, another client might engage a DMC to provide only a select few components of the event.

DMC VERSUS DESTINATION MARKETING ORGANIZATION

The realm of DMC services is sometimes likened to, and frequently intermingled with, the functions provided by a **destination marketing organization** (DMO), occasionally referred to as a "**convention and visitors bureau**" (CVB). Although their roles are distinct, the services they offer have noteworthy similarities. DMOs are dedicated to elevating the exposure of a specific destination. They engage in pioneering efforts to curate unique experiences for visitors and foster the development of a sustainable tourism and travel infrastructure within the community. Typically operating as quasigovernment, not-for-profit entities, DMOs have a dual funding stream, comprising both tax dollars and membership fees, which enables them to remain impartial when it comes to their destination's suppliers and vendor members.

DMOs collaborate closely with event planners, facilitating site visitations, disseminating informative marketing materials, and guiding planners to local suppliers of meeting services and venues. For a more comprehensive exploration of DMOs, refer to Chapter 3.

In contrast to DMOs, DMCs operate as for-profit entities. They possess the unique capability to negotiate and execute supplier contracts on behalf of their meeting clients. Leveraging their deep knowledge of the destination, DMCs expertly recommend and secure special event venues, transportation services, tour guides, and restaurant reservations. DMCs deliver exceptional value by acting as their clients' representatives, sourcing a wide array of products and services. At the core of their effectiveness are the strong relationships they nurture with suppliers.

Modern consumers demand a destination that tailors its product and service offerings to align with their expectations. Destinations that successfully enhance customer satisfaction levels and provide support throughout the buying process will not only endure but also reap substantial benefits. Consequently, DMOs collaborate with both the broader community and private companies that offer these services. The pivotal distinction between a DMO and a DMC lies in their roles: a DMO represents the destination to the client, whereas a DMC represents the client to the destination.

BUSINESS STRUCTURE OF DMCS

Some prerequisites are essential to the destination management process:

- staff
- temporary "**field staff**"
- office
- technology
- licenses and insurance
- community contacts
- customer contacts
- history
- destination resources

Staffing stands out as one of the most apparent prerequisites for running a successful DMC. An effective team encompasses office personnel responsible for sales, marketing, logistics, accounting, and administrative duties. Moreover, temporary field staff positions, such as tour guides, greeters, and on-site supervisors, are essential. These individuals often work on a contract basis for each specific event and may be hired temporarily by other DMCs as well.

A strategically positioned office is a fundamental necessity for any DMC. Proximity to major hotels, convention facilities, tourist attractions, and event venues is vital. In today's fiercely competitive landscape, access to cutting-edge technology is imperative. DMC clients typically include associations and major corporations that are tech savvy and expect DMCs to excel in electronic communications. Standard tools for modern DMCs include top-notch communications equipment, imaging software, high-speed internet, and office computers with capabilities such as database and customer relationship management. DMCs also frequently employ computer-aided design programs to efficiently and creatively design meetings. The ability to swiftly process information, make real-time adjustments, and produce professional documents and graphics has evolved into an industry standard and a necessity for DMCs.

Given the nature of DMC services, adequate legal insurance coverage is essential. This encompasses business liability insurance and standard coverage, such as workers' compensation and automobile insurance. Each destination imposes unique laws and licensing requirements governing DMC services. Event professionals must ensure that their chosen business partners possess sufficient insurance coverage and comprehensive knowledge of local ordinances that could influence the smooth operation and execution of their events.

Much like many businesses in the service sector, DMCs thrive in an industry where relationships are paramount. Clients and professionals put their reputations and careers on the line when choosing a DMC. DMC management and staff must boast an extensive network of contacts within the community, spanning hotels, attractions, convention bureaus, airports, law enforcement agencies, and the broader supplier community. Articulating a commitment to fostering and sustaining positive relationships with clients is crucial. It is through these collaborative business partnerships, nurtured via repeated work experiences, that a DMC can effectively cater to the diverse needs of its clients.

The reputation of a DMC within the client community, beyond the destination itself, is significant to the long-term success of the company. The most valuable asset a DMC possesses is its track record of success, which is the most reliable validation when selecting a DMC partner.

The destination community must possess the necessary resources to support the DMC in executing a well-organized program or event. It should feature a competitive service environment with numerous reputable suppliers.

THE DMC ORGANIZATION

DMCs come in various sizes and organizational structures. Due to their low overhead requirements and traditional, albeit modest, profit margins, it is feasible to enter this business with minimal startup funding. In the following section, we will delve into the spectrum of organizations that function as DMCs.

INDEPENDENT OPERATOR

Independent DMCs are locally owned and operated small businesses that frequently began their journey as "ground operators." For many years, these DMCs formed the bedrock of destination management and primarily offered a limited selection of specialized services, such as transportation, tour organization, staffing, or special event management. Today, independent DMCs continue to be influential in the industry, and many have broadened their service portfolios to compete with larger national DMCs. The enduring success of independent DMCs largely hinges on the owner's capacity to cultivate enduring relationships and goodwill by consistently exceeding client expectations. Although starting such a business might be relatively straightforward, the hours and challenges can be demanding.

MULTISERVICES OPERATOR

DMCs that provide a multitude of services are typically larger organizations, in contrast to independent operators. Over time, these entities establish extensive networks of service offerings. To manage complex and diverse client programs effectively, they employ well-trained professionals. Frequently, larger multiservices operators maintain staff and offices in multiple destinations. This enables them to offer clients a distinct advantage in securing high-quality services at a cost lower than what is typically available through independent operators. Examples of such organizations include Hosts Global Alliance, which serves over 300 destinations, and Allied PRA, serving more than 100 domestic destinations along with numerous global partners.

DESTINATION MANAGEMENT NETWORKS

Local "one-destination DMCs" face a challenge due to their lack of the economies of scale enjoyed by national or international DMCs. In response, networks of DMCs have emerged. One notable example is "DMC Network," created to consolidate resources from individual one-city DMCs, primarily for sales and marketing purposes. Similar DMC groups exist with the primary aim of sharing mutual sales and marketing efforts and expenses.

Destination management networks consist of independent DMCs that pay a fee or commission to be affiliated with a national or regionally based organization.

These networks offer peace of mind to event professionals when working with DMCs in unfamiliar locations. This arrangement allows smaller, independent DMCs to maintain their autonomy while gaining significant advantages typically reserved for larger, multiservice, multidestination DMCs.

Sometimes, especially within DMC networks, it is valuable to engage professional representation firms to target specific market segments. Typically contracted for particular geographic locations, such as New York, Chicago, or London, these firms reach out to potential and existing customers in the area on behalf of a DMC network. They introduce professionals to the network while identifying potential leads for future business. These firms may also serve as local intermediaries between customers and DMC partners.

BUSINESS MODEL OF DMCs

DMC clients are individuals or organizations responsible for planning a wide range of events, including meetings, exhibitions, events, conventions, and **incentive travel programs**. When discussing the business model of DMCs, you will often encounter terms like "customer," "client," and "professional" to describe the various individuals, organizations, or companies involved in receiving DMC services. In some cases, these roles may be fulfilled by separate entities. The **customer** is the organization that will be securing and paying for the services. The **client** is the representative of the organization who is in a leadership role when deciding to purchase DMC services. The **professional** representing the customer organization, is the person (or persons) whom the DMC works directly with in planning and coordinating events.

Those involved in planning the services provided by a DMC are typically internal staff, such as corporate sales personnel or account representatives/managers. Although DMCs primarily serve corporate clients, they are increasingly recognized for their value by large tour operators. These operators often contract DMCs to assist with transportation and tours for sizable groups. For instance, a cruise ship might engage a DMC to manage land tours, transportation, and excursions, showcasing the versatile range of services offered by DMCs.

A DMC can enter into a contract directly with an organization whose employees or members will participate in the program. Alternatively, the DMC may engage with a third party or an independent professional meeting planner who offers their services to the participating organization or customer (see Figure 7-1).

For most event professionals, DMCs serve as a local extension of their own office and staff during their stay in the destination. They expect the DMC to function as their "eyes and ears" on the ground, always acting in their best interests. DMCs provide unbiased, experience-based recommendations on logistics, venue selection, event concepts, and social program content. Event professionals rely on DMCs to assist them in designing programs that precisely align with their unique requirements, which can vary in size, budget, duration, and purpose.

Scenario A

Destination management company

Hired by . . .

Company or organization that is planning a meeting or event . . .

Scenario B

Destination management company

Hired by . . .

Professional meeting or event planning company which is hired by . . .

Company or organization that is planning a meeting or event . . .

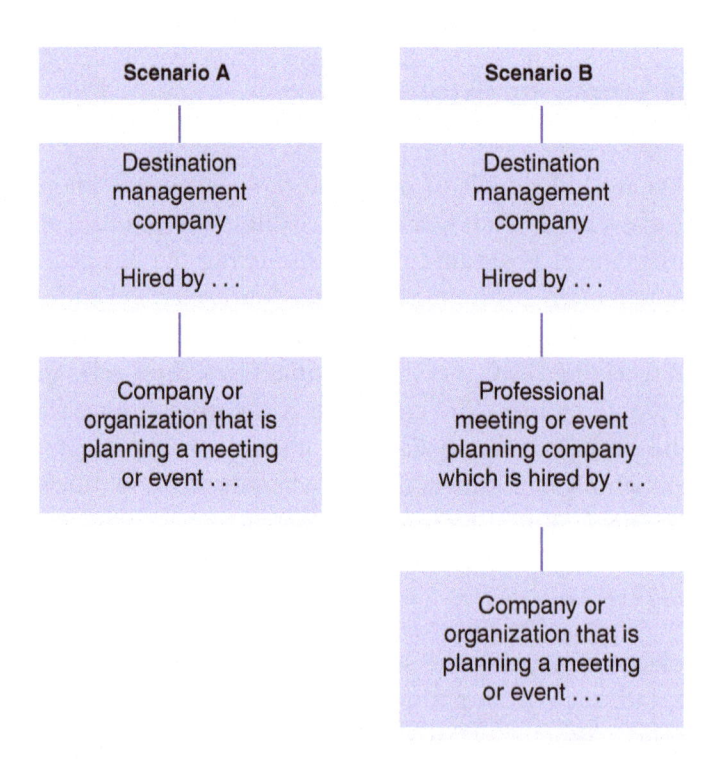

FIGURE 7-1 Sample DMC flow chart

CLIENTS

DMCs serve a wide range of customer categories, each with its unique requirements. Their programs encompass corporate, association, incentive-based, and **special event clients**.

Corporate Accounts

Corporate clients organizing meetings are under increased scrutiny, reflecting recent global economic challenges. In the past, corporate events that combined a half-day of meetings with leisure activities, such as golf, did not attract much attention. However, today, even the choice of location can generate negative publicity. DMCs need to be highly attuned to the constraints and increased scrutiny that these clients face when planning and organizing meetings.

Furthermore, corporate clients are reevaluating the value of in-person meetings. It is essential for DMCs to collaborate closely with their clients to ensure that these meetings and events offer value that exceeds what could be achieved through virtual alternatives. In a world where virtual meetings have become more prevalent, DMCs must strive to demonstrate the unique advantages of face-to-face events.

The following is a list of sample event programs that DMCs work on with corporate clients:

- national sales meetings,
- training meetings,
- product introductions,
- dealer and/or customer meetings, and
- team-building activities.

Association Accounts

Associations are organizations established to champion an industry, shared interest, or activity. They span the spectrum from local and state levels to regional, national, and even international groups. Most associations provide networking and educational opportunities to their members; they regularly organize a variety of meetings, conventions, and conferences.

In today's highly competitive landscape, individuals considering attending conferences and conventions are becoming increasingly discerning. Traveling to an event outside of the local area demands a significant investment of both time and money. Attendees weigh the ROI they expect to gain from their participation. DMCs play a pivotal role in providing substantial resources and support to assist clients in crafting events that offer their members the greatest impact. The following is a list of sample event programs that DMCs work on with association clients:

- industry trade shows (food, construction, aircraft, etc.),
- professional trade shows and conferences (for architects, doctors, teachers, etc.),
- fraternal organizations (VFW, Lions, etc.),
- educational conferences (medical symposia, other professional groups), and
- political conventions.

INCENTIVE-BASED ORGANIZATIONS

Incentive-based meetings and events are meticulously crafted to acknowledge and reward employees who have not only met but often exceeded company targets. This segment of the meetings and events market is experiencing remarkable growth. Modern organizations increasingly recognize the significance of offering incentives and recognition to employees. These events are typically 3–6 days and can range from modest, meaningful getaways to extravagant experiences for employees and their companions. DMCs excel in providing clients with a range of services tailored to their budget and employee preferences. The following is a list of sample event programs that DMCs work on with incentive-based clients:

- sales incentives,
- dealer incentives, and
- service manager incentives.

SPECIAL EVENT CLIENTS

Local corporations, associations, and for-profit and not-for-profit organizations often turn to DMCs for stand-alone events that can encompass a wide range of celebrations, including galas, fundraisers, anniversary celebrations, and walk/run challenges. DMCs provide their expertise in managing local resources and logistics to ensure these events are executed seamlessly.

DMC OPERATIONS

Unlike hotels, resorts, convention centers, and restaurants, DMCs do not require extensive capital investments to establish and operate a businesses. This is because they do not produce or manufacture any products. Typically, DMC offices are strategically located near the primary venues for meetings and events. Proximity to major airports can be advantageous, given that many program services involve group arrivals and departures.

The specific responsibilities and job titles within a DMC can vary by company. Many DMCs are small, locally owned, stand-alone businesses with a single office. In contrast, larger companies may have offices in multiple destinations, each with local staff managing responsibilities at all levels. (Refer to Table 7-1 for a breakdown of job responsibilities.)

To achieve success, DMCs must handle various tasks, including generating business leads, proposing suitable services, contracting services, coordinating group arrivals, delivering contracted services, and handling billing and program reconciliation. These tasks often involve partnering with supplier companies, hiring temporary field staff, and assigning program staff. Field staff, responsible for functions such as tour guiding, hospitality desk operations, and airport "meet-and-greet" services, are typically temporary contract employees hired for the duration of a specific program. It is common for field staff in a destination to work for multiple DMCs.

Management and Administration	Operations and Production
• General Manager	• Director of Operations
• Office Manager	• Director of Special Events
• Accounting Manager	• Operations Manager
• Executive Assistant	• Production Manager
• Administrative Assistant	• Transportation Manager
• Receptionist	• Staffing Manager
• Research Assistant	
	Field Staff
Sales and Marketing	• Meet-and-Greet Staff
• Director of Sales	• Tour Guide
• Director of Marketing	• Transportation Manager
• Director of Special Events	• Event Supervisor
• Sales Manager	• Field Supervisor
• Sales Coordinator	• Equipment Manager
Account Representative/Manager	
• Proposal Writer	
• Research Analyst	

TABLE 7-1 Categories of DMC Job Responsibilities, with Sample Job Titles

The job titles can differ by DMC. However, all DMCs share fundamental responsibilities that fall into three main categories: sales and promotion, **operations and production**, and management and administration. Although these core areas are consistent, the levels of authority and reporting structures often vary, influenced by the company's size and the qualifications of its staff. For instance, the title "director of special events" might appear under both sales and marketing functions and operations and production. This duality depends on the company's structure and the expertise of the individual executive.

In many cases, DMCs do not own transportation equipment, props, décor, or other supplies that they package and offer. Instead, they commonly procure these items from selected suppliers and manage them within the context of the broader event program. In essence, the DMC acts as a "contractor" for the services provided by numerous local suppliers.

A crucial element for the sustained success of DMCs is their capacity to impartially recommend and select service suppliers. The value proposition of a DMC to event professionals hinges on their ability to identify the most suitable providers that align with the client's budget and program requirements. Clients must have confidence that the DMC earns its compensation through its management services rather than inflated financial "arrangements" with suppliers.

THE SALES PROCESS

For DMCs to thrive, they must consistently seek out and secure new business ventures. Opportunities may arise through various avenues. Not all DMCs serve all the client categories mentioned earlier in this chapter. Some have built prosperous enterprises by specializing in niches, such as associations' convention business, corporate meetings, or international travel groups. Others may cater to individual travelers, and some concentrate primarily on the domestic incentive market. Nevertheless, the majority of DMCs operate across multiple markets, a determination usually driven by the characteristics of their chosen destination.

In essence, a destination's infrastructure and allure often determine which market segments DMCs engage with. That infrastructure, including convention centers, convention hotels, resorts, and airport facilities, significantly influences the decision. Additionally, other destination assets, such as natural and manufactured attractions, play a pivotal role in whether corporations choose a location for important meetings or incentive travel rewards. Factors such as picturesque beaches, lush forests, favorable weather, recreational amenities, fishing opportunities, cultural attractions, gaming facilities, and theme parks all contribute to a destination's overall appeal.

IDENTIFYING NEW BUSINESS OPPORTUNITIES

The initial phase of the sales process involves uncovering fresh business opportunities and actively pursuing these leads. These opportunities usually arise from engaging with customers in places where they conduct business, such as industry trade shows or conferences. Notable examples of these trade shows include the American Society of Association Executives (ASAE) Annual Meeting and Exposition, IMEX America (Las Vegas), IMEX Frankfurt, and Holiday Showcase (Chicago). Sales executives representing DMCs must meticulously research these trade shows to optimize their sales and marketing resources. Being aware in advance of which potential customers will be present and understanding the business opportunities they represent significantly enhances a DMC's chances of establishing new relationships.

DMCs often acquire **leads** for new accounts through requests from event professionals who have collaborated with a DMO. Once the DMO passes on the lead, the DMC's account representative or manager initiates communication through direct and electronic means, including presentations that frequently showcase the DMC's competence, highlighting examples of its successful programs. After establishing that the DMC possesses the expertise to meet the client's requirements, it responds to the client's **request for proposal (RFP)**.

Certain customers, particularly corporate clients, incentive companies, and meeting management firms may designate a "preferred" DMC in specific destinations. In the world of DMCs, this is commonly referred to as a "**house account**." When house account planners require services, their chosen DMC can assist them without having to undergo the often-arduous competitive bidding process. These accounts are important and require meticulous care and maintenance. They are highly sought after, with rival DMCs constantly vying for them. Maintaining these relationships necessitates periodic visits to the customers and maintaining open lines of communication and may involve joining the same industry organizations; attending conferences and meetings that they host enables DMC representatives to connect and network with existing and potential planner clients.

For most DMCs, sales efforts at the destination level are important within their sales strategy. Establishing relationships with local industry representatives who engage with the same customers and planners is an effective method to uncover new business opportunities. This involves networking at local hospitality industry events, such as monthly meetings hosted by the Hospitality Sales and Marketing Association International or convention bureau mixers.

Successful DMCs often stay informed about industry developments, the professionals involved, and any changes in services and staffing within the local industry.

Comprehensive sales and marketing plans for DMCs rely on essential collateral materials. These materials encompass brochures, letterheads, business cards, proposal templates, and fact sheets detailing the various activities and services offered by the DMC. DMCs also often produce company newsletters to enhance their image and recognition in the industry. Electronic media is increasingly used, but a consultative selling approach remains indispensable. The effectiveness of a DMC hinges on its ability to cultivate and nurture enduring relationships with both suppliers and clients or professionals.

RFP

Typically, potential customers will request bids from two or more DMCs based on a set of specifications outlined in their RFP. Each DMC then crafts detailed and imaginative proposals for services that align with the client's specific requirements. These proposals are typically created at no cost to the client, a significant consideration.

For DMCs, responding to a client's RFP often entails substantial expenses, including staff time dedicated to creating customized proposals. Consequently, DMCs must make prudent choices when selecting which business opportunities to pursue. The cost associated with collecting and submitting bids in response to client RFPs is regulated by the adoption of standards for electronic RFP submissions. The **Event Industry Council** has played a leading role in developing these standards, and templates for the electronic formats can be accessed under the **APEX** guidelines, which are essentially best practices encompassing glossaries, forms, and procedures embraced by the industry for various event planning components.

DMCs meticulously prepare detailed service proposals tailored to the planner's specifications and budget. Event professionals provide DMCs with information to facilitate creating a proposed itinerary that best aligns with the group's objectives, demographics, psychographics, behaviors, and expectations. Initial proposals often feature multiple suggested itineraries, offering the client various options, cost breakdowns, and comprehensive details regarding the proposed services.

Once a DMC has secured the sales lead, contacted the customer, and convinced that client to consider the DMC, the DMC will be asked to provide a proposal of services. The following items must be considered and addressed in this proposal stage:

- project specifications
- research and development
- creativity and innovation
- budgets
- response time
- competition

As a DMC begins to determine exactly what to offer a customer, the project specifications become a valuable tool. A great deal of detailed information is usually included in them:

- group size
- choice of hotel, resort type
- meeting space allotments
- dates of service
- types of services required
- demographic, psychographic and behavioral information about the attendees
- management's goals for the meeting or event
- approximate budget
- history regarding past successes and challenges
- deadlines for completion and proposal submission

Equipped with the client's specifications and pertinent information, the DMC formulates a proposal for services that align seamlessly with the client's expectations. The first step often involves a series of creative brainstorming sessions within the DMC's team, where ideas are explored. Following these discussions, the research and development phase commences; the DMC assesses the availability of suppliers, venues, transportation options, and entertainers. It also gathers bids for services, such as catering, transportation equipment, and venue costs. It is imperative to identify the costs associated with each component for precise budgeting.

In the realm of winning proposals, creativity and innovation carry significant weight. The selected program should reflect the client's company, making creativity, innovation, and a meticulously designed program pivotal for success. Response time is a critical factor. However, a trade-off exists between speed and creativity, as innovative ideas take time to develop. A proposal that fails to meet the client's deadline is unlikely to secure the business.

A final and critical step in the proposal process is pricing. Several factors must be considered:

- total estimated costs for delivering the proposed services;
- staff time and involvement necessary before, during, and after the program;
- amount of DMC resources necessary to operate the program;
- unknown costs, which are factored into the planning and contingency stages;
- supplier choice and availability;
- time of the year and local business activity during a particular season;
- costs of taking staff and company capacity off the market for this customer; and
- competitive bids on the project.

The following questions are the type that a DMC should ask itself prior to making a final decision on how much effort to dedicate to a given opportunity. The answers may show that ultimately the best decision is for a DMC to choose not to bid on a client's RFP.

- What is the revenue potential of the business opportunity?
- What is the value of a future relationship with the customer?
- How much proposal work will be involved in the bid?
- How many companies are bidding?
- Which competitors are bidding?
- What success rate does it have on similar projects?
- What success rate does its competitors have?
- What time of year will the program be operating?
- What are the approximate odds of winning the program?
- How profitable will the program be?

Given the variety among proposal elements offered by the competing DMCs, a client may not choose a winning bid based solely on price but may consider other important factors:

- Is the proposal feasible?
- What is the perceived value of services offered?
- Will the participants appreciate the suggested program?
- Will the quality be sufficient to make the program or even a success?

- Is the DMC capable of producing the program or event in an acceptable manner?
- Is the program creative enough that it will meet the needs/appetite of the participants?

One of the changing dynamics of DMCs in recent years is their degree of legal awareness because, over the years, potential clients (prospects) receive proposals but then decide not to proceed with any DMC at all. Rather, they take the information and advice and create their own event. Financially and ethically, this can create problems; in response, the DMC adds confidentiality agreements to its proposal to protect itself from idea theft, etc.

SITE INSPECTIONS

Although DMCs may be involved in **site inspections**, they typically do not organize or sponsor them. This responsibility falls to the DMOs in the locale (see Chapter 3 for more information).

PROGRAM DEVELOPMENT

The execution and professionalism of business transactions within the meetings and events industry heavily relies on contractual agreements. This holds true for various entities, including hotels, convention centers, cruise ships, airlines, and DMCs. Each of these stakeholders enters contracts with its clients, meticulously outlining the specifics of the purchase and responsibilities of both parties. The size and complexity of these contracts can vary depending on the scale and scope of the program and services offered by the DMC.

Following the contract signing, a pivotal transition takes place, shifting the focus from active program selling to executing the program. All suppliers, who have been contracted by the DMC, are promptly notified that the program has received approval, and their services are officially confirmed. Typically, in larger DMCs, the operations team, distinct from the sales team, collaborates with the sales representatives, which involves reviewing the customer's requirements, objectives, and any intricate details critical to seamlessly delivering the program.

Throughout this phase, the roster of actively engaged participants may vary, necessitating vigilant cost monitoring and meticulous attention to detail. With the client actively involved, activities and services can be added or removed. Hence, it is imperative for DMC representatives to remain accessible, responsive, and diligent in recording and implementing these changes. As integral members of the customer's team, DMCs manage the destination aspect of the broader customer event. Therefore, flexibility and cooperation are paramount. A designated program manager, often an operations or events manager, assumes primary responsibility for overseeing the entire event. During the setup phase, every activity and service is meticulously reviewed and confirmed. Full- and part-time professional program managers, supervisors, tour guides, and escorts are diligently scheduled well in advance. Moreover, during the program development phase, the event manager institutes a comprehensive system of checks and balances to ensure thorough coverage in all aspects.

PROGRAM EXECUTION

DMCs are tasked with the intricate coordination of staff and suppliers, forming a unified program of products and services. They identify opportunities, craft proposals, earn the trust of professionals, secure program contracts, and prepare meticulously. It then falls to the operations, logistics, and production staff to ensure seamless delivery. The image of the customer organization, planner's reputation, prospects for the DMC with the planner, DMC's standing within the destination, and opportunity to profit from the contract all hang in the balance.

Successfully executing a program is immensely significant. Consider, for instance, conventions hosted by prominent associations, such as the American Medical Association, Radiological Society of North America, and National Automobile Dealers Association, all of which use a DMC. Professionals overseeing these associations manage substantial events with thousands of participants on an ongoing basis. The attendees' perception of the organization is on the line. Attendees' experiences can be significantly impacted by various factors, including the quality of shuttle transportation to and from the convention hall, networking events, cocktail parties, meal service, and activities, such as the annual golf tournament and optional sightseeing tours—many of which potentially fall under the DMC's purview. Ensuring these services meet or exceed expectations is imperative. Activities and tours must be both entertaining and impeccably organized. After all, the participants represent the association planner's clientele, and the quality of program delivery significantly influences membership renewals and convention attendance.

Similar dynamics come into play in the realm of corporate programs. Participating in trade shows provides corporations with an opportunity to captivate their customers through special event programs meticulously curated by their contracted DMCs. Insurance companies, for instance, use incentive programs to acknowledge and reward their top sales producers, effectively demonstrating the value their top executives place on these contributions. Additionally, computer and software companies frequently host events to introduce new products, either as stand-alone occasions or in conjunction with industry conventions. Their success often has significant implications for the sponsoring companies' futures.

Through these examples, the immense pressure of executing a flawlessly organized and high-quality program becomes evident. These pressures weigh heavily on event professionals and DMCs. The operations and production staff of DMCs have only one opportunity to deliver the program flawlessly. Mistakes or missteps are not easily rectified, and events cannot be rescheduled. If bus and limousine suppliers fail to provide the equipment as ordered, departure times cannot be adjusted. Thus, the linchpin of program success is the reliability of execution, with cost considerations a distant second. However, not all DMCs are identical, and selecting the most suitable one for a specific program is paramount. Cultivating a close working relationship characterized by trust, seamless communication, and mutual understanding necessitates the immediate availability of the planner's DMC contact, just as the planner must remain readily accessible to the DMC's operations manager throughout the program's duration.

TRANSPORTATION SERVICES

Transportation management frequently constitutes a significant portion, if not the primary component, of a DMC's operations. This facet encompasses various aspects, including route planning, vehicle use, staffing needs, special venue considerations, staging areas for equipment, staff scheduling and briefings, maps, and signage. Transportation scenarios and requirements are typically interspersed throughout the program itinerary.

Meeting and greeting guests and arranging their transportation is only one of many services provided by a DMC, with transportation coming in all shapes and sizes

Although most DMCs do not book flights, a few do. However, a DMC's largest component is ground transportation. When beginning the event process, the DMC will need to assess the travel and transportation requirements of the client by identifying the following:

- type of event
- size of event
- scope of event
- type of attendees/audience profile
- arrival/departure service
- continuous or timed shuttle service
- transfers (from hotel to conference, etc.)
- any mobility/disability issues
- bundling of transportation services
- special transportation needs of VIPs, performers/entertainers, or major sponsors (limos or town cars)

DMCs often secure or provide the appropriate transportation for the event. They will need to provide the appropriate equipment, coordinate transportation types, and supervise on-site services. DMCs offer local transportation coordination and other local travel needs:

- group tours/chartering,
- group transfers,
- shuttle scheduling, and
- special event arrangements.

When a DMC sends out an RFP for transportation services, selecting a provider becomes crucial for the successful execution of an event. DMCs require specific information to assess the vendor's suitability, such as the size of the fleet, the condition of the vehicles, whether the equipment is owned or subcontracted, the drivers' possession of current commercial driver's licenses, the presence of a driver drug and alcohol testing program, annual bus inspections, the amount of public liability insurance, and the existence of notification procedures for roadside emergencies and breakdowns, as outlined by the Federal Motor Carrier Administration.

Once a company is selected, the DMC's process unfolds in three stages. First, the DMC coordinator must consider factors such as the number of people requiring transportation (travel demand), transfer timings (referencing travel manifests and arrival times), and types of vehicles suitable for the transfers.

Second, during arrivals and departures, a DMC may organize various services, including meet-and-greet services, specialized baggage handling, motor coach transfers, shuttle services, courtesy cars, and a fleet of limousines for VIPs, entertainers, dignitaries, etc. In many cases, especially for conferences or conventions using multiple hotels for accommodations, a continuous or timed shuttle service between the airport and hotels is essential. The meet-and-greet and arrival transfer is the first impression a DMC makes on attendees, and the departure transfer is the last impression. Effective execution relies on dispatchers, directional staff, radios, cell phones, and signage to ensure the success of each transfer.

Third, during the conference, continuous or scheduled shuttle services between the hotels and the event venue may be required, along with transportation for evening functions and dine-arounds, among other activities. Similar to arrival and departure logistics, the success of these transfers depends on the presence of dispatchers, directional staff, communication tools, such as radios and cell phones, and appropriate signage.

Effective traffic management is essential when planning group transfers, especially when the DMC is dealing with multiple hotels. DMCs collaborate closely with transportation companies to assess traffic patterns and route options for transferring large numbers of attendees to and from various venues. Avoiding traffic congestion, road construction, accidents, competing events that cause significant traffic, and rush hour is crucial for not only the smooth operation of the event but also attendee satisfaction. Consequently, DMCs and transportation companies often establish a traffic control plan well in advance of the event to address these concerns.

DMCs also charter motor coaches for various purposes, such as remote tours, additional trips before and after conferences, sightseeing tours, team-building activities, sporting events, educational programs, and off-site company events. This is a safe, cost-effective, and environmentally friendly option. Businesses often prefer luxury motor coaches over public transportation or school buses because they come equipped with extra features, such as reclining seats, stereo music, video/TV monitors, a DVD player, Wi-Fi, device charging outlets, luggage space, restrooms, and air-conditioning.

When selecting a motor coach service provider, DMCs consider factors such as location, reputation, insurance requirements, safety records, availability, reviews, and estimated costs. They carefully review contracts and often negotiate on behalf of the planner. Once the service provider is chosen, the tour is planned and total cost calculated. Costs can fluctuate leading up to the tour date due to changing fuel prices and fuel industry volatility.

Each bus will have signage displayed in the windows, and name badges may be provided for each guest. Tour guides or group escorts are often used to enhance the tours and ensure the group stays on schedule. Box lunches may be provided or meal stops included, especially on longer journeys. Occasionally, shopping opportunities may be added. At the conclusion of the tour, the DMC typically presents each guest with a gift or memento to commemorate the experience.

Sporting events, such as the Tour de France, represent ideal opportunities for DMCs to showcase the destination experiential benefits of in-person meetings

MEETINGS, EXPOSITIONS, EVENTS, AND CONVENTIONS

Transportation services can significantly impact the success of an event. DMCs orchestrate personalized and meticulously planned transportation services that prioritize attendee safety and timeliness, starting from their arrival until departure. Given that transportation is often the most substantial component of a DMC's business, they must carefully evaluate and execute every detail, ensuring that attendees have a memorable and seamless experience from start to finish.

PRODUCTION OF EVENTS

Event production is also typically a major part of a DMC's services. Events can be large or small, on a hotel property, or in a remote location, such as the following:

- cocktail receptions and networking events;
- breakfasts, luncheons, and dinners;
- dining events at unique venues;
- gala dinner events;
- extravagant theme parties;
- outdoor and indoor team-building events; and
- guest and children's programs.

Operational staff must possess in-depth knowledge of municipal regulations for insurance, fire safety codes, permitting crowd control, and police requirements. Experience is irreplaceable, and collaborating with a DMC known for its successful track record becomes crucial.

Whether coordinating sightseeing tours, organizing a scavenger hunt, managing a golf tournament, or overseeing a hospitality desk, a DMC operations manager must possess strong organizational skills, thorough preparation, and a profound sense of commitment and responsibility. When the success of the event hinges on the DMC's performance, planners often establish a strong bond with the managers, relying on them as on-site consultants.

Event professionals will often have to deal with on-site questions and requests for VIP arrangements with little advance notice, and the DMC staff will support them in doing so. Last-minute requests that DMCs are asked to take care of include the following:

- "Where can I send my VP of marketing and her husband for a romantic dinner? She just realized that today's their wedding anniversary!"
- "My company president is arriving early in the corporate jet. Can we get a limo to the executive airport in forty-five minutes?"
- "The boss just decided he wants a rose for all the ladies at tonight's party."
- "Can we get Aretha Franklin to sing 'Happy Birthday' to one of our dealers during her performance at the party tonight?"

As a wise person once said, "It is often the little things, the details, which separate great events from ordinary ones." Knowing someone's favorite wine, song, or dessert can transform an ordinary event into one that will be remembered forever. These are the things that are not explicitly written into the contract but add special touches. They provide excellent opportunities for the production staff to showcase their commitment to serving the client passionately. A production manager who has cultivated strong relationships with suppliers can often rely on them to get involved in the process and suggest ideas for program improvement voluntarily. Suppliers do this because they want the event to be exceptional, establishing an ongoing relationship with the DMC for potential future events. Planners are usually delighted to have additional options presented to them, such as confetti cannons for the dance floor, extra accent lighting, or separate martini bars as on-site event upgrades.

Much of an operations or production manager's day is spent confirming and reconfirming services. Maintaining constant communication with vendors and suppliers is crucial to ensure that final participant counts, and timing, are accurate. One common task to ensure the success of events is the **advancing of a venue**: DMC staff arrive well ahead of a group to ensure that the service staff and the event location are adequately prepared and set up. Details such as the number of seats, room temperature, serving instructions, menu, and beverage service are all examples of items that should be verified when advancing a dinner event.

Throughout each event, operations and production managers must vigilantly oversee the originally contracted services and any changes after the initial itinerary and contracts are established. Every addition, including modifications in participant counts, service times, and services, should be

Sporting venues, such as the new Sofi stadium in Los Angeles, are increasingly being chosen by delegates for interesting places to meet and conduct business

meticulously documented. Precise, real-time records of the services provided must be maintained for billing purposes. To prevent billing disputes, it is crucial to verify that an authorized representative of the client has endorsed the change or addition, ideally in writing and granted in advance by the client.

WRAP-UP AND BILLING

The final invoice should accurately reflect the contracted services agreed upon before the program's execution. It should itemize the actual services provided, including the number of participants for each charged item. Typically, items are billed either at fixed "lot" costs, which are independent of the number of participants (e.g., bus tours, entertainer fees, or ballroom décor packages) or per person, which is based on the actual number of participants (e.g., food and beverage at a luncheon billed at a fixed price per person, plus tax and gratuities).

Any additions or deletions to the originally contracted services must be clearly listed on the invoice, which should also display the "grand total," including all deposits and payments received prior to the final billing. Typically, around 90% of the bill is paid 30 days in advance. Whenever possible, it is advisable to review and approve the final billing details with the planner or on-site representative immediately upon completion, while all details, additions, and changes are still fresh in everyone's memory. The longer the time between completion and the receipt of the final invoice, the greater the likelihood of disputes regarding program details, such as participant counts, timings, and approved additions.

FINDING AND SELECTING A DMC

When event professionals need to find and select a DMC, several steps and guidelines can ensure a successful outcome. To begin the search, it is advisable to reach out to industry professionals who regularly manage and execute meetings and events. Networking offers the advantage of having contacts who can provide valuable advice and guidance. If an event professional lacks suitable connections, they can explore industry groups, such as the Professional Convention Management Association, Meeting Professionals International, International Live Events Association, and ASAE, as valuable resources. Additionally, the destination's CVB or DMO will have listings of DMCs operating in and around it.

ASSOCIATION OF DESTINATION MANAGEMENT EXECUTIVES

An invaluable resource for finding a DMC is the **Association of Destination Management Executives International (ADMEI)**. Established in 1995, ADMEI is dedicated to the principle that professional destination management plays a pivotal role in the success of every meeting or event. One of its primary objectives is to continually emphasize and advocate for the significance of destination management as an essential resource for planners of meetings, events, and incentive travel programs. Furthermore, ADMEI strives to be the definitive source for information, education, and discussions centered around destination management within the meetings, events, incentive, and hospitality industries.

Professionals in the field of destination management can become a *destination management certified professional*, introduced by ADMEI in January 2000, is a prestigious certification available only to individuals who successfully pass an extensive examination administered by ADMEI. Applicants undergo a rigorous screening process, which includes a detailed questionnaire that outlines their experience and industry education. ADMEI has also developed the Destination Management Company Accreditation (ADMC) program, which is designed to promote professional standards and recognize DMCs that demonstrate excellence in destination management while adhering to the standards set forth by ADMEI. The ADMC designation is a valuable resource for the meeting planning community, helping them identify DMCs that meet the high standards of practice, ethics, and industry knowledge established by ADMEI.

Once a list of DMCs has been identified through references or research of the various industry associations, it is time to identify the best of the group. Factors that may be important before soliciting the RFP selection include the following:

- How long the company has been in business?
- What are the experience levels of the management and staff?
- What are the perceptions of the planner of the personalities of the management team?
- Is the DMC an affiliated member of any relevant professional organizations?
- Is the DMC adequately bonded, relative to the size and complexity of the program?
- What is the quality of the references provided by the DMC in size of previous programs and ranking of professional providing the references?

The next step in the process is to select a DMC that best aligns with the needs and budgetary guidelines. Event professionals should formally notify DMCs by issuing a RFP. Once the final selection has been made, it is crucial to initiate collaboration with the chosen DMC. This ensures it has access to information related to the organization's participants, which can significantly impact the successful execution of the program.

BEST PRACTICES IN DMCs

The diverse representatives in the destination management industry recognize the importance of evolving with the times. DMC operators should prioritize eight key areas to enhance their leadership and reputation in the field, both now and in the future:

1. *Take the Lead in Green Practices.* Be proactive in initiating sustainable practices by implementing leading-edge methods for leaving a smaller carbon footprint, educating other parts of the hospitality industry through professional training activities and developing and distributing training materials. In addition, DMCs should develop new partnerships

to share these activities and materials with other businesses in both the private and public sectors.
2. *Work Together in Consortia.* The DMC industry will continue to see a consolidation of service organizations. It will be important for smaller, niche DMCs to bond together in consortia to ensure that business remains in the local community and that the overall experience for event professionals is seamless from planning, execution, and payment.
3. *Identify and Develop New Business From Drive-To Markets.* Given the uncertainty of the economy and the unfriendly skies, businesses will begin to look for more local and regional sites for holding their meetings and events. This should lead DMCs to focus on developing new clients from locations that are closer to their destinations.
4. *Develop Crisis Networks.* Issues surrounding the safety and security of meeting attendees will continue to be a concern for corporations and associations. Successful DMCs will develop, implement, and execute risk and crisis management plans and business continuity networks in partnerships with other organizations within their communities.
5. *Emphasize Standards of Conduct and Operations.* DMCs will continue to be scrutinized about the behavior of staff used to provide client services. It will become increasingly important that DMCs implement high standards of conduct for their employees and operations. These policies should be defined, recognized, and understood by every employee, clients, and the general public as part of an established image and reputation.
6. *Have a Relationship Management Strategy.* Corporations and associations that conduct business and meeting travel are quickly consolidating their travel, meeting, and event expenses into a more economically efficient model. Local and niche DMCs will need to use consultative selling techniques to build strong, lasting relationships with event professionals to ensure that they are on the list of approved vendors.
7. *Attend to Competitive Forces.* Given the ubiquity of the internet, and its convenience, successful large DMCs no longer need a continuous presence in a local market. Local, niche DMCs will need to increase the quality of customer contacts and services to meetings and events professionals and their attendees to remain relevant in a competitive marketplace.
8. *Use Ethical Business Protocols.* DMCs rely heavily upon their confidential intellectual property, creative ideas, and research conducted for a specific client program. The industry's (DMCs, planners, and suppliers) adherence to the ADMEI Code of Ethics is vital for its continued growth and professionalism.

THE COVID-19 IMPACT ON BUSINESS DESTINATIONS AND DMCs

Although leisure travel has experienced a robust rebound, with major destinations, such as Orlando and Las Vegas, surpassing expectations, the success of virtual meetings on platforms such as Zoom and Teams has hindered the recovery of business travel. The business market has become more discerning in its travel decisions. Work-related trips are still ongoing, as observed by the bustling activity at most U.S. airports. In 2019, business travel injected approximately $334 billion into the U.S. economy and supported around 2.5 million jobs. Therefore, even a slight decline could adversely affect the economy, causing DMCs to need to highlight the positive aspects of business travel and the advantages of being physically present. Although videoconferencing and virtual meetings are here to stay, they do have limitations and often lack the personal touch of face-to-face interactions. The segment most at risk appears to be short, single-day trips. However, the market for trips lasting more than 1 day is expected to endure and possibly even grow. Business professionals are seeking alternative and more stimulating environments than their offices, moving beyond the confines of a screen and a square block on it.

The evolving landscape of business travel presents numerous opportunities. However, destinations and DMCs must adapt by offering enhanced experiences, paying meticulous attention to detail, and refocusing on encouraging repeat visits. They can also explore expanding into the "Bleisure" market, being more flexible with pricing, and creating versatile packages in collaboration with major stakeholders, such as airlines, hotels, Airbnb, restaurants, and entertainment providers. Furthermore, DMCs can contribute to the remote work trend by promoting their destinations as appealing remote workplaces. They can develop programs and packages for newcomers in the business world who are eager to work from home but still want to engage in local networking.

One promising aspect for the future is human nature. Despite the abundance of virtual platforms that reduce the need for physical travel, most of us still crave new experiences, value face-to-face interactions, and believe that in-person meetings enhance long-term business success. Therefore, the future of business travel remains promising, as long as DMCs adapt to the changing nature and expectations of business travelers.

SUMMARY

The role that DMCs play in the MEEC industry is crucial for event professionals. These organizations provide an essential service because the companies and organizations that sponsor meetings and events always require access to local expertise. The depth of local destination knowledge, extensive network of local contacts and connections, strong community standing, purchasing influence, and hands-on experience in implementing programs and events are resources not readily available to nonlocal organizations. DMCs have undergone interesting transformations over time. Many of the early DMCs specialized in providing tours and transportation services for visiting travel groups. However, as the demand for association and high-end corporate programs grew in the late 1950s, DMCs expanded to include dining programs, a wider range of activities, and the coordination of special events.

In today's competitive landscape, DMCs are found in the form of multidestination, national firms operating extensive networks worldwide. However, much like individual, distinctive hotels that thrive alongside major chains, specialized one-destination DMCs also continue to flourish. The services requested by event professionals are continually evolving, with destination management services recognized as a pivotal element for success in the MEEC industry.

Professionals working within the destination management segment of the MEEC industry have access to a wide array of industry associations that offer support, as well as trade shows and conventions for marketing their services. Notably, the ADMEI and its DMC accreditation and executive certification programs play a central role in this network.

The long-term prospects for DMCs are promising, provided they adapt to the changing expectations of business travelers. The meeting and event industry that DMCs support remains robust, with many established firms maintaining financial stability and poised to expand their market share and brand recognition, notwithstanding occasional threats and business slowdowns. The industry continues to offer abundant opportunities for long-term, successful careers for both new and experienced professionals.

Cannes, France, home of the International Film Festival, one of the most enticing convention destinations in the world

CASE STUDY WORKING WITH A DMC

Natalie works for a professional association of financial managers in Chicago and has booked her conference of 1,000 participants for the late spring in San Diego. This is the first time the event or Natalie has used that destination. To familiarize herself with the city, she arranged for a site visit, where she was escorted by a member of the sales team of the San Diego Tourism Authority (a DMO). They visited many hotels, attractions, special event venues, and golf courses and discussed how it could help market the conference to her membership. It also provided a directory of member suppliers (tour and transportation companies, golf courses, décor companies, event venues other than hotels and restaurants). Before signing hotel contracts, she worked with the DMO in narrowing venues down to four properties; she eventually chose two.

Now that Natalie had firm dates and a location, she began to think about a number of special events and activities her planning committee had recommended. As she considered it and the additional workload involved, it became clear that she needed a partner. The DMO could only point her in the direction of suppliers. It was not a planner, and to be fair to all of its members, it could not negotiate contracts or recommend one supplier over another.

Natalie turned to a DMC. She referred to the DMO's membership directory, asked for recommendations from industry colleagues, and sent a RFP to her top three choices. Natalie was planning the following:

1. A golf tournament, where she needed a golf course, transportation, awards, tournament planning, continental breakfast, lunch, and on-site supervision.
2. An adventure tour; they had done desert jeep tours, horseback riding, and swamp tours with airboats. She needed venue recommendations, transportation, a place for lunch, and supervision.
3. The opening reception at one of the hotels, but she needed theme décor and entertainment.
4. A historical cultural tour of the city, requiring a planned route, bus transportation, qualified tour guides, and on-site supervision.
5. Two VIP dinners at high-end restaurants for 35 people each on two different nights, requiring a private room; she needed floral arrangements and transportation.
6. Private transportation for the president, chairman of the board, and keynote speaker to and from the airport.

Once the DMC's proposals arrived and after a careful review, Natalie chose to interview two of them during a site visit. The DMCs met with her, clarified the objectives and the audience for each event, and used their expertise of the city to develop a total program for the association. Rather than Natalie having to manage negotiations and contracts for each of these events and the many suppliers, she turned to a one-stop shop. She was able to develop a trusted partnership; the DMC became her eyes and ears in San Diego. In essence, she hired an event planner for herself.

1. Did Natalie do a complete job?
2. What would you have done differently?
3. What else would you have done?

KEY WORDS AND TERMS

For definitions, see glossary or http://www.conventionindustry.org/APEX/glossary.aspx.

Association of Destination Management Executives
Advancing of a venue
APEX
client
client project
convention and visitors bureau
customer
destination management company
destination management networks
destination marketing organization
Event Industry Council
field staff
ground operator
house account
incentive travel programs
International Association of Professional Congress Organizers
leads
operations and production
professional
professional congress organizer
request for proposal
site inspection
special event clients

REVIEW AND DISCUSSION QUESTIONS

1. What is a DMC?
2. What services are offered by DMCs?
3. Compare and contrast a DMC and a DMO.
4. Create an organizational chart for a DMC.
5. How do DMCs generate their business leads?
6. What are the resources DMCs provide to event professionals?
7. Describe the differences between the types of accounts that use DMCs.
8. What professional organizations support the professionals who work in the destination management industry?
9. List the services provided by ADMEI.
10. Describe key factors that are considered when event professionals are selecting a DMC.
11. Outline the important role, and financial contribution, that transportation plays in the workings of a DMC.

ABOUT THE CHAPTER CONTRIBUTORS

Dr. Alan Fyall is the associate dean of academic affairs and Visit Orlando Endowed Chair for Tourism Marketing at the Rosen College of Hospitality Management, University of Central Florida. He has published widely in the areas of tourism and destination marketing and management, including 23 books. Dr. Fyall is a former member of the Bournemouth Tourism Management Board (DMO) and has conducted numerous consulting and applied research projects for clients around the world. He teaches International Tourism Management and Destination Planning for Events, both at the graduate level.

Steve Brinkman received both his bachelor's and master's in education from Illinois State University. Before UCF, he spent 24 years in the tourism and hospitality industry, working in sales and marketing. He was also instrumental in developing the first commission-free group travel website, Group Travel Odyssey. He has been on numerous sales and marketing boards and committees. The most notable boards and committees included Visit Florida's International Tourism Board, Visit Orlando's Marketing Committee, Domestic Group Travel Agency Board of Directors, American Bus Association Marketing Advisory Committee and cochairman of the American Bus Association Marketplace Convention.

Previous Edition Chapter Contributors

Brian Miller, associate professor, University of Delaware

Terry Epton, executive vice president, Host Global Alliance

William R. Host, associate professor, Roosevelt University, Chicago, Illinois

CHAPTER 8

SPECIAL EVENTS MANAGEMENT

WEDDINGS ARE "VERY SPECIAL" EVENTS

CHAPTER OBJECTIVES

- Provide an overview of the history, definition, and main components involved in special event planning.
- Outline several helpful special event planning tools.
- Discuss the many different considerations that go into special event marketing.
- Clarify the steps in preparing for a special event.
- Discuss the elements of a special event budget.
- Articulate the steps in breaking down a special event.

Contributed by David Smiley. © Kendall Hunt Publishing Company.

HISTORY AND OVERVIEW OF SPECIAL EVENTS

A WORKING DEFINITION OF A SPECIAL EVENT

"*Special event*" is a broad term that encompasses all gatherings designed to unite people for a unique purpose. Most events necessitate careful planning by the organizer. Special events, whether city festivals, fairs, or even smaller-scale gatherings, can involve coordinating with **community infrastructure**, handling merchandising, promotion, and, in some cases, managing media relations. These events can vary widely in scale, from the local Kiwanis picnic to the grandeur of the Olympics. Special events are woven into a tapestry of **meetings, expositions, events, and conventions** and amusement parks, parades, **fairs, festivals,** and **public events**.

The Events Industry Council glossary provides the following definition for special events:

- *Special Event:* A one-time celebration or unique activity.
- *Special Events Company:* These companies may be contracted to organize an entire event or specific components of one. Special events *production companies* may specialize in presenting special effects and theatrical acts and also hire speakers as part of their contractual obligations.

Special events serve various purposes, such as bringing organizations together for fundraising, establishing a city or community as a local, regional, or national destination, and stimulating the local economy. These events also present opportunities for associations and corporations to establish favorable relationships with communities or the wider consumer audience. Sponsoring a particular type of event can provide a competitive marketing advantage and an additional channel for reaching customers. For instance, Mercedes-Benz sponsors numerous PGA golf tournaments, aligning with the demographic of its target clientele. It also sponsors the U.S. Open tennis tournament. Other examples include Coors Light sponsoring NASCAR races, Allstate sponsoring the Sugar Bowl football game, and Macy's sponsoring the Thanksgiving Day parade.

Orchestrating a special event goes beyond just having an idea. It requires meticulous planning, a deep understanding of your target audience, fundamental operational knowledge, effective communication skills, collaboration with volunteers or volunteer organizations, adherence to a budget, event promotion, and even the logistics for event breakdown. In essence, an event professional must grasp the "who, what, where, and why" of the special event.

HISTORY AND BACKGROUND

Festivals and special events have been integral parts of human history since time immemorial. Humans have celebrated significant life events, such as births, weddings, and funerals, and organized special gatherings, such as the Olympics and gladiatorial contests. However, most historians attribute "special event" in its modern context to a Disney "imagineer" named Robert Janni. Disney faced a challenge; families visiting the theme park would often tire out and leave by 5 p.m., despite the park staying open for several more hours. To keep attendees engaged, Janni proposed a nightly "Main Street Electric Parade," featuring a multitude of illuminated floats. It proved highly successful in retaining visitors during the evening hours. When asked by a reporter what he called this parade, he simply replied, "A Special Event." Using special events to attract and retain crowds remains a valuable strategy in the present day.

> **USING FESTIVALS IN THE OFF-SEASON: "ROCKIN' MOUNTAINS"**
>
> The stereotypical image of the Rocky Mountains and Colorado conjures up visions of snow-covered peaks in the winter, adorned with skiers. However, what happens when the summer season arrives, and skiing is no longer an option? Do the ski resorts shut down? The emphatic answer is "No!" Instead, they transform into vibrant venues for music festivals, using the same facilities that winter sports enthusiasts enjoy. The setting is nothing short of idyllic, with music resonating through the crisp mountain air against the breathtaking backdrop of towering peaks.
>
> Repurposing Colorado's mountain ski facilities traces its roots back to 1949, when concerts graced the town of Aspen. Back then, it was known as the "Goethe Bicentennial Celebration." Some of these events featured the Minneapolis Symphony Orchestra performing in a tent that accommodated 2,000 attendees. Over time, this special event

evolved into the Aspen Music Festival and School. In recent years, it has featured more than 800 international musicians participating in over 400 events throughout its 8-week session. Of the festival's four major **venues**, the largest is the Benedict Music Tent, capable of hosting over 2,000 people, constructed from the same material as Denver airport's terminal.

Another ski resort that has embraced musical events to entice visitors during the off-season is Telluride, Colorado. Nearly every weekend during the summer, it hosts various musical events. The crown jewel among them is the Telluride Bluegrass Festival, a tradition spanning over 40 years. Held over 4 days in June, it restricts daily attendance to 11,000 people. Telluride also has a Jazz Festival, Chamber Music Festival, and Blues and Brews Festival.

In Winter Park, located just west of Denver, many weekends come alive with the sounds of music festivals. Enthusiastic concertgoers settle on the slopes to enjoy performances by various bands set against the stunning backdrop of the Continental Divide. The Winter Park Music Festival stands out with a lineup of "old-school" music acts, such as Molly Hatchet and Cheap Trick. During July, the Winter Park Jazz Festival unfolds over 2 days, treating audiences to artists spanning a wide range of musical genres, and the Winter Park 30 Solshine Music Festival, a free event showcasing local, spans two weekends.

Breckenridge, too, hosts a summer concert series that runs from late June through mid-August. This series encompasses an eclectic mix of musical genres, ranging from classical to rock. What sets it apart is its unique funding structure; a quarter of its budget is raised through the Bon Appetit Series, which includes intimate gatherings that encompass everything from country music concerts, wildflower hikes, and scavenger hunts on Peak 7, to tours of SouthPark, cabaret evenings, and Texas Hold'em tournaments.

IT ALL BEGINS WITH A RELATIONSHIP

What do wedding receptions, 5K charity runs, the Macy's Thanksgiving Day parade, and company picnics all have in common? They are all exceptional events, albeit quite distinct. Yet, they are meticulously planned by individuals who must thoroughly grasp the goals, needs, and desires of their clients. The event professional must do everything possible to achieve these objectives while operating within the constraints of the location, city, or facility.

So, how does the event professional embark on the journey of truly comprehending the client's vision? And, in turn, how does the client come to trust in their efforts? The art of special events management begins and thrives through cultivating a relationship. The event professional's role is to not only listen to the clients but to truly understand their words and envision their desires. They must possess the expertise and professionalism to transform that vision into reality, aligning it with the client's goals and aspirations. This harmonious partnership and the ability to translate vision into execution form the bedrock of successful special event planning.

Effective communication is essential. Through dialogue and active listening, a viable plan can take shape. The event professional must always bear in mind that any successful event is built upon a solid relationship. This involves attentively hearing the client's needs, delivering on promises, attending to even the smallest details, and maintaining unwavering communication.

Regardless of the event's profile, every special event holds great significance for one or many individuals. The challenge lies in meeting and surpassing the client's expectations, a fundamental responsibility of the event professional.

A shining example of a highly successful event that draws over 100,000 visitors to Central Pennsylvania is the summer Central Pennsylvania Festival of the Arts™ at downtown State College and the University Park campus of Penn State. It is renowned for its nationally recognized Sidewalk Sale and Exhibition, a gallery exhibition, and a rich tapestry of music, dance, and theatrical performances hosted in a variety of traditional and unconventional venues. Founded in 1967, it recently achieved the top spot on *Sunshine Artist* magazine's list of the 100 Best Fine Arts and Design Shows in America.

The Presidential Inauguration Day Parade

Although the tradition of the inaugural parade traces its roots to the inauguration of George Washington, the first organized parade officially took shape at the inauguration of James Madison in 1809. Madison was escorted to the Capitol by a troop of cavalry. Following the oath of office, he observed a parade featuring various militia units. Over time, the parade evolved. Notably, in 1841, during William Henry Harrison's inauguration, floats made their debut. Military bands, political groups, and college organizations eventually joined as participants.

A significant moment occurred when African Americans participated in Abraham Lincoln's parade, marking an expansion of diversity. In 1873, Ulysses S. Grant reordered the schedule, placing the parade *after* the inaugural ceremony rather than *before*, which persists to this day.

In 1881, for James Garfield's inauguration, reviewing stands were constructed. To shield attendees from the often harsh and cold weather conditions, these grandstands were eventually enclosed. Additionally, reviewing stands were erected to accommodate visitors.

In 1917, women took part in the parade, marking a significant inclusion. Then, in 1921, Warren Harding broke tradition by becoming the first president to ride in an automobile. This set a precedent that held until 1977, when Jimmy Carter chose to walk alongside his wife and daughter from the Capitol to the White House. The first televised inaugural parade was held in 1949 for Harry S. Truman.

The largest parade on record was in 1953 for Dwight D. Eisenhower. This grand spectacle featured an astounding 73 bands, 59 floats, and horses, elephants, military units, and a variety of civilian and military vehicles. It lasted for over 4.5 hours.

Over the last 200 years, the size and complexity of the parade has grown tremendously, transforming it into a nationally acclaimed special event. At the 2009 inaugural parade, Barack Obama hosted 15,000 participants, which included 2,000 military personnel. From the 1,000 bands that applied, 46 were selected to take part. Today, millions of Americans can witness the parade, whether through television broadcasts, internet streaming, or in-person attendance. It has truly become a cherished celebration tradition.

The Armed Forces Inaugural Committee oversees the parade's organization, and the Presidential Inaugural Committee selects all parade participants.

Lauderdale-by-the-Sea Arts festival

EXAMPLES OF SPECIAL EVENTS

For movie enthusiasts, a film festival can be a dream come true, offering the chance to rub shoulders with renowned actors who might be strolling alongside them, as often happens on the streets of Park City, Utah, during the Sundance Film Festival. Established in 1981, it has burgeoned into the largest independent film festival in the United States, attracting tens of thousands of visitors each year, all eager to view over 3,000 film submissions.

These remarkable events trace their origins to a historical tradition that gradually evolved to captivate hordes of visitors, even in some of the most remote locations. To sustain this allure, thorough planning and strategic tools come into play, encompassing an understanding of the community's infrastructure, the art of merchandising and event promotion, forging valuable sponsorships, and adeptly navigating media relations. This amalgamation of art and science constitutes the essence of special events management.

At its core, a special event is a celebration, which is precisely what makes it special. Figure 8.1 provides some examples of special events.

Civic Events
- Centennials
- Founders' Day

Megaevents
- Olympics
- America's Cup
- United Nations Assembly's
- World Expo's
- World Cup

Festivals (for profit) and Fairs (not for profit)
- Marketplace of ancient days
- Community Events

Expositions
- Where suppliers meet buyers
- Education
- Entertainment

Sporting Events
- Super Bowl
- World Series
- Masters Golf Tournament
- FIFA World Cup

Social life-cycle events
- Wedding
- Anniversary
- Birthday
- Reunion
- Bar/bat mitzvah

Meetings & Conventions
- Political National Convention
- National Restaurant Association convention in Chicago
- PCMA annual conference

Retail Events
- Long-range promotional event
- Store opening

New product launches
- X-box
- Apple

Religious Events
- Papal Inauguration
- Hajj (Mecca)
- Easter
- Kwanzaa

Corporate Events
- Holiday parties
- Annual dinner
- Company picnics
- Conferences/meetings

FIGURE 8-1
Examples of Special Events

PLANNING TOOLS FOR SPECIAL EVENTS

Special events management, akin to other forms of management, requires planning tools. The first and foremost is a vision statement, which should meticulously outline the "who, what, when, where, and why." As the event takes shape, it remains crucial to keep all parties aligned with this vision, which requires continuous monitoring, assessment, and, whenever possible, quantifiable measurements of progress toward the objectives (refer to Chapters 13 and 14 for more details).

The "who" in the equation comprises the individuals or organizations seeking to host and orchestrate the event. For instance, for the St. Patrick's Day Parade in Chicago, Illinois, the city itself is the host and orchestrator, overseeing the coordination of marchers, floats, and bands. The "what" encapsulates the essence of the event (a parade that celebrates Irish pride and local traditions). As for the "where," it is in downtown Chicago, with floats and bands traversing Michigan Avenue. Finally, the pivotal "why" revolves around tradition, community pride, enjoyment, and tourism promotion, all of which bolster the local economy. When the city elected to host this event, it became imperative to employ the tools of special event management.

Several management tools are key in orchestrating successful events, including the following:

- Flow charts and graphs for scheduling: If you examine any program for a meeting or event, you will notice it comprises start and end times, intervals for coffee breaks, designated lunch periods, and the resumption and conclusion times. A flowchart can take various forms, from the structured schedule of a wedding ceremony to the ordered sequence of floats for a parade, program rundown for a talent show, or comprehensive **agenda** for a weeklong international conference. These visual representations serve as navigational aids for attendees and guests, ensuring the smooth flow and execution of the event. **Gantt Charts** are frequently employed for managing tasks within these schedules.
- Clearly defined setup and breakdown **schedules**. These allow the event manager to determine tasks that may have been overlooked in the initial planning process.
- Policy statements developed to guide in the decision-making process. These provide a clear understanding of commitments and what is expected to fulfill them, such as human resources, sponsors, security, ticketing, volunteers, and paid personnel.

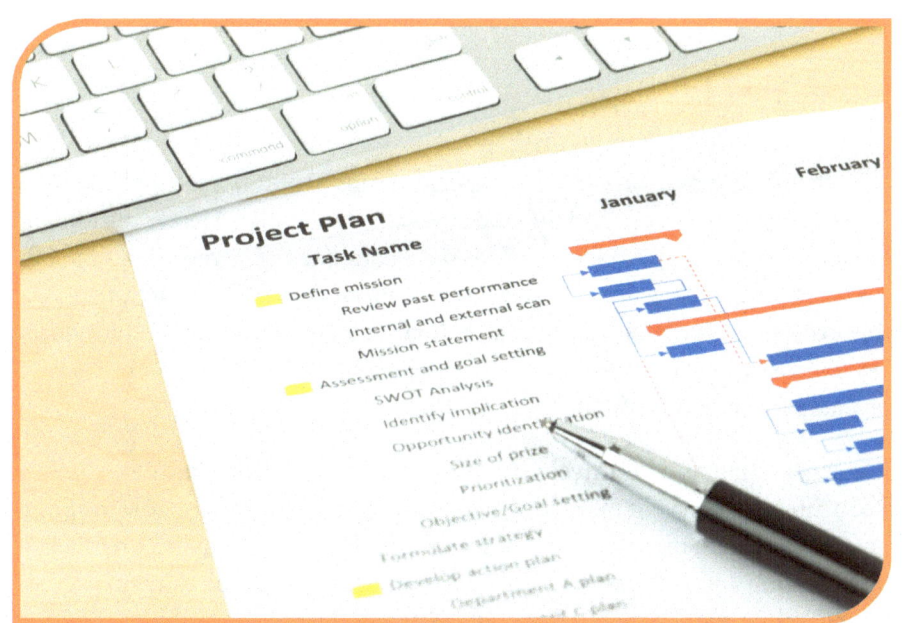

Gantt Chart Project Plan

© Casper1774 Studio/Shutterstock.com

CHAPTER 8 SPECIAL EVENTS MANAGEMENT

251

UNDERSTANDING COMMUNITY INFRASTRUCTURE

Another crucial aspect in planning a successful event is comprehending the infrastructure within the community where it is scheduled. This may encompass the CEO of the company, politicians, influential local business leaders, civic and community groups, the media, and other community figures. Without buy-in from city leadership, a community may be less inclined to provide essential support. Business leaders may offer sponsorships, donations, staff, or potentially workplace facilities for event coordination. Frequently, community groups are volunteer workers and an extension of the promotional efforts.

Early in the planning process, it becomes imperative to determine whether a community or company is genuinely committed to hosting a special event that will require its support, which extends beyond mere financial commitment; it also entails the physical and emotional commitment essential to steer an event from inception to conclusion. For a promoter or special events management company to maintain a positive reputation, a solid infrastructure is indispensable.

SPECIAL EVENT MARKETING CONSIDERATIONS

MERCHANDISING AND PROMOTING

Merchandising and promoting a special event serve as essential planning tools to draw attendees and enhance overall profitability. Merely deciding to host a craft fair or street festival does not guarantee the necessary attendance to meet the needs of vendors and visitors. Profit for vendors and a memorable experience for attendees are the primary objectives, so the event requires an exhaustive promotional effort, leveraging all available resources from an event management company or civic group.

Understanding and effectively using the **promotional mix model** is pivotal for achieving the event marketing plan's objectives. Promotion's role in special events management involves coordinating all efforts to establish channels of information and persuasion. Traditionally, the mix had four elements: advertising, sales promotion, publicity, and personal selling. However, direct marketing and interactive media have been added. The latter encompasses social media platforms, such as LinkedIn, Facebook, and Twitter. Modern-day event marketers employ a plethora of means to engage with their target markets. Each element in the promotional mix functions as an integrated marketing communications tool, serving a distinct role in attracting attendees to the special event. Each element can take on various forms and presents distinct advantages.

PROMOTIONAL MIX

Advertising is any paid form of nonpersonal communication about an event. The term "nonpersonal" signifies that advertising uses mass media channels, such as TV, radio, magazines, mobile phones, websites, and newspapers. Advertising is renowned as the most prominent and extensively analyzed form of promotion due to its exceptional persuasive power, particularly when targeting a broad consumer audience, as seen in events such as home and garden shows. It can shape brand images, employ symbolic appeals, and elicit rapid responses from potential attendees.

The many elements of the promotional mix for special events include the following:

Direct marketing is a form of advertising that establishes direct communication with the target customer, aiming to generate a response. It extends far beyond direct mail or catalogs, encompassing a range of activities, including database management, direct selling, telemarketing, direct-response ads, online marketing, and various broadcast and print media. The internet, in particular, has significantly amplified the growth of direct marketing, offering distinct advantages such as the ability to measure response rates.

Engagement marketing, sometimes referred to as "experiential marketing," is a strategic approach that involves inviting consumers to participate in a brand experience. This creates face-to-face opportunities for event designers. Cobranding is also employed to boost responses. An example of a highly successful campaign is Zappos' "Google Cupcake Ambush," where Zappos offered free pairs of shoes to customers who received a cupcake while trying out Google's new photo app.

Interactive or internet marketing facilitates a dynamic exchange of information. Users can engage with and modify the form and content of the information they receive in real time. Unlike traditional one-way forms of communication, such as advertising, this type of media empowers users to perform various functions. It enables them to receive and customize information and images, make inquiries, respond to questions, and even make purchases. Many attendees turn to websites for information about special events, such as concerts, and directly purchase their tickets online. For instance, attendees of the Aspen Music Festival can visit the official website to access schedules, gather event details, explore the surrounding area, buy tickets, and request additional information. Interactive media extends beyond the internet, encompassing devices such as flash drives, kiosks, and interactive television.

Sales promotion typically refers to marketing activities that employ incentives or discounts to boost sales or attendance. A widely used form is the coupon. Many events leverage two-for-one attendance coupons to stimulate attendance on slower days. Additionally, event organizers often offer merchandise when customers purchase multiple tickets simultaneously.

Publicity and public relations consist of two distinct components. Publicity is neither directly paid for nor sponsored by an identified entity. When an event planner secures media coverage or garners a favorable story, it significantly impacts attendees' awareness, knowledge, and opinions. Publicity is regarded as a credible form of promotion, although it is not always within the planner's control. For instance, in the case of South by Southwest (SXSW), organizers release press releases in advance, highlighting the participating performers or acts. During the event, reporters and camera crews provide daily coverage.

Social media has emerged as a predominant strategy, offering extensive reach with minimal expense and relatively effortless execution. This approach is often referred to as "viral marketing." Although various social media platforms exist, the more frequently used ones include Facebook, blogging, LinkedIn, Pinterest, and Twitter. Each of these platforms allows for reaching numerous individuals simultaneously, projecting a carefully crafted and positive message to the audience. Furthermore, the message is delivered instantly (for more information, refer to Chapter 11).

Various special events are organized to promote destinations or occasions, with one prominent example being the annual SXSW event held in March in Austin, Texas. Spanning 9 days, it is the foremost congregation of professionals in the Music, Film, and Interactive industries.

Public relations, in essence, involves systematically planning and disseminating information to exert influence over the image and publicity of an event. Its primary aim is to cultivate beneficial relationships with stakeholders and consumers, and it encompasses a broader objective than publicity. Public relations and publicity are favored by festival and event directors due to their efficacy in reaching the desired audience. Public relations can be the driving force behind hosting the special event itself. For instance, tobacco companies have employed special events, such as NASCAR races or tennis tournaments, to enhance their image among consumers.

Personal selling is the final component of the promotional mix model, characterized by person-to-person communication (a seller endeavors to assist and persuade prospective attendees). Group tour sales often represent one of the most promising avenues. Numerous touring companies purchase substantial blocks of tickets. Unlike advertising, personal selling entails direct interaction between the event buyer and seller, typically through face-to-face interactions. It is also the most expensive form of promotional activity when considering the number of consumers reached. Examples of events that attract group tours include the Indianapolis 500, Kentucky Derby, or Jazz Fest in New Orleans. Group tour organizers engage in face-to-face meetings or telephone discussions with event professionals to secure tickets for their groups.

Branding a Destination

SXSW

SXSW comprises a series of festivals and conferences held annually in Austin, Texas, during the spring season. This multifaceted event encompasses music, film, and interactive technologies. Originating as a modest gathering in 1987, it is now the largest music festival of its kind worldwide, featuring over 2,200 bands performing on 113 stages. The film festival primarily aims to attract emerging directors, and the interactive portion focuses on cutting-edge technology. SXSW has served as the launchpad for several groundbreaking products, with Twitter and Foursquare among the most prominent examples. It was also pivotal in propelling John Mayer's career; he made a significant breakthrough by performing at the festival.

Although the core mission is promoting the three industries, the event has also evolved into a major catalyst for tourism. It is consistently the most lucrative event for Austin's hospitality industry. In 2019, it generated significant economic impact on the local economy (totaling $335.9 million):

- 12,800 individual hotel registrations, totaling over 55,300 room nights ($1.9 million in occupancy tax revenue)
- 280,000 conference and festival participants
- a direct economic impact of $264.6 million (directly related to the local economy)
- an indirect impact of $157.1 million (increases in sales, income, and jobs associated with companies that benefit from SXSW expenditures); and
- induced impacts of $16.7 million (spending by individuals because of increased earnings as a result of the conference).

SXSW Registration booth

MEETINGS, EXPOSITIONS, EVENTS, AND CONVENTIONS

SPONSORSHIPS FOR SPECIAL EVENTS

Sponsorships play a pivotal role in ensuring the profitable success of an event. They represent an innovative way for event organizers to secure funding and offset costs. Sponsorships should be viewed not merely as acts of charity by companies but as potent marketing tools.

Event sponsors contribute funds or provide "in-kind" contributions and receive recognition through logo usage and association with the event. Recent sponsorship trends indicate rapid growth in this practice. It can take various forms. For instance, a large corporation may offer financial sponsorship. In contrast, midsized and smaller organizations might need to adopt more creative approaches. A smaller organization could, for example, offer products instead of a financial contribution; its banner might not be visible, but attendees will have its product in hand.

Many types of special events rely on sponsorship for their success. Sporting events have traditionally led in securing sponsorships for teams and athletes. Nevertheless, their market share has declined as companies increasingly allocate funds to other events, such as city festivals and the arts. This shift over the past decade is due to companies recognizing the effectiveness of sponsorships in their overall marketing strategies. Sponsors are starting to acknowledge that festivals can be as attractive as sports events in generating a return on investment (ROI).

NAPLES, FLORIDA

The Annual Naples Winter Wine Festival is the nation's premier charity wine auction. This remarkable event unfolds in Naples, Florida, spanning 3 days each January.

Inaugurated in 2001, the festival is a charitable endeavor to benefit the Naples Children & Education Foundation and, in turn, the children of Collier County, Florida. In recent years, the live auction held during this event has raised more than $12.8 million. Since its inception, it has amassed over $176 million in support of its charitable mission.

The event's auction entices participants with a captivating array of items to bid on, including ski trips, vintage wines, hotel stays, and luxury cars. A Rolls Royce Phantom once claimed the highest bid at an impressive $780,000.

The festival exudes ceaseless excitement. A "Fund-a-Need" initiative raised over $2.4 million to benefit underserved children in need of oral healthcare and hunger relief. The online auction, which concluded a few days later, contributed an additional $170,275.

For the Naples Winter Wine Festival, the paramount focus remains on charity. The event champions children's mental health, affording auction-goers the opportunity to interact with some of the young beneficiaries. Furthermore, it consistently attracts new attendees each year, with first-time visitors accounting for 40–50% of attendees.

Company sponsorships are an important option to consider for five compelling reasons:

1. economic changes (both upturns and downturns),
2. ability to target market segments,
3. ability to measure results,
4. fragmentation of the media, and
5. growth of diverse population segments.

Changes in the country's economic climate inevitably impact the goals, spending strategies, and expectations of sponsoring organizations. During periods of economic prosperity, both large and small companies may be more inclined and financially able to allocate their promotional budgets generously. Conversely, in downturns, organizations tend to scrutinize the ROI more closely. In essence, sponsorship is perceived as an investment, and organizations confirm that they are reaping a solid ROI. During challenging times, such as the COVID-19 pandemic or a recession, sponsors often reduce the scale of their investments. Regardless of the economic climate, sponsorships effectively promote intangible benefits, such as company visibility and overall goodwill.

When seeking sponsorships for a special event, organizers must evaluate whether it aligns with the company's objectives. Event professionals must thoroughly understand the company's goals and conduct comprehensive competitive research. Organizers should offer sponsors innovative promotional concepts to help them achieve their objectives. It is imperative for event promoters to ensure that sponsors receive commensurate value for their financial commitment and remember that sponsors target both internal and external audiences, and the appeal must resonate with both.

"Cross-promotional opportunities" enable sponsors to maximize their visibility by leveraging multiple promotional avenues within a single event. For instance, if PepsiCo sponsors an event, it can expect substantial visibility through banners, logos, and other promotional means. However, PepsiCo might also propose that only Pepsi products be available for sale. This would not only increase its visibility but also generate revenue, yielding a triple benefit. A corporation's internal audience includes its employees, who must also be onboard with the sponsorship. Companies should provide opportunities for employee engagement. For example, if the event involves a charitable marathon, employees may be encouraged to participate in it or raise funds for the charitable cause and then be featured in promotional materials or press releases.

New York City Marathon

Sponsorship

The New York City Marathon boasts over 50,000 runners with more than 2 million spectators and is one of the largest live sporting events in the world, broadcast to over 330 million viewers in more than 154 territories. Television coverage includes a live 5-hour telecast on ABC Channel 7 in New York, a 2-hour national telecast on ESPN, and various live and highlight shows internationally. For the first time, the event awarded prize money for nonbinary athletes, with a top prize of $5,000 for the fastest nonbinary finisher. The prize money for the nonbinary category was awarded by New York Road Runners; the World Marathon Majors awarded prize money for athletes in the male and female gender categories.

New York Road Runners and the New York City Marathon are fortunate to have the support and commitment of sponsors and strategic partners.

Their continued support makes the New York City Marathon a world-class event year after year.

Sponsors

Title Sponsor:

Tata Consultancy Services

Additional Sponsors

Airbnb
United Airlines
New Balance
The Rudin Family
Mastercard
Flow water
iFIT
Michelob Ultra
Norquain
Hospital for Special Surgery
Science in Sport
STRAVA

Reaching the external audience of the corporation, which includes consumers, involves various strategies. First, the company can showcase its logo by featuring it on outdoor banners and promotional items, such as T-shirts, caps, or sunglasses, effectively promoting its association with the special event. The range of specialty products for advertising is virtually limitless and offers excellent avenues for brand promotion. Additionally, the company might consider designating an employee spokesperson for radio or television interviews.

WORKING WITH THE MEDIA FOR AN EVENT

Securing media coverage for a special event rank among the most effective methods for attracting attendees. Ideally, event organizers aim to gain free exposure on television, radio, and in print. To capture the media's attention, event promoters must have a solid grasp of what constitutes compelling coverage and what does not.

When a camera crew is dispatched by assignment editors at a TV station, it seeks a compelling story that can be effectively conveyed through visual footage. It also aims to find a captivating vignette that can engage viewers within a brief time frame, typically 30 seconds or less. If an organizer desires television or radio stations to cover their event, they must bring it to the stations' attention through a press release or a press conference. They have no guarantees that a station or newspaper will air or publish the story, but the chances improve if a camera crew captures footage or a reporter conducts an interview. Special events often offer ideal subjects for evening news, such as interviews with attending celebrities or sneak peeks at art exhibitions.

Event organizers strive to present something out of the ordinary to the media. For instance, Nike, a major player in the athletic shoe market, employs creative advertising campaigns to compete effectively. To draw attention to its brand and promote its shoes, it installed an interactive advertising sign equipped with a built-in camera. Passersby were challenged to sprint past the sign at maximum speed, with their times recorded. The fastest runner was rewarded with the latest pair of Reebok shoes.

Reebok: Are you fast enough campaign

This also resulted in the story being carried on national news broadcasts and a multitude of media coverage over the next several weeks. Promoters of special events have long recognized what TV and radio coverage can do for an event.

Here are some helpful hints for attracting television and radio coverage:

1. Early in the day is considered the best time. A crew must come out, film, get back to the studio, edit the film, and have the segment ready for the 5:00 or 6:00 p.m. newscast that night.
2. The best day of the week is Friday because it is usually a quiet news day. Saturday and Sunday have even fewer distractions, but most stations do not have enough news crews working.
3. Giving advance notice is very helpful to assignment editors. It is nice to give about 3 days' notice, with an explanation of the event via a press release and telephone follow-up. If an interview is involved, a 7-day notice is good.

UNDERSTANDING THE TARGET MARKET FOR YOUR SPECIAL EVENT

Bringing special events to a community has not significantly changed over the years, but consumer expectations and preferences have evolved. Modern consumers are more selective and sophisticated. Given the rising costs of attending events, people are discerning about how they allocate their entertainment budgets, which places a premium on event quality.

Understanding the target market is a pivotal factor in overall success. Event marketers and professionals must possess a deep understanding of the participant audience and of factors such as age, gender, religion, and ethnicity. Depending on the nature of the event, professionals must also consider participant restrictions (e.g., religious or dietary) and needs. The event should be designed to cater to the overall requirements and desires of the target market.

The most valuable outcome a special event can generate for a community is positive word of mouth. To achieve this, organizers acknowledge that an event cannot be all things to all people. Instead, they identify the specific target market that the event is intended to serve.

Target marketing involves precisely identifying the audience that is likely to be interested in a particular event. For instance, a Justin Bieber concert primarily appeals to female audiences aged 12–16. To ensure a profitable concert, event promoters will focus their advertising efforts on this target demographic and tailor all promotional materials and strategies to cater to this age group.

A Very Special Wedding

Let's look at a real-life example involving a couple planning a wedding in New Orleans. They were captivated by the city's charm, such as moss-draped oak trees, antebellum homes, and horse-drawn carriages. They decided to invite 100 guests and hired a local destination management company (DMC). Their request was for the DMC to arrange a rehearsal dinner for 12 people and reception for 100. Costs related to transportation to New Orleans, hotel accommodations, and the church were not included in the bid. Remarkably, their budget was a whopping $350,000. Yes, that is over a quarter of a million dollars or $3,500 per guest! When the event professional learned of this budget, she had a twofold reaction: (a) how could she possibly create this event while spending that much money, and (b) if that was their budget, she would aim to upsell them.

The rehearsal dinner took place in a private dining room at the renowned Arnaud's restaurant in the French Quarter. However, the real expenditure was reserved for the reception. They secured the art deco Saenger Theater for the evening, but it had a slight issue: The floor was sloped toward the stage, a common feature in theaters. To overcome this, they went to great lengths and removed all the seats, constructing a new, level floor. Remarkably, the theater's interior was so stunning that it required minimal additional decoration. To preserve the period ambiance for the couple and their guests, the New Orleans Police Department was enlisted to close the street between the church and the theater to traffic. This allowed the group to be transported in horse-drawn carriages without disturbance. When the couple and their guests arrived at the theater, they were welcomed by models dressed in period costumes, served mint juleps, and treated to a gospel performance. A blues band followed, and the night reached its peak with not one but two sets by Jennifer Lopez, who owns a home in New Orleans. The event was catered by the renowned Emeril Lagasse and featured heavy hors d'oeuvres, without a formal sit-down dinner. The final cost for this extravagant event came to nearly $395,000, much to the delight of the couple.

The planner was Nanci Easterling of Food Art, Inc.

Many communities recognize that hosting a special event can have a positive economic impact on both the local community and the broader region. Consequently, competition is fierce among cities. To entice special events, cities often offer incentives, which might include free event space, security services, parking facilities, and even symbolic gestures, such as awarding the "key to the city" to celebrity performers or organizers. The term "citywide" is frequently used to describe large events or conventions that affect the whole city, which are significant contributors to urban economics. A major event or convention typically results in several positive economic effects. Hotel rooms may be fully booked throughout the city, restaurants experience increased business, and retail and cultural attractions can thrive due to the influx of visitors.

Success hinges on two critical factors. First, the community must be supportive and welcoming. Second, it must align with attendees' needs and interests. For example, New Orleans hosts the annual "Southern Decadence" over Labor Day weekend. This 3-day event, drawing over 150,000 attendees from the LGBTQIA1 community, generates over $150 million in economic impact.

PREPARING FOR THE SPECIAL EVENT

Basic operations for staging an event need to be established and include the following:

- Secure a venue.
- Obtain **permits**:
    - Parade permits,
    - Liquor permits,
    - Sanitation permits,
    - Sales permits or licenses, and
    - Fire safety permits.
- Involve **government agencies** where necessary (i.e., if using city recreation facilities, work with the department of parks and recreation).
- Involve the health department if food and beverage (F&B) will be involved.
- Meet all relevant parties in person so that any misconceptions are cleared up early.
- Secure all vendors and suppliers.
- Recognize the complexities of dealing with the public sector. Sometimes, public agencies have a difficult time making decisions.

- Recognize the logistics that a community must contend with for certain types of special events, such as street closures for a marathon.
- Set up a security plan, which may include venue-supplied security and professional law enforcement. (Pay attention as to which organization takes precedence.)
- Secure liability insurance (the most vulnerable areas are liquor and liquor laws).
- Determine ticket prices and sale distribution if the special event involves ticketing.

The type of special event will determine the degree of preparedness needed. The larger it is, the more involved the checklist. Preparedness should produce a profitable and well-managed event.

SOFTWARE AND TOOLS FOR SPECIAL EVENTS

Event planners are confronted with a wide array of tasks, with a plethora of tools available to assist. Despite the many options to choose from, it is crucial to identify the specific types of tools you need based on your event's requirements. Are you looking for project management assistance or tools to enhance attendee engagement?

One of the most common management tools is Google Drive. Planners can use the features for managing documents, folders, spreadsheets, and collaboration. If you are looking for an overall event management software, Whova makes software that handle everything from registration, on-site check-in, attendee polling, name badge creation, and an event app.

If you typically use an Excel spreadsheet for managing tasks, you might want to consider Smartsheet, which also allows live collaboration and communication. The program has a very easy-to-use dashboard, despite a short learning curve for new users.

Basecamp is another good management software. Although not as new as some of the others, it is still a very solid performer.

If you have mastered project management but need communication, you might want to consider a program such as Slack. It allows users to share and discuss ideas from anywhere and is a great way to keep your team informed.

F&B events require some separate tools. Caterease is one of the industry leaders. Ticketing is another area that planners are commonly looking for help. TicketSpice is one of the most powerful ticketing solutions available.

Floor plan design programs are also an important tool. AllSeated makes a program that allows the user to design floor plans, manage guests lists, and create visual seating charts.

For multiple events, Trello is a great program for creating boards for each event to help with organization. It is otherwise very easy with multiple events to forget some of the minor details.

Finally, audience engagement is the latest area that event planners are attempting to influence. EventMobi is one of the leaders; it has a customizable app, built-in audience response tracking, gamification, registration, and reporting tools. We have only touched on a small portion of the range of products available, but it is clear that help is available for any task you might have.

Getting a Permit

San Diego, California's event permitting process is quite typical for many moderate-sized cities. The city has published a guide to inform event organizers about the necessary permits, and the city's website provides a planning guide and access to all the forms that might be required.

Events or organized activities that involve 75 or more people, require street closures, or entail components that necessitate coordination across multiple city departments or other agencies (such as alcohol service, on-site cooking, food sales, or large-scale temporary structures) are typically subject to the Citywide Special Event Permit Process. Examples of such events include festivals, parades, runs/walks, farmer's markets, and other organized group activities.

To ensure that an application is considered complete, applicants must provide the following minimum information in the sections of the Citywide Special Event Permit Application, with sufficient detail for assessment and understanding:

- Host Organization Section (Complete)
- Event Summary Section (Complete)

- Event Infrastructure Section (All aspects that relate to the specific event)
- Operational Plan Section (All aspects that relate to the specific event)
- Site Plan/Route Map Section (Complete)
- Community Outreach Section (Complete)
- Insurance Section (Complete including all required certificates of insurance and endorsements)
- Signature Section (Complete)
- Any required documentation relevant to the permit application processes and requirements in the Special Events Planning Guide and Citywide Special Event Permit Application (Complete)

Applicants are responsible for obtaining all permits, authorization, and/or exemptions required by other agencies with jurisdiction for any element of the event (e.g., Alcohol Beverage Control Permits, Health Permits, California Coast Guard, California Coastal Commission approval).

https://www.sandiego.gov/sites/default/files/legacy/specialevents/pdf/planningguide.pdf

THE BUDGET

For an event to be considered successful, it must also be profitable. Achieving profitability necessitates a solid understanding of budgeting and financial concepts related to events (for more information, see Chapter 13). The fundamental elements that constitute the costs of a special event include the following categories.

RENTAL COSTS

The cost of renting a venue or space is a significant component. Depending on the type of event, you may need to rent facilities, such as a convention center or open ground space for erecting a tent. Convention centers typically charge based on the square footage used, and this charge often applies even on move-in and move-out days. Events that span multiple days may have the opportunity to negotiate rental discounts.

Rental costs can vary based on the type of event and venue. For instance, if an association is hosting a conference in a hotel, it might receive the event space at no cost or a reduced rate if it commits to booking a certain number of rooms for their participants. Additionally, if the group requires catering services, the rental space might be provided at a reduced rate or even complimentary in exchange for meeting an **F&B minimum**.

SECURITY COSTS

Convention centers, rental halls, hotels, and similar venues typically provide basic security services, which may involve stationing guards at the primary entrances and exits. However, the level of security required can vary significantly depending on the nature of the event. For instance, a rock concert by a band with passionate fans might necessitate additional security measures. Events such as European soccer (football) matches often demand even more extensive security arrangements. The actual costs will depend on factors such as the city where the event is held and the specific security needs associated with it.

PRODUCTION COSTS

Production costs pertain to the expenses involved in organizing and staging. These costs can vary considerably by type of special event. For example, a large home and garden show has various expenses associated with setting up the trade show booths. Many such shows feature exhibitors who create intricate garden landscapes, which require significant time and labor for both setup and teardown. The costs for decorators' labor must be factored in and can vary by booth type and size. Additionally, these shows may incur expenses related to electrical and water services, which must be included in the production costs. Other production-related expenses may include creating signage or banners for individual booths and fees for items such as pipe and drape.

LABOR COSTS

The location can affect labor costs, especially in unionized cities, where strict labor unions may dictate event logistics. For example, exhibitors might be limited in what they can transport. These union-driven practices can increase event costs. Organizers often pass these expenses on to exhibitors or raise ticket prices. Therefore, when choosing a location, it is crucial to consider the local union environment's impact on budgets and planning.

MARKETING COSTS

Attracting attendees can be a significant budgetary consideration. Organizers must evaluate the most effective methods for reaching their target audience. Mass advertising, such as television commercials, can be costly; a mix of promotional approaches, including advertising, direct marketing, publicity, sales promotion, interactive marketing, and personal selling, is common.

TALENT COSTS

Most events involve talent or performers, such as speakers, bands, or sports teams. However, organizers must balance their aspirations for talent with budget constraints. Booking A-list performers might not align with the event's financial reality.

Event professionals must create detailed cost and revenue projections before, during, and after an event; these are vital for deciding whether to host future events. Consistent billing updates and transparent communication with clients are essential to avoid cost surprises at the end.

BREAKDOWN OF THE SPECIAL EVENT

Special events have one thing in common: They all come to an end! Taking down or **breaking down** the event usually involves many steps. Once the attendees have gone, the organizer has a variety of closing tasks.

First, the parking staff should expedite the flow of traffic; community police can sometimes assist.

Staff should be debriefed to determine what did or did not happen. Issues may be pending that will need documentation. It is always best to have written reports to refer to for next year's event. Consider having the following sources add information to the report:

- *Participants:* Interview some of the participants. A customer's perception and expectation is an invaluable insight.
- *Media and the Press:* Ask why it was or was not a press-worthy gathering.
- *Staff and Management:* Get a variety of staff and other management to give feedback.
- *Vendors:* Exhibitors and vendors *must* complete a survey. Because of their unique perspective, they can provide outstanding and constructive feedback for the next event.

The following should also be included in a final report on the event:

- Finalize the income and expense statement. Did the event break even, make a profit, or experience a loss?
- Finalize all contracts. Fortunately, almost everything involved will have written documentation. Compare final billing with actual agreements for any discrepancies.
- Send the media a final press release on the overall success of the event. Interviews with the press could be arranged. This could be especially newsworthy if the event generated significant revenues for the community.
- Provide a written thank-you to volunteers who were involved in any way and perhaps include a celebration, especially if the event was financially and socially successful.

Once the elements of breakdown have taken place, the organizers can examine the important lessons of staging the event. What would they do or not do next year?

TRENDS AND BEST PRACTICES IN SPECIAL EVENTS

- Less is the new more. Clients are seeking the simple with a "flair."
- Clients want to appear to be responsible in their spending. Excessive overspending is no longer the desirable trend.
- "Stylish minimalism" refers to the idea that clients still want style, flair, and innovation in the overall event but choose to uphold a conservative budgetary perception.
- Quality is paramount, at a cost that the client sees as a "value."
- Frivolous events are seen as wasteful; events should have a purpose.

- Many events are now targeted toward service or charitable causes. This provides purpose. Events may target medical concerns (i.e., cancer research, heart disease, autism awareness) or national or international relief (i.e., Haiti Relief, Hurricane Katrina Relief).
- Clients are looking for an entire "package." The event planner is truly planning an experience—often referred to as "experience management." Some planners believe that a good event should captivate the audience and offer "change" every half hour.
- Going green—environmentally, event professionals are urged to consider green solutions. Earthy, environmentally friendly efforts are becoming the expectation. Interestingly, because of the perceived lack of sophistication, "eco-friendly" efforts are more likely to be incorporated into an event rather than a primary means of service. For example, recycled coffee cups may be offered at a coffee station along with china cups and saucers.
- Technology is key in promotional efforts. More internet promotions are desired, as event managers can quantify the number of "hits" that they receive.
- Technology will also impact the meeting space. Google Glass can create a more personal, staged, and shared attendee experience.
- Gamification—adding games can create healthy competition and measurable ROI.
- Every client has its own unique set of needs and wants. Every client wants the undivided attention of the event professional; its needs must be recognized throughout the entire planning and execution.
- Quality, cost, and relationship must be in balance for every special event.
- Although face-to-face events are still occurring, many events will continue with some virtual portion. Organizers have realized that adding an additional virtual component can increase participant numbers and revenue. This trend is here to stay.

SUMMARY

Creating a memorable event necessitates not only meeting but surpassing attendees' expectations. Whether it is a meeting, parade, festival, fair, or exhibit, understanding the objectives is key. Effective planning tools and a grasp of community infrastructures are crucial for event success.

Failure to decide on the promotional mix model's components in advance can lead to costs. This model includes advertising, direct marketing, interactive/

internet marketing, sales promotion, publicity/public relations, and personal selling. Sponsorships can help offset expenses and are a valuable marketing tool for sponsors. Generating local and national media coverage is vital for attracting attendance, requiring an understanding of what constitutes effective media coverage for print or broadcast. Always keep the target market in mind when setting objectives, planning promotions, and ensuring the event's longevity.

After the planning and promotion stages, the event's basic operations and logistics come into play. Event professionals should maintain checklists to ensure all necessary tasks are addressed. These checklists are crucial for developing the event budget, which must be continuously reviewed to track revenues and expenditures. The final step involves a checklist for closing the event. Do not forget to appreciate your volunteers; they are essential to the success of your event!

CASE STUDY

Navigating Crisis: A Wedding Planner's Last-Minute Catering Catastrophe

Unexpected obstacles are not uncommon, and professional adaptability is a necessity. One such event organizer, Jane Harper of "Harper Wedding Planners," recently faced a daunting challenge. A highly reputed wedding planner with a decade of experience, Jane found herself grappling with a last-minute cancellation from the caterer just days before a grand wedding.

The Situation:

The event was a luxury wedding, scheduled to host 300 guests. The menu, meticulously planned in coordination with the client and caterer, was a crucial element. The wedding was only 3 days away when the caterer unexpectedly pulled out due to unforeseen personal circumstances, leaving Jane with an enormous problem to solve. The couple was understandably devastated, and the pressure was on Jane to rectify the situation promptly.

The Challenge:

Finding a new caterer on such short notice was a daunting task. Besides availability, the new caterer would need to match the quality and style of the previous one and adapt to the predetermined menu that was tailored to the couple's tastes and dietary restrictions. Moreover, budget constraints added another layer of complexity to the situation.

The Action:

Jane sprang into action immediately. She reached out to her extensive network of event industry professionals for potential caterer recommendations. Simultaneously, she reassured the couple, taking full responsibility for the situation and promising to find a solution that would not compromise the quality of their wedding day.

Jane shortlisted three potential caterers who were available on the wedding date. She arranged urgent meetings to discuss the menu and logistics. She made sure to discuss the couples' preferences, style of food, and exact requirements for each dish. To mitigate the risk of another cancellation, Jane also identified a backup caterer.

The Result:

After a grueling 48 hours, Jane managed to secure Gourmet Delights, a catering service known for its versatility and high-quality food. It was not only able to match the previous menu but also offered to provide a few upgrades at no extra cost as a goodwill gesture, considering the circumstances. The backup caterer, "Cuisine Creations," was kept on standby.

The wedding day arrived, and Gourmet Delights exceeded expectations. The food was exquisite, the presentation was impeccable, and the service was seamless. The couple and their guests were thrilled, and what could have been a disaster turned into a triumph.

Lessons Learned:

This case study serves as a reminder of the unpredictability inherent in event planning. It underscores the value of a well-maintained professional network, the importance of contingency planning, and the need for exceptional problem-solving skills.

Jane's proactive approach, backed by her experience and relationships in the industry, allowed her to turn a potential catastrophe into a success story. Her transparency and communication with the couple also maintained their trust, further enhancing her reputation as a dependable and resourceful wedding planner.

This case study epitomizes the mantra that every crisis is an opportunity. For Jane Harper and her company, handling this last-minute cancellation became a testament to their resilience, resourcefulness, and commitment to delivering unforgettable events against all odds.

Questions:

Question 1: How did Jane Harper manage to reassure the couple after the unexpected cancellation of the caterer, and why was this step important?

Question 2: How did Jane's professional network contribute to resolving the crisis, and what does this case study suggest about the importance of networking in the event planning industry?

Question 3: What steps did Jane take to ensure that the same quality and style of catering was delivered by the new caterer?

KEY WORDS AND TERMS

For definitions, see glossary or http://www.eventscouncil.org/APEX/glossary.aspx

agenda
breaking down
community infrastructure
fairs
festivals
food and beverage minimum
Gantt Chart
government agencies
meetings, expositions, events and conventions
permit
promotional mix model
public events
schedule
venues

REVIEW AND DISCUSSION QUESTIONS

1. Discuss the types of events that a city might host.

2. What does the vision statement of an event provide for an organizer?

3. Discuss the importance of the event professionals' client relationship in event planning.

4. Discuss the types of planning tools that aid in successful event management.

5. What are the distinctive roles of the promotional mix model?

6. What are the benefits of sponsorships at a special event?

7. What are some tips for working with broadcast media?

8. What are some basic operations for staging an event?

9. Discuss costs associated with the event budget.

10. Outline the elements of breakdown for a special event.

11. Consider special event opportunities for your community. How would you offer advice as an event professional to encourage attendance?

ABOUT THE CHAPTER CONTRIBUTOR

David Smiley received his M.S. in hospitality and tourism management from the University of Central Florida and a bachelor of science in recreation and park management from Pennsylvania State University. He is a senior lecturer in the School of Public Health at Indiana University Bloomington after serving 22 years in the industry, including 10 years with Rosen Hotels & Resorts. He is also the coordinator of the Tourism, Hospitality, and Event Management program in the new department of Health & Wellness Design.

Previous Edition Chapter Contributors

Joy Dickerson, Widener University

Cynthia Vannucci, emeritus, Metropolitan State College in Denver Emeritus

CHAPTER 9

FOOD AND BEVERAGE (F&B)

MEAL FUNCTIONS CAN MAKE OR BREAK YOUR EVENT

CHAPTER OBJECTIVES

- Clarify the different types and requirements of catered events.
- Discuss specific requirements and considerations related to beverage events.
- Outline items to consider when choosing, planning, and arranging rooms for an event.
- Outline important service requirements to consider when planning and producing an F&B event.
- Name current trends and best practices in F&B practices for events.
- Be knowledgeable regarding the effects of COVID-19 on F&B in MEEC.

Contributed by George G Fenich. © Kendall Hunt Publishing Company.
Contributed by Kristin Malek. © Kendall Hunt Publishing Company.

F&B at events is often organized by outside planners or in-house contractors. But many event planners do not know what they can discuss with the caterers, how they set their prices, and when they might agree to something.

According to the EIC glossary, a **caterer** provides food services, especially for big parties or special themes. They can be either a special F&B vendor or the main provider for a place that hosts events.

The quality of F&B can really affect how people feel about a meeting or event. When you're getting ready to plan a catered event, the first thing to think about is "what's the main goal?" Are you trying to satisfy hunger, give people a break, help them socialize, give out awards, show respect to important people, or keep everyone interested while a speaker talks?

Even though some people see food as just something to fill them up, for others, it is a big part of the whole experience. Planning what food to serve and figuring out the cost is not something to leave to chance. It is one of the biggest expenses, and things might not always go perfectly. Also, the choices and preparation are important. Things have changed quite a bit—you can choose organic food, different cultural foods, or vegetarian options. People seem to be spending more on food because more choices are available now. But the money from drinks might be going down because event sponsors do not want to be responsible for problems related to alcohol.

CATERED EVENTS

Catered events generally have one host and one bill, and most attendees eat the same meal (exceptions would be vegetarian, gluten-free, or other special meals). A mandatory gratuity or service charge of typically 18–24% is added to the check, and taxes can add another 5–9%. The distribution of the charge varies widely among venues and companies. A gratuity differs from a tip, which is voluntary and at the discretion of the client for service over and above expectations. A gratuity is generally 100% distributed to team members. A service charge includes a percentage distributed to team members (which may include servers, bartenders, and sometimes management team) and a percentage that is retained by the property. When in doubt, ask. In many countries and cultures, service charges and tips do not exist.

QUESTIONS TO ASK WHEN PLANNING FOR F&B:

1. Whom will I work with planning the event?
2. Who will be on-site during the event?
3. When can I expect your written proposal?
4. What is your policy regarding deposits and cancellations?
5. When is the final payment due?
6. Do you have other charges for setup, delivery, overtime, and so on?
7. Do you take credit cards? PayPal? Online payment?
8. When must I give you my final head count guarantee?
9. What percentage is overset above the guarantee?
10. What is the sales tax, and what are your gratuity and/or service charge policies?
11. What is the chef's best menu items?
12. What are your portion sizes?
13. Will wine be poured by the staff or placed on the tables?
14. How many staff will be working at the event?
15. What are your substitution policies for vegetarian plates and special meals?
16. Could you pass wine or champagne as guests arrive?
17. How many bartenders will be used during the cocktail hour?
18. Do you provide table numbers?
19. What size tables do you have?
20. What are the options for linen, chair covers, china, stemware, flatware, and charger plates?
21. What decorations do you provide for the banquet room, tables, buffets, and food stations?
22. Are you Americans with Disabilities Act compliant?
23. What are your "green" initiatives?

FIGURE 9-1 Questions to ask when planning for F&B

ON-PREMISE CATERING

On-premise catering is defined as taking place in a facility that has its own permanent kitchens and function rooms, such as a hotel, restaurant, or convention center. This means that the food is prepared and served on-site. Usually, the facility would not rent the equipment but would keep permanent furniture, such as banquet-style tables and chairs. If a venue has on-premise catering, event professionals are almost always required to use this option. In a citywide convention, one hotel is usually named the host hotel and holds most of the food functions, although some events move attendees to a variety of venues.

Most meals are catered on-premise during a meeting. Serving attendees all at once prevents strain on the restaurant outlets, keeps attendees from leaving the property, and ensures that everyone will be back on time for the following sessions.

Conference centers offer a complete meeting package, which includes meals. Breakfast, lunch, and dinner are generally available in a cafeteria-type setup at any time the group decides to break. This keeps the group from having to break just because it is noon if it is in the middle of a productive session. If more than one group is in the facility, they will each be assigned different areas of the dining room. Refreshments are usually available at any time as well, allowing breaks at appropriate times. Conference centers can also provide banquets and receptions on request.

Convention centers and stadiums usually have concession stands open. More and more, exhibitions are holding their own opening reception or providing lunch on the show floor to attract attendees into the exhibits. Most convention centers are public entities, and the food service is contracted out to companies, such as ARAMARK or Sodexo. These companies often have exclusive contracts and other vendors or caterers are not allowed to work in the facility.

Thesw venues may also have full-service restaurants on the property. If the group will use the restaurant, check the capacity and hours. For example, ICHRIE held one of its annual conventions at a major hotel in Palm Springs, California, during late July. It attracted about 700 attendees and was virtually the only people in the 1,500-room hotel. ICHRIE felt that the five freestanding restaurants would be more than adequate to meet its dining needs (dining off-site was not a practical option). This would normally be true. However, as it was low season for the hotel, it closed all but two of the restaurants; convention attendees were faced with waits of over 2 hours to be seated for dinner.

OFF-PREMISE CATERING

Catered events can be held in just about any location. **Off-premise catering** requires transporting food to a location, such as a tented area, museum, park, or attraction. Food can be prepared in a kitchen and transported fully cooked, partially prepared in a kitchen and finished at the site, or prepared from scratch at the site. Mobile kitchens can be set up just about anywhere using generators and/or propane and butane as fuel to heat cooking equipment. Usually, off-premise caterers must provide their own equipment (or rent it), including tables, chairs, chafing dishes, plates, flatware, and

Gas Lamp District, San Diego

glassware. You may be responsible for simultaneously coordinating both on-premise and off-premise catering events. In this case, a shuttle bus system should be set up to transport attendees back and forth to off-premise events, which can be expensive.

Many excellent restaurants have banquet rooms, and bigger restaurants have banquet sales managers. Arnaud's restaurant in New Orleans has a six-person sales staff, so banquets are big business. In Las Vegas, a trend is for celebrity chefs to create their own signature restaurants within the hotel that are separate from the hotel's own food service operations. These restaurants, such as Spago in the Forum Shops at Caesars Palace or Delmonico's at the Venetian, also have their own banquet sales staff. Websites such as *Opentable* make it easy to research what local restaurants have to offer.

For an off-premise event, the first step for an event professional would be to create a request for proposals (RFP) and send it to event managers or caterers in the area. The RFP would include basic information such as the objectives, information on the company, workable dates, number of attendees, approximate budget, and any special requests, such as the need for a waiter-parade area. Many catering companies have online RFPs. Once the event professional reviews the proposals, an interview and, if possible, a site inspection would follow. During the site inspection, the event professional should look at the ambiance, the level of cleanliness and maintenance, and other amenities that may be required, such as parking and restrooms.

Often, off-premise events will be outsourced through a destination management company (DMC). DMCs are familiar with the location and have relationships established with unique venues in the area. For example, in Las Vegas, the Liberace Mansion is available for parties. In New Orleans, Mardi Gras World, where the parade floats are made, is an outstanding setting for a party. Just about every destination has some distinctive spaces for parties: Southfork in Dallas, the Rock and Roll Hall of Fame in Cleveland, and the Getty Museum in Los Angeles.

DMCs also know the best caterers, decorators, shuttle companies, entertainment, and any other supplier of products or services you may require. Although DMCs charge for their services, they often can get quantity discounts because of the volume they purchase annually. DMCs can also usually resolve problems faster because of the amount of business that would be jeopardized.

Two of the challenges with off-premise events are transportation and weather. Shuttle buses are an additional expense. Weather can spoil the best-laid plans, so contingency measures must be arranged. Backup shelter should be available, whether it is a tent or an inside function room. For example, outdoor luaus in Hawaii are moved inside at the last minute because of the frequent tropical storms that arise there.

During the initial site inspection, obtain a copy of the facility's banquet menus and policies. Does it offer the type of menu items that would be appropriate for your group? Ask if it is prepared to handle custom menus if you decide not to use its standard offerings. When planning custom menus, always check the skill level of the culinary team in the kitchen and the availability of special products that may be required.

Other important considerations include the demographics of the group. Menu choices would be different for the American Truck Drivers Association versus the International Association of Retired Persons. The typical truck driver would probably prefer a big steak, and a retired person would likely prefer a smaller portion of chicken without heavy spices. You need to consider gender, age, ethnic background, profession, and so on.

Many meetings/events have at least one off-premise event, often the opening reception, closing gala, or a themed event. Attendees want to experience some of the flavor of the destination and often get cabin fever if they never leave the hotel. Events can be held at an aquarium, a museum, a winery, or a historic mansion. For example, in St. Louis, many events are held at Busch stadium, home of the world champion Cardinals baseball team. In San Diego, some large conventions actually take over the entire Gas Lamp District for an evening.

STYLE OF SERVICE

Many ways to serve a meal exist, from self-service to VIP white-glove service (see Table 9-1). Given some disagreement on a few of the following definitions, the following are based on the EIC glossary. This book also follows White House protocol (the White House publishes the *Green Book*, which explains how everything is to be done for presidential protocol). However, because of confusion in the area, it is important to be sure that the event professional and catering representative agree on what the service styles mean. (Unfortunately, the *Green Book* is not available to the public, as it also includes information on presidential security.)

Continental breakfast	Typically an assortment of breads and pastries, juice, and coffee, although it can be upgraded by adding sliced fruit, yogurt, and/or cold cereals. Most are self-service with limited seating unless an additional fee for "seated continental service" is assessed. Continental breakfast is excellent for budgets, speed, and efficiency.
Full, served breakfast	Entrees plated in the kitchen and would normally include some type of egg, such as eggs Benedict, a meat, such as bacon or sausage, a potato item, such as hash browns, fruit, and coffee. When deciding on breakfast service, planners need to consult their history and guarantee accordingly, as attendance is invariably lower because not everyone indulges in breakfast and many will use the time to visit the gym or to catch up on work.
Breakfast buffet	A wide assortment of foods, including fruits and fruit juices, egg dishes, meats, potatoes, and breads. Buffets are good because the time food is out can be longer, allowing for latecomers to be accommodated, and can be cheaper than a full, served breakfast.
Refreshment breaks	Often beverages only but may include snacks such as cookies, bagels, or fruit. Remember that such breaks are to refresh and energize. The F&B selection should reflect this objective. If your breaks are put out longer, make sure the food items selected can accommodate this length and not dry out or lose quality. Refreshment breaks are often themed.
Brunch	A late-morning meal and includes both breakfast and lunch items. A brunch can be a buffet or a plated, served meal.

TABLE 9-1 Types of Functions (continued)

Buffet lunch	A cold or hot buffet, with a variety of salads, vegetables, meats, and so on. A deli buffet may include a make-your-own sandwich area.
Box lunch	Normally only available for carrying away from the hotel to an off-premise location. They can be eaten on a bus during a long ride to a destination (such as a ride from San Francisco to the Napa Valley for a day's activities) or at the destination (such as a picnic area to hear the Boston Pops Orchestra). Box lunches can also be provided to attendees at a trade show.
Full, served lunch	A plated lunch, usually a three-course meal that often includes a salad, a hot/cooked main course, and a dessert. A one-course cold meal is sometimes provided, such as a grilled chicken Caesar salad.
Receptions	Networking events with limited seating, which allow for conversation and interaction during the event. Food is usually placed on stations around the room and may also include butler-style service. Beverage service is always offered. Light receptions may only include dry snacks and beverages and often precede a dinner. Heavy receptions would include hot and cold appetizers and perhaps an **action station** and often replace a dinner.
Dinner buffet	A variety of salads, vegetables, entrees, desserts, and beverages. Often, meats are carved and served by attendants.
Full, served dinner	A three- to five-course meal, including an appetizer, soup, salad, main course, and a dessert. Food is plated in the kitchen and served to each guest seated at round tables in the dining room. This is often referred to as "American Style Service."
Off-site event	Any event held away from the host hotel. It could be a reception at a famous landmark, such as the Queen Mary in Long Beach, or a picnic at a local beach or park.
Theme party	A gala event with flair. It can be a reception, buffet, or served meal. Themes can vary widely. An example would be an international theme, where different stations are set up with food from Italy, China, Japan, Mexico, Germany, and so on.

TABLE 9-1 Types of Functions

The style of service will often influence the types and varieties of foods offered. The common service styles that can be used include the following:

BUFFET

Food is attractively arranged on tables. Guests serve themselves and take their plates to a table to sit and eat. Beverages are usually served at the tables. Buffets are generally more expensive than plated served meals because there is no portion control and surpluses must be built in to assure adequate supplies of each food item. However, staffing costs are lowered by 8–10% or more. Be sure to allow adequate space around the table for lines to form and for efficient

Dessert buffet table

replenishment by the service staff. Consider the flow, and do not make guests backtrack to get an item. For example, place the salad dressings after the salad so that guests do not have to step back on the next guest. Provide one buffet line per 100 guests, with 120 guests being the point to break into two lines.

ATTENDED BUFFET/CAFETERIA

Guests are served by chefs or attendants. This is more elegant and provides better portion control.

COMBINATION BUFFET

Inexpensive items, such as salads, are presented buffet style; guests help themselves. Expensive items, such as meats, are served by an attendant for portion control.

ACTION STATIONS

Sometimes referred to as "performance stations" or "exhibition cooking," **action stations** are similar to an attended buffet, except food is freshly prepared as guests wait and watch. More flair and more interaction make action stations part entertainment. Some common action station themes include

CHAPTER 9 FOOD AND BEVERAGE (F&B)

285

pasta, quesadilla, fajita, sushi/sashimi, oyster shucking, lettuce wrap, panini, French fries, mashed potato, comfort foods, soups, espresso, pizza, s'mores, chocolate dipped fruit, grilled meats or shrimp, omelets, crepes, Caesar salad, Belgian waffles, carved meats, and flaming desserts such as Baked Alaska, crepes suzette, or bananas foster.

Reception

Light foods are served buffet style or passed on trays by servers (**butler service**). Guests usually stand and serve themselves and do not usually sit down to eat. Receptions are often referred to as "Walk and Talks." Small plates should always be included for these events, as some cost control can be managed by selecting the appropriate service pieces. Some receptions serve only finger food, and others offer fork food.

Family Style/English Service

Guests are seated, and large serving platters and bowls of food are placed on the dining table by the servers. Guests pass the food around the table. A host often will carve the meat. This is an expensive style. Surpluses must be built into the price to account for potentially high food costs and additional service equipment.

Sliders are one of many food items that can be served at a reception

© LaineN/Shutterstock.com

MEETINGS, EXPOSITIONS, EVENTS, AND CONVENTIONS

Plated/American Style Service

Guests are seated and served food that has been portioned and plated in the kitchen. Food is served from the left of the guest. The meat or entree is placed directly in front of the guest at the six o'clock position. Beverages are served from the right of the guest. When the guest has finished, both plates and glassware are removed from the right. **American Service** is the most functional, common, economical, controllable, and efficient type of service. It usually has a server/guest ratio of 1:20 or 1:30, depending on the level of the facility.

Preset

Some foods are on the table when guests arrive. The most common items are water, butter, bread, appetizer, and/or salad. At luncheons, where time is of the essence, the dessert is often preset. These are all cold items that do not lose quality from sitting out for 30–60 minutes.

Butler Service

At receptions, hors d'oeuvres are passed on trays, and the guests help themselves.

Russian Service

(1) Banquet Russian: The food is fully prepared in the kitchen. All courses are served either from platters or an Escoffier dish. Tureens are used for soup and special bowls for salad. The server places the proper plate in front of the seated guest. After the plates are placed, the server returns with a tray of food and, moving counterclockwise around the table, serves the food from the guest's left with the right hand. The server controls the amount served. (2) Restaurant Russian: Guests are seated. Foods are cooked tableside on a *réchaud* (portable cooking stove) on a *gueridon* (tableside cart with wheels). Servers place the food on platters (usually silver), and guests serve themselves. Service is from the left.

Banquet French

Guests are seated. Platters of food are assembled in the kitchen; servers take them to the tables and serve from the left, with two large silver forks or one fork and one spoon. Servers must be highly trained; using the forks and spoons together in one hand is a skill that must be practiced, and many hotels are now permitting silver salad tongs.

Food on a réchaud

Cart French

Less common for banquets except for small VIP functions, this style is used in fine restaurants. Guests are seated, and foods are prepared tableside using a réchaud on a gueridon. Cold foods, such as salads, are prepared on the gueridon, sans réchaud. Servers put the finished foods directly on the guest's plate, which is placed in front of the guest from the right. Bread, butter, and salad are served from the left, and beverages are served from the right. All are removed from the right.

Hand Service or Captain

Guests are seated, with one server for every two guests. Servers wear white gloves. Foods are preplated. Each server carries two plates from the kitchen and stands behind their assigned guests. At a signal from the room captain, all servings are set in front of all guests at the same time, synchronized. This can be done for all courses, just the main course, or just the dessert. This is a very elegant and impressive style of service used mainly for VIP events because of the significant additional labor required.

A La Carte

Guests are given a choice of 2–3 entrees, with a minimum of two predetermined courses served before the entree choice.

Waiter Parade

Waiter Parade

An elegant touch in which white-gloved servers march into the room and parade around the perimeter carrying food on trays, often to dramatic music and lighting. This is especially effective with a flaming Baked Alaska. The room lighting is dimmed, and a row of flaming trays carried by the waiters slowly encircles the room, after which the music stops and service starts. (Flaming dishes should never be brought close to a guest. After the parade, the dessert is brought to a side area, where it is sliced and served.)

Mixing Service Styles

The event professional can change service styles within the meal. For example, the appetizer can be preset, with the salads "Frenched" (dressing added after they are placed on the table), the main course served American, with a dessert buffet.

MENUS

In times past, menus rarely changed. Today, change is necessary to keep pace with the shifting tastes of the public. Most food trade journals run features on "What's Hot and What's Not." Tables 9-2 and 9-3 list items that are generally always "hot" and consumption guidelines, respectively.

Seasonal food	In-season locally grown produce is served at the peak of flavor, enhancing the quality of the event.
Ethnic foods	With the influx of people from other cultures into many countries has come the unique cuisine of many areas of the world. The American palate has grown beyond the ethnic foods of the past, such as Italian, Chinese, and Mexican, to include the foods of many Asian countries, the Middle East, and South America.
High-quality ingredients	People may pinch pennies at the grocery store, but when they eat out at a banquet, they want the best. No longer satisfied with frozen, sweetened strawberries, they want fresh Driscoll strawberries on their shortcake. They want giant Idaho baked potatoes and prime Angus beef.
Fresh ingredients	Frozen, canned, and dried foods, once seen as the newest, greatest technology, have worn out their novelty. The loss of flavor during preservation has made fresh food highly prized. This also means local sourcing, with many establishments naming the specific farms.
New and unusual ingredients	With improvements in production, technology, and transportation, foods have appeared in marketplaces that were unknown to many people. These include artisanal breads and cheeses, heirloom tomatoes, lemon grass, Yukon Gold potatoes, purple potatoes, and blood oranges.
Safe foods	Organic foods and foods free from pollution and pesticides are served.
Highly creative presentations	Plate presentations are increasingly important. We eat with our eyes before anything hits our taste buds. Contemporary presentations should focus on the primary menu components, and garnishes should be minimal (based on the time food might be on display or stored in a hot box).
Excellent service	Food served promptly (while still hot) and friendly, courteous service are important considerations in the enjoyment of a meal.
Sustainable	For consumers, sustainability means food sourced that promotes good health, helps protect the environment, is fair to workers, and addresses animal welfare.

TABLE 9-2 "Hot" Menu Items

FOOD CONSUMPTION GUIDELINES

Type of Reception	Type of Eaters	Number of Hors D'Oeuvres per Person
2 hours or less (dinner following)	Light Moderate Heavy	3–4 pieces 5–7 pieces 8+ pieces
2 hours or less (no dinner)	Light Moderate Heavy	6–8 pieces 10–12 pieces 12+ pieces
2–3 hours (no dinner)	Light Moderate Heavy	8–10 pieces 10–12 pieces 16+ pieces

TABLE 9-3 Food Consumption Guidelines

The most important information in deciding how much food to order is the history of the group: Who are they? Why are they here? A pretty good determination can be made based on previous years. If this is a new group or the history is not available, consider its demographics.

Some General Guidelines

Guests generally eat more during the first hour of a reception (an average of seven hors d'oeuvres per person). These general guidelines will vary by group demographics.

The amount of food consumed may also depend on how many square feet of space is available for guests to move around in (smaller equals less consumption).

In general, menu offerings tend to lend themselves toward assembly-line production and service. Certain delicate items cannot be produced and served in quantity without sacrificing culinary quality. For example, lobster, soufflé, rare roast beef, medium-rare tuna, rare duck breast, or salmon steak are difficult to prepare and serve satisfactorily to more than a handful of guests at a time. One technology that has grown in popularity that has addressed this concern is sous vide (the phrase means "under vacuum"), which involves vacuum sealing foods in plastic, then cooking at a precise temperature in a water bath. The result is a consistent product, excellent taste because the food cooks in its own natural juices, ease of cooking because no attention is needed while cooking, and reduced waste because nothing is dried out.

Menu Restrictions

Banquet servers should know the ingredients and preparation method of every item on the menu. Many attendees have allergies or are restricted from eating certain items, such as sugar or salt, nuts, or gluten due to health concerns. Others do not eat certain foods due to their religious restrictions, and others are vegetarians who do not eat meat. The question of allergies and food restrictions should be posed as early as possible. For conventions, attendees are asked to provide information on food restrictions on the convention registration form. The caterer will never know if these are by choice, for allergy reasons, or for religious reasons. Dietary preferences should never be thought of as optional, as the guest could have severe allergies.

Guests with special diets will influence the types of foods served. Some people cannot tolerate monosodium glutamate or MSG (allergic reactions), onions and garlic (digestive problems), certain spices or peanuts (allergic reactions), sugar (diabetes), salt (high blood pressure, heart problems), fat (weight problems, high cholesterol), and wheat, rye, or barley (celiac disease). Other dietary restrictions include lactose intolerance, which means someone has difficulty digesting anything containing milk or milk products. Sometimes, the restrictions are not the content of the food but the frequency. Those with hypoglycemia must eat every few hours.

According to the FDA, the eight most common food allergies are milk/dairy, egg, fish, shellfish, tree nuts, peanuts, wheat, and soy. An acute allergic reaction may manifest as swelling of the eyelids, face, lips, tongue, larynx, or trachea. Other reactions can include difficulty breathing, hives, nausea, vomiting, diarrhea, stomach cramps, or abdominal pain. Anaphylactic shock is a severe whole-body reaction that can result in death.

Today, people have also chosen dietary restrictions in an effort to eat in a healthier fashion, including low-carbohydrate and high-fiber diets. Others choose certain dietary lifestyles to align with their beliefs. Vegetarians often make up approximately 10–15% of a group and come in three basic types: will not eat red meat but will eat chicken and fish, lacto ovo (will not eat anything that has to be killed but will eat animal by-products, such as cheese, eggs, and milk), and vegans (will not eat anything from any animal source, including animal by-products, such as honey, butter, and dairy). When in doubt, assume attendees who identify as vegetarian are vegan, and serving them a plate of vegetables with butter and cheese would not be appropriate.

Religious restrictions may also impact food and diet. For example, people who maintain a kosher diet will not eat anything that does not follow kosher guidelines, not mix dairy products with meat products, and keep separate china and separate kitchens for dairy and meat. Kosher food must follow stringent rules and pass the approval of a *mashgiach*, who does not have to be a rabbi but must be recognized in the community as a person authorized to give certification for *kashruth*. Kosher food conforms to strict Judaic laws regarding the type of food that may be eaten and can be combined during a meal. In addition to the kinds of animals considered kosher, the laws state that animals must be killed in a specific manner. In kosher service, with the exception of glass and silverware that can undergo a curing period, meat products must not be served on any plate that has ever had dairy products on it. Pork, shellfish, rabbit, and hindquarter cuts of beef and lamb are examples of foods that are not allowed for various reasons. As these meals oftentimes have to be prepared in a specialty kitchen, they can be considerably more expensive. The conference organizer can choose to pass that cost on to the attendee or absorb it.

It is a good idea to have attendees fill out a form indicating if they have menu restrictions. This information can be communicated to the catering manager, who will ensure that the proper number and type of alternative menu items are available. At meetings of the National Association of Catering Executives, attendees are provided with complete menus of every event, along with a form where they can indicate which meals they need to have changed.

CONTRACTS

Normally, formal catering contracts are required. Sometimes they may be forgone in place of a signed **banquet event order** (BEO) or a signed letter of agreement. A BEO, sometimes referred to as a "function sheet," is a venue's internal communication system between departments. It is also the building block upon which accounting and record keeping systems are constructed. A resume is a summary of function room usage for a particular convention or meeting. The resume usually includes all BEOs. The resume focuses on the major highlights and defers to the pertinent BEOs for specific details. A catering contract, or letter of agreement, usually contains a combination of standard, boilerplate language, plus language specifically tailored to the event.

F&B Attrition

Most event professionals do not like **attrition** clauses, although these benefit both event professionals and venues by setting legal obligations for both sides and establishing liability limits. When a contract is signed, both parties want the F&B **guarantee** to be met. The difference is that caterers want to be certain and up-front, but event professionals want to wait until the last minute to give the final guarantee. If it is too high, they might have to pay for it as attrition. They agree in the contract to buy a specific number of meals or spend a specific amount of money on group F&B; the caterer's obligation is to provide the service and the food. If the guarantee is not met, the professional must pay the difference between it and the actual amount or an agreed-on percentage of the actual amount (see Chapter 10 on legal issues for more information on attrition).

BEVERAGE EVENTS

REASONS FOR A BEVERAGE EVENT

Beverage events are popular and include refreshment breaks and receptions. Beverage breaks not only provide liquid nourishment (and possibly a snack) but also allow the attendee to get up, stretch, visit the restroom, check text messages and email, call the office, check-in on social media, and possibly move into another room for the next breakout session.

Receptions are slightly different because most include alcoholic beverages and potentially more variety and quantity of food options. Reasons for receptions include the following:

- *Socializing:* To provide a relaxed atmosphere that encourages interaction among guests.
- *Networking:* To provide an opportunity to discuss business and develop new contacts.

Planners typically plan and purchase for only three main types of beverage functions with alcohol: cocktail receptions, hospitality suites, and poured wine service. A key consideration in finalizing a beverage menu is based on the demographics and history of the group.

CATEGORIES OF LIQUOR

The categories of alcoholic beverages offered for a catered event are liquor (distilled spirits), wine, and beer. The caterer typically offers tiers of these options, representing different price and quality levels: well, call, and premium brands. The event professional will choose the tier most appropriate for their guests and the event budget.

- *Well Brands:* These are sometimes called "house liquors" and less expensive, such as Kentucky Gentleman Bourbon. Well brands are served when someone does not "call" for a specific brand.
- *Call Brands:* These are priced in the midrange and generally asked for by name, such as Jim Beam Bourbon or Beefeater's Gin.
- *Premium Brands:* These are high-quality, expensive liquors, such as Crown Royal, Chivas Regal, or Tanqueray Gin.

SPIRITS

All premium brands are available in 750-ml and 1-liter bottles. One 750-ml bottle equals 20 (1 1/4-ounce) servings; a 1-liter bottle equals 27 (1 1/4-ounce) servings (see Table 9-4). Consumption will average three drinks per person during a normal reception period.

		1 Ounce	1¼ Ounce	1½ Ounce
1 Liter	33.8 ounces	33	27	22
750 ml	25.3 ounces	25	20	16

TABLE 9-4 Number of Drinks per Bottle

WINE/CHAMPAGNE

All premium brands are available in 750-ml bottles and many in 1.5 liters (magnums). There are other sizes as well:

Split (187-ml)
Half bottle (375-ml)
Bottle (750-ml) = five 5-ounce servings
Magnum (1.5-liter bottle) = 10 5-ounce servings
Double magnum (3-liter)

CHAPTER 9 FOOD AND BEVERAGE (F&B)

Jeroboam (3-liter for sparkling, 4.5-liter for still)
Imperial (6-liter)
Methuselah (6-liter)
Nebuchadnezzar (15-liter)

Consumption will average three glasses per person during a normal reception period. Assuming that 50% of the people will order wine, you would order 30 750-ml bottles for every 100 guests.

Champagne should be served in a flute glass instead of the classic coupe because it exposes less surface to the air; the bubbles do not escape as fast, causing the champagne to go flat much later (see Figure 9-2).

Beer

The caterer should always offer a variety of domestic and imported choices and a contemporary list of "craft" beers from small, independent, and traditional brewers (i.e., Dogfish Head 60 Minute IPA, Bell's Two Hearted Ale).

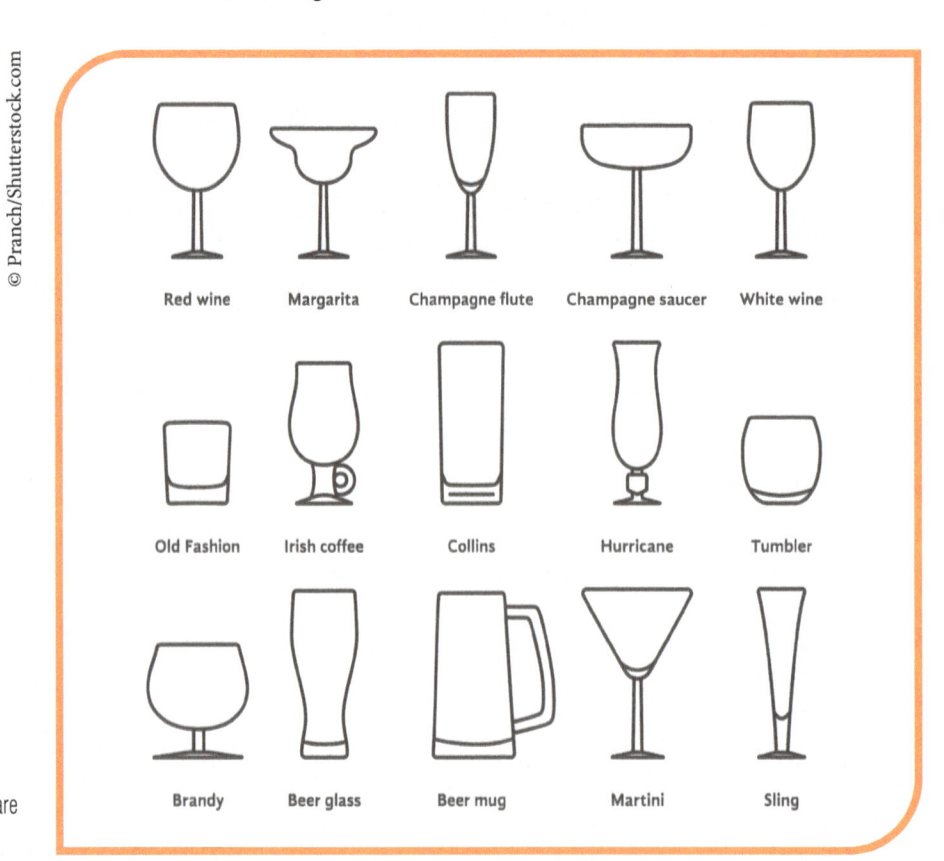

FIGURE 9-2 Pack of different thin line stemware

HOW BEVERAGES ARE SOLD

By the Bottle

This is common for open bars and poured wine at meal functions. The event professional pays for all of the liquor bottles that are opened. A physical inventory is taken at the beginning and end of the function. Most venues charge for each opened bottle, even if only one drink was poured from it. This method saves money but is inconvenient to monitor and calculate. The event professional will not know the final cost until the event is over. Usually, the group history will give some indication of how much consumption to expect.

Open bottles may not be removed from the property unless the venue has an off-sale liquor license. You can, however, have them delivered to a hospitality suite or to the room of a VIP to use during the meeting. This method is less and less common, except for wine.

By the Drink

Also called "Consumption Bar," the host is charged for each individual beverage consumed. Normally, the price per drink is high enough to cover all relevant expenses (limes, stirrers, napkins, etc.). Individual drink prices are set to yield a standard beverage cost percentage set by the venue (the amount of profit the venue expects to make). Cost percentages are 12–18% for spirits and usually around 25% for wine. The event professional will not know the final cost until the event is over.

Per Person

This method can be more expensive but involves less work and aggravation. The event professional chooses a plan, such as premium liquors for 1 hour, and then tells the caterer how many people are coming ($25 per person × 500 guests = $12,500). Costs are known ahead of time with no surprises. Tickets are collected from attendees at the door and the guarantee monitored. The key to selecting this, or any other method, is to know your group. Know their drinking capacity and pattern by reviewing their past history.

Charge Per Hour

This is similar to per person. This method often includes a sliding scale, with a higher cost for the first hour. This is because guests usually eat and drink more during the first hour, then level off. You must provide a firm guarantee before negotiating a per-hour charge. Or, you can combine per person and per hour: $25 per person for the first hour, and $20 per person for the second hour, so hosting 100 guests for a 2-hour reception would cost $4,500 [$25 × 100 = $2,500 (+) $20 × 100 = $2,000 (=) $4,500]. No consideration is given for those who arrive late or leave early; the fee is $45 per person regardless.

Open Bar

Also called a "hosted bar," this is when a host or sponsor pays for drinks. Guests usually drink as much as they want of what they want. Consumption is higher because someone else is paying. The sponsor can be the meeting itself, an exhibitor, an external party, or a similar organization. For example, at the Super Show, which features sporting goods, Nike may sponsor a bar.

Cash Bar

Also called a "no-host bar," this is when guests buy their own drinks. Guests usually purchase tickets from a cashier to exchange with a bartender for a drink. At small functions, the bartender may collect and serve, eliminating the cost of a cashier. Cashiers are usually charged as extra labor but can provide better control and speed up service. This also prevents bartenders from having to handle dirty money and then glassware and garnishes, such as lemons/limes.

Combination Bar

This is a very common format where a host purchases tickets and gives each attendee a certain number (usually two). If the guest wants another drink, they must purchase it themselves. This could also be set up by time—the host could pay for the first hour and then revert to a cash bar for the rest of the time. This method provides free drinks but retains control over costs and potential liability for providing unlimited drinks.

Limited Consumption Bar

Alcohol is priced by the drink. The host establishes a dollar amount; when the cash register reaches that amount, the bar is closed. The host may decide to reopen as a cash bar.

CALCULATE TOTAL COST TO DETERMINE THE BEST OPTION

A bottle of bourbon yields 27 14-ounce drinks. If guests are expected to drink two drinks per hour, for a 1-hour reception for 1,000 people:

Purchasing by the bottle, at $80 per bottle, it would cost $6,000.

Purchased by the drink, at $4.00 per drink, the same group would cost $8,000.

Purchased at $10 per person, it would cost $10,000.

The hotel makes more money selling per person; by the bottle is becoming less common.

LABOR CHARGES

Extra charges are usually levied for bartenders and/or **barbacks**, cocktail servers, cashiers, security, and **corkage** fees. These items are negotiable, depending on the value of the business. For example, if a bar sells over $500 in liquor, the bartender charge may be waived.

A "barback" is the bartender's helper. They restock liquor, keep fresh ice filled, and make sure clean glasses are available. This saves the bartender from having to do it during service.

One of the authors attended a wedding at Cornell University with the reception at Statler Hall. It was a small wedding, so only one bartender was provided with no barback. Many of the attendees were snow skiing instructors who consumed more alcohol than the typical person. Partway through the reception, the bar was running low on some types of liquor. As the bartender had to leave the bar to obtain the supplies, he asked two men in the wedding party to cover the bar. They did, but they filled each glass with extra liquor. When the bartender returned, the bar was low on other alcohol inventory.

"Corkage" is the fee added to liquor brought into but not purchased from the venue. The venue charges it to cover the cost of labor, glasses (which must be delivered to the room, washed, and placed back in storage), mixers, olives, lemon peels, and so forth. Corkage is not available at all properties and depends on venue policy.

Considerations for the number of bartenders include the number of bars scheduled, types of drinks, number of attendees, hours of operation, amount of barback work, and applicable union or company human resources policies. The standard ratio is one bartender for every 100 attendees. If guests all arrive at the same time, a ratio of 75 (or down to even 50) is appropriate. At large events with over 1,000 attendees, a ratio of 100 is appropriate. To alleviate pressure on bartenders, ask for a few servers to pass glasses of champagne, still wines, bottled waters, or juices. This will also add an extra touch of elegance to the event. Unless the event is very small, at least one barback is needed. Considerations for the number of barbacks include the number of bars scheduled, capacity of each bar setup, distance between bars and kitchen, ease in retrieving stock, hours of operations, number of attendees, variety of liquor stock, glasses and garnishes, and the applicable union or company human resources policies.

HOSPITALITY SUITES

Hospitality suites are places for attendees to gather outside of the meeting events. They are normally open late in the evening, after 10:00 p.m., but occasionally around the clock. Three types of hospitality suites are the following:

- *Morning:* Continental breakfast
- *Afternoon:* Snacks and sodas
- *Evening:* Liquor and snacks

Hospitality suites can be hosted by the sponsoring organization, a chapter of the organization, an exhibitor, a nonexhibiting corporation, an allied association, or a person running for an office in the organization. They can be held in a client or partner's suite on a sleeping room floor. Usually, these are handled by room service and sold by catering. Sometimes, they are held in a public function room and are both sold and serviced by catering.

Some suites offer a full bar, but some are beer and wine only. Some have lots of food, and others have only dry snacks. Some offer desserts and specialty coffees. Consider ordering more food if the attendees have had an open evening.

Watch for "underground hospitality suites" (unofficial parties), where you gain legal liability and lose revenue. The court case resulting from the Tailhook Scandal, in which a women was groped in a hallway at a military meeting at the Las Vegas Hilton, set a precedent that a hotel can no longer claim that it does not know what is going on within the property.

Make sure to have the appropriate alcohol licenses. There are on-sale licenses, off-sale licenses, and beer and wine licenses. Licenses also stay with the property. For example, if your hotel has a liquor license, it is not valid in the public park across the street. The caterer would need to obtain a special temporary permit. Another factor to keep in mind is that liquor laws vary by state, county, and country. You should always check the laws in the specific location where your event is being held. Event professionals who wish to bring their own liquor into an establishment must check local laws and be prepared to pay the establishment a per-bottle corkage fee.

EXAMPLES

In Las Vegas and New Orleans, liquor can be sold 24/7 and carried and consumed in public places.

In California, liquor cannot be sold between 2 a.m. and 6 a.m.

In Atlanta, liquor may not be served until 11 a.m. on Sundays.

In some states, liquor may not be sold at all on Sundays.

There are generally four types of illegal liquor sales, wherever you are located:

- to minors,
- to intoxicated persons,
- outside legal hours, and
- with an improper liquor license.

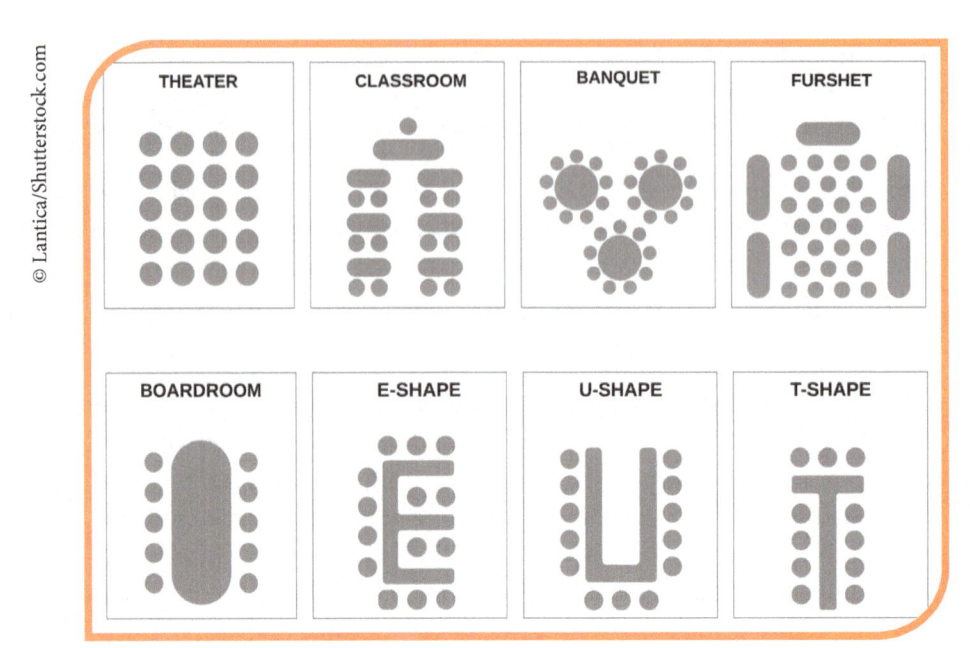

FIGURE 9-3
Sample room layouts

ROOMS

ROOM SETUPS

The way the room is set up is critically important to the success of any event. It can affect the flow of service, amount of F&B consumed, and even guests' mood. The ambiance can make or break a meal function, whether it is a continental breakfast or a formal dinner.

Room setup includes tables, chairs, décor, and other equipment, such as portable bars, stages, and audiovisual equipment. It is essential that the event professional communicate *exactly* how they want the room to be set to the banquet setup manager. This is accomplished on the BEO form and by using room layout software. These types of programs allow the placement of tables, chairs, and other equipment into a meeting room plan. Room software demos may be viewed on a number of websites, including Social Tables, Meeting Matrix, All Seated, and Room Viewer.

Aisle Space

Aisles allow people to move easily around the room without squeezing through chairs and disturbing seated guests. They also provide a buffer between the seating areas and the F&B areas. Aisles between tables and around F&B stations should be a bare minimum of 36 inches wide (3 feet), but 48 inches is preferable. Also, leave a 3-foot minimum aisle around the perimeter of the room. Cross aisles should be 6 feet wide. Check with the local fire marshal for local rules and regulations, as these vary from location to location.

Per Person

Remember to deduct space for furniture before calculating the number of people. Include large sofas found in many hospitality suites, buffet tables, portable bars, plants, décor and props, and check-in tables. Allow 10 square feet per person at rectangular banquet tables. Allow 12.5 square feet per person at rounds (this assumes the facility is using standard 20- by 20-inch chairs). Allow 3 square feet per person for dance floors. These are numbers you can reference later in an internet search, but the key to remember is to always check local fire codes.

TABLESCAPES

The tabletop should be seen as a stage—it sets expectations and should reflect the theme of the event. Once guests are seated, the focus is mainly on the table, so it is imperative that it not be overlooked.

- The centerpiece should not block sight lines for people sitting across the table. Centerpieces should be low or high with a Lucite or slender pole in the middle portion.
- The *cover* is the place setting and includes placement of flatware, china, and glassware.
- "Napery" includes all table linens, such as tablecloths, overlays, napkins, and table skirting.
- Other décor may include ribbons, greenery, or items relating to the theme of the meal.

A "wow" tablescape presentation

CHAPTER 9 FOOD AND BEVERAGE (F&B)

Examples

- trailing flower garlands or ribbons between place settings,
- different-colored napkins at each cover,
- creative napkin folds at each cover, and
- creative centerpieces.

Large or specifically themed props for **tablescapes** can be rented from prop houses, service contractors, or party stores or be provided by the venue, hotel, or club. Other props that are small, decorative pieces can be found in many places, such as the following:

- auto supply stores
- toy or crafts stores
- garden centers
- ethnic food stores or import shops
- travel agencies (destination posters)
- sports clubs or stores
- medical supply stores, and
- military surplus stores.

ROOM RENTAL CHARGES

Can they be waived? It varies by venue. If the function is part of an event that also requires the sleeping rooms, it is easier to negotiate the room rental charge from the hotel. When undertaking catering events at hotels that are handled by the catering department rather than the sales department because no room nights are involved, an event professional rarely encounters a rental fee. Rather, a minimum revenue requirement will be based on the amount of space needed for the event. The group may have to spend $50,000 in F&B to secure a ballroom for an event, which frequently means that guests eat *very* well.

In off-premise venues, it depends on how they have set up the charge/profit schedule. Most charge a rental fee. Some charge a rental fee, some an admission fee per guest, and a few charge both and then add on catering, rentals, and service costs. The types of charges are almost always dependent on the size or projected profitability of the event. However, everything is negotiable. At several venues, it may be possible to negotiate removing the rental charge when bringing a large or highly profitable event to the property; it varies by venue.

SERVICE REQUIREMENTS

Labor is a major cost for catering. Most properties use a staffing guide to formalize policies in an effort to contain labor costs.

One bartender per every 100 guests is standard. If guests will arrive all at once or you do not want long lines, you could have one bartender for every 50 or 75 guests, but there may be an additional labor charge. If a dinner involves a wine pairing for each course or has three or more wines, a dedicated wine service team is commonly added.

Service is critical. Many excellent meals are ruined by poor service. Meal service levels can run from one server per eight guests to one per 40 guests. Most staffing guides allow for a ratio of 1/32, but most event professionals want 1/20 or 1/16 with either poured wine or French Service.

Savvy event professionals negotiate for the following:

General
Rounds of 10: one server for every two tables, busser for every six tables
Rounds of 8: one server for every five tables, busser for every eight tables

With poured wine or French Service
Rounds of 10: two servers for every three tables
Rounds of 8: one server for every two tables

Buffets
One server per 30–40 guests
One runner per 100–125 guests

French or Russian Service
Rounds of 8 or 10: One server per table, busser for every three tables

Supervision
One room captain. One section captain for every 250 guests (25 rounds of 10).

Space Requirements for Tables			
Rounds	60-inch round =	5-foot diameter =	Round of 8
	72-inch round =	6-foot diameter =	Round of 10
	66-inch round =	Compromise size	Seats 8–10
Rectangle	6-foot long	30 inches wide	Banquet 6
	8-foot long	30 inches wide	Banquet 8
Schoolroom or classroom	6 or 8 feet long	18 or 24 inches wide	
Half-moon table	Half of a round table		
Serpentine	¼ hollowed-out	round table	
Space Requirements for Receptions			
Minimum (tight)		5.5–7 square feet per person	
Comfortably crowded		7.5 square feet per person	
Ample room		10+ square feet per person	

TABLE 9-5 Space Requirements

SET OVER GUARANTEE

This is negotiable, depending on the property. It is the percentage of guests that the hotel will prepare for beyond the guarantee, in case additional, unexpected people show up. Below are **set over guarantees** at a major Las Vegas property:

Average overset is 3%, but you must look at the numbers, not just the percentages.

<100 guests = the guarantee is the set
100–1,000 guests = 3% overset with a maximum of 50
Over 1,000 guests = 3% overset

COCKTAIL SERVERS

Cocktail servers can only carry 12–16 drinks per trip. Counting the time to take the order, the time to wait for the drinks at the service bar, and the time it takes to find the guest and deliver the drink, it takes at least 15 minutes per trip to the bar. This only makes it possible to serve 48–64 drinks per hour. Cocktail servers are usually only used at small or VIP functions.

SERVICE TIMING

Fifteen minutes before you want to start serving, dim the lights, ring chimes, start music, open doors, and so on to get guests to start moving to their tables.

The salad course should take 15–20 minutes, depending on dressing or service style. The main course should take 30–40 minutes from serving to plate removal. Dessert should take 20–30 minutes.

A typical luncheon will last about 1 hour and 15 minutes and a typical dinner about 2 hours.

TRENDS AND BEST PRACTICES BEFORE COVID-19

Event professionals also need to stay abreast of food trends. They do so by reading trade journals, such as *Meeting News, Successful Meetings, Convene,* or *Meetings & Conventions*. Many of the event and food trade publications, such as *Event Solutions, Special Events, Event Manager Blog, Bizbash, Meetings & Conventions, Catersource,* and *Smart Meetings*, are wonderful resources as well and can be accessed online. Identified below are trends and practices that the authors identified prior to COVID-19.

- Global and sustained efforts to embrace and integrate "green" products and practices.
    - Instead of "just" recycling—focus more on reducing and repurposing.
    - Donate leftover food to local shelters and organizations to distribute to the community.
    - Use compostable utensils and plateware.
    - Organic décor: Use cotton tablecloths instead of linen and low-cost candlescapes instead of laurels.
- Use fresh, locally/regionally sourced, sustainable foods and products.
    - Include the "story" of where their food came from (on printed menus, in presentations, etc.).
- Rethink breakfast.
    - Some venues are allowing multiple groups to share the same breakfast buffet, thus saving cost.
    - Another trend is to consolidate breakfast and lunch into brunch, yielding cost savings.

- Use clean/slick/simple presentations and efficient service.
- Focus on food flavors and options.
  - Fads are on hold. People are looking for sophisticated interpretations of familiar food.
  - Focus on big/bold flavor profiles.
  - Include a signature portfolio of "house-made" items (potato chips, jams, jerky, olives, etc.).
  - Make strategic use of well-known branded products (Boars Head, Starbucks, Evian, Pellegrino).
- Consider food service options.
  - Food trucks continue to be popular! An interesting addition to receptions as a themed station.
  - More meals are focusing on networking opportunities in lieu of a large, long, sit-down meal.
  - Lunches are going to a more "grab and go" style or small, tapas-style items.
  - Dinners are often replaced by receptions.
- Consider tapas-style small plates.
  - Small plates allow attendees to taste more with every meal.
- Craft beer options and bolder options for varietal wines are being included in most bars.

SUMMARY

F&B is an integral part of most meetings and events. Astute planning can save a tremendous amount of money. Knowing what is negotiable and how to negotiate is critical. F&B functions create memories and provide a necessary service beyond being a refueling stop. Although most attendees do not specify F&B as a reason for attending a meeting, when asked later about a meeting, they will often rave (or complain) about it. Catered events often set the tone of the meeting and create great memories that can result in future business, not only from the event professional but also from every guest in attendance.

CASE STUDY: ENHANCING F&B SERVICE IN A HOTEL

Background: You are a group of students participating in a hospitality management program. Your task is to analyze and provide recommendations for improving the F&B service at the midsized Harmony Haven Hotel. It has been receiving feedback from guests about its dining experiences, and the management is eager to address these concerns to enhance overall guest satisfaction.

Scenario: Harmony Haven Hotel is a popular destination for both business travelers and tourists. It offers a variety of rooms and services, including a restaurant that serves breakfast, lunch, and dinner. The restaurant's ambiance is inviting, but recent guest reviews and surveys indicate a few areas of concern related to the F&B service.

Issues Raised:

1. Limited Menu Variety: Guests have mentioned that the restaurant's menu lacks diversity, especially for guests with dietary restrictions and preferences. Some guests feel that the menu could offer more vegetarian, vegan, and gluten-free choices.

2. Slow Service: Several reviews have highlighted instances of slow service during peak hours. Guests have expressed frustration with long wait times for both placing and receiving orders.

3. Inconsistent Food Quality: Some guests have commented that the taste and quality of dishes can vary from one visit to another, leading to uncertainty about the overall dining experience.

4. Undertrained Staff: A few guests have noted that the restaurant staff seemed untrained or unfamiliar with the menu, resulting in inaccurate recommendations and incorrect orders.

Your Task:

1. Menu Enhancement: Propose specific additions and modifications to the menu that cater to a wider range of dietary preferences, including vegetarian, vegan, and gluten-free options. Explain how these changes can attract more guests and increase satisfaction.

2. Service Efficiency: Suggest strategies to improve the speed of service during peak hours. Consider technology solutions, staff training, and kitchen management techniques that could streamline the process.

3. Quality Assurance: Develop a plan to ensure consistent food quality across all visits. This could involve implementing quality control measures in the kitchen and providing chefs with guidelines for maintaining consistent flavors.

4. Staff Training: Outline a training program for restaurant staff that focuses on menu knowledge, customer service skills, and handling dietary requests professionally. Highlight the benefits of well-trained staff on guest satisfaction.

5. Feedback Mechanism: Propose a system for collecting guest feedback on their dining experiences. Explain how this system will help the hotel monitor improvements and make necessary adjustments over time.

Deliverables:

Prepare a comprehensive report addressing the above points. Include well-reasoned explanations for your recommendations and consider the potential challenges of implementation. Your report should reflect a deep understanding of the importance of F&B service in hospitality and how it contributes to guest satisfaction.

KEY WORDS AND TERMS

For definitions, see glossary or http://glossary.conventionindustry.org.

action stations	corkage
American Service	guarantee
attrition	on-premise catering
banquet event order	off-premise catering
barbacks	room setup
butler service	set over guarantee
catered events	tablescapes
caterer	

REVIEW AND DISCUSSION QUESTIONS

1. What is the first step for an event professional when planning for an off-premise event? List five types of functions, and give a brief description of each.

2. Describe how Family Style/English Service and Plated/American Style service differ.

3. What is the most important information to consider when deciding how much food to order for a group?

4. What is the average number of hors d'oeuvres a guest will eat during the first hour?

5. What are the three categories of liquor?

6. What is the function of a hospitality suite, and what are the three types?

7. What are the important aspects of an event that are affected by how the room is set up?

8. When catering an event at a hotel, and no room nights are involved, which department handles the booking of the event?

9. Why is it imperative that the tabletop not be overlooked?

CHAPTER 9 FOOD AND BEVERAGE (F&B)

ABOUT THE CHAPTER CONTRIBUTORS

Kristin Malek, Ph.D., CMP, CED, DES, CHE is an event management extension specialist and assistant professor in the hospitality, restaurant, and tourism management program at the University of Nebraska—Lincoln.

George G. Fenich, Ph.D. is a professor emeritus in the School of Hospitality Leadership at East Carolina University in North Carolina.

Previous Edition Chapter Contributors

Donnell Bayot, Ph.D., CHE, CPCE, CFBE, director of academic affairs for the International School of Hospitality in Las Vegas

Gary L. McCreary, CPCE, CMP, CSEP, vice president of catering and convention operations at the Venetian/Palazzo Resort Hotel & Casinos in Las Vegas

Perry Lynch, faculty at the Rosen College of Hospitality Management at the University of Central Florida

Patti J. Shock (deceased), academic consultant for TISOH and emeritus professor and chair in the Harrah College of Hotel Administration at the University of Nevada—Las Vegas.

CHAPTER 10

LEGAL ISSUES IN THE MEETINGS, EVENTS, EXHIBITIONS, AND CONVENTIONS (MEEC) INDUSTRY

CONTRACTS ARE A CRITICAL LEGAL FACTOR IN MEEC

© panitanphoto/Shutterstock.com

CHAPTER OBJECTIVES

- Cover the most important elements of negotiation in MEEC.
- Note the specifics to consider when dealing with contracts in this industry.
- Discuss the importance of crisis preparedness and management.
- Clarify the points and impact of Americans with Disabilities Act as it pertains to MEEC.
- Articulate the legal importance of intellectual property as it has to do with this industry.
- Outline potential labor issues to consider in the industry.
- Discuss important ethical concerns to consider in MEEC.
- Outline current trends and best practices regarding legal issues in MEEC.

Contributed by Tyra Warner. © Kendall Hunt Publishing Company.

Legal aspects and issues permeate almost every facet of our work as meeting planners and organizers. Contracts, often characterized as lengthy and verbose, are not, as the joke goes, "bloated" because lawyers are compensated by the word count. Instead, the verbosity arises from a concerted effort by the parties to eliminate as much ambiguity as possible from the contract's language. Ideally, contracts should be clear and comprehensible to the average person upon reading. Regardless of our role as buyers (meeting organizers) or suppliers (hotels, DMCs, caterers, audiovisual [A/V], production, etc.), we invariably engage in negotiations. Our concerns extend to a multitude of risks, including **force majeure** events (emergencies, crises, or disasters), incidents causing injury, and instances of nonperformance. Additionally, we must remain vigilant regarding national, state, and local laws that influence how we orchestrate an event, whom we employ, and the entertainment we incorporate. This chapter delves into many of these issues and offers valuable insights into legal matters, but it is not a substitute for consulting with an attorney well-versed in MEEC law and licensed to practice in your specific jurisdiction. Furthermore, legal and ethical concerns can vary significantly by one country. Although this chapter adopts a U.S.-centric framework, its principles are broadly applicable across the globe.

NEGOTIATION

Negotiation is the process through which a meeting planner and a hotel representative (or other supplier) come to an agreement regarding the terms and conditions that will govern their relationship before, during, and after a meeting, convention, exposition, or event.

Planning and executing a meeting may entail negotiating several contracts. Undoubtedly, the primary—and arguably the most critical—agreement pertains to the hotel and/or trade show facility. Nevertheless, agreements may also encompass a wide array of supplementary services, such as temporary personnel, security, A/V equipment, destination management (e.g., tours and local transportation), entertainment, external catering, exhibitor services or decorations, and housing bureaus. Negotiations might extend to "official" transportation providers, such as travel agencies, airlines, and rental car companies.

GENERAL NEGOTIATION STRATEGIES

Although many believe that the objective of a negotiation is to establish a win-win scenario, some contend that true win-win situations are rare because one or both parties usually must make concessions. The actual "winner" is often the party who enters the negotiation well prepared and has the strongest bargaining position. Hotel representatives typically hold an advantage over planners, as hotels typically have more information about the planner's organization than the planner has about the lodging industry or specific hotel. Negotiating contracts is frequently a more significant aspect of a hotel salesperson's role than it is for a meeting planner, so familiarity with the negotiation process also plays a pivotal role.

Negotiating strategy encompasses a multitude of approaches, each as diverse as the negotiators themselves. Here are some valuable tips from an experienced negotiator:

- *Do your homework.* Develop a "game plan" of the outcomes sought, and prioritize your wants and needs. Learn as much about the other side's position as you can.
- *Keep your eyes on the prize.* Do not forget the outcome sought.
- *Leave something on the table.* It may provide an opportunity to come back later and renew the negotiations.
- *Do not be the first one to make an offer.* Letting the other person make the first move sets the outside parameters for the negotiation.
- *When you hit a roadblock, find a more creative path.* Thinking outside the box often leads to a solution.

Some people think there is no win-win outcome to negotiations. What do you think?

- *Timing is everything.* Remember that time always works against the person who does not have it and that 90% of negotiation usually occurs in the last 10% of the time allocated.
- *Listen, listen, listen … and do not get emotional.* Letting emotions rule a negotiation will cause you to lose sight of what result is important.

When negotiating meeting contracts, or indeed any type of contract, it is prudent to adhere to some fundamental rules. These general guidelines can greatly assist in the negotiation process:

- *Go into the negotiations with a plan.* A skilled negotiator knows their bottom line: what is really needed, what is just wanted, and what can be given up to reach a compromise result.
- *Always go into a contract negotiation with an alternative location or service provider in mind.* Bargaining leverage is better if the other party knows you can go somewhere else.
- *Be thorough.* Put everything negotiated in the contract. Develop your own if necessary.
- *Do not assume anything.* Put it in writing. Meeting industry personnel change frequently, and oral agreements or assumptions can be easily forgotten or misunderstood.
- *Beware of language that sounds acceptable but is not specific.* For example, what does a "tentative first option" mean? Words such as "reasonable," "anticipated," and "projected" should be avoided, since they mean different things to different people.
- *Do not accept something just because it is preprinted in the contract or the proposal is given to you by the other party.* Everything is negotiable. (See Case 1. SXSW Entertainment Contract.)
- *Read the small print.* For example, most contracts come with standard clauses that are copied and pasted from contract to contract, also known as "boilerplate" language. This can include indemnification of parties in the event of negligence, which can make a major difference in the resolution of liability after an accident or injury.
- *Look for mutuality in the contract's provisions.* For example, do not sign a contract in which the indemnification clause only protects one of the parties and never give one party the unilateral right to do anything, such as change the location of meeting rooms without the consent of the meeting organizer.

CASE 1. SXSW ENTERTAINMENT CONTRACT

In 2017, the United States was in the wake of a change of power in the federal government. This change in power brought declarations of sweeping changes in immigration policy among many other policies. SXSW, an annual music, media, and film festival, came under fire during this time because of a controversial clause in its contract with musicians who wanted to play at the festival. The clause read in part:

> "Foreign Artists entering the country through the Visa Waiver Program (VWP), B visa or any non-work visa may not perform at any public or unofficial shows, DAY OR NIGHT, in Austin from March 10-19, 2017. Accepting and performing at unofficial events (including unofficial events aside from SXSW Music dates during their visit to the United States) <u>may result in immediate deportation, revoked passport and denied entry by US Customs Border Patrol at US ports of entry</u>." (emphasis added) (Strauss & Yoo, 2017)

One entertainer declined to participate in the event because of this language that he (and others) perceived as threatening to non-U.S. artists, despite the fact that the language had been in previous year's contracts but gone unnoticed.

SXSW, in crisis management mode after the debate over this language went public, reiterated their support of foreign artists and their stance on government issues. They claimed to have put this in the contracts as a reminder of the responsibility of the artists traveling to the U.S. and to protect SXSW in the event of "egregious acts" by foreign entertainers. Although it was too late at the time of the public backlash to go back and change all of the existing contracts, SXSW indicated that it would consider whether to modify the contract language in the future. Everything truly is negotiable.

NEGOTIATING HOTEL CONTRACTS

In addition to the general "rules" that apply to all contract negotiations, it is crucial to keep some specific rules in mind when dealing with hotel contracts:

- *Understand revenue streams.* Recognize that a meeting contract represents a comprehensive financial package for the hotel. Consider the hotel's overall financial gain, including room rates, food and beverage (F&B) income, and other revenue sources, and negotiate terms that benefit your organization accordingly.

- *Finalize details.* Avoid signing contracts that leave critical elements, such as room rates, for future negotiation. Future rates can typically be defined as a percentage of the current "rack" rate or a maximum increase over the current "group" rates. This principle should extend to rooms, catering services, A/V equipment, and other expenses.
- *Specify special room rates.* Clearly outline any special room rates, such as those for staff and speakers, and specify whether these are part of the complimentary room formula. Define the formula if necessary.
- *Specify when function space will be finalized.* Determine when the allocation of function and meeting rooms will be finalized. Although it is preferable to have specific rooms designated in the contract, consider a secondary negotiation position that ensures rooms are assigned at least 12 months in advance, depending on the timing of the first promotional materials. Additionally, establish conditions for changing assigned meeting rooms, requiring approval from the meeting organizer. Be open to alternative space or payment for the original space if the group size significantly decreases.
- *Get changes in writing.* Insist on your documenting any changes or amendments to the contract. Ensure that all modifications are clearly outlined in the original contract or an addendum. For the latter, make sure it references the primary agreement and supersedes any conflicting language. Additionally, ensure that all documents are signed by authorized representatives of the contracting parties.

NAMING NAMES

One of the frequently overlooked yet crucial aspects of a hotel contract is identifying the contracting parties. Although the meeting organizer's name is typically included (for independent planners, it is advisable to sign as an agent for the organizer or have an authorized representative of the organizer sign), the name of the hotel is almost always instances, listed merely as the name displayed on the hotel marquee, such as "Sheraton Boston."

However, the hotel's name is essentially a trade name, representing the identity under which the property's owner or management company conducts business. In today's diverse landscape, a given hotel may operate as a franchise within a national chain, managed by a company that might not be familiar to the planner. For instance, one of the nation's largest hotel management companies is Interstate Hotels & Resorts, Inc. The 300-plus hotels it manages operate under various chain names, including Marriott, Holiday Inn, Hilton,

Sheraton, and Radisson. Hence, if a contract with one of Interstate's properties simply identifies it as the "Gaithersburg (MD) Marriott," the planner might not realize that the actual contracting entity is Interstate Hotels & Resorts. This highlights the critical need for clarity and precision in specifying the parties in hotel contracts to avoid misunderstandings and ensure legal accountability.

Every contract should contain the following provision, usually as the introductory paragraph:

"This Agreement dated _____ is between (official legal name of entity), a (name of state) (corporation) (partnership) doing business as (name of hotel) and having its principal place of business at (address of contracting party, not hotel) and (name of meeting organizer), a (name of state) (corporation) (partnership) having its principal place of business at (address of meeting organizer)."

Sleeping rooms generate the major share of hotel revenue, so this is often their biggest concern.

Catered F&B are also important but only if it is the "right" kind of F&B function, since not all functions are equal in value. For example, a seated dinner for 100 people is worth more—in revenue and profit—than a coffee break or continental breakfast for the same number of people.

The type of entity organizing the meeting. Hotels know from experience that certain types of attendees are likely to spend more at hotel food outlets (restaurants, room service, etc.) than others, who may venture outside the property for meals at more expensive restaurants. From experience, a hotel is also able to estimate the number of attendees who will not show up or will check out early; both deprive the hotel of expected revenue.

To effectively negotiate with a hotel, meeting planners should grasp how a hotel assesses a meeting as a business opportunity, considering all the revenue streams it generates. Additionally, understanding the competitive landscape in which the hotel operates, including its strengths, weaknesses, and occupancy patterns, is essential.

- Meeting planners play a pivotal role in showcasing their event in the best possible light. This involves using comprehensive data and insights from prior meetings to support their approach. When a hotel is evaluating a meeting, particularly one it has not hosted, it may rely on its perception of the industry or profession associated with the organizer. Consequently, meeting organizers can counter any negative perceptions or emphasize positive aspects by providing the hotel with ample information about their **meeting history**. Sharing details about room block use, total expenditures on accommodations, F&B, equipment rentals, and additional services, such as recreational activities or in-room entertainment, can be highly beneficial; it enables the hotel to appreciate the full value of the meeting and facilitates a more constructive negotiation process.

Many seasoned hoteliers often encapsulate meeting negotiations with a straightforward principle: "dates, rates, and space—you can only have two" (refer to Exhibit 1). Following this principle, a planner might secure their preferred meeting dates and space but might need to be flexible on the rate. However, much more than just these factors are open to negotiation. Various terms can be negotiated, including provisions for earning complimentary rooms based on the number of reserved rooms, cutoff dates, rates applicable after the cutoff date, attrition and cancellation clauses, fees for meeting or exhibit space rental, complimentary suites, staff rates, limo service, A/V rates, VIP amenities, parking fees, and F&B arrangements. In essence, virtually *every* aspect of a hotel contract, and contracts with other vendors or suppliers, can be negotiated. This insight underscores the breadth of flexibility available, allowing meeting planners to tailor contracts to their specific needs and achieve the best possible terms.

Exhibit 1

Rates, Dates, and Space ...You Can Only Have Two

The Cocoa Society wants to meet in Portland, Oregon, ideally the week after Memorial Day. They would like to keep their rates under $200 a night. They need 20,000 sq. ft. of meeting space. In a negotiation, they may get options like the following.

Rates	Dates	Space
$199.00/night Run of House	June 1–4	12,000 sq. ft. at a rental of $2500/day total
$199.00/night Run of House	May 15–19	20,000 sq. ft. complimentary
$289.00/night Run of House	June 1–4	20,000 sq. ft. complimentary

The meeting planner should assess areas where flexibility is possible for the meeting organizer. Successful negotiations often entail concessions from both parties to achieve an equitable and acceptable agreement. For instance, when a planner recognizes that the space-to-room ratio for the meeting exceeds the standard, they can strengthen their position by adjusting the program format or removing 24-hour "holds" on meeting or function spaces, allowing the hotel to use them during unused hours. A planner who refuses to adapt may not secure the most favorable deal. Another effective strategy is to consider altering the arrival and departure dates to better align with the hotel's occupancy patterns. Shifting the schedule by a week or more can also yield cost savings, particularly if the preferred timing coincides with high demand for sleeping rooms.

To understand how a hotel approaches a meeting negotiation, the planner must first know about the hotel. Some of the necessary information is obvious:

- Location—is it near an airport, downtown, or close to a convention center?
- Type—is it a resort with a golf course, tennis court, and other amenities; a "convention" hotel with a great deal of meeting space; or a small venue with limited meeting facilities?

However, some crucial information is not immediately evident and might even vary with the time of year. For instance, understanding the balance between the hotel's transient business, originating from individual business travelers or tourists, and group bookings is vital. Within the group segment, it is valuable to discern the proportion of business from corporate, government, and association sources. Equally important is grasping the hotel's definition of "high" season, marked by peak room demand, and "low" season, when demand reaches its annual nadir. This information is pivotal in helping the planner gauge the hotel's position in the negotiation process and offers valuable insights for structuring a proposal that aligns with the hotel's requirements.

Seasonal variations can be influenced by external factors, such as events in the city. For example, a knowledgeable planner will be aware that securing rooms in New Orleans during Mardi Gras or the annual Jazz Fest (late April and early May) can be challenging due to hotels capitalizing on individual tourist rates over group rates. Similarly, numerous hotels in Ft. Lauderdale, Florida, experience high occupancy rates during spring break.

New Orleans during Mardi Gras is a very busy time for the city

Understanding the typical arrival and departure patterns of a hotel's guests is equally essential for planners. For instance, securing bookings for weekend meetings at a Las Vegas hotel can be challenging, as the city tends to attract a large influx of individual visitors seeking weekend getaways. Conversely, a hotel catering predominantly to individual business guests may have greater availability on Friday and Saturday nights, when they are less frequent. National surveys have indicated that, for most hotels, occupancy rates tend to be at their lowest on Sunday evenings and peak on Wednesdays.

Although hotels derive revenue from various sources and have increasingly sophisticated methods for analyzing these "profit centers," the primary income source remains sleeping rooms; one industry research report estimates that this is over 67% of a hotel's total revenue.

Hotels establish their sleeping room rates, particularly the published or **rack rates**, through several approaches. Initially, hotels aim to attain a satisfactory return on their investment. However, given that nearly 50% of all rooms are sold at lower rates, actual rates can vary considerably based on various supply and demand factors, including seasonal fluctuations.

Many hotels have adopted the concept of **yield management**, also known as "revenue management," which was originally pioneered by the airline industry. They adjust their rates almost daily, depending on the current and anticipated demand for rooms at specific times. However, this approach may have some adverse effects on meeting planners. For instance, a planner who books a meeting 15–18 months in advance may discover that as the meeting date approaches, the hotel's room use is lower than expected. To generate additional revenue, the hotel may promote special pricing that turns out to be lower than what was initially offered to the planner. To mitigate this, including a contractual provision prohibiting this practice (referred to as a "lowest rate clause")—although many hotels may be unwilling to agree to it—or at least providing the planner with credit for its room block on rooms booked at these reduced prices can help offset the impact of yield management practices.

CONTRACTS

Contracts for meetings, conventions, trade shows, and the associated services provided often contain self-serving statements, lack specificity, and fail to accurately reflect the full negotiations. This is understandable, given that neither meeting planners nor hotel sales representatives typically receive training in the legal aspects governing these agreements.

By definition, a contract represents an agreement between two parties that outlines their intentions to undertake or refrain from certain actions. For instance, in its simplest form, a meetings contract delineates that the organizer commits to using a specified number of rooms and services, and the hotel undertakes to furnish these as outlined.

A contract need not necessarily be called a "contract"; it can also be referred to as an "agreement," a "letter of agreement," a "memorandum of understanding," and sometimes a "letter of intent" or "proposal." The nomenclature is not the critical factor; its substance is. For instance, if a document labeled a proposal sets out the details of a meeting and incorporates the essential legal elements of a contract, it becomes legally binding once both parties have signed it. Therefore, it is essential not to be misled by the title at the top.

The essential elements of a contract are the following:

- an **offer** by one party.
- **acceptance** of the offer as presented by another party. This is typically done by signing the contract.
- **consideration** (i.e., the price negotiated and paid for the agreement). Although consideration is usually expressed in monetary terms, it need

not be—for example, mutual promises are often treated as consideration in a valid contract.
- **capacity.** The parties must have legal capacity to enter into the contract. This includes both mental capacity (e.g., they must not be mentally incapacitated) and authority.
- **legal subject**. The contract must be for a legal subject. So, a contract between parties that has all of the other legal components but is for illegal drugs would not be valid.

Offers can be terminated prior to acceptance in one of several ways:

- at the expiration of a specified time (e.g., "This offer is only good for 24 hours." After 24 hours, the other party cannot accept it because it expired.).
- at the expiration of a reasonable time period.
- on specific revocation by the offeror. In this case, however, the revocation must be communicated to the offeree to be effective.

Rejecting an offer by the offeree or the presentation of a counteroffer effectively terminates the original offer. However, a mere request for additional information about the offer does not constitute rejection. If an individual responds to an offer by stating, "I accept, with the following addition," this is not a true acceptance but rather a counteroffer. The original offeror must then evaluate this counteroffer and decide whether to accept or reject it.

There are many good reasons to put contracts in writing, and sometimes they are legally required to be in writing

Frequently, a meeting contract proposal from a hotel will include a specified termination period. These "offers" are typically framed with terms such as "tentative first option" or similar wording. As the planner does not make any payment or commitment for this "option," it essentially amounts to a contract offer, which the planner must explicitly accept. The hotel is under no legal obligation to keep the option or offer open for the stated time period.

The hotel, venue, or vendor is typically the offeror. After some initial negotiations, it usually proposes a written agreement to the planner, who assumes the role of the offeree, although a counteroffer is frequently introduced.

For an offer to be considered accepted, the acceptance must be clear and must mirror the terms of the offer precisely. Any deviation from the offer's terms constitutes a counteroffer, effectively nullifying the original offer. This switch in roles between offeror and offeree requires that the counteroffer be accepted by the original offeror for a valid contract to be established.

Acceptance must be communicated to the offeror using the same medium that the offeror employed. In simpler terms, if the offer was made in writing, the acceptance must also be in writing. Mere silence on the part of the offeree can never be interpreted as acceptance, and an offeror cannot impose an agreement on the other party by stipulating that the contract will be assumed if no response is received by a specified date.

As mentioned, consideration represents the price negotiated and paid for the agreement. Although it typically involves monetary compensation for the other party's commitment to providing specific services—such as payment to a hotel for sleeping rooms, meeting space, and F&B services—it can also involve exchanging mutual promises, as in a barter arrangement.

Consideration, in legal terms, must be deemed "sufficient" by the law, not solely from a monetary perspective but based on whether the act or reciprocal promises result in either a benefit to the promisor or a detriment to the promisee. The fairness of the agreed-upon exchange holds no legal relevance. Therefore, the law does not concern itself with whether one party "overpaid" for what it received. An affirmative promise or payment of money is not the sole form of consideration; for example, forbearance, which means refraining from doing something that someone is legally entitled to do, can also constitute consideration.

Both promises within a contract must be legally enforceable to establish valid *consideration*. For instance, a promise to engage in an illegal act does not qualify as *consideration*, as the law will not compel anyone to commit an unlawful act.

In contract law, a party must possess the mental *capacity* to comprehend the implications of entering into the agreement and the terms to which they are consenting. Mental incapacity can result from factors such as mental illness drug use. Additionally, society establishes a minimum age requirement, rendering minors incapable of contracting.

Even if all of the other components of a contract are present, the law will not enforce a contract if the subject of that contract is illegal.

STATUTE OF FRAUDS

Although a contract does not necessarily require a written form to be legally enforceable, law students are taught that having a written document is preferable, as it minimizes the chances of misunderstandings regarding the terms of the agreement. However, certain contracts must adhere to what is known as the "Statute of Frauds" and be in writing to be legally binding. This statute was initially enacted in England in 1677 and has, in various forms, become a fundamental component of the laws in nearly every U.S. state, with the exception of Louisiana, which follows the French Napoleonic code.

Contracts under the Statute of Frauds include agreements for the sale or lease of real estate and those not to be performed within 1 year from the date of agreement. The latter category encompasses contracts for meetings and other events scheduled far in the future. The former category could also include a meeting contract because it might be interpreted as a "lease" of hotel space. These contracts are required to be in writing because they are considered more substantial documents compared to "ordinary" agreements. Nonetheless, it is strongly advised for planners to document all contracts in writing to mitigate the risk of misunderstandings.

A valid written contract should include the identification of the involved parties, a clear description or recitation of the subject matter and terms of the agreement, and a statement regarding the consideration. If the latter may not be readily apparent, the contract often states that it is entered into for "good and valuable consideration, the receipt and sufficiency of which are acknowledged by the parties."

When a contract is in writing, it is typically subject to the "**parol evidence**" or "four-corners" rule of interpretation: When it is intended to serve as the comprehensive and definitive expression of the rights and obligations of the parties, any evidence of prior oral or written negotiations or contemporaneous oral agreements cannot be considered by a court tasked with interpreting it. Many contracts incorporate what is commonly referred to as an "entire agreement" clause, explicitly stating that the written document constitutes the entire agreement between the parties, superseding all previous oral or written negotiations or agreements.

PAROL EVIDENCE

Parol evidence, or evidence of oral agreements, can be admitted in limited circumstances, particularly when the plain meaning of words in the written document is in question. Courts generally interpret a contract most favorably for the party who did not prepare the written document. For conflict between printed and handwritten words or phrases, the handwritten portion takes precedence.

Many contracts, particularly meeting contracts, often include addenda prepared concurrently with or after the signing. When the terms of an addendum differ from those in the main contract, the addendum typically takes precedence. However, it is advisable, when using an addendum, to explicitly state that, in the event of any discrepancies, the addendum will prevail.

KEY HOTEL GROUP MEETING CONTRACT CLAUSES

Provisions related to attrition, cancellation, and force majeure in a hotel contract can often be perplexing. If not carefully drafted, they can lead to various complications (and substantial expenses) if a meeting organizer fails to meet room block requirements or decides to make changes for any reason. For further insights into these and other crucial clauses in hotel group meeting contracts, you can refer to the Events Industry Council's Accepted Practices Exchange (https://insights.eventscouncil.org/Portals/0/APEX_Contracts.pdf).

ATTRITION

Attrition clauses, sometimes referred to as "*performance clauses*," outline the payment of damages to the hotel when a meeting organizer falls short of using the room block specified in the contract. Most hotels view the room block as a commitment to fulfill the specified number of room nights. However, in at least one case, a court determined that the room block did not represent a commitment, influenced, in part, by contract language indicating that room reservations would be made by individual attendees rather than by the meeting organizer.

A well-crafted attrition provision should grant the organizing entity the flexibility to reduce the room block by a predetermined amount (slippage)—for example, 10–20%—up to a specified time before the meeting, without incurring damages. Subsequently, damages should only be applicable if the organizer fails to either pay for or occupy the remaining percentage—(e.g., 85–90%) of its adjusted room block. **Pickup**, which encompasses all the room nights used or paid for by the meeting organizer or its attendees, can be measured on either a cumulative room night basis or a night-by-night basis, leading to significantly different financial implications.

As hotels occasionally provide rates to the general public as part of special promotional packages that are lower than those offered to meeting attendees, it becomes crucial to measure meeting room pickup based on the total attendance, regardless of the rate paid. This may require some additional effort from both the hotel and the meeting organizer. However, the outcome could lead to cost savings for the organization, particularly if meeting attendance falls short of expectations. For instance, the contract might incorporate language similar to the following:

> Group shall receive credit for all rooms used by attendees, regardless of the rate paid or the method of booking. Hotel shall cooperate with Group in identifying these attendees and shall charge no fee for assisting Group.

Using this language, an organization would submit its meeting registration list to the hotel and request that the hotel cross-reference the list with the guests in house. An alternative approach, often rejected by many hotels, involves both the hotel and the group sitting down with the registration list to jointly review the hotel's in-house guest list for matching.

Damages from a failure to meet a room block commitment should be clearly specified in dollars rather than based on a percentage of an ambiguous figure, such as "anticipated room revenue." The latter approach may allow the hotel to incorporate "ancillary revenue," which includes estimated spending on items such as telephone calls and in-room movies. The specified damages should be calculated based on the hotel's lost profit, not lost revenue. For instance, within the sleeping rooms segment, the average industry profit margin stands at approximately 75% (slightly higher for resorts and slightly lower for limited-service properties). Therefore, the attrition fee per room should not exceed 75% of the group's single room rate. The industry standard for catered F&B profit is about 35%, with slight variations by property type.

As attrition damages are considered a form of liquidated damages, the hotel is typically not required to mitigate these damages by providing credit for any unused sleeping rooms that can be resold. If the meeting organizer seeks credit for resold rooms, a specific contract clause must impose a clear obligation on the hotel to make efforts to resell the rooms and credit the proceeds against the group's attrition damages (See Exhibit 2).

Exhibit 2

Calculating Attrition Damages

A contract between The Cocoa Society and the Fountain Hotel initially includes the following attrition clause (it is not favorable to the Group):

Clause 1. This Agreement is therefore based on Group's use of 200 total room nights. Group agrees that if Group uses less than the room block established in this agreement, Hotel will be harmed. Hotel will allow Group 10% room block shrinkage without any liquidated damage payment. For shrinkage over and above this allowance, the Hotel will require payment from Group for each unused room night at the confirmed group average rate plus applicable tax for Group's committed room block. This payment will not be in effect with respect to any unused room nights within your committed block for any night during your stay in which all of the available rooms in the Hotel are sold.

After modification by The Cocoa Society, the clause reads as follows:

Clause 2. This Agreement is therefore based on Group's use of 200 total room nights. Group agrees that if Group uses less than the room block established in this agreement, Hotel ~~will~~ may be harmed. Hotel will allow Group ~~10%~~ 20% room block shrinkage without any liquidated damage payment. For shrinkage over and above this allowance, the Hotel will require payment from Group for each unused room night at 75% (profit margin) of the confirmed group ~~average~~ Run of House rate plus applicable tax for your committed room block.

~~This payment will not be in effect with respect to any unused room nights within your committed block for any night during your stay in which all of the available rooms in the Hotel are sold.~~ <u>Group will receive credit against attrition damages for all room nights Hotel is able to resell. The parties understand the Hotel will resell Group rooms only after the rest of its inventory has been sold.</u>

To see how significant a few changes to an attrition clause can be in terms of financial damages, compare the calculations with Clause 1 and Clause 2. Examples assume that the Group picked up 150 room nights.

Clause 1.

200 – 150 room nights = 50 room nights unsold
Shrinkage (200 × 10%) = 20 room nights shrinkage
50 room nights unsold – 20 room nights shrinkage = 30 room nights for attrition damages
30 room nights × $235/night = US **$7,050** attrition damages

Clause 2.

200 – 150 room nights = 50 room nights unsold
Shrinkage (200 × 20%) = 40 room nights shrinkage
50 room nights unsold – 40 room nights shrinkage = 10 room nights for attrition damages
10 room nights × ($200/night × 75% profit margin) = US **$1,500** attrition damages

Attrition clauses are often found in the section of a contract that discusses meeting room rental fees. Typically, the contract states that these fees will be applied on a sliding scale if the room block is not fully occupied. If this clause is mentioned in conjunction with meeting room rental, it should not be duplicated elsewhere in the contract, resulting in a double charge. Language should be included to clarify that the meeting room rental fee is the sole charge to be imposed if the room block is not fully used.

CANCELLATION

The cancellation provision outlines damages that may be incurred if the meeting is canceled for reasons not covered by the force majeure provision. Frequently, in a hotel-provided agreement, this is one sided, offering damages to the hotel in case the meeting organizer cancels. A well-drafted agreement should specify damages if either party cancels without a valid reason. However, as mentioned, some contract drafters believe that damages should not be specified for a hotel cancellation, as it could give the hotel an amount to use as a buyout option. An alternative approach is to outline what the group's damages will be if the hotel cancels. This is referred to as an "actual damages clause" (as opposed to liquidated damages, discussed later). It includes items such as increased F&B costs or rooms at an alternative hotel, additional marketing materials, and expenses for site inspection trips to find a new meeting venue. Although it may seem counterintuitive for a hotel to cancel a meeting, it does occur (see Case 2).

The meeting organizer should not possess the unilateral right to cancel a contract solely to book the meeting in another hotel or city, nor should the hotel be permitted to cancel to make way for another, more lucrative event.

Cancellation damages imposed by the group are often outlined on a sliding scale, with higher damages closer to the meeting date. These damages should be framed as "liquidated damages" or a cancellation fee, rather than as a penalty, as contract law typically does not recognize penalty provisions. Like damages specified in an attrition clause, they should be expressed in dollar amounts rather than room revenue (to avoid sales tax implications) and only be payable if the hotel is unable to resell the space.

CASE 2. SYLVANIA V. BOCA RATON RESORT & CLUB

Osram Sylvania, Inc. signed a contract with the Boca Raton Resort & Club for a national sales meeting to take place in October 2007. Sylvania had a long history with the hotel, having held 17 meetings at the hotel since 1984. Imagine Sylvania's surprise when, in 2007, the hotel cancelled the contract for the 2007 national sales meeting that had been negotiated and signed in 2004! Because the contract was signed during a recession period for the U.S., the rates Sylvania was able to negotiate in 2004 may have been more favorable than the market rates in 2007. This is why negotiating contract clauses is so important - you may think the hotel will never cancel (it is unusual), especially if you are a long-standing client, but it does happen. Sylvania never got to meet at the Boca Raton Resort & Club in 2007, but through a settlement, they did return in 2008.

Bassett, M. (2007, August 1). The seller's market strikes again. *MeetingsNet*. Retrieved from http://www.meetingsnet.com/checklists/sellers-market-strikes-again

MeetingsNet. (2007, September 21). OSI Settles Meeting Flap. *Corporate Meetings & Incentives*. Retrieved from http://www.meetingsnet.com/corporate-meetings/osi-settles-meeting-flap

FORCE MAJEURE

Sometimes referred to as an "**Impossibility**" or "**Act of God**" clause, this provision allows either party to terminate the contract without incurring damages if the fulfillment of the obligations outlined are made illegal, impossible, or, depending on the clause's wording, impracticable due to events beyond the control of either party. Such events typically include labor strikes, severe weather conditions, and transportation disruptions. Commonly, the clause states that performance will be excused when circumstances beyond the control of the parties render the meeting "illegal or impossible." The provision may also employ the term "impracticable," signifying that, although it may not be absolutely impossible, it is functionally unfeasible.

A meeting organizer has several reasons to desire the ability to terminate a contract without incurring damages, including changes in hotel ownership, management, or brand affiliation; the event's size outgrowing the hotel's capacity; fluctuations in the hotel's quality rating, as measured by organizations such as the American Automobile Association; or other circumstances that make it unsuitable or unfeasible. The language in the termination clause should be broad enough to encompass situations where objectionable policies

Force majeure incidents are beyond the control of the parties to the contract

or laws render the choice of location inappropriate. For instance, an organizing entity canceled a major shooting sports trade show after the city hosting it filed lawsuits against gun manufacturers, which happened to be the show's primary exhibitors.

Due to the variations in contracts offered by hotels and the ease with which even experienced planners can overlook crucial elements in a contract, many meeting organizers are now crafting their own standard contracts. Although some organizers might be uncertain about the cost of having a competent attorney draft such a document, these expenses are relatively minimal when compared to the time (and thus the expenses) incurred in reviewing each contract proposed by a hotel, whether that is by an attorney or a meeting planner or another staff member.

Creating their own contract allows organizers to ensure their specific needs are met and reduces the likelihood of legal issues arising from misunderstandings regarding the agreement's terms.

CASE STUDY

In January 2019, the U.S. federal government shut down due to failure to come up with a federal budget. The American Astronomical Society was not a government entity, but some of its annual meeting attendees were. Out of 3,200 attendees, the association expected to lose 300–450 furloughed government workers. With a loss of 10–15% of its attendees, the conference could likely go on, so a complete termination would not be necessary. Whether the organization considered language addressing a *partial* force majeure that excused performance damages in a situation beyond their control would be helpful in this kind of situation.

DISPUTE RESOLUTION

No matter how meticulously a contract is drafted, disputes may still arise. These disputes can stem from disagreements between parties regarding their respective rights and obligations or when one party fails to meet its commitments. Such conflicts typically do not revolve around groundbreaking legal issues but rather require assessing facts and interpreting contract terms. When such differences surface, parties often prefer to resolve them privately and informally, in a businesslike manner that fosters ongoing business relationships.

However, in some instances, private resolution is unattainable. The "aggrieved" party is left with three options: relinquish the prospect of a resolution and walk away from the issue, initiate legal proceedings and file a lawsuit, or explore alternative dispute resolution methods.

Turning to the court system can be expensive and time consuming. Overcrowded court dockets may lead to months or even years of delays before a decision. Attorney fees can accumulate rapidly, especially if extensive pretrial procedures are necessary. Depending on the court's location, one or both parties may incur additional expenses for travel. Furthermore, as court cases are public records, adverse publicity is possible.

"Arbitration" is increasingly gaining favor as an alternative method for resolving disputes: One or more arbitrators are selected to hear each party's arguments and render a decision. Under rules administered by the American Arbitration Association, arbitration is designed for swift, practical, and cost-effective resolutions and follows a structured process guided by procedural rules and legal standards of conduct. Although either party can choose to have legal representation, it typically involves minimal pretrial procedures. When arbitration is designated as the dispute resolution mechanism in the contract, the parties generally agree that the outcomes are binding, meaning they cannot be appealed to a court of law. The contract should also specify the location. As arbitration is typically not public record, the entire process can remain confidential.

If the parties opt for arbitration to resolve disputes, this decision should be made proactively, before any disagreements emerge. The contract should include language outlining the arbitration option. If it is not selected, the contract should clearly state which state's law (e.g., where the meeting took place or where the meeting organizer is based) will be applied.

In the American legal system, each party involved in a court case or arbitration proceeding is generally responsible for covering its own attorney's fees, unless the agreement explicitly stipulates that the winner has the right to recover its attorneys' fees and costs from the loser.

Last, a well-crafted contract should specify the damages to be awarded in case of a breach by either party. This approach removes the decision-making burden from a judge or arbitrator, leaving the dispute resolver only to determine whether a breach occurred. Damages are usually expressed as "liquidated damages," which means they are predetermined and agreed upon in advance as the consequence of a breach. Courts typically do not enforce contract provisions that impose a "penalty" for a breach, so it is advisable to avoid using that term. For instance, during a conference held at a Las Vegas hotel, the meeting organizer failed to settle the $57,000 master bill. After multiple unsuccessful attempts to secure payment, the hotel contemplated billing individual attendees for their proportionate share of the master bill. This decision led to considerable dissatisfaction among the attendees and garnered negative media attention. The hotel reversed its stance and returned to pursuing payment from the meeting organizer.

CRISIS PREPAREDNESS AND MANAGEMENT

WHAT IS RISK? CRISIS PREPAREDNESS?

All meetings inherently involve an element of **risk**, which can be defined as the potential for experiencing loss or harm. *Risk management* is the process of evaluating, analyzing, and mitigating these risks, aiming to reduce the likelihood of adverse events. Realized risks, those that materialize, are categorized based on their scope and impact, which can range from minor incidents to emergencies, crises, or even disasters; they may manifest as minor mishaps within the intricate process of planning and managing events.

For instance, envision an outdoor exhibition where torrential rains unexpectedly occur during setup, rendering it impossible to complete the preparations or hold the exhibition. Inclement weather serves as a prime example of a risk. Depending on the severity, it could lead to a business incident, such as a delayed opening, escalate to an emergency if lightning strikes a would-be exhibitor, or even spiral into a full-blown crisis if the lightning ignites exhibitor materials, resulting in an uncontrollable fire. Now, consider a scenario in which a prudent exhibition planner has arranged for rented tents to shelter exhibits, allowing the show to proceed despite adverse weather conditions. This demonstrates an essential facet of crisis preparedness.

CASE STUDY

In October 2017, during the Route 91 outdoor music festival in Las Vegas, a tragic incident unfolded. Stephen Paddock, who had checked into the Mandalay Bay Resort and Casino, broke a window in his hotel room and opened fire on attendees, comprising around 22,000 people. This horrifying act resulted killed 59 people and injured approximately 500. Despite exhaustive investigations, no clear motive was determined for his actions. In the aftermath of this devastating incident, extensive efforts were made to understand how he managed to bring a large number of weapons into his hotel room and to enhance security measures for outdoor events.

Many lessons can be learned from a tragic event, such as the Route 91 Harvest Festival shooting

CRISIS MANAGEMENT

Once the meeting professional has assessed and analyzed risks, they will have determined which crises have (a) the highest probability of occurring or (b) the greatest impact if they do occur. This is when crisis preparedness and management kicks in. Crisis management can be broken down into four stages:

1. mitigation,
2. preparedness,
3. response, and
4. recovery.

The outdoor exhibition example can be used to illustrate the steps of emergency management.

Mitigation

Conducting a risk assessment and analysis also aids the planner in determining which mitigation measures should be employed. Here are examples of some common mitigation measures:

- contracts: Signed prior to the meeting or event, contracts mitigate risk by narrowing or shifting liability to the responsible party for injuries or damages or specifying the monetary damage fees (e.g., attrition or cancellation) for contract underperformance.
- insurance: This shifts some of the financial liability to the insurance company. By paying a premium, the meeting/event organizer ensures that the insurance company will cover claims for loss or damage within the policy's defined limits.
- security: Employing security guards to provide physical security and/or monitor a property is a means of mitigating the risk of injury or loss.

In our rain example, during the mitigation stage, the planner would identify strategies for risk reduction, with a focus on decreasing the probability of rain (despite recognizing the challenges of controlling the weather!). Simultaneously, the planner would aim to mitigate the crisis by minimizing the consequences if it were to rain. Recognizing the latter aspect as more manageable, the planner might have arranged for a tent rental company to be on standby (or proactively rented tents if budget constraints allowed), secured a backup indoor venue through contractual agreements, and obtained event cancellation insurance as a safeguard.

Preparedness

In the preparedness stage, the planner initiates various activities, including staff training, conducting emergency drills, and preparing essential documentation, such as a crisis plan and an incident report form. The individuals involved—such as meeting organizer staff, facility staff, and vendor staff—are allocated specific roles that typically involve monitoring emergency indicators and collecting information that would be crucial in a crisis. This information may include a list of contact details for both staff and attendees.

In our rain example, the *preparedness* stage would entail designating someone to closely monitor weather reports in the days leading up to the exhibition.

Response

If a crisis adversely impacts a meeting or event, despite meticulous planning, it is essential for the event professional to have an emergency response team ready to take action. The response required depends on the nature of the crisis. It could be as straightforward as sending a notice to participants regarding a change in the program or as complex as coordinating an evacuation and providing first aid to the injured. The complexity of the response should align with the crisis.

Determining *when* and *how* to respond can be challenging. For instance, if the weather forecast, two days before the event, indicates a 60% chance of rain on the date, should the planner activate the rain plan? Does this involve securing tents or merely informing exhibitors about the potential change in plans? Alternatively, should the planner wait until the morning of the exhibition to make a decision, and would this provide sufficient time to implement the rain plan? The answers hinge on factors such as the event's size, scope, and specifics of the contingency plan.

Recovery

Recovery also varies depending on the nature of the crisis. In our ongoing example with the rain, if the inclement weather is so severe that the exhibition must be canceled, the recovery process would encompass several facets. This includes insurance claims to compensate for the losses incurred by the organizer and proactive actions they took to mitigate any negative publicity.

A crisis often results in various forms of loss or harm, potentially causing damage to property, harm to individuals, or impacting more intangible elements, such as the reputation of the organizer or planner. For the outdoor exhibition, the recovery phase might involve an insurance claim or refunding fees to exhibitors or attendees who were unable to participate. However, for a major disaster or crisis, the recovery stage can be substantially more serious and protracted.

AMERICANS WITH DISABILITIES ACT

The U.S. **Americans with Disabilities Act** (ADA) of 1990 makes it illegal to discriminate against individuals with disabilities or fail to provide them with "reasonable accommodation." ADA places the responsibility on the owners and operators of public accommodations, such as hotels, restaurants, convention centers, retail stores, zoos, and parks, to ensure equal enjoyment for individuals with disabilities.

A **disability**, according to ADA, is defined as "a physical or mental impairment that substantially limits a major life activity of an individual." **Major life activities** encompassed tasks such as performing manual tasks, walking, seeing, hearing, speaking, breathing, learning, and working. The ADA Amendment Act of 2008 modified and broadened these definitions, as discussed later.

The ADA covers a wide range of disabilities, including those affecting mobility, hearing, or vision, as well as "invisible disabilities," such as multiple sclerosis, epilepsy, or other conditions that may not be immediately apparent to others.

Title III of the ADA, which applies to places of public accommodation, such as hotels, restaurants, convention centers, and retail stores, requires reasonable accommodations for individuals with disabilities unless it imposes an undue hardship. The ADA Technical Assistance Manual and case law provide guidance on what qualifies as undue hardship (that an accommodation, such as sign language interpreters or large-print materials, might be costly does not automatically qualify).

The following is the stated purpose of ADA:

1. to provide a clear and comprehensive national mandate for the elimination of discrimination against individuals with disabilities;
2. to provide clear, strong, consistent, enforceable standards addressing discrimination against individuals with disabilities;
3. to ensure that the federal government plays a central role in enforcing the standards on behalf of individuals with disabilities; and
4. to invoke the sweep of congressional authority, including the power to enforce the Fourteenth Amendment and to regulate commerce, to address the major areas of discrimination faced day-to-day by people with disabilities.

For more information on the Americans with Disabilities Act, see the U.S. government's ADA website, www.ada.gov.

The ADA Amendment Act of 2008, which came into effect on January 1, 2009, was introduced because the U.S. Justice Department recognized that the ADA was sometimes being used to exclude individuals rather than include them.

Individuals might be denied accommodation based on the argument that their disability was not explicitly listed. However, ADAAA changed this approach. It provides a nonexhaustive list of major life activities and major bodily functions that qualify as disabilities and now encourages a broad and inclusive interpretation rather than a narrow one, as was the case under the original ADA. This expanded scope means that certain issues, such as food allergies and dietary restrictions, are now included. (See Case 3.)

CASE 3

J.D. is a child who went on a school trip to Colonial Williamsburg. While there, the group went to a restaurant for a meal. J.D. has a gluten sensitivity and brought his own special meal to ensure that he did not get sick from eating restaurant food with gluten in it. The restaurant's policy did not allow people to bring in outside food, and J.D. was told he would have to eat his special food outside. J.D.'s family sued for discrimination under ADA. The lower court, the federal district court, sided with Colonial Williamsburg. The appeals court found that because J.D. had reactions to restaurant food that was supposed to be safe before, a jury might agree that he must bring his own food and reversed to allow J.D. to go back and try to prove his ADA claim. Imagine if J.D. were a meeting attendee instead of a restaurant guest?

Title III of ADA covers public accommodations, which applies to meeting planners and organizers as well as facilities and vendors. Organizers must (a) determine the extent to which attendees have disabilities and (b) make reasonable efforts to accommodate their special needs at no cost to them. As a result, we now see sections on registration forms asking if the attendee has any special needs, such as a hearing impairment. The planner would have to provide a sign language interpreter, large-print materials, or another accommodation that allows them to fully participate in the meeting to the extent possible. Readers may have seen these interpreters in class or during important speeches. For those with vision impairment, the planner may have to provide documents with extralarge type or Braille. Failure to accommodate attendees with disabilities can result in legal action and fines. The accommodations requirement also applies to employees.

The planner must be aware of the ramifications of ADA and be sure that all facilities, activities, and programs meet its guidelines. Be aware, however, that this act only applies to U.S. events and meetings. Accessibility and accommodation vary significantly from country to country.

INTELLECTUAL PROPERTY

Three main areas of intellectual property exist: **patents**, **trademarks**, and copyrights.

PATENTS

Patents represent property rights for inventions, providing inventors with a means to safeguard their creations for a specific duration, and come in three primary types:

Utility—cover new and useful processes, machines, articles of manufacture, compositions of matter, or any innovative improvements thereof.

Design—pertain to new, original, and ornamental designs for articles of manufacture.

Plant—apply to the invention or discovery of a distinct and new variety of plant.

One particular area of intellectual property that meeting planners should be aware of is music copyright and licensing

Patents are not widely discussed in the meetings industry, although a claim was once made by a company that they had invented the online registration process. It sent demands for money to associations who were using online registration for their meetings. ASAE and the Center for Association Leadership got involved, and the issue ultimately went away.

CHAPTER 10 LEGAL ISSUES IN THE MEETINGS, EVENTS, EXHIBITIONS, AND CONVENTIONS (MEEC) INDUSTRY

TRADEMARKS

Trademarks (or service marks) are identifiable elements, such as words, names, symbols, or devices, associated with goods or services. They signify the source of goods and distinguish them from others in the market. For instance, Campbell's Soup® labels its cans with its name, ensuring consumers recognize its product. Similarly, Ritz-Carlton® affixes its name to its hotels, indicating the brand and expected quality. For more information, refer to the U.S. Patent & Trademark Office website (www.uspto.gov).

COPYRIGHTS

Copyright safeguards "original works of authorship," encompassing literary, dramatic, musical, artistic, and certain other intellectual creations, whether published or not. In the meetings industry, copyright applies to various aspects, such as event proposals, music, photographs, and videos. Copyright protection becomes effective when the work is "fixed in a durable medium." For example, a singer might compose an original song during a performance, but it is only copyrightable once the lyrics are transcribed or the music recorded. To find comprehensive information on copyrights, visit the U.S. government's copyright website, www.copyright.gov.

Music Copyright

Many meetings and trade shows incorporate musical elements, whether performed live or prerecorded. Music can serve as background ambiance, as at a cocktail reception, or take center stage, such as during a dinner dance or concert. In trade shows, both individual exhibitors and the organizing body may use music.

According to the federal copyright act, when music is played, it is considered a "performance." Many court rulings have established that the entity organizing the event is seen as controlling this "performance," even if that control merely involves hiring an orchestra without specifying the playlist. The sole recognized exception to this rule is for music played via a single receiver (radio or TV) typically found in homes.

Today, multiple **performing rights organizations** (PROs) act as intermediaries to collect royalties for the public performance of copyrighted music on behalf of artists, authors, composers, and publishers within their membership. Notable PROs include the American Society of Composers, Authors and Publishers

(**ASCAP**), Broadcast Music, Inc. (**BMI**), SESAC, SoundExchange, and Global Music Rights. These organizations exist to obtain licensing fees from entities that "perform" copyrighted music, including radio stations, retail establishments, hotels, and organizations involved in planning meetings, conventions, and trade shows. ASCAP, BMI, and SESAC were the initial PROs, and a U.S. Supreme Court decision in 1979 granted them a special, limited exemption from standard antitrust laws that has allowed them to establish "blanket" licensing agreements for various industries that use live or recorded music. In the late 1980s, after negotiations with major meeting industry organizations, such as the International Association of Exhibits and Events and the American Society of Association Executives, both ASCAP and BMI developed special licensing agreements and fee structures tailored for meetings, conventions, trade shows, and expositions that replaced earlier arrangements where hotels paid licensing fees for meetings held on their premises by others. Although these negotiated agreements were technically set to expire at the end of 1994, ASCAP and BMI have extended them annually, typically with slight increases in licensing fees. Due to court decrees, ASCAP and BMI cannot offer special agreements to individual meetings. Consequently, the agreements are uniform for all meetings. Failing to sign these agreements with *both* organizations could expose a meeting or trade show organizer to costly and embarrassing legal action for copyright infringement.

According to copyright law, an organization cannot fulfill its obligation by mandating that musicians performing the music or the booking agency or hotel that arranged for the musicians obtain ASCAP and BMI licenses. Instead, it is the responsibility of the entity organizing the event to secure the necessary licenses.

CASE 4. TRADEMARK INFRINGEMENT AT AN EXHIBITION

Jibbitz, Inc., the official maker of snap-on accessories for Crocs (shoes), attended the World Shoe Association trade show as an exhibitor. At the trade show, the Jibbitz exhibit staff noticed another exhibitor promoting the sale of snap-on accessories for Crocs. Because Jibbitz (as a wholly owned subsidiary of Crocs, Inc.) was the only official maker of these accessories, it filed a copyright and trademark infringement lawsuit against the other exhibitor. Jibbitz was awarded $56 million in damages.

https://www.law360.com/articles/56002/crocs-awarded-56m-in-suit-over-shoe-charms

Speaker/Entertainment Copyright

An organization will often want to make audio or video recordings of certain speakers or programs at its meeting, to sell copies to those who could not attend or for archival purposes.

Speakers or program participants have a common law copyright interest in their presentations, and the law prohibits the organization from selling audio or video copies without obtaining the written permission of the presenter. Many professional speakers who also market books or recordings of their presentations frequently refuse to provide consent to be recorded.

Permission can be obtained by having each speaker whose session is to be recorded sign a copyright waiver, a simple document acknowledging that the session is going to be recorded and giving the organizing entity permission to sell the recordings made of it. If the recording is to be done by a commercial A/V company, a sample waiver form can usually be obtained from that company, or the sample form following this summary can be used.

LABOR ISSUES

Preparation for on-site work at meetings and trade shows often involves long hours and temporary or part-time personnel for administrative or other support. It is, therefore, crucial for organizations to understand how federal employment law requirements impact these situations.

The U.S. Federal Fair Labor Standards Act (FLSA), enacted in 1938, is often recognized for setting a minimum wage for a significant portion of the workforce. However, another important aspect of FLSA, and one that is frequently misunderstood, mandates that all workers covered by its minimum wage provisions must receive overtime pay at a rate of 1.5 times their "regular" rate of pay *unless* they fall under specific exemptions outlined in the statute.

Numerous common misconceptions exist among employers regarding FLSA's overtime provisions, including the following:

- Only hourly employees (and not those paid a regular salary) are eligible for overtime.
- Overtime pay can be avoided by giving compensatory time off (comp time) instead.
- Overtime need only be paid to those who receive advance approval to work more than 40 hours in a week.

Over the years, Department of Labor regulations and court decisions have clarified that overtime pay cannot be circumvented by offering comp time in a different workweek, even with the employee's consent. According to the Department of Labor, comp time is only legally permissible if it is provided in the same week or within the same pay period and sufficient to offset the overtime worked, typically at the time-and-a-half rate.

The use of comp time is a frequent violation of FLSA overtime pay requirements. This is because many employees, especially those on salary, may prefer to have an extra day off for various personal reasons, such as medical appointments, holiday preparations, or simply "attitude adjustment." Comp time is also often provided, albeit unlawfully, when a nonexempt employee works long hours in connection with a meeting or convention and is given extra time off during a different pay period.

Overtime pay is not contingent on the approval of extra work in advance. According to the law, it pay must be provided whenever an employee works more than 40 hours in a week or is on call for additional work, even if this was not explicitly approved. Therefore, if a nonexempt employee works additional hours leading up to a meeting, they must be receive overtime.

Overtime pay is not restricted to lower-salaried or hourly employees. The FLSA mandates it for *all* employees unless they qualify for one of the law's specific exemptions. The most commonly used are the white-collar exemptions, which pertain to professional, executive, and administrative employees. To determine whether an employee qualifies for one of these exemptions, a thorough review of FLSA, relevant regulations, and interpretations is necessary. The exemptions apply based on an employee's actual job duties; job titles alone are not sufficient. As of 2020, to be eligible for a white-collar exemption, an employee typically must meet specific criteria related to their job duties and receive a salary of at least $684 per week.

It is important for all employers to know which of their employees are exempt from overtime pay requirements and which are not. This is especially significant when employees are asked to work long hours at meetings or conventions, particularly those held out of town, or to "pitch in" and help complete a large project. When in doubt about overtime, an organization should review job descriptions with a competent human resources professional or experienced counsel.

ETHICS IN MEEC

The previous section of this chapter primarily addresses legal issues, and event professionals can seek guidance from legislation or legal advisers to navigate them. However, within the MEEC industry, numerous other actions, practices, or activities may be legal but could raise ethical questions. Ethics serve as a guiding principle in our personal and professional lives. In recent years, ethical concerns have gained significant attention due to unethical practices by various businesses and public figures, such as Enron, Tyco, and Martha Stewart, and are now a prominent topic in the media.

The nature of the MEEC industry provides ample opportunities for ethical dilemmas or misconduct. How individuals respond to ethical issues is often influenced by their personal values and cultural backgrounds. What is considered ethical behavior in one community or society may be deemed unethical in another. Ethical dilemmas in the MEEC industry can also involve choices between loyalty to personal friends and loyalty to an employer. Ethical issues and personal conduct are essential aspects of any industry. Given the complexity of this topic, readers are encouraged to explore additional sources of information and guidance. Ethical decision-making is a vital skill for professionals in the MEEC industry, and continued learning and reflection on ethical issues are crucial for maintaining integrity and professionalism.

A person's ethics say a lot about their core values and should match the core values of their organization

SUPPLIER RELATIONS

In the MEEC industry, planners can sometimes think that suppliers and vendors are primarily driven by profit and may make exaggerated promises to secure a contract. Conversely, suppliers and vendors may believe that event professionals tend to overstate their needs or potential business. These situations raise ethical questions related to honesty and transparency in business dealings. Although making ambitious promises may not always be illegal, it may not align with ethical business practices. Similarly, exaggerating event details, such as the number of rooms needed or projected F&B expenses, raises ethical concerns. To address these issues and build a strong foundation of trust, it is essential for both parties, the buyer (planner or organizer) and the seller (vendor or supplier), to clearly document their agreements in a contract.

Even with a contract in place, open, forthright, and honest communication is crucial. Trust forms the core of any business relationship; without it, the relationship becomes fragile. In today's business landscape, where relationship marketing is gaining significance, maintaining ethical and honest conduct can not only lead to successful transactions but also foster business opportunities based on trust and integrity.

Another ethical issue deals with the ownership and use of intellectual material. Destination management companies (DMCs) often complain that meeting planners submit requests for proposals to many suppliers and the DMCs spend quite a bit of time, energy, and money to develop creative ideas and programs to secure the planners' business. However, in many cases, a planner will take the ideas developed by one DMC and have another implement them, or the planner may then do this on their own. Is this legal? Probably. Is it ethical? No.

Still another issue for suppliers relates to offering gifts. Should an event professional accept gifts and privileges from a supplier or vendor? If so, is the planner obligated to repay the supplier by steering business in the vendor's direction? When does one cross the line from ethical to unethical behavior? Is it proper to accept a Christmas gift but not football tickets? Event professionals working for the U.S. government are prohibited from accepting any gift with a value of $50 or more.

Another ethical question regards so-called familiarization or "fam" trips: potential clients are invited on an all-expenses-paid trip to a destination in the hope of winning their business. But what if a planner or organizer is invited on a fam trip but has no intention of ever holding a MEEC gathering in that location? Should the planner accept the trip? If accepted, is there some implicit expectation that the planner *will* bring business? Although it is perfectly legal to accept a trip in this situation, is it ethical?

The planner or organizer of a large MEEC gathering wields significant influence and power, stemming from the event's substantial economic and social impact. This influence can be leveraged for legitimate purposes, such as negotiating favorable room rates, catering fees, and complimentary services that benefit the group as a whole. However, an ethical question arises when they seek personal favors that exclusively benefit themselves. Is it ethically justifiable for them to request or accept such favors?

The MEEC industry presents numerous ethical dilemmas and questions. Individuals are expected to uphold a personal code of ethics, and many industry associations have established their own codes that members must adhere to. Recognizing the importance of ethics, colleges and universities have introduced courses on the subject. This chapter's discussion of ethics aims to highlight the crucial role it plays in the study of the MEEC industry without aspiring to be an exhaustive treatise on the topic.

TRENDS AND BEST PRACTICES REGARDING LEGAL ISSUES IN MEEC

- Third-party beneficiary contract issues will continue to grow in importance with the growing number of independent meeting planners, professional congress organizers, and the like. Where two parties have signed a contract but commission issues affect a third party, the law recognizes the third party's rights to the benefit outlined in the contract.
- New and unexpected force majeure issues, such as the COVID-19 pandemic, will continue to challenge our interpretation of existing force majeure clauses, statutes, and interpretation of case law. Clearly, not everything can be anticipated, and this clause is not meant to cover everything that can possibly happen.
- The protection of intellectual property becomes a greater challenge as technology makes it easier to take photos (including by drone), make copies, or "snip" a piece of writing that is meant to be protected.
- Who has the upper hand in negotiation—the organizer or the vendor—will depend upon the economy. In a good economy, where demand is strong, the supplier has the upper hand; in a weak economy, it is the organizer or buyer.

- The line between ethics and law will continue to be gray, but more organizations will formalize ethics policies to avoid public relations nightmares, especially via social media, and bolster their stance that they do not want to do business with certain parties who operate against their established code of ethics.
- Fees and surcharges in contracts, especially those that are not so obvious, will become a serious negotiation point as suppliers unbundle services to charge separately for them and use fees and surcharges to keep up with increasing costs.

SUMMARY

Legal issues are an increasingly important factor in the MEEC industry. This chapter is meant to provide insights into some of these issues, such as negotiation, contracts, statutes, labor, and intellectual property. Other issues that were not discussed, and entire books are devoted to them. Readers are reminded to seek legal counsel whenever appropriate.

KEY WORDS AND TERMS

For definitions, see the glossary or https://insights.eventscouncil.org/Industry-glossary.

acceptance	legal subject
Act of God	major life activities
Americans With Disabilities Act	meeting history
American Society of Composers, Authors and Publishers	offer
	parol evidence
attrition	patent
Broadcast Music, Inc.	performing rights organizations
capacity	pickup
consideration	rack rates
contract	rates
copyright	risk
dates	space
disability	trademark
force majeure	yield management
Impossibility	

CASE STUDY

Max West was looking forward to attending the annual meeting for the National Association for the Study of Sea Creatures (NASSC). The convention was always highly educational and a great place to network with other people interested in marine life. Furthermore, this year, it was being held at a very nice coastal resort in North Carolina. Another thing to look forward to!

Max West planned carefully for his trip, including his travel, the clothes he would take, and the social events that he would participate in. Most of all, however, he planned his food. Max has a serious peanut and tree nut food allergy. Eating just a little bit of nuts can cause him to go into anaphylactic shock, where his throat swells shut, blocking off his airway, or cause vomiting and hives. He carries an epinephrine auto-injector with him wherever he goes.

Max checked the box on the NASSC registration form that asked if he had ADA special needs. He then indicated that he had dietary restrictions and specified peanuts and tree nuts. A member of the NASSC meetings staff called him and discussed his dietary restriction, including verifying that it was ingestion-based and not airborne. Furthermore, the meeting staff sent ingredient lists for the catered meals, so Max could double-check and order a special meal when necessary. He was particularly concerned about the Jamaican veggie patty being served at lunch one day, but he did not see any nuts on the ingredient list for it.

When Max arrived on-site at the NASSC meeting, he was given a special bright blue card to put out at meals that said "Nut-Free." As he routinely did, Max made sure that his servers knew that he could not eat nuts and asked them to confirm that there were no nuts in any of the meals (unless he was already getting a special meal because of the nuts in the regular meal).

The day of the Jamaican veggie patty lunch arrived. Max felt okay about it because he had reviewed the ingredient list himself, but he still asked the server about any nuts in the patty. Deborah, the server who had worked at the resort for over 10 years, assured him no nuts were in the lunch. Max took only two bites before he felt the onset of an allergic reaction—his throat tightened, his eyes watered. He administered his epinephrine, and an ambulance was called.

REVIEW AND DISCUSSION QUESTIONS

1. Discuss the negotiation process. What are the important points for each party to be aware of?

2. What are the five elements of a legal contract?

3. What are the most important clauses in hotel group sales contracts? Why?

4. Discuss negotiating contracts.

5. Discuss three strategies for negotiating attrition clauses.

6. What is the difference between cancellation and force majeure regarding events?

7. Choose one type of crisis, emergency, or disaster, and discuss what you should do at each of the four stages of crisis management to reduce the likelihood of occurrence or minimize the impact.

8. What is the ADA, and how does it impact events and gatherings?

9. What are the three types of intellectual property? Give an example of something event related that might be protected under each type.

10. What are some of the labor issues unique to MEEC?

ABOUT THE CHAPTER CONTRIBUTOR

Tyra Warner, Ph.D., J.D., CMP is the department chair of Hospitality, Tourism, & Culinary Arts at the College of Coastal Georgia. She has also served as an attorney representing meeting organizers and specializing in meeting and event contracts. She has been published and widely quoted in academic and trade publications, and her expertise is in legal and crisis preparedness issues for the meetings, events, and hospitality industries. Her 30-year meetings industry career has included management roles in hotels, travel, destination marketing, associations, catering, law, and academia. Dr. Warner has received national recognition for her contributions to best practices initiatives with the Events Industry Council and Meeting Professionals International. She is one of only two people in the world who has been a practicing attorney, has a Ph.D. in hospitality, and has earned the Certified Meeting Professional designation.

Contact Information:

Tyra Warner, Ph.D., JD, CMP
Associate Professor and Chair
Department of Hospitality, Tourism, and Culinary Arts
College of Coastal Georgia
One College Drive
Brunswick, GA 31520
Phone: (912)279-4568
twarner@ccga.edu
http://www.ccga.edu

Previous Edition Chapter Contributor

James M. Goldberg, PLLC

CHAPTER 11

TECHNOLOGY AND THE MEETING PROFESSIONAL

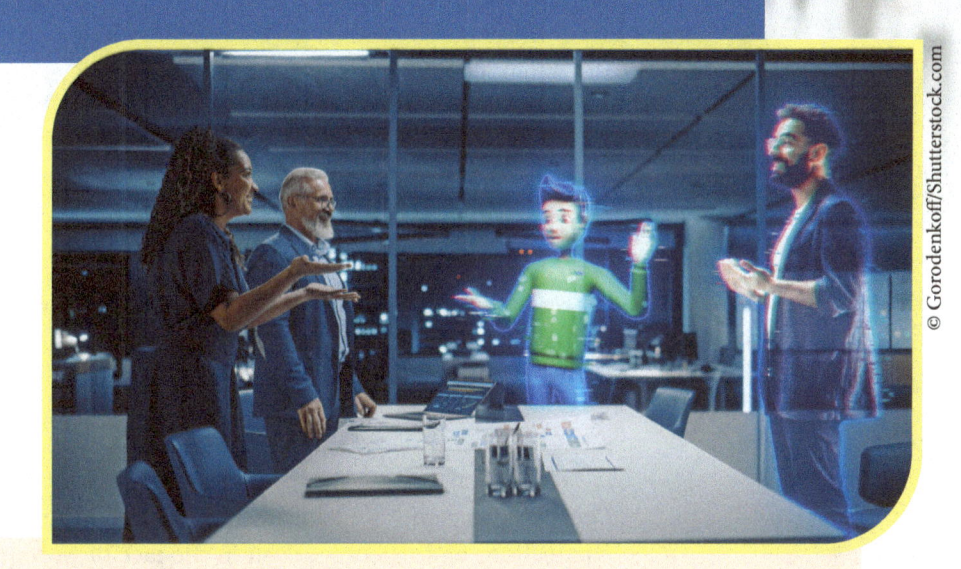

CHAPTER OBJECTIVES

- Recognize how technology historically has supported meetings and events industry.
- Understand the critical technology terms that apply to the hospitality industry.
- Recognize how the maturing technologies, such as artificial intelligence, can and will impact the work done in the hospitality industry.
- Understand the postpandemic changes to the meetings industry and how technology applications can help the industry move forward.

Contributed by James Spellos. © Kendall Hunt Publishing Company.

Chapter Outline

- Introduction
- Virtual Site Selection & Research
- Marketing & Communications
- Social Media
- Event Apps
- Desktop & Mobile Tools
- On-Site Event Tech Infrastructure
- Attendee Interaction and Communications
- Postconference Applications
- Mixed Reality
- Artificial Intelligence
- Virtual & Hybrid Meetings
- The Roaring Tech Twenties
- Conclusion
- Critical Terms

INTRODUCTION

As we witness the gradual return of business operations to a semblance of normalcy, albeit a new one, following the significant disruptions caused by the pandemic, a few noteworthy developments have emerged. First and foremost, it is abundantly clear that people still have a fundamental need for in-person interactions, which remains an intrinsic aspect of human nature.

On the other hand, we have also discovered innovative ways to sustain our connections and meetings, even in the face of widespread travel restrictions and canceled on-site events. New tools and platforms have arisen to bridge the gap. (Remember the relatively obscure Zoom of 2019?) Technological advancements have surged at an unprecedented pace. It is been estimated that the pandemic accelerated the rate of technological adoption by 5–10 years. For an industry that often prided itself on its traditional, low-tech approach, technology was thrust upon it in a manner that will undoubtedly reshape its future. Both the technological tools and the economic landscape of events and society will ensure that the industry can never revert to its previous state.

Technology has undeniably played a pivotal role in shaping the meetings and events industry throughout its history. It began with automating the registration process, extended into the early days of the internet era with the advent of virtual, albeit limited, site inspections, progressed through the proliferation of **social media** and conference apps during the 2010s, and has now arrived at generative **artificial intelligence** (AI; including ChatGPT) and mixed reality as the latest tech trends. These transformations have collectively propelled our industry forward.

Integrating technology has been a turbulent journey, especially given that our industry has not typically embraced adding it to what is widely perceived as a "people business." Nevertheless, technology has consistently excelled in one critical aspect: facilitating and enhancing people's ability to connect and convene. It is worth examining the various technological components that have defined our industry's landscape, many of which continue to shape it today. This analysis becomes even more relevant in the context of the current landscape, where tools, such as AI, can further augment and redefine how, where, and why we gather.

Technology itself is not inherently good or bad; it is simply a tool, albeit an incredibly powerful one. The sooner we all align ourselves with this notion and dedicate more time to embracing new possibilities, the more effectively our industry can remain relevant in the years ahead.

VIRTUAL SITE SELECTION AND RESEARCH

In the not-so-distant past (although it may seem like countless eons ago), event planners relied on encyclopedic books with essential information about meeting facilities. The landscape transformed dramatically in the 1990s with the advent of searchable CD-ROMs and the internet. Hotels and convention and visitors bureaus (CVBs) recognized the value of replacing their conventional marketing methods with these tools, vastly expanding the toolkit available to planners for research.

Today, we find ourselves on the cusp of yet another transformation. AI offers a glimpse of a future where research is conducted not primarily through search engines but through interaction with **chatbots** and similar AI-driven systems. The site selection and research aspect encompasses more than just hotels and physical conference venues; it also includes the capabilities and constraints of virtual spaces that have become indispensable for the continuation of meetings and events in the 2020s.

ONLINE RFPS

During the evolution of the internet in the mid- to late 1990s, one of the initial tools to emerge was the ability, available through CVB websites and hotel and third-party planning platforms, to create efficient online **requests for proposals** (RFPs). This allowed event planners to streamline the process of disseminating information to potential hotels about upcoming meetings. Although the model has shifted from a fee-based RFP system to a free approach, the fundamental concept remains unchanged: It empowers planners to easily input their specifications and leverages the internet to distribute this information to prospective cities and hotels.

Without standardization, each RFP possesses its own unique nuances, potentially demanding extra time for each one. Planners must still grapple with the decision of which channel to pursue for distributing their meeting specifications, whether through CVB/destination marketing organizations, hotel-specific platforms, or third-party services. This lack of uniformity has, and will likely continue to, pose challenges. However, from a broader perspective, it underscores the distinctiveness of each event and emphasizes the critical role of a professional planning team in comprehending the fundamental objectives of each gathering.

Some planners opt to bypass traditional RFP forms altogether, relying on email and the internet to expedite their process by distributing an office-based specification sheet. Regardless of the approach, technology is undeniably key to significantly reducing the time required.

VIRTUAL TOURS

Industry statistics have estimated that over half of all meetings are arranged without the necessity of a formal site inspection. Although recent data are not widely available, it is a reasonable assumption that this has increased in the new reality of the pandemic. Nothing can truly replace physically visiting a venue, but the visual capabilities offered by the web have empowered planners to gain at least a preliminary sense of a facility when time or budget constraints make on-site inspections challenging. Tools such as **virtual** and **augmented reality**, although not yet extensively used, are poised to deliver site inspections directly to a planner's desktop.

The virtual site inspection has evolved significantly over the years, progressing from its humble beginnings, featuring only static images of meeting rooms. Several years ago, the introduction of videos and 360° panoramic tours showcasing meeting spaces and sleeping accommodations marked a significant leap forward. Ongoing developments in virtual reality, enabling immersive virtual walkthroughs, promise to elevate it even further. Effective virtual tours, which can also illustrate how a hybrid meeting can be organized, are becoming increasingly indispensable.

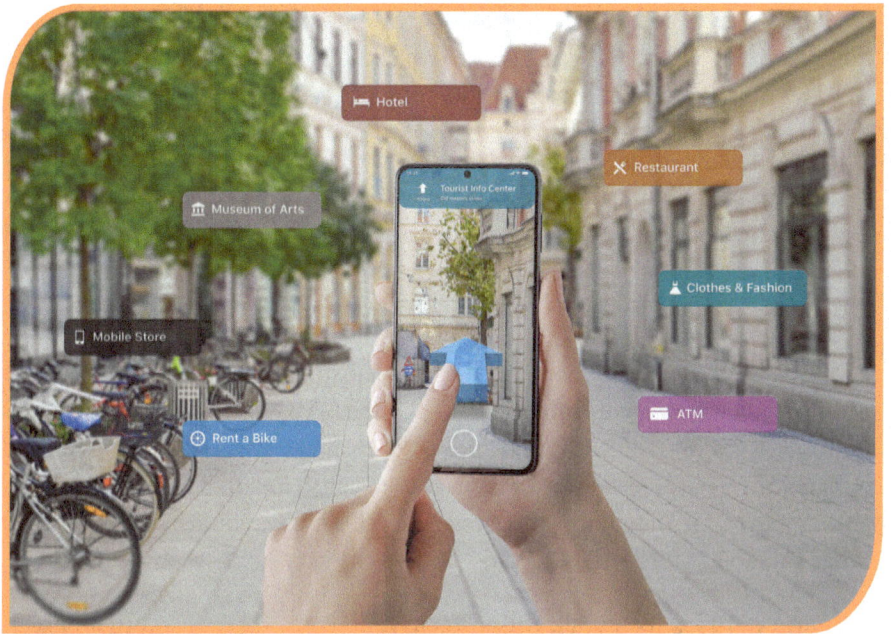

More than a decade ago, a virtual world called "Second Life" generated considerable excitement within the tech-savvy segment of our industry, sparking discussions about the future of site selection and related services. Starwood Hotels' Aloft brand used it as a platform to showcase design concepts to potential customers. However, Second Life, although innovative, was significantly ahead of its time and often exceeded computers' processing capabilities. Consequently, it never achieved widespread adoption. Considering the evolution of virtual reality (VR) and augmented reality (AR) devices that are available or on the horizon, it would unsurprising if forward-thinking properties soon begin to embrace these tools.

As for whether an AI tool will eventually become the industry's primary choice for virtual site inspections, it is not quite the norm yet. It may be a matter of time until a groundbreaking application emerges. Nonetheless, the value of physically visiting a space (and the corresponding city) remains unparalleled when making the ultimate decision.

MEETING INDUSTRY PORTALS AND INFORMATION RESOURCES

Although they may be less sophisticated in design, industry information **portals** continue to thrive, providing an immensely valuable resource. Search engines are undoubtedly valuable for general research, but our industry benefits from an abundance of information readily accessible to savvy web users who can find resources and tools with just a few clicks. This is specifically referring to websites that do not require registration or a paid subscription.

ChatGPT will be discussed more later on. The current version relies on information that has not been updated in nearly 2 years. Although this will change and has already been updated to some extent by incorporating **generative AI** and more traditional web searching techniques, users must remain aware of the accuracy and timeliness of the information they are researching.

When discussing information portals for the hospitality industry, Corbin Ball's website (http://www.corbinball.com) is crucial. His favorites page provides visitors with access to nearly 3,000 industry-related websites, neatly organized by categories. He consistently updates the site, ensuring that it remains a valuable resource for meeting professionals. Additionally, you can find plenty of other valuable information for those in the industry on his website.

Liz King Caruso's techsytalk (http://techsytalk.com) serves as both an excellent tech resource and a portal for event planners. It also stood out as one of the industry's premier tech conferences. Although the conference briefly ceased to operate for a few years, 2020 witnessed its revival. Liz was among the first to demonstrate to the industry how to successfully run an all-virtual conference during the early stages of the COVID-19 pandemic.

Although not a traditional portal, another invaluable site to explore is the Event Manager blog (http://www.eventmanagerblog.com/). Curated by Julius Solaris, it is a treasure trove of excellent articles and resources for meeting planners. It serves as a critical tech resource for our industry, offering valuable insights and information.

Social media platforms are often rich sources of information, especially for those skilled at sifting through content to find the signal amidst the noise. Our industry boasts some exceptional Facebook communities where professionals help one another by sharing insights and knowledge. Liz King contributes to this space with her techsytalk Facebook community. Tracy Stuckrath, a trailblazer in the realm of food safety for event attendees, has established the highly successful Eating at a Meeting Facebook community. Additionally, for those focused on supporting the return of live events, the Facebook Live Events Coalition boasts over 20,000 members actively engaging in discussions and sharing updates.

For those seeking nontraditional destinations, the Unique Venues website (https://www.uniquevenues.com/) is valuable. It opens up a world of possibilities, including college campuses, cruise ships, and business offices, making it a rich resource. It offers an informative blog and a traditional magazine to complement the wealth of information available. Additionally, it distinguished itself as one of the most successful organizations in delivering content to its community through virtual meetings during the early stages of the pandemic.

Google Groups (http://groups.google.com) serves as a hub for ongoing dialogue within the meeting industry. Two notable groups, the Meeting Industry Forum and Meetings Community, provide platforms for planners and suppliers to exchange ideas and best practices. Many users appreciate that this space strictly prohibits sales or marketing, fostering a productive and collaborative environment for industry professionals.

MARKETING AND COMMUNICATIONS

The increasing number of new events emphasizes the growing importance of effectively marketing your brand and conference. Undoubtedly, the most potent marketing tool is successfully executing a conference that not only meets but exceeds the expectations of its audience. However, attracting attendees has become increasingly task. Most planners and suppliers now acknowledge that their customers' decision-making process occurs later in the selling cycle. People no longer commit to attending events months in advance, making marketing an indispensable component of a successful planner's toolkit. Technology often serves as the primary, if not the sole, medium for distribution in these efforts, and it is likely that the decision-making cycle may continue to shrink over time.

Today, a significant portion of the marketing process unfolds through social media channels. The following section, dedicated to social media, delves into these components in more detail.

WEBSITES AND STRATEGIC COMMUNICATIONS

It used to be all about one-way communication—information sent from organizers to (potential) attendees. However, over the past decade, with the rise of websites and social networks as hubs for real-time communication, the model has clearly evolved into a two-way exchange.

Websites still play a crucial role in the landscape; they are the event's true landing page. They not only need to embrace a two-way communication model but must also efficiently deliver essential information to conference attendees. The most successful online event models incorporate effective social media strategies alongside user-friendly event websites that are easy to find, navigate, and purchase from.

In this decade, one critical realization for all event marketers is the need to prioritize mobile devices. We find ourselves squarely in a mobile-first world (rapidly transitioning toward a voice-reliant, mobile-first world), where the focus has shifted from large-screen websites to ensuring that content is readily accessible on smaller screens.

EVENT WEBSITES

The event website of today serves a role similar to that of a conference marketing brochure from a generation ago. It is a platform for providing information, sparking interest, and, ideally, persuading people to register for the conference.

The most effective websites employ a two-way strategy, offering interactive communication and perhaps a live social stream, along with clear links to all essential social channels. However, the paramount requirement for a successful website is comprehensive information about the event.

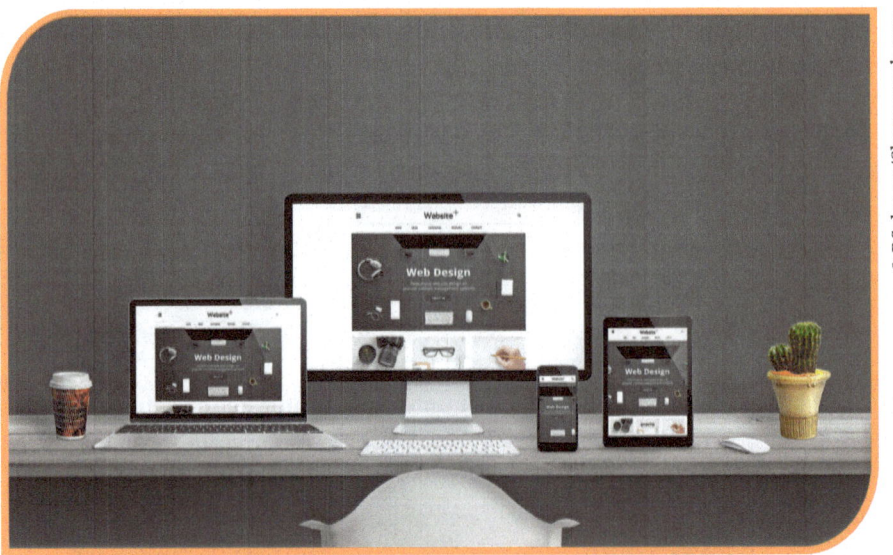

The fundamental principles for a successful conference website include the following:

- The need for the clear, easy-to-find information;
- Focus on the 5 Ws about the conference (who, what, where, when, and why);
- Easy access through any device (smartphone, tablet, laptop/desktop, with a potential eye to engaging content through wearable devices and through voice access);
- The ability to make the sale (the payment process on the registration form).

With the increasing use of what you see is what you get or low-code tools, such as Wix and SquareSpace, website development has become accessible and cost effective for most groups. Larger meetings with more complex requirements may still necessitate a higher level of customization and development.

Furthermore, AI-based web development tools have emerged in 2023, potentially simplifying and expediting the process. These tools handle all the heavy lifting to create various types of websites, including those for conferences, in less than a minute. It might seem hard to believe, but tools such as Mixo (https://www.mixo.io) demonstrate that it is indeed possible.

Event organizers often face a common issue: not getting information onto their websites early enough. Despite no set time frame, if you are running an annual event, details about next year's meeting should be ready to go live on the day this year's meeting concludes. It is simply common sense. If attendees are pleased with the conference, why not allow them to register for next year while their memories are still fresh? Yet, many planners do not establish their websites as early as they should. Perhaps this ties into the issue of the shorter sales/purchase cycle.

MOBILE WEBSITES

As mentioned, any web strategy must place a clear emphasis on mobile accessibility. Unfortunately, some planners and suppliers still allocate most of their website efforts as if the desktop or laptop platform is the sole focus. Mobile usage has now surpassed traditional computer usage. This highlights the importance of a well-designed mobile site, which some argue could be the primary focus for planners today, alongside effective use of social channels.

"Responsive web design" is commonly used to describe a website that adapts itself to the platform, whether it is a desktop, tablet, or phone. Although this approach ensures that the content is displayed clearly on each screen, it does not fully address the fact that mobile and desktop users often have different content needs when they are searching.

The critical question that planners should be asking themselves, or discussing with their web designers, is "what content is most vital for mobile users?" This should invariably encompass easy access to registration and other essential information, all without burdening users with slow-loading videos or resource-heavy elements that might strain their bandwidth. Planners cannot assume that users are have adequate bandwidth. Therefore, content must reach potential customers efficiently. The "6-second rule" remains a valuable tool for planners. If a mobile page takes longer than 6 seconds to load, it might be time to reassess the content and trim accordingly. Even in the age of Wi-Fi and **5G**, large files, such as videos, could lead to slow page loading.

E-BLASTS

Thirty years ago, Jane Planner used to send out as many direct mail pieces as her budget allowed. The more information that a buyer received, the higher the likelihood that they might attend.

Twenty years ago, Jane shifted to email as her primary marketing tool. When used correctly, a well-orchestrated e-blast strategy could yield substantial benefits.

However, as mentioned, the landscape has evolved. We are now bombarded with spam, with some experts estimating that as much as 85% of our daily email consists of spam. Consequently, sending multiple unsolicited emails can have the opposite effect, causing people to tune out those communications or relegate them to the promotions or, worse, spam folder.

Rather than bombarding the audience with a barrage of emails, Jane Planner would be wise to follow a different set of marketing principles to effectively promote her conference.

- *Opt-in*: Having an email address is not an open invitation for spamming. The Federal Trade Commission's CAN-SPAM act of 2009 (https://www.ftc.gov/tips-advice/business-center/guidance/can-spam-act-compliance-guide-business) requires all businesses, including events, to adhere to proper rules regarding email marketing. In a technology-savvy and ethical approach, it is advisable to initiate a dialogue and confirm that the recipient genuinely wishes to receive future mailings.

- *General Data Protection Regulation (GDPR)*: In 2018, European Union countries implemented this regulation, mandating opt-in consent for all email marketing activities, with substantial financial penalties for violation. Although it is a European regulation, its global impact is significant, as it applies to any individual residing in one of the E.U. countries. By early 2020, GDPR had already triggered over 160,000 data breach notifications, and Google faced a hefty fine of over 50 million euros.

- *Do Not Overdo It*: Once you have the green light to send emails, it is essential not to inundate recipients with an unending stream of mindless communications. We receive a multitude of messages daily, so we are actively seeking ways to reduce the number that demand our attention. It is wiser to invest time in crafting useful, occasional messages rather than sending repetitive, mundane reminders.

- *What's in It for Me (Technology Version)*: From your customer's perspective, why should they bother reading your emails? If all you do is inundate them with information about the conference, it comes across as a constant hard sell. Given that email is a marketing medium (and one that can seal the deal), leverage it to establish a meaningful dialogue. Provide educational content, involve customers in the event before they arrive, and inform them about tools to enhance their professional skills. Of course, you can also communicate the benefits of your conference, but this information is better received within an environment of trust rather than persistent sales pitches.

- *Keep It Simple*: Avoid lengthy emails. People have become accustomed to quick soundbites, and they do not have time for extensive reading; TLDR ("too long, didn't read") seems to be the standard response. Keep your messages concise and easy to read. Videos tend to capture more attention than photos, which are, in turn, more engaging than plain text. Additionally, if you include links, ensure that they function correctly.

- *Make it Visually Appealing*: Our responses are often more drawn to visuals than words, and videos tend to outperform static images. Maintaining this approach is likely to lead to greater success in your email marketing efforts.

VIDEO MARKETING

We have unmistakably evolved into a video-centric generation. The remarkable success of platforms such as YouTube, Instagram, and, more recently, TikTok (although TikTok's future availability in the United States is uncertain), underscores the importance for planners to disseminate content as short-form videos as extensively as they do through email blasts. It would not be surprising if, by the end of this decade, video marketing becomes the preferred and more effective choice for planners and suppliers, surpassing text-based options.

ROOM DESIGN SOFTWARE

Taking communication efficiency to another level involves how planners convey information to the facility to ensure that their requirements are precisely executed. Conference resumes and run of show documents are effective flow charts outlining what needs to occur and when. (As a side note, a standard database is excellent for producing a professional-looking resume, although most planners still rely on Excel.)

Certain aspects of your event, such as themed parties, banquets, or unique setups, can be challenging to convey effectively through written descriptions alone. In such cases, planners turn to computer-aided design **room design software** to enhance their communications.

Our industry boasts a range of options for this purpose, typically user friendly but varying in price. Two prominent providers are Social Tables (https://www.socialtables.com/) and All Seated (http://www.allseated.com/). Some solutions are better suited for meetings, and others specialize in special events. Social Tables operates on a premium model, whereas All Seated is free. Both platforms feature 3D room tour capabilities, and many venues have used these tools to virtually showcase their spaces on their websites.

SELLING THE SHOW FLOOR

The return of large-scale trade shows remains uncertain. However, when they do make a comeback, technology will be key to enhancing communication and marketing. One significant advancement is the assistance to trade show managers in selling exhibit space. Traditionally, this relied on documents such as the Exhibit Prospectus and a generic show floor layout.

By posting the show floor diagram on the web and making it interactive, trade show managers can provide potential buyers with a comprehensive view of available booth locations. This approach offers several advantages, including real-time updates to layouts, helping buyers choose spaces in proximity to or far from competitors based on their strategy. Color coding for booths can effectively differentiate between available spaces and premium cost areas.

Virtually every trade show now incorporates some form of virtual enhancement into the exhibit floor selling process. These online platforms also include downloadable versions of the Exhibit Prospectus and other pertinent information for exhibitors.

A deeper dive into virtual trade shows is provided in the upcoming **webinars** and virtual events section. This will explore how the actual event can transform into an immersive online experience for both attendees and exhibitors.

ONLINE REGISTRATION

Online registration is one of the most mature technologies in our industry, possibly surpassed only by the site selection and RFP process. Although this is rare, some meetings still do not embrace it. Many, particularly internal meetings with mandatory attendance, opt to avoid the expense of a professional online registration system, preferring traditional or email-based approaches. In this age of virtual pivoting, online registration for virtual events can be seamlessly managed within the virtual platform itself, such as Zoom's webinar functionality.

However, despite the maturity of online registration, planners still face several challenges when establishing it. One of the most significant challenges is data integration. Even under the best circumstances, not all attendees will use an online service. Therefore, planners must ensure that data integration is accurate and has no record duplication. It is crucial to ask service providers if their online registration system can seamlessly export data into the tools you use to maintain the remaining records, such as Excel. This ensures a smooth and error-free registration process.

Organizations using online registration services often encounter unexpected expenses, particularly creating additional reports. Planners have two strategies to mitigate this issue. One approach involves thoroughly understanding all the reports they might require and negotiating them into the service package during the purchase phase. The other, more tech-savvy option is to familiarize themselves with report writing features. Many online registration services use SAP Crystal Reports to generate customized reports for clients.

When it comes to selecting an online registration service, countless options are available. Researching through industry portals, such as Ball's website (http://www.corbinball.com), and exploring industry favorites will yield a wide array of choices.

SOCIAL MEDIA

Has social media surpassed websites as the primary go-to information tool for events? Although it might be a stretch for some to believe (and not so much for others), the combined power of a well-designed website (optimized for both mobile and desktop) along with the use of multiple social channels significantly enhances a planner's marketing and communication efforts. Can a planner even imagine hosting an event without, at the very least, a Facebook page (and possibly an event-specific Facebook page) as part of their communication strategy? These digital tools have become indispensable in reaching and engaging with today's audience.

PRIMARY SOCIAL CHANNELS

The past decade has witnessed the rise and dominance of social media services. At the core of this industry's success has always been social networks. A conference gathering, such as the Annual Widget Convention, essentially represents a vast social network of professionals convening to exchange knowledge and insights.

The key difference now is that this social network extends beyond face-to-face interactions and has grown exponentially in the pandemic era. Over the past decade, various applications have emerged, facilitating real-time communication within this sphere. Facebook, Instagram, **Twitter**, YouTube, and LinkedIn are the dominant general social channels employed by planners. Additionally, tools such as Snapchat and TikTok have showcased their value for events, particularly when the audience's demographics align with these newer technologies.

- Facebook's event pages, viral marketing capabilities, and social interaction features make it an excellent platform for communication and marketing related to meetings. A well-crafted event page can generate excitement, particularly when supported by an engaged community. The key is for planners to understand their specific audience to determine what strategies work best. As the social channel with the largest community, Facebook is an essential component of the marketing strategy for all groups.
- Instagram, owned by Facebook, reigns supreme as the ultimate visual tool, primarily focused on photos and videos. Surprisingly, in 2023, many planners have yet to fully tap into its potential for promoting and enhancing their events. Its hashtag-centric approach aligns perfectly with conferences and events, offering a valuable tool for engaging attendees. Furthermore, with the ongoing obsession with food photography, Instagram is an indispensable resource for promoting aspects such as meals and culinary experiences.
- Twitter, despite making efforts to keep pace with Facebook, lags behind in terms of user numbers. Recent management changes have also alienated some users. However, Twitter's true strength, especially for savvy social media users, lies in its ability to curate content from its user stream. Features such as hashtags and lists can transform the social media noise into meaningful nuances. Twitter walls, particularly popular at larger conferences and events in the late 2010s, aggregate and exclusively display posts using the event's hashtag. It will be intriguing to observe how newer microblogging social platforms, such as Bluesky (https://account.bsky.app), may vie for Twitter's audience.
- Owned by Google, YouTube is the foremost video channel available. Savvy planners often create a dedicated YouTube channel containing videos to promote and highlight their events. Google's rules have imposed more regulation on the monetization of YouTube channels, prompting

many planners to host their videos on other platforms, such as Vimeo (http://www.vimeo.com). YouTube, much like Facebook, supports 360-degree video, which is explored further in the section on mixed reality.
- LinkedIn is primarily regarded as a business network rather than a social one. It is more oriented toward individual networking. Although it features groups, which are valuable tools, it has no dedicated space for direct event promotion. However, LinkedIn hosts vibrant meeting communities, such as the Senior Planners Industry Network, and remains a valuable platform for networking within the meetings and events industry.

Twitter, Facebook, and LinkedIn are not the only social networks available to event planners. Platforms such as TikTok and Twitch, which focuses more on the gaming community, offer potential value for specific audiences and event types. Customizable networks, available in both free and premium versions, have gained favor among many groups; these enable planners to tailor the layout and content to suit the specific needs of their events.

LIVESTREAMING

Livestreaming has become a standard mode of communication since the introduction of Meerkat in February 2015. Platforms such as Facebook, YouTube, and Instagram Live have been pivotal.

However, the landscape changed dramatically in March 2020, when the pandemic hit. Almost overnight, organizations widely embraced tools such as Zoom for their connectivity needs. These platforms served a dual purpose, functioning as virtual staff meetings and livestreaming hubs for educational content. Zoom experienced exponential growth, becoming an invaluable resource for many planners and suppliers. Alternative products also exist, such as Microsoft Teams, which some organizations favored, especially during the pandemic's early stages, when concerns arose about Zoom's privacy and security (which ultimately proved more than sufficient for most).

The events industry has had mixed responses to livestreaming. Supporters highlight its ability to effortlessly extend meetings to those who cannot attend physically, but opponents raise concerns about broadcasting content for which individuals lack the rights or permissions. However, this capability became a crucial part of our response to the pandemic. Now, the challenge is to understand how planners will incorporate it into true hybrid events.

No matter where you stand in the livestreaming debate, it is undeniable that it has become increasingly prevalent within social channels. The value of video content on social platforms far surpasses other types of posts. Therefore, the conversation about livestreaming in meetings has only just begun. The events of 2020, driven by the pandemic, have further accelerated the adoption of livestreaming in our industry and many others.

BLOGGING

A "blog," short for "web log," is essentially an online diary. Although considered an "old-school" social channel, blogs remain an effective means of conveying information to customers and followers. Blogging inherently fosters two-way communication, as successful blogs encourage readers to respond and contribute to the discussion on the posted topics.

In conference marketing, blogs serve a straightforward purpose: to create a dialogue between organizers and their audience. With built-in comment functionality, blogs become tools that allow organizers to gauge the thoughts and sentiments of their attendees. Savvy planners have also enlisted external bloggers to share content with those unable to attend physically. Whether such bloggers will continue to be sought after in a postpandemic rebound remains to be seen.

Despite blogs being an easy entry point into social media and an effective way to bolster web presence, it is surprising how few planners and suppliers maintain and regularly update them. In part, the rise of platforms such as Facebook and Twitter may be responsible for this decline. Nonetheless, planners would be wise to create and maintain blogs as part of their event communications strategy. As mentioned, Julius Solaris' Event Manager's Blog (http://www.event-managerblog.com/) is an excellent example of a successful industry blog.

PODCASTING

Podcasts, much like blogs, are considered an old-school tool in the realm of social media. However, their popularity has steadily increased, with over 5,000,000 podcasts and more than 70 million listeners worldwide in 2023. The pandemic played a significant role in normalizing daily podcast use for people worldwide, and the content available for our industry is abundant.

The event podcast essentially represents an evolution of what planners have been doing for years. In the past, they would record sessions on audiotapes and distribute or sell them to those unable to attend in person. Podcasts digitize this recording process. However, as our attention spans have shortened, and with the proliferation of freely available podcasts online, event podcasts may function more as a marketing tool than a revenue stream. Nevertheless, they serve as an excellent means to extend events to those who could not attend in person.

Popular podcast listening platforms include Spotify, Apple's iTunes and iOS, and Apple-based services, such as Stitcher. Moreover, as we enter the age of personal AI devices, such as Google Home and Amazon Alexa, podcasts are becoming accessible on these, expanding their reach.

HASHTAGS

No discussion about social media is complete without addressing the importance of hashtags. Essentially, these are keywords or phrases that help direct social posts to a specific and interested audience. Although they are widely used across various social channels, they play a predominant role in driving engagement on Twitter and Instagram.

On Twitter, hashtags are the threads that establish and fuel conversations. Many events create a single hashtag, using it to disseminate information before and during the event. This also enables attendees to actively participate in these discussions. In some cases, particularly with larger and tech-savvy groups, events may use multiple hashtags, facilitating more focused dialogues.

On Instagram, hashtags are the primary means of reaching a wider audience, with no strict limit on the number of hashtags that can be used. Many proficient Instagram users believe that incorporating 15–20 or even more hashtags is the key to maximizing its reach and visibility.

Hashtags, also increasingly common in Facebook and even LinkedIn posts, are key in content curation. They streamline content to reach those who are interested. In our industry, hashtags go beyond conferences; they are essential for curating and accessing content. For instance, #eventprofs is one of the most respected tags. Tools such as Hashtagify.me (http://hashtagify.me/) help users discover relevant hashtags by showing which ones are commonly used alongside their known hashtags. Hashtagify used to be free, but it has become primarily premium, emphasizing the importance of understanding critical hashtags.

SOCIAL SELLING

The fusion of event marketing and social channels is incomplete without acknowledging the role of advertising within these platforms (and, of course, on Google). Paid social media advertising is an often-underused tool that can cut through the noise of social channels, ensuring your content reaches the screens of potential attendees.

Targeted ads, notably prevalent on Facebook and often referred to as "retargeting," empower organizations to identify specific demographics, such as 35–44-year-olds in New York and Connecticut interested in widgets, and serve ads to them. As Facebook curates the content users see (you do not see all posts from everyone you follow), businesses are increasingly relying on ads or boosted posts to maximize the visibility of their messages among their desired audience.

Apart from Facebook, most other social channels accept paid placement. Twitter offers a tool called "Promoted Tweets," which allows event organizers to expand the reach of their posts. Like Facebook, it provides targeting options. Instagram and LinkedIn also incorporate ad functionality within their platforms.

In comparison to more traditional advertising methods, ads on social channels tend to be much more budget friendly. Following the successful Google model, these tools empower tech-savvy planners to promote their conferences without exhausting their marketing budgets.

EVENT APPS

Is the printed program guide a thing of the past? Well, that depends on whom you ask, but the rise of event-specific apps has allowed planners to deliver event content directly to attendees' mobile devices. This approach is not only more environmentally sustainable but has also become an industry standard.

Event apps offer various content sections, which planners can customize based on budget constraints. Common sections include Program, Maps, Local Information, Social Media, and Gamification, among others. By integrating social posts into the app, event organizers can encourage attendees to share content about the event, enhancing event marketing and awareness.

Cvent has made significant acquisitions over the past few years, consolidating its position as a key player (https://www.cvent.com/en/event-marketing-management/mobile-event-apps). Other companies, such as Results Direct's

RD Mobile (https://www.resultsdirect.com/rdmobile) and EventMobi (https://www.eventmobi.com/), also offer viable options.

Moreover, with Google's increasing ability to index content on mobile devices, event organizations need to consider the value of not only event-specific but also organization-level apps to maintain digital relevance.

In 2019, a group of entrepreneurs, some with experience at Microsoft, introduced Glide (https://go.glideapps.com), an app creation tool. This innovation aligns with the growing trend known as "low code," which empowers nonprogrammers to create apps and other mobile tools that were once the exclusive domain of technical coders. Think of platforms such as Wix and SquareSpace as low-code tools for website creation. In recent years, major players, including Google and Microsoft, and third-party companies have developed drag-and-drop, low-code tools that extract data from spreadsheets or databases to create mobile apps in just minutes.

DESKTOP AND MOBILE TOOLS

The MS Office Suite remains a cornerstone for event professionals, offering a robust set of tools, including Word, Excel, PowerPoint, and Access, to manage various aspects of events.

However, some planners find these tools overly complex or outdated. Online collaborative office tools, such as Google Drive (https://drive.google.com), offer ample functionality and superior collaboration features. Notably, Google Forms, a hidden gem in Google Drive, allows planners to create surveys, evaluations, and questionnaires at no cost.

During the lockdown, productivity tools, such as Slack and Microsoft Teams, gained significant traction by streamlining communication and reducing email overload. These tools offer add-on communities to boost productivity, and their usage is expected to rise as remote work persists. Yet, for some planners, general packages, such as Microsoft and Google, may not meet every requirement. In organizations with decentralized meeting departments, tools that support information sharing across the organization are essential. The industry offers various solutions to enhance information centralization.

One critical aspect of centralizing information is the ability for organizations to gain purchasing leverage. Individual planners organizing small meetings within large organizations often face challenges in negotiations. However, third-party software tools can provide a significant advantage over Microsoft or Google options, albeit at a higher cost. These tools can enable organizations to bundle their purchasing needs, resulting in cost savings.

ACCEPTED PRACTICES EXCHANGE (APEX)

The Events Industry Council has been a leader in establishing APEX, which aims to enhance industry efficiency by creating a set of accepted standards that all industry stakeholders can adopt. APEX covers various areas, including technology, with white papers and resources related to event bandwidth, RFPs, event sustainability, and certified meeting professional resources. (See the Events Industry Council website: https://www.eventscouncil.org/Industry-Insights/About-Industry-Insights.)

VIRTUAL TRADE SHOWS

The COVID-19 pandemic forced the events industry to rely heavily on virtual platforms, which created an expectation that virtual events would shine. However, the reality has been more complex. One significant reason for this is that the technology was not mature enough to meet the diverse needs of different meetings.

Virtual meetings and trade shows continue to show promise but with a learning curve in determining when and how to use these tools effectively.

At its core, a **virtual trade show** can be a digital floor plan with hyperlinks to exhibitor sites. Some virtual trade shows aim to create a fully immersive experience, allowing attendees to navigate a virtual event space and engage with exhibitors through chats or interactions.

ON-SITE EVENT TECH INFRASTRUCTURE

Event professionals understand the importance of negotiating with hotels on various aspects, including rates, dates, and space. Knowledge and information about the event and the destination are key in facilitating productive discussions with hotels to create win-win events.

However, many planners, out of either fear or a lack of awareness of technology, tend to omit any discussion of it during the planning process. This can prove to be quite costly. On the other hand, a technology-savvy planner understands the essential technologies well enough to add them in the initial planning stages, sometimes even negotiating to include them.

FACIAL RECOGNITION AT ON-SITE REGISTRATION

The next topic might raise red flags for some individuals, but **facial recognition** as part of on-site registration check-in has been in practice for over 5 years now. The concept is straightforward: no more enduring long lines for check-in. Your photo is preuploaded to the server. As you approach the line, the system recognizes your face, and your personalized information is swiftly provided. Is it convenient? Undoubtedly. Is it creepy? For many, absolutely.

Many companies that had promoted facial recognition for registration have quietly shifted their focus toward solutions such as "Ethical Facial Analysis." This is the current message featured on Zenus.ai's landing page (https://www.zenus.ai/), an early provider of the software for events. Privacy concerns among the public have cast a shadow over the idea of facial recognition, even though it can be more secure and private than the social networks that attendees frequently use.

Nevertheless, it is challenging to envision a future for events where these tools are not in use, possibly to a significant extent. The necessary information and technology are readily available. However, as a society, we have reservations, especially with the prevalence of deep fakes. As always, time will reveal the path we take.

BANDWIDTH

Bandwidth represents the volume of information that can flow through a communication line. More bandwidth means more simultaneous activities, such as sending emails or accessing social networking sites. Bandwidth can be a costly consideration for event planners, particularly for convention centers rather than hotels.

In 2023, obtaining the necessary bandwidth itself is not as much of an issue at most properties and locations as the associated cost passed on to planners is. With improved and more seamless connectivity within properties via Wi-Fi, coupled with the ongoing expansion of 5G networks, attendees often have access to the bandwidth they require. Consequently, the prevailing challenge primarily revolves around its cost. Planners should proactively negotiate this up-front, particularly when dealing with convention centers and nonhotel venues, to avoid unexpectedly high expenses when requesting it at the last minute.

Determining the exact amount of bandwidth required for an event can be complex. Planners may seek assistance from their IT professionals, provided they have a comprehensive understanding of their on-site needs, and must factor in the requirements for issues such as the following:

- Registration networking (for the planner)
- Internet cafes (including email access)—these were very popular in 2010–2019 but are no longer as essential in the age of smart devices and widespread connectivity,
- HQ office and press room bandwidth for office communications,
- Speaker internet access for presentations
- Attendee bandwidth for interactive elements
- Live streaming for sessions and events
- Social channel content distribution, and
- Hybrid meetings.

The final item might be debatable for some. However, hybrid meetings in the upcoming decade are likely to demand bandwidth for not only content dissemination to remote audiences but also real-time interactivity. Live attendees are quite likely to engage with the virtual stream in real time, creating an additional bandwidth requirement.

So, how much bandwidth will you need? The answer depends on various factors, including those listed and others unique to your event. Talking with your

IT team or a third-party organization you have contracted before finalizing contracts will allow you to ensure that the facility can meet your requirements and help you negotiate more reasonable costs.

Although you can find bandwidth calculators for meetings through online searches, the pandemic technological landscape may render these estimation models somewhat marginal, if not entirely obsolete. As technology evolves, it is essential to stay flexible and adapt to the changing needs and demands of your event.

As we embark on this decade's shift toward virtual and hybrid meetings, the demand for bandwidth at events will increase. Whether it is Wi-Fi, provided either by the hotel or third-party organizations, or the emerging 5G cellular technologies, the battle for dominance in event connectivity will unfold in the years ahead.

WIRED VERSUS WIRELESS

The majority of attendees expect seamless access to their email and social media channels wherever they are, whether in a hotel or elsewhere. With the widespread adoption of 5G networks, replacing 4G/4G LTE, attendees can often rely on their mobile devices without needing to connect to Wi-Fi. However, certain scenarios, such as meetings held below ground (where cell signals may be weak) or in international destinations with limited device compatibility, may still necessitate stable hardwired connections.

The introduction and expansion of 5G wireless capabilities in the United States and globally have spurred technological advancements in various domains. This progress could reduce the need for expensive venue-provided Wi-Fi. Nevertheless, the monetization of 5G will be a significant factor in its full-scale deployment, and whether costs for customers and planners will be lower than those for Wi-Fi remains uncertain. The evolution of connectivity options will continue to shape the landscape of event technology in the years ahead.

Many guest rooms nowadays offer wired access, but wireless connectivity has become the standard. Although wireless access in guest rooms has seen significant improvement over the last decade, the ever-increasing demand for digital connectivity has posed challenges for hotels in keeping up with guest expectations.

Ubiquitous connectivity also carries the persistent risk of digital security threats. Planners, attendees, and anyone carrying a tech device (which is practically everyone) should remain vigilant against phishing and malware scams and ransomware threats that can disrupt an entire network within seconds. Although delving into the intricacies of the issue is beyond the scope of this chapter, awareness of digital attacks and the use of software to mitigate their impact have become essential aspects of conducting business in 2023 and beyond.

The wireless standard is defined by an engineering specification (802.11) that was adopted in the late 1990s. However, the standard has several variations, each offering different potential bandwidths to users. It is advisable to consult with your IT department to understand the limitations and capabilities of standards such as 802.11n, 802.11ac, 802.11n, and the latest 802.11ax, as this knowledge can greatly inform your event's technology planning.

To add a layer of complexity for nontechnical individuals, the Wi-Fi Alliance, which names these specifications, has decided to change their names. For instance, 802.11ac is now Wi-Fi 5, 802.11n is Wi-Fi 4, and 802.11ax is Wi-Fi 6. With these name changes, it is no wonder that having a friend in the IT department can be incredibly helpful!

When you ask many speakers who rely on high-speed access for the success of their presentations, they often prefer hardwired connections (an Ethernet cable attached to their computer) over going wireless. Although our industry is advancing to create a more seamless broadband experience, wireless remains the standard. However, a savvy planner should always have a hardwired backup plan in case the wireless signal proves inadequate and ensure that the bandwidth allocated to the speaker is dedicated solely to their device(s) and not shared by attendees. Otherwise, a busy online audience could adversely affect the speaker's needs.

STREAMING MEDIA

Thanks largely to the pandemic, livestreaming has become an integral part of our daily lives. Although it was gaining momentum before 2020, the reliance on technology for information, education, networking, and various other purposes skyrocketed during that time.

Although Zoom continues to be the go-to platform for most groups, when looking to enhance your livestream capabilities, planners now have more options than they did in 2020. Streamyard (https://streamyard.com) and ReStream (https://restream.io) are two prominent livestreaming solutions. They offer both webinar-style experiences and the ability to stream content to an organization's social media channels. Additionally, a multitude of companies now offer specialized solutions catering to various niches within our industry.

DIGITAL RECORDINGS OF SESSIONS

The general session is immensely significant in any annual meeting or conference. The marketing success of many conferences hinges on the quality and often the name recognition of the keynote speakers, who set the tone for the event.

However, numerous individuals who cannot physically attend still want to watch or listen, either in real time or on an archived basis. To reach this broader audience, organizations can extend the reach of their keynotes and other meeting components by recording and/or livestreaming them. This allows more people to access valuable content and engage with the event remotely.

If you have never done this at a meeting, be aware that a lot of extra coordination and support is required, especially with video content. You will need to have cameras and good room lighting (and video/audio engineers) to ensure the recorded material is good quality. You will need a company to digitize the video into a format that can be electronically distributed. You will need to determine whether the event should be streamed live (always more risky) or archived. And will people have free access to it, or will the organization charge a fee to virtually attend?

Or, of course, have a single person with a phone and a livestreaming app stand up and provide real-time content at no cost (although clearly not at the same quality). The choice is yours.

In addition to the technical considerations, planners must also understand their audience. Age and demographics can play a significant role in deciding whether to digitize an entire session or opt for a highlights approach. The adage "know your group" applies to all aspects of meeting planning, including the technological side. Understanding your audience's preferences and needs is essential for delivering a successful and engaging virtual experience.

DRONES

For outdoor events, drones can be a valuable tool for capturing aerial photography. A drone is an unmanned aircraft that can be maneuvered via remote control. Although initially employed primarily by the military for aerial reconnaissance, drones have now become mainstream. They are significantly regulated by the Federal Aviation Administration, so flying them indoors, even in a spacious convention center with high ceilings, is generally not recommended. Nonetheless, many tech-savvy photographers now offer drone photography as part of their services.

ATTENDEE INTERACTION AND COMMUNICATIONS

The era of paper badges is seen by many as a relic of the past, particularly as technology has transformed the humble name badge into a multifunctional tool that can interact with various planner tech tools and, eventually, even other badges.

© Mathlaul Anwar/Shutterstock.com

BEACONS

A beacon is a Bluetooth-based tool that broadcasts small pieces of information directly to a Bluetooth-enabled device, such as a smartphone. Typically, the content is location specific and tailored to the individual user. In the context of meetings and events, beacon technology can interface with phones or even "smart badges" (equipped with tiny beacon receivers). This technology enables event organizers to convey content, track attendance for continuing education credits, promote sponsors, and serve various other purposes. Beacons offer a versatile means of enhancing attendee engagement and communication.

Two-way beacon technology represents the next frontier in this field. Typically a wearable device, such as on a lanyard around the neck, these devices operate independently of a smartphone (many people often keep their Bluetooth turned off for various privacy and battery-saving reasons). They can both send and receive data directly. This opens up a wide range of possibilities for wearable social media integration and direct communications between wearable devices. Looking further into the future, these tools may even integrate with AR to provide floating information above attendees' heads, enhancing networking opportunities. It is indeed a fascinating prospect!

NEAR FIELD COMMUNICATIONS (NFC) AND RADIO FREQUENCY IDENTIFICATION (RFID)

NFC is a short-range, high-frequency wireless technology that enables information exchange between compatible devices. RFID refers to the tags (readers) used to access these signals. Many of us are already familiar with RFID tags, as they are used for purposes such as paying tolls on bridges and tunnels in some cities (known by various names, such as EZPass or SmartPass) and inventory management in warehouses, allowing companies to track their products more efficiently. In the events and conference industry, RFID and NFC technologies are being used primarily in **interactive nametags** and other applications, offering enhanced engagement and convenience for attendees.

LEAD RETRIEVAL SYSTEMS

For many years, trade shows and exhibits have employed **lead retrieval** systems to gather customer information. The process typically begins with the meeting organizer asking specific questions during registration to help identify information of interest to exhibitors, often about the attendee's purchasing responsibilities and products or services they might be interested in.

The information collected is encoded onto a badge, although it does not necessarily have to be RFID technology. From the 1990s to today, many groups still use simple barcoding on badges or even credit card-based systems to store this information.

When attendees enter the trade show floor and engage with exhibitors, staff can request to scan the badge using their handheld lead retrieval device. Typically, these devices are rented for the duration by a supporting vendor. The attendee's information is stored in the device. Exhibitors can download these data into their spreadsheets or databases and send customized thank-you notes before wrapping up their work for the day. This process not only facilitates better follow-up but also provides exhibitors with valuable insights into prospective clients.

The planner's role in this process is to identify and select a system or service that can support the lead retrieval process. As exhibitors often require this level of information to assess the potential benefits of participation, lead retrieval systems are primarily used for trade shows. However, they have also been used to facilitate attendee surveys through automated kiosks placed throughout the event venue.

Another tool available to event planners is the reverse lead retrieval system. In this scenario, instead of the exhibitor scanning the attendee's badge, the planner uses a handheld device to scan information provided by the exhibitor. This approach is often employed at larger shows, where the volume of exhibitors and their information is substantial.

AUDIENCE RESPONSE SYSTEMS (ARSs) AND SPEAKER INTERACTION

ARSs have evolved significantly over the past few decades. Initially, handheld devices were distributed to audience members to allow them to interact with questions posed from the front of the room. However, the prevalence of smartphones and the development of conference apps have rendered separate devices nearly obsolete while still enabling robust interactivity.

ARS systems could be costly, but advancements in technology have made them more affordable and, in today's two-way communication era, a more essential part of many meetings. One such service is Poll Everywhere (www.polleverywhere.com), which uses SMS (texting) in addition to web and Twitter voting, interfacing with a real-time web-based poll. Audience members respond, and the data are instantaneously updated and displayed for all to see. Many event apps now incorporate ARSs, making it more user-friendly and controllable for event organizers. It enhances engagement and interactivity during presentations and sessions.

Twitter has been widely employed to facilitate interactivity during sessions, whether for audience chat discussions or to send messages and questions directly to speakers. Texting questions to a session moderator, is another method through which these technologies have fostered real-time connections between speakers and their audiences.

This technology enables meeting organizers and speakers to gain instant information, including demographic data, about attendees. It can be used to highly customize the content and direction of educational sessions, enhancing the overall attendee experience.

POSTCONFERENCE TECHNOLOGY APPLICATIONS

Technology serves a valuable role not only in the marketing and execution of meetings but also after the event has concluded. From the postconference evaluation process to the creation of digital highlights that seamlessly integrate into marketing efforts for the next conference, several technology applications are worth exploring in the postconference phase. Technology continues to be key in enhancing the overall conference experience from start to finish.

EVALUATIONS AND SURVEYS

Many organizers have transitioned from paper-based, on-site evaluations (which can also be digitized) to postconference online approaches for gathering attendee feedback. Debate is ongoing about whether these provide a sufficiently large sample size compared to on-site evaluations, which tend to have a higher response rate. Both digital and physical survey deployment and collection methods are used. Some planners strongly believe that embedding session and event surveys into conference apps does not yield the depth of feedback they require.

Nevertheless, many planners use this system. Most small to midsize meetings use free tools, such as Google Forms to manage their digital surveys and evaluations. These web-based services not only distribute and collect evaluations but also aggregate the data and provide planners with easily digestible analyses of the questions. Furthermore, many integrated online solutions for meeting professionals now include event survey functionality.

With the integration of AI into digital tools and services, AI-based surveying tools have become more prevalent. These enable conference organizers to have AI analyze larger data sets, identifying relevant trends and information. As the landscape of companies in this space is continually evolving, leveraging your network and using resources such as Google (and perhaps ChatGPT) can help you identify the current players and the most suitable tools for your needs.

Online surveys should not be limited to conference evaluations. Any meeting professional involved in programming understands that gaining insights into the needs of their audience is valuable tool identifying program elements that provide greater value to attendees. Conducting online surveys independently of conference evaluations can provide substantial support.

MARKETING THE MEDIA

The essence of postconference technology is to extend the event beyond its traditional time limits. It is no longer confined to Monday–Thursday; many digital-only conferences last multiple weeks. It can commence with attendee networking months before the opening session, using tools such as the pre-event networking features discussed earlier. After the conference, planners can continue to provide content to those who did not attend or wish to revisit it.

When planners arrange for video recording and streaming activities, they also need to consider how this information will be delivered. Questions related to cost and delivery are significant parts of this conversation. Planners must decide whether to charge for virtual attendance. In the COVID-19 environment, organizations are grappling with the concept of how much to charge, as people have grown accustomed to accessing online content for free. This presents challenges for event organizers seeking to monetize their content fully. Finding the right balance between providing value and generating revenue is an ongoing consideration.

Regarding delivery, especially in a live environment, planners must ensure that they have the necessary servers and technology infrastructure, including adequate bandwidth, to support seamless access for all viewers. This responsibility typically falls to the IT department, whether internal or external, rather than the planner.

As mentioned, the success of previous events is one of the planner's most potent marketing tools. The digitization and distribution of event content are critical for generating revenue from the current event and for continuing to attract attendees in future years.

MIXED REALITY

In the realm of game-changing technology for meetings and events, one of the most prominent areas to watch is **mixed reality**, which encompasses

AR and VR. These technologies could revolutionize the industry, although they are still finding their footing. They are relatively new, and their usage is somewhat limited. Early tech adopters are exploring various ways to integrate them successfully into events, and their full potential is yet to be realized. Nevertheless, they offer exciting possibilities for enhancing attendee experiences and engagement.

In June 2023, Apple made a significant move into the space by unveiling its first mixed reality device, the VisionPro (https://www.apple.com/apple-vision-pro). It is scheduled for release in late 2023, albeit with a hefty price tag (~$3,500). The VisionPro glasses offer a mixed reality experience, combining elements of traditional VR glasses (such as Oculus) while allowing users to see and interact with the real world. Apple has also teased the development of a dedicated AR device, which is expected to be released at a later date, likely a year or more away.

AR

Many experts, including Apple CEO Tim Cook, anticipate that AR will prove to be the more practical and useful technology. AR enables users to see content that is not visible to the naked eye. By looking through a device, such as a smartphone, tablet, or wearable headset or glasses, users can view and interact with digital content seamlessly integrated into the real world. One notable example of AR's impact is the 2016 breakout app, Pokémon Go. Despite initial skepticism, it has achieved remarkable success, with over 1 billion cumulative downloads and user spending exceeding $1 billion since its launch. These figures underscore the potential and significance of AR beyond its initial impression as a game.

Many people still associate AR with QR codes but on a much more advanced level. With AR, users point their devices at something and digital content comes to life, transforming the way we interact with our surroundings. Unlike QR codes, AR can be applied to almost anything.

In 2009, Layar (http://www.layar.com/) introduced the first AR browser, allowing users to use their mobile devices equipped with built-in GPS and cameras to display real-time information on top of live images. Some forward-thinking hotel companies followed suit by adding an augmented element to their magazine advertisements, providing users with "second-screen" content to enhance their experience. For event planners, a simpler use of AR is to augment traditional session signage at meetings, making it interactive. When attendees hover their phones over the sign, they can watch a short video clip of the session or speaker in action.

The tech industry's ever-evolving nature, along with the financial challenges of creating and monetizing a user base, often leads to the rise and fall of various tech products and services; for example, Layar is no longer on the market. However, user-friendly AR tools, such as Roar (https://theroar.io) and ZapWorks (https://zap.works), empower planners and everyday tech users to create simple and cost-effective AR experiences. The real challenge in using AR effectively is not the technology itself but rather the creativity to develop experiences that resonate with customers and enhance their engagement.

VIRTUAL REALITY/360° VIDEOS

VR provides an immersive experience in which users wear goggles to view 360°content. Users see only what is projected inside the device. VR devices have traditionally fallen into three categories: phone-based, computer-based, and stand-alone. However, in recent years, phone-based devices have become obsolete due to the cost and technical advancements of the other categories. Computer-based VR devices, such as the HTC Vive Pro, are powerful tools that connect to a high-performance PC, offering a rich VR experience. Stand-alone VR headsets, which are completely untethered, are dominated by the Meta Quest Pro. Other companies, such as HTC Vive, are also entering the stand-alone market.

For the events industry, VR has numerous applications. Special events can allow attendees to experience various forms of content, including multimedia, photos, videos, and games. Integrating VR into event gamification is expected to enhance the user experience significantly. In the late 2010s, several hotels and CVBs used VR to promote destinations at trade shows and during sales calls. Although the postpandemic future of VR remains uncertain, 360° video in both VR and web-based applications is likely to continue growing. Major platforms, such as Facebook and YouTube, support 360° content on their pages, facilitating broader accessibility and adoption.

As technology matures, prices tend to decrease, and the quality often improves. This trend is evident in the 360° camera market. Companies such as Matterport (https://go.matterport.com) have become leaders in providing 360° tours for hotels. They offer products that allow users to shoot and create 360°

videos using their smartphones. Products such as the Insta360 (https://www.insta360.com/) have made 360° video creation accessible to a wider audience due to their affordability compared to higher-end cameras. These products often come with basic editing software, and more advanced editing tools, such as Adobe Premiere Pro, have incorporated this functionality. The value of these cameras extends beyond just viewing with VR goggles; these videos can be shared on destination websites and social media channels, enhancing the overall experience for users.

AI

AI is poised to have a significant impact on the meeting, events, and hospitality industry. In the events and hospitality industry, AI can be used to personalize the guest experience by analyzing data on past behavior, preferences and interactions. AI-powered chatbots and virtual assistants can also improve communication and streamline operations, allowing for more efficient and effective event planning.

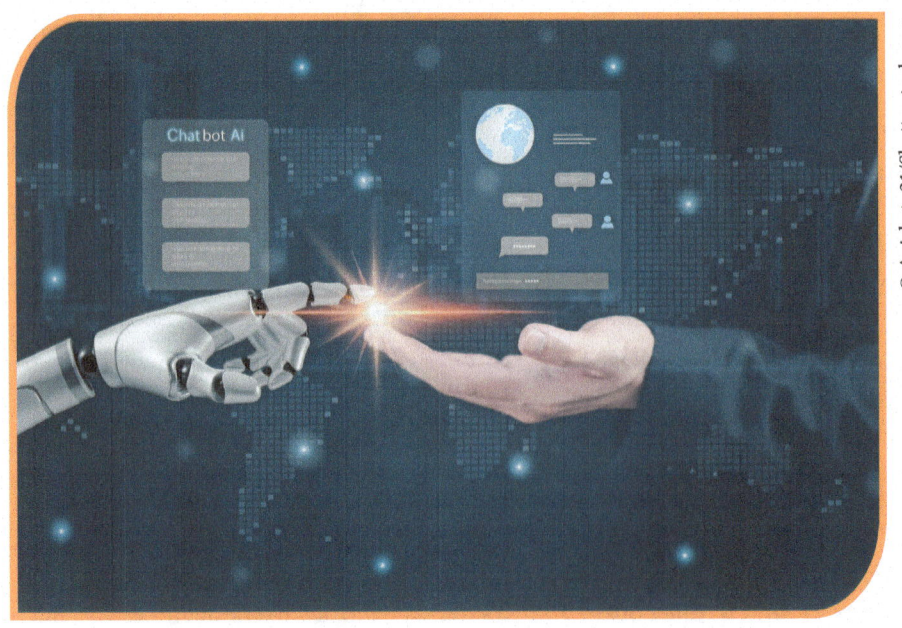

Wait a minute. Who wrote that paragraph? Was it . . . **ChatGPT**? In either case, 2023 marked a significant year for the widespread impact of AI on various industries, including hospitality. Although suppliers have been leveraging big data and AI for years, the advent of what could be termed "desktop AI" has democratized AI tools and brought them into the hands of a broader user base. The market for AI tools and solutions is expanding rapidly, and the potential applications across different sectors, including hospitality, are vast. AI is poised to continue transforming the way businesses operate and interact with customers in the coming years.

Hmmm . . . maybe that first paragraph was written by AI . . . if so, what else does it think about this topic?

> *In addition, AI can be used in the meeting industry to enhance event planning, attendee engagement and postevent analysis. For example, AI-powered matchmaking tools can help connect attendees with similar interests or job roles, while facial recognition technology can automate check-ins and reduce wait times. Overall, AI has the potential to revolutionize the meeting, events, and hospitality industry by providing personalized and streamlined experiences for guests and event planners alike.*

Cannot really argue much about that paragraph either. The business world is undergoing a profound transformation due to the capabilities and limitations of AI, and we are just scratching the surface of this journey.

The exponential growth of data creation, fueled by both human activities and AI-generated content, is a remarkable trend. The sheer volume of data generated today presents opportunities and challenges for AI to extract valuable insights and patterns from it.

AI is indeed integrated into our daily lives more than we might realize. Personalized recommendations on platforms, such as Netflix, voice-activated assistants, such as Alexa and Google Home, and even automated responses from chatbots on websites and event apps are all examples of how AI is applied to improve user experiences and streamline processes.

Chatbots, in particular, have found early applications in the events industry. These are computer programs trained to engage in conversations with humans using natural language. They can provide quick and automated responses to inquiries, enhancing customer support and engagement during events. The potential for AI in meetings and events is vast, with the ability to automate tasks, provide real-time information, and enhance attendee experiences.

AI chatbots have proven to be incredibly valuable for event planners in handling inquiries efficiently. They can address common questions, such as event schedules, keynote speakers, Wi-Fi passwords, and venue locations, relieving planners of the burden of these repetitive queries.

Another direct application of AI in the events industry is the service Wordly (https://wordly.ai), which specializes in language translation at events. It is tailored to the specific needs of the events industry, offering simplicity and the ability for multiple users to receive translations simultaneously based on their preferences. It has gained significant traction in international conferences and can revolutionize traditional approaches.

Popular video conferencing platforms, such as Zoom and Teams, have integrated various AI services. These integrations enhance internal functionality and allow connections to third-party AI services. One notable service is Otter.ai (https://otter.ai/), an AI-based meeting assistant that automatically records meetings and provides summaries of the conversation. It simplifies the task of capturing key information and can be a valuable tool for event organizers.

CHATGPT

Although AI has been in existence for some time, the standout representation of it in 2023 is undoubtedly ChatGPT. Understanding what it is, deciphering

© MMD Creative/Shutterstock.com

the acronym, and exploring how it can benefit our industry are all important questions.

ChatGPT is an exceptionally powerful example of a chatbot. It has been trained on an extensive data set and is a large language model (LLM), a type of AI that employs deep learning techniques to comprehend and respond in natural language. Although the intricate technical details are beyond the scope of this book, LLMs will become increasingly prominent.

"GPT" stands for Generative PreTrained Transformer, with "generative" being a key term. To oversimplify, this means that the tool generates responses to your queries word by word, selecting the next word based on the current question's context, primarily relying on what words naturally follow in a sentence. Unlike Google searches, which retrieve webpages matching your request, ChatGPT processes data and language on a much deeper level.

AI, CHAT GPT, AND HOSPITALITY

What does the industry landscape look like for ChatGPT and the plethora of AI desktop tools entering the market in 2023? To simplify, ChatGPT seamlessly integrates in several ways. It can serve as a valuable tool to kickstart the site or destination selection process. Another practical use is requesting it to distill industry trends and information. Furthermore, the trend of using it to craft content for event websites and digital media is expected to continue growing.

One essential point is that ChatGPT, and any chatbot or AI application, can produce inaccurate information just as often as good content without human intervention. Any meeting professional, or any person for that matter, who believes that AI will entirely replace the need for the human touch is missing the fundamental point. Although our roles may evolve significantly due to AI, it is unlikely that we will lose our jobs to it. Instead, our roles will adapt to these changes.

Giving ChatGPT the last word, I asked it what AI and the chatbot look like in 2030:

> *In 2030, AI and chatbots like ChatGPT will likely become even more sophisticated and intelligent, have a deeper understanding of natural language and context, and be used in a wider range of industries and applications.*

I think it is underestimating itself a bit. Do you agree?

VIRTUAL AND HYBRID MEETINGS

Although face-to-face interactions remain the preferred choice for most individuals, both for networking and education, the meeting industry has undeniably transformed due to the pandemic. However, it is apparent that the concept of truly effective hybrid meetings is not readily embraced by many industry professionals. This could be attributed to factors such as cost, the evolving nature of tech platforms, and, quite possibly, people's longing for in-person gatherings. The realization of the full potential of hybrid meetings still seems somewhat distant.

HYBRID MEETINGS

When executed skillfully, a hybrid meeting effectively broadens the reach of your live events to accommodate those who cannot attend in person. As the name implies, a hybrid meeting combines a live event with a remote component. Successful hybrid events go beyond simply streaming video content from the event to remote attendees. They are meticulously designed to offer unique and enriching experiences for both audiences. Striking a delicate balance to cater to the needs of both groups is crucial in crafting and delivering these sessions.

Hybrid meetings come in various types, ranging from town halls to technical trainings. As long as you can cater to the requirements of both live and remote audiences, you can be successful. These events can be quite costly, as they demand audiovisual and content delivery tools that engage the remote audience in real time and enhance the live audience's experience.

We are on the cusp of an era where hybrid meetings will become more prominent. However, several challenges and limitations must be addressed and overcome on both the planner's and supplier's sides. Event planners face hurdles related to crafting and executing engaging content and interactivity that can captivate both in-person and virtual audiences. Achieving this balance is no small task. Suppliers have the challenge of creating a virtual environment that not only mimics the feel of a live event but also provides an immersive experience for virtual participants. This entails overcoming technical and logistical obstacles. As we embrace the potential of hybrid meetings, it is essential to recognize and work through these challenges to ensure their success.

ONLINE MEETINGS AND WEBINARS

If one company can claim that the pandemic had a profoundly positive impact on its business, it is undoubtedly Zoom. A combination of user-friendly functionality and being in the right place at the right time propelled Zoom into becoming the default tool for the majority of meetings in 2020. Although imperfect, it offered a straightforward interface, reliable connectivity, reasonable pricing with its freemium model, and features that ensured not only its widespread adoption but also a touch of weariness (as humans tend to feel when exposed to too much of a good thing).

Creating a successful webinar differs significantly from organizing a live event. All-day online events rarely achieve success (after all, who wants to remain tethered to their desk all day for a virtual meeting?). Short, concentrated training sessions, some as brief as 15–20 minutes, can prove equally, if not more, effective than the more traditional 60–90-minute durations. Presenters, who lack visual and auditory cues from their audience, must possess the skill to keep their viewers engaged. Q&A sessions are typically scheduled after the main presentation or, more effectively, integrated into the platform's Q&A and chat functionality (unless you want a cacophony of 100 voices speaking simultaneously!).

Is Zoom the sole option? Certainly not. Numerous webinar providers are available for event planners to choose from. It is crucial for planners to ensure that the service they select aligns with their budget and requirements. Considerations should include how the service handles audio (via computer or phone), the maximum capacity it can support for virtual events (noting that platforms such as Zoom differentiate between meetings and webinars), whether it offers interactive features, such as chat and polling, and how easily event organizers and speakers can transition between the platform and their desktop to showcase applications and browsers.

Our industry is increasingly focused on refining the management of these virtual gatherings. An excellent resource on this topic is *Engaging Virtual Meetings* by industry veteran John Chen, available at https://engagingvirtualmeetings.com/. This book is a must-read for those interested in effectively organizing virtual and hybrid events. John Chen also maintains an active presence on various social platforms, including Facebook.

LARGE-SCALE VIRTUAL MEETINGS

Although Zoom and similar platforms excel at hosting individual meetings, many event planners require more extensive capabilities. What if you need to host multiple simultaneous sessions? How about running a virtual trade show? What if you want to offer attendees a single landing page where they can choose which segment of the meeting to attend? This is where more advanced event industry virtual meeting tools are rapidly emerging to meet these demands.

At the onset of the pandemic, it became evident to many in our industry that these services, although valuable, were not prepared to meet the demand or sophistication required and desired. Conversations with many company owners echoed similar sentiments. First, they were often understaffed, resulting in months-long waitlists for new clients. Second, their infrastructure required substantial upgrades.

The realm of large-scale virtual events and meetings has no one-size-fits-all solution. Each product has its strengths and areas for improvement, and providers are diligently working to enhance their offerings. Event planners seeking more robust solutions should explore these products to see if they align with their modified event objectives. Some notable options to consider include MAP Digital (https://mapdigital.com), Notified (https://www.notified.com), and an especially intriguing example of a purely virtual meeting and trade show digital space showcased by Meetaverse (https://meetaverse.com/).

THE ROARING TECH TWENTIES

If there ever was a decade that started with more questions than answers about its future, it is undoubtedly the 2020s, or the Roaring Tech Twenties. We find ourselves in an era where the future of meetings remains uncertain, except for the undeniable fact that change is inevitable. This is a time when new technologies continue to emerge while older ones mature and finally begin to fulfill their technological promises.

A century ago, the Roaring Twenties bore a striking resemblance to the present day. A global pandemic had swept across the world, reshaping lives. Technological breakthroughs were fundamentally altering the landscape of business, and once these tools were adopted, there was no turning back. These transformative technologies included commercial radio stations, sound movie films, and the nascent stages of commercial aviation, to name a few.

So, which technologies are likely to define this current decade? It will likely be a combination of innovations we have not even heard of yet and those that find a perfect fit in our daily lives, both at work and at home. Although it is challenging to predict the technologies that have not been created yet, here are some noteworthy ones (some of which have already been mentioned) that planners, suppliers, and indeed, everyone should keep a close eye on.

- **AI:** It is no surprise that AI is first, is it? As of mid-2023, we are only scratching the surface of "desktop AI"—tools that the average person can use, in contrast to the big data AI tools that have been in use for many years. The fascinating development to observe over the next few years will be how both planners and suppliers harness these tools. Currently, the landscape of potential tools includes ChatGPT, Bard, MidJourney, Dall-E, Kaiber, and Pictory. The question remains: Which ones will stand the test of time, and what new tools are on the horizon?
- **5G:** This game-changing cell technology is poised to redefine the speeds we experience on our devices without relying on Wi-Fi. Clearly, this will significantly impact the further development of **autonomous vehicles** (discussed separately). The landscape of Wi-Fi at hotels and conferences may, and should, never be the same again. Although its rollout

has commenced (albeit slower and more limited than what phone companies may lead you to believe), 5G can render Wi-Fi obsolete, offering wide-reaching, seemingly unlimited bandwidth. The only foreseeable concerns revolve around monetization discussions and the technology's ability to benefit everyone, not just those who are financially fortunate. In fact, we must remain cognizant of the digital tools' role in exacerbating economic disparities.

- **Mixed Reality:** How will AR and VR become integrated into events and various aspects of our lives? With Apple's involvement, notably the impending release of Vision Pro, it is intriguing to anticipate when one of these tools, likely AR initially, will experience its "killer app" moment in our industry. It is not a matter of if but when. At some point, AR technology could become synonymous with wearable tech.
- **Autonomous Vehicles:** Building upon the discussion of AI, the focus shifts to one of its byproducts, the autonomous car. Our industry might consider its application as a driverless shuttle bus. In 2023, most event planners would not seriously contemplate driverless group ground transportation. However, as the technology matures, coupled with the development and implementation of 5G, its safety and capabilities could meet and even exceed those of human-driven vehicles. A controversial idea? Perhaps.
- **Blockchain:** Although primarily associated with cryptocurrency, blockchain could become integral in areas such as securing online data and registration, as well as automated digital contract enforcement. Numerous obstacles must be surmounted before it becomes standard, but as blockchain gains ground in industries such as finance, it is wise to monitor its progress.
- **3D Printing:** This technology has left a significant footprint, albeit not yet in the meetings industry, except for niche applications, such as customized giveaways at events. Could 3D printing of food, a concept explored for well over a decade, become a frontier we explore in this decade?
- **Virtual/Hybrid Meetings:** We are already in the era of virtual meetings. What comes next, and how the live and virtual worlds will seamlessly integrate, remains a significant question. Keep an eye out for companies striving to blur the line between these two realms. Is it possible that hybrid events will become the dominant approach in our industry in the next 10 years? Absolutely.

SUMMARY

Do you think technology has evolved rapidly up until now? Well, you have not seen anything yet. In retrospect, 2023 may be regarded as a pivotal moment in the impact of technology on our lives, primarily due to the maturation of desktop AI. This is a remarkable consideration, given all the technological changes we have witnessed over the past two generations.

But how will all this affect meetings and events? The pandemic demonstrated not only the potential of new technologies to influence our daily work but also the challenges in achieving substantial change. Moreover, our industry's core essence revolves around people, not technology, which might suggest that technological developments could progress at a slower pace in our field compared to many others.

However, the AI revolution is upon us. It appears that, ready or not, significant changes are looming on the horizon for all aspects of our personal and professional lives, and that certainly includes the events industry.

So, buckle up for what might be a turbulent journey. Change is happening all around us, and we should watch to see which tools will ultimately have the most significant impact on what we do.

KEY WORDS AND TERMS

3D printing
5G
APEX
artificial intelligence
audience response systems
augmented reality
autonomous vehicles
blockchain
blogging
chatbots
ChatGPT
facial recognition
generative AI
hybrid meetings

interactive nametags
lead retrieval
mixed reality
near field communications
podcasting
portals
radio frequency identification
request for proposals
room design software
social media
Twitter
virtual reality
virtual trade shows
webinars

ABOUT THE CHAPTER CONTRIBUTOR

James Spellos is the president of Meeting U in New York City. The website is "meeting-u.com." He is a consultant and frequent speaker on technology issues in the MEEC industry.

CHAPTER 12

SUSTAINABLE MEETINGS AND EVENTS

SUSTAINABILITY IS A CRITICAL ELEMENT OF THE MEEC INDUSTRY

© FLUKY FLUKY/Shutterstock.com

CHAPTER OBJECTIVES

- Define sustainable meetings.
- Describe best practices in sustainable meetings.
- Outline sustainable event standards and guidelines.
- Describe the benefits of sustainable meetings and events.
- Identify sustainable trends in the MEEC industry.

Contributed by Carole Sox. © Kendall Hunt Publishing Company.

Riverbanks Zoo & Garden Offers a Green Event Venue

In addition to being home to over 3,000 magnificent and fascinating animals, Riverbanks Zoo and Garden offers the perfect setting for weddings, corporate events, and social gatherings. It is a prominent provider of unique, enjoyable, and environmentally friendly events in the capital city of Columbia, South Carolina. Its flagship restaurant, Tuskers, has earned recognition as one of the greenest restaurants in the state by the Green Restaurant Association.

"We take pride in our sustainable efforts," declared Thomas Stringfellow, president and CEO. "As leaders in the field of conservation, we consider all environmental factors in our endeavors and are excited to encourage our community to join us by offering sustainable options at their events."

Sustainable initiatives implemented at Riverbanks's events and throughout the park include introducing green alternatives to its 1.4 million annual guests. Riverbanks has eliminated single-use plastic lids and straws from its concession stands, instead offering guests a product from Strawfish that enables guests to sip sustainably, using biodegradable straws made from oyster shells. In 2023, Riverbanks began offering guests Bird Friendly coffee at its concessions and catered events. This coffee is certified to have been grown in ways that protect critical habitat for birds and wildlife and promote sustainable agricultural practices. Both of these examples not only benefit wildlife but also serve as educational opportunities regarding issues affecting wildlife and sustainable replacements for everyday products.

Riverbanks' cooking oil goes through a complete storage, filtering, and disposal system. This process not only enhances its longevity by removing fine particles but also reduces landfill waste by eliminating the need for plastic jugs. Moreover, it eliminates the emission of harmful greenhouse gases by reducing excessive transportation. When the oil reaches the end of its useful life, it is transported to an off-site facility for recycling.

Riverbanks has recently introduced solar power at the zoo and installed energy-efficient lighting throughout the park. It also promotes sustainable seafood choices by participating in the Monterey Bay Aquarium's Seafood Watch Program, helping patrons and consumers make informed decisions.

Riverbanks leads regular river sweeps as part of the Adopt-A-Waterway program. It has removed over 5,000 pounds of toxic trash from the banks of the Saluda River, recycling more than 2,100 pounds. The zoo has invested over a million dollars in local and global conservation efforts through the Satch Krantz Conservation Fund and continues to explore ways to reduce catering and concession waste with sustainable alternatives.

About Riverbanks Zoo & Garden

Riverbanks is one of the nation's most beautiful and inspiring botanical gardens. Spanning 170 lush acres, the site boasts dynamic natural habitat exhibits, scenic river views, spectacular valley overlooks, and significant historic landmarks. From small-scale initiatives to large efforts aimed at promoting and maintaining a sustainable environment, Riverbanks Zoo and Garden takes pride in being a green destination for year-round events and everyday visitors. For more information, please contact planyourevent@riverbanks.org

INTRODUCTION TO GREEN & SUSTAINABLE MEETINGS

Green meetings are defined in various ways, but "green" is commonly used to describe a meeting's environmental practices. Policies such as recycling, using energy-efficient lighting, or serving pitchers of water instead of bottled water typically determine how green a meeting is considered by the venue and client. The emphasis on protecting the environment often serves as a key indicator for green meetings.

Green meetings are those designed to mitigate harmful effects on the environment (e.g., minimizing waste, reducing single-use plastic). Although they take the current state of the environment into account, they are not usually associated with the overall impact on future generations or the triple bottom line.

The industry began referring to green meetings approximately 10–12 years ago when the concept of being environmentally friendly gained popularity in the lodging sector. The movement is evolving to include efforts that affect the human aspect of meetings and events, such as taking care of employees working at the meetings and events, attendees, and those who are impacted in the community where an event may occur—all while also turning a profit. This is often referred to as the "triple bottom line" or "sustainability."

Although sometimes used interchangeably, "green meetings" and "sustainable meetings" have different meanings.

"Sustainable meeting" is more comprehensive; it encompasses implementing and executing a plan to conserve resources while improving the performance of a meeting or event. It implies that the impact of a meeting on the environment, society, and the economy has been taken into consideration. According to the Events Industry Council, "sustainability for events means taking action toward preserving our natural environment, promoting a healthy, inclusive society, and supporting a thriving economy." The council identifies four principles of event sustainability:

1. Both event planners and suppliers have shared responsibility for employing and communicating sustainable event practices to all stakeholders.

2. Basic environmental practices include conservation of resources; waste management; carbon emissions reduction and management; responsible purchasing and supply chain management; and biodiversity preservation.

3. Basic social considerations include universal human rights, community impacts, labor practices, respect for culture, safety and security, and health and well-being.

4. Sustainable events support thriving economic practices through collaboration and partnerships, local support, stakeholder participation, equitable economic impact, and transparency and responsible governance.

The widely recognized Brundtland Report, created after the 1983 World Commission on Environment and Development, defines **sustainability** as "development that meets the needs of the present without compromising the ability of future generations to meet their own needs." This definition is one of the most frequently cited and focuses on three aspects of sustainable development: economic development, social development, and environmental protection. These three aspects, often referred to as the "three pillars of sustainability"—profit, planet, and people—are interconnected; none can exist without the others.

> **TIDBIT**
>
> Coordinated primarily by the World Wildlife Fund, Earth Hour began in Australia in 2007 to combat the effects of global warming and conserve energy by encouraging people to turn off their lights from 8:30 p.m. to 9:30 p.m. toward the end of March. In 2022, 192 countries and territories supported it, generating a record-breaking 10.1+ billion social media impressions worldwide.

The movement toward sustainable meetings in the Meetings, Events, Exhibitions, and Conferences (MEEC) industry is impacting all aspects of meeting planning. As more planners strive to minimize the environmental footprint of their events, suppliers are also making efforts to offer more eco-friendly products and services. Event professionals are actively learning how to organize sustainable meetings, and meeting suppliers are aligning with this trend. When meeting professionals embrace sustainable planning, it has a positive ripple effect on all involved parties.

WHY DO IT?

THE TRIPLE BOTTOM LINE

Perhaps addressing the question of "why?" involves considering more than a single response. Some experts propose the "**triple bottom line**" as a more comprehensive measure of a company's achievements and a better response to this question. This concept considers people (social impact), planet (environmental impact), and profit (economic impact). It broadens the definition of success to encompass environmental and social achievements alongside financial ones. Research suggests that many forward-thinking organizations, associations, and companies are adopting this approach to assess their success and report to stakeholders.

PROFIT (ECONOMIC IMPACT)

Economic sustainability pertains to a meeting's ability to use resources efficiently and responsibly to meet all financial obligations over time. In the MEEC industry, this is crucial for both planners and the organizations hosting or requesting the meetings. This approach not only makes sound business sense but also leads to higher reported gross profit margins, return on sales, return on assets, and stronger cash flow compared to less sustainable competitors. Economic sustainability examples encompass return on investment (ROI), fair trade, supporting the local economy, fostering growth, and enhancing business performance. Once a company commits to becoming more sustainable, it becomes easier to apply these principles to its meetings and events.

Taking small steps toward sustainability can result in significant improvements in a company's bottom line. For instance, one large event saved $1.5 million by eliminating bottled water during a 5-day event attended by 40,000 people. Another group saved over $1,500 in 1 year by reusing badge holders. Beyond cost savings, these initiatives significantly reduce waste going to landfills. Oracle's sustainability efforts during its annual OpenWorld event saved it $1.7 million over 5 years. Among its numerous green initiatives, reevaluating signage policies alone saved $420,000. Its signage now consists of lighter, reusable materials sourced from local companies.

Planet (Environmental Impact)

Many efforts related to economic impacts and savings through sustainability are inherently linked to environmental initiatives and cost-saving measures. This underscores the interconnected nature of the triple bottom line; it is challenging to focus on one aspect without considering the others. The aspect that is often easiest to comprehend is environmental sustainability. Many in the MEEC industry primarily associate it with actions aimed at reducing the negative impact of meetings and events on the environment; they have numerous avenues to address environmental concerns and minimize the impact of their events. For instance, they can reduce printed materials, such as program guides, venue maps, or exhibition materials. This yields not only environmental benefits but cost savings. Many organizations have moved away from the traditional practice of automatically printing conference and meeting programs for every attendee. Instead, they leverage technology to encourage

Event Apps have replaced paper programs

attendees to use mobile apps. These event apps have evolved over the years to offer features such as daily schedules, speaker and exhibitor information, social media tools, calendars, personal customization options, and user-friendly interfaces. All the information typically found in a printed program guide is now readily accessible through these digital tools.

Carbon Offsets

Large trade shows and conventions now provide attendees with the opportunity to purchase a **carbon offset**, allowing them to mitigate their environmental impact. Given that attendees often need to use various forms of transportation, such as airplanes, cars, or trains, to reach these events, they inevitably generate emissions that harm the environment. Transportation is the largest contributor to an event's environmental footprint, accounting for approximately 90% of emissions produced by events worldwide. A carbon offset compensates for carbon dioxide and greenhouse gas emissions produced during travel by balancing or canceling them out. Officially, a carbon offset is defined as a method to "reduce or offset carbon emissions through the funding of activities and projects that improve the environment." For instance, if an individual flies round-trip from Phoenix to New York for a meeting or event, it results in approximately 806 pounds of carbon emissions, assuming the flight is at full capacity. The impact is even greater on less populated flights. By purchasing a carbon offset, individuals can help minimize this impact by contributing to projects that reduce carbon and greenhouse gas emissions, such as tree planting, investment in renewable energy sources, such as windmills, or alternative fuels. Meeting professionals now offer attendees the option to voluntarily purchase carbon offsets; the associated costs can vary. Although it may not be the most preferred method for reducing environmental impact, it represents a proactive option that is certainly better than taking no action.

> #### Tidbit
>
> You can calculate your event's carbon footprint using tools, such as *Terrapass's* online **carbon footprint calculator**. This calculator considers factors such as attendee profiles, number of attendees, their travel distances, origins, number of meals served, and water consumption at the event. Based on the results, attendees can determine how many carbon offsets to purchase.

People (Social Impact)

In addition to the environmental and economic factors of sustainability, it also encompasses people, including those who attend meetings and events, work at them, organize them, and live in the communities where they are held. This is "realized by equitably meeting the needs of all people affected by the planning or activation of an event." The question that meeting planners must ask themselves is how their events impact not only their own employees but also attendees and the local communities. Is that impact a positive one?

To provide a framework for this concept of working with and for people, many companies have embraced the idea of **corporate social responsibility** (CSR). It has been in existence since the 1950s and referred to in a number of different ways (e.g., "corporate responsibility," "corporate accountability," "corporate ethics," "corporate citizenship," "corporate sustainability," and "responsible business"). According to the World Business Council for Sustainable Development, CSR is the "continuing commitment by business to behave ethically and contribute to economic development while improving the quality of life of the workforce and their families, as well as the local community and society at large." This aligns perfectly with the people side of sustainability. Another appropriate definition comes from Simply CSR: "a long-term approach to business that addresses the needs of communities, people, and their employers. CSR provides frameworks for a successful enterprise that is harmonious with its surroundings. It is an opportunity to generate honest, authentic good-news stories that a business and its community can be proud of." At the core of CSR are individuals doing the right thing.

How does this translate to action in the MEEC industry specifically? Internally, employees of organizations that support sustainability efforts can experience several benefits. Their health may improve as they work in naturally lit and well-ventilated offices designed for energy efficiency. They might also be encouraged to adopt healthier habits, such as taking the stairs or riding a bicycle to work, which contributes to their personal well-being. Additionally, fostering a culture of sustainability can enhance employee satisfaction. Encouraging employees to actively participate in sustainability initiatives often means promoting a healthier and more active lifestyle, resulting in happier and more productive individuals. Moreover, these efforts can positively impact a company's bottom line, such as by providing paid time off for volunteering at local charities or matching employee donations to a charity of their choice.

Externally, event attendees also benefit from sustainable efforts, especially when participating in programs focused on reducing, reusing, and recycling. These initiatives often extend beyond the event venue and encourage participants to engage with the local community or support local charities. The expectation is shifting from providing attendees with the same old experience to introducing them to the city and demonstrating how their presence affects it and its residents.

These activities can take various forms. Some organizations encourage attendees to actively engage in community projects while attending an event, but others may simply request donations or make contributions on behalf of the entire organization. Some examples include the following:

Oracle—Oracle's annual OpenWorld conference exemplifies its commitment to sustainability and community engagement. It collaborates with local agencies and charities to make various contributions. For instance, in 1 year, it donated 1,135 pounds of event furniture to a local chapter of Habitat for Humanity, along with 1,268 pounds of essential items, such as backpacks, socks, toiletry sacks, and office supplies. Furthermore, it contributed 1,621 pounds of food and 150 pounds of lightly used soaps and room amenities to aid those in need.

Clean the World—This third-party company partners with hotels to recycle soap and partially used toiletries. During events, attendees can dedicate a few minutes to assemble small toiletry kits, which are distributed to local homeless shelters and other organizations serving those in need.

Tee It Up for the Troops—This is an organized run held during the annual Club Management Association of America's World Conference and Business Club Expo. The proceeds from this event are entirely donated to this charitable organization, and it consistently sells out every year.

Food Runners—In San Francisco, this initiative provides an avenue for anyone hosting a meeting or event to donate leftover food. It collects and distributes this surplus food to feeding programs throughout the city, delivering an impressive 17 tons of food per week, which translates to approximately 20,000 meals per week.

These initiatives highlight the positive impact that the MEEC industry can have on local communities and charitable causes.

BENEFITS OF SUSTAINABILITY

In an industry as fast paced and detail oriented as MEEC, where every aspect is significant, it is understandable that planners, suppliers, vendors, and facility managers seek efficiency and streamlining. So, why should industry professionals take on the added challenge of embracing sustainability? Because doing the right thing is simply the right thing to do.

Enhanced Brand Image

Planning and executing sustainable events are not just good for the planet; they are also good for business. This is particularly crucial for large corporate and association events worldwide. When attendees recognize the positive impact that organizers are making on both the environment and communities, it enhances the organization's image and fosters repeat attendance. Attendees also feel good about participating, knowing they can minimize their environmental footprint while contributing to local communities.

Differentiation

One of the challenges in the MEEC industry is keeping meetings and events engaging and relevant, especially for attendees who return year after year. Sustainability provides a unique selling point, offering something new and exciting each time, giving attendees a fresh perspective and something to look forward to.

Cost Savings

Sustainability practices, such as waste reduction, energy conservation, sourcing local food, and eliminating bottled water, result in cost savings, benefiting both the organization and the environment.

Raise Awareness

The MEEC industry presents a remarkable opportunity to educate attendees every time sustainable practices are integrated into an event. Attendees come from all corners of the world and may not be familiar with such practices or their benefits. This can inspire people to make decisions that reduce their own environmental footprint, in both their business and personal lives, creating a ripple effect of positive change.

Social Benefits

When carefully planned and executed, meetings can bring about significant social advantages for the local region. They can create job opportunities, support regional suppliers, encourage better working conditions, and act as a catalyst for promoting environmental best practices throughout the region (UNEP, Green Meeting Guide).

SUSTAINABLE MEETING STANDARDS AND GUIDELINES

The MEEC industry is rapidly progressing toward realizing sustainable meetings as the norm in the future. Evidence supporting this trend is the growing number of guidelines and certifications available that play a pivotal role in identifying, unifying, and standardizing sustainability efforts.

SUSTAINABLE MEETING STANDARDS

In 2022, the Events Industry Council (EIC), in collaboration with 100 industry experts, revised internationally accepted industry standards (the APEX/ASTM Environmentally Sustainable Meeting Standards from 2019). These updated standards are now the *2022 EIC Sustainable Event Standards*, covering eight distinct sectors:

1. event organizer,
2. accommodations,
3. audiovisual and production,
4. destination,
5. exhibitions,
6. food and beverage,
7. integrated property, and
8. venue.

Event organizers undergo assessments across various domains, including internal practices, climate action, supply chain management, accommodations, venue, food and beverage, destination, audiovisual (A/V) and production, and exhibitions if these elements are part of their event. Suppliers, on the other hand, are assessed in categories such as organizational management, air quality management, community engagement, climate action, water management, energy efficiency, waste management, marketing and communications, and supply chain management.

For more detailed information regarding these standards, you can visit the EIC website https://www.eventscouncil.org/.

UNITED NATIONS (UN) SUSTAINABLE DEVELOPMENT GOALS

UN crafted the 2030 Agenda for Sustainable Development, which garnered unanimous adoption by all UN member nations in 2015. It "provides a shared blueprint for peace and prosperity for people and the planet, now and into the future." It represents a pressing call to collaborate on a global scale to achieve the 17 Sustainable Development Goals (SDGs) that constitute the core of this agenda. EIC has also embraced these goals as the foundation upon which it has constructed its four principles of event sustainability.

ISO 20121

ISO 20121 is an international management system created to assist MEEC organizations in enhancing the sustainability of their events, encompassing products, services, and related activities. It originated as a British standard in 2007 and was adapted internationally, particularly to coincide with the 2012 London Olympics. It aims to comprehensively address all facets of the industry. Organizations that successfully implement it can pursue certification through an independent accrediting body. ISO 20121 and the EIC Sustainable Event Standards offer distinct approaches to defining sustainable events, but they can function independently or collaboratively.

Sustainable Development Goals

> ### Global Experience Specialists (GES) Achieves Environmental Sustainability Recertification
>
> In 2015, GES became the first general service contractor to achieve certification according to an international sustainability standard specific to the meetings and events industry. GES has been recertified at Level 2 of the EIC Sustainable Event Standards, pertaining to evaluating and selecting exhibits for environmentally sustainable meetings, events, trade shows, and conferences.
>
> GES has maintained a strong and ongoing commitment to sustainable practices. Its U.K. operations are ISO 20121 certified (a complex and demanding international standard focused on adopting a management systems approach to organizing more sustainable events) (GMIC, 2017).

In addition to the EIC Sustainable Event Standards and ISO 20121, many eco-friendly, third-party certifications are recognized within the MEEC industry. The following is a list of some various certifications or awards that apply primarily to suppliers.

A. Accommodations/Venues
- Green Key Global's Green Key Meetings
- Audubon Green Lodging Program
- Green Globe
- Leadership in Energy & Environmental Design (LEED)
- Energy Star Qualified Buildings
- ISO 20121
- Green Seal

B. Catering/Food and Beverage
- Marine Stewardship Council
- Fair Trade Certified
- USDA Certified Organic
- Green Restaurant Association
- Rainforest Alliance Certification

C. Printing/Promotional/Gifts

- Forest Stewardship Council
- The Programme for the Endorsement of Forest Certification
- The Sustainable Forestry Initiative(r)
- American Tree Farm System
- Waterless Printing Association

Not all meeting industry certifications are covered here, and the landscape is continually evolving. New certifications emerge, some are amalgamated, and others become obsolete, replaced by more meaningful alternatives. Gaining a deep understanding of the requirements for each certification is crucial. Planners must conduct due diligence and ensure that the it holds value. Each certification has its unique prerequisites, but the overarching aim is to maintain a standard of quality in the ever-evolving practice of integrating environmentally friendly approaches. Such thoroughness on the part of meeting professionals guarantees no misrepresentation to attendees and that the sustainability goals for the meeting are achieved.

GREENWASHING

These certifications play a vital role in assisting MEEC professionals in identifying companies genuinely committed to sustainability. As consumer awareness of sustainable practices grows, companies are responding by integrating more sustainability efforts into their business standards. However, in the competitive landscape, some companies may be too eager to promote their sustainability initiatives, achievements, or standards. As awareness spreads, even consumers find it increasingly challenging to distinguish between companies genuinely implementing sustainable practices and those involved in **greenwashing**.

Greenwashing is any misrepresentation by a company that leads consumers to believe its policies and products are environmentally responsible when such claims are false, misleading, or unsubstantiated. It is also used to describe companies that spend more on advertising their environmentally friendly efforts than on the efforts themselves. This phenomenon underscores the importance of discerning certifications and ensuring their legitimacy.

Greenwashing began in the mid-1960s, when companies were eager to align themselves with the emerging environmental movement. As these practices evolved, they eventually became known as "greenwashing," coined in an essay by environmentalist Jay Westerveld in 1968 that reviewed the practice of placing a card on the pillow in each hotel room, explaining that the hotel encourages guests to reuse towels for environmental responsibility. Upon closer examination, Westerveld concluded that, in most cases, hotels were making minimal efforts to reduce energy waste with these programs and primarily using them as profit-driven strategies.

For planners, being well informed about sustainability standards is a crucial way to educate themselves and their clients. As part of their due diligence, planners should include a back-of-the-house tour, which can be instrumental in validating (or disproving) green claims. For instance, if a venue claims to offer readily available recycling opportunities for all attendees, this should be evident during the tour. Planners should be able to witness where recycled materials are stored and the processes involved once they are removed from the event space. Similarly, if a venue claims to use local produce for all meals, evidence should be apparent during the tour. Furthermore, planners should practice sustainability within their own departments and organizations, setting an example and advocating for green practices. Although numerous checklists are available to assist them in planning green events, the one at the end of this chapter serves as a good starting point. By becoming aware of the challenges posed by greenwashing, planners can more effectively identify areas of concern and proceed positively with the planning of sustainable events.

CREATING A PROCESS FOR SUSTAINABLE PRACTICES

Studies indicate that over half of all meeting professionals are now considering environmental practices. It is no longer sufficient to limit these considerations to sleeping rooms. At major events organized by Meeting Professionals International (MPI), for instance, the board of directors intentionally considers the seven areas of sustainable meetings defined by EIC's standards.

Planning, managing, and assessing a sustainable meeting were once seen as challenging and costly endeavors. It may be as straightforward as carefully considering decisions related to company policies. Here are some simple steps that professionals can follow to make their next meeting more sustainable, as recommended by EIC.

Step 1: Create a plan. Develop a management system approach for defining the sustainability objectives. This plan should outline how you intend to achieve these objectives and specify the key performance indicators for measuring the plan's success. Identify precise activities (such as achieving a certain percentage of waste diversion or serving a percentage of local or organic meals), metrics for monitoring progress, desired outcomes for each objective, and the individuals responsible for achieving these results.

Step 2: Engage internal stakeholders in supporting your plan. Establish or formulate a sustainable meeting policy for your team, department, or event. Ideally, this policy should reflect your company or organization's internal values to ensure alignment with your event efforts.

Step 3: Engage vendors in supporting your plan. Encourage your vendors to support your plan, ideally at cost savings or cost-neutral pricing. Incorporate language into your request for proposals process and contracts that requires vendors to provide the data you need to track your performance. The first year can serve as a benchmark for evaluation and future growth.

Step 4: Track your performance. Just as we meticulously monitor our event budgets, it is essential to track the performance of our sustainability action plans. After the event, ensure accurate reporting so that you can build on the results and use them in your site selection process.

Step 5: Communicate the results, celebrate the success. Although continuous improvement is a primary goal for sustainability professionals, it is important to pause, acknowledge, and share the success of your action plan with attendees, vendors, the media, and the industry. The more you can quantify your results in human-scale terms (e.g., amount of money saved, number of trees preserved, amount of CO_2 reduced), the more engaged you and your stakeholders will be in supporting the plan in the following years.

Step 6: Be innovative, and have fun! Although this is not strictly part of the environmental management action plan, event professionals must enjoy what they do. The goal is to create fulfilling experiences for attendees. Therefore, if it aligns with your organization's goals, be creative and incorporate elements such as yoga breaks, human-powered energy stations, or networking events that serve the local community. Remember to allocate outdoor or unscheduled activity time, as attendees will appreciate your efforts to address their sustainability needs.

Habitat for Humanity

BEST ENVIRONMENTAL PRACTICES

Now that best sustainable practices have been established, here are some specific actions that meeting professionals can take to incorporate them into their meetings.

Use Technology: Leverage technology to reduce the need for paper. With user-friendly apps or registration companies, you have virtually no need to produce printed materials. To cut down on travel costs, use podcasting, webinars, and video streaming. These approaches can increase attendance by making it easier for more people to participate.

Choose a Local Destination: Approximately 90% of an event's carbon footprint results from air travel. Whenever feasible, event professionals should select a destination close to where participants reside. If air travel is necessary, opt for a venue or hotel near the airport or within walking distance of off-site events. Research public transportation options in the host city.

Reduce, Reuse, and Recycle: Include proper recycling bins on the event supplies list, and ensure that staff are trained in the correct procedures. Request that venues provide visible and accessible recycling services for paper, metal, plastic, and glass. Inquire with banquet managers about composting options or giveaway programs. Explore the possibility of using real china for meals; if this is not feasible, select disposable plates made from renewable resources that will biodegrade in a landfill. Collect name badge holders and lanyards for reuse.

Volume Up: Encourage food and beverage providers to use bulk dispensers for sugar, creamer, and other condiments instead of individual packets. Look for hotels that use dispensers for shampoo and lotions rather than small bottles. Request water stations rather than bottled water and provide attendees with a reusable bottle, which can also present a sponsorship opportunity.

Eat Local: Engage with the banquet manager to incorporate local, in-season fruits and vegetables. Include more vegetarian meals, as they have a lower carbon energy footprint. Ensure an accurate headcount before finalizing food orders to minimize food waste.

Decorate with Nature: Use local flowers, plants, and succulents for table decorations, leaving them in pots so they can be repurposed as gifts or prizes, reducing waste. Some cities have local charities that collect event flowers and donate them to churches or assisted living facilities.

Decorating with nature

Use Paper Wisely: If print materials are essential, use chlorine-free, recycled paper and vegetable inks. Print on both sides of the paper, and only print materials for participants upon request. Consider using "print-on-demand" stations rather than printing copies for each attendee.

Save Energy: Seek venues and hotels that prioritize energy efficiency and have energy-saving policies. Coordinate with them to ensure that lights, A/V equipment, and air-conditioning in meeting spaces are turned off when not in use. Remind attendees to conserve energy in their rooms by turning off lights when leaving and avoiding electronic devices left plugged in and powered on.

Inform Everyone: Communicate your sustainability efforts and expectations to participants, speakers, suppliers, vendors, and the media. Clear communication is essential to encourage and secure active participation from all involved parties. For instance, ensure that green expectations are explicitly stated in speaker contracts, so speakers do not arrive with printed handouts.

Repurposing: Consider repurposing items such as meeting banners into useful and creative products, such as messenger bags, wallets, tote bags, or laptop sleeves. This approach reduces waste and promotes sustainability.

EVALUATION OF SUSTAINABLE EFFORTS

If you can measure it, you can manage it. This is a common mantra in many sectors of the business world. It applies equally well to sustainable meetings and sustainable efforts. It is important for meeting professionals and companies to set clear goals in the beginning so that it is possible to measure event success or failure. Fortunately, because of the growing interest in conducting green meetings, a few tools have been created to help in the measurement/evaluation process.

MEETGREEN® CALCULATOR 2.0

Measuring the impact of sustainable efforts can be challenging, but *Meet-Green* has developed a calculator to address this issue. It is a comprehensive tool for benchmarking the sustainability aspects of events, regardless of their size. It enables event professionals to gather valuable information throughout the planning process, making it easy to assess achievements and areas for improvement. The tool evaluates event management practices and measurable outcomes in 14 key categories to audit the environmental impact of conference activities. It integrates elements of ISO 20121 and the EIC Sustainable Event Standards.

SUSTAINABLE MEETING PROFESSIONAL

MPI offers a Sustainable Event Strategist Certification program that teaches planners how to approach event planning with a sustainability perspective. It covers tactical best practices for reducing the environmental impact of events and guides participants in creating a culture of sustainable decision-making throughout the planning process. The program uses the EIC Sustainable Event Standards and ISO 20121 to achieve these goals.

The following three examples provide insights regarding sustainable efforts in practice.

Grand Carolina Resort and Spa

The resort was selected to host 1,000 delegates over 6 days. Initially, it was not particularly environmentally friendly, but in response to the client's green requirements, management changed standard operating procedures and implemented capital improvements, such as installing solar panels. Delegates also contributed by reducing their own consumption while on-site.

Throughout the event, daily data on utility usage and waste generation was collected and reported the following morning during general sessions. Total consumption was compared to the average of a similar convention held the previous year. The results were impressive: Electricity consumption decreased by 21%, water use by 48%, and solid waste by 34%. These green initiatives were estimated to save the resort over $1 million per year.

As the demand for measurable outcomes continues to grow and companies seek a ROI for green strategies, the ability to measure sustainability factors will become increasingly important. Expect to see new and more sophisticated tools for tracking carbon, energy, water footprints, and overall conference achievements. These newer tools will complement established ones, such as paper savings calculators and the MeetGreen Calculator.

A Look Into the Oregon Convention Center (OCC)'s First-of-Its-Kind Waste Diversion Policy

OCC in Portland is renowned for its sustainability efforts and holds LEED® Platinum certification, signifying its dedication to environmentally responsible practices. OCC strives to not only minimize its own impact but also set a new standard for sustainability in the convention industry.

Convention centers are known to generate substantial waste, much of it stemming from event organizers' decisions. This waste often includes materials, such as banners and cardboard boxes, that are typically discarded and end up in landfills.

In 2015, OCC took a pioneering step by introducing a waste diversion policy designed to reduce event waste, foster innovation, and promote reuse. Developing it was a significant undertaking, given no industry precedents. OCC embarked on extensive research and engaged in discussions with both internal staff and external partners to craft a comprehensive strategy.

Today, the policy is fully integrated into OCC's contracts and operational procedures, covering every stage from event inception to conclusion. One aspect that OCC takes pride in is its commitment to donation. Many leftover convention items can be repurposed, and OCC collaborates with local nonprofit organizations in need of them. For example, in partnership with its catering provider, Pacificwild, OCC donates tens of thousands of meals each year to the nonprofit social services organization Blanchet House. It partners with FreeGeek, a local nonprofit, to recycle used electronics. Through these partnerships, OCC has donated over 120,000 pounds of reusable goods and provided 46,600 meals to combat food scarcity in the Portland area.

OCC has set an ambitious long-term goal of achieving at least an 80% diversion rate for waste. Impressively, as of now, 94% of events held at OCC follow its waste diversion policy. Over the past year, OCC has made significant strides in its sustainability efforts, recycling over 400 tons of materials and diverting 122 tons of food scraps from landfills through composting.

OCC is an environmentally conscious facility owned by Metro and managed by the Metro Exposition and Recreation Commission. OCC regularly hosts groups and events from around the world, contributing significantly to the economy of Portland and the broader state of Oregon.

FREEMAN

Since Freeman was founded as a family-owned event company in 1927, one of its core values has been ethical business conduct and a strong commitment to the well-being of its employees, communities, industry, and environment. Today, the Freeman family and employees continue that legacy every day through a variety of activities, programs, and, most of all, a spirit of caring. In 2019, Freeman earned the APEX/ASTM Sustainable Meetings Certification.

In fiscal year 2018:

- More than $700,000 in goods and services were donated to charities.
- Employees volunteered 5,010 hours to organizations.
- 229 individual programs or events were held in 2017–2018.

Organizations it has worked with include American Heart Association, local schools and school districts, local food banks, Veteran's Stand Down, Boys & Girls Club, BL Duke, Goodwill, Salvation Army, and blood donation drives.

TRENDS AND BEST PRACTICES

GreenMatch gained insights from 42 professional experts to determine the global sustainability trends for 2023. Although these trends were not event specific, they can certainly be implemented within the event arena, and some have already taken hold.

1. Reuse and repurpose
2. Recycle
3. Renewable energy sources
4. Transport transformed
5. Reduce food waste
6. Remote work
7. Brand responsibility and transparency
8. Plant-based diets
9. Increase in technology efficiency
10. Standardized sustainable materials

In addition to current trends, the following are some of the best practices in MEEC sustainability.

- Increasing numbers of planners will have sustainable meeting policies that will extend to suppliers.
- Sustainable meeting practices will increasingly be incorporated into events.
- Increasing numbers of groups will have meeting and event policies associated with all three factors of sustainability—people, profit, planet.
- Many national governments and large corporations are likely to demand that the meetings and events they organize and sponsor incorporate sustainable elements.
- There will be increasing "accountability" and requirements that planners "prove" their meetings and events are sustainable.

- An increased focus on cost versus benefits of sustainability will continue. Being able to document and calculate the true cost and true benefits will be crucial.
- Some sustainable activities that are now voluntary will become legal requirements.
- Educational training and certification programs for providers of sustainable events will become more abundant.

SUMMARY

This chapter summarizes the most recent developments in the MEEC industry related to sustainability. Sustainability is not a fad; it is a fact of life in the 21st century. The challenge is how to incorporate it into meetings and events and show how those efforts impact the bottom line, the environment, and the people, while also providing attendees with a good experience.

Now that you have completed this chapter, you should be competent in the following Meeting and Business Event Competency Standards.

(MBECS)—SKILL 2: DEVELOP SUSTAINABILITY PLAN FOR MEETING OR EVENT

	Subskills	Skills (standards)
A2.012	Implement sustainability management plan	
A2.02	Demonstrate environmental responsibility	

CASE STUDY SUSTAINABLE OPTIONS AT RIBALD EVENTS

(Produced by Scott Turner and Ariel Prescott of Ribald Events and Dr. Carole Sox of Columbia College, SC)

Ribald Farms was established in 2006 by Scott and Shawna Turner as a small full-time nursery selling an assortment of plant species, including various potted plants. In 2007, cut flowers were added, which helped their floristry business bloom. Soon after, Ribald began fulfilling floral needs for special events, such as weddings, dances, and birthday celebrations. Then in 2010, Scott and Shawna decided to add event rentals to their brand and became a one-stop shop for floral and event rental needs. The convenience of having a "two in one" store helped to build their reputation in the event world and became their primary focus. Shawna, a seasoned florist and Scott, a wise businessman, were truly excited for new business opportunities and to bring each client's vision to life. In 2020, Ribald moved forward with specializing in only event rentals and changed the company name to "Ribald Events." Since this decision, Ribald has continued to exceed its client's expectations and remain competitive within the event rental industry.

Ariel Prescott, a graduate of the hospitality, tourism and event program at Columbia College in South Carolina, was hired by Ribald Events right after graduation. She is an event rental agent and works directly with all event planners and brides to assist them in determining what they might need. She receives many requests per year for sustainable options. Ariel goes through options with her clients and provides information on sustainable options, a few of which are listed below.

- China dishware versus plastic,
- Linens (washed using energy-efficient washers), and
- Reusable miscellaneous décor (vases, table centerpieces, etc.).

Although these are all good options, Ariel is considering adding information on the website about all of the sustainable options available for planners and brides. Ribald Events provides rental options, such as draping, lighting, chairs, tables, bars, dance floors, dishware, tents and more. Go to their website https://www.ribaldevents.com/ to see more of what they offer.

1. After viewing their website, create a page to be added to it explaining green meetings, sustainability, the benefits, and what Ribald Events can offer to satisfy any green and/or sustainability requests from planners.

KEY WORDS AND TERMS

For definitions, see the Glossary, or https://insights.eventscouncil.org/Industry-glossary.

carbon footprint calculator
carbon offset
corporate social responsibility (CSR)
green meeting
greenwashing
sustainability
sustainable meeting
triple bottom line

REVIEW AND DISCUSSION QUESTIONS

1. Discuss the economic advantages of a sustainable event.
2. How does a meeting manager evaluate sustainable efforts?
3. Explain the difference between the terms "green meetings" and "sustainable meetings," and give examples for each that support your answer.
4. Describe how an event planner can ensure that a venue is not greenwashing.
5. What is CSR? What role does CSR play in the MEEC industry?
6. What is the triple bottom line, as applied to the MEEC industry?
7. Define sustainability.
8. Describe best practices for incorporating sustainability into your meeting or event.

RECOMMENDED WEBSITES

EIC: http://www.eventscouncil.org/

EIC Centre for Sustainability & Social Impact:

https://www.eventscouncil.org/Sustainability/CSE

UN SDGs: https://sdgs.un.org/goals

ISO 20121: http://www.iso20121.org/

MeetGreen: https://meetgreen.com/

Sustainable Event Professional Certificate Program:

https://www.eventscouncil.org/Sustainability/SEPC

Terrapass: https://www.terrapass.com/

ABOUT THE CHAPTER CONTRIBUTOR

Carole Sox, Ph.D., CHE, is an associate professor and the department chair of the Undergraduate Business Program at Columbia College in South Carolina. Dr. Sox started the hospitality, tourism, and event management concentration and hospitality minor at Columbia. She teaches courses in hospitality and business. She earned her master's from Southern Wesleyan University and her Ph.D. in hospitality management from the University of South Carolina. Dr. Sox has almost 20 years of corporate experience and 17 years of academic experience at higher learning institutions, and she is the author and coauthor of nationally and internationally presented research on various hospitality topics. Dr. Sox was the recipient of the Faculty Excellence Award (Columbia College, 2023), Educator of the Year Award (South Carolina Restaurant and Lodging Association, 2020), and Rookie Innovative Educator Award (Columbia College, 2019).

Green Event Checklist

15 THINGS YOU CAN DO TODAY

MeetGreen

1. Ask for recycling at the facility
2. Ask for a towel reuse program at the hotel
3. Request no bottled water be served
4. Ask for all condiments and beverages to be served in bulk
5. Request leftover food be donated
6. Request water glasses not be pre-filled at banquets
7. Request china and linens for meals, no disposables
8. Ask if there is electronic signage in the meeting venue
9. Ask about sustainable local food
10. Reuse signage and create using sustainable material
11. Reduce printed material and use recycled content where possible
12. Reduce conference swag and use a sustainable source for any swag
13. Minimize packaging on all purchased products
14. Find a donation stream for leftover materials (think of end use when making purchases)
15. Communicate sustainability efforts and options to attendees

Copyright © 2023 by MeetGreen. Reprinted by permission.

CHAPTER 12 SUSTAINABLE MEETINGS AND EVENTS

CHAPTER 13

PLANNING MEEC GATHERINGS

WELCOME AND REGISTRATION AREA FOR A CONVENTION

CHAPTER OBJECTIVES

- Discuss the importance and process of setting goals and objectives when planning Meetings, Expositions, Events, and Conventions (MEEC) gatherings.
- List the considerations to keep in mind during the site selection planning process.
- Articulate the areas of concern when program planning for an event.
- Outline the many logistical considerations to keep in mind when planning a MEEC gathering.
- Discuss the main considerations in direct and indirect marketing and promotion that a MEEC professional must consider when planning a gathering.

Contributed by Amanda Cecil. © Kendall Hunt Publishing Company.
Contributed by Erica Shonkwiler. © Kendall Hunt Publishing Company.

An event professional may possess familiarity with all the elements of the MEEC industry. However, effective planning, organization, direction, and control are required to bring together these diverse elements and make them work seamlessly. The organizer must gain a deep understanding of the group and its desires and needs. Who are they, and why are they attending? Once these questions are answered, objectives can be established to guide the program delivery, aligning it with these desires and needs while adhering to budget constraints. This chapter provides a broad overview of planning a MEEC event. Two additional textbooks are available for those seeking more detailed information, intended to be read sequentially: The first focuses on *Planning and Management of MEEC* and the second on *Production and Logistics in MEEC*. Keep in mind that the planning "process" and steps discussed here are applicable to any event, whether for business or leisure, recreation, or entertainment.

NEEDS ANALYSIS

As a crucial component of setting objectives for a meeting, a **needs analysis** must be conducted. It serves as a method for understanding the expectations surrounding a particular meeting and can be as straightforward as consulting with senior management to determine their goals for the event and then structuring it around those expectations. The needs of corporate and association meeting attendees differ significantly (refer to Chapter 2). The first step in this process is to identify the attendees by asking the fundamental question: "Who are they?" An event professional must gather demographic information on both past and potential attendees. This task is more straightforward for annual events, such as association meetings or corporate management gatherings. The event professional maintains a detailed **group history** of attendees, their preferences, dislikes, and any pertinent information that can enhance future meetings. Questions to consider include the following:

- What is the age and gender of past attendees?
- What is their level of expertise—beginner, intermediate, advanced?
- What is their position within the organization's hierarchy—new employee, junior management, or senior management?
- How is the content best delivered? Only face to face? Hybrid? Virtual only?

- What hotel amenities are preferred—indoor pools, spas, tennis courts, exercise rooms, wireless internet access?
- Do attendees have specific dietary restrictions (i.e., kosher, Muslim, vegetarian, and low-carb, low-sugar, gluten-free food, specific medical conditions or health issues, such as allergies, diabetes, or celiac disease)?
- Who is paying the expenses? Most people are more cost conscious if they are paying out of their own pocket rather than a company expense account.
- Will meeting attendees bring guests or children to the event?
- Are networking opportunities important?
- How far are attendees willing to travel to attend the meeting?
- Will international guests who require interpreters attend?
- Are special accommodations needed for people with disabilities?
- What are the educational outcomes expected at the meeting?

Certain information can be obtained through questions on the event registration form, and other details can be sourced from association membership or company records. Most event professionals routinely conduct evaluations after an event to gather feedback that can be instrumental in enhancing subsequent meetings, which will be discussed later in this chapter.

In the evaluation of the event process, it is also important for the event professional to identify the event **stakeholders**: someone with a vested interest in an enterprise. Typical stakeholders include the organizing entity, decision-makers, sponsors, exhibitors, organizational members (for events hosted by associations or membership organizations), beneficiaries (for benefits or events promoting a cause), and various categories of participants, such as attendees, speakers, presenters, volunteers, and performers. Some event professionals prioritize these stakeholders and their needs throughout the planning process.

SETTING GOALS AND OBJECTIVES

Determining the Meeting and Event Goal(s)

The first step for a event professional is to answer two fundamental questions: (a) Who constitutes the group, and (b) What is the objective of the event? These seemingly simple questions form the foundation of the entire planning process.

A meeting's *goal* defines the purpose behind it and offers a clear direction for the organizer. It essentially clarifies "why the organization exists and the event is taking place."

An *objective* is a specific achievement or goal to strive for. Every meeting and event should commence with clear, concise, and measurable objectives. These serve as the bedrock for virtually all facets of the planning process, regardless of event type, be it corporate meetings, association meetings, special events, exhibitions (formerly trade shows), or virtual meetings conducted over the internet. The meeting's objective will influence decisions related to venue selection, food and beverage (F&B) requirements, transportation logistics, communication channels, and, most notably, program content.

Most attendees participate for three primary reasons: education, networking, and conducting business. Some attend association **annual meetings** to benefit from networking opportunities and educational offerings. Others may primarily attend to cultivate business relationships, generate leads, or make sales. Failure to tailor program content and scheduling to align with these objectives may lead to attendee dissatisfaction.

Furthermore, program planning, especially for association meetings, often is months or even years before the actual event. The average attendee may not fully grasp the considerable effort involved for even seemingly straightforward events, let alone the complexity of an association's annual meeting and trade show/exhibition. Much like the hospitality industry, the real work occurs behind the scenes.

Effective meeting objectives should center on the attendees. What will entice attendees to participate in the meeting? What will be their **return on investment (ROI)**? What sets this event apart from competitors' offerings? The following are some key components of meeting planning directly influenced by meeting objectives.

Developing Specific, Measurable, Attainable, Measurable, Relevant, Time-Based (SMART) Objectives

Once the event professional has identified the needs of the attendees and sponsoring organization, it becomes crucial to clearly and concisely formulate, ensuring that all parties involved in the planning process understand and align with common goals. A common method for crafting effective meeting objectives is the **SMART** approach. Each letter in SMART serves as a reminder of essential elements for constructing a well-defined objective.

After defining the event goals, the next step is to develop one or multiple SMART objectives for each goal. These are essential for assessing whether the goal has been achieved.

Example Goal: Improve Event Attendee Registration Profits

Now, let's explore how a event professional can work toward this goal. They can enhance attendee registration revenue, reduce attendee-related expenses, or both. Let's proceed by crafting a SMART objective specifically focused on revenue:

> ***Specific:*** Only one major concept is covered per objective. For example, instead of *make the event more profitable,* state *generate more event revenue.*
>
> ***Measurable:*** Must be able to quantify or measure that objectives have been achieved. For example, instead of *generate more revenue,* state *generate 100% more revenue.*
>
> ***Achievable:*** Is it possible to accomplish the objective? So, instead of *generate 100% more revenue,* state *generate 30% more revenue.*
>
> ***Relevant:*** Is the objective a relevant way to determine whether the goal is accomplished? For example, instead of *generate 30% more revenue,* state *generate 30% more revenue from attendee registrations.*
>
> ***Time-related:*** Include when the objective must be completed. So, instead of *generate 30% more revenue from attendee registrations,* state *generate 30% more revenue than last year from attendee registrations in the 6 months that registration is open.*

Starting meeting objectives with an action verb (e.g., *achieve*, *promote*, *understand*, *design*) and incorporating cost factors, where relevant, is a valuable practice. Furthermore, it is important to specify the individual or department responsible for achieving each objective. The art of crafting well-structured meeting objectives is important for event professionals. These objectives serve as guiding beacons, maintaining a clear and focused trajectory throughout the planning process. Postevent, the event professional can effectively communicate to management which objectives were successfully met or surpassed and which were not, along with the reasons for any shortfalls. Incentives or performance reviews, whether at an individual or team level, can be centered around the attainment of these objectives. Achieving objectives showcases the tangible ROI that the event professional delivers to the organization. Conversely, if objectives are not met, this provides an opportunity for management to explore innovative approaches to achieving desired outcomes in future meetings. next meeting.

> **MEETING GOAL: Increase revenue for the annual meeting**
>
> SMART Objective: The Meetings Department of the International Association of Real Estate Agents will "generate attendance of 7,500 people at the 2024 annual meeting to be held in Orlando, Florida, U.S."
>
> **MEETING GOAL: Host successful sales training event**
>
> SMART Objective: The Brettco Pharmaceutical Corporation will "execute a 2-day 2024 sales training conference for 12 regional sales managers to launch five new products where total meeting costs do not exceed $15,000."

Site Selection

The site selection process commences once meeting objectives are established. These goals and objectives serve as guiding principles for event professionals in determining the physical location, type of facility, transportation options, and other critical components of the event. Site selection can occur anywhere from days to weeks, months, or even years in advance. Major conventions often choose their city 3–10 years in advance, and some prominent associations, such as the American Library Association, plan decades into the future. Conversely, small corporate meetings typically have a much shorter lead time, often just a few weeks or months.

In the context of association meetings, the event professional usually does not have the final say in selecting the host city. Typically, that is a collective decision made by a volunteer committee, with significant input from the board of directors and association staff. The meeting professional will conduct thorough research, consult with fellow event professionals, and may offer recommendations. For corporate events, the event professional may wield more influence over site selection, particularly for smaller gatherings (for larger events, the CEO or chairman of the board might make the final decision). Occasionally, location choices are influenced by the availability of recreational activities, such as golf, shopping, or spa facilities, rather than the exceptional quality of meeting facilities. It varies from one organization to another.

Large travel expos, such as IMEX in Frankfurt, Germany or IMEX America in Las Vegas, Nevada, present excellent opportunities for event professionals to gather information about potential locations. These expos implement a "hosted buyer" strategy in which exhibitors cover the travel expenses of event professionals (buyers) in exchange for guaranteed appointments (for more details, see Chapter 5).

Several other factors warrant consideration during site selection, including the rotation of locations and the geographical distribution of attendees. U.S. event professionals might opt to rotate their conventions across different regions. For instance, they could host a major convention in the East (e.g., Boston) 1 year, the South (e.g., New Orleans) the following year, the West (e.g., San Francisco) the third year, and the Midwest (e.g., Chicago) the fourth year. This approach allows attendees to experience a diverse range of destinations and ensures that those living on one side of the country do not consistently face long journeys across multiple time zones. However, if a majority of attendees reside on the East Coast, it may be more convenient to select a location there. Nonetheless, some conventions, such as the National Association of Broadcasters, MAGIC Marketplace, International Builder's Show, or the Consumer Electronics Show, are so massive that their choice of cities is highly restricted due to the substantial requirements for sleeping rooms, meeting spaces, and exhibition areas.

Cost is another critical factor to consider. Apart from the expenses incurred for essentials, such as meeting space, attendee costs should also be taken into account. Certain cities, especially first-tier ones, are known for their high cost of living and travel expenses (for instance, New York City has an average daily rate of over $250 per night, plus taxes). The choice between cost and location largely depends on what holds greater significance for the attendees. An alternative approach is to hold a meeting in a first-tier city and at a first-class property but during the off-season or slower periods, such as around major holidays, when many hotels offer discounted rates. As seen during the global economic downturn that began in 2008, most hotels had to reduce their rates to entice a shrinking number of MEEC gatherings. As economies rebounded and people have become more willing to spend on travel, the prices for various services have been increasing and will likely continue to rise.

The mode of travel is another key consideration in site selection. How will attendees reach the location: by air, road, or rail? In recent years, major airline carriers have faced significant challenges, leading to mergers and acquisitions. Many individuals remain cautious about air travel due to concerns about terrorism, airport security, crowded planes, additional baggage fees, food expenses, and government-imposed travel restrictions. The availability of flights (**airlift**) is also crucial role. Cities with the most flight options include Chicago, Atlanta, Dallas, and New York. On the other hand, some convention destinations that boast convention centers may lack airlift options, such as Anchorage, Alaska; Huntington, West Virginia; Davenport, Iowa; and Wheeling, West Virginia.

Another significant consideration is the type of hotel or meeting facility. You have various options, including metropolitan hotels, suburban hotels, airport hotels, resort hotels, and casino hotels. Additionally, specialized facilities are designed exclusively for hosting meetings, known as "conference centers." The International Association of Conference Centers is an association where member facilities must meet over 30 criteria to qualify as approved conference centers. For more information, you can visit its website at https://www.iacconline.org/. Other alternatives include full-service convention centers, cruise ships, and university campuses (see Chapter 4).

Meeting space requirements play a pivotal role in the site selection process. Determining the number of meeting or banquet rooms needed and allocating space for staff offices, registration areas, and prefunction spaces is crucial. You can easily access floor plans with room dimensions through the facilities' sales brochures or their websites. Comprehensive diagrams should also provide information on ceiling heights, seating capacities, entrances, exits, and the location of columns and other potential obstructions. Most major hotel chain websites offer direct links to their hotels and detailed specification information.

Once the meeting objectives are clearly defined and the basic location and logistics outlined, the meeting professional creates a **request for proposals (RFP)**. It serves as a written description of all the key requirements for the meeting. The Events Industry Council (EIC), a federation comprising over 30 MEEC industry associations, has developed a standardized format for RFPs, which is copyright free and available for use. An RFP can also be employed for selecting other suppliers that provide services such as audiovisual (A/V) arrangements, transportation, special event venues, registration contractors, and virtual event platforms.

Once the RFP is complete, it is time to share it with hotel properties and convention facilities that might be interested in bidding. Typically, the event professional can distribute the RFP via the internet, directly to preferred hotels and the destination marketing organization (DMO) or convention and visitor bureaus (CVBs) of appealing cities, with the option for them to forward it to all properties. Alternatively, the RFP can be submitted through the DI website. Planners may also choose to send their RFP directly to national hotel chains, such as Marriott or Hyatt. The RFP enables hotels to assess the potential economic impact of the meeting and decide whether to submit a bid. DI offers its members access to an economic impact; for instance, if the group has limited resources and can requires an $89 room rate, it is less likely to attract interest from major luxury hotels. However, smaller properties or hotels in second-tier cities might eagerly vie for the opportunity. If a facility decides to submit a proposal, its sales department will carefully review the meeting specifications and craft a response accordingly.

COVID-19 LESSONS LEARNED FOR RFP ADDITIONS:

- Cancellation and termination (act of God, force majeure) clause requirements;
- Commitment to adhering to federal/state/local health and sanitation mandates or guidelines from government, health organizations, or industry best practices/standards; and
- An outline of current facility upgrades and operational procedures undertaken to ensure maximum health and safety of event attendees—describing what the guest experience will be and how it is affected based on these procedures.

Once the event professional has reviewed the proposals and conducted any necessary site visits, whether in person or virtually, negotiations with the facility's sales department can commence. This process can be quite intricate, and it is crucial to maintain well-documented records of all communications, concessions, and financial expectations.

> Freeman used drones and its PLATOUR Application to conduct a virtual site tour of the Omni Dallas: https://www.youtube.com/watch?v=FHS0oy2Vpb4.

Another method of promoting a destination or specific facility to event professionals is through **familiarization** or **(fam)** trips, which are typically no- or low-cost excursions arranged by the local DMO or CVBs or directly by the hotel. Event professionals personally assess sites for suitability. The hotel or convention facility aims to impress them by showcasing its property, amenities, services, and overall quality. Throughout the visit, the professional should explore all F&B outlets, recreational areas, various types of sleeping rooms, and meeting spaces, assess the efficiency of the front desk and other personnel, evaluate cleanliness and overall appearance, and, if possible, meet with key personnel. Experienced professionals often prepare a comprehensive list of questions, as hotel selection involves numerous considerations.

EVENT BUDGETING

Budgetary considerations typically follow as the next major step. Questions such as how much it will cost, who will bear these costs, how much attendees will be charged for registration (if at all), the nature of planned F&B events, whether meals will be complimentary or offered at an additional cost to attendees, and identifying potential revenue streams all need to be addressed. Sponsorships may also be explored. For first-time events, event professionals often rely on estimation for expenses and potential revenues, and repeated events benefit from historical data for cost comparisons and projections. Developing a meeting budget typically involves establishing financial goals, identifying expenses, and pinpointing revenue sources.

ESTABLISH FINANCIAL GOALS

Financial goals are of paramount importance and should be easily measurable. These goals can be established by the event professional, association management, or corporate mandates. Essentially, they answer the question:

What are the financial expectations for the event? Not every event is planned with profit as the primary objective. For instance, a company may organize an awards ceremony to honor top achievers, which represents a cost. Similarly, a corporate sales meeting may not be geared toward generating immediate profits; rather, its primary aim could be to strategize on increasing future business and overall profitability. The meeting itself is considered an expense. By contrast, many association meetings heavily rely on conventions to generate operating revenue (for more details, see Chapter 2). For most associations, the annual meeting, often accompanied by a trade show, ranks as the second-highest revenue generator, following membership dues. The financial goals for an annual meeting can be influenced by factors such as fluctuations in membership numbers, prevailing economic conditions, political climate, competition from other events, and location. Any event has three possible financial goals:

- *Break-even:* Revenues collected from all activities cover the expenses. No profit is expected.
- *Profit:* Revenues collected exceed expenses.
- *Deficit:* Expenses exceed revenues.

IDENTIFY EXPENSES AND REVENUE SOURCES

Expenses should be categorized by their different functions:

- *Fixed costs* are expenses incurred regardless of the number of attendees, such as meeting room rental or A/V equipment.
- *Variable costs* can vary based on the number of attendees (e.g., F&B).
- *Indirect costs* should be listed as overhead or administrative line items in a program budget. These are expenses of the organization not directly related to the meeting, such as staff salaries, overhead, or equipment repair.

Expenses will vary according to the overall objectives of the meeting and be impacted by location, season, type of facility, services selected, and other factors. For example, a gallon of Starbucks coffee in San Francisco at a luxury hotel may cost $90 or more. A gallon of coffee at a moderate-priced hotel in Oklahoma City may only cost $25 or less. Hosting a meeting includes many areas of expense:

- meeting space,
- F&B

- A/V
- shuttle service
- production
- speakers
- internet
- temporary staff
- staff travel general service contractor (exhibitions)
- volunteers
- décor/rentals
- signage
- security
- insurance
- licenses and permits
- marketing
- registration system/services, and
- event tech/apps/virtual platforms.

Various avenues exist for funding meetings and events, each tailored to different circumstances. Corporations, for example, typically include meeting costs in their operating budgets, and corporate event professionals must operate within these predefined boundaries. On the other hand, associations often need to be more resourceful in securing funding for planning and executing events. They must justify the expense by demonstrating the expected ROI for attendees. Attending association meetings can be quite costly. For a hypothetical example: transportation ($500), three nights of accommodations ($700), F&B expenses ($300), registration fee ($500), and miscellaneous costs ($200), totaling $2,200. Depending on the city and the association, this amount could easily double. Balancing the creation of an exceptional event with affordability is a complex undertaking. If the registration fee is too high, it discourages attendance; if it is too low, the organization may fall short of revenue expectations. However, multiple potential funding sources are available beyond registration fees:

- corporate or association funding;
- private funding from individuals;
- exhibitor fees (if incorporating a trade show/exhibition);
- sponsorships;
- selling logo merchandise;
- advertising fees, such as banners or ads in the convention program;
- local, state, or national government assistance;
- banner ads or links on the official website or on social media platforms;

- membership contact lists rented for marketing purposes;
- "official partnerships" with other companies to promote their products for a fee or percentage of their revenues; and
- contributions in cash or in kind (services or products).

Estimating expenses and revenues can be accomplished by first calculating a break-even analysis. The simple way of doing this is to determine the total all of your expenses (e.g., $300,000) and then recognizing you will need at least that same amount (e.g., $300,000) in revenue to have no profit or loss.

However, a event professional is not often asked to consider break-even so simply. Instead, leadership will often ask: How many attendees do we need to break even, or what do we need our registration fee to be in order to break even?

A couple of simple formulas help us to answer these more specific questions.

How many attendees do we need to break even?

For this, you need to know total fixed costs, variable costs per attendee, and an idea of what the attendee registration fee will be.

Total Fixed Costs / (Registration Fee − Per-Attendee Variable Costs)

What do we need our registration fee to be in order to break even?

If instead you are trying to determine what you should charge for attendee registration, you need to know total fixed costs, variable costs per attendee, and an estimation of how many attendees will come to the event.

(Total Fixed Costs/Estimated Number of Attendees) + Per-Attendee Variable Costs

BUDGET ASSEMBLY

Event professionals must gather all expected revenue and expense items for each event and compile them into a budget. Multiple budgets may then be consolidated to represent an entire department. However, detailed information specific to each event is essential for the review and approval processes within an organization. Microsoft Excel is the most commonly used software. For repeat events, finance departments and organization leaders may request including the previous year's budget and actual expenditure data in the new budget as a reference point. For significant deviations, event professionals should be prepared to provide explanations. It is also beneficial to include the percentage of total revenue (as a percentage of the overall revenue) and percentage of total expenses (as a percentage of the overall expenses) for each line item. This information allows the budgeting team to identify the most significant areas of revenue and expenses, facilitating adjustments if needed. For instance, if cost reductions are necessary, it is easier to make changes to a major expense category, such as F&B, than to a smaller, more inflexible expense category, such as shipping.

Once the budgets are compiled, organizations often convene internal budget meetings for review and discussion. These meetings enable the leadership team to assess each department or project budget in the context of the organization's overall operating budget. Edits and adjustments are frequently required as outcomes of these meetings. Final budgets are typically submitted to organization leadership and the Finance Department for approval.

Sample association event budget format:

This budget assumes attendees are paying for their own registration, housing, and travel.

PROGRAM PLANNING

Once the basic objectives of the meeting have been identified, the site selected, and the budget set, the program can be developed in detail. Some major concerns involved in this process are the following: Is the programming to be designed to facilitate communication between departments within a corporation? Is it geared toward training new employees to use a particular computer system? Is it intended to educate the members of a professional association and lead toward a certification? To address these concerns, the event professional must consider several factors, including the following:

- program type
- content, including track and level
- session scheduling
- speaker arrangements
- refreshment breaks and meal functions
- ancillary events
- evaluation procedures

REVENUE	2024 Budget Amount	Percent of Total	2023 Actual Amount	2023 Budgeted Amount	2023 Actual/2024 Budget Variance
Registration	$ 700,000	70%	$ 668,750	$ 625,000	$ 31,250
Sponsorships	$ 150,000	15%	$ 139,100	$ 130,000	$ 10,900
Exhibits	$ 100,000	10%	$ 96,300	$ 90,000	$ 3,700
Merchandise	$ 25,000	3%	$ 18,000	$ 20,000	$ 7,000
Advertising	$ 25,000	3%	$ 20,400	$ 20,000	$ 4,600
TOTAL REVENUE	$ 1,000,000		$ 942,550	$ 885,000	$ 57,450

VARIABLE EXPENSES

Food and Beverage	$ 420,000	59%	$ 401,250	$ 375,000	$ 18,750
Registration Fees	$ 31,500	4%	$ 29,960	$ 28,000	$ 1,540
TOTAL VARIABLE EXPENSES	$ 451,500	63%	$ 431,210	$ 403,000	$ 20,290

FIXED EXPENSES

Venue Rental	$ 30,000	4%	$ 25,000	$ 25,000	$ 5,000
Exhibit Materials	$ 50,000	7%	$ 46,258	$ 45,000	$ 3,742
Signage	$ 12,000	2%	$ 10,723	$ 10,000	$ 1,277
Merchandise	$ 17,500	2%	$ 16,050	$ 15,000	$ 1,450
Rentals/Décor	$ 25,000	3%	$ 19,759	$ 22,000	$ 5,241
Technology	$ 15,000	2%	s 12,432	$ 10,000	$ 2,568
Audio Visual	$ 25,000	3%	$ 21,400	$ 20,000	$ 3,600
Speakers/Entertainment	$ 30,000	4%	$ 23,476	$ 25,000	$ 6,524
Staff Expenses	$ 15,000	2%	$ 15,164	$ 15,000	$ (164)
Volunteer Expenses	$ 5,000	1%	$ 5,350	$ 5,000	$ (350)
Shipping	$ 3,000	0%	$ 2,349	$ 2,500	$ 651
Supplies	$ 2,500	0%	$ 2,045	$ 2,200	$ 455
Insurance	$ 1,500	0%	$ 1,250	$ 1,250	$ 250
Permits	$ 500	0%	$ 450	$ 450	$ 50
Security	$ 5,000	1%	$ 4,280	$ 4,000	$ 720
Medical/First Aid	$ 2,000	0%	$ 1,605	$ 1,500	$ 395
Transportation	$ 25,000	3%	$ 24,610	$ 23,000	$ 390
TOTAL FIXED EXPENSES	$ 264,000	37%	$ 232,201	$ 226,900	$ 31,799
TOTAL EXPENSES	$ 715,500		$ 663,411	$ 629,900	$ 52,089
NET INCOME/LOSS	**$ 284,500**		**$ 279,139**	**$ 255,100**	**$ 5,361**

CHAPTER 13 PLANNING MEEC GATHERINGS

Putting together a good meeting program requires the event professional to select appropriate program types, understand the content appropriate and interesting to attendees, and scheduling the different formats into a master agenda.

PROGRAM TYPES

Different types of programs or sessions are designed for specific purposes, which can range from disseminating information to all attendees, fostering discussions on current events in small groups, providing hands-on training, to hosting panel discussions. The following are typical descriptions of the major program types and formats.

A **general** or **plenary session** is primarily used as a platform to communicate with all conference attendees at one time in one location. It usually inaugurates the meeting and features welcoming remarks from management or association leadership. It outlines the purpose and objectives, introduces notable officials, recognizes major sponsors or contributors to event planning, and covers other significant topics of general interest. General sessions typically last 1–1.5 hours. Oftentimes, a distinguished industry leader or a well-known personality delivers a **keynote address**, setting the tone for the meeting. In the context of a corporate meeting, this could be the CEO or the chairman of the board. Associations may engage professional speakers with expertise in specific subject areas, such as business forecasting, political analysis, leadership and change, technology, or motivational topics. Many event professionals also leverage the appeal of highly recognizable figures from politics, sports, and entertainment. For instance, a recent association convention featured the famous former basketball player Magic Johnson. Some associations have even hired former presidents. These individuals are selected not solely for their familiarity with the association and its professions but often to attract attendees. It is common to spend $75,000–100,000 or more (plus travel expenses) to secure a well-known sports or entertainment figure as a speaker. Closing general sessions may also be held at the end of a convention to provide a sense of closure, recap meeting achievements, and present awards while recognizing sponsors. Attendance is typically smaller, as attendees often begin making travel arrangements to return home early.

A **concurrent session** or breakout session is designed for professional development and career enhancement. They are led by qualified speakers who provide education on specific topics in a conference-style format. Alternatively, several speakers may form a panel to offer various perspectives on the topic. Some sessions may include group discussions at individual tables. Typically, these sessions are 30–90 minutes.

Workshops provide a more intimate and interactive learning experience within smaller groups. Participants can delve into the latest trends, challenges, and technologies in a particular field. Workshops are often led by experienced members or peers of the association and may involve a variety of instructional methods, such as lectures, role-playing, simulations, problem-solving, or group work. They are typically tailored to accommodate 150 attendees or fewer. Workshops are a fundamental component of any convention, and the number offered depends on the event's size. For instance, a large association, such as the American Library Association, offers more than 1,000 at its annual convention. Workshops generally last 50–60 minutes.

Roundtables and **discussion groups** are small, interactive sessions designed to delve into specific topics of interest. Typically, 8–12 attendees gather around a large, round table with a facilitator. Several discussions may occur simultaneously in a single location, such as a large meeting room or ballroom. Attendees can join or leave different groups as they see fit. Roundtables can also provide an opportunity for continued and more intimate conversation with workshop speakers. The facilitator's role is to steer the discussion in the right direction and prevent anyone from dominating the conversation. Sometimes, roundtables may enlist a **subject-matter expert** to both inform and moderate the group.

TEAM OF PEOPLE COLLABORATING IN A WORKSHOP

Poster sessions are commonly used in academic or medical conferences to offer a more intimate experience. Instead of employing various meeting rooms for speakers or panels, display boards are provided for presenters that showcase charts, photographs, and research synopses of research. Presenters are scheduled to be at their display boards during specified times, enabling interested attendees to engage in informal discussions about the presentations.

General or Plenary Session	High-level broad, motivational topics; shorter session
Concurrent or Breakout Session	Ankle-deep, more information, mid-high-level topics; shorter session
Workshop	Deep-dive, hands-on, very specific; longer session
Roundtable	Collaborative, peer-to-peer learning of application of a specific topic
Poster Session	Very deep dive into a specific topic and the research performed/outcomes related to the topic

Types of sessions

PROGRAM CONTENT

The typical attendee can only attend 3–6 sessions in a single day. Therefore, it is crucial for attendees to be well informed about what each session offers and whether it aligns with their objectives for attending the meeting. In association meetings, programming objectives are established months in advance and play a significant role in marketing the convention to potential attendees. Program content should not follow a "one-size-fits-all" approach. Instead, it should be meticulously designed to meet the specific needs of the audience. For example, a presentation on "Basic Accounting 101" might be suitable for a junior manager but completely inappropriate for a chief financial officer. To assist attendees in selecting the most relevant programs to attend, it is beneficial to categorize sessions into tracks and levels. **Track** refers to classifying programs under specific topics, such as computer skills, professional development, marketing, personal growth, legal issues, certification courses, or financial matters. Various workshops can be developed that focus on these specific areas. **Levels** pertain to the skill level—beginner, intermediate, or advanced—for which the program is designed. This allows speakers to tailor their content to a particular audience, and attendees can easily determine if a session matches their level of expertise. Most programs offer multiple tracks and levels.

The following is an example of typical description of a session.

> **SESSION DESCRIPTION**
>
> Workshop 14: Effective Marketing through Social Media and Email Marketing:
> Frank Wise, PhD
> 3:30 p.m. to 4:45 p.m. (1530–1645)
> Room 314
>
> With over 132 billion email messages sent daily and billions of users on thousands of social media platforms, how can your company develop an effective marketing strategy to capitalize on these technologies? What are the most effective options to do so?
>
> Attend this session to
>
> - Discover the top 10 steps in developing effective electronic media marketing messages.
> - Discuss a variety of delivery platforms.
> - Enhance your own effectiveness with social media.
>
> Track: Marketing
>
> Level: Intermediate

SESSION SCHEDULING

The event professional must meticulously plan every minute of each day to ensure the meeting runs smoothly and stays on schedule. Each day's agenda should offer an exciting array of activities that captivate attendees, leaving them eager to participate in subsequent events. One of the most significant mistakes is double-booking events. For instance, if workshops are scheduled from 8:00 a.m. to 1:00 p.m. and a celebrity golf match tees off at 12:30 p.m., attendees interested in golf may skip the workshops. Trade shows and exhibitions present another challenge. When workshops overlap with the show floor's opening hours, attendees are forced to make a choice. If they opt for education sessions, exhibitors may experience lower than expected foot traffic. Conversely, if they prioritize the trade show, meeting rooms may sit empty with frustrated speakers.

Another significant issue is allocating enough time for attendees to engage in customary activities. It is unrealistic to expect 5,000 people to transition from a general session to breakout sessions on the opposite side of the convention center in just 10 minutes. Thoughtful planning is essential. Adequate time should be allocated for attendees to use restrooms, check emails, messages, or voicemails, reconnect with old friends, and comfortably make their way to their next workshop. Failing to account for these natural delays in advance could result in attendees disrupting workshop sessions by arriving late or, in some cases, skipping sessions altogether.

Recent scheduling trends include incorporating microsessions, time for self-care, outdoor activities, and corporate social responsibility projects.

The following is a description of the schedule for an association meeting.

Example of an Association Meeting Schedule

Although no two conventions are the same, the following timeline provides a good idea of a typical meeting's flow.

Day 1
8:00 a.m. Staff office and pressroom area setup
    Exhibition setup begins
    Preconvention meeting with facility staff
    Registration setup

Day 2
8:00 a.m. Association board meeting
    Registration opens
    Staff office opens
    Exhibition setup continues
    Set up for preconvention workshops
1:00–4:00 p.m. Preconvention workshops (with break)
    Various committee meetings
    Program planning committee finalizes duties for meeting

5:00 p.m. Private reception for board members and VIPs
7:00–9:30 p.m. Opening reception

Day 3
6:30 a.m. Staff meeting
8:00 a.m. Registration opens
Coffee service begins
9:00 a.m. General session
10:30 a.m. Break
10:45 a.m. Concurrent workshops
12:00 p.m. Registration closes
12:00–1:30 p.m. Lunch
1:30–3:00 p.m. Exhibition open
3:00–4:30 p.m. Closing session
    Pack up staff office
    Pressroom closed
5:00 p.m. Postconference Meetings

LOGISTICAL CONSIDERATIONS

REGISTRATION

For most conventions or exhibitions, registration is a necessary step. Even weddings require an RSVP. Registration is the comprehensive process of collecting all essential information and fees required for an individual to attend an event. It goes beyond merely collecting money; registration data are a valuable asset for the sponsor. The registration process typically commences several weeks or even months in advance and continues up to the final day. Discounts are often provided to attendees who register in advance. They are offered an **early-bird rate** incentive. The event professional can determine if registration numbers are at anticipated levels. Also, this income allows for a positive **cash flow** so that advance deposits and expenses can be paid. If not, the sponsor can increase marketing or negotiate with the hotel or meeting facilities about lowering expectations and financial commitments.

Information gathered on registration forms typically includes name, title, occupation, address, email, phone, fax, membership category, preferred workshop sessions, attendance at social functions, optional events, chosen payment method, special medical or dietary requirements, and a liability waiver. Some organizations have also started asking about lodging arrangements and length of stay, helping determine the event's impact. Questions about company size, employee count, or attendees' financial responsibilities, such as decision-making authority for purchases, may also be included. These registration data serve a purpose before, during, and after the meeting.

Before the meeting, the data can be provided or sold to exhibitors or advertisers, enabling them to promote their companies, products, and services in advance. They can also be leveraged for marketing to potential attendees who are yet to commit. For instance, advertising "we have 7,500 qualified buyers attending this year's convention" can entice more companies to register or exhibit. Preregistration data can also help the event professional gauge interest in special events or specific workshops that may be in high demand. If so, adjustments can be made, such as moving them to a larger room or increasing seating.

During the meeting, registration data serve as a promotional tool for the press, helping gain media attention for the organization, sponsors, and exhibitors. They can also assist the local DMO in justifying the costs associated with marketing and attracting groups to its city. Concrete figures, such as 3,000 rooms and 200,000 square feet of meeting space, are particularly appealing to hospitality companies. Attendees can now easily access, via smartphone or computer, a list of who is attending a specific meeting and save it for future use.

Both before and during the meeting, QR codes have gained widespread adoption within registration systems and areas. Although QR codes existed well before COVID-19, their adoption by restaurants for touchless menu access helped familiarize a large portion of the public with them. Many event professionals offer a QR code on printed materials that links to the registration form for convenient access. Additionally, QR codes are extensively employed at on-site registration areas to access registration records, information, and materials. Beyond convenience, QR codes have reduced signage and printed materials.

After the meeting, registration data continues to be valuable. They can be used to update association membership records and attract new members. Alternatively, they can be sold to interested parties. Most importantly, these data helps the event professional with logistics and promotes the next meeting. A thorough analysis of registration data provides the organization with a clearer understanding of the meeting's attendees, revealing trends in key areas, such as gender, age, education, and organizational position.

Registration Fees

Registration fees can vary widely and are usually structured differently for different groups. For association meetings, members often receive a discount as an incentive to join. However, within the member category, not all members pay the same price. For example, the Professional Convention Management Association (PCMA), in a recent year, charged different rates for various membership types: professional members (event professionals) paid $1,095; suppliers (hotel salespeople, CVBs) paid $1,295; university faculty members paid $525, and student members paid $275. These rates were for early-bird preregistration, available until about 6 weeks before the convention. After the preregistration **cutoff date**, prices increased by $50–100. Registrants who did not stay in the designated hotel were subject to an additional fee of $200. All attendees, regardless of registration, had the same educational and networking opportunities and meals, breaks, and receptions. However, certain special activities, such as golf, tours, or entertainment functions, might incur extra charges.

For events such as the Exhibitor Show, an annual trade show for professionals in the exhibition industry, registration fees are often tailored to attendees' preferences. Entrance might be free, but educational sessions could cost $295 or more per workshop. Separate charges may apply for additional events, such as dinners and receptions. An all-inclusive option is also available, typically costing well over $1,500, providing access to all education programs and activities. Allowing attendees to choose event activities a la carte provides flexibility in scheduling and price, but it may result in lost revenue for the event and can be inconvenient for attendees who cannot make on-site adjustments to their event activities.

Associations often provide significant registration discounts to their members, which can make joining the association an attractive proposition. The "nonmember" rate may even exceed the difference between the cost of membership and the member rate. This approach is an effective way for associations to grow their base and offers opportunities to promote other products and services to new members. Registration fees are typically waived for certain groups, including press, speakers, and local dignitaries. However, complimentary registrations need to be carefully monitored, as costs may still be involved if the meeting includes F&B or other events.

Corporate events designed for internal stakeholders or employees generally do not require registration fees, with exceptions. Some companies, such as Do It Best (hardware stores) or McDonald's, invite their franchise store owners to attend training and recognition events. Franchisees are often expected to pay a registration fee and cover their own travel expenses.

HOUSING

Not all meetings require housing (overnight arrangements) for attendees, exhibitors, sponsors, suppliers, speakers, or staff. However, four methods of handling it exist:

1. Attendees arrange for their own rooms. Lists of hotels may be provided, but the meeting owner makes no prior arrangements regarding price negotiations or availability.
2. A group rate is negotiated by the event professional at one or more properties, and attendees respond directly to the reservations department of their choice.

3. The meeting host handles all housing, and attendees book rooms through them. Then the meeting host provides the hotel with a **rooming list** of confirmed guests.
4. A third-party **housing bureau** (outsourced company) handles all arrangements either for a fee or is paid by the DMO. The meeting owner pays them to manage the entire process.

Having attendees make their own hotel reservations is the easiest method, as it removes that responsibility and shifts the contract liability away from the organization. However, hotels typically base their pricing on the anticipated total revenue from the group, and sleeping rooms represent a significant portion of that. When rooms are not blocked (set aside for the group), the organization may face premium charges for renting meeting space and other services, such as F&B and A/V equipment. Therefore, the room block is a crucial negotiation tool.

The last three options mentioned involve the event professional setting a rate for attendees that reflects negotiations with the hotel's sales department, taking into account the total value of the meeting for the facility. A specific number of rooms are reserved, forming a "block," and rooms are subtracted from this inventory as attendees request them. This can be a challenging aspect for event professionals, as they need to estimate the number of attendees accurately. If, for instance, 100 rooms are blocked, but only 75 are used, the event professional may be held responsible for the cost of the unused rooms. The difference between the rooms blocked and rooms "picked up" is **attrition**, and it can have financial implications (see Chapter 10).

A significant challenge facing event professionals is attendees booking rooms outside the designated block, sometimes even cheaper options within the host hotels. For instance, if the host hotel charges $199 per day, but a smaller and less luxurious hotel down the street charges $99, a certain percentage of attendees will choose it. Attendees may also secure better prices in the same hotel by contacting it directly or using online discount hotel brokers, undercutting the negotiated rates. If a large number of attendees do so, the event professional could end up responsible for paying for a significant number of unused rooms. One effective strategy to mitigate this potentially costly issue is to incorporate review dates into the hotel contract, which would enable the event professional to adjust the **room block**, increasing or reducing it by a certain percentage at specified times. Another method is offering incentives and penalties to attendees based on their choice to book inside the designated block. Incentives might include participation in drawings for room discounts, VIP experiences, special access to speakers, or discounts for the following year's event. Penalties, although somewhat challenging to enforce, could involve a higher registration fee. It is crucial to verify such penalties through delayed credit card charges and clearly outline these policies in the registration materials. Keep in mind that the closer the event date, the less likely the hotel will permit reductions in the room block. The hotel needs time to attempt to sell any unused rooms and recover potential losses. A hotel room is a perishable commodity; if it remains unsold one day, that revenue is lost forever.

Offering attendees the option to make their room reservations directly with the hotel, either by calling or booking online, is a convenient choice. This approach ensures that attendees can take advantage of the negotiated room rates, and the hotel manages the reservation process directly, reducing the need for significant involvement from the event professional or their team. For larger gatherings involving multiple properties, it is advisable to offer a range of hotel prices to cater to the varying budgets of attendees.

Registration and Housing Companies

Several companies have evolved that specialize in handling both conference registration and housing, such as ConferenceDirect and Experient.

Outsourcing the housing process to a third-party vendor or DMO is most prevalent with medium and large meetings. Some groups, such as the National Association of Broadcasters or Consumer Electronics Show, are so large that they require most of the hotel rooms in the city. Housing for a *citywide* meeting is best left to professionals who have the most current technology and are well equipped to handle thousands of housing requests. The housing bureau may charge a fee per transaction, which may be paid by the sponsoring organization; the local DMO may absorb some or all of the costs. Many DMOs and even hotels operate their own housing bureaus as a service to event professionals. Third parties may manage or assist with registration components. The scope of their services can range from only their registration platform, to managing all preregistration, to being on-site to supervise and assist with the registration process.

When it comes to handling attendee reservations internally, it is feasible but works best for smaller groups. For small, high-profile events, event professionals can have attendees reserve rooms through the organization. In this case, a rooming list is created and provided to the hotel, detailing room preferences, ADA requests, smoking or nonsmoking preferences, arrival and departure dates, names of additional guests in the room, and any special requests. Managing reservations in house can be time intensive and may require additional staffing. Alternatively, engaging a housing bureau can provide valuable assistance.

REFRESHMENT BREAKS AND MEAL FUNCTIONS

Just as with scheduling workshops, it is essential to allocate time for attendees to eat and relax throughout the day. Planning F&B functions requires careful consideration, as they are crucial yet costly (see Chapter 9). Nevertheless, it can be more productive to provide meals to attendees rather than having them wander around a convention center or leave the property in search of food. Refreshment breaks offer valuable opportunities to reconnect with old friends, make new business contacts, network, and enjoy a quick meal or recharge with a cup of coffee or tea. Both breaks and meals present excellent sponsorship opportunities, enabling companies to gain recognition among attendees.

SPEAKER ARRANGEMENTS

For large conventions, it becomes nearly impossible for the event professional to independently organize all the various sessions and speakers. Typically, the meeting department collaborates with the education department to develop the educational content. Additionally, a program committee, consisting of industry leaders and individuals with a vested interest in education, volunteers to support the event professional. These volunteers work diligently to determine suitable session topics and potential speakers. The committee's responsibility is to safeguard the quality of educational content. Subcommittees may be formed to focus on finding speakers for general sessions, workshops, concurrent sessions, student member events, and so forth.

Most associations are unable to cover the costs of all speakers at a large convention and rely on volunteer speakers. A moderate-sized convention with

2,500 attendees might offer more than 100 sessions during a 3-day event. Compensation can vary, ranging from no assistance at all to covering a speaker's fee and all associated expenses, as with general-session speakers.

Benefits of Using Volunteer Speakers

- Reduces expenses (the person may already have budgeted to attend the meeting, so no housing or transportation costs are required).
- They are knowledgeable about important industry topics.
- Popular industry leaders may increase attendance at sessions.
- Builds relationships between speaker and event sponsor.

Challenges of Using Volunteer Speakers

- May not adequately prepare for presentation.
- May not be a good presenter, even if they are knowledgeable about topic.
- May have a personal agenda; may use the session to promote self or company.

Another, more expensive yet often a more dependable source of speakers is to use a **speaker bureau**, which is essentially a professional talent broker, skilled at finding the ideal speaker to align with your objectives and budget. Typically, speaker bureaus maintain a roster of highly qualified professionals capable of addressing a wide range of topics. The fees and additional offerings span from budget-friendly to extravagant. If you represent a small Midwestern association of county clerks, it is improbable that you can afford a globally renowned athlete as your keynote speaker for your annual meeting. However, you might be able to secure a gold-medal Olympian from the 1990s who can share insights on teamwork and determination, all for a more affordable price of $4,000.

Speaker Giving a Talk at Corporate Business Conference

Bringing in popular, highly paid, and sought-after speakers is likely to boost attendance. A strategic approach to securing such talent is to have the speaker's expenses sponsored by a key exhibitor or an industry leader. The general session is a high-profile event, and it could be cost effective for a company to cover the keynote speaker's costs as a means of promoting itself to a maximum number of attendees. For example, a $30,000 speaker for a group of 5,000 attendees amounts to just $6 per attendee. This might be more cost effective than designing and distributing traditional mailings!

Another valuable source for speakers is local dignitaries, industry leaders, and university professors. You will not incur transportation and lodging expenses, and their services are often either free or very affordable. To find willing individuals, you can enlist the assistance of the local DMO or contact nearby universities. It is customary to offer a small gift or honorarium to express gratitude for their time and effort.

Developing speaker guidelines is essential to ensure that both paid and non-paid speakers are well informed about the logistical requirements and clearly outline the organization's expectations. Although specific guidelines may vary, most should include the following:

- background information about the association
- date and location of meeting
- special events or activities the speaker may attend
- date, time, and location of speaker's room for presentation
- presentation topic and duration
- demographics and estimated number of attendees for the session
- room setup and A/V equipment requests and availability
- request for short biography
- names of other speakers, if applicable
- remuneration policy
- dress code
- location of **speaker-ready room**, where the speaker can practice or relax prior to speaking
- instructions for preparing abstracts or submitting final papers (typically for academic conferences)
- instructions for having handouts available
- transportation and lodging information
- maps and diagrams of hotel or facility

- deadlines for all materials that must be returned
- hints for speaking to the group (i.e., attendees are very informal; attendees like time for questions and answers at the end of session)

It is common to include a variety of contractual agreements that must be signed by the speaker.

A **presenter contract** is a formal written agreement between the presenter and the sponsor, outlining the presentation of a specific topic at a designated time. It is essential to use a contract, whether the speaker is compensated or not. It documents and clarifies various aspects, including covered expenses, relationship between the parties, promotional materials required for session advertising, deadlines for A/V and handout materials, disclosure statements for potential conflicts of interest, restrictions on selling or promoting products or services, penalties for failure to fulfill the contract, and permissible conditions for contract termination.

If the session will be recorded in any digital format and made available on a website or online video platform, it is imperative to inform the speaker and obtain their signed consent for *recording internet authorization, and/or waiver*. Some speakers prefer not to have their presentation materials accessible on the internet, where their content could be easily duplicated and used by others. Selling digital recordings of sessions can also serve as an additional revenue stream for associations. Attendees who missed certain sessions due to scheduling constraints can purchase these recordings to access the information they missed.

INCLUSION THROUGH SPEAKER SELECTION

Incorporating diversity through speaker selection is crucial, whether speakers are paid or volunteers. Subject matter experts and professionals available to speak on various topics reflect as much diversity as in the general public. As a event professional, it is important to declare from the outset of the speaker selection process that fostering diversity is a priority for both you and the organization. This clear intention and commitment will guide your planning committee, teams, and speaker bureaus in sourcing a more diverse group of speakers.

PANEL OF SPEAKERS AT BUSINESS CONFERENCE

Why is diversity in speakers important? First, diversity enhances quality. Having speakers with varied life experiences and perspectives provides unique and varied insights, even on the same topic. Second, event attendees come from diverse backgrounds and cultures. Offering them the opportunity to learn from professionals they can personally relate to enriches their experience. Third, it makes the event more appealing to a diverse audience. Often, planners are tasked with assessing and improving the diversity of event attendees, and having speakers from various backgrounds is a positive step in that direction. Last, it transforms your event into a place where the professional achievements and contributions of all individuals are celebrated and acknowledged—this embodies inclusion. Event professionals should continually strive to design events and spaces that are welcoming and inclusive to all people.

Many industry organizations offer resources to support this commitment. For example, PCMA provides a platform to connect with speakers from diverse backgrounds, searchable by topic area, through its Ascent Initiative: www.pcma.org/ascent/pass-the-mic/.

A/V EQUIPMENT

Most hotels and meeting facilities do not permit event professionals to bring their own A/V equipment, such as LCD projectors, television monitors, and media players. Renting and servicing this equipment constitute a significant revenue stream for these facilities. Renting it can be prohibitively expensive; often, the cost equals or even surpasses that of purchasing it outright. For instance, a 40-inch television, which might be available for purchase at a discount store for $350, could cost the event professional that amount in rental fees *each day*!

Hence, controlling A/V costs is important. Event professionals may consider informing speakers that only an LCD projector and a laptop computer are available. This allows speakers to tailor their presentations. Providing speakers with a template for preparing overheads and handouts is also a practical idea. You can request that all slides and handouts adhere to specific guidelines, including font choices such as Arial or Times New Roman, prescribed text and background colors, and a clear organization or event logo. This promotes a consistent visual identity for your meeting. Additionally, some organizations may impose strict deadlines for content review and approval.

To reduce expenses and conserve resources, many groups have chosen to place all handouts on an event app, a cloud service, such as Dropbox, or a flash drive, offering them for free or at a nominal charge. Similarly, some groups opt to post all handouts on their company website instead of distributing them. Others provide "print on demand" stations for attendees who prefer hard copies. If handouts are used, remember to request a master copy well in advance.

MARKETING AND PROMOTION
(adapted from *Planning and Management of MEEC* by Fenich)

Planning an event does not automatically guarantee attendance. Right? Indeed, not necessarily. The costliest mistake in event management is failing to attract an audience. No amount of lavish decorations, fine cuisine, effective room design, engaging speakers, lively entertainment, impeccable A/V, or elaborate staging can compensate for an event attended by only a handful of people. Despite meticulous efforts to organize and manage a well-executed event, if attendance is low or nonexistent, the event will not be considered a success. The importance of event marketing and communication cannot be underestimated.

Marketing encompasses far more than mere communication. The application of marketing principles begins right at the inception of a new event, involving identifying the event's audience (**target market**) and determining how the event will be positioned to meet its needs. Subsequently, the marketing mix, often referred to as the "4Ps" of marketing, plays a pivotal role in shaping our event design and strategy: product, price, place, and promotion. In the context of the event industry, we delve into the first three using industry-specific questions:

Product

- What does the target market want from the event? What need is met?
- What event features meet those needs?
- What does the event look like? How will it be experienced?
- What should the look/feel be?
- How is it different from competitors?

Price

- What is the value of the event to the attendee?
- Is the attendee price sensitive?
- What discounts should be offered?
- How will the price compare with competitors?
- What price generates a profit?

Place

- Where/when will the event be? Is that good for attendees?
- How and when will potential attendees register?

The final P where the communication plan comes together. It outlines the when, where, and how of communicating the event details to potential attendees. The promotional mix is the combination of channels used to disseminate information. Event professionals often face constraints in terms of human and financial resources, preventing them from promoting their event through every channel. Consequently, they must make decisions about the most effective channels for reaching the target audience, whether it is event attendees, exhibitors, or sponsors. Numerous options are available, some of which can be blended, including the following.

Promotional Mix

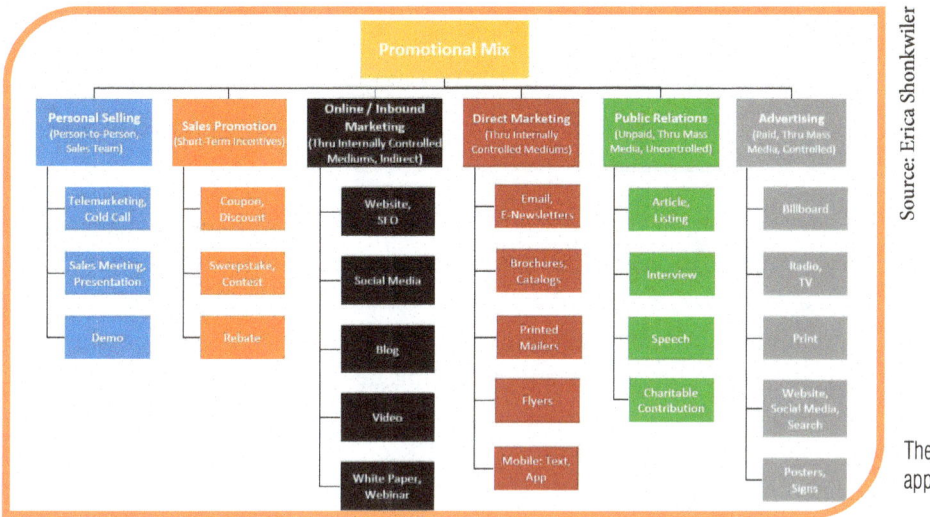

Personal Selling (Person-to-Person, Sales Team)	Sales Promotion (Short-Term Incentives)	Online / Inbound Marketing (Thru Internally Controlled Mediums, Indirect)	Direct Marketing (Thru Internally Controlled Mediums)	Public Relations (Unpaid, Thru Mass Media, Uncontrolled)	Advertising (Paid, Thru Mass Media, Controlled)
Telemarketing, Cold Call	Coupon, Discount	Website, SEO	Email, E-Newsletters	Article, Listing	Billboard
Sales Meeting, Presentation	Sweepstake, Contest	Social Media	Brochures, Catalogs	Interview	Radio, TV
Demo	Rebate	Blog	Printed Mailers	Speech	Print
		Video	Flyers	Charitable Contribution	Website, Social Media, Search
		White Paper, Webinar	Mobile: Text, App		Posters, Signs

Source: Erica Shonkwiler

The promotional mix as applied to events

Certain events and meetings rely on a minimal set of promotional channels. For instance, a corporate sales meeting, where attendance is mandatory, might necessitate only an email notification. Social events, such as weddings, birthday parties, or anniversaries, may only require printed or emailed invitations. Events dependent on attendee registration, exhibitor participation, and sponsorship contributions demand a more extensive promotional effort to ensure a substantial audience.

In some organizations, event marketing is handled by an entire team of event professionals, who may also hire specialized contractors for marketing, public relations, and promotional campaigns. In contrast, some organizations entrust a single event professional with sole responsibility for all event marketing efforts. In both cases, it is logical for the professional to be actively involved in all marketing activities to ensure that objectives are accurately represented and the design, theme concepts, and overall look and feel are all consistent.

TYPES OF PROMOTION FOR EVENTS

PERSONAL SELLING

Personal selling encompasses three primary promotional channels: phone calls (telemarketing or cold calling), presentations, and demonstrations. These channels are typically carried out by the sales professionals within the team supporting a event. They are most commonly employed to persuade exhibitors or sponsors, groups with substantial event-related costs, to participate in the event in various capacities.

Sales Promotions

All sales promotion channels are designed to emphasize special deals, rates, or incentives to arouse excitement and motivate attendees to register. These channels are often integrated with other promotional methods. For instance, an event might distribute discount codes through its social media event page, engaging existing followers and attracting new ones, all while encouraging event registration.

Online/Inbound Marketing

Content disseminated through online/inbound marketing channels is entirely controlled by the organization hosting the event. However, readers/viewers access this content voluntarily. These channels may include the organization's or event's website, social media accounts, blog, or YouTube channel. Some associations even offer digital magazines and resources for their members that could feature event promotional content. These channels are considered "inbound" because potential attendees or viewers choose to visit source independently, seeking information, because they already enjoy engaging with the organization for entertainment or information purposes. Their visit it presents the perfect opportunity to promote and highlight an upcoming event hosted by the organization. Delivering high-quality content that avoids being overly sales oriented is crucial for success in these channels.

Direct Marketing

Unlike inbound marketing, direct marketing involves pushing information directly to the reader. The organization has complete control over the content, which is delivered to the target market (potential attendees) through various channels, such as email, e-newsletters, brochures or catalogs, printed mailers, digital or printed flyers, and mobile communications via text or an app. Printed materials, such as save-the-dates, invitations, and reminders, can be quite expensive to produce and mail. However, for smaller groups or VIPs, a well-designed hardcopy piece or package can generate excitement. Digital options are more cost effective and offer broader reach, but to stand out amidst the deluge of email and digital communications, content should be concise, engaging, tailored to the audience, and able to drive readers to the website for more information. The frequency is crucial; sending messages too often can cause readers to disengage and possibly opt out of future communications. By law, opt-out options must be included in these communications, and it is important to be aware that these laws vary by country and should be researched to ensure compliance.

Public Relations

Public relations involves effectively managing relationships and communications to influence behavior and achieve objectives. In the meetings/events industry, public relations can be described as the "presentation of an event via the media or other outlets, stressing the benefits and desirability of such event" (CIC, 2011). All events employ public relations strategies, albeit at varying scales, with some events requiring more extensive efforts than others.

Event professionals must consider multiple public relations strategies to engage with the media before, during, and after the event. Additionally, different categories of media need to be taken into account. Although most events involve industry or trade media related to their topics, many also need to consider engaging local, state, and even national news media if the content is significant for the public.

When employing public relations as part of the promotional mix, event professionals do not have control over how the media reports on the event. Their responsibility is to provide the media with information, highlight newsworthy content, and offer access to spokespersons to convey the intended message. However, the media retains the final say in how it communicates this to its audiences. Although public relations is an unpaid promotional effort, associated costs may need to be included in the event budget, such as a dedicated staff person, hiring of a PR consultant or firm, the development of media materials, and on-site support for media engagement during the event.

Advertising

An advertisement is a public notice. In most cases, advertising refers to paid forms of commercial promotion (also known as "ads"). The most common forms of commercial advertising include print media ads, such as those in newspapers and magazines; broadcast media ads, such as television and radio commercials; and online media, such as ads on websites, search engines, social networking sites, and web video commercials. Commercial advertising can take numerous other forms, ranging from billboards to mobile phone screens, bus stop benches, aerial banners, balloons, individuals wearing signs (human billboards), and bus and subway train signs.

Given that advertising can be costly, event professionals aim to allocate their budget effectively by targeting individuals most likely to attend the event. Ads may be placed in relevant trade magazines, journals, or publications, to not only promote the event but also raise the organization's profile. For instance, if an event is tailored for an audience of event professionals, suitable trade journals might include *Convene, Successful Meetings,* or *Meetings and Conventions Magazine.* If the event's target audience is bankers, it may be advertised in the American Bankers' Association publication, *ABA Banking Journal.*

Some media outlets may offer trade-out advertising arrangements in exchange for services provided by the event organization. For example, a large exhibition's event manager might exchange exhibit space for an advertisement in a publishing company's publication. Similarly, a radio or television station might be willing to become a sponsor, granting them marketing exposure at the event in return for free advertisements.

SUMMARY AND BEST PRACTICES

Planning a event is a lengthy process that often necessitates input from numerous individuals or committees. Establishing goals and clearly defined objectives is the initial and crucial step in crafting effective program content and managing logistics. These objectives affect city selection, type of facility, and required services. Additionally, the event professional must comprehend attendee motivations: Why should they attend? Is attendance voluntary or mandatory? Planning a corporate event can differ significantly from an association event. Education typically supersedes recreation as the primary driving force behind most meetings.

Once the objectives are clearly defined, a needs analysis should be conducted to further guide the event professional in selecting suitable meeting space, speakers, and amenities expected by the attendees. Demographics of the attendees must also be taken into account. Meetings and conventions represent significant economic potential for cities. During the site selection process, the RFP announces the event professional's requirements. DMOs and individual hotels must evaluate the meeting's potential and respond accordingly. Properties that express interest may invite the event professional for a familiarization trip to visit their venue.

Education and networking re the most important elements for most meetings. However, people also seek entertainment along with education, so event professionals must cater to all attendees' needs, providing a balance of both. The format of education sessions and the setup of meeting spaces should align with the meeting's objectives. Program content should be designed with specific tracks and levels to cater to the majority of attendees. Housing and registration are vital components in executing the event plan. Both paid and voluntary speakers can be employed, each with its own advantages and disadvantages. Careful consideration is needed to ensure speakers are adequately prepared to address the group and are contractually obligated to perform. Last, ancillary activities, such as shopping trips, tours, childcare, and other services that enhance attendees' meeting experience, should be thoughtfully planned to avoid interfering with the scheduled programming.

Due to the intricacies of the meeting planning process, this chapter can only provide a brief overview. For more in-depth information on planning and production in MEEC, two books are available: *Planning and Management of Meetings, Expositions, Events and Conventions* and *Production and Logistics in Meetings, Expositions, Events and Conventions*, both by Fenich.

CASE STUDY MEETING PLANNING BASED ON STAKEHOLDER ANALYSIS

Meeting stakeholders are anyone impacted by the positive/negative outcomes of the meeting—attendees, exhibitors, sponsors, the organization holding the meeting and its staff, volunteers, meeting suppliers, media, and even the community where the meeting is held. The stakeholders for different meetings have different values and interests. A meeting professional should always consider the specific needs of their stakeholders when making all of the planning decisions for an event covered in this chapter. How do you understand your stakeholders? For attendees, why are they coming to the meeting? What do they hope to get out of their money and time spent? What are their demograpics (characteristics categorized by distinct criteria—such as age, gender and income) and psychographics (qualitative psychological characteristics and traits such as values, desires, goals, interests, and lifestyle choices)?

Let's consider the attendee stakeholder groups for two very different meetings:

America's Beauty Show (www.americasbeautyshow.com/)
America's Beauty Show is one of the largest annual events in the United States for the professional beauty industry. Owned and produced by salon professionals, America's Beauty

Show drives the salon industry by monitoring and lobbying for professional licenses and providing advanced education and and the latest on all products related to the cosmetology industry. Its mission is to give back to the industry by educating all professionals and improving the cosmetology profession by helping those in need.

Fire Department Instructors Conference, FDIC (https://www.fdic.com/)
FDIC International offers thousands of fire and rescue professionals worldwide quality world-class instructors, classrooms, workshops, and the most innovative products and services available to the industry displayed by over 800 exhibiting companies.

1. Why are the attendees coming to these meetings? What do they hope to take away?
2. What are the attendee demographics and psychographics for these meetings? *Note: think of the most common attendee. Although events want to be inclusive and create welcoming spaces for all demographics/psychographics, it is helpful to consider the majority.*
3. How would the difference of attendees in these two meetings cause you as the planner to make different choices in the planning of each of them? *Consider: meeting location/venue, programming/schedule, types of education sessions, F&B selection, registration fee, housing needs, speakers, and types of promotion.*

KEYWORDS AND TERMS

For definitions, see glossary or https://insights.eventscouncil.org/Industry-glossary.

airlift	poster sessions
annual meetings	presenter contract
attrition	request for proposal
cash flow	return on investment
concurrent session	room block
cutoff date	rooming list
discussion groups	roundtables
early-bird rate	SMART
familiarization (fam) trip	speaker bureau
general session	speaker-ready room
group history	stakeholder
housing bureau	subject-matter experts
keynote address	target market
level	track
needs analysis	workshops
plenary session	

REVIEW AND DISCUSSION QUESTIONS

1. What is the difference between a meeting goal and a SMART objective?

2. What is the purpose of using program formats, levels, and tracks in designing effective meeting programming?

3. What are the benefits and challenges of using volunteer versus paid speakers?

4. What are the benefits and limitations of outsourcing components of a meeting, such as housing or registration?

5. How can event professionals use registration data before, during, and after a convention?

6. How does preregistration assist the event professional in planning a meeting?

7. Describe the four different methods of housing.

8. Think of a MEEC event you have attended. Who was the target audience? What marketing strategies did the organizer use?

ABOUT THE CHAPTER CONTRIBUTORS

Amanda Cecil, **Ph.D.**, is a professor in the Department of Tourism, Event, and Sport Management at Indiana University (IUPUI). Her teaching and research focuses on event tourism and business travel.

Erica Shonkwiler, M.B.A., is a lecturer in the Department of Tourism, Event, and Sport Management at IUPUI. Her teaching and scholarship focuses on event design and management.

CHAPTER 14

PRODUCING MEETINGS AND EVENTS

ERECTING TRADE SHOW BOOTHS IS A MAJOR COMPONENT OF THE MEEC INDUSTRY

CHAPTER OBJECTIVES

- Discuss the basic requirements of producing an on-site meeting or event.
- Outline strategies and considerations for managing the on-site team.
- Discuss the various considerations and specifics that go into on-site communications.
- Cover the specific considerations to keep in mind when planning and executing public relations when producing an event.
- Articulate the reasons and important elements of preconvention meetings.
- Specify the elements needed for a successful postconvention review.

Contributed by Amanda Cecil. © Kendall Hunt Publishing Company.
Contributed by Erica Shonkwiler. © Kendall Hunt Publishing Company.

Producing meetings and events is a sequential part of the planning and execution process. "Producing" or production and logistics are often associated with "on-site" activities. In large convention hotels, the sales team handles the planning, and convention services manage the production. These are distinct departments with separate teams.

ON-SITE MANAGEMENT

Several crucial areas require meticulous on-site management for every event. These include registration, housing, food and beverage (F&B), speakers and entertainers, audiovisual, and **ancillary** events. Effective management of each area demands a skillful approach to ensure flawless logistics, cost control, and the achievement of strategic goals and outcomes. The following sections explain each key area.

REGISTRATION AND HOUSING

Similar to a hotel's front desk, the registration area serves as attendees' first interaction with an event. A slow or inefficient registration process can significantly impact the entire event. To create a positive first impression, it is essential to adequately staff the registration area on the first day and keep it open throughout the event. If international guests are expected, consider translating registration materials and providing interpreters to ensure a smooth check-in process. For events involving exhibitions, a separate area for exhibitor registration is advisable.

Event professionals often outsource registration, especially for large events, due to its complexity, which necessitates thorough training for registration attendants. Some hotels or convention centers partner with temp agencies that provide staff experienced in registration services, and some registration management companies handle housing as part of their services.

For an efficient event experience, the registration area should be thoughtfully designed, minimizing wait times for check-in or inquiries. Electronic kiosks are increasingly being used to streamline the registration process. For significant issues with an individual's or a group's registration, a dedicated staff member should be available to meet with them; it is advisable to allocate a private meeting room or create a hospitality area near the registration desk for this.

Moreover, questions and concerns related to housing should be promptly addressed at the registration area. If the registration staff cannot assist, they should guide attendees to the appropriate resource. If someone has issues regarding accommodations or service quality at the hotel, they should be directed to its designated contact person. If the problem remains unresolved, the meeting planner or a third-party representative should step in to assist.

You should request final registration and housing reports before departing from the event location. These reports contain crucial information necessary for future negotiations with hotels, venues, and suppliers. Furthermore, it is advisable to discuss these reports in all subsequent strategic follow-up meetings.

F&B

At this stage, all F&B orders, room locations and designs, food providers, and permits should be finalized. Most facilities typically provide a **banquet event order (BEO)** for each function where F&B services are provided. This document outlines details such as F&B quantities, timing, logistics, staffing requirements, and service type. Upon arrival on-site, the event planner should meet with the catering manager or convention services manager (CSM) to review each BEO and address any inaccuracies or necessary updates.

One crucial aspect that requires finalization is the **guarantee**. This is the contracted number of meals or items the organization will pay for, regardless of actual attendance. The timing for submitting it may vary, typically ranging from 48 hours to 2 weeks in advance, depending on the group's size and menu complexity. This process can significantly impact the budget if the event professional overorders, and it could lead to embarrassment for the host if F&B is insufficient. Therefore, having a clear understanding of the event's history and projected attendance is imperative to accurately determine the guarantee.

Other essential on-site considerations include verifying that all vendors and the organization possess the necessary permits and licenses for operation and conducting a thorough evaluation of the space before the actual event to ensure that room setups are appropriate. Additionally, discussions about service expectations should take place with the banquet or F&B captain. Furthermore, it is vital to review all policies and procedures related to food safety and liability issues, especially when alcohol is being served (see Chapter 9).

FUNCTION ROOM LAYOUTS

When selecting a venue, one key consideration is how each room will be arranged. Several factors influence the layout, including the number of attendees, type of meeting, attendee learning styles, A/V and technology requirements, speaker tables, refreshment tables, and the physical attributes or obstacles within the room. Traditional layouts include auditorium/theater, banquet, reception, classroom, cocktail, boardroom, hollow square, exhibit, conference, and U-shape. Most venues can provide planners with renderings depicting how each room can be configured using these different layouts.

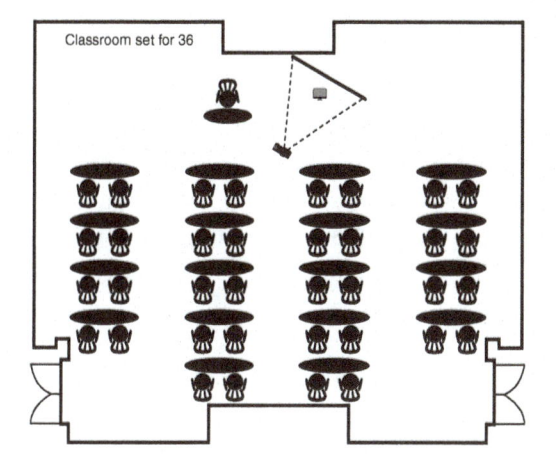

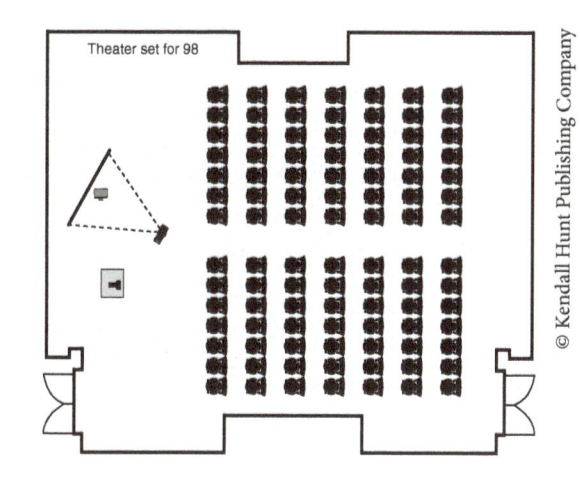

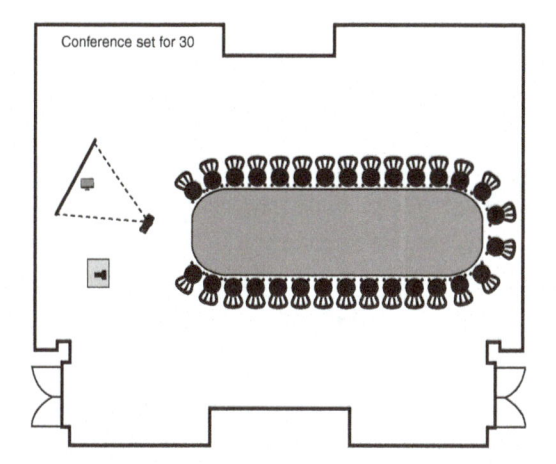

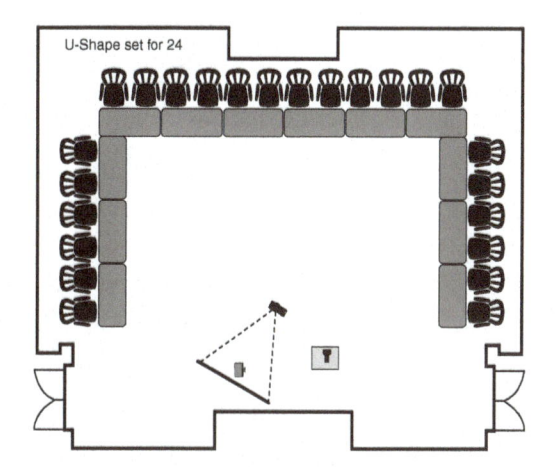

FIGURE 14-1 Traditional venue layouts

AUDITORIUM OR THEATER STYLE

Perhaps the most commonly used seating arrangement for meetings is the auditorium or theater design. An **auditorium-style** room setup proves particularly effective when attendees do not need to interact with each other during the session. Its primary purpose is to maximize seating capacity within a room. Chairs are neatly aligned in rows, all facing the same direction. Typically, these rows are directed toward the front of the room, which may be indicated by a stage, head table, lectern, or screen. The meeting is typically led by a speaker or panel who often lecture while attendees may take notes based on the information being presented.

CHAPTER 14 PRODUCING MEETINGS AND EVENTS

Classroom Style

Meetings may require tables for attendees to complete tests, take notes, or collaborate with one another to solve presented problems. This is where the **classroom-style** setup becomes valuable. Chairs are arranged similarly to an auditorium, but tables are provided for each row of chairs. These tables are typically 6 or 8 feet long and 18 inches deep. If attendees sit on both sides of the table, 30-inch-deep tables (or two 18-inch tables placed back to back) are used to ensure adequate space. Tables are draped, and each place setting has notepads and pens or pencils.

Like auditorium setups, classroom setups can be adjusted as needed. At times, classrooms are arranged diagonally toward the head table or even perpendicular to the front of the room. However, perpendicular room setups can pose challenges, as it may require a significant number of attendees to have their backs turned to the speaker. This arrangement may work when the purpose of the session is to collaborate with table partners but is generally not advisable when attendees need to focus on the individual on stage.

Rounds

Round tables are occasionally used for meetings but most commonly employed for dining functions. They prove particularly valuable in smaller breakout sessions or meetings that necessitate substantial interaction among attendees. Round tables promote and facilitate communication because all individuals seated at the table can easily see and engage with their table companions, fostering collaboration.

Many meeting venues offer 6-foot rounds (72 inches in diameter) or, less frequently, 5-foot rounds (60 inches in diameter). The diameter of the tables is significant because it determines how many individuals can comfortably sit. Five-foot rounds can accommodate 6–8; 6-foot rounds can seat 8–10.

In the image provided, eight guests were seated at each 6-foot round table. An alternative to full rounds is the **crescent round**. Crescent rounds may use full-sized round tables but will not have seats all the way around the table. This design ensures that no one is seated with their back to the head table, and everyone at the table enjoys an unobstructed view of the speaker.

Another variation of round tables serving the same purpose is the sunburst setup. Rectangle tables can be used, or a combination of rectangles and rounds can create a more diverse spatial layout while still supporting interaction at the tables. Rectangles can evoke the feeling of gathering around a home dinner table, fostering a more intimate and contemporary atmosphere.

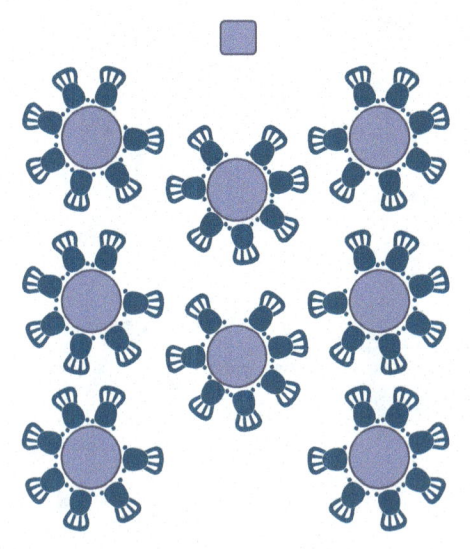

FIGURE 14-2 Additional Seating Layouts

Nontraditional Room Setup

As attendee and meeting planner expectations evolve to demand more interactive meeting spaces, several innovative room layouts have emerged. These fresh designs aim to foster connections among attendees and prioritize engagement. Casual layouts, featuring comfortable seating, such as couches and buffets served at action stations, are just the beginning of the future of meetings. Event professionals should also consider the diverse learning styles of attendees when determining room setups. Blended setups have become increasingly popular, allowing attendees to choose seating that best suits their needs. For instance, some setups include countertop-level tables where attendees can stand while taking notes or stools at the back of the room to accommodate those who prefer to move or stand or have difficulty sitting for extended periods. In the middle of the room, round or classroom-style tables are available for those who prefer a conventional seating arrangement. Finally, at the front of the room, options such as soft couches, benches, bean bags, and coffee tables are provided for attendees seeking a more comfortable and relaxed setting. A single meeting room for an educational session offers options to accommodate multiple learning styles and attendees' physical needs, all while presenting a unique and engaging atmosphere. Many of these distinctive setups require renting special furniture, which is typically available at an additional cost from venue vendors. Therefore, a venue's setup can be customized to align with the event planner or client's unique vision.

CHAPTER 14 PRODUCING MEETINGS AND EVENTS

Source: Erica Shonkwiler

Source: Erica Shonkwiler

476

MEETINGS, EXPOSITIONS, EVENTS, AND CONVENTIONS

COMMON ISSUES FACED ON-SITE

Regardless of where an event is held, all events have some issues in common. Many of these issues are based around logistics, such as transporting attendees from the airport. The following list includes issues that are common to most, if not all, meetings.

OBSTACLES

One of the primary challenges for event planners is overcoming obstacles that could hinder the attendees' success during the meeting. These obstacles can originate from various sources within the event venue, such as an understaffed or undersized registration desk, insufficient parking space for attendees who drive to the event, or noise ordinances restricting loading and unloading activities between 10:00 p.m. and 6:00 a.m. Physical obstacles are not limited to considerations related to disabilities. Logistical concerns also exist, such as how attendees will travel from their rooms to a gala dinner in formal attire during inclement weather or whether buses transporting guests to an off-site venue can conveniently access the venue's entrance.

POWER

Many outdoor special events and even some gatherings in smaller indoor venues often require power capacities that surpass what is readily available. Generators are typically used, but they can be quite expensive. Properly anticipating power requirements is even more crucial in these events than in traditional meeting venues. With a generator, the planner incurs not only the daily rental cost but also a fuel charge. The fuel expenses depend on three key factors: the fuel's price per gallon, the generator's runtime, and the amount of power drawn. The planner can control two of these elements. Generator usage is billed based on fuel consumption, and even an idling generator consumes fuel. Turning off a generator when it is not needed can save money.

For any meeting or special event featuring video displays or name entertainment, particularly those with numerous trade show booths or large scenic units, special power requirements become essential. Power can be a costly component. Surprisingly, the expenses tied to running a sound system can even surpass the equipment rental costs. Many convention centers offer discounts if power requests are made well in advance. Technical vendors can typically calculate power requirements with relative ease. When a 30% discount for early power requests is available, a prudent strategy is to order approximately 10–15% more power than initially estimated. This ensures that ample power is available at a cost lower than if the power order were placed after all detailed requirements had been calculated.

Power charges are based not on consumption but rather on the maximum amount of power that can be delivered at any given time. In many states, it is illegal to meter actual consumption and charge accordingly, as this would categorize the facility as a utility company subject to rate regulations.

Event professionals engaged in global events must remain acutely aware of local differences. Voltage standards can vary significantly; for instance, North America typically uses 110 volts, but much of the rest of the world relies on 220 volts. The style of electrical outlets and corresponding plugs also exhibit wide variation, with over 10 different configurations in use.

Rigging

Plaster ceilings can be the production rigger's worst nightmare, closely followed by precast concrete roofs with no steel support. Any event involving more than a few hundred people or video image magnification often requires ceiling-mounted lighting. Unless a facility is exceptionally well equipped for it, the task typically involves hanging trusses, which requires rigging. Although theaters usually have adequate provisions for lighting without hanging trusses, hotels may not be as well prepared.

The hotel's contracted rigging company will require access to all floor plans not less than 2 weeks in advance. Although that lead time should be simple for an event contracted a year in advance, generating an accurate floor plan turns out to be a challenge many planners cannot accommodate. In some jurisdictions, the fire marshal, building code inspector, or safety officer can

Lighting Rigging

refuse to allow a show to be hung without a detailed hanging plan. Having to cancel a show at the last minute due to failure to submit paperwork can be a career-ending mistake.

Most venues choose to contract rigging services to external companies for liability protection. This decision aligns with the standard practice of outsourcing tasks that venue management may not have sufficient expertise to oversee effectively. Rigging professionals, who regularly handle the responsibility of suspending "live loads" above the general public, approach their work with a strong commitment to safety. Their aim is to ensure safety, not to hinder the event. Providing adequate advance notice of schedules and requirements can help ensure that the event venue is properly rigged on time and in compliance with safety standards.

Floors

It is not safe to assume that merely because a building has a ground-level loading door spacious enough to accommodate a tractor-trailer, the floor can automatically support it. Even if the floor is four inches of steel-reinforced concrete at ground level, the utility boxes within it may not have been designed with the same strength in mind. To illustrate, one facility in the Orlando area had to excavate and repour concrete around several floor pockets due to the constant traffic of forklifts causing them to sink into the ground. Additionally, it is unwise to assume that a particular scissor lift can be easily maneuvered into a ballroom. For events where these considerations are relevant, planners should include inquiries about floor load capacity during site inspections because this information is seldom readily available.

Ballrooms are typically carpeted, and many hotels stipulate that plastic sheeting must be placed over the carpet during the move-in and move-out processes. If so, it is crucial for the **event services contractor** and all technical vendors to be informed in advance. The demand for covering the floor with materials such as Polytack is increasingly common. Neglecting to submit a proper floor plan to those responsible for applying the floor covering or failing to schedule the installation properly can lead to costly delays.

Many academic theaters feature polished wood floors on their stages. It is strongly discouraged to nail or screw into these floors, as it can quickly lead to the venue refusing to host future events. These floors are not designed to withstand heavy loads, such as scissor lifts or forklifts, and adjustments may be necessary in terms of staffing and equipment requirements.

Access

Ensuring that attendees, technical support teams, and catering staff can easily locate the venue and its entrance is crucial. The design of loading access can significantly impact an event's financial considerations. For instance, a facility in South Florida has the sole loading access to the ballroom via backing a truck along a sea wall for a hundred yards. A 21-foot truck cannot make the corner, but a 17-foot truck can. The closest parking for a tractor-trailer is a quarter mile away. An event relying on a tractor-trailer for technical support equipment would need to unload off-site and transport it to the loading dock using a smaller truck, incurring significant additional expenses. Another facility on Florida's west coast has loading access to the ballrooms through an open-sided elevator without a top attached, on the exterior of the building. In this region, summer rains are frequent, making a load scheduled for 4:00 p.m. in July susceptible to complications.

Having truck-height docks is not always sufficient to ensure smooth loading. Some facilities, such as the WDW Dolphin and the Gaylord Palms, feature elevators from the docks to the ballrooms. Access to the theater at the Orange County Convention Center requires two elevators and a push down the hall between them. The number and placement of docks play a significant role, such as the Morial Convention Center in New Orleans, which is entirely on one level with loading docks lining an entire side of the building.

For even more "common issues" in producing meetings and events, see the book in this series called *Production and Logistics in Meeting, Expositions, Events, and Conventions* by Fenich.

SPEAKERS AND ENTERTAINERS

For a large meeting featuring multiple speakers and entertainers, managing the logistics of who is where and what is happening can be an immense undertaking. Enlisting the help of volunteers or hiring temporary staff can make a significant difference. One of the worst scenarios is having a speaker fail to show up for the meeting, unbeknownst to the event professional. Additionally, it is essential to recognize that most speakers and entertainers expect acknowledgment for their time and effort. They may have specific requirements and contractual expectations that need addressing on-site, particularly in the case of musicians.

Once everyone is on-site, a collaborative effort between the planner, facility manager, and speaker/entertainer is crucial during rehearsal. The presenter should practice their presentation on the stage (or in the room) with all the necessary A/V, lighting, and music elements in place. Adjustments to the session should be made as necessary. This rehearsal provides an opportunity to address any lingering questions from the speaker or entertainer or their support team.

A new trend is emerging where attendees preselect sessions or activities featuring speakers and entertainers of interest, enabling them to come better prepared for large events. Social media platforms, such as Facebook, Twitter, LinkedIn, Pinterest, Tumblr, and blogs, play a pivotal role in facilitating discussions on various topics months in advance. Speakers can actively participate in these conversations and tailor their actual presentations based on the insights gained. Similarly, some speakers use this intelligence to gauge the attendees' level of knowledge within the group. After the session concludes, attendees can be reassessed, measuring their learning.

ON-SITE A/V

Effectively managing the technology needs and program design on-site requires a carefully planned approach. Meeting planners are no longer limited to basic tools, such as flip charts and projectors; they now seek sophisticated technology options, including plasma screens, digital signage, LCD projectors, and intelligent lighting.

A crucial aspect of planning and managing the A/V requirements is the selection of a key supplier. This A/V provider may or may not be in-house. Some planners prefer to bring their own trusted supplier who is familiar with the event and the organization's specific needs. The primary aim of this partnership is for the supplier to assist the organization in conveying its messages effectively. The emphasis is not solely on equipment selection but on achieving the meeting's goals and desired outcomes. Sound, lighting, staging, and other equipment needs should be discussed within this broader context.

During the planning process, a group of key individuals will come together to create a **production schedule** (see Chapter 11), an overview of the production for each function, from installing equipment to dismantling the stage or room setup. This timeline serves as a detailed, step-by-step plan that all parties should follow on-site. Typically, an event assigns a production or technical director to oversee all technical aspects of the meeting and lead a team of skilled professionals. The director's responsibility includes ensuring that objectives are met, safety and security standards are adhered to, and the program runs smoothly.

ANCILLARY EVENTS

Various activities can be incorporated before, during, and after the main scheduled program. Many event sponsors and exhibitors extend corporate hospitality offers to attendees, which may include golf outings, exclusive dinners, or tickets to local sports or cultural events. Moreover, in today's fast-paced business environment, attendees often try to incorporate a short vacation into their meeting schedules. It is becoming increasingly common for spouses, significant others, and children to accompany attendees as guests. Some meeting participants may add a few extra days to their trip to spend quality time with family and friends. While attendees are engaged in workshops and trade shows, guests typically seek activities to keep themselves occupied. Options include tours, shopping excursions, cultural events, sports events, dinners, museum visits, festivals, and theatrical shows. Every city, regardless of its size, offers something of interest to explore. The key consideration is to ensure that these **ancillary activities** do not detract from the overall program objectives. They should not be more attractive than the primary program. Additionally, they should be suitable for the age, gender, and interests of the guests.

Consider limiting participation in planning ancillary activities for two important reasons: additional effort and liability concerns. As an event professional, your primary focus should be on the proceedings within the meeting facility. You should not have to worry about the punctuality of the bus to the mall or similar logistical matters. Where feasible, it is advisable to attendee the management of ancillary activities to a local **destination management company (DMC)**. A DMC specializes in organizing activities and possesses in-depth knowledge of the local area (see Chapter 7). Moreover, in the unfortunate event of injuries at an event, you would not want to be burdened with liability issues. An excellent example is when childcare services are provided by the sponsoring organization; it is essential to consider additional insurance coverage to shield against liability issues. Childcare should be outsourced to a professional service, given the specialized licensing required to ensure the safety and security of children.

The safest approach is to furnish attendees with a list of local activities and the website address of the destination marketing organization (DMO). This enables attendees to plan their own activities. A word of caution: When hosting meetings in popular resort destinations, such as Orlando or Las Vegas, the various "attractions" available can quickly become "distractions." It is not uncommon to lose a few attendees in Las Vegas when the call of the slot machines is louder than an hour-long workshop on a dry topic.

MEETING AND EVENT SPECIFICATION GUIDE

One of the significant challenges in the meeting and events profession has been the historical lack of standardized policies, procedures, and terminology. To address this issue and initiate the codification of definitions and standardized practices, an industry-wide task force, the **APEX Initiative,** was established. As mentioned in Chapter 1, APEX stands for Accepted Practices Exchange. One of its initial accomplishments was developing accepted practices related to terminology. The committee discovered that many terms were used interchangeably to describe the document used by meeting and event professionals to communicate specific requirements for a function. Some of these terms included "catering event order," "meeting résumé," "event specifications guide," "staging guide operations manual," "production schedule," "room specs," "schedule of services," "working agenda," "specifications sheet," and "group résumé." After considerable effort and input from various meeting and event professionals, hotel convention service managers, DMCs, exhibit managers, and DMOs, the panel created a format that significantly improved communication between event professionals and service providers.

The panel introduced the term **Event Specification Guide**, defined as a "comprehensive document outlining all the requirements and instructions for an event. Typically authored by the event professional, this document is shared with all relevant vendors to communicate service expectations for a project." The industry-accepted practice is to use the APEX Event Specifications Guide (ESG), available on the Events Industry Council website.

The ESG is a three-part document that includes the following:

1. **The Narrative:** general overview of the meeting or event,
2. **Function Schedules:** timetable outlining all functions that compose the overall meeting or event, and
3. **Function Setup Orders:** specifications for each separate function that is part of the overall meeting or event. This is used by the facility to inform setup crews, technicians, catering and banquet staff, and all other staff regarding what is required for each event.

A standardized timetable exists for communication between event professionals and the facility and service providers. Although these guidelines may vary depending on the size, timing, and complexity of each event, they do offer a helpful general framework.

The ESG contains a substantial amount of detailed information. It is essential for event professionals, catering and convention services staff, and key suppliers to have access to a copy. Any modifications should be documented in all copies. Fortunately, with advancements in technology and connectivity, maintaining and updating this document has become more manageable. What was once a cumbersome five-pound, three-ring binder filled with paper forms has now been transformed into a mobile app. This allows for easy modifications to the ESG, which can be accessed by the relevant parties. Changes to the ESG are inevitable for all meetings. One of the primary responsibilities of a skilled event professional is to respond to and effectively manage changes, often unforeseen ones.

Size of Event	Submit ESG in Advance	Receive Return from Facility and Vendors
1–500	4 weeks	2 weeks
501–999	6 weeks	4 weeks
1,000+	8 weeks	6 weeks

CONTROLLING COSTS

To adhere to the budget and achieve financial objectives, it is crucial to implement cost control measures. These measures serve as tools for monitoring the budget. For a large event catering to thousands of attendees, it is common for only a handful of meeting planning staff to oversee it. This situation presents numerous opportunities for costly mistakes. The key factor here is ensuring that the event facility understands which individual within the sponsoring organization possesses the authority to make additions or changes to the orders placed. Typically, this authority rests with the CEO and the designated meeting planning staff. For instance, if an association board member decides to have an expensive dinner at the hotel restaurant and requests it to be charged to the association's account, the restaurant cannot proceed without approval from a person who holds this "**signing authority**." This practice helps minimize unexpected expenses. A daily review of expenses is essential, and any disputes should be promptly addressed. After the event concludes, invoices or cost projections should be thoroughly examined to prevent conflicts once the event location has been left.

MANAGING THE ON-SITE TEAM

The organization must determine how to adequately staff its meeting or event, considering full-time employees, temporary staff, and volunteers. Regardless of the staff type, all individuals need to be properly trained, supervised, motivated, and evaluated. The size of the team required will be contingent upon the event's size and complexity. Once again, the decision regarding staffing types and service levels should align with the meeting's goals and objectives. Furthermore, it is imperative to ensure that staffing needs are incorporated into the budget, with appropriate resources allocated to prepare the on-site team adequately. Orientation sessions for employees, temporary staff, and volunteers should be conducted on-site or virtually, followed by a tour of the meeting space and an opportunity for the team to address any questions they may have. Additionally, it is advisable to distribute a handbook to all team members, providing comprehensive information about the event, their roles and responsibilities, a key contact list, answers to frequently asked questions, facility maps, and other pertinent details.

EMPLOYEES

The planning team should meticulously assess which organizational employees should attend the event and how they will be deployed on-site. Full-time staff members should assume supervisory roles across various areas, including registration, educational sessions, and the exhibition or trade show. These individuals are already well versed in the attendees' needs, group's characteristics, organization's culture, and expectations set by its leadership. They should serve as invaluable sources of information for temporary staff and volunteers, aiding with training and supervision and serving as role models.

The organization must allocate funds for employee travel. In most instances, this includes air travel, ground transportation, hotel accommodations, and meals. The organization should establish a clear travel policy and transparently communicate whether additional expenses, such as dry cleaning, phone or internet charges, and airport parking, will be reimbursed. Depending on the event's location, these extra costs can accumulate swiftly. Hence, it is imperative for the organization to conduct a cost–benefit analysis to determine which employees need to be on-site.

Not all positions can be adequately filled by temporary employees or volunteers. The organization should bear in mind that crucial on-site roles require full-time employees: overseeing registration, managing high-profile functions, coordinating the production of general sessions, handling logistics for the exhibition, and ensuring F&B commitments. These areas can significantly impact the outcome of the meeting and have substantial budget implications.

TEMPORARY STAFF

Temporary staff members offer a viable solution for positions that require specialized training, such as expertise in registration software, accounting, or security. Some facilities may mandate temporary staff for roles related to safety and security. Medical and security personnel, if necessary, typically consist of local, hourly workers or contractors who are familiar with the facility and local services, such as hospitals and medical clinics.

Temporary staff will represent the organization to attendees and may appear to be official employees. Therefore, it is imperative that they are trained on the service expectations of the group, briefed on attendee demographics and needs, supervised by employees aligned with the meeting's goals and objectives, equipped with guidance on policies and procedures, and are evaluated for performance. Clearly define the roles of temporary staff to prevent conflicts in various scenarios. For instance, they should know if they have the authority to issue attendee refunds (registration) or remove an exhibitor for inappropriate behavior (security). Effective communication between them and key employees is vital to success.

The DMO or event facility can offer recommendations for staffing agencies that supply temporary employees. As mentioned, these should complement rather than replace key employees. They should be assigned specialized service roles to support event operations. Planners can contract with agencies or individuals, which can help reduce travel expenses.

VOLUNTEERS

Most events heavily rely on volunteers (who generously donate their time and expertise to assist with event operations without charge). Volunteers should not be placed in roles demanding specialized services, such as security, nor should they replace essential employees. However, volunteers can be used in various capacities, such as welcoming attendees at main entry points, offering directions or facility information, assisting in the registration area by distributing badges or materials, or monitoring educational sessions.

Volunteers still require training, supervision, and evaluation. Like temporary employees, volunteers need to be well informed about the organization's history, goals, and objectives. They should receive detailed attendee and guest profiles, clear role expectations, instructions regarding their level of authority, contact information for questions or assistance, and guidance on attire and working hours. Volunteers can be recruited from many sources, including (a) members of the association or organization assisting for reduced registration rates or simply to "give back," (b) local professionals, (c) community members who are retired and interested in serving the destination, or even (d) college students looking for professional experience. The DMO or local contacts can provide recruitment options.

Volunteers may not receive an hourly wage, but there are associated expenses to consider. Planners should thoroughly address and communicate whether they provide uniforms, meals, reimburse parking costs, or cover other related expenses. Clarity is essential to prevent any confusion. Additionally, planners should specify if a minimum number of hours expected. For example, volunteers might be required to commit to two shifts, each lasting 4 hours. This not only justifies the effort put into training and providing basic services but also ensures their commitment to the event.

Another critical consideration is motivating volunteers. Organizations should aim to retain their volunteers for future events, emphasizing the importance of creating a meaningful experience for them. Recognizing their efforts, either during the event or afterward, is vital to show appreciation for their time and expertise. Even a simple certificate, small gift, or thank-you can have a significant impact. Some organizations go the extra mile by hosting volunteer appreciation events and designating a "volunteer of the year" award to honor outstanding contributions.

ON-SITE COMMUNICATIONS

PERSONAL COMMUNICATIONS

Event professionals must be mindful that they will invariably engage in personal types of communication, which can be categorized into two techniques: formal and informal. Although these techniques are self-explanatory, event professionals and their constituents must understand when and how to use each appropriately. Formal communication occurs in business settings, when interacting with officials and dignitaries, etc. Informal communication occurs within groups of peers in nonbusiness settings.

Written	Verbal	Visual	Behavioral
Training manual	Briefings	Photographs	Videos
Memo	Meetings	Displays	Working practices
Letters	Radio conversations	Models	Role modeling
E-mail	One-to-one discussions	Demonstrations	Nonverbal communication
Handbooks	Instruction	Printed slogans	Social networking
Staff newsletters	Telephone conversations	Posters	
Reports	Training	Videos	
Information bulletins	Word-of-mouth messages	Internet	
Checklists			

FIGURE 14-3 Communication Strategies

Here are some guidelines for improving communication within the event team.

Establish the Level of Priority. It is crucial to establish the level of priority promptly. Emergency situations, understandably, pose the highest risk during any event. Therefore, communication related to an incident or potential incident should be given top priority.

Identify the Receiver. Identifying the receiver allows the event professional to tailor their message to the receiver's needs, demonstrating empathy. It also ensures that the message reaches the correct target audience.

Know the Objective. Clarity often stems from a well-defined action objective. When the event professional knows what they want to achieve, expressing themselves becomes more straightforward. Describing a problem and its consequences is typically just the initial stage. By specifying the necessary actions, the event professional can more effectively achieve the objective and attain a mutually agreed-upon outcome.

Review the Message in Your Head. Before sending a message, it is essential to structure it effectively. Additionally, considering the likely response from the receiver can be valuable in preparing the message.

Communicate in the Language of the Other Person. Using examples and illustrations that the receiver can understand makes the message more comprehensible.

Clarify the Message. If the receiver's nonverbal behavior suggests a lack of understanding, clarification becomes essential.

Do Not React Defensively to a Critical Response. Asking questions can help understand why the receiver responded defensively, fostering mutual understanding and effective communication.

TECHNOLOGY

DETERMINE AND ACQUIRE COMMUNICATION EQUIPMENT AND RESOURCES

The event professional must possess a comprehensive understanding of communication equipment and resources, including what is required and where to source them—identifying reliable suppliers, all while being mindful of budget constraints. It is imperative for the event professional to establish realistic concepts and expectations, never presenting unattainable pipe dreams that the client cannot afford. The event professional must analyze the unique needs of the event, considering factors such as the type and size of the venue, the attendees, staff, volunteers, and users. This holistic assessment is critical to effective planning.

The following strategies can help to develop effective communications between users:

- Identify specific information needs of group members.
- Use simple words in the language of the conference and/or host country.
- Allocate buddies or partners to develop subteams.
- Use graphics to impart information.
- Rotate roles.
- Provide all users with opportunities to participate in the group.
- Develop groups' rituals and a group identity.

Specialized communication equipment and resources may need to be allocated for emergency personnel. They require dependable, battery-powered devices and sometimes nonpowered tools, such as semaphores, reflective batons, and signs, to facilitate communication and direction during emergencies. Additionally, the event professional should evaluate the adequacy of emergency lighting and illuminated directional signage (including battery-powered exit signs) within the venue, recognizing that these elements are also forms of communication equipment.

Communication with attendees typically involves written and digital text, such as programs, activity schedules, and signage indicating ongoing events and their locations. Presentations often require A/V equipment, including microphones and amplification systems, and projection equipment. For more extravagant events, special effects lighting and signage may be employed. Public address systems can also play a crucial role in ensuring effective communication.

Determine Technology Appropriate for the Event

The growing emphasis on sustainability has compelled event professionals to streamline on-site communication efficiently and effectively. As technology continues to advance, one of the principal objectives and challenges is adapting content for mobile platforms. With the proliferation of smartphones and tablet computers designed for mobility, stakeholders now anticipate that communication will be readily available and accessible on these devices.

The effectiveness of mobile communication devices is underscored by the increasing adoption of meeting-enhancing online and social networking tools, such as Twitter.

- more demands from meeting professional for innovative technology, such as polling tools;
- a broadening scope of event technologies, such as RFP and bidding software;
- demands from attendees and speakers—especially younger ones who have grown up in a digital world for increasing the use of sophisticated multimedia and other technologies that facilitate the flow of ideas between them and their audiences;
- the growing prominence of mobile applications;
- the growing adoption of events that combine in-person and virtual aspects; and
- given the extensive use of the internet, sufficient bandwidth to handle the traffic.

Types of Equipment

- Smartphone: The primary communication tool used by event professionals and attendees is the smartphone. Larger events commonly develop apps that consolidate essential event information. Text messaging is routine, and phone calls are made when necessary. Organizations may opt to rent smartphones to address employee privacy concerns.
- PA system: PA systems are vital for communicating with large groups. Typically, these systems are hardwired, ensuring their reliability regardless of usage intensity. Event professionals should verify that venues they use have backup power supplies for the PA system, ensuring it remains functional during emergencies.
- Walkie-talkies: These two-way radios provide secure, reliable, and instant communication between event professionals.
- Hard landline: This may be needed for the operational and/or media room and would be critical in a crisis or during loss of cell phone service.
- Computers: Computers and their equivalents are the cornerstone of modern communication. Proficiency in desktop publishing software, such as the Microsoft Office Suite, is invaluable for event professionals and essential for effective written communication. Event professionals should also consider data storage solutions beyond the device itself. External options, often using USB ports, offer one solution. Another option is web storage, commonly referred to as "cloud computing"; information is stored on remote servers and accessed via the internet. Although this approach provides the advantage of accessibility from anywhere, it does rely on internet connectivity.
- Touchscreen kiosks. Many organizations now employ touchscreen kiosks in high-traffic areas to expedite attendee service needs. These kiosks serve various purposes, such as facilitating registration for badge printing and providing information. They should complement, not replace, human assistance for guest support.
- Digital signage. The era of printing all wayfinding and promotional signage is drawing to a close. Most convention centers and hotels are equipped with some form of digital signage that allows meeting planners to submit content for display. Digital signage offers several advantages, including the flexibility to make last-minute changes and contributing to sustainability efforts.

Woman using smartphone application and check-in machine at the airport For additional information on technology, see Chapter 11

Monitor On-Site Communications

The final facet of on-site communication at meetings and events is *monitoring*. Event professionals must stay vigilant and stay informed about what, when, and how information is being conveyed. It is imperative to adhere to established policies, protocols, and hierarchies. Additionally, equipment must be readily available and in good working order. If any of these elements are lacking, event professionals must promptly make necessary adjustments and corrections. Ultimately, they are responsible for every aspect of the event.

A critical aspect of monitoring involves responding to social media accounts. Although many meetings and events still provide a dedicated phone number for attendees to call with questions before and during the event, younger generations prefer alternative modes of communication. They are more inclined to post questions privately or publicly to the event, host organization, or even CEO on their social media platforms, with a clear and measured expectation that these inquiries will receive swift and comprehensive responses. Moreover, social media posts serve as one of the quickest and easiest ways to disseminate announcements to attendees. To meet these demands, event professionals must ensure the presence of dedicated staff or volunteers tasked with monitoring social media platforms. Equipping them with the necessary talking points and responses to frequently asked questions is essential to efficient engagement.

PUBLIC RELATIONS

WHAT IS PUBLIC RELATIONS?

Public relations is the art of effectively managing relationships and communication to influence behaviors and achieve objectives. In the MEEC industry, public relations can be defined as the "presentation of an event via the media or other outlets, stressing the benefits and desirability of such event" (CIC, 2011). All events, whether large or small, involve public relations strategies.

Public relations activities extend beyond media relations. It encompasses all forms of communication and the development of relations with all event *publics*, from attendees, to sponsors, speakers, the community where the event is being held, the government, and the organization members and leadership. It also involves adept crisis management to preserve the event's positive image and attractiveness to constituents during unexpected situations.

Just as in friendships, professional relationships thrive and strengthen through time and collaboration. Therefore, the relationships established today with the community, media, organization members, attendees, sponsors, vendors, and other event stakeholders are likely to endure for years. Nurturing these relationships contributes to the smooth execution of events and potentially enhances their success year after year.

DEVELOP AND MANAGE MEDIA RELATIONS

Media plays a pivotal role in our publicity plan, as it is responsible for generating the desired publicity. We cannot control their support for our event, but we can influence their decision by cultivating positive and, hopefully, enduring relationships with them.

One fundamental aspect of working with media is understanding that writers and editors specialize in different areas. Therefore, the contact person responsible for an event may not be the same as the one covering political events or other subjects. It is imperative to establish a connection with the right individual. In essence, the editor will only consider covering our event if it aligns with their audience's interests and their expertise. Sending communications to any random editor often results in the message being overlooked. Depending on the nature of our event, media may exhibit varying levels of interest, ranging from intense coverage to complete disinterest. We can employ different strategies to keep them informed and engaged.

NEWS RELEASES

A news release, or press release, is a third-person narrative that conveys essential information to the media, enabling them to report on a specific event. Throughout the event planning process, we can send a series of these releases to the media to generate interest and anticipation. These releases can be emailed individually or included in a comprehensive press kit.

1. Think like a reporter. Reporters receive a deluge of messages daily and are unlikely to pay attention unless provided with something that genuinely simplifies their work, such as a compelling story that captivates their audience. Without this, event professionals risk being ignored by reporters who will not return their calls or cover the event.
2. Develop the story from the reporter's perspective. When we write, we sometimes assume that others possess the same level of knowledge we do, which is not accurate. Reporters may not be familiar with the event name when they receive the release, and even if they are, they will not have the details, as they have not been involved in the planning process.
3. Make sure to include all of the relevant and important details:
    a. What is the event all about?
    b. When will the event take place?
    c. Where will it take place?
    d. Why is this newsworthy?
    e. Who will be there?
4. Get to the point, and provide unique information. Sometimes, including a quote from a well-recognized industry leader can be attractive to the media. Twisting the story to touch people's hearts is almost always a winning formula.
5. Make sure the message sent is clear, easy to understand, and accurate.
6. Write persuasively, but do not lie. Lying is not ethical and will put you in a difficult position sooner or later.
7. Make sure the communication does not have grammatical errors. Sending communications with errors looks unprofessional.

After crafting the news release, the next step is distribution.

- Ensure you have a well-organized database containing the names and contact information of media outlets you intend to approach. It should, at the very least, include the reporter or editor's name, area of expertise, email, phone number, and preferred mode of communication. Gathering this information can be time consuming and sometimes frustrating. Therefore, it is wise to collect it in advance, so it is readily available when you need to send your communication.
- Send out your communications promptly after drafting the release. This ensures that the information remains fresh when it reaches the media.
- Respect the preferences of the media outlets when it comes to communication. If they prefer fax, then use that method.
- Address communications to the correct person.
- Follow up with a phone call the next day to confirm receipt of the news release. This not only gauges their interest in covering the event but also offers an opportunity to address any queries. Keep in mind that reporters are often inundated with calls and may not respond to every voicemail. Be patient, respectful, and professional.
- Regularly monitor the media outlets you have approached to check for any editorials or event announcements. This provides another gauge of the plan's effectiveness.

ATTRACT AND ACCOMMODATE MEDIA

Regrettably, the media cannot cover every event, so the event professional's task is to grab their attention. The key to achieving this? Provide them with something genuinely newsworthy.

The most effective way to pique media interest is by creating a series of stories and events surrounding the main event. These activities must be carefully outlined in the event plan. For instance, when an event professional manages a citywide convention, they can calculate and communicate the impact on the local economy, which can be fascinating to the community and may garner their support. Moreover, if the event is linked to a local charity, a compelling story can be crafted around that, generating interest among prospective attendees or sponsors.

Once media attention is secured, the event professional must be prepared to respond to inquiries and accommodate their needs. A staff member should be assigned to promptly address media inquiries. Voice messages and emails should be returned within 24 hours, as media coverage occurs daily, even on holidays. On-site media's expectations include the following:

- Have a media registration area, separated from attendee registration.
- Have someone on staff assigned to accommodate media needs. That person should receive the media during registration and introduce themselves as a facilitator.
- Provide the media with complimentary tickets to enter the event, and give them preferential access to special events, speakers, and sponsors.
- Prepare a media or press room with access to computers, internet (Wi-Fi), phone, fax, electric outlets where they can connect their electronic devices, tables, and chairs where they can sit and write their stories, and a small table in a quiet place to conduct interviews. It is always nice to provide refreshments in the media room.
- Have someone ready to provide the latest, most accurate news as quickly as possible.

After the event concludes, it is essential to send a news release to the media, effectively communicating the most significant outcomes. Including high-quality pictures that media outlets can use is highly recommended. However, for event professionals to use an image, they must obtain permission from not only the photographer but also the individuals featured.

When people have been following a specific event for months, it is highly likely that they are eager to learn about its outcomes. If it is a fundraiser, the event professional should provide details on the amount of money raised and how it will be used. This transparency helps establish credibility, which, in turn, paves the way for smoother interactions when seeking media attention and community support in the future.

Additionally, expressing gratitude is always advisable. It is important to extend thanks not only to the media but also to all constituents. Thank-you letters or emails can greatly strengthen relationships with supporters and even increase the likelihood of their continued support. Table 14-1 provides some tips to accommodate and manage media before, during, and after the event.

Public relations activities involve much more than media relations; they include all communications and the development of relations with all event publics. Public relations are a fundamental element of the event's marketing plan and will help control people's perceptions.

Before the Event
• Editors and reporters focus on different industries. Make sure to communicate with the right person.
• Use their preferred way of communication.
• Follow up by phone after sending a news release.
• Build interest by creating stories around the event.
• Treat media with respect and professionalism.
• Follow protocols and make media aware of them.
• Appoint someone to be the contact person for all media inquiries.
• Answer media inquiries immediately
• Invite media to the event and provide them with complimentary tickets
During the Event
• Have a media registration area, separated from attendee registration.
• Make sure someone is available on staff to accommodate media needs and provide latest news.
• Have a pressroom equipped with Internet, phone, fax, computer access, electric outlets, etc.
• Have a quiet place available to conduct interviews
• Provide access to speakers, sponsors, and other VIPs.
• Provide preferential access to special events.
After the Event
• Send a press release with event's most important outcomes.
• Send pictures to reporters and editors.
• Call supporters and thank them for their help.

TABLE 14-1 Tips to Accommodate and Manage Media Before, During, and After the Event

MEDIA OUTLETS

Various traditional and advanced media, including podcasting, mobile advertising, YouTube, and social media, can reach a wide audience of consumers. The MEEC industry can harness the power of the internet to effortlessly broadcast its messages, provided that the content is well crafted and prewritten. These messages can be produced by independent creators and distributed on a modest budget, especially when leveraging social media channels that are easily accessible to the public. For instance, podcasting allows for one-click downloads to mobile devices, making it convenient for audiences to access both audio and video content. These messages can also be shared through file exchanges on blogs or by gaining followers and "likes" on platforms such as Facebook. Podcasting, in particular, can yield a high return on investment due to its potential for attracting a large volume of listeners.

Increasingly, groups are using social media for daily communications and announcements regarding their activities. Companies, in particular, have reaped the benefits of word-of-mouth marketing when their advertisements are posted on platforms or linked to websites. Facebook has fostered a sense of community among its users. Blogs allow individuals to freely share their thoughts and event-related activities with a global audience. Interactions among members can amplify the popularity of social media and enhance the visibility of advertisements and promotional activities. Customers often rely on product or service reviews from fellow customers. However, the credibility of these reviews has come into question, as some "fake" customers have posted misleading reviews. To address this concern, many online platforms now only allow reviews from individuals who have actually purchased or booked products, services, or events through the specific platform, such as Expedia.

SELECT AND MANAGE SPOKESPERSONS

Not everyone can effectively articulate a message or remain composed and professional, especially in a crisis. Therefore, it is crucial to designate a spokesperson (in house or outsourced) responsible for communicating with the media. The selection of the spokesperson should align with the event's scale and nature. It may be the president of the hosting organization, or a dedicated public relations manager assigned to oversee all event communications. In some cases, organizations opt for a celebrity speaker or a well-known personality, with the expectation that they will attract both the public and media attention. For instance, if an event professional is organizing a National Culinary Fest, they might choose a nationally renowned chef as the spokesperson. For a nonprofit event, the organization's executive director may assume this role, and for an event such as the Olympic Games, the president of the Olympic Committee could be the appropriate spokesperson. In any case, the person in charge should

- be knowledgeable and available to speak about any situation or detail of the event when needed.
- understand the message that is to be sent and the image it is meant to portray.
- review the talking points scripted by the communication specialist.
- have an image that is aligned with the hosting organization and the event.

- be a good communicator, capable of communicating an idea clearly verbally or in writing and able to control their facial expressions and remain calm before any situation.
- have the right combination of knowledge and character to establish a healthy relationship with the media.

If the spokesperson is not involved in planning the event, event professionals must meet with them regularly to inform them of updates and how the organization would like to handle it.

PRECONVENTION MEETINGS

A day or two before the actual start of a meeting, the event professional should participate in a preconvention (**precon**) meeting. It includes key individuals representing all departments within the facility and external vendors or suppliers who will be part of the team. In addition to the CSM, who is the primary contact, the following representatives may be requested to attend the meeting: catering or banquet manager or F&B director; A/V representative; sales manager; accounting manager; front desk manager; bell staff or concierge; housekeeping manager; security manager; engineering manager; switchboard manager; recreation manager; and all outside service providers, such as transportation, special events, and decorators. Often, the general manager of the facility will make an appearance to introduce themselves and extend a welcome to the event professional. The meeting allows the event professional to meet and establish visual connections with all supporting individuals. In many cases, this will be the first time they interact with many of them. Each representative is introduced, and any changes or additional responsibilities in their respective departments are reviewed, after which, the event professional can release each person to return to their duties.

During this meeting, the ESG is reviewed page by page with the CSM. Any necessary changes are made, guarantees are confirmed, and last-minute instructions are communicated. The precon meeting is essentially the final opportunity to make significant changes without disrupting the facility. Once an event is underway, major changes become very challenging and potentially costly. For instance, deciding an hour before a session that the room should have only chairs instead of tables and chairs as specified in the Function Sheet or BEO can create chaos. Additional staff may be required to remove the tables, incurring labor changes. Sometimes, last-minute requests cannot be accommodated. If, for example, 50 additional tables are requested, the hotel may not have them available or may not have scheduled staff for the setup.

POSTCONVENTION REVIEW

At the conclusion of a major meeting, the event professional should create a comprehensive postconvention report that serves as a record of all key events and includes vendor reports and meeting data. Its primary purposes are to aid in planning for future meetings and provide a "report card" for both the facility and the meeting manager. It should encompass both successes and challenges. Following this, a postconvention (postcon) meeting is convened, typically on a smaller scale than the precon meeting. Attendees may include planning staff, the CSM, the F&B director, the A/V manager, and a representative from the accounting department. This meeting offers an opportunity to address any billing discrepancies, service shortcomings, or issues encountered. It also provides a platform to commend facility staff for exceptional performance. Although most major meetings have a postcon meeting, smaller meetings may not require one. If the organization plans to return to the same destination or venue in the following year, it is crucial to openly discuss the "lessons learned" on both sides to ensure that any issues are identified and rectified. Conversely, if the event will be held in a different city, this is the time to recap the event and make note of areas for improvement.

EVALUATION

Creating and executing successful meetings is a collaborative effort. It is advisable for all event professionals to conduct evaluations after each event to gather feedback from attendees, exhibitors, facility staff, and any other individuals involved. These evaluations can be used to assess the effectiveness of individual sessions, quality of speakers, and appropriateness of the educational content. Overall event evaluations should gather data on various aspects, including the comfort of the hotel, transportation convenience, desirability of the location, quality of F&B services, special events, networking opportunities, and number and quality of exhibitors at trade shows or conventions. Feedback can be collected through written questionnaires distributed after the event, telephone interviews, the association or corporate website, or web-based data collection. An efficient and cost-effective method is to send an email with a link to an electronic questionnaire. Numerous software packages are available to design, distribute, collect data, and analyze the results. The information collected about speakers and logistical aspects will assist the event professional and program planning committee in enhancing the program. It is a valuable tool for continuous improvement and ensuring that future events meet the needs and expectations of all stakeholders.

The electronic **audience response systems (ARS)** has witnessed a surge in popularity as a means of engaging session participants. ARS enables event professionals to survey stakeholders through handheld devices or a dedicated smartphone event app. It transmits information in real time, allowing for on-the-fly adjustments and collecting valuable data for future events.

Evaluations, although essential, can be both time consuming and costly to design and implement. Regrettably, the data sometimes remain underused, especially when the results cast a negative light on the event. Boards of directors and CEOs are understandably hesitant to receive feedback indicating that the venue fell short of attendees' expectations. However, negative feedback can be transformed into a valuable marketing tool. A well-crafted evaluation form should be straightforward, concise, and quick to complete. A good source of questions is the event's goals and objectives. For annual events, it is advisable to include consistent questions each year. This allows for accumulating data over time, facilitating meaningful analysis.

The timing of administering individual session or event evaluations is a critical consideration. Collecting data on-site during or immediately after an event may lead to a higher response rate. Event professionals can remind attendees to complete and submit their evaluations before transitioning to the next session or event. Alternatively, some prefer to wait a few days. This allows attendees to reflect on the event's proceedings and form an objective opinion that is not clouded by the excitement of the moment. Incorporating ARS and thoughtful evaluation strategies can greatly enhance the overall effectiveness of meetings and events while ensuring that valuable feedback is leveraged for continuous improvement.

Evaluating the overall meeting should commence during the early stages of meeting planning and align closely with the meeting's objectives. The questions should encompass various aspects, such as the registration process, housing options, overall functionality of the meeting space, and F&B options, which should be factored into the meeting budget, covering costs associated with development, dissemination, analysis, and reporting. The evaluation process is a valuable component of a meeting's historical record, documenting what aspects did and did not succeed. It is cyclical, with the results of each evaluation directly informing the objectives of the following year's meeting. As most large meetings are organized by committees, evaluation results play a crucial role in transferring information from one committee to the next, ensuring that lessons learned are applied for continuous improvement.

SUMMARY AND BEST PRACTICES

The successful production of a meeting or event necessitates a skilled team to meticulously carry out the meeting plan. Every facet—from registration and F&B to A/V, housing, speakers and entertainers, and ancillary events—must be expertly managed on-site. Vital information for the on-site team to reference is conveniently compiled in the ESG. The event team comprises a blend of full-time staff members, temporary and contracted staff, and volunteers. Together, they undertake multifaceted roles to execute the meeting plan with precision. Effective communication is paramount, requiring a deliberate strategy, adept professionals, and allocated resources. Throughout the entire life cycle—before, during, and after the event—regular team meetings are essential. These meetings provide a forum to discuss achievements, concerns, lessons learned, and enhancements to the event plan.

Given the intricate nature of the meeting production process, this chapter offers only a glimpse into some of the activities involved. For a more comprehensive understanding, see *Production and Logistics in Meetings, Expositions, Events and Conventions*.

CASE STUDY STAFFING A LARGE CONVENTION

Ann is the director of meetings and events for the Association of Women in Business. The organization is headquartered in Portland, Oregon and has a 10 full-time staff members. Its annual convention is being held in Georgia this year at the Atlanta Convention Center. The event attracts 2,500 women from all over the United States and another 300–500 from outside of the country. It has contracted several hotels in the downtown area and has a special networking event in Centennial Park.

Ann has been asked to put together a comprehensive staffing plan and she must consider where to place the nine other staff members. Additionally, the chief financial officer needs to understand if she will need to hire temporary employees in key areas. The local Atlanta chapter has offered to recruit 20 volunteers to help during the conference, as well.

These areas will need to be staffed during the event:

Day 1:

Registration
Information Desk
Board Meeting and Lunch
Opening Network Reception

Day 2:

Registration
Information Desk
Membership Lounge
Opening General Session
Breakout Sessions
Networking Lunch
Exposition

Day 3:

Information Desk
Exposition
Tours of the City

Questions:

1. What areas must have a full-time association employee present to assist attendees? Explain why it is important to have an employee from the organization in these key areas.

2. What areas should the organization pay to have local, temporary employees? Explain why it is important to use someone from the local area in these key areas.

3. What areas can Ann use volunteers to assist in event-related tasks? Explain why these areas make the most sense to staff with a volunteer.

4. What can Ann offer volunteers because they are not being paid?

5. What training will temporary staff and volunteers need prior to the start of the event?

KEY WORDS AND TERMS

For definitions, see the glossary or http://glossary.conventionindustry.org

- ancillary activities
- ancillary events
- APEX Initiative
- audience response system
- auditorium style
- banquet event order
- classroom style
- crescent round
- destination management company
- event services contractor
- event specification guide
- guarantee
- precon
- postevent report
- production schedule
- public relations
- signing authority

REVIEW AND DISCUSSION QUESTIONS

1. What is the difference between the F&B projection and the final guarantee?

2. Describe the benefit of the meeting planner managing ancillary events.

3. What roles should volunteers and temporary (paid) staff be assigned on-site? What roles are critical that a full-time staff member perform?

4. How has technology advanced to better communicate with attendees or the public?

5. Articulate the key principles of a good press release.

6. What is the primary purpose of the preconference meeting and the post-conference meeting?

ABOUT THE CHAPTER CONTRIBUTORS

Amanda Cecil, Ph.D., is an associate professor in the Department of Tourism, Conventions and Event Management at Indiana University (IUIU). Her teaching and research focus on event tourism and business travel.

Erica Shonkwiler, M.B.A., is a lecturer in the Department of Tourism, Event, and Sport Management at IUIU. Her teaching and scholarship focus on event design and management.

Previous Chapter Contributor

Curtis Love, Ph.D., emeritus associate professor at the William F. Harrah Hotel College at the University of Las Vegas

CHAPTER 15

INTERNATIONAL ASPECTS IN MEEC

MEEC EVENTS ARE HELD AROUND THE GLOBE. BERLIN IS THE HOST DESTINATION FOR THE WORLD'S LARGEST TOURISM TRADE FAIR.

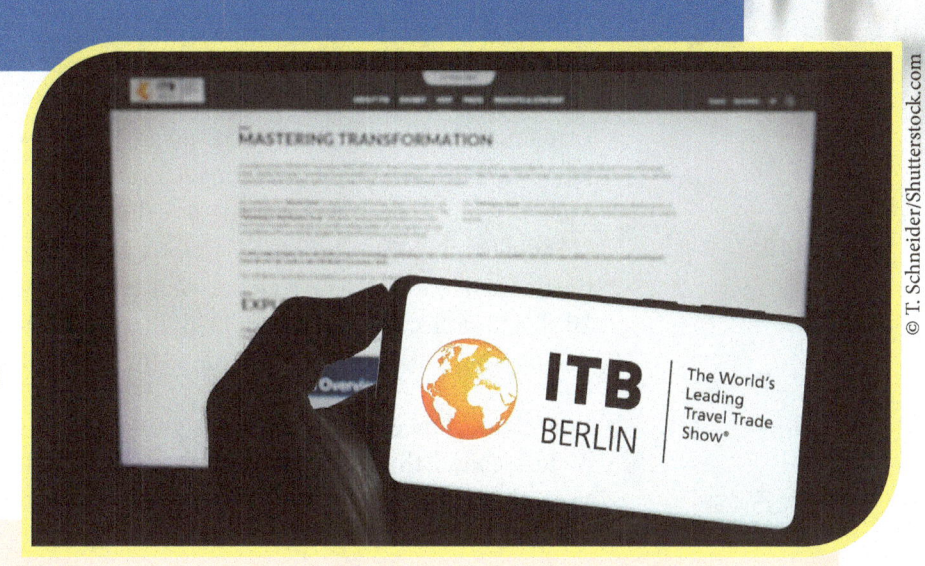

CHAPTER OBJECTIVES

- Articulate ways in which MEEC varies around the globe.
- Discuss ownership, sponsorship, and management models important for international meetings and gatherings.
- Recognize important international meeting and trade fair associations.
- Name some specific considerations that are necessary to think through for successful international MEEC events.

Contributed by Mady Keup. © Kendall Hunt Publishing Company.

The expansion of international communications and travel has brought about significant changes in the way the world conducts business. Thirty years ago, only the largest companies were considered "international." Today, few large companies do not have a global presence.

As a result, the Meetings, Expositions, Events, and Conventions (MEEC) industries have also expanded internationally. In this chapter, we will explore how the international scope of MEEC has evolved and how it varies in different parts of the world.

The Union of International Fairs (UFI) regularly publishes impressive statistics about the international **trade fair** industry. In its 23rd edition of the Global Exhibition Barometer, released in July 2019, UFI estimated that 32,000 exhibitions are held annually, attracting 4.5 million exhibitors and welcoming 303 million visitors. The market value of exhibitions was estimated at $14 billion U.S. dollars in 2021. The MEEC market is the largest revenue contributor to the tourism industry, with a global value of $805 billion in 2017, $916 billion in 2019, and projected to reach $1,439 billion in 2025 and $1,780 billion in 2030, despite a temporary dip in 2020 due to the COVID-19 pandemic (CBI, 2021).

International meetings also play a significant role in employment. Regardless of the location, the purposes of international meetings and exhibitions remain the same: communication, learning, networking, trading, and marketing.

HOW MEEC VARIES AROUND THE GLOBE

Although the purpose remains similar, cultural and business influences have given rise to diverse models for MEEC events across the world. Consider Chinese incentive travel, which can be grand in scale. In 2015, Tien's Group treated 6,400 of its employees to a 3-day excursion in France, celebrating the company's 20th anniversary. The trip featured exclusive access to the Louvre Museum in Paris and creating a beachfront human-made phrase in Nice, recognized by Guinness World Records as the largest of its kind, reading "Tien's Dream is Nice in the Côte d'Azur." The estimated cost of this incentive trip was a staggering $18 million.

Another example of a globally impactful business event is the legendary Stratos brand-activation experience, orchestrated by the Austrian multinational Red Bull. After 5 years of planning, involving a team of 300, including 70 scientists and engineers, Felix Baumgartner made a daring jump from the stratosphere in 2012, at an altitude of 128,100 feet (four times higher than most passenger jets fly). He set a new speed world record at 833.9 miles per hour. Although the freefall occurred in New Mexico, it was broadcast by 40 TV stations worldwide and became a sensation on YouTube, watched by eight million followers. All of this aimed to prove that "Red Bull Gives You Wings."

This chapter primarily concentrates on conventions and exhibitions due to their remarkable and consistent growth over the past few decades. When analyzing 50 years of international association meeting data, the International Congress and Convention Association (ICCA) noted a consistent pattern: The number of regularly occurring, internationally rotating, association meetings doubled every 10 years. This trend persisted until 2019, when the organization declared the "highest ever recorded annual figure in its yearly statistics," including 317 additional congresses compared to the "record-breaking figures" of the previous year. A similar trend holds for trade fairs. According to Kai Hattendorf, managing director of UFI, the global association for trade show stakeholders, the data from the Global Exhibition Barometer in 2019 underscores the resilience and consistent growth of exhibitions in core markets worldwide. However, the pandemic significantly impacted this industry, which had relied solely on face-to-face gatherings, revealing the sensitivity of MEEC to health, economic, and political challenges.

This chapter examines the various types of exhibitions and conventions in Europe, Asia, Australia, Africa, and the Middle East. It delves into their scope, operations, and the cultural nuances that shape them. To conclude, we provide a concise list of international trade fair and meetings organizations.

One of the many buildings where the Canton Fair is held in Guangzhou, China

The World's Largest Fairs

The Canton Fair

The China Import and Export Fair (the Canton Fair) has been a biannual event held in Guangzhou since 1957, taking place every spring and autumn. In spring 2023, it spanned an impressive 16 million square

feet. However, Western visitors decreased, mainly due to escalating geopolitical tensions between China and Western countries, notably the United States, Canada, and the European Union (Pao, 2023). In response to the pandemic, the fair transitioned online for its 2020–2022 editions (see the final section of this chapter).

The Hannover Messe is a biennial industrial fair located in Northern Germany. In 2023, the organizers, Deutsche Messe, reported that the event saw participation from 4,000 international exhibitors, with over 130,000 visitors attending in person. Another 15,000 participants registered for the online component. The year 2020 posed a unique challenge, as the physical fair had to be canceled due to the pandemic. However, the conference element was successfully transformed into the Hannover Messe Digital Days, held in July of that year. For a comprehensive discussion of the Digital Days, please refer to the final section of this chapter.

In 2023, the fair focused on core industrial technology in

- artificial intelligence,
- hydrogen,
- energy management,
- connected and intelligent production, and
- the new manufacturing-X data ecosystem.

Aerial view of Hanover Messe

EUROPE

The roots of the trade fair industry trace back to Europe. In the Middle Ages, the concept began with farmers and craftsmen gathering in town centers to showcase their products and connect with customers. Despite temporary setbacks during the wars of the last century, Europe has reemerged as the epicenter of international trade fairs and exhibitions.

Two primary factors contribute to its prominence. First, its strategic location has always made it the crossroads of the world. International hub airports in Frankfurt, London, Amsterdam, Paris, and Madrid facilitate easy access for visitors and cargo worldwide. Additionally, Europe boasts an exceptional rail network that allows swift connectivity between many cities. For instance, the Eurostar train links London to Paris and Brussels within just 2 hours and extends to Amsterdam in under 4 hours. The second key factor is its robust industrial base. With assistance from the United States in post–World War II reconstruction, Europe swiftly recovered its manufacturing and distribution capabilities. European governments also played a crucial role in developing top-tier trade fair facilities in their industrial centers.

For industry and trade fairs in Europe, Germany typically comes to mind. The segment of business travel related to trade fairs and other MEEC events contributed a significant 2.1 million trips to the German incoming business travel market (German Convention Bureau, 2021). Germany is home to four of the world's 10 largest exhibition centers, including Hanover, Frankfurt, Cologne, and Düsseldorf.

The Largest Exhibition Venue

The Hannover Fairgrounds is the world's largest exhibition site, boasting nearly 11 million square feet of exhibit space spread across 27 exhibit halls and an open-air display area. The site also features a convention center with 35 conference rooms, 42 restaurants with a total seating capacity of 14,000, parking facilities for 50,000 vehicles, banks, laundry services, a pharmacy, and even the Münchner Halle—the world's largest trade fair beer hall. What sets Hannover Fairgrounds apart is its ability to host multiple events concurrently, thanks to separate units equipped with their own infrastructure. Moreover, the regional government and management company have collaborated to establish outstanding transportation and lodging facilities.

United Kingdom

Prominent exhibitions included the Farnborough International Air Show, International Spring Fair (Birmingham), World Travel Market (London), and London Fashion Week.

London Fashion Week

MEETINGS, EXPOSITIONS, EVENTS, AND CONVENTIONS

MEEC events have significant impacts on employment, gross domestic product, and direct and indirect contributions to the overall economy, including participating companies. The total impact is estimated at £11 billion (or nearly $14 billion).

https://cdn.asp.events/CLIENT_AEO_6F6DAB1E_5056_B739_5434F-CD30E5F9143/sites/AEO/media/Research-reports/EIA-Economic-Impact-Study.pdf

Italy is another hub of international trade fair activity, with Milan serving as the fashion trade fair center of the world. Other essential trade fair centers can be found in Bologna and Verona. In Spain, trade fair activity is concentrated in Barcelona, Valencia, and Madrid. The Benelux nations (*Be*lgium, *Net*herlands, and *Lux*embourg) also have a robust trade fair program, with excellent facilities in Amsterdam, Rotterdam, Brussels, and at Schiphol Airport. Paris, too, hosts numerous international events. The growth of the European Union, adoption of the Euro as its common currency, and removal of trade barriers and tariffs have all contributed to the growth of the European trade fair and exhibition industry.

The most significant growth in trade fairs in Europe is in Eastern European countries. New facilities have been established in Zagreb, Belgrade, Warsaw, Moscow, and St. Petersburg, with the ExpoForum center launching in 2014. Other large Russian cities, such as Kazan, Yekaterinburg, Kaliningrad, and Perm, have successfully hosted various international and domestic business events. However, the conflict with Ukraine has led to widespread sanctions against Russia, resulting in the suspension of U.S. airlines flying to Russia as of May 2023. Boycotts in protest against Russian aggression may also impact other international events, such as the Paris Olympics in 2024, where reports indicate that the United States and 34 other nations are opposing the participation of athletes from Russia and Belarus (Roush, 2023).

Europe also hosts numerous international association meetings. According to ICCA statistics for 2021, 16 of the top 20 destinations worldwide were European cities. Vienna claimed the top spot among destinations for international association meetings in 2021 (ICCA, 2022).

The European Society of Cardiology (ESC) Congress

One of these prominent international association meetings is the ESC Congress. The ESC, a not-for-profit medical federation comprising national cardiology associations and individual members from around the world, represents a community of over 100,000 professionals united by a common mission: "to reduce the burden of cardiovascular disease." The organization orchestrates 15 international meetings, each focusing on different cardiology topics. Among them, the ESC Congress stands out as the world's largest cardiovascular event, an annual tradition that commenced in 1962. This prestigious gathering spans 5 days, usually in late August or early September, and changes its location every year.

The planning cycle for an event of this magnitude is extensive and intricate, in line with the scale of a major medical convention. It commences with the request for proposals several years before the event itself. The cycle culminates with a postmortem reporting on the convention. Traditionally, the process of selecting the destination typically kicks off 3 years in advance, and the format of the event starts to take shape approximately 18 months before. During this phase, the layouts of lecture halls and exhibition rooms are designed and the scientific program and abstract policies defined. The focus shifts to operational logistics and supplier selection around 10 months before. A few months later, the scientific program is developed, and marketing efforts ramp up.

In 2016, the congress convened in Rome, and the statistics were nothing short of impressive. Attendees included a record-breaking 33,000 health professionals and stakeholders, including clinicians, scientists, epidemiologists, nurses, technicians, healthcare industry executives, opinion leaders, media representatives, and policymakers from more than 140 countries. The event centered around themed scientific villages at the Fiera di Roma exhibition and conference center. The congress also hosted an exhibition featuring over 200 companies showcasing their goods and services, spread across an expansive 120,000 square feet. The event culminated in a historic address by Pope Francis.

International meetings now increasingly use technological tools to communicate even more widely. The audience was not limited to on-site participants, as the events had a virtual reach:

- Over 100+ resources were consulted on ESC Congress 365 (the ESC Congress scientific content platform) between its launch in January 2013 and September 2016.
- Over 66,000 resources were consulted during the 5 days of ESC Congress, including more than 35,000 presentation slide sets.

The ESC Congress changes venues within Europe every year. Destinations have included the Fira Gran Via 2 in Barcelona, the ExCeL Centre in London, and the RAI in Amsterdam. In 2023, the congress returned to Amsterdam. The information presented here has been adapted from documents graciously provided by the ESC management.

Paris, France—September 1, 2019: Congress of the ESC at the Porte de Versailles Convention Center in Paris

ASIA

The growth of trade fairs and exhibitions in Asia over the past two decades has been nothing short of astonishing. New facilities and government promotions have transformed the industry from its infancy into a world-class phenomenon in just a little over a decade. Traditionally, Asian trade fairs have focused on technology, consumer electronics, and food. However, they now encompass all types of manufacturing and service industries. They are typically sponsored either by trade organizations, such as the world trade centers, or by individual governments.

Taiwan and Singapore have emerged as leaders. Taiwan boasts excellent facilities and regularly hosts trade fairs in sectors such as semiconductors, consumer electronics, and food industries. It is also a significant exhibitor at trade fairs and exhibitions in North America and Europe.

Singapore is a prominent "destination" city, drawing numerous visitors to its textile, fashion, food, and electronics trade fairs. The city offers multiple facilities, all seamlessly connected to outstanding shopping and entertainment complexes. It also stands out for its top-notch transportation infrastructure, including a world-class airport. Moreover, the government actively promotes the city as a preferred destination for exhibitions. Enterprise Singapore (formerly International Enterprise Singapore) collaborates with the Singapore Exhibition and Convention Bureau to position Singapore as an international exhibition hub. They provide financial and marketing support for trade fairs by both Singaporean and international organizers.

China

The growth of China's economy, the world's second largest, has been extraordinary. Business events in China have greatly benefited from major sporting events and Expos there, leading to infrastructure development and skills enhancement. Beijing hosted the Olympics in 2008, and Shanghai hosted the Expo in 2010. In 2022, China hosted both the Winter Olympics (in Beijing) and Asian Games (in Hangzhou). These events not only boosted corporate hospitality but also contributed to an increase in corporate meetings and the establishment of event service companies in China. Hosting crucial political meetings, such as the APEC and G20 summits in 2014 and 2016, respectively, has also elevated China's reputation as a meeting destination.

Exhibitions are well established in China, seen as an extension of trading. Corporate meetings and incentives are relatively newer concepts, and association conventions face challenges, as most associations in China are government managed. The government holds a significant role in Chinese business affairs; all international events require approval from both the central government and the provincial government or relevant ministry. Large international congresses with a high proportion of international participants must gain approval from the central government and the state council.

However, as mentioned, Chinese events may continue to face challenges due to Western reactions to geopolitical tensions, including concerns over alleged government interference and espionage in Western democracies, human rights issues related to the Uyghur ethnic minority in China, and ongoing geopolitical disputes, particularly concerning the island of Taiwan, which China does not recognize as a separate country.

Convention and Exhibition Industries in China

In 1978, China hosted just six international conventions and exhibitions and participated in only 21 exhibitions abroad. The first exhibition company in China, SIEC, was established in 1984. Since then, the number and scale of exhibitions have grown exponentially, permeating all sectors of the national economy. Each industry now boasts its own international professional exhibitions. According to UFI, as of December 2018, China's main venues have nearly 62 million square feet of indoor exhibition space, accounting for roughly 17% of the world's total. China ranks second globally, following only the United States. Moreover, China has become the world's largest business travel market, surpassing the United States (now in second position), as per the Global Business Travel Association. In 2017, Chinese business travelers collectively spent a staggering $346 billion USD during their trips. Beijing and Shanghai are pivotal contributors to China's room supply and meeting space. Additionally, robust hotel construction has been observed in secondary markets, including Macau, Guangzhou, Shenzhen, Sanya, and Wuhan. These markets now offer a growing array of top-tier hotel options, catering to the needs of MEEC buyers.

Destination	Convention Center Space (million sq. ft.)	Major Airport(s)	Total Hotels	Total Sleeping Rooms	Destination Marketing Organization link
Beijing	3.43	PEK	703	120,521	https://english.visitbeijing.com.cn/
Guangzhou	1.3	CAN	343	66,885	NA
Hong Kong	Over 7.5	HKG	318	90,000	https://mehongkong.com/eng/home.html
Macau	2.15	MFM	NA	35,000	http://www.mice.gov.mo/en/index.aspx
Shanghai	42.8	PVG SHA	657	124,618	https://www.meet-in-shanghai.net/

Adapted from CVENT and DMO sources. Developed by Mady Keup

Table 15-1 Hotel Capacity in Major Chinese Cities

Five economic belts dedicated to conventions and exhibitions have been established on the Chinese mainland: the Yangtze River Delta, Zhujiang Delta, Bohai Bay Area, and Northeast and Central China. Many trade shows have extended their reach to the western regions, including Chengdu in Sichuan Province, Chongqing City, and Xi'an in Shaanxi Province. When it comes to the scale and impact of exhibition projects, Beijing, Shanghai, and Guangzhou have emerged as the most pivotal cities. Some cities have grown into regional centers, serving as hubs for economic activity: Dalian, Shenzhen, Chengdu, Hangzhou, Nanjing, Ningbo, Suzhou, Qingdao, Xiamen, Xi'an, Wuhan, Nanning, Kunming, and Chongqing.

Both Hong Kong and Macau, as Special Administrative Regions of China, are significant in the international MEEC landscape. Hong Kong, as a free port with a major international airport hub, has consistently ranked among CVENT's Top Meeting Destinations in the Asia Pacific for several years. Key venues include the Hong Kong Convention and Exhibition Center, Asia World Expo, and Hong Kong International Trade and Exhibition Center. Macau has become a favored incentive destination, with its numerous casinos attracting international travelers to the "Vegas of the East." As in the rest of China, the government plays a pivotal role in Hong Kong, exemplified by initiatives such as the visa-free scheme that allows nationals from 170 countries to visit Hong Kong without a visa for 7–180 days.

Although the Chinese exhibition and meetings industry is rapidly evolving, organizing an event in China remains administratively and legally complex. The UFI Special Interest Group on China has highlighted key points that international organizers should consider when planning events:

- need to understand local regulations and licensing requirements,
- importance of a local partner,
- rise of e-commerce and online competitors,
- rising labor costs, and
- challenge to find skilled and professional managers.

However, Chinese companies and the government are increasingly recognizing the necessity for greater internationalization. For instance, the China Convention and Exhibition Society and China Association for Exhibition Centers have collaborated with international organizations to provide training and promote their members. Numerous other Chinese cities have started to realize the significance of meetings in contributing to the balanced development of the convention and exhibition industries.

Incentive Travel in China

Incentive travel is a relatively new sector in the Chinese tourism industry, but it holds immense potential. As more Chinese organizations and companies embrace incentive travel, several traditional travel agencies, including Ctrip, Tuniu, and JD, have adapted their business models or introduced new services. Economic prosperity has led to a surge in incentive travel, with Chinese companies hosting more frequently, traveling to a wider range of destinations, and involving a greater number of employees. This trend is expected to continue with the rise of small corporate meetings. These are predominantly commissioned by companies in the pharmaceutical/medical, IT, direct selling, automotive, and financial sectors.

Several professional trade shows represent the incentive events sector, with the largest being the China Incentive Business Travel & Meetings Exhibition and Incentive Travel & Convention Meeting IT & CM China. The former, the first international exhibition dedicated to business travel, incentives, and conferences, was launched in 2005. Both allow exhibitors to connect with qualified buyers interested in various business travel products and services.

With abundant tourism resources, competitive pricing, and a positive tourism image, China is poised to become one of the world's most popular incentive travel destinations. However, recent geopolitical challenges (discussed earlier) have somewhat slowed down this trend.

Thailand

Thailand is pivotal in hosting a wide array of trade shows, including those dedicated to clothing, textiles, food, agribusiness, and automotive and engineering. Bangkok, with its excellent transportation infrastructure, serves as a convenient gateway for visitors from across the globe. The crown jewel of its exhibition and convention facilities is the IMPACT Exhibition and Convention Centre, Thailand's largest. It offers a staggering total indoor space exceeding 1.5 million square feet, spread across five expansive venues. The IMPACT Challenger conference venue is particularly notable, with three interconnected halls providing a colossal column-free space exceeding 645,000 square feet, earning the distinction of the world's largest column-free hall. Its ambition, as stated on the company's website, is to secure a place among "Asia's Top 5 Venues." Adjacent to the IMPACT complex, the IMPACT Lakefront development on Muang Thong Thani Lake provides an open-air venue suitable for corporate, private, and public events and spans more than 1.6 million square feet (impact.co.th).

Korea

Korea boasts three prominent exhibition centers: COEX, Kintex (Korea International Exhibition Center), and Songdo Convensia. All are strategically located in or near the capital city of Seoul and regularly host a diverse range of events, including exhibitions and meetings. COEX distinguishes itself as not only an events venue but also a multifaceted complex, offering nearly 5 million square feet of floor space. It features Asia's largest underground mall, three luxurious five-star hotels, office buildings, a department store, and even a subway station. Kintex is situated in Goyang City. Its exhibition and meeting space underwent significant expansion in 2011, culminating in an impressive floor space of nearly 1.2 million square feet. It operates as a partnership between the Korean national government investment agency and regional and municipal administrations. Finally, Songdo Convensia, conveniently located next to Korea's primary international airport, Incheon, is managed by the local tourism organization.

India

In April 2023, India claimed the title of the world's most populous country, according to the United Nations (2023). India not only has a massive population but is an economic powerhouse. Research conducted in 2018 highlighted India's resilience, as it was projected to "remain the fastest growing major economy amidst heightened concerns over global trade wars and oil price fluctuations" (Sharma, 2018). Looking ahead to 2025, it is forecasted that a remarkable 99% of India's workforce will possess valuable skills, solidifying its position as the world's youngest nation, with an average age of just 29. The Indian Exhibition Industry Association, responsible for commissioning this study, estimated the economic impact of the Indian exhibition sector in 2018 to be an impressive 649 billion Indian rupees (~$8.8 billion U.S.). The government's proactive approach adds an interesting dimension to this economic landscape. As this chapter addresses with Australia, the Indian government has identified key industry sectors to support, and the exhibition calendar aligns seamlessly with these sectors. This government initiative is aptly named

"Make in India," with a vision to transform the country into a global hub for design and manufacturing.

Sharma (2018) identified the following trends in the Indian exhibition industry:

- shift in focus from general events to specialized exhibitions,
- increasing emphasis on quality of participants, better services,
- industry consolidation through acquisition of local organizers,
- incorporation of technology/digitalization,
- introduction of global events, and
- rise in international participation for exhibitions as well as visitors (~15% share)
Source: Adapted from Sharma (2018).

In India, the MEEC sector predominantly thrives in several key business cities, including New Delhi, Mumbai, Bangalore, Hyderabad, Chennai, and Goa. With ongoing foreign direct investments, particularly in sectors aligned with "Make in India," the country is also witnessing a surge in outbound MEEC trips. A DPI Research study from 2018 boldly predicts that the "India Outbound Meetings, Incentives, Conferences and Exhibitions tourism market is expected to reach nine billion U.S. dollars by 2025."

Make in India logo as a colorful statue

OTHER ASIAN COUNTRIES

Other countries actively nurturing trade fair programs with strong government backing are Vietnam, Malaysia, and Indonesia. In these nations, government ownership and operation of facilities are common, and promotional efforts receive substantial support from various government agencies. For instance, Vietnam has carved a significant niche in clothing and food trade fairs, and Indonesia's Ministry of Tourism and Creative Economy has recently appointed a deputy responsible for tourism products and events, with a clear goal of boosting foreign earnings through increased business events in the country.

AUSTRALIA

Australia has a rich history of hosting prestigious international events, particularly association congresses and incentives. A study commissioned by the Business Events Council of Australia in 2020 reveals that a staggering 484,000 business events took place there in 2019, generating an estimated direct industry expenditure of AUD 17.2 billion (~$11.5 billion U.S.). Remarkably, 19% of attendees hailed from outside Australia, underscoring its global appeal.

Australia's major cities, including Melbourne, Brisbane, Perth, and Adelaide, are home to world-renowned conference and exhibition centers. In 2016, the Brisbane Convention & Exhibition Centre won the coveted AIPC Apex Award for the "Best Client Rated Convention Centre." In Sydney, the International Convention Centre (ICC) at Darling Harbour stands out, offering an exhibition capacity of 376,000 sq. ft., meeting space of 86,000 sq. ft., an expansive external event deck of 54,000 sq. ft., a theater accommodating 8,000, and an adjacent headquarters hotel offering 590 rooms.

The Image of the Sydney Opera House in Australia is known worldwide. It is actually an event center putting on not only operas but also orchestra recitals, theater performances, meetings, and special events

AFRICA

With a population of 1.4 billion as of 2022, as reported by Galal (2023), Africa is experiencing rapid economic growth. In May 2019, the agreement establishing the expansive African Continental Free Trade Agreement came into

Sandton Convention Centre in Johannesburg, where the annual Meetings Africa MEEC Trade Fair is held

effect for the initial 24 signatory countries, and trading officially commenced on January 1, 2021. As of March 2023, all 54 African Union member states have embraced this agreement. Much like its European counterpart, it aspires to establish a unified, continent-wide market for goods and services, streamlining the flow of capital and people. This, in turn, is expected to foster and encourage business travel and events, both within Africa and with global trade partners.

The following economies in Africa were the following, in order of highest GDP in 2021:

1. Nigeria,
2. South Africa,
3. Egypt,
4. Algeria,
5. Morocco,
6. Ethiopia,
7. Kenya,
8. Ghana,
9. Tanzania, and
10. Ivory Coast.

List adapted from Tradingeconomics.com.

TOURISM GRADING COUNCIL OF SOUTH AFRICA (2019) CORE GRADING REQUIREMENT, downloaded from https://www.tourismgrading.co.za/assets/Uploads/10031125-TGCSA-Grading-Criteria-Booklet-REV-20.pdf on August 27, 2020

In a news release from March 30, 2023, Meetings Africa organizers discuss a recent study by the South African National Convention Bureau. Participants believe that some African destinations already possess positive characteristics that attract meeting and business events:

- good air connectivity (Ethiopia and South Africa),
- unique leisure options (South Africa, Kenya, Egypt), and
- high-quality MEEC services and infrastructure (South Africa, Kenya, Tanzania).

Potential barriers to doing business on the African continent were the following:

- Strict import regulations for products for trade shows;
- strong regulations in business sectors, such as pharmaceutical and defense; and
- length of travel from main Western markets.

Another challenge respondents mentioned is a perceived lack of safety in some destinations.

The MEEC industry is developing at pace within Africa, both for corporate and association events. In 2015, the African Society of Association Executives was successfully founded. Four conventions centers opened their doors in 2016:

- Calabar, Nigeria: Calabar ICC: 377,000 square feet, capacity for 5000 delegates.
- Algiers, Algeria: Centre International Conference d'Alger: 2,900,000 square feet, auditorium for 6,000.
- Cape Town, South Africa: Century City Conference Centre: on a precinct that combines residential, commercial, and leisure components; capacity of up to 1,900 in 20 spaces.
  - Cape Town, South Africa: ICC expanded in 2017 to offer an extra 10,000 sq. m. of multipurpose space.
- Kigali, Rwanda: Kigali Convention Centre: auditorium for 2,500 and on-site hotel with 292 rooms.

Africa stands out as the sole "growing continent," housing some of the world's fastest-expanding economies. With its burgeoning population and ongoing urbanization, the continent anticipates significant improvements in life expectancy and a substantial increase in per capita disposable income. This transformative development is reflected in Meetings Africa, a specialized exhibition within the MEEC industry. Organized by South African Tourism since 2004, Meetings Africa is a pan-African event. Although it was canceled during the COVID-19 pandemic, it successfully ran in 2022, drawing participation from 161 global buyers and 216 exhibitors representing 13 African countries (Van Wyk, 2023).

MIDDLE EAST

Dubai and Abu Dhabi in the United Arab Emirates prominently feature trade fairs and exhibitions due to robust government promotions, modern facilities, and seamless travel accessibility. Both cities boast international airports with connections worldwide. The concept of being a global "crossroads" is heavily emphasized in promotional materials. These cities actively promote the duty-free zones near their airports and the extensive duty-free shopping available on-site. Additionally, the regional market for consumer goods remains robust.

Dubai gained international acclaim by hosting Expo 2020, a 6-month event spanning 2021 and 2022, albeit postponed due to the pandemic. It marked the first time a Middle Eastern nation was chosen to host a World Expo. According to the Bureau International des Expositions (2023), Expo 2020 attracted over 25 million visitors and is projected to AED 155 billion (~$42 billion U.S.) in gross value added to the UAE's economy from 2013 to 2042. As part of the preparations for Expo 2020, a new convention center in Al Jaddaf, near Dubai Creek, was constructed, offering a spacious 592,000 square feet of event space.

Qatar has been diligently working to attract both exhibition and meeting planners. The Qatar National Convention Centre, which opened in 2011, was constructed in accordance with the U.S. Green Building Council's Leadership in Energy and Environment Design gold-certification standards. Furthermore, in 2022, Qatar successfully hosted the FIFA World Cup. In August 2016, the Oman Convention & Exhibition Centre marked its inauguration with the Oman 2016 event, one of the Middle East's largest building and construction exhibitions.

Across the entire Middle East region, new hotel properties continue to be built.

LATIN AMERICA

Latin America, with its substantial population base, offers an ideal environment for trade fairs and exhibitions; most of these were regional. However, recent investments in new facilities and promotional efforts are setting the stage for significant growth in international exhibitions. Key hubs for this activity include new facilities in Sao Paulo, Brazil, and Mexico City. The Las Americas Exhibition Center in Mexico City, for instance, is situated within an entertainment complex featuring a horse racing track, restaurants, hotels, and a shopping center.

Brazil, between 2010 and 2020, was in the global spotlight as it hosted both the World Cup in 2014 and the Olympic Summer Games in 2016. The impact of the World Cup was substantial, contributing over $60 billion U.S. to the country's economy and generating 3.63 million jobs. Additionally, these events played a pivotal role in reshaping Brazil's image from being solely associated with soccer and samba to that of an innovative nation with a strong focus on research and development, a robust economy, and modern cities.

Table 15-2 shows a list of international top cities for meetings and events, according to the 2020 American Express Global Meetings and Event Forecast report.

Top Cities Based on Meetings and Events Activity			
Rank	Europe	Latin America	Asia- Pacific
1	Madrid, Spain	Bogota, Colombia	Tokyo, Japan
2	Barcelona, Spain	Mexico City, Mexico	Osaka, Japan
3	London, United Kingdom	Cartagena, Colombia	Sydney, Australia
4	Paris, France	Buenos Aires, Argentina	Seoul, South Korea
5	Manchester, United Kingdom	Cancun, Mexico	Taipei, Taiwan

Source: Adapted from 2023 Global Meetings and Events Forecast (2023).

Table 15-2 Top International MEEC Cities

OWNERSHIP, SPONSORSHIP, AND MANAGEMENT MODELS

In the United States, many trade shows are linked to association meetings and typically owned by the associations. Some may be sponsored by private entrepreneurial firms and run for profit. The management and ownership often involve two distinct companies collaborating to ensure the show's success. Additionally, various service companies assist both the trade show management company and exhibitors.

This model, however, is not universally adopted for trade fairs and exhibitions worldwide. Although several commercial trade show organizing companies hold significant influence, especially in the United Kingdom, other countries, such as Germany and Italy, have venues that organize the fairs while also providing space for rent. Frequently, governments, in partnership with organizing companies, assume pivotal roles in sponsoring and operating trade fairs. For instance, the Chinese government is key in supporting most trade fairs held in Beijing, Hong Kong, and Shanghai.

PROFESSIONAL CONGRESS ORGANIZER (PCO)

PCOs represent a crucial service provider in the global event industry, although the term is not as commonly used in the United States. PCOs act as intermediaries between organizers, sponsors, and large congresses worldwide. They advocate for their clients when dealing with DMOs, DMCs, hotels, restaurants, transportation providers, and other suppliers. PCOs handle negotiations with vendors on behalf of their clients and are well versed in international issues, such as customs, taxation, and government regulations. Additionally, PCOs may take charge of financial transactions, letters of credit, and foreign bank accounts. They often shape the content of events and work closely with speakers, entertainers, and performers. PCOs have their own professional association, the International Association of Professional Congress Organisers.

Global Commercial Exhibition Organizing Companies

A leaderboard exists of global commercial exhibition organizing companies. The companies are truly global trade fair organizing companies, which operate across the world in all main markets: Informa Markets, Reed Exhibitions, Comexposium, Clarion Events and Messe Frankfurt.

IMPORTANT INTERNATIONAL MEETING AND TRADE FAIR ASSOCIATIONS

All associations offer members the opportunities for knowledge exchange and training/professional certification, thereby playing an important role in the advancement of professionalism and international networks in international MEEC business.

Name of organization	Membership: Event managers (EM) or event suppliers (ES)	Membership	HQ location	Notes, goals and website address
AIPC (Association Internationale des Palais de Congres)	ES	180 centres in 57 countries	Brussels, Belgium	*In English: International Convention Centre Association *Goals: AIPC is committed to encouraging and recognizing excellence in convention centre management, while at the same time providing the tools to achieve such high standards through its research, educational and networking programs. *https://aipc.org/about-aipc/
International Association of Professional Cogress Organisers (IAPCO)	EM	138 companies in 30 countries	Zurich, Switzerland	*"The IAPCO mission is to raise the standards of service amongst its members and other sectors of the meetings industry by means of continuing education and interaction with other professionals." *https://www.iapco.org/about-iapco/
International Congress and Convention Association (ICCA)	ES (recently also EM)	Over 1100 member companies and organizations in over 100 countries	Amsterdam, The Netherlands	* ICCA tracks over 18,000 regularly occurring association meetings that rotate between at least three countries. Access to this data and association clients is the primary reason why companies and organizations belong to ICCA. * https://www.iccaworld.org/abouticca/
Meeting Professionals International (MPI)	EM (predominantly) & ES	60,000 individual event professionals in 70 chapters and clubs worldwide	Dallas, Texas, USA	*Mission: MPI will connect the global meeting and event community to learn, innovate, collaborate and advocate. * https://www.mpi.org/about/who-we-are
UFI – Union des Foires Internationales	EM & ES	1100 member companies	Paris, France	In English: The Global Association of the Exhibition Industry *"UFI's main goal is to represent, promote and support the business interests of its members and the exhibition industry […] UFI offers reliable data and insights for members and the industry at large as research is a core element of our association's mission" * https://www.ufi.org/about/

Professional associations are an important part of doing business in international MEEC

PROFESSIONAL ASSOCIATIONS

INTERNATIONAL MEEC CONSIDERATIONS

LESSONS TO BE LEARNED

Trade fair, event, and exhibition managers should strive to understand the key factors contributing to success in various aspects of the international marketplace. For instance, North American trade show managers and destination representatives can gain valuable insights from their European counterparts in three crucial areas:

- Infrastructure excellence: European public transportation systems excel in providing crucial support for trade fairs and exhibitions.
- Logistics: International trade fair organizers have honed their expertise in logistics, as they understand that international exhibitors are the lifeblood of many shows. Consequently, many of these organizers maintain specialized departments dedicated to assisting exhibitors in overcoming the unique challenges in their respective countries. These agencies streamline shipping and storage procedures, making it as effortless as possible for exhibitors to participate.
- Support organizations: Although many U.S. trade shows are sponsored and organized by associations, in other parts of the world, trade promotion organizations, such as world trade centers or government agencies, typically take on this responsibility.

METHODS OF EXHIBITING

Significant distinctions exist between U.S. trade shows and international trade fair or exhibition. Organizations must incorporate these differences into their foundational research.

Companies usually have several options. The U.S. government, for instance, sponsors pavilions at many trade fairs, allowing U.S. companies to collaborate with it; the U.S. Department of Commerce can provide substantial support. Alternatively, companies can choose to exhibit under another company that organizes a pavilion. The private company often serves as the primary interface, and contractual arrangements are established with them. Companies should conduct thorough *due diligence* when considering this approach to ensure that the organizing company is reputable, experienced in the host country, and well versed in the desired trade fair.

Companies often consider forming joint ventures, particularly when one of them possesses prior experience in exhibiting at a specific trade fair. In such cases, it is crucial for companies to ensure that their products or services do not compete with each other. This collaborative approach thrives when their products are complementary, providing an excellent means for a company to enter the international trade fair arena and gain invaluable experience.

Another option is to "go it alone." This path is often chosen by larger companies with the financial resources and personnel to manage the intricacies of international exhibiting. However, smaller companies must meticulously assess all requirements, costs, and timelines. For instance, they need to account for the time and expenses associated with ensuring that all tasks are completed. Incorrectly assuming that if the preparation time for an international trade show mirrors that of a domestic trade show can lead to costly mistakes.

TERMINOLOGY

Terminology can vary significantly across different parts of the world. For example, in many regions, an exhibit is referred to as a "**stand**." Depending on the location of the trade fair and its management, participating companies must familiarize themselves with these differences.

For example, in Germany the following terms must be understood:

- **Ausstellung:** Consumer show
- **Kongress:** Meeting or convention
- **Gesellschaft:** Company or society
- **GmBH:** Limited liability company
- **Messe:** Trade fair
- **Messegelaende:** Fair site

And in the United Kingdom:

- **PLC:** Public limited company
- **Trade Exhibition:** Trade show
- **Delegate:** Attendee at conference
- **Accommodation:** Housing
- **Value-Added Tax** (VAT): VAT is typically incorporated into the price of retail products but is itemized separately on quotes and invoices for services provided by suppliers. In the United Kingdom, the VAT rate for 2023 is 20%. The country has established procedures that permit international event organizers to recover VAT on legitimate business expenses.

CONTRACTUAL AND PROCEDURAL ISSUES

Beyond differences in terminology, significant disparities exist in contractual and procedural aspects. Labor regulations in the United States differ markedly from those in Europe or Asia. In Asian countries, unions and jurisdictional issues are relatively rare, granting exhibitors more latitude in their exhibit activities. In Europe, unions do exist, but they tend to be more adaptable compared to many in the United States.

Companies must not assume that setup or logistical contracts in international settings mirror those in their home country. Substantial variations exist not only from one country to another but also from one trade fair to the next. Companies should meticulously scrutinize each contract and comply with all stipulated requirements. Any unclear or ambiguous aspects should be promptly brought to the attention of show management.

CUSTOMS CLEARANCE

At international exhibitions, organizers provide access to experienced international freight forwarders, who also serve as customs brokers, ensuring that all preparations are in order and that shipments arrive punctually. They possess in-depth knowledge of the customs regulations in the host country and work diligently to apprise exhibitors of every requirement and deadline.

Typically, goods can be temporarily imported to an international show site without incurring duties or taxes, through a **carnet** or a **trade fair bond**. Obtaining a carnet can be a complex process, often necessitating a substantial bond. However, most trade fair venues offer straightforward bonds that are easy to arrange. Once again, international freight forwarders serve as the primary point of contact. It is essential to inquire about the host country's rules regarding giveaways and promotional materials. Some countries impose duties when the value exceeds a certain threshold, but others do not.

PROTOCOL

Business etiquette encompasses the guidelines that help individuals navigate appropriate behavior in various situations. Event organizers must thoroughly research the business customs of the host country. Staff members should receive comprehensive training on these cultural differences in advance. What is considered acceptable in one country may be offensive in another or at a different trade fair. Language is one of the most apparent distinctions: Although English typically serves as the "official" language of international business, it is unwise to assume that all attendees or suppliers are fluent in English. Prudent companies ensure that at least some of their staff are bilingual, especially in the language of the host country. Furthermore, different cultures exhibit varying levels of communication directness. Hall (1976) categorized communication behavior as "low context" in cultures like Scandinavia and North America (information is conveyed explicitly). In contrast, cultures such as Chinese and Arabic are "high context" (information must be deduced from context and nonverbal cues).

Staff members at international events will interact with people from diverse countries. Therefore, they must acquaint themselves with appropriate greetings for different cultures and understand the various forms of address. Although most participants may not take offense if protocol is not strictly adhered to, observing their cultural norms leaves a positive impression. Culture can be defined as the collective programming of the mind that distinguishes one group or category of people from others. Next, we explain these dimensions and provide examples of how business etiquette should be adapted accordingly.

Identity (Individualism Versus Collectivism)

This dimension revolves around an individual's position in society. In collectivist societies, people primarily identify themselves as members of powerful groups, such as extended families, and prioritize maintaining group harmony. Conversely, individualist societies emphasize independence, with individuals encouraged to express their thoughts freely.

For instance, in collectivist countries, such as China, building robust, mutually beneficial relationships, known as "guanxi," is paramount. It is considered impolite to outright decline in negotiations, as this can disrupt group harmony. It is advisable to present multiple alternatives, allowing Chinese negotiators the opportunity to decline options gracefully. Additionally, maintaining a consistent negotiating team throughout the process is crucial.

Hierarchy (Power Distance)

This dimension pertains to the acceptance of authority inequalities in a society or institution, such as a family. A high level of power distance indicates that a society expects top-down authority as the norm.

In the Netherlands, characterized by low power distance, it is essential to avoid projecting an air of superiority. Egalitarianism holds a central place, with everyone in a Dutch company, from the boss to laborers, regarded as valuable and deserving of respect. Traditionally, the United States has also adhered to a low power distance model.

When engaging with French business contacts, refrain from using first names or the informal *tu* unless expressly permitted to do so. France has a relatively high-power-distance culture, emphasizing respect for hierarchical structures within the same company. In Korea, age and rank carry significant weight, making it advantageous to establish relationships with business counterparts of a similar age.

Gender Association (Masculinity Versus Femininity)

This dimension categorizes societies as either more achievement oriented (masculine) or more care oriented (feminine), reflecting the prevalence of presumed masculine or feminine values.

Japan ranks highest in the masculinity dimension. Japanese culture is renowned for its strong work ethic and high competitiveness. When engaging with Japanese stakeholders, it is crucial to exercise care in selecting and presenting business gifts. In Japanese etiquette, it is essential not to discard or tear up the gift wrapping, as it is considered an integral part of the gift. The United States also scores notably high in masculinity, as per Hofstede's research.

Truth (Uncertainty Avoidance)

This factor relates to the extent to which a society can tolerate ambiguity. Does society seek a single, absolute truth (high uncertainty avoidance), or is it comfortable in a less structured or even unstructured environment (low uncertainty avoidance)?

In countries with high uncertainty avoidance, such as Germany and Greece, meticulous planning is essential for meetings. These nations also tend to have numerous official rules and legal regulations concerning contracts and import/export procedures. In contrast, the United States scores below average on uncertainty avoidance.

Aside from these dimensions, several other factors must be considered. Food and beverage (F&B) often hold more significance than in the United States. In many parts of Asia, extended business dinners with numerous toasts to hosts and VIP guests are integral to enduring business relationships. In Japan, the host typically covers the expenses during outings. Allow your host to order for you, display enthusiasm while eating, and express gratitude afterward. In Russia, it is customary for everyone at a dinner to consume vodka in shots, not sipped. With each shot, a different guest proposes a toast, with toasts becoming progressively longer with each round. In Saudi Arabia, coffee is frequently served toward the end of a meeting, signaling its conclusion.

Differences in the perception of punctuality exist across cultures. For instance, in Switzerland or Germany, a meeting should unquestionably commence on time, but in countries such as India or Nigeria, event project milestones may be viewed as more flexible.

Significant disparities also arise in individuals' expectations regarding "personal space" and their comfort levels with physical proximity. Anglo-Saxons tend to require the largest personal space, followed by Asians, whereas Mediterraneans and Latin Americans are more accustomed to close proximity. In many countries, public contact between individuals of different sexes is limited, aside from handshakes. It is important to refrain from kissing or hugging a different-sex person in public, even if they are your spouse. Conversely, in some cultures, physical contact between individuals of the same sex is permissible and often regarded as platonic. For instance, men may hold hands or walk with their arms around each other, which is seen as a sign of friendship.

- When giving gifts in Switzerland, avoid knives—it is considered bad luck.
- In many Asian countries, do not pat people on the shoulder or initiate any physical contact.
- In China, avoid the colors blue, black, and white for gift wraps, as they are associated with disease, funerals, and death, respectively.
- Do not give chrysanthemums in Spain or France or carnations in Germany, where they are used for funerals.
- In most Arabic countries, the left hand is considered dirty; never eat or accept anything with it. Be sure when giving gifts or promotional materials to do so with the right hand.
- The number 8 is the luckiest number in China, as its pronunciation is close to a word meaning "to make a fortune," whereas the pronunciation for 4 sounds like "death."
- In Japan, business cards are presented after a bow or handshake. Present your card, using both hands, with the Japanese side facing your colleague, in such a manner that it can be read immediately. Handle cards very carefully, and do not put them in your pocket or wallet. Never write on a person's business card in their presence.

Last, some symbols/colors/numbers and gestures to avoid:

In the United States, the hand gesture where the thumb and forefinger are forming a circle with the other three fingers raised is considered the "OK" sign.

- In Brazil, it is considered a vulgar or obscene gesture.
- In Greece and Russia, it is considered impolite.
- In Japan, it signifies money.
- In southern France, it means zero or worthless.

In the United States, waving the hand back and forth is a means of saying hello.

- In Greece, it is called the *moutza* and is a serious insult. The closer the hand is to the face of the other, the more threatening it is.
- In Peru, waving the whole hand back and forth can signal "no."

In most of the world, making a fist with the thumb raised means "OK." In Australia, Greece or the Middle East, it is a rude gesture.

These are just a few of the cultural considerations that foreign businesspeople must navigate. Before traveling to any country, it is prudent to consult multiple sources to gain insights into its appropriate business and social etiquettes. Dedicate time to understanding the expected behavior in the host country and the greetings anticipated for potential visitors at the trade fair.

Diversity and cultural differences are not solely relevant when conducting international events. They should also be considered when designing events for diverse participants, as highlighted by respondents to the American Express Global Meetings and Events Forecast. The link below will take you to the image (p. 40) that illustrates this phenomenon.

https://www.amexglobalbusinesstravel.com/meetings-events/meetings-forecast/

The following are aspects of international trade fairs that are different from U.S. exhibitions; these are generalizations and do not apply to all situations.

- Hospitality events are generally held on the exhibit floor, with many companies providing F&B as a matter of course in their exhibit.
- Height restrictions may be nonexistent. Many large exhibits may be two or three levels.
- The exhibit hall may have no rules on smoking; many exhibitors and attendees may do so.
- Some trade fair organizing companies may not offer "lead retrieval" systems that U.S. companies are accustomed to. It is always wise for a company to bring its own method.
- International trade fairs are often longer than U.S. trade shows and open on weekends as well. Although a European show may run from 9 a.m. to 6 p.m., in Brazil or other Latin American countries, it is common for them to open at 2 p.m. and run until 10 or 11 p.m.
- Be aware that most of the world outside the United States uses the metric system. Voltages may differ, and exhibitors may need plug-in adapters or transformers.

Other Considerations

- Visas may be required for entry and exit.
- Items that U.S. residents take for granted may have to be declared upon entry to a country. For example, brochures and written materials must be declared and taxes paid on them.
- Many international destinations require payment of departure taxes.
- Most countries require that payment be made to ensure that goods exhibited at a trade show are exported and not sold within the country. A freight handling company can arrange a bond as security.
- AND many more! When in doubt, ask.

VIRTUAL AND HYBRID EVENTS

As a consequence of the COVID-19 pandemic, many MEEC organizers found it imperative to incorporate information technology, transitioning to fully virtual or hybrid formats. The following examples illustrate how various international events handled this adaptation.

ESC CONGRESS 2020—THE DIGITAL EXPERIENCE

In response to pandemic concerns and global travel restrictions, ESC made the decision to transform its annual congress in 2020 into a virtual event. To further support healthcare professionals worldwide during these challenging times, it took the exceptional step of offering complimentary registration.

Much like their traditional face-to-face gatherings, participants had a range of options. They could attend live studio speeches with dedicated question hotlines or explore an extensive on-demand playlist of recorded presentations. They retained the ability to interact with their peers through related forums and engage in simultaneous industry Q&A sessions. To foster more in-depth discussions within specialist disciplines, the ESC organized all congress sessions into separate channels or tracks based on topic. Even in the on-demand program, which remained accessible for some time following the congress, users could connect with abstract presenters, rate presentations, and engage in discussions with fellow participants.

Furthermore, all abstracts presented at ESC Congress 2020—The Digital Experience were published in the *European Heart Journal* Supplement, Vol. 41, October 2020. This publication is significant for the continuing medical education requirements of physicians and was instrumental in substantiating credentials for medical researchers.

To maintain effective communication with its members and congress participants, the ESC employed a range of social media platforms, each associated with a variety of hashtags. These platforms included Facebook, Twitter, LinkedIn, Pinterest, and YouTube.

CANTON FAIR

In a similar vein, the world's largest trade exhibition, the Canton Fair, made the significant move to shift its 127th edition entirely online in June 2020. Leveraging tools such as livestreaming, exhibitor and exhibit search functionality, messaging, and virtual events, both buyers and exhibitors could conduct their trades remotely.

However, the industrial manufacturing trade event Hannover Messe did not take place in 2020. In the organizers' news release Jochen Köckler, Chairman of the Board of Management, Deutsche Messe AG stated, "We firmly believe that nothing can replace direct, person-to-person contact, and we are already looking forward to the time after Corona, but especially in times of crisis, we must be flexible and act pragmatically. As organizers of the world's most important industrial trade fair, we want to offer orientation and sustain economic life during the crisis. We are doing that with our new digital offering. Next year, they will then present themselves with the latest products and solutions for Industry 4.0 and the energy system of the future" (Hannover Messe News, March 26, 2020, *No Hannover Messe in 2020*).

Replacing the physical exhibition, Messe presented its conference content during the "Digital Days" over 2 days in July 2020. This program featured approximately 200 speakers and 100 partner companies and attracted more than 10,000 participants.

UFI GLOBAL CONGRESS 2020

UFI opted for a slightly different way to deliver its annual congress in 2020.

The organization offered a glocalized (a mixture of global and local) events that took place in different destinations as well as online during the course of 1 week:

- In Dubai, UAE (Sunday, November 15 to Monday, November 16),
- In Basel, Switzerland (Wednesday, November 18 to Friday, November 20),
- In Hong Kong (exact dates to be confirmed), and
- Online (Sunday, November 15 to Friday, November 20).

This event provided a networking platform to meet face-to-face AND digitally—on-site and online. It allowed participants to attend one or more destination(s) of their choice in person as well as being connected digitally. Alternatively, it was possible just to log in online.

SUMMARY AND BEST PRACTICES

The expansion of international trade fairs, exhibitions, and meetings has been nothing short of remarkable in recent decades. Europe, with its historical roots in trade fairs, maintains its dominant position in hosting the world's largest trade fairs, many of which wield substantial economic influence. Meanwhile, Asia has made remarkable progress by constructing cutting-edge facilities and promoting its offerings on a global scale. In parallel, the Middle East, Africa, and Latin America have all launched robust initiatives aimed at securing a larger share of the international trade fair, exhibition, and convention market.

Worldwide communications, easy travel access, and open markets have been a boon to the international event industry. Few large companies can afford **not** to be in the international marketplace today. What was once the playground of only the world's largest companies is now a necessity for most companies of any size. Trade fairs and exhibitions are the easiest method for these companies to enter the marketplace and meet their potential customers.

Nonetheless, exhibiting at international trade fairs is not without its challenges. Cultural and business disparities present exhibitors with new hurdles, and logistical and travel procedures become more intricate. Companies must thoroughly analyze all factors before committing to an international trade fair program, hosting of an international meeting, or a global convention.

CASE STUDY

An International Event Management Agency, adapted from Suder and Keup (2011).

MCI is a very large, globally integrated event management company, specialized in creating events for corporate and institutional clients, with headquarters in Switzerland and 60 offices in 31 countries and a staff of around 1,500 in 2021.[1]

In 1987, Roger Tondeur and Ursula Wigert created MCI, which then stood for "Meetings, Conferences and Incentives." The company was launched in Geneva, Switzerland as a DMC and congress organizer.[2] By 1999, MCI had become the number 1 of its sector in

---

[1] MCI Annual Report 2021
[2] Company media file 2010, downloaded from http://www.MCIevents.com/Country_Navigation/Countries/Switzerland/~/media/MCI/LocalFiles/Switzerland_Geneva/MCI_in_the_press/2010/dossier_de_presse_MCI.ashx

Switzerland. Soon after this, the first international office was launched in Lyon, France, initiating a fast and successful program of internationalization that lasts until today. MCI, a privately held company, proudly reached a turnover of €242m in 2021.[1]

MCI's employees help clients when acting as

- Event organizer.
- PCO.
- DMC (or specialized incoming ground handler).
- Technology and production company.
- Association management company (AMC), "a professional service company that specializes in providing management services for associations on a fee-for-service basis."[3]

AMCs provide expert staff, administration support, office space, technology and equipment. Event solutions proposed by MCI include congresses, conferences, meetings, seminars, roadshows, exhibitions, incentive programs, and product launches.

MCI has three main competitors, AIMS International Congress Services, CIMGlobal, and Kenes Group. All three have also internationalized.

In 1999, right after opening its second Swiss office in Zurich, MCI acquired a company in Lyon, France. The success of this first cross-border office encouraged MCI to take a next step, a little further away: In 2002, MCI acquired a corporate event management agency in the United Kingdom, then expanded to Brussels, Belgium in 2003,[4] followed by establishing offices in Paris, France and Berlin and Stuttgart, both in Germany. By 2021, MCI was established all over Europe, Asia, Australia, and the Americas.

To guide growth, MCI's executive committee created a hit list of markets for expansion, based on research of industry statistics. They used data from the International Association Meetings Market report published by ICCA and similar sources.

Jurriaen Sleijster, president and COO of MCI Group, stresses that the expansion was not meant as an "ice cold, calculated, machine way of conquering the market" but rather a question of "whom do we know, whom have we been working with in the past, who are our friends and where do you build the relationships. The people element is very, very important." Clients wished, for example, to see MCI teams help them in Paris (MCI office

---

[3] ASAE, The Center for Association Leadership
[4] Brussels is the location of the European Union's main institutions.

established in 2003) and in Singapore: The Singapore office was MCI's first in Asia, in 2005, and first step outside Europe.

"We had two clients for whom we had provided association management services who said, we need to be closer to our members in Asia, can you please open an office there as well," Jurriaen remembers. Initial business was thus ensured by existing clients—also, their wishes illustrated that they found no similarly suitable event management companies in the area.

Clients asked if MCI would serve them in Latin America; this request led to growth there in 2009. "Brazil is a key growth economy and the main economic motor of Latin America. São Paulo and Rio de Janeiro host some of the leading companies headquarters and several of MCI's institution clients have expressed an interest to expand in Brazil," noted Roger Tondeur, president and founder of MCI, at the time.[5]

Internationalization was also driven by the need to stay close to clients and deliver international services for an increasingly globalized clientele. "Being international, being local," Jurriaen stresses, is crucial to MCI's services: on one hand, clients are looking for a multinational presence from MCI; it helps it rationalize costs, simplify contracting, and standardize the quality of its live communication internationally. On the other hand, MCI needs to establish trust-based relationships with in-destination suppliers to the industry, such as convention centers, carriers, hotels, and caterers.

Jurriaen highlights another effect of internationalization: "We do recognize (…) differences within one client company where people from different offices in different parts of the world do different business. We recognize that and we have to respect that. It is sometimes a challenge both for us and for our clients to make sure that a contract which is written with certain rules and guidelines in mind is being executed or respected or interpreted in the same way both by the client and by the supplier all over the world."

---

[5] MCI Group News Release, September 3, 2009, http://www.MCI-group.com

KEY WORDS AND TERMS

For definitions, see glossary, https://www.iapco.org/publications/on-line-dictionary/dictionary/, or http://www.eventscouncil.org/APEX/glossary.aspx

- accommodation
- Ausstellung
- carnet
- delegate
- Gesellschaft
- GmBH
- International Congress and Convention Association
- Kongress
- Messe
- Messegelaende
- PLC
- trade exhibition
- trade fair
- trade fair bond
- stand
- Value-Added Tax

REVIEW AND DISCUSSION QUESTIONS

1. List some ways that international trade fairs may differ from U.S. trade shows.

2. What are two reasons for Europe's strength in the international trade fair industry?

3. What is the purpose of UFI, AIPC, or ICCA? Make sure to follow the website links to get detailed information on each association.

4. What are some of the complexities that a company must consider before taking part in an international event in China?

5. In the chapter, you read about how external events can influence MEEC. Identify one such external event from the chapter, and discuss why this is particularly important in the case of international MEEC.

6. Before proceeding with your exhibition or conference outside of North America, list at least five pieces of knowledge you will require before moving ahead. Where will you get the information?

ABOUT THE CHAPTER CONTRIBUTORS

Mady Keup is a partial-load professor (postsecondary education) at Algonquin College in Ottawa, Canada and former course director for the master of science programs in strategic event management and tourism management and in international hospitality management at SKEMA Business School in France. She was head of the London Convention Bureau (now London & Partners) for 5 years, and she is accredited by Meeting Professionals International as a trainer and an instructor for Destination Sales Training in Europe & the Middle East on behalf of Destination Marketing Association—International. She has traveled extensively for consultancy and training in Europe, the Middle East, and North America.

The case study is adapted from a published case by the contributor and the lead author:

Dr. Gabriele Suder, associate deputy vice-chancellor, academic, Federation University, Australia.

The section on China is based on previous contributions by

Jenny Salsbury, CEO at IMC Convention Solutions, formerly senior director, International, China National Convention Centre

Dr. Chunlei Wang, associate professor in the Department of Event Management, School of Tourism and Event Management, Shanghai University of International Business and Economics, Shanghai

CHAPTER 16

PUTTING IT ALL TOGETHER

MEEC EVENTS ARE LIKE PUZZLES—EVENTUALLY THEY HAVE TO BE PUT TOGETHER

CHAPTER OBJECTIVES

- List items needed to understand the event's organizing association.
- Articulate the event's goals.
- Articulate specific items to consider when determining the event's budget.
- Discuss the elements to keep in mind considering the event's income.
- Specify the necessary components involved in the request for proposal.
- Discuss the main considerations for conducting the first site inspection.
- Outline the important steps in the destination selection.
- Articulate the importance and the considerations necessary for the second site inspection.
- Discuss the part played by the marketing committee.
- Cover the steps involved in the creation of the conference program.
- Outline the importance of partnerships.
- Clarify the considerations involved in handling the event's contract.
- Specify the events and sequencing determined by the meeting timeline.
- Discuss the important items to consider after the meeting.

Contributed by M.T. Hickman. © Kendall Hunt Publishing Company.

Many books conclude with a chapter that recaps and synthesizes earlier content. In this textbook, we employ a fictitious case study of a citywide convention to serve the same purpose. It aims to unify the concepts presented in the preceding chapters. Throughout this text, you have explored various aspects of meeting and event planning. With this case study, you will gain deeper insights into these topics as they apply to a citywide annual conference with 3,000 attendees. The primary goal is to help you grasp the multitude of tasks that planners or event professionals (we use these terms interchangeably in this chapter) must successfully execute to ensure a meeting, exposition, event, or convention (MEEC) is a triumph. Furthermore, this case study will shed light on the intricacies of budgeting, scheduling, and the extensive communication required when working as an event professional.

CASE STUDY

This case study employs a 3-year planning timetable for a single citywide conference. The process of meeting planning is ongoing, and two key skills essential for an event professional are organizational prowess and the ability to multitask. Typically, event professionals manage 3–5 meetings or events simultaneously, each at varying stages of development.

When examining the budget aspect of this case study, note that numerous variables come into play, including current economic conditions, timing of the event, planner's negotiation skills, facility's interest in the business, and trade-offs involved. The budget is comprehensive and underscores the multitude of details that planners must consider.

THE ASSOCIATION

As a meeting or event planner, understanding your audience—the event attendees—is paramount. For association meeting planners, this understanding is especially critical, as they are responsible for marketing the conference to both existing and potential members. Furthermore, the planner must effectively communicate information about their association's members to suppliers for the convention. The more comprehensively a supplier grasps the audience profile, the better they can cater to their needs. For instance, if a hotel is aware that most attendees are women, it might consider adding targeted amenities to enhance the guest experience.

MEETINGS, EXPOSITIONS, EVENTS, AND CONVENTIONS

Consider the American Small Animal Association (ASAA) as an illustrative example of a typical association in the United States, although it is a fictitious entity. ASAA is an 8,000-member nonprofit association, comprising veterinarians specializing in small-animal care. The organization's funding primarily derives from membership dues, publication advertisements, and the annual conference, the latter of which contributes 40% of its income.

ASAA was founded a decade ago by a group of veterinarians who recognized the need for updated research and networking opportunities within the small-animal-care field. A substantial portion, over 60%, of its membership operates independently owned veterinary clinics. The remaining members are suppliers, including pharmaceutical companies, prescription food providers, and product suppliers. Although the number of female members is on the rise, the majority (60%) are male. The ethnic makeup is 55% Caucasian, 30% African American, and 15% a mix of Latino, Asian, and Native American. Understanding the composition of the organization is vital to ensure that the event can effectively cater to its attendees' desires and requirements. Event planners or organizers must ask two fundamental questions: Who constitutes the group, and why have its members chosen to attend?

ASAA is governed by an executive committee and a board of directors. The day-to-day operations are overseen by the executive director and seven committee members. The board of directors is comprised of members elected from seven established regions, each serving 2-year terms. All board elections take place during the annual meeting and are officially announced on the final night. Sue Rodriguez is director of meetings at ASAA. Among the organization's five full-time employees, Sue's responsibilities include coordinating the seven regional meetings and the annual conference. She reports directly to the executive director. Planning for the annual conference commences 3 years in advance. Over the past 5 years, attendance has seen a consistent 5% annual increase, with 37% of the membership attending last year. This remarkable growth is attributed to the success of the trade show segment, introduced 5 years ago.

Logo for the (fictitious) ASAA.

CHAPTER 16 **PUTTING IT ALL TOGETHER**

549

GOALS

Sue begins by reviewing conference evaluations provided by attendees and members of the board of directors. Although the board initially considered cost-cutting measures for networking activities, feedback from members underscored the importance of providing opportunities to connect with professionals nationwide. The board also aims to increase the revenue generated by 10%, recognizing that, aside from membership dues, the annual conference represents the association's largest income source. Last year, ASAA introduced the Small Animal Preventive Disease Certificate (SAPDC) program during the annual convention. It allows veterinarians to earn 25 continuing education units and gain knowledge about preventive medicines crucial for saving the lives of small animals. Additionally, the board of directors has requested the inclusion of a **corporate social responsibility (CSR)** segment in the annual conference. Once the destination for the annual meeting is determined, Sue will collaborate with the local community to identify not-for-profit organizations in need of assistance.

To provide clarity and direction to her efforts, Sue revisits the ASAA mission statement: "The mission of ASAA is to provide an educational forum for members to exchange ideas and develop ways to ensure the health of small animals." This mission is fulfilled by delivering high-quality education to members, offering support to new clinics, and creating a platform for members to collaborate on emerging technologies.

Sue has established operational and educational objectives to measure the **return on investment** (ROI) effectively. The operational objective is to increase conference profits by 5% compared to the previous year, and the educational objective aims to boost the enrollment of attendees in SAPDC classes by 10%. The overarching conference objective, which is "to host a 4-day educational conference for veterinarians and suppliers to the veterinary industry that will result in a 10% increase in attendance and 5% increase in profit from last year's conference" has been shared with Sue's team and all conference partners.

BUDGET

Sue initiates the budgeting process by examining previous meeting budgets (see Tables 16-1 and 16-2). Her expense considerations encompass marketing materials, the convention center, the host hotel, the decorator, **audiovisual**

(A/V) equipment, speakers, entertainment, and staff costs. Furthermore, Sue must align her budget with the operational objectives set for the meeting. In the pursuit of income sources, Sue examines records of past meeting **sponsors** and exhibitors. This year, the marketing strategy will feature an expanded presence on social media platforms and active solicitation of technology sponsors to help offset Wi-Fi expenses.

Budget	Income	Registration
		3,000 attendees
Members		1,680 attendees
Early (at 60% = 1,008 people)	$700 p/p	$705,600
Late (at 40% = 672 people)	$900 p/p	$604,800
Nonmembers		600 attendees
early (at 50% = 300 people)	$800p/p	$560,000
late (at 50% = 300 people)	$1,000 p/p	$300,000
Student (at 5% = 120 people)	$300 p/p	$30,000
Speakers (100 people)	400 p/p	$40,000
Exhibitors	Included in exhibit fee	
Registration Total		**$2,246,400**
SAPDC (500 people)	$300p/p	$150,000
Exhibitors	$3,500 p/exhibit	$1,750,000
Sponsors (500 exhibitions)		$150,000
Bookstore/Gift Shop		$10,000
Other		$5,000
Total Income		**$2,040,000**
Expenses		$2,322,807
Net Income		**$1,963,593**

TABLE 16-1 Budget Income

The hotel budget comprises expenses related to meeting room rental, food and beverage (F&B), staff sleeping rooms, and service charges and gratuities. While developing the budget, Sue is aware that negotiation opportunities will arise from the sleeping and meeting room usage ratios. The closer meeting room use aligns with the hotel's ideal sleeping room to meeting room ratio, the more favorable the negotiation terms can be. To assist in managing hotel room blocks efficiently, Sue relies on a housing bureau.

Regarding the convention center, expenses encompass space rental for meeting rooms, the exhibit hall, electricity, internet connectivity, garbage disposal, security services, and staffing for coffee and food stations. To optimize budget allocation, Sue strategically schedules most educational events there. This approach not only allows her to leverage the daily rate for convention center rooms but also serves as a compelling selling point for exhibitors who seek proximity to attendees during the trade show.

Sue must also identify a **general services contractor** (GSC) to handle decorations and set up the trade show. Additionally, she needs to assess A/V requirements for both the hotel and convention center. The GSC will provide staging for various events, including the reception, general session, trade show, and awards night, and the A/V company will be responsible for sound and lighting. To provide accurate quotes, the GSC needs information on carpeting preferences, number of trade show booths, estimated freight use, and specific staging requirements for the opening session, general session, and awards dinner. The A/V company requires details on sound and lighting requirements for each venue and the type of production needed for the general session, opening reception, and awards dinner. Notably, the general session will be webcast for members unable to attend in person, so Sue lists this as a separate expense (refer to Table 16-2).

Sue addresses the transportation budget by analyzing previous budgets to gauge the number of attendees who used the shuttle service for airport transfers. However, she acknowledges that this expense can fluctuate significantly based on the infrastructure of the host city. She allocates funds for a comprehensive shuttle service, covering each day of the conference, VIP transportation, and transportation to off-site events and the golf tournament. In addition to ground transportation, Sue's transportation budget incorporates air travel expenses for staff and VIPs and freight shipping costs.

Budget	Expenses
Convention Center	$495,000
Host Hotel	$343,907
GSC	$112,470
Signage	$88,000
Audiovisual	$275,000
Webcasting	$66,000
Transportation	$55,000
Off-Site Venue	$82,500
Golf Event	$22,000
Marketing Committee	$209,000
Program Committee	$22,000
Speakers	$92,000
Entertainment	$33,000
Security	$198,000
Insurance	$110,000
Special Services	$5,500
Printing	$11,000
Temporary Staff	$73,920
Gifts	$22,000
Site Visits	$2,310
Other	$6,000
Total Expenses	$2,322,807
Total Expenses	$2,081,188

TABLE 16-2 Budget Expenses

Sue determines the marketing budget by examining past cost history. This year, she plans to reduce expenses related to physical items, such as brochures and direct mail pieces, opting to allocate more resources to electronic marketing, social media campaigns, and engaging bloggers.

Approximately 75% of speakers are association members presenting research papers. To incentivize member participation in presentations, ASAA offers a 50% discount on the early registration fee. However, a substantial portion of the speaker budget is allocated for a keynote speaker and entertainment. To source these, Sue engages the services of a speaker's bureau, with the fee included in this expense category.

To ensure the event runs seamlessly, Sue anticipates the need to hire temporary staff. This budget item encompasses the cost of registration personnel, staff for on-site assembly of attendee packets, room monitors, and individuals responsible for distributing evaluations and fulfilling various duties. Sue plans to bring in temporary staff 1 day before the meeting for training and compensate them for their time.

As an ongoing necessity, security remains a crucial budget consideration. Given the association's increased involvement in new, confidential, and sometimes controversial small-animal research, additional security measures will be required.

Insurance is another expense that is on the rise. Sue includes insurance coverage to mitigate attrition and potential revenue loss due to unforeseen circumstances, such as acts of God, terrorism, and liability issues.

Sue incorporates a special services category that will support members who require services such as translators, materials in Braille, sign language interpreters, and accommodations for Seeing Eye dogs.

During the budgeting process, Sue contacts city officials in the host city. Although ASAA enjoys nonprofit status and is exempt from most city and state taxes, it is essential to complete the necessary paperwork to secure these exemptions. Additionally, Sue must provide documentation proving ASAA's nonprofit status, which will also be shared with suppliers.

Sue includes certain expenses in the budget, even though she expects sponsors to cover them. Each year, finding sponsors for items such as tote bags distributed to all attendees, transportation, the opening reception meal, and VIP dinner entertainment poses no challenge. Nevertheless, Sue adds these items to maintain a clear record of them.

To account for unexpected costs, Sue establishes an "Other" category, reserved for unforeseen or irregular expenses that do not occur annually or are not part of the initial plan. For example, it serves as a contingency fund for unexpected increases in shipping costs.

INCOME

The income (see Table 16-1) will offset the expenses for the meeting, which are estimated to be $2,322,807. To achieve the financial objectives and generate a profit, Sue must not only cover all expenses but also build in a profit margin.

When determining income, Sue begins with the revenue generated from registration fees. She starts with an expected attendance of 3,000 and subtracts 500 exhibitors, whose registration fees are included in the exhibitor package, and the 100 speakers who qualify for reduced registration rates. ASAA offers three categories: members, nonmembers, and students. Data indicate that 70% are members, 25% are nonmembers, and 5% are students. To incentivize early registrations and reduce attrition fees, Sue establishes both early and late registration fees for members and nonmembers. It is projected that 60% of members and 50% of nonmembers will register early. With the goal of covering expenses through registration fees alone, Sue calculates that the per-person fee must be set at $729. Accordingly, Sue's fee structure is $700 for early members, $800 for early nonmembers, $900 for late members, and $1,000 for late nonmembers. Students are offered a reduced rate of $300, encouraging them to join when they enter the field. Sue estimates the total registration income to be $2,246,400.

Exhibitors represent the next largest single source of income. Renting convention space, GSC services, and A/V equipment costs ASAA approximately $15 per square foot. ASAA, in turn, sells trade show space for $35 per square foot. Historical data reveals a steady 10% annual increase in exhibitors. In the previous conference, approximately 450 companies secured booth spaces. Sue's estimate for exhibitor income this year is $1,750,000 (calculated based on 500 exhibitors each spending $3,500 for a ten-foot by ten-foot booth).

Sue collaborates with the marketing team to create sponsorship opportunities aimed at offsetting expenses while providing companies with increased exposure to attendees. This year's sponsorship goal is set at $125,000 and will be achieved by offering the following tiers: (1) Title $15,000, (2) Signature

$10,000, (3) Gold $7,000, (6) Silver $5,000, (6) Bronze $3,000, (12) Scavenger Hunt, and (30) Gift of Love at $100 each.

The title sponsor's logo will receive prominent placement on all digital and hardcopy promotional materials, and the other sponsorships will involve opportunities to underwrite various aspects, such as lunches, coffee breaks, and tours. The sponsors' logos will also feature prominently on printed materials and the mobile app. The Scavenger Hunt sponsorship is exclusively available to exhibitors and designed to enhance the visibility and traffic around their booths. For the Gift of Love sponsorship, which is affordable for any attendee, participants have their names displayed on an electronic reader board at the exhibition hall entrance.

Additional income sources included in the budget encompass rebates from hotel rooms, the transportation company, and the GSC. Instead of accepting commissions, ASAA negotiates rebates per room night, effectively creating an income stream. A modest sum is generated from the sale of bookstore products, including books, shirts, and branded items.

Last year, 454 individuals enrolled in classes to earn the SAPDC. Anticipating a 10% increase, Sue estimates that 500 individuals will pursue the certification this year. The fee will remain unchanged at $300, as it did last year, to encourage participation; it is separate from the registration fee.

REQUEST FOR PROPOSALS (RFP)

After outlining the meeting objectives and establishing a budget, Sue proceeds to create an RFP. Her aim is to provide comprehensive information within the RFP, aiding hotels and cities in submitting well-informed proposals. The RFP contains detailed meeting specifications related to ASAA and clarifies that it is sent out 3 years in advance of the annual conference date. Although most RFPs are transmitted electronically, Sue compiles a hard copy to ensure consistent information dissemination to potential vendors. Once venues and destinations respond to the RFP, Sue, in collaboration with Dave Rogers, the executive director, and Elizabeth Rice, a board member and convention chair, reviews the submitted information. They select two cities for an initial site inspection. After these preliminary site visits are completed, a final decision is made. If a city is chosen, Sue and Dave proceed with a second site inspection to commence contract negotiations. To maintain impartiality, ASAA covers the expenses of the initial site inspections, with the understanding that the selected host city will reimburse these costs.

The RFP includes a list of cities under consideration and the preferred dates for the event. Although the dates may vary within March and April, the event must be Thursday to Sunday. The annual conference is held in different regions across the country, typically in large cities near the residences of board members.

Sue's RFP includes a comprehensive meeting room grid outlining specific requirements. It features special requests, such as two chairs per 6-foot table in classroom setups and a water station stocked with recyclable cups at the rear of each room. Additionally, Sue provides an F&B summary highlighting special dietary considerations for attendees. The grid contains key details, including the event name, expected attendance, and room setup.

ASAA's preference is to work with no more than five hotels in each city. A dedicated grid in the RFP requests information about the number of suites, single rooms, and double rooms that ASAA anticipates using at each hotel. When evaluating potential host cities, Sue seeks downtown hotel properties that offer a range of room prices and are near each other. The selected hotel should be willing to reserve a minimum of 900 rooms. In addition to providing sleeping rooms, it will host the opening night reception and provide breakout rooms for special-interest groups. Sue includes a detailed overview in the RFP, covering the past 3 years, that presents information on peak room nights, meeting room block, sleeping room block, and pickup figures for the host hotel, its room block, and each nonhost hotel; an F&B section illustrates reported usage. ASAA has reported a consistent 10% annual increase in meeting attendees over the last 2 years, and its attrition rate remains at a low 2%.

The final section of the RFP consists of a two-page questionnaire to be completed and submitted by the hotel along with its proposal. This questionnaire covers various aspects, including green initiatives, safety and security plans, the comp room policy, deposit policy, the definition of "sold out," attrition policy, master accounts, split folios, shuttle service availability, tax rates, nonprofit tax policies, service charges, gratuity distribution, internet connection and associated fees, phone charges, and fees for fitness facilities. Additionally, Sue includes inquiries regarding the hotel's handling of "in conjunction with" and exhibitor room blocks and whether the hotel is willing to prioritize housing for ASAA members over nonmembers. Sue has found that this questionnaire serves as a useful tool for efficiently comparing hotels.

To streamline the process, Sue uses the RFP link provided on the destination marketing organization (DMO) or **convention and visitors bureau (CVB)** website. She enters meeting details and attaches a questionnaire for the DMO to complete that covers various aspects, such as state, local, and hotel room taxes, holidays, union contracts, available special venues, services offered by the DMO, and any citywide events or holidays occurring during the meeting dates.

FIRST SITE INSPECTIONS—EXPLORING TWO POSSIBLE CONFERENCE LOCATIONS

Sue, Dave, and Elizabeth have reviewed the proposals and identified two potential host cities: Chicago and Dallas. Sue initiates contact with the DMOs in both cities to arrange a 3-day visit. During these visits, the team intends to conduct a detailed site inspection, assessing various aspects, such as hotels, off-site venues, and golf courses. Sue also provides the DMOs with the site inspection form that the team will use to evaluate the city and its properties. She clarifies that the team plans to stay at the potential host hotels and conduct brief tours of nonhost hotels that are being considered. For the nonhost properties, the team's requirements are limited to meetings with their sales contact, a view of a standard room, and a tour of the retail outlets.

DAY 1

Mark Tester, vice president of sales at Choose Chicago DMO, warmly welcomes Sue, Dave, and Elizabeth at Chicago's O'Hare Airport. Mark provides a comprehensive driving tour of downtown Chicago, passing by all the hotels under consideration. The group enjoys lunch at the Chicago Museum of Art, where Kesha Evans, the owner of Windy City, a **destination management company (DMC)**, joins them. Kesha outlines the array of services her company can offer, including transportation arrangements, off-site event planning, spouse tours, and private dining experiences. Tom Delaney, the catering manager at the Chicago Museum of Art, introduces himself and guides the group on a tour of its private function areas. He recommends the best area for an off-site event and uses his tablet to showcase various meeting setups and décor options. Tom provides Sue with a sales packet featuring sample menus and pricing details and says he will send an email containing a link to more detailed information.

After lunch, Mark Tester takes the inspection team to the Hyatt Regency McCormick Place to meet with its sales manager, Bob Taylor, and general manager, Larry Rose. Together, they embark on a comprehensive property tour, meticulously exploring the sleeping rooms, suites, singles, and doubles. They also assess the suitability of the meeting rooms and ballrooms as potential locations for the opening reception, special-interest group meetings, and various available outlets. They convene in one of the conference rooms for an in-depth discussion covering available dates, rates, and bandwidth.

Sue, Dave, and Elizabeth gather again at 6:00 p.m., this time in the hotel restaurant for dinner. During the meal, they keenly observe how guests are treated, assess the quality and timing of food service, and evaluate the attentiveness of the waitstaff. In their commitment to thorough assessment, they order different entrées to sample the diverse food offerings that their attendees might select. After dinner, Sue takes the opportunity to stroll through the meeting spaces, peering into the meeting rooms to gauge their setup and layout.

DAY 2

The following day at 8:30 a.m., Mark meets the team members, who have already enjoyed breakfast and checked out of the hotel. Mark has thoughtfully arranged a 9:00 a.m. meeting with Randy Moses, the senior sales manager of McCormick Place Convention Center. Randy offers an insightful tour of the facility, highlighting the most suitable locations for their functions, loading docks, shuttle drop-off and pickup points, and areas where sponsored items, such as banners, can be displayed. Sue queries Randy about available dates, F&B concession hours, internet/Wi-Fi charges, taxes, union regulations, and contract renewal dates. Randy promptly provides this information and discusses security protocols and medical and emergency procedures. Both Mark and Randy elucidate how the DMO and convention center collaborate as a unified team to effectively market the Chicago meeting to attendees. They delve into marketing strategies, encompassing premailers, email campaigns, social media initiatives, and on-site promotions in the year leading up to the event.

For lunch, Mark treats the group to a memorable experience aboard the Golden Princess, an opulent yacht owned by ABC Charters, which specializes in dinner tours of Lake Michigan. Rich Cunningham, the general manager of ABC Charters, warmly welcomes them. They partake in a special lunch designed for meeting planners to sample the menu and enjoy a minicharter experience. Deborah Adams, the president of Chicago DMC Services, elucidates her services and showcases videos on her tablet featuring off-site locations that Sue may wish to consider.

The afternoon is dedicated to forging connections and conducting tours of the hotels under consideration. Mark skillfully arranges 30-minute tours of each nonhost hotel, clearly outlining the team's focus on viewing sleeping rooms and restaurant areas only. By 4:00 p.m., Sue, Dave, and Elizabeth are prepared to check into the Hyatt Regency Chicago, the second hotel under consideration as headquarters. They are met by Rachel Monroe, the associate sales manager, who commences the tour. Rachel is enthusiastic about a recently added ballroom and discusses its use for the opening reception. Following the tour, Richard Moore, the general manager, joins the group to discuss available dates and rates. Sue, Dave, and Elizabeth take a 1-hour break and reconvene in the restaurant for dinner, where they meticulously review all the notes collected over the past 2 days. Subsequently, Sue embarks on her tour of the meeting rooms.

DAY 3

The team checks out early and gathers in the hotel lobby. While checking their emails, they notice a line forming as guests check out. They make mental notes of the checkout duration and the courtesy of the employees at the front desk and bell stand. Mark arrives at the hotel and escorts the group to their first destination, the Harborside International Golf Center, a four-star course located just 12 miles from downtown Chicago. The group meets with the special events manager to discuss the optional golf outing planned as part of the ASAA event. The tournament is scheduled for Thursday afternoon, preceding the opening reception. After this, Mark guides the group to another golf course and two more hotel site inspections before they head to the airport. Sue, Dave, and Elizabeth extend their gratitude to Mark for his time, and they inform him that they will be touring Dallas next month. Their plan is to make a decision within 2 months and communicate it to the bureau.

One month later, Sue, Dave, and Elizabeth embark on a 3-day site inspection in Dallas. Patty Brown, the sales manager at Visit Dallas DMO, arranges for the group to meet with staff from the hotels, convention center, and various off-site locations. Patty highlights the significant developments in Dallas, including the Omni Dallas Hotel connected to the Dallas Convention Center and the upcoming expansion of the Convention Center.

DESTINATION SELECTION

After both site inspections, the team convenes to review their notes. They decide to schedule their meeting on St. Patrick's Day, notwithstanding potential conflicts with other industry events. In their evaluation of Chicago, they express concerns about room availability, the renewal dates for certain union contracts, and the cost (25% more). Although this cost increase might be justified by some attendees preferring Chicago, the meeting is expected to attract a larger number of attendees seeking the SAPDC certification, making location less of a determining factor. Consequently, Dallas was chosen. Sue contacts Mark from Choose Chicago to convey their concerns and provides a detailed explanation for selecting Dallas. She reminds Mark that it has not held a meeting in Chicago for 5 years but expresses a desire to explore opportunities.

SECOND SITE INSPECTION: FINALIZING DETAILS

DAY 1

Sue sends a letter of intent to Patty Brown, expressing the intention to hold the conference in Dallas. She contacts Patty to coordinate a second site inspection, which will include only Sue and Dave and span 3 days. The objectives are to finalize nonhost properties, select off-site venues and a golf course, choose the DMC and transportation company, initiate contract negotiations, and identify an organization for the CSR project. Upon arrival, Sue and Dave rent a car and embark on a self-guided tour of the city. They then check in at the downtown Omni Hotel Dallas, designated as the headquarters hotel.

At the Omni, Sue and Dave meet with Loretta Jones, the global director of sales, and Vicki Wall, the **convention services manager (CSM)**. Once the contract is signed, Sue will collaborate with Vicki for the event planning. During this meeting, Sue and Loretta commence negotiations for sleeping rooms, meeting rooms, shuttle service, and other logistics.

Sue meets with Sonja Miller, the sales manager of the Dallas Convention Center, along with Erika Bondy, CMP, the senior event coordinator, and Bill Baker, the director of catering. Once the contract is finalized, Sue will collaborate with Erika on all meeting details and work closely with Bill to plan the F&B aspects. Today, Sue initiates negotiations on rates with the Dallas Convention Center. During the meeting, she reviews her requirements and aims to find the best win-win arrangement for both her attendees and the convention center.

Sue and Dave take a lunch break at the Dallas Museum of Art, where they meet with Cindy Hartman, the catering sales manager, to discuss rates for hosting the VIP dinner in its restaurant. Later, Carolyn Petty, the president of EMC (a DMC), joins Sue and Dave during lunch to explore the offerings EMC can provide for the ASAA meeting, including gift baskets and comprehensive transportation services.

In the afternoon, Patty has organized meetings with two nonhost hotels under consideration for sleeping room space. At each hotel, Sue meets with the sales manager to negotiate rates and amenities. For dinner, Patty treats Sue and Dave to a delightful local Mexican restaurant, a favorite among the locals, where she discusses the range of services that Visit Dallas can offer, including registration personnel, marketing, social media packages to promote the meeting, supplier leads, transportation services, internet access, and on-site concierge support to assist attendees with local dining and sightseeing activities. She also mentions that Visit Dallas will set up a promotional booth at the meeting preceding the one in Dallas.

Registration company trains temporary staff before the opening of the conference

DAY 2

The morning is dedicated to touring and re-establishing contact with the remaining hotels providing sleeping rooms. Sue and Dave enjoy a leisurely lunch at the Perot Museum of Nature while scouting for a lively venue for the VIP meeting. Their meeting with Nicole Benson, event sales manager, involves a tour and a discussion about potential dining options. Although they consider this option, it might be deemed too casual for the group. Nicole, however, brings her tablet to showcase pictures of events hosted at the museum, which alleviates Sue's concerns.

In the afternoon, Sue and Dave explore two golf courses; Sue makes contacts, arranges for the event sales manager to lead them on a nine-hole tour, and initiates discussions about pricing. Sue also pays attention to potential areas where the group could convene before and after the tournament, ensuring suitable spaces for postgame gatherings.

DAY 3

Sue and Dave commence their day with a meeting with the GSC contact, Jack Boyd, an account executive for the Freeman Companies. They are also joined by Mark Lee, the director of sales at PSAV, Dallas, an AV company. The initial meeting takes place at the Dallas Convention Center before moving to the Omni. The focus of their discussions revolves around GSC and audiovisual equipment requirements. They tour each venue, delving into specific details regarding staging, setup, Wi-Fi capabilities, and other essential needs for each event.

Their final stop of the day is at the Dallas SPCA, where they meet with Iris Henderson, volunteer coordinator. Sue discovered it while researching potential meeting sites for the CSR event. She learned about their program that allows groups to volunteer time to sanitize the shelter.

MARKETING COMMITTEE

ASAA has both an in-house marketing department and an outside advertising agency, and they collaborate to develop the marketing campaign. Upon Sue's return from the second site inspection, she convenes a meeting with George Day, the ASAA director of marketing, and Julie Love, the account manager from Idea Maker, Inc., an advertising company. During this meeting, George and Julie present the results of a member survey, which revealed that members are actively using Facebook, LinkedIn, and Twitter. They emphasize the significance of incorporating social media into the marketing strategy. Sue discusses the convention's location and objectives, underscoring the importance of promoting the new SAPDC. Two weeks later, Sue reconvenes with George and Julie. Julie comes prepared with theme ideas and visuals for the marketing materials. After evaluating several themes, they settle on "Power of Prevention." They decide to employ three marketing tools. First, they plan to create a four-color, postcard-sized mailer as a teaser, which will be sent to all previous conference attendees and targeted potential members. It will also double as an advertisement to be placed in industry newsletters and digital magazines. The second element is an email announcement for all association members. It will contain a link to the convention website, which will feature a comprehensive convention agenda listing dates, times, and speakers, along with a program-at-a-glance grid, current sponsors, and convention and housing registration forms. The final component is the social media campaign for Facebook, Instagram, TikTok, LinkedIn, and Twitter. Working alongside popular convention speakers, the marketing committee will disseminate information on Facebook and LinkedIn and use Twitter to broadcast updates about conference activities.

Additionally, TikTok and YouTube videos will be incorporated into the conference website to generate excitement and encourage early registration. Bloggers will also be hired to write about and share their conference experiences. This year, with the aim of reducing paper usage, they will create a one-sheet program detailing the location of exhibitors in the trade show and summarizing the conference activities. Upon registering, attendees will have the option to download the conference app, which will include comprehensive information on the program, speakers, educational sessions, exhibitor locations, and detailed product information. Furthermore, the app will provide a platform for attendees to interact with each other and feature an electronic game designed to facilitate networking and engagement with exhibitors.

George is enthusiastic about the app and explains to Sue and David that the game developed for it will highlight key sponsors, thus introducing a new source of revenue for the conference.

During each conference, a new board of directors is introduced, awards are presented, and crucial announcements are made. Sue, George, and Dave convene to discuss the types of presentations to be delivered and the scripts that

George and his team will prepare. Sue's responsibility includes scheduling rehearsal time for each presentation.

The marketing committee is tasked with crafting press releases to be distributed to professional publications. With each conference, a new research piece takes the spotlight, and the marketing committee works diligently to promote this research to the public.

CREATION OF THE CONFERENCE PROGRAM

Upon Sue's return from the Dallas site inspection, she meets with the program committee to begin developing the meeting's educational content. The program committee comprises Doug Walker, a board member and chair of the SAPDC; Dan Dearing, chairman of the board of directors of the program committee for the annual convention, and his appointed committee members, Liz Stewart and Mark Collins; and Donna Smith, ASAA administrative assistant. These five individuals, alongside Sue, will collaborate to shape the meeting's content.

Sue commences the meeting by offering each committee member the option to receive either a hard copy or an electronic notebook containing their respective responsibilities, past convention notes, and the meeting theme, "Power of Prevention." Sue's primary goal is to ensure that the committee members comprehend the objective, which is to boost SAPDC member attendance by 10% by providing a 4-day conference focusing on educational content, ultimately increasing meeting profits by 5%. The committee unanimously agrees to adhere to the same meeting agenda as in previous years: an opening reception, a general session, concurrent sessions, an awards dinner, and a **poster session** in the middle of the trade show. The conference will encompass an ASAA VIP dinner, a golf tournament, and 120 60-minute education sessions in 2 days. The sole schedule modification is the addition of two 4-hour segments dedicated to the SAPDC class. The committee's primary responsibility is to secure speakers for SAPDC classes and all breakout sessions. ASAA members will present 100 of the educational sessions. To assist the program committee, the Paper Review Committee is established to issue the call for papers, evaluate and grade the submissions, and inform the program committee of the final selections for the presentations and poster session. For various key events, such as the opening reception, general session, awards dinner, ASAA VIP dinner, and entertainment, Sue will use a speaker's bureau. Sue has provided the committee with a timeline for reference. Using abstract management software, the Paper Review Committee will call for papers 1 year before the meeting. Six months before, the program committee will receive the final selections and make initial contact with presenters and speakers. It will also provide speaker recommendations for all sessions. Once speakers and backup speakers have been identified, Sue will send out invitation letters. These letters will request the speaker's commitment, outline A/V options, and mandate submitting an abstract for the presentation, along with a biography and a photo.

The committee will contact all the selected speakers and conduct follow-ups with those who have not responded. A point person will be designated to address any speaker inquiries. Sue's will then collect information, allocate time slots, and maintain correspondence with the speakers. This includes sending letters of acceptance and reminders.

One crucial aspect is the exhibitors. Jill Kochan, an ASAA staff member, serves as the trade show manager. Her responsibilities encompass all communications with exhibitors and the GSC during the trade show setup. Jill will work closely with Sue to relay exhibitor needs and collaborate with the GSC to establish specifications for the exhibitor prospectus.

The newly formed CSR Committee will collaborate with the Dallas SPCA to create a program that allows attendees to volunteer at the new shelter. Additionally, the committee will partner with the marketing team to craft an announcement encouraging attendees to bring items for donation to the SPCA. As a gesture of gratitude to ASAA for its support, the SPCA will organize a "puppy petting" session in the lobby on the first day of the conference.

PARTNERSHIPS

As Sue prepares for this meeting, she recognizes the significance of her collaborative partners. Throughout the conference, Sue relies on numerous companies to deliver exceptional service and contribute to a memorable experience for ASAA members. She reviews her contact list, acknowledging the many companies she will partner with.

Although most housing bureaus offer complete housing packages, including hotel selection, negotiation, and contract management, Sue prefers to engage the housing bureau's services after selecting the hotels. Once the hotel choices are finalized, the housing bureau sends a confirmation letter. It creates a dedicated website for attendees to book rooms online, along with a downloadable form for attendees to complete, scan, and email. One of the most advantageous aspects of the partnership is room block management. Instead of contacting all the hotels being used, Sue relies on the housing bureau to provide monthly, weekly, and daily rooming reports as needed, including managing the exhibitor room block.

Sue prefers to collaborate with a local DMC. She uses its services to arrange airport meet and greets, hotel transfers, VIP transportation, and shuttle services from hotels to the convention center. The DMC handles all logistical aspects of the VIP dinner, allowing Sue to focus on invitations and content. Sue values the DMC's network of motor coach suppliers, as transportation has been a concern in the past. She recalls an incident in Washington, D.C., where a motor coach contracted by her company broke down with all attendees on board, with no backups available. This led to a nearly hour-long wait for rescue and transportation to the event.

Sue's busy schedule leaves her with insufficient time to research potential speakers and entertainers. The speaker's bureau provides recommendations for the best candidates. Once Sue makes her selections, it handles all necessary arrangements. It ensures that speakers arrive promptly at the meeting and can swiftly arrange for backup speakers if unforeseen issues arise.

Sue opts for an online registration company to establish the meeting registration site and manage registration fees. The company accepts registrations, automatically sends attendees confirmation letters containing links to the housing bureau, and stores registrations for easy retrieval to create name badges. It also offers on-site registration services, staffing, and financial reporting. This ensures a consistent experience for attendees and provides Sue with rapid access to reports for monitoring registration activity and income.

Sponsors are integral partners for the ASAA conference. Sue collaborates closely with all sponsors to ensure they receive exposure to members in exchange for their financial and/or in-kind support. Sue recognizes that without annual conference sponsors, ASAA would struggle to meet its financial objectives for the convention.

Although ASAA has always provided meeting security for attendees' safety and exhibitor product protection, Sue plans to enhance security measures. An animal rights association has contacted ASAA with plans to protest a new laboratory rat testing procedure. Sue acknowledges the need to allow this group to express its views but wants to ensure that its protest is peaceful and does not disrupt meeting attendees.

Key partners in the conference's success include the GSC, responsible for decorations, and the A/V company, providing electronic equipment. Sue views the GSC as the partner responsible for bringing the conference theme to life, so the decorations must captivate attendees visually. Sue understands the GSC's crucial role in keeping exhibitors happy, as exhibitors contribute significantly, generating 44% of the conference's revenue.

Sue values her collaboration with the A/V company, recognizing its essential role in every aspect of the meeting. Proper projection and sound are vital for attendee learning. Sue works closely with the A/V company's staff during the event, understanding that even a single malfunctioning microphone or burned-out light bulb can disrupt a breakout session.

To ensure efficient operations during the conference, Sue hires temporary staff early and builds strong partnerships with them. They become integral members of the team, representing ASAA.

CONTRACTS

Sue ensures that she has a contract for each convention partner and service provider, specifying the expected services and outlining penalties for unmet expectations. Early in her career, Sue encountered an association that signed a contract without a realistic attrition clause. It did not meet its room block and paid over $50,000 for unused rooms. At least 1 year in advance, Sue meticulously reviews each contract. Long before the conference, she finalizes contracts with numerous entities, including the host hotel, housing bureau, registration company, airlines, off-site venues, golf courses, speaker's bureau, security, A/V companies, DMCs, and GSCs.

MEETING TIMELINE

1 YEAR TO 6-MONTH COUNTDOWN

Sue glances at her **meeting timeline**, realizing that she is 12 months away from the Power of Prevention annual conference. She retrieves her meeting resume and meticulously examines all contracts. She also schedules a meeting with George and Julie from the marketing committee to review both electronic and hardcopy marketing materials. Sue knows that any missed educational session or grammatical error in these materials becomes part of the final product. If a significant mistake is identified, the piece is reprinted and the expenses added to the conference's cost. Fortunately, electronic materials allow for quick and cost-effective changes.

Sue also arranges a meeting with Doug and Dan from the program committee to select speakers for the convention. After that, Sue sends acceptance emails with requests for them to confirm their commitment. She asks them to provide an electronic biography, a digital photo, a presentation abstract, and an A/V needs form. Sue proactively contacts the speaker's bureau to verify the status of the motivational speaker and entertainment. She emphasizes the importance of identifying all A/V needs 8 months before the meeting to establish a more accurate budget.

Sue secures 10 sponsors, including Small Vets Plus, a company that supplies vaccines for small animals (for tote bags); Hoover Pharmaceuticals, a producer of small-animal antibiotics (for transportation); LabSmlab, a provider of medical instruments used in animal surgery (for the opening night reception); Mix-a-vet, a developer of special food for small animals (sponsoring the conference app); and Smalco, a pet store specializing in small-animal products. Small Vets Plus will cosponsor the VIP entertainment and awards dinner. Sue will reach out to each sponsor to confirm their commitment and have it sign the contract. During these discussions, Sue emphasizes that sponsors must return a form with the exact spelling of their company name and the design of their signage or logo in a format suitable for mobile apps.

The trade show floor plan for the Dallas conference was created and approved 14 months in advance. Exhibit space was sold on-site at the ASAA conference preceding Dallas, boasting an 87% exhibitor retention rate. Nine months prior, the GSC updates the floor plan and emails electronic exhibitor links to potential exhibitors. ASAA employs exhibition software to generate an electronic floor plan, manage booth sales, facilitate exhibitor registration, and provide financial reports for sales monitoring.

In addition to the trade show, Sue collaborates with the GSC to finalize the setup for the opening reception, general session, and awards dinner. She determines the location of the media center and registration area. Sue relies on the GSC's expertise to recommend the best spots for sponsor banners, gobos, and signage. Most convention centers enforce strict rules regarding banner and signage placement, and GSCs that regularly work with convention centers are well versed in these regulations and often have creative ideas for recognizing sponsors.

6 MONTHS BEFORE TO DAY OF THE MEETING

Fast forward to the 6-month countdown. The marketing committee steps up its efforts by drafting and sending out press releases. It also increase its presence on various social media platforms, including Facebook, Instagram, and LinkedIn.

Early registration forms begin to arrive within weeks of being sent out. During her review of these forms, Sue notices that three attendees have indicated that they have mobility disabilities and will require special accommodation. In adherence to the Americans with Disabilities Act, Sue initiates collaboration with all meeting partners to ensure that these attendees can fully participate. This entails arranging for handicapped rooms and configuring meeting rooms with appropriate aisles to accommodate them.

Sue receives the menus from the hotel catering manager and selects the meals. She makes a conscious effort to choose menus that cater to the diverse tastes of all attendees. In feedback from the previous year's conference evaluations, attendees expressed a desire for more healthy and vegetarian options.

To compile information for the convention program and app, Sue contacts the host hotel and convention center to obtain the names of the designated meeting rooms. This information is crucial, although hotels and convention centers are often hesitant to provide it early, as they prefer not to commit to specific rooms that might be reserved by other event planners. Effective communication and flexibility are key in managing such situations.

Sue collaborates with the DMC to review the menu and with the GSC to plan the VIP dinner at the Perot Museum of Nature and Science. The dinner will be hosted in a room with a picturesque view of downtown Dallas, and the evening will include a private tour of the museum, along with an opportunity for attendees to create a new virtual species of bird and test its ability to fly. Additionally, Sue contacts Larry Grant, the event organizer at Tenison Golf Course, to finalize tournament rules. The event is off to a promising start, with 30 people already registered. Sue provides Larry with the names and disabilities of the participants.

During this time, Sue also collaborates with the DMC to finalize shuttle routes for all events, allowing her to initiate the order of transportation signage. Sue recognizes that even highly educated individuals sometimes struggle with directions at meetings, so she ensures that all event details, locations, and shuttle service times are clearly listed in the program and on the app. Signage plays a crucial role in enhancing the overall conference experience.

MONTH 5

Five months in advance, Sue sends out reminders to all speakers. She collaborates with the marketing committee to finalize and distribute the brochure and update social media promotions. Following a period dedicated to proofreading meeting materials, she establishes a comprehensive work schedule for staff, temporary employees, and volunteers. Sue also orders name badges and necessary supplies and contacts the security company to review her requirements.

MONTHS 4 AND 3

During the fourth and third months leading up to the event, Sue monitors registration weekly. When the third month arrives, she assesses registration numbers and makes adjustments to her room block. This flexibility was negotiated in her hotel contract as a means to manage attrition.

Sue reviews her initial room block (refer to Table 16-3) and compares it with current hotel registrations. Historical data indicate that 60% of attendees register early, ideally resulting in a reserved block of 600 rooms at the host property. However, Sue notes that all rooms at the Hyatt Regency Downtown Dallas are fully booked, and securing additional rooms is not possible; she must close reservations for the Hyatt Regency. On the other hand, the Hilton Anatole and W Hotel remain on track and require no adjustments. The Holiday Inn has 50 rooms fewer than expected, prompting Sue to reduce the block by 40%. She is now committed to 60 rooms instead of the initial 100. Conversely, the host Omni Dallas Hotel has 100 rooms more than anticipated. Sue opts for a conservative increase of 5% in the block, obligating her to 954 rooms.

Hotel	Omni Hotel Dallas	Hyatt Regency Downtown Dallas	Hilton Anatole	W Hotel	Holiday Inn
Initial Room Block	900	800	1,000	200	100
90-Day Room Block Review	700	500	500	150	50
Room Block Adjustment	Over—will add 54 rooms	No change	On Schedule	On schedule	Under—will remove 40 rooms
New Room Block	954	800	1,000	200	60

TABLE 16-3 ASAA Hotel Room Blocks

Sue has received calls from the convention center requesting the relocation of several meeting rooms and calls from speakers needing to cancel. These changes have a ripple effect on the one-page printed program, the website, and the conference app, necessitating revisions. Sue views this as a period of numerous changes, all part and parcel of her job. To manage speaker cancellations, she reaches out to the program committee to identify potential backup speakers.

Month 2

Two months before the event, Sue arranges another trip to Dallas. Patty, the CSM at Visit Dallas, facilitates meetings with all the key contacts to ensure the success of the conference. Vicki, the director of CSM at the Omni, conducts a property walk-through with Sue. During this visit, Sue meets with various hotel staff, including the catering manager to discuss the menu, the accounts receivable contract for a bill review process explanation, the front desk manager to confirm prekey guests and the check-in and checkout procedures, and the director of security and medical staff to review emergency procedures. The CSM serves as the primary hotel contact and will assist Sue in acquiring the necessary information from the hotel, ranging from room pickups to bill reviews. Vicki and Sue establish a close working relationship.

At the Dallas Convention Center, Sue conducts a walk-through with Erika Bondy, senior event coordinator. She also invites the GSC and AV contacts to join her. This collaborative approach allows Sue to have multiple perspectives looking for potential issues. Additionally, Sue dedicates time to meeting with the catering manager to review the menu for the lunch and awards dinner.

Sue conducts a meeting with the DMC representative to walk through the hotel transportation routes and finalize details related to menus, decorations, and entertainment for the VIP dinner at the Perot Museum of Nature and Science. Following this, she meets with the event coordinator at Tenison Golf Course to update the player list and review pairings.

Upon her return, Sue collaborates with the marketing team to update the app and sends the one-page program to the printer. She also arranges for materials to be shipped to the convention site, works with the marketing committee on finalizing scripts, and reviews her staging guide, which contains all her contacts, timelines, contracts, menus, and notes.

Month 1

One month before the event, Sue continues to monitor registrations weekly and sends reminder emails to all speakers. She collaborates with the advertising firm to approve press releases announcing research findings to be presented at the conference. She also works with her staff to finalize work schedules, marketing efforts, scripts, and rehearsal times. Sue creates a checklist and prepares her convention materials. Her meticulous planning includes contingency plans for various activities. For instance, if the golf tournament is disrupted by rain, the group will spend the morning on a sports tour of Cowboy Stadium.

Sue likens the month leading up to the meeting to a tennis match. She anticipates that emergencies may feel like multiple balls coming across the net at the same time. She ensures she is prepared with her racket in hand to successfully respond to these challenges and remain ready for the next volley of issues.

Premeeting Activities

Three days before the event, Sue and her staff arrive in Dallas to establish the meeting headquarters. Sue is delighted to find that all her convention materials have arrived intact. She schedules meetings with all key contacts to finalize event plans and organizes a comprehensive walk-through of the host hotel and the convention center, involving her staff, temporary employees, and volunteers. The hotel facilitates a preconvention meeting, bringing together everyone involved to review the meeting resume for any last-minute changes or concerns.

Sue closely oversees the setup of all events and actively engages in on-site troubleshooting. Something always requires adjustment, whether it is correcting an error on a sponsor sign, necessitating a call to the GSC, or addressing more complex issues, such as inadequate space for registration. This period demands constant problem-solving.

Sue also joins George and the marketing staff as they rehearse for the general session, prepare the pressroom, and conduct a press conference. George goes over the press list with Sue, as she needs to be familiar with the names to ensure prompt assistance from ASAA staff upon their arrival. Positive publicity can significantly contribute to the success of future conferences.

MEETING DAY ACTIVITIES

The meeting commences, and Sue is actively engaged in ensuring that all meeting rooms are set up correctly and all speaker materials and evaluations are prepared. Her role is primarily behind the scenes, focused on making the attendees' experience flawless. She is the first to arrive on-site and will be the last to leave. The day is filled with questions she must address and problems that require solutions. This is the time that truly excites Sue—the moment when she witnesses all her hard work come to life. She uses the contacts she has cultivated to swiftly resolve issues. For instance, if equipment in one of the rooms malfunctions, she promptly contacts the A/V company. At the start of each day, Sue meets with the hotel CSM and the accounts receivable department for a bill review. She also coordinates with the housing bureau to cross-reference ASAA registration with the in-house guest list, ensuring proper coding for ASAA attendees, which aids in future event accommodations.

A dedicated ASAA exhibitor headquarters office opens at the convention center. Jill, ASAA's trade show manager, remains in this office to address any issues that may arise during the trade show and accept exhibitor bookings for next year's conference.

AFTER THE MEETING

IMMEDIATE POSTMEETING ACTIVITIES

After an exhausting day, Sue reflects on the successes and areas for improvement at the conference. Before departing Dallas, she organizes a postconference meeting, involving those who attended the preconvention meeting. The aim is to discuss any challenges encountered and brainstorm ways to enhance future conventions. Sue collaborates with the hotel and vendors to reconcile registration numbers, review all pickups, and estimate ancillary business.

Sue works for an association that focuses on small animals, so she often jokes that her job is like "pulling a rabbit out of a hat"

Planning a convention is a collective effort, and Sue takes the time to express gratitude to all speakers, sponsors, committee members, and facilitators for their contributions to the conference's success. She also rewards her staff with a free day in Dallas to unwind and relax.

2-MONTH POSTMEETING ACTIVITIES

After thoroughly reviewing the statistics and evaluations, Sue begins her report to the executive director and the board of directors concerning the Power of Prevention conference's ROI. It is crucial to conduct an evaluation after each conference. Sue and her team established specific objectives: to increase SAPDC attendance by 10% through a 4-day conference focused on education and networking, ultimately boosting conference profits by 5%. What is the purpose of organizing a convention if its success is not measured? Part of the meeting planner's role is to illustrate how a convention or meeting contributes to achieving organizational goals. By setting objectives and assessing ROI, a planner can demonstrate their role in supporting company objectives and financial performance.

Sue is thrilled with the outcome. The industry press provided outstanding premeeting coverage, resulting in over $50,000 worth of tracked nonpaid advertising. The marketing committee's decision to invest in push ads on Facebook and Instagram and hire bloggers significantly contributed to its success. Sue believes that this third-party endorsement played a key role in boosting attendance. She also credits the marketing committee for introducing the exhibitor Scavenger Hunt in the conference app. It generated $18,000 in additional sponsorship revenue, with 12 exhibitors purchasing sponsorships at $1,500 each. Both attendees and exhibitors enjoyed the experience. Attendees loved participating in the game and competing with each other, and sponsors benefited from increased booth traffic. The meeting's objectives were achieved: SAPDC class enrollment increased to 500 attendees (a 10% rise from the previous year's 454), and meeting profits grew from $1,865,413 to $1,963,593 (a 5% increase).

Attendees participate in app scavenger hunt

Sue finishes her report and takes a call from the Orlando Convention Center, the location for next year's annual conference. She is 12 months away from the conference and receiving the names of the meeting rooms that will be used. The meeting cycle continues.

SUMMARY

In this chapter, you have learned about the process of creating a citywide meeting. This is a large task for one person and requires many partners to achieve success. Through this case study, you have been able to see the life of a meeting planner and the many tasks leading up to the conference. The chapter began with creating conference objectives and budgets, and it ended with evaluating ROI to determine the success of the meeting.

REVIEW AND DISCUSSION QUESTIONS

1. What is the operational and conference objective of ASAA?
2. Review Table 16-1 (income) and Table 16-2 (expenses) and answer the following. In addition to registration, what are three sources of income included in the ASAA budget? Identify and explain which expenses you think are too low or too high.

3. Starting with creating the meeting objective, what steps does Sue go through to plan and execute this meeting?
4. Which destination did ASAA select, and why? List the suppliers and vendors that Sue used for the meeting.
5. Do you think that in-person inspections are still needed?
6. Review the types of sponsorships. Is there anything that you would change, and why?

KEY WORDS AND TERMS

For definitions, see glossary or http://glossary.conventionindustry.org.

audiovisual
convention services manager
convention and visitor bureau
corporate social responsibility
destination management company
destination marketing organization
general services contractor
meeting timeline
poster session
request for proposals
return on investment
sponsors

ABOUT THE CHAPTER CONTRIBUTOR

M. T. Hickman, CMP, CSECP, is a senior lecturer in the Department of Hospitality, Event and Tourism Management at the University of North Texas. She was the lead faculty and head of the Hospitality, Exhibitions, and Event Management Dallas College—Richland Campus in Dallas, Texas, for 20 years. Her career began at the Irving, Texas CVB, where she worked in many departments, including tourism sales, convention sales, and special events. She has been a director of marketing for the National Business Association and proposal writer for WorldTravel Partners. She is active in the meeting and exposition planning associations, including MPI, PCMA, IMEX, and IAEE. In 2023, she was named the PCMA Educator Lifetime Honoree.

Previous Edition Chapter Contributors

Roy T. Benear, divisional director of sales and events divisional director of sales—Association Meetings, Tradeshows, Exhibit Design Agencies; Events SmartSource

Laura Jordan, CMP, CTA, events consultant, Health Care Service Corporation

Patty Stern, chief creative officer, PattyStern.Com Creative Marketing & Event Concepts

David Gisler, (retired) director of sales and training, Total Show University, Freeman Companies

Bitsy Burns, CMP, (retired) director of operations, Southwest Veterinary—Symposium

Erin Donahue, vice president, Global Accounts Shamrock Innovation

Patty Towell, senior sales manager, San Antonio CVB

Dana Rhoden, CMM, founder and CEO, Veterinary Education Network

CHAPTER 16 PUTTING IT ALL TOGETHER

REFERENCES

2023 global meetings and events forecast. (2023, February 21). Amex GBT—United States. https://www.amexglobalbusinesstravel.com/meetings-events/meetings-forecast/

Bureau International des Expositions. (2023, March 31). *Expo 2020 Dubai impact drives decades-long growth in UAE.* Bureau International des Expositions. https://www.bie-paris.org/site/en/news-announcements/expo-dubai-2020-2/expo-2020-dubai-impact-drives-decades-long-growth-in-uae#:~:text=One%20year%20after%20the%20closing,period%20from%202013%20to%202042.

Business Events Council of Australia. (2020, March 20). *Value of business events to Australia: FY19 high-level update.* Kingston.

Galal, S. (2023, April 23). Total population of Africa 2000–2030. Statista.com. https://www.statista.com/statistics/1224168/total-population-of-africa/#:~:text=As%20of%202022%2C%20the%20total,increased%20annually%20from%202000%20onwards.

German Convention Bureau. (n.d.). *Newsroom.* gcb.de. https://www.gcb.de/en/media/news-room/#/pressreleases/hybrid-formats-drive-transformation-of-the-event-market-results-of-meeting-und-eventbarometer-2021-strich-22-3178209

Hannover Messe. (2023, April 21). *Hannover Messe News: Industry in upbeat mood at Hannover Messe.* https://www.hannovermesse.de/en/news/news-articles/industry-in-upbeat-mood-at-hannover-messe

International Congress and Convention Association (ICCA). (2022a). ICCA DPI 2021. Amsterdam.

Pao, J. (2023, April 24). *U.S. sanctions turn away Canton Fair's western buyers.* Asia Times. https://asiatimes.com/2023/04/us-sanctions-turn-away-canton-fairs-western-buyers/

Roush, T. (2023, February 20). *U.S. and 34 other nations "do not agree" Russian athletes should be in 2024 Olympics—Boycott Brewing.* Forbes. https://www.forbes.com/sites/tylerroush/2023/02/20/us-and-34-other-nations-do-not-agree-russian-athletes-should-be-in-2024-olympics-boycott-brewing/?sh=376854796320

Sharma, N (2018) A Snapshot of the Indian Exhibition Industry downloaded from http://www.iaee.com/wp-content/uploads/2018/12/Indian-Exhibition-Industry-Snapshot.pdf on August 24, 2020

South African Tourism. (2023a, March 30). *New study reveals Africa's potential in hosting business events*. https://www.indaba-southafrica.co.za/news/new-study-reveals-africas-potential-in-hosting-business-events.aspx

Suder, G., & Keup, M. (2011). *Expanding event management across and beyond Europe: The MCI Group*. European Case Clearing House.

Trading Economics. (n.d.). GDP—Countries—List/Africa. Tradingeconomics.com. https://tradingeconomics.com/country-list/gdp?continent=africa

United Nations. (n.d.). *India to overtake China as world's most populous country in April 2023, United Nations projects*. United Nations. https://www.un.org/en/desa/india-overtake-china-world-most-populous-country-april-2023-united-nations-projects#:~:text=24%20April%202023%20%2D%20China%20will,the%20population%20of%20mainland%20China.

Van Wyk, M. (2023, January 30). *Meetings Africa 2022—Recap*. Uwin Iwin Incentives. https://uwin-iwin.co.za/meetings-africa-2022-recap/

INDEX

A

Acceptance, 323, 325
    terminated prior to, 324
Accepted practices exchange (APEX), 5, 19, 53–54, 374
    guidelines, 222
    Initiative, 483
Accounting, 193
Accreditation, 94
Action stations, 285–286
Act of God clause, 332
ADA Amendment Act of 2008, 339
"Advancing" of venue, 232
Advertising, 155, 164, 253, 463–464
AfCFTA. *See* African Continental Free Trade Agreement (AfCFTA)
Africa, 523–525
    MEEC industry in, 525
African Continental Free Trade Agreement (AfCFTA), 523
African Society of Association Executives (AfSAE), 525
AfSAE. *See* African Society of Association Executives (AfSAE)
Agenda, 251
Agreement, 323
AI. *See* Artificial intelligence (AI)
Air lift, 436
Air transportation, 8
A La Carte, 288
AMC. *See* Association management company (AMC)

American Association of Oral and Maxillofacial Surgeons (AAOMS), 114–117
American Astronomical Society, 333
American Hotel and Lodging Association (AHLA) Career Development Resources, 21
American Small Animal Association (ASAA), 549–550, 553–554, 556
    hotel room blocks, 570–571
    meeting dates, 557
    members, 566
    mission statement, 550
American Society of Association Executives (ASAE), 234, 341
    Association Career HQ, 22
American Society of Composers, Authors and Publishers (ASCAP), 343
Americans with Disabilities Act (ADA), 338–341, 454
    public accommodations, 340
    purpose of, 339
    ramifications of, 341
American legal system, 334
American Truck Drivers Association, 282
Amphitheaters, 132–133
Ancillary activities, 482
Ancillary events, 470
Ancillary revenue, 329
Annual conference, 550
    reviewing, 550
Annual meetings, 432
Annual Naples Winter Wine Festival, 257–258
Anticipated room revenue, 329
APEX. *See* Accepted practices exchange (APEX)

AR. *See* Augmented reality (AR)
Arbitration, 334
Arenas, 132–133
ARS. *See* Audience response systems (ARS)
Artificial intelligence (AI), 354, 388–390, 395
    ChatGPT, 388, 390–391
    generative, 358
ASAA. *See* American Small Animal Association (ASAA)
ASAE. *See* American Society of Association Executives (ASAE)
ASCAP. *See* American Society of Composers, Authors and Publishers (ASCAP)
Asia, MEEC international aspects in, 515–516
    China, 516–519
    India, 520–521
    Korea, 520
    Thailand, 519–520
Assembly, 6
Association management company (AMC), 22, 64–65
Association meetings, 50, 58
    decision-making process for, 51
    professional, 434–435
Association of Australian Convention Bureaux Inc (AACB), 95
Association of Collegiate Conference and Events Directors-International (ACCED-I) Career Center, 22
Association of Destination Management Executives International (ADMEI), 234
Associations, 50–52, 548–549
    accounts, 217–218
    gatherings and events-purposes and objectives
        board meetings, 54
        committee meetings, 54
        conventions, 53–54
        regional conferences, 54
    marketing and attendance, 55–56
    medical/health, 52
    professional, 52
    SMERFs, 52–53
    trade, 52
    types of, 52–53

Attendance, 55–56
Attended buffet/cafeteria, 285
Attendees, 69
    interaction and communications
        audience response systems and speaker interaction, 382–383
        beacons, 381
        lead retrieval systems, 382
        NFC and RFID, 381
    personalization, 68
Attorney fees, 334
Attrition, 122, 294, 328–330, 452
    damages, 329–330
Audience engagement, 266
Audience response systems (ARS), 382–383, 501
Audiovisuals (AV), 470
    company, 552
    equipment, 458–459
Auditorium/theater style, 473
Augmented reality (AR), 70, 191, 386–387
Australia, international visitors in, 522
Autonomous vehicles/AI, 395–396
AV. *See* Audiovisuals (AV)
Available air lift, 51

B

Bandwidth, 376–377
Banquet event order (BEO), 302, 471–472
Banquet French, 287
Banquet Russian, 287
Bar backs, 299
Basecamp, 265
B2B. *See* Business-to-Business (B2B)
B2C. *See* Business-to-Consumer (B2C)
BCEC. *See* Brisbane Convention and Exhibition Centre (BCEC)
Beacons, 381
Beer, 296
BEO. *See* Banquet event order (BEO)
Best Client-Rated Convention Centre, 522

Beverage
- by bottle, 297
- cash bar, 298
- charge per hour, 297–298
- combination bar, 298
- by drink, 297
- event, reasons for, 294
- labor charges, 299–300
- limited consumption bar, 298
- open bar, 298
- per person, 297

Big data, 389, 395
Billing, 233–234
Blockchain, 396
Blogging, 369–370
BMI. *See* Broadcast Music, Inc. (BMI)
Board meetings, 46–47, 54
Boardroom, 106–107
Brand image, 409
Breaking down, 269–270
Breakout rooms, 107
Break-out sessions, 6, 444
Brisbane Convention and Exhibition Centre (BCEC), 522
Broadcast Music, Inc. (BMI), 343
Brundtland Report, 403
Budget assembly, 441–442
Budget/budgeting, 550–554
- concepts of, 267
- contracts, 567
- expenses, 552
- income, 551, 554–555
- meeting timeline, 567–569
- request for proposal (RFP), 555–557
- transportation, 552

Buffet, 284–285
Busch Stadium, 283
Business
- opportunities, 221–222
- relationships, 334
- services, 194
- transactions, 189

Business-to-Business (B2B)
- exhibitions, 151, 162
- shows, 152–155

Business-to-Consumer (B2C)
- exhibitions, 162
- public shows, 155–156

Business destinations, COVID-19 impact on, 237
Butler service, 287

C

CAD programs. *See* Computer-aided design (CAD) programs
CAEM. *See* Canadian Association of Exposition Management (CAEM)
California's event permitting process, 266–267
Canadian Association of Exposition Management (CAEM), 198
Cancellation, 330–331
Canton Fair, 509–510, 540
Capacity, 324
Carbon offsets, 406
Careers
- American Hotel and Lodging Association (AHLA) Career Development Resources, 21
- American Society of Association Executives (ASAE) Association Career HQ, 22
- Association Management Company (AMC) Institute Talent Center, 22
- Association of Collegiate Conference and Events Directors-International (ACCED-I) Career Center, 22
- Financial & Insurance Conference Professionals (FICP) Mentorship Programme, 22
- Hospitality Sales & Marketing Association International (HSMAI), 22
- IACC scholarships and internships, 23
- Incentive Research Foundation (IRF), 23
- International Association of Exhibitions and Events (IAEE) Career Center, 23
- International Association of Venue Managers (IAVM) Career and Learning Resources, 23
- Meeting Professionals International (MPI) Resources, 23

Professional Convention Management Association (PCMA) Recovery Discovery, 24
Society of Incentive Travel Excellence (SITE), 24–28
Carnet, 533
Cart French, 288
Cashiers, 299
Catered events, 278–279, 280
    A La Carte, 288
    off-premise catering, 280–283
    on-premise catering, 279–280
    style of service, 283–284
Caterer/catering, 194
    definition of, 278
CEMA. *See* Corporate Event Marketing Association (CEMA)
Center for Association Leadership, 341
Center for Exhibition Industry Research (CEIR), 151–152, 198
Central Florida Home and Garden Show, 156
Certified destination management executive, 92
Certified Meeting Professional (CMP)
    examination, 10
CEUs. *See* Continuing education units (CEUs)
Chatbots, 389
ChatGPT, 388, 390–391
China, 516
    convention and exhibition industries in, 516–517
    hotel capacity in, 517
    incentive travel in, 518–519
China Association for Exhibition Centers (CAEC), 518
China Convention and Exhibition Society (CCES), 518
Classroom style, 474
Cleaning services, 194
Clean the World, 408
Clear span tents, 139–140
Clients, 215–216
    association accounts, 217–218
    corporate accounts, 217
    incentive-based organizations, 218
    special event clients, 218

Clinic, 6
Clothing trade fairs, 522
CMP Code of Ethics, 20
CMP-HC program. *See* CMP healthcare subspecialty (CMP-HC) program
CMP healthcare subspecialty (CMP-HC) program, 16–17
CMP international standards
    benefits of certification, 15
    created by and for meeting professionals, 15–16
    healthcare subspecialty (CMP-HC) program, 16–17
Cocktail servers, 299, 306
Collateral materials, 222
College and universities, 133–134
    negotiating your event, 134
        food and beverage, 134–135
Combination buffet, 285
Committee meetings, 54
Committee members, 50
Communications
    with attendees, 489
    guidelines for improving, 488
Community infrastructure, 244
Company sponsorships, 258
Complete meeting package, 122
Complimentary meeting space, 110
Computer-aided design (CAD) programs, 212
Computers, 194, 491
Concessionaires, 108
Concurrent session, 444
Conference, 6, 119
Conference centers, 119–120, 280, 436
    associations and consortiums, 121
    food and beverage, 121
    meeting room spaces, 119–120
    negotiating your event, 122
Conference locations, 557
    day one, 557–558
    day three, 559
    day two, 558–559
Conference program, creation of, 564–565
Congress, 6

Consideration, 323–325
Consortiums, 121
Consulting, 194
Consumer shows, 48
    types of, 156
Continuing education units (CEUs), 54, 550
Contract/contractors, 323–326, 567
  budget
    components of, 326
    differences in, 334
    elements of, 323–324
    and event organizers, 197–198
    food and beverage, 293
    MEEC industry, legal issues in, 323–326
    negotiating meeting, 315
    organizer's development of, 333
    well-crafted, 335
Convention and Visitor Bureau (CVBs), 12, 211, 437
  websites, 355
Convention centers, 111–117, 133
    expenses, 552
    financial structure, 117–118
    negotiating for your event, 118–119
    prices, 51
    and stadiums, 280
    in United States, 112–113
    in world, 112
Convention marketing and sales
    sales processes, 85–86
    site inspections, 88
    site review and leads process, 86–88
Conventions, 4, 50, 53–54, 508, 525
Convention service managers (CSMs), 483, 560
Copyrights, 342
    law, 343
    music copyright, 342–343
    speaker/entertainment copyright, 344
Corbin Ball website, 358
Corkage fees, 299
Corporate accounts, 217
Corporate Event Marketing Association (CEMA), 198
Corporate gatherings and events, 45
Corporate meetings, 45, 58

Corporate social responsibility (CSR), 200, 407, 550
Corporations, 44–45, 440
    board meetings, 46–47
    corporate gatherings and events, 45–46
    department/individual responsible for organizing and planning, 49–50
    incentive trips, 48
    management meetings, 46–47
    public shows, 48–49
    sales training and product launches, 47–48
    stockholder meetings, 46
    training meetings, 47–48
Cost, 435
    savings, 409
COVID-19, 29, 116, 151
    Business Recovery Task Force, 29
    destination management companies (DMCs), 237
    Requests for proposals (RFPs), 437
    virtual and hybrid events, 539–540
    and virtual trade shows, 374
Creativity, and innovation, 223
Crescent round, 474
Crisis management, 166
    mitigation, 337
    preparedness, 337
    recovery, 338
    response, 338
Crisis networks, 236
Crisis preparedness and management
    mitigation, 337
    preparedness, 337
    recovery, 338
    response, 338
    risk, 335–336
Cross-promotional opportunities, 259
Cruise ships, 122–126
    negotiating your event, 126–127
    seasonality, 127–128
CSMs. *See* Convention service managers (CSMs)
Customer, 215
Customer relationship management (CRM), 212
Customizable networks, 368
Customs clearance, 533

D

Damages, 328–329
    payment of, 332–333
Décor, 194, 239
Department/individual responsible for organizing and planning, 49
Design patents, 341
Desktop and mobile tools, 373–374
    APEX, 374
    bandwidth, 376–377
    digital recording, 379
    drones, 380
    on-site event tech infrastructure, 374–380
    virtual tradeshows, 374
    wired *vs.* wireless, 377–378
Destination, 27
    community, 213
Destination and Travel Foundation, 93
Destination Management Certified Professional (DMCP), 234–235
Destination management companies (DMCs), 282, 347, 482–483, 557–558, 567
    for annual conference, 552–553
    association of, 234–235
    best practices in, 235–236
    business model of, 215–216
    business structure of, 212–213
    changing dynamics of, 225
    clients. *See* Clients
    COVID-19 effect on, 237
    definition, structure, and services, 208–209
    vs. destination marketing organization, 211–213
    effectiveness of, 222
    finding and selecting, 234
    flow chart, 216
    job responsibilities, 219
    leads, 257
    management, 226
    networking among attendees, 226–227
    operations, 218–220
        identifying new business opportunities, 221–222
    production of events, 231–233
    program development, 225–226
    program execution, 226–227
    request for proposal (RFP), 222–225
    sales process, 220
    site inspections, 225
    transportation services, 227–231
    wrap-up and billing, 233–234
    organization, 213
        destination management networks, 214–215
        independent operator, 214
        multi-services operator, 214
    sample event programs, 217
    services provided by, 209–211
    suppliers contracted by, 225–226
Destination management networks, 214–215
Destination management organization (DMO), 486
Destination Marketing and Management Organizations (DMMOs), 96–98
Destination marketing organization (DMO), 12, 76–77, 211–212, 355, 437, 486–487, 556–559
    attracting leisure travelers, 79–80
    business case for, 83
    changing scope of responsibilities, 90–91
    charge for services, 78–79
    convention marketing and sales
        sales processes, 85–86
        site inspections, 88
        site review and leads process, 86–87
    departments and staff, 84
    Destinations International (DI), 91–92
        accreditation, 94
        certified destination management executive, 92
        Destination and Travel Foundation, 95
        event impact calculator, 94
        PDM Program, 92
        professional development offerings, 92
        research, 93
    meeting planners need to know about, 81–83
    promoting destination, 80–81
    purpose of, 77–78
    research and advocacy, 93

services for meeting professionals, 89
trends, 96–101
website, 80–81
DestinationNEXT Futures Study, 93
Destination selection, 560
Destinations International (DI), 91–92
    accreditation, 94
    certified destination management executive, 92
    Destination and Travel Foundation, 95
    event impact calculator, 94
    PDM Program, 92
    professional development offerings, 92
    research, 93
Destination stewardship, 98–99
Destination weddings, 138
DI. *See* Destinations International (DI)
Differentiation, 409
Digital recording, 379
Direct mail, 63–64
Direct marketing, 253, 462–463
Disability, 339
Dispute resolution, 333–335
Distributor of products, 152–153
Diversity, 69
DMCs. *See* Destination management companies (DMCs)
DMO. *See* Destination marketing organization (DMO)
Drayage, 182
Drive-to markets, 236
Drones, 380

E

EACA. *See* Exhibitor-Appointed Contractors Association (EACA)
EACs. *See* Exhibitor-appointed contractors (EACs)
Earth Hour, 404
EDPA. *See* Exhibit Designers & Producers Association (EDPA)
Educational seminars, 54

EEAA. *See* Exhibition and Event Association of Australasia (EEAA)
EIC. *See* Events Industry Council (EIC)
Electrical, 194
E-mail, 63–64
Emotional commitment, 252
Employees, 485–486
Engagement marketing, 253
Entertainers, 470, 480–481
Entertainment, 8
Entertainment Agency, 194
"Entire agreement" clause, 327
Environmental practices
    decorate with nature, 417
    eat local, 417
    inform everyone, 418
    local destination, 416
    reduce, reuse, and recycle, 416–417
    repurposing, 418
    save energy, 418
    technology, 416
    use paper wisely, 418
    volume up, 417
ESC. *See* Exposition Service Contractors (ESC)
ESG. *See* Event Specification Guide (ESG)
Ethics, 346
Europe
    international association meetings, 513–514
    MEEC, international aspects in
        European Society of Cardiology (ESC) Congress, 513–514
        Hannover Fairgrounds, 511–513
    trade fairs in, 513
European Society of Cardiology (ESC) Congress, 513–514
Event budgeting, 438
    establish financial goals, 438–439
    identify expenses and revenue sources, 439–441
Event Industry Council, 11
    member organizations, 12
EventMobi, 266
Event organizers, contractors and, 197–198

Events, 5
- apps, 372–373
- attendee registration profits, 433–438
- design, neuroscience in, 68
- impact calculator, 94
- management circles, 235–236
- meetings and. *See* Meetings
- outdoors, 138–139
- planners, 106–107
- production of, 231–233
- professionals, 283
- services, 192
- sponsors, 257
- technology, 69–70, 192

Events Industry Council (EIC), 19, 222, 410, 436–437
- standards, 414–415

Event Specification Guide (ESG), 483–484
Exclusive services, 196–197
Exhibit Designers & Producers Association (EDPA), 199
Exhibition, 4–5, 63, 150, 508, 527, 531
- at American tradeshow, 530–531
- in Asia, 515–516
- halls, 113
- managers, 164
- organizers, 157, 166–167
- programs, 152–153, 157

Exhibition and Event Association of Australasia (EEAA), 199
Exhibition management, 156
- companies, 62–64, 157–158, 161–162, 164
- exhibition organizer, 157
- facility manager, 157–158
- knowledge, skills, and abilities (KSAS) of exhibition manager, 159–161
- official service contractor (OSC), 158–159

Exhibition management companies (EMCs), 62–64
Exhibitions and trade shows
- business-to-business (B2B) Shows, 152–155
- Business-to-Consumer (B2C) public shows, 155–156
- considerations in managing
  - location, 161–163
  - marketing and promotion, 164–165
  - risk and crisis management, 166–167
  - shipping and storage, 163
  - technology, 165–166
- consolidation shows, 156
- exhibitor perspective, 167
  - exhibit design principles, 167–171
  - return on investment (ROI), 173–174
  - staffing the exhibit, 171, 173
- history, 150–152

Exhibition Services & Contractors Association (ESCA), 199
Exhibit layout, 169
Exhibit manager, 169
Exhibitor-appointed contractors (EACs), 196–197
Exhibitor-Appointed Contractors Association (EACA), 198
Exhibitor perspective, 167
- exhibit design principles, 167–171
- return on investment (ROI), 173–174
- staffing the exhibit, 171, 173

Exhibitors, 151, 174, 185, 551
- service manual, 183

Expenses, 439–441
Experiential marketing, 253
Exposition, 4, 5
Exposition Service Contractors (ESC), 23, 109

F

Facebook, 367
Facial recognition, 375
Facility, 27
- manager, 157–158

Fairs, 244
Familiarization, 347, 438
Family style/English service, 286
Fam trips, 347, 438
F&B. *See* Food and beverage (F&B)

Federal Fair Labor Standards Act (FLSA)
    attitude adjustment, 345
    overtime pay requirements, 344
    overtime provisions, 344
Federal procurement policies, 60
Festivals, 244
Film festival, 349
Finance, 193
    concepts of, 267–269
Financial goals, 438–439
Financial & Insurance Conference Professionals (FICP) Mentorship Programme, 22
Financial structure, 107–108
    convention centers, 107–108
Fire safety permits, 264
5G, 395
    wireless capabilities, 377–378
Fixed costs, 439
FLSA. *See* Federal Fair Labor Standards Act (FLSA)
Food and beverage (F&B), 8, 107–108, 109, 471–472
    attrition, 294
    categories of liquor, 295
        beer, 296
        spirits, 295
        wine/champagne, 295–296
    catered events, 278–279
        off-premise catering, 280–283
        on-premise catering, 279–280
        style of service, 283–289
    contracts, 293
    events, 266
    food consumption guidelines, 291
        menu restrictions, 292–293
        some general guidelines, 291–292
    menus, 289–290
    minimum, 267–268
    quality of, 278
    reasons for beverage event, 294
    service requirements, 305–306
        cocktail servers, 306
        service timing, 307
        set over guarantee, 306
    trends and best practices before COVID-19, 307–308

Food consumption guidelines, 291
    menu restrictions, 292–293
    some general guidelines, 291–293
Food Runners, 408
Food trade fairs, 522
Force majeure, 332–333, 348
Formal communication, 487–488
Formal meeting, 10
Forum, 6
"Four-corners" rule of interpretation, 327
4G/4G LTE mobile phones, 377
Frame tent, 139
Frauds, statute of, 326–327
Freeman Companies, 421
Function room layouts, 472–473
    auditorium or theater style, 473
    classroom style, 474
    round tables, 474–476
Functions, types of, 283–284
Funding of activities and projects, 406

G

Gamification, 165
Gantt charts, 251
Gatherings
    association management companies, 64–65
    economic and social impact of, 347
    exhibition management companies, 62–64
    independent meeting managers, 66–67
    meeting-management companies, 65
    organizations arranging
        labor unions, 61–62
        political organizations, 61
    professional congress organizers, 65–66
    trends and best practices, 67–70
GBAC. *See* Global Biorisk Advisory Council (GBAC)
GBTA. *See* Global Business Travel Association (GBTA)
General/plenary session, 444

General service contractor (GSC), 180–185, 189, 552
    business of, 189
    definition of, 180–181
    responsibilities, 181–185
    software, 191
General Sponsorships, 164
Generative AI, 358
Giraffe Manor, Nairobi, 136
Global business events
    direct impacts of, 3
    total impacts of, 4
Global Business Travel Association (GBTA), 516–517
Global commercial exhibition organizing companies, 528
Global Consortium of Entrepreneurship Centers (GCEC) conference, 133–134
Global Exhibition Barometer in 2019, 508
Global Experience Specialists (GES), 163, 412
Goals, 432, 550
Go LIVE Together (GLT) Coalition, 151
Google, 367, 391
Google Drive, 265, 373
Google Forms, 373
Google Groups, 359
Government, 58–59
    agencies, 264
    department/individual responsible for organizing and planning, 60–61
    financial rules and regulations, 59–60
    meetings, 58
    security, 60
Government-sponsored meetings, 60
Grand Carolina Resort and SPA, 419–420
Green and sustainable meetings, 401–404
    benefits of sustainability, 409
        cost savings, 409
        differentiation, 409
        enhanced brand image, 409
        raise awareness, 409
        social benefits, 410
    definition, 401
    evaluation of sustainable efforts, 418
    greenwashing, 413–414
    ISO 20121, 411–413
    Meetgreen^r Calculator 2.0, 418–419
    process for sustainable practices, 414–415
        best environmental practices, 416–418
    professional
        Freeman, 421
        Grand Carolina Resort and SPA, 419–420
        Oregon Convention Center, 420–421
    standards, 410–411
    trends and best practices, 422
    triple bottom line, 404
        people (social impact), 407–408
        planet (environmental impact), 405–406
        profit (economic impact), 404–405
    United Nations sustainable development goals, 411
Greenwashing, 413–414
Gross domestic product (GDP), 3, 513
Ground operator, 208
Ground transportation, 8, 162
Group history, 430
GSC. *See* General service contractor (GSC)
Guarantee, 294, 472

H

Hand service or captain, 288
Hannover Fairgrounds, 511
Harborside International Golf Center, 559
Hard land line, 491
Hashtags, 370–371
HCEA. *See* Healthcare Convention and Exhibitors Association (HCEA)
Healthcare Convention and Exhibitors Association (HCEA), 199
Heavy Equipment Operators Union, 187
Hierarchy (power distance), 534–535
Holograms, 200–201
Hospitality Sales & Marketing Association International (HSMAI), 22
Hospitality suites, 300–301

Hosted buyer exhibition, 153
Hotels, 106, 107, 355–356
    attrition, cancellation, and termination provisions in, 328–329
    budget, 551
    contracts, negotiating, 317–318
    financial structure, 107–108
    negotiating your event, 108
        food and beverage, 109
        local meetings and events, 110
        revenue generating departments, 109–110
        room rates, 108–109
        seasonality, 110–111
    physical characteristics, meeting room spaces, 106–107
    rooms, 555
    sleeping room rates, 322
    type of, 436
    yield management, 322–323
"Hot" menu items, 290
House account, 221
Housing, 451–454, 470–471
HSMAI. *See* Hospitality Sales & Marketing Association International (HSMAI)
Hundredweight, 182
Hybrid events, 69
Hybrid meetings, 356–357, 376
    types of, 392

I

IACC. *See* International Association of Conference Centers (IACC)
IACC scholarships and internships, 23
IAEE. *See* International Association of Exhibitions and Events (IAEE)
IAPCO. *See* International Association of Professional Congress Organizers (IAPCO)
ICCA. *See* International Congress and Convention Association (ICCA)
ICHRIE. *See* International Council on Hotel, Restaurant and Institutional Education (ICHRIE)

Identity (individualism *vs.* collectivism), 534
IEIA. *See* Indian Exhibition Industry Association (IEIA)
ILEA. *See* International Live Events Association (ILEA)
IMEX Group, 153, 435
    hosted buyers, 154
Immediate post-meeting activities, 573–574
IMPACT Exhibition and Convention Centre, 519
Impossibility, 332
Incentive-based organizations, 218
Incentive Research Foundation (IRF), 23
Incentive Travel Index, 48
Incentive travel programs, 215
Incentive trips, 48
Inclusion, 69
Income, 554–555
    sources of, 554
"In conjunction with" (ICWs), 556
Independent meeting managers, 66–67
Independent operator, 214
India, 520–521
    lion logo, 521
    MEEC activity in, 521
Indian Exhibition Industry Association (IEIA), 520
Indirect costs, 439
Individual contractors, 183
Industry standardization, 356
Industry trade shows, 218
Informal communication, 488
Information resources, 357–359
In-line exhibit, 170
Innovation, creativity and, 224
Instagram, 367
Institute, 7
Insurance, 553
Intellectual property
    music copyright, 342–343
    patents, 341
    protection of, 348–349
    speaker/entertainment copyright, 344
    trademarks, 342
Interactive/internet marketing, 253–254

Interactive learning, 445
Internal meeting planners, 62
International Association of Conference Centers (IACC), 121, 436
International Association of Exhibitions and Events (IAEE), 23, 61, 63, 151, 199
International Association of Professional Congress Organizers (IAPCO), 208
International Association of Retired Persons, 282
International Association of Venue Managers (IAVM) Career and Learning Resources, 23
International Congress and Convention Association (ICCA), 509, 513, 542
  International considerations MEEC, international aspects in
    contractual and procedural issues, 532–533
    customs clearance, 533
    lessons to be learned, 530–531
    methods of exhibiting, 531–532
    protocol, 533–538
      hierarchy (power distance), 534–535
      identity (individualism *vs.* collectivism), 534
      truth (uncertainty avoidance), 535–538
International Council on Hotel, Restaurant and Institutional Education (ICHRIE), 280
International freight forwarders, 533
International Live Events Association (ILEA), 234
International meetings, 514
International trade fair, 531
  activity, 513
Interstate Hotels & Resorts, Inc., 318–319
IRF. *See* Incentive Research Foundation (IRF)
Island booths, 170
ISO 20121, 411–413

J

Joint ventures, 531

K

Kansas City Chiefs, 128–132
Kansas Sports, Boat & Travel Show, 156
Keynote address, 444
Key partners, 567
Knowledge, skills, and abilities (KSAs), 13
  of exhibition manager, 159–161
Korea, 520
KSAs. *See* Knowledge, skills, and abilities (KSAs)

L

Labor charges, 299–300
Labor costs, 268–269
  for decorators, 268
Labor issues, 344–345
Labor Management Relations Act, 186
Labor practices, 186
Labor/trade unions, 185–187
Labor union market, 61–62
Latin America
  MEEC, international aspects in, 527
  population base of, 526
Leadership in Energy and Environment Design (LEED), 525–526
Lead retrieval systems, 165, 382
Lecture, 7
LEED. *See* Leadership in Energy and Environment Design (LEED)
Legal subject, 324
Leisure travelers, attracting, 79–80
Letter of agreement, 323
Letter of intent, 323
Levels, 446
Liability insurance, 265
Lighting technology, 171
LinkedIn, 368
Liquidated damages, 335
Liquor, 295
  beer, 296
  call brands, 295

permits, 264
premium brands, 295
spirits, 295
well brands, 295
wine/champagne, 295–296
Live streaming, 368–369
Liz King Caruso's techsytalk, 358
Local contacts, 487
Local event, 110
Local meetings and events, 110
Lodging, 7
Logistical considerations
    housing, 451–454
    refreshment breaks and meal functions, 454
    registration, 449–450
        fees, 450–451
    speaker arrangements, 454–457
Logistics, 192
London Fashion Week, 512

M

Major life activity, 339
Management
    companies, 155, 164–165
    meetings, 45–47
    models, 527
Mandatory attendance, 58
Marketing, 55–56
    committee, 562–564
    and communications, 359–366
        E-blasts, 362–363
        event websites, 360–361
        mobile websites, 361–362
        online registration, 365–366
        room design software, 364–365
        selling show floor, 365
        video marketing, 364
        websites and strategic communications, 359
    costs, 268–26
    funds for, 553

    and promotion, 459–461
        advertising, 463–464
        direct marketing, 462
        online/inbound marketing, 462
        personal selling, 461–462
        public relations, 463
        sales promotions, 462
Material handling, 180–183, 192, 194
McCormick Place Convention Center, 558
Meal functions, 454
Media
    attract and accommodate, 495–497
    outlets, 497–498
    relations, develop and manage, 493–494
    special events working with, 260–262
    streaming, 379
MEEC gatherings
    associations, 50–52
        marketing and attendance, 55–56
        medical/health, 52
        professional, 52
        SMERFs, 52–53
        trade, 52
    corporations, 44–45
        board meetings, 45
        orporate gatherings and events, 45
        department/individual responsible for organizing and planning, 49
        incentive trips, 48
        management meetings, 46–47
        public shows, 48
        sales training and product launches, 47–48
        stockholder meetings, 46
        training meetings, 47–48
    entities help organize gatherings, 62
    government, 58–59
        department/individual responsible for organizing and planning, 60–61
        financial rules and regulations, 59–60
        security, 60
    organizations arranging gatherings
        labor unions, 61
        political organizations, 61

Meetgreen® Calculator 2.0, 418–419
Meeting Professionals International (MPI), 61, 234, 414
    Sustainable Event Strategist Certification, 418–419
Meeting Professionals International (MPI) Resources, 23
Meetings, 4–6, 392
    contract, 328
    and event goal(s), 431–432
    and event specification guide, 483–484
    facility, type of, 436
    history of, 10
    industry portals, 357–359
    managing on-site team, 485
        employees, 485–486
        temporary staff, 486
        volunteers, 486–487
    on-site communications
        personal communications, 487–489
        use of technology, 489–492
    on-site management
        ancillary events, 482–483
        common issues, 477–480
        controlling costs, 484
        function room layouts, 472–476
        on-site audiovisual, 481–482
        registration and housing, 470–471
        speakers and entertainers, 480–481
        specification guide, 483–484
    planners, 28, 49–51, 56, 58, 60–62, 64, 81–85, 106, 108–111
    planning, 10
    postconvention review, 500–502
    public relations
        attract and accommodate media, 495–497
        definition of, 493
        develop and manage media relations, 493–494
        media outlets, 497–498
        news releases, 494–495
        preconvention meetings, 499–500
        select and manage spokespersons, 498–499
    services for, 27–28
    sponsor, 26
Meetings and Business Events Competency Standards (MBECS), 13
Meetings, expositions, events, and convention (MEEC) industry, 2–4, 314, 508, 548
    academic community, 18
    Africa, 523–525
    Americans with Disabilities Act (ADA), 338–341
    Asia, 515–516
        China, 516–519
        India, 520–521
        Korea, 520
        Thailand, 519–520
    associations, 18
    attrition, 328–330
    Australia, 522
    cancellation, 330–331
    Canton Fair, 540
    career planning, 28
    careers in
        American Hotel and Lodging Association (AHLA) Career Development Resources, 21
        American Society of Association Executives (ASAE) Association Career HQ, 22
        Association Management Company (AMC) Institute Talent Center, 22
        Association of Collegiate Conference and Events Directors-International (ACCED-I) Career Center, 22
        Financial & Insurance Conference Professionals (FICP) Mentorship Programme, 22
        Hospitality Sales & Marketing Association International (HSMAI), 22
        IACC scholarships and internships, 23
        Incentive Research Foundation (IRF), 23
        International Association of Exhibitions and Events (IAEE) Career Center, 23

International Association of Venue
  Managers (IAVM) Career and Learning
  Resources, 23
Meeting Professionals International (MPI)
  Resources, 23
Professional Convention Management
  Association (PCMA) Recovery
  Discovery, 24
Society of Incentive Travel Excellence
  (SITE), 24–28
CMP code of ethics, 20
contracts, 293
COVID-19, impact of
  changes to event protocols and design in
    response to, 30
  increase in advocacy for events industry's
    workforce, 30
crisis preparedness and management
  mitigation, 337
  preparedness, 337
  recovery, 338
  response, 338
  risk, 335–336
direct impacts of global business events, 3
dispute resolution, 333–335
diversity, equity, inclusion, and accessibility,
  32–33
ESC Congress 2020, 539
ethics in, 346
  supplier relations, 347–348
Europe, 511
  European Society of Cardiology (ESC)
    Congress, 513–514
  Hannover Fairgrounds, 511–513
Events Industry Council (EIC), 19
evolution and maturation of, 13
  CMP international standards, 15–16
  Meetings and Business Events Competency
    Standards (MB), 13–14
force majeure, 332–333
history of, 9–12
industry terminology and practice, 4–7
intellectual property
  copyrights, 342
  music copyright, 342–343
  speaker/entertainment copyright, 344
  patents, 341
  trademarks, 342
international considerations
  contractual and procedural issues, 532–533
  customs clearance, 533
  lessons to be learned, 530–531
  methods of exhibiting, 531–532
  protocol, 533–534
  terminology, 532
international scope of, 508
key hotel group meeting contract clauses, 327
labor issues, 344–345
Latin America, 526
meetings/events professionals, 17–18
Middle East, 525–526
models for, 508
negotiation
  contracts, 317–318
  naming names, 318–323
  strategies, 315–317
organizational structure of tourism and
  hospitality industry
  food and beverage, 8
  lodging, 7
  tourism and recreation, 8
  transportation and travel, 8–9
ownership, sponsorship, and management
  models, 527
  global commercial exhibition organizing
    companies, 528
  Professional Congress Organizer (PCO),
    527–528
parol evidence, 327
professional preparation for career in, 71–72
social impact, 33
statute of frauds, 326
sustainability, 32
total impacts of global business events, 4
transforming role of technology
  content and community, 31

INDEX

595

data security, trust, and responsibility, 31
increased technology use for engagement, 30
pivot from event logistics to event strategists, 31–32
transition to omni-channel events, 31
trends and best practices regarding, 348–349
UFI global congress 2020, 540
varies around globe, 508–510

Meetings, expositions, events, and conventions (MEEC) industry, 244
Meetings/less presentations, 69
Meeting space, 107
    requirements, 436
Meeting timeline
    meeting day activities, 573
    one year to six months countdown, 567–569
    pre-meeting activities, 572–573
    six months to day of meeting, 569–572
Mega convention centers, 158
Memorandum of understanding, 323
Mental capacity, 326
Menu choices, 282
Merchandising, 252–253
Michigan Golf Show, 156
Microsoft, 373
Middle East, trade fairs and exhibitions in, 525
Mixed reality, 385–386, 396
    augmented reality, 386
    virtual reality/360 videos, 387
Mixing service styles, 289–291
Mobile communication, 490
Mobile devices, 360
Mobile kitchens, 280
Monitor on-site communications, 492
Multilevel exhibits, 170
Multi-services operator, 214
Multiuse facility, 133
Music copyright, 342–343

N

NAICS codes. *See* North American Industry Classification System (NAICS) codes

National Association of Broadcasters, 435
National Association of Convention Bureaus, 150
National Association of Exposition Managers, 151
National Western Stock Show, 163
Natural attractions, 8
Needs analysis, 106, 430–431
Negotiation
    contracts, 317–318
    naming names, 318–320
    strategies, 315–316
Negotiator, 315
News releases, 494–495
New York City Marathon, 259–260
Nonresidential conference centers, 121
Nontraditional destination, 358–359
Nontraditional room setup, 475
North American Industry Classification System (NAICS) codes, 9

O

Objective, 432
OCEC. *See* Oman Convention and Exhibition Centre (OCEC)
Offer, 323
Official service contractor (OSC), 156, 158–159
Off-premise events, 281–282
Oman Convention and Exhibition Centre (OCEC), 525–526
"One-size-fits-all" proposition, 446
One-way communications, 359–360
Online/inbound marketing, 462
Online meetings, 393–394
    creation of, 393–394
Online RFPS, 335–336
On-site audiovisual, 481–482
On-site communication, 492
    equipment and resources, 489–492
    meeting/convention/event, 490
    monitor on-site communications, 492
    personal communications, 487–489

use of technology
- equipment, 491
- equipment and resources, 489–490
- meeting/convention/event, 490
- monitor on-site communications, 492

On-site event tech infrastructure, 374–380
- bandwidth, 376–377
- digital recordings, 379
- drones, 380
- facial recognition, 375
- streaming media, 378–379
- wired *vs.* wireless, 377–378

On-site management
- ancillary events, 482–483
- common issues
  - access, 480
  - floors, 479
  - obstacles, 477
  - power, 477–478
  - rigging, 478–479
- controlling costs, 484
- food and beverage, 471–472
- function room layouts, 472–473
  - auditorium or theater style, 473
  - classroom style, 474
  - round tables, 474–475
- meeting and event specification guide, 483–484
- on-site audiovisual, 481–482
- registration and housing, 470–471
- speakers and entertainers, 480–481

On-site promotion, 183–184
On-site team, managing, 485
- employees, 485–486
- temporary staff, 486

Oracle, 408
Orange County Convention Center, 480
Oregon Convention Center, 420–421
Organizations, 44–45
- of company, 191–193

OSC. *See* Official service contractor (OSC)
Osram Sylvania, Inc., 331

Outdoor events, 138–139
- tents, 139–140
- venue challenges, 139
- venue permits, 140

Outdoor sports, 139
Overtime pay, 344–345
Ownership, 527

P

Paid attendees, 51–52
Panel discussion, 7
Parade permits, 264
Parol evidence, 327
"parol" evidence, 327
Partnerships, 565–567
PA System, 491
Patents, 341
PCOs. *See* Professional congress organizers (PCOs)
PDM Program, 92
Peninsula booths, 170
People (social impact), 407–408
Per diem rates, 59
Performance clauses, 328–329
Performing rights organizations (PROs), 342–343
Permits, 264
Personal selling, 255, 461–462
Person-made attractions, 8
Physical commitment, 252
Pickup, 328
Planet (environmental impact), 405–406
Planning MEEC gatherings
- budget assembly, 441–442
- event budgeting, 438
  - establish financial goals, 438–439
  - identify expenses and revenue sources, 439–441
- logistical considerations
  - audiovisual equipment, 458–459
  - housing, 451–454
  - inclusion through speaker selection, 457–458

refreshment breaks and meal functions, 454
registration, 449–450
fees, 450–451
speaker arrangements, 454
marketing and promotion, 459–461
advertising, 463–464
direct marketing, 462–463
online/inbound marketing, 462
personal selling, 461–462
public relations, 463
sales promotions, 462
needs analysis, 430–431
program planning, 442–446
content, 446–447
session scheduling, 447–448
types, 444–446
setting goals and objectives
improve event attendee registration profits, 433–438
meeting and event goal(s), 431–432
Plant patents, 34
Plated/American style service, 287
Podcasting, 370
Pole tent, 139–140
Policy statements, 251
Political events, 61
Post-conference technology applications, 383
evaluations and surveys, 383–384
marketing media, 384–385
Postconvention review, 500
evaluation, 500–502
Poster sessions, 446
Potential exhibitors, 155
Practices implementation, 19
Pre-convention (precon) meeting, 499–500
Prefunction space, 107
use of, 107
Pre-meeting activities, 572–573
Presenter contract, 457
Preset, 287
Presidential Inauguration Day Parade, 247–248
Press, 61

Price, 325
Primary social channels, 366–368
Production, 192
costs, 268
of events, 231–233
schedule, 481–482
Product launches, 47–48
Professional, 214–215
Professional congress organizers (PCOs), 65–66, 208, 348, 527–528
Professional Convention Management Association (PCMA) Recovery Discovery, 24, 61, 234
Professional development offerings, 92
Professional relationships, 493
Professional speaker, 444
Profit (economic impact), 404–405
Program development, 225–226
Program execution, 226–227
Program planning, 432, 442–444
content, 446–447
session scheduling, 447–448
types, 444–446
Promoting, 252–253
Promotional items sponsorship, 164
Promotional mix, 252–255
Proposal, 323
process, 224
PROs. *See* Performing rights organizations (PROs)
Protocol
gender association (masculinity *vs.* femininity), 535
hierarchy (power distance), 534–535
identity (individualism *vs.* collectivism), 534
truth (uncertainty avoidance), 535–538
Proxy statement, 46
Public address systems, 490
Public event, 244
Public exhibitions, 155–156
Publicity, 254
Public relations, 254, 463
activities, 496
attract and accommodate media, 495–496
definition of, 493

develop and manage media relations, 493–494
media outlets, 497–498
news releases, 494–495
preconvention meetings, 499–500
purpose of, 254–255
select and manage spokespersons, 498–499
Public shows (expositions), 48–49, 62
Public spaces, 107

Q

QR codes, 450

R

Rack rates, 322
Radio coverage, 262
Radio frequency identification (RFID), 165, 381
Real estate, 326
Reasonable accommodation, 338–339
Reception, 286
Recreation, 8–9
Red Bull, 508
Refreshment breaks, 107
and meal functions, 454
Regional conferences, 54
Registration, 449–450, 470–471
desks, 107
fees, 440–441, 450–451, 554
Registration and Housing Companies, 453–454
Relationship, 246–249
management strategy, 236
marketing, 182
Rental costs, 267–268
Requests for proposals (RFPs), 197, 222–225, 281, 347, 436–437, 490, 555–557
COVID-19 lessons learned for, 437
final portion of, 556
Residential conference centers, 121
Restaurants, 137
Retreat facilities, 135–137

Return on investment (ROI), 173, 188, 217, 257, 432, 550
calculating, 173, 175
measuring, 174
Revenues
generating departments, 109–110
sources, 439–441
RFID. *See* Radio frequency identification (RFID)
RFPs. *See* Requests for proposals (RFPs)
Risk, 335
management, 335
Riverbanks Zoo and Garden, 400–401
Robert Morris University (RMU), 33–39
Rocky Mountains and Colorado, 245–246
ROI. *See* Return on investment (ROI)
Room block, 452
Rooming list, 452, 454
Rooms
layouts, 119–120
rates, 108–109
rental charges, 304
setups, 302
aisle space, 303
per person, 303
Rotation of locations, 435
Round tables, 474–476
Roundtables and discussion groups, 445
Route 91 outdoor music festival, 336
Russian service, 287

S

Sales, 192
efforts, 257–258
permits or licenses, 264
process, 85–86, 220
promotion, 254, 462
training, 47–48
Sanitation permits, 264
SAPDC. *See* Small Animal Preventive Disease Certificate (SAPDC)
Schedules, 251

SDGs. *See* Sustainable Development Goals (SDGs)
Seasonality, 110–111
Second Life (virtual world), 357
Second site inspection
 day one, 560–561
 day three, 562
 day two, 562
Security, 299
 costs, 268
Self-service, 283
Seminars, 6, 54
Service companies, 164
Service contractors, 186–187
 best practices, 200–201
 evolution of, 188–191
 exhibitor-appointed contractor (EAC), 196–197
 general services contractor (GSC)
  definition of, 180–181
  responsibilities, 181–185
 labor/trade unions, 185–187
 organization of company, 191–193
 organizer and, 201
 relationship between contractors and event organizers, 197–198
 sales representatives of, 189
 specialty service contractors, 193–196
Service timing, 307
SESAC. *See* Society of European Stage Authors and Composers (SESAC)
Session
 scheduling, 447–448
 typical description of, 446–447
Set over guarantee, 306
SGMP. *See* Society of Government Meeting Professionals (SGMP)
Shoulder, 107
Show/event organizers, 184–185
Show management, 155
Signing authority, 484
SITE. *See* Society of Incentive Travel Excellence (SITE)
Site inspections, 88, 225

Site review and leads process, 86–87
Site selection process, 434–438
Skill level, 446
Small Animal Preventive Disease Certificate (SAPDC), 550, 555
SMART objectives, 432–433
Smartphones, 491
Social channels, 369
Social event, 7
Social impact, 33
Social interaction, 367
Social media, 63, 254, 358, 366
 blogging, 369–370
 hashtags, 370–371
 live streaming, 368–369
 podcasting, 370
 primary social channels, 366–368
 social selling, 371–372
Social networking, 366–367, 490
Social selling, 371–372
Society, 326
Society of European Stage Authors and Composers (SESAC), 343
Society of Government Meeting Professionals (SGMP), 61
Society of Incentive Travel Excellence (SITE), 24–28
Sourcing, 67
South Africa, MEEC industry in, 525
South by Southwest (SXSW), 255–256
Space sizes, 113
Speaker, 480–481
 arrangements, 454–457
 bureau, 455
 copyright, 344
 interaction, 382–383
 ready room, 456
Special communication equipment, 490
Special events, 244
 breakdown of, 269–270
 budget, 267
 clients, 218
 company, 244
 examples of, 249–250

history and background, 245–246
labor costs, 268–269
management, tools of, 250–251
marketing costs, 269
merchandising and promoting, 252–253
planning tools for, 250–251
preparing for, 264–265
production costs, 268
promotional mix, 253–256
relationship, 246–249
rental costs, 267–268
security costs, 268
software and tools for, 265–267
sponsorships for, 164, 257–260
talent costs, 269
trends and best practices in, 270–271
types of, 257
understanding community infrastructure, 252
understanding target market for, 262–264
working definition of, 244–245
working with media for event, 260–262
Specialty service contractors, 193–196, 198
Specific-use facilities, 132
    financial structure, 132–133
Spirits, 295
Spokespersons, select and manage, 498–499
Sponsors, 551, 553, 566
    gatherings, 58
Sponsorships, 259–260, 527
    for special event, 258
    for special events, 257–260
Sports facilities, 132
Stadiums, 132–133
Staffing, 212
Stakeholders, 4, 431
Stand, 532
Standard booth, 169
Statute of frauds, 326–327
Stockholder meetings, 46
Streaming media, 378–379
Stronco, 193
Style of service, catered events, 283–284
    action stations, 285–286
    attended buffet/cafeteria, 285
    Banquet French, 287
    buffet, 284–285
    butler service, 287
    Cart French, 288
    combination buffet, 285
    family style/English service, 286
    hand service or captain, 288
    preset, 287
    reception, 286
    Russian service, 287
    style of service
        A La Carte, 288
        mixing service styles, 289
        plated/American style service, 287
    waiter parade, 289
Subject-matter expert, 445
Supplier relations, 347–348
Suppliers for convention, 548
Sustainability, 32, 200, 403
    benefits of, 409
        cost savings, 409
        differentiation, 409
        enhanced brand image, 409
        raise awareness, 409
        social benefits, 410
Sustainable Development Goals (SDGs), 411
Sustainable efforts, evaluation of, 418
Sustainable meetings, 403
Sustainable practices, process for, 414–416
SXSW. *See* South by Southwest (SXSW)
Symposium, 7
Systems integrator, 157

T

Tablescapes, 303–304
    examples, 304
Taft-Hartley Act of 1947, 186
Talent costs, 269
Target audience, 65
Targeted electronic communication, 155

Target market, 460
  for special events, 262–264
Technology, 191, 354–355
  artificial intelligence and big data, 388–391
  attendee interaction and communications
    audience response systems and speaker interaction, 382–383
    beacons, 381
    lead retrieval systems, 382
    NFC and RFID, 381
  desktop and mobile tools, 373–374
    APEX, 374
    bandwidth, 376–377
    digital recording, 379
    onsite event tech infrastructure, 374–375
    streaming media, 378–379
    virtual tradeshows, 374
    wired *vs.* wireless, 377–378
  event apps, 372–373
  marketing and communications, 359
    E-blasts, 362–363
    event websites, 360–361
    mobile websites, 361–362
    online registration, 365–366
    room design software, 364–365
    selling show floor, 365
    video marketing, 365
    websites and strategic communications, 359–360
  mixed reality, 385–386
    augmented reality, 386–387
    virtual reality/360 videos, 387–388
  on-site communications
    equipment, 490–492
    meeting/convention/event, 490
    monitor on-site communications, 492
  post-conference technology applications, 383
    evaluations and surveys, 383–384
    marketing media, 384–385
  social media, 366
    blogging, 369–370
    hashtags, 370–371
    live streaming, 368–369
    podcasting, 370
    primary social channels, 366–368
    social selling, 371–372
  transforming role of
    content and community, 31
    data security, trust, and responsibility, 31
    pivot from event logistics to event strategists, 31–32
    transition to omni-channel events, 31
  virtual and hybrid meetings, 392
    hybrid meetings, 392
    large-scale virtual meetings, 394–395
    online meetings and webinars, 393–394
    roaring tech twenties, 395–396
  virtual site selection and research, 355
    meeting industry portals and information resources, 357–359
    online RFPS, 355–356
    virtual tours, 356–357
Television, 262
Temporary staff, 212, 486
Terrapass, 406
Thailand, 519–520
Theaters, 132
Third parties, 65
3D Printing, 396
Total fixed costs, 441
Tourism, 8–9
Track, 446
Trade fairs, 150, 527
  in Asia, 515–516
  bond, 533
  industry, 508, 511
Trademarks, 342
  infringement at exhibition, 343
Trade publications, 155
Trade show (exhibition), 5, 62–64
  exhibitions and. *See* Exhibitions and trade shows

Traditional planning, 68
Traditional venue layouts, 472–473
Training meetings, 47, 54
Transportation, 8
    company, 555
    services, 227–231
Travel, 8
    mode of, 436
Travel and Tourism Satellite Accounts (TTSAs), 9
Trends and best practices before COVID-19
    Food and beverage (F&B), 307–308
Triple bottom line, green and sustainable meetings, 404
    people (social impact), 407–408
    planet (environmental impact), 405–406
    profit (economic impact), 404–405
Truth (uncertainty avoidance), 535–538
TTSAs. *See* Travel and Tourism Satellite Accounts (TTSAs)
Twitch, 368
Twitter, 367, 490
Two-month post-meeting activities, 574–575
Two-way communication model, 360

U

UFI. *See* Union of International Fairs (UFI)
Unforeseen calamities, impact of
    changes to event protocols and design in response to, 30
    increase in advocacy for events industry's workforce, 30
    responding to environmental, social, and cultural occurrences, 29
Union of International Fairs (UFI), 508, 199
    global congress 2020, 540
United Nations sustainable development goals, 411
Unusual venues, 137–138
Utility patents, 341

V

Variable costs, 439
    per attendee, 441
Vienna Convention Bureau, 100–101
Viral marketing, 367
Virtual and hybrid meetings, 392
    hybrid meetings, 392
    large-scale virtual meetings, 394–395
    online meetings and webinars, 393–394
    roaring tech twenties, 395–396
Virtual events, 394
Virtual/hybrid meetings, 396
Virtual Reality (VR), 387–388
Virtual site inspection, 356
Virtual site selection and research, 355
    meeting industry portals and information resources, 357–359
    online RFPS, 355–356
    virtual tours, 356–357
Virtual tours, 356–357
Virtual trade shows, 374
Volunteers, 486–487
    motivating, 487
Volunteer speakers
    benefits of using, 455
    challenges of using, 455–457
VR. *See* Virtual Reality (VR)

W

Waiter parade, 289
Walkie talkies, 491
Warehousing, 192
Water transportation, 8
Webinars, 365, 393–394
    creation of, 393
Well-drafted contract, 335
White-collar exemptions, 345
WHO. *See* World Health Organization (WHO)
Wine/champagne, 295–296
Wired *vs.* wireless, 377–378

Workshops, 6, 445, 446
World-class exhibitions, 150
World Commission on Environment and Development 1983, 403
World Health Organization (WHO), 151
Wrap-up, 233–234
Written agreement, 325
Written contract, 326
Written document, 327

Y

Yield management, 322
YouTube, 367–368

Z

Zoom, 393